Ken Greenwood

SAMS
Teach Yourself
ABAP/4®
in 21 Days

SAMS

A Division of Macmillan Computer Publishing
201 West 103rd St., Indianapolis, Indiana, 46290

Sams Teach Yourself ABAP/4 in 21 Days

Copyright © 1999 by Sams

International Standard Book Number: 0-672-31217-4

Library of Congress Catalog Card Number: 97-69119

Printed in the United States of America

First Printing: September 1998

00   4   3

Trademarks

Warning and Disclaimer

EXECUTIVE EDITOR
Bryan Gambrel

ACQUISITIONS EDITOR
Angela Kozlowski

DEVELOPMENT EDITOR
Nancy Warner

MANAGING EDITOR
Patrick Kanouse

PROJECT EDITOR
Rebecca Mounts

COPY EDITORS
Heather Kaufman Urschel
Carol Bowers

INDEXER
Becky Hornyak

PROOFREADER
Linda Knose

TEXT TECHNICAL EDITORS
Nam Hunyh
Brian Bokanyi

CD TECHNICAL EDITORS
Deepak Bapna
Barry Fewer

SOFTWARE DEVELOPMENT SPECIALIST
Andrea Duvall

INTERIOR DESIGN
Aren Howell

COVER DESIGN
Gary Adair

LAYOUT TECHNICIANS
Tim Osborn
Staci Somers
Mark Walchle

Contents at a Glance

Contents

About the Author

KEN GREENWOOD is the President of Ontario, Canada-based SAP consulting firm Modus Novus, Inc. He is also an ABAP Certification instructor at SAP America's ABAP/4 Academy in Boston, Lambton College in Ontario, and has recently taught ABAP/4 at SAP America in Foster City.

JACOB J. BOLOTIN is a SAP consultant for PricewaterhouseCoopers LLP and has been involved in many upgrade and implementation projects on the West Coast. In his spare time he enjoys working on his Cadillacs, swimming in the ocean, and listening to Sublime. Questions for Jacob can be sent to `cadillac@mindless.com`.

Dedication

This book is dedicated to my parents,
Marian and Vern Greenwood
(a.k.a. Mommy and Daddy Greenwood.)
Thanks for everything.

Tell Us What You Think!

As the reader of this book, *you* are our most important critic and commentator. We value your opinion and want to know what we're doing right, what we could do better, what areas you'd like to see us publish in, and any other words of wisdom you're willing to pass our way.

As the Executive Editor for the Client/Server Database team at Macmillan Computer Publishing, I welcome your comments. You can fax, email, or write me directly to let me know what you did or didn't like about this book—as well as what we can do to make our books stronger.

Please note that I cannot help you with technical problems related to the topic of this book, and that due to the high volume of mail I receive, I might not be able to reply to every message.

When you write, please be sure to include this book's title and author as well as your name and phone or fax number. I will carefully review your comments and share them with the author and editors who worked on the book.

Fax: 317-817-7070

E-mail: cs_db@mcp.com

Mail: Bryan Gambrel
          Executive Editor
          Programming
          Macmillan Computer Publishing
          201 West 103rd Street
          Indianapolis, IN 46290 USA

Introduction

Having taught the ABAP/4 certification course to hundreds of beginners and experienced developers at both at SAP and at other institutions, I know the kind of problems and questions you will have when learning this powerful language. By incorporating all the best techniques that I have encountered into this book, I hope to impart that same learning experience to you as well. To that end, this book is chock full of detailed diagrams, full-screen snapshots, working sample programs, narrated screencams, and step-by-step procedures. All the sample programs are also supplied on the CD-ROM so that you can upload and run them on your own system. In addition, the utilities that I supply to all of my classes are included on the CD-ROM, plus some new ones that I have written specifically for the buyers of this book.

ABAP/4, for all of its simplicity on the surface, is a complex language underneath. Because of that, the beginner is often bewildered by its behavior. By understanding how it works below the surface, you will be able to master this language. By understanding the hows and whys, you will gain an understanding few have in this exciting field.

This book will guide you through the intricacies of the ABAP/4 language and environment one step at a time. After you complete each chapter, you will be presented with exercises to reinforce your learning. Working solutions are provided for all exercises on the CD-ROM.

As experienced programmers know, and beginners soon find out, creating ABAP/4 programs often means creating more than just a program. It frequently involves the creation of development objects to support it. Procedures for creating these objects are all explained in exquisite detail using a list of numbered steps. Each step contains the title of the screens you encounter and the expected responses to each command. All procedures are accompanied by a screencam showing you exactly how it is done. Now, not only can you learn by watching me, but you can fast forward and rewind me as well.

The sheer volume of information needed to master ABAP is a daunting task for most, but I have taken the most vital information that you need and separated it into 21 manageable bites. With the knowledge you gain using this book, you will be able to branch out to complex ABAP/4 tasks with a solid understanding as your foundation.

As you go through the material, if you have problems or questions please visit the Internet site http://www.abap4.net. There I will post answers to frequently asked questions, and problems you may encounter that have not been covered. If you find an error in this book, or suspect there may be an error, you can find and post errata there.

I hope you will find using this book as enjoyable as I have found writing it. Cheers. Here's to *your* ABAP/4 in 21 days!

Conventions Used in This Book

Text that you type and text that you see onscreen appear in monospace type

```
It will look like this
```

to mimic the way the text looks on your screen.

Variables and placeholders (words that stand for what you will actually type) appear in *italic monospace*.

Each chapter ends with questions pertaining to that day's subject matter, with answers from the author. Most chapters also include an exercise section and a quiz designed to reinforce the day's concepts. (The answers appear in Appendix B.)

Note
A note presents interesting information related to the discussion.

Tip
A tip offers advice or shows you an easier way of doing something.

Caution
A caution alerts you to a possible problem and gives you advice on how to avoid it.

Do	Don't
These Do/Don't sidebars give you tips for what to do and what not to do with ABAP/4.	

SCREENCAM Many of the procedures in this book are demonstrated using *screencams*. Screencams are like movies; they show a series of screens, including keystrokes and mouse movements, with a descriptive voice-over.

NEW TERM New terms are introduced using the New Term icon.

The Syntax icon alerts you to the proper syntax usage for the code.

INPUT The Input icon highlights the code to be input.

OUTPUT The Output icon highlights the output produced by running the code.

ANALYSIS The Analysis icon designates the author's line-by-line analysis.

WEEK 1

At a Glance

You begin Week 1 by learning about the R/3 environment, including Basis, logon clients, the ABAP/4 Development Workbench, and the Data Dictionary. Within the dictionary, you create transparent tables using data elements and domains, add foreign keys to validate input, and create secondary indexes or buffering to speed up data access. You also learn how to create F1 and F4 help for the user, begin to write simple ABAP/4 programs, and become familiar with the ABAP/4 editor.

- Day 1, "The Development Environment," explains what an R/3 system is and how it looks and feels to the user. You learn about the system architecture in which ABAP/4 programs run.

- Day 2, "Your First ABAP/4 Program," teaches you to create and modify simple ABAP/4 programs. You also display a table and its contents using the Data Dictionary, as well as add comments and documentation to your programs.

- Day 3, "The Data Dictionary, Part 1," describes the differences between transparent, pooled, and cluster tables. You also learn to create domains, data elements, and transparent tables in the Data Dictionary.

- In Day 4, "The Data Dictionary, Part 2," you create foreign keys, create and use text tables, describe the difference between a structure and a table, and create structures in the R/3 Data Dictionary.

- During Day 5, "The Data Dictionary, Part 3," you create and use secondary indexes appropriately, set up the technical attributes for transparent tables, and set up buffering for tables.

- In Day 6, "The Data Dictionary, Part 4," you use the database utility to perform consistency checks, display database-specific table information, and drop and re-create tables in the database.

- After Day 7, "Defining Data in ABAP/4, Part 1," you understand the elements of ABAP/4 syntax, describe the concept of data objects and their visibility, use literals and understand how to code each type, and define and use constants.

DAY 1

The Development Environment

Chapter Objectives

After you complete this chapter, you should be able to answer the following questions:

- What is an R/3 system?
- What is an R/3 instance?
- What is Basis?
- What platforms does R/3 support?
- What are the possible R/3 system configurations?
- What is the R/3 server architecture?
- What is a logon client?

What Is R/3?

R/3 is an integrated suite of applications designed to handle the data processing for large corporations. It was developed in Germany by the company named SAP (an acronym for Systems Applications and Products for data processing).

> **Tip**
>
> When you see the word SAP by itself, it is pronounced *"ess-ay-pea."* When it is combined with another word, it is pronounced *sap*, as in "tree sap." You should never say *"sap"* when referring to the company SAP. Always pronounce it as *"ess-ay-pea."* Saying *"sap"* is the surest way to say, "I don't know anything about SAP."

Within R/3 is a runtime environment and an integrated suite of application programs written in SAP's 4GL—ABAP/4. These application programs are designed to meet the data processing needs of very large businesses. R/3 and its predecessor R/2 are particularly popular with the manufacturing sector.

R/3 is the system in which your ABAP/4 programs will run. Logically, it looks like Figure 1.1.

Figure 1.1.

Application modules are all written in ABAP/4, which is interpreted by Basis executables, which in turn, run on the operating system.

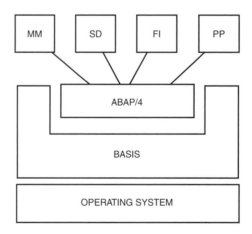

What Is the Purpose of R/3?

The sole purpose of an R/3 system is to provide a suite of tightly integrated, large-scale business applications. A few of these can be seen at the top of Figure 1.1. The standard set of applications delivered with each R/3 system are the following:

- PP (Production Planning)

- MM (Materials Management)
- SD (Sales and Distribution)
- FI (Financial Accounting)
- CO (Controlling)
- AM (Fixed Assets Management)
- PS (Project System)
- WF (Workflow)
- IS (Industry Solutions)
- HR (Human Resources)
- PM (Plant Maintenance)
- QM (Quality Management)

These applications are called the *functional areas,* or *application areas*, or at times the *functional modules* of R/3. All of these terms are synonymous with each other.

Traditionally, businesses assemble a suite of data processing applications by evaluating individual products and buying these separate products from multiple software vendors. Interfaces are then needed between them. For example, the materials management system will need links to the sales and distribution and to the financial systems, and the workflow system will need a feed from the HR system. A significant amount of IS time and money is spent in the implementation and maintenance of these interfaces.

R/3 comes prepackaged with the core business applications needed by most large corporations. These applications coexist in one homogenous environment. They are designed from the ground up to run using a single database and one (very large) set of tables. Current production database sizes range from 12 gigabytes to near 3 terabytes. Around 8,000 database tables are shipped with the standard delivery R/3 product.

Why Do You Need to Know This?

This is important for you, as an ABAP/4 programmer, to know because these applications are all written entirely in ABAP/4. These are the applications you must understand to be a proficient developer in R/3.

For example, assume you know ABAP/4 and you have been asked to write a financial report summarizing debits and credits by fiscal year for each vendor in the enterprise. You might know how to code in ABAP, but would you know how to begin to solve such a request?

Or perhaps your job entails new development in ABAP/4. You are asked to design a system that provides stock quotations to potential buyers. If you do not know the financial and sales and distribution systems, you won't know if you are creating something that already exists in R/3. Nor can you know if there are R/3 tables that already contain data similar to or identical to the type of data you want to store. These applications are highly integrated. A developer who takes the approach "I'll build my own tables and keep my own copies of the data," might soon find his data is redundant and must be routinely synchronized with the rest of the database. He has built an application that does not take advantage of the highly integrated nature of the R/3 environment.

I only point this out because many developers who wish to become independent consultants think that learning ABAP/4 is all they need to develop in the R/3 system. It is certainly a great start, but it is only the start. The importance of training in a functional area can be overlooked or unknown to those interested in becoming proficient ABAP/4 consultants. Obviously, much of this learning can and will be done on the job. However, I hope to illustrate the point that learning the ABAP/4 language is only the beginning of a long journey into SAP. If you desire to be successful as an independent consultant, you will eventually need to acquire functional area knowledge.

Tip

> You can learn about the functional areas by reading the R/3 online reference (R/3 menu path Help->R/3 Library). It contains tutorials and information for all of the functional areas. If you have access to a system with IDES data (International Demo and Education System), you can work through the R/3 Library exercises as well. For availability of training courses, contact SAP (http://www.sap.com) or Lambton College (http://www.lambton.on.ca).

Discovering What R/3 Looks Like

In a Windows environment, you will sign on to R/3 either by choosing a menu path from the Start menu, or by double-clicking on an R/3 icon, such as the one shown below in Figure 1.2.

The R/3 system will prompt you for a user ID and password. The logon screen appears in Figure 1.3. You will fill in these two fields and then press Enter.

The R/3 system will then display a copyright screen, and when you press Enter, the system will display the R/3 main menu as shown in Figure 1.4.

FIGURE 1.2.

The R/3 icon on the desktop.

1

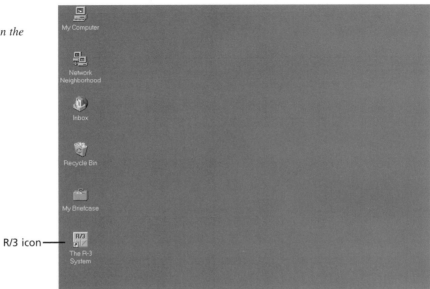

R/3 icon ——

FIGURE 1.3.

The R/3 logon screen prompts you for a password.

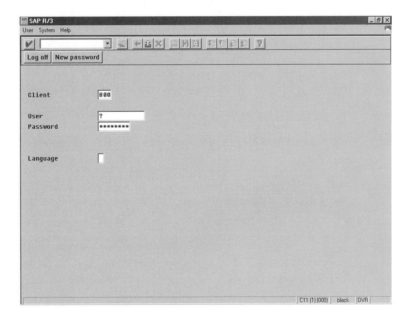

FIGURE **1.4.**

The R/3 main menu.

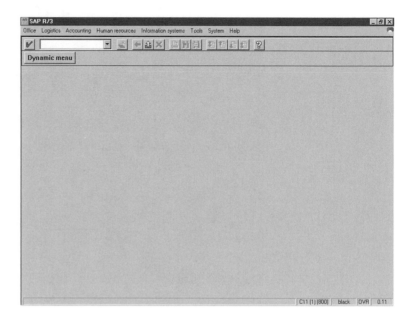

Using the R/3 System Conceptual Areas

From the main menu, you can go to three conceptual areas in the R/3 system:

- the Applications area
- the Basis area
- the Development Workbench

In the Applications area, you initiate transactions for the functional areas within R/3. To access these, from the R/3 main menu choose one of the following: Logistics, Accounting, Human Resources, or Information Systems.

In the Basis area, you can run transactions that monitor the R/3 system itself. To access the Basis area, from the main menu choose the menu path Tools->Administration. Here you will find many performance, tuning, and database administration tools.

The Development Workbench is used to create and test ABAP/4 programs. As an ABAP/4 programmer, you will spend most of your time within the Workbench. To access the Development Workbench, choose the menu path Tools->Development Workbench. However, your code will most probably read or update application data, and so it will be destined to become part of the application area. With that in mind, let's have a look within an Applications area first.

For our example, imagine that you are a clerk working in an accounts payable department. A vendor calls to say his address has changed. You put a bookmark in the magazine article you were reading (*A Criminologist's View of the Problems with Creative Accounting*) and proceed to update his address in the R/3 system. First, you reach the Accounts Payable menu by choosing the menu path Accounting->Financial Accounting->Accounts Payable (see Figure 1.5).

FIGURE 1.5.

The menu path to update a vendor master record (part 1).

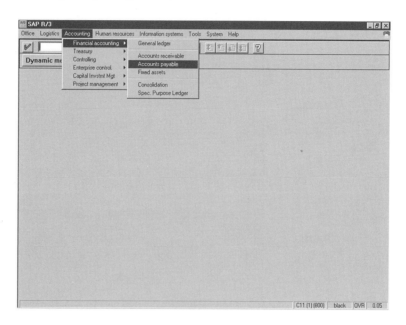

You then bring up the vendor master record maintenance transaction by choosing the menu path Master Records->Change (see Figure 1.6). You will see the Change Vendor: Initial screen.

From the Initial screen shown in Figure 1.7, you type his vendor number, tickmark the Address check box, and press the Enter key. You will then see the Address screen (see Figure 1.8).

You change his address and press the Save button (see Figure 1.9).

Upon saving, the system returns you to the Change Vendor: Initial Screen. It also displays a success message within the status bar located at the bottom of the screen (see Figure 1.10).

FIGURE 1.6.

The menu path to update a vendor master record (part 2).

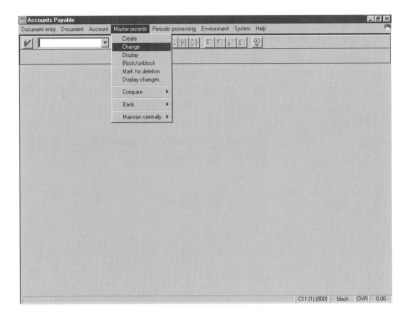

FIGURE 1.7.

The Vendor Master Update Transaction: Initial Screen.

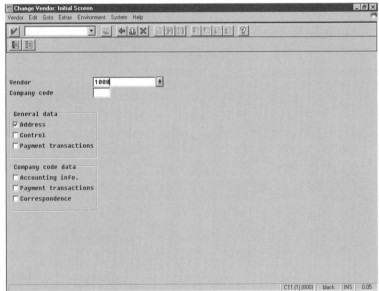

FIGURE 1.8.

The Vendor Master Update Transaction: Address Screen.

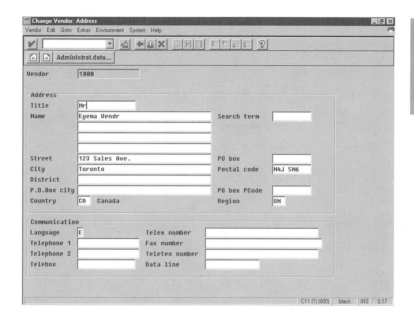

FIGURE 1.9.

Saving changes to the vendor's address.

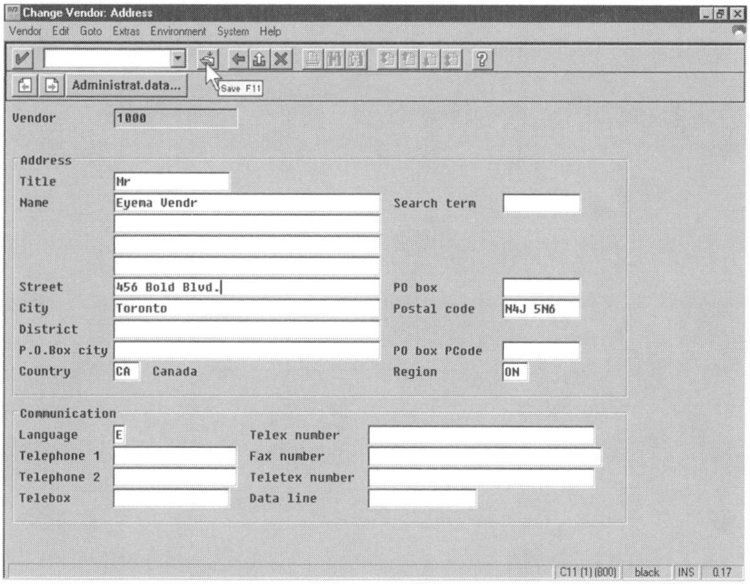

FIGURE **1.10.**

*The Initial Screen
gives verification that
the address change
was made.*

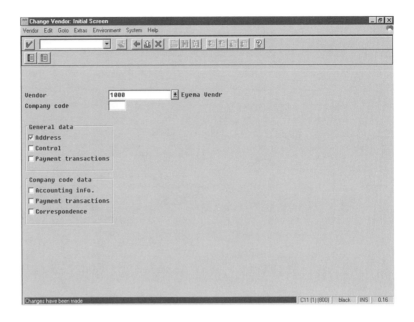

This transaction is representative of many of the transactions in the R/3 system. Most master data transactions have a similar look and feel.

Discovering the R/3 User Interface

Figure 1.11 shows the main menu again, with the important screen areas identified.

Every R/3 screen contains these elements:

- *Title bar:* Contains the title of the current screen.

- *Menu bar:* The contents of the menu bar change with each screen. By browsing the menus within it, you can discover all functions that are possible on the current screen. The System and Help menus are present on every screen and the menu items they contain never change.

- *Command field:* Here you enter commands to be executed. For example, you can log off by typing /**nex** in this field and pressing the Enter key. The section "Using the Command Field" describes this field in more detail.

- *Standard toolbar:* Contains the Command field and a series of buttons. They will never change in appearance, position, or function, and they will be present on every screen. Some might be grayed out if their functionality is currently unavailable.

- *Application toolbar:* Changes with each screen. Displays buttons that give you quick access to menu items for that screen.

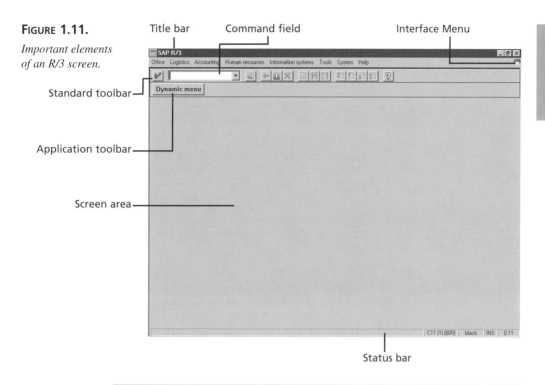

FIGURE 1.11.

Important elements of an R/3 screen.

Title bar   Command field   Interface Menu

Standard toolbar

Application toolbar

Screen area

Status bar

> **Tip**
>
> If you position your mouse pointer over any button and let it rest there for a few seconds, R/3 will display a tool tip describing its function. In R/3 it is called *quick info*. It contains a brief description of the button and the function key assigned to it.

- *Interface Menu:* Enables you to customize the characteristics of the user interface, access the Windows clipboard, and generate graphics. The following section will cover more features of the Interface Menu in depth.

- *Screen area:* This is the big area in the middle of the screen that displays the report data or a screen from a dialog program.

- *Status bar:* Displays messages, the system ID, session number, client number, insert/overtype mode indicator, and the current time.

You can turn most screen elements on and off. If your screen does not look or behave like the one described in this chapter, follow the instructions in the next section to correct it.

Working with the Interface Menu

The icon with three colored circles in the upper right-hand corner of the R/3 window is called the *Interface Menu.* With it, you can customize user interface settings such as screen colors, font sizes, and cursor behavior. To accomplish this, click once on the icon in the upper right-hand corner of the R/3 window (see Figure 1.12). A menu will appear; click on the Options menu item.

FIGURE 1.12.

The Interface Menu with the Options menu item highlighted.

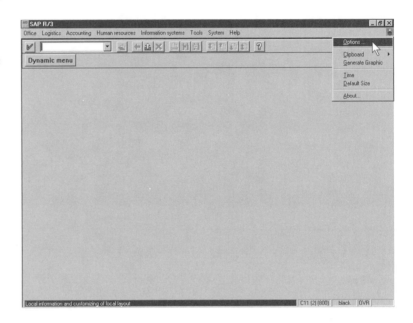

Click on the General tab and change your settings to match those shown in Figure 1.13. Doing so will ensure that your user interface will look and behave as described in this book.

Turn on all of the toolbars (tickmark them all) and set Quick Info to Quick. Tickmark the first and last of the message check boxes as shown. Click Apply.

Tip
> You must click the Apply or OK button before choosing another tab. If you do not, your changes will not take effect.

Click on the Colors In Lists tab and tickmark the Lines In Lists check box as shown in Figure 1.14. Click OK to return.

FIGURE 1.13.

The General Interface options.

FIGURE 1.14.

Tickmarking the Colors In Lists *check box.*

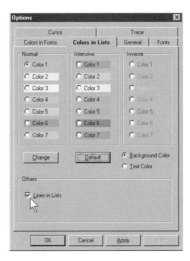

The Lines In Lists option turns on or off the display of horizontal and vertical lines in your report output. It should be checked so that you will see the effect of the line graphic statements you will code later in this book.

Tip

Display all function key (or *f-key*) settings by right-clicking anywhere in the screen area. This works on all screens. Function keys 1 through 12 are the top row of keys on your keyboard. Function keys 13 through 24 are those same keys with the Shift key held down. For example, F13 is Shift+F1. For f-keys 25 through 36, use Ctrl instead of Shift. For 37 though 48, use Alt. For f-keys higher than 48, hold down Ctrl and type the key number on the numeric keypad. For example, for F50, hold down Ctrl and type **50** on the numeric keypad.

Using the Command Field

In the Standard toolbar is an input area called the Command Field. Here you can enter system commands. For a list of the commands you can enter here, put your cursor in the command field and press the F1 key.

This field is most often used to start a new transaction.

 Note   For now, think of a program as a transaction. The two are roughly equivalent. When you start a transaction, you are starting a program.

NEW TERM   Instead of choosing a menu path to start a transaction, you can enter its *transaction code* into the command field. A transaction code is a 3 or 4 character code associated with a transaction—you can use it to start the transaction without using a menu path. Every transaction has a *transaction code* (also called a *tcode*).

To find the transaction code for any transaction, you would invoke the transaction and then choose the menu path System->Status. The System:_Status screen will be displayed. The transaction code appears in the Transaction field.

For example, from the R/3 main menu, choose the menu path Accounting->Financial Accounting->Accounts Payable. You will see the Accounts Payable screen. From here, choose the menu path Master Records->Display. You will see the Display Vendor: Initial Screen. Choose the menu path System->Status. You will see the System:_Status screen. In the Transaction field is the transaction code for this screen: FK03.

Now that you have the transaction code, you can start this transaction from any screen by entering in the command field **/n** followed by the transaction code.

For example, return to the main menu (click the Cancel button twice and then click the Back button). In the command field type **/nfk03**, then click the Enter key. You will immediately see the Display Vendor: Initial Screen.

On any screen, you can find the transaction code of the current transaction. To do this, choose the menu path System->Status.

Understanding Basis

 Basis is like an operating system for R/3. It sits between the ABAP/4 code and the computer's operating system. SAP likes to call it *middleware* because it sits in the middle, between ABAP/4 and the operating system.

Note

The predecessor to R/3 is R/2. R/2 is mainframe-based, and SAP ported it to the client/server environment. To do this, SAP created Basis. Creating Basis enabled the existing ABAP/4 code to run on other platforms.

If you turn back to Figure 1.1, you can see Basis sitting between ABAP/4 and the operating system. ABAP/4 cannot run directly on an operating system. It requires a set of programs (collectively called Basis) to load, interpret, and buffer its input and output.

Basis, in some respects, is like the Windows environment. Windows starts up, and while running it provides an environment in which Windows programs can run. Without Windows, programs written for the Windows environment cannot run.

Basis is to ABAP/4 programs as Windows is to Windows programs. Basis provides the runtime environment for ABAP/4 programs. Without Basis, ABAP/4 programs cannot run. When the operator starts up R/3, you can think of him as starting up Basis. Basis is a collection of R/3 system programs that present you with an interface. Using this interface the user can start ABAP/4 programs.

To install Basis, an installer runs the program r3inst at the command-prompt level of the operating system. Like most installs, this creates a directory structure and copies a set of executables into it. These executables taken together as a unit form Basis.

To start up the R/3 system, the operator enters the startsap command. The Basis executables start up and stay running, accepting requests from the user to run ABAP/4 programs.

ABAP/4 programs run within the protective Basis environment; they are not executables that run on the operating system. Instead, Basis reads ABAP/4 code and interprets it into operating system instructions.

ABAP/4 programs do not access operating system functions directly. Instead, they use Basis functions to perform file I/O and display data in windows. This level of isolation from the operating system enables ABAP/4 programs to be ported *without modification* to any system that supports R/3. This buffering is built right into the ABAP/4 language itself and is actually totally transparent to the programmer.

Basis makes ABAP/4 programs portable. The platforms that R/3 can run on are shown in Table 1.1.

TABLE 1.1 PLATFORMS AND DATABASES SUPPORTED BY R/3

Operating Systems	Supported Hardware	Supported Front-Ends	Supported Databases
AIX SINIX	IBM SNI SUN	Win 3.1/95/NT	DB2 for AIX
SOLARIS HP-UX	Digital HP	OSF/Motif	Informix-Online
Digital-UNIX	Bull	OS/2	Oracle 7.1
		Macintosh	ADABAS D
Windows NT	AT&T Compaq	Win 3.1/95/NT	Oracle 7.1
	Bull/Zenith	OSF/Motif	SQL Server 6.0
	HP (Intel) SNI	OS/2	ADABAS D
	IBM (Intel)	Macintosh	
	Digital (Intel)		
	Data-General		
OS/400	AS/400	Win95 OS/2	DB2/400

For example, if you write an ABAP/4 program on Digital UNIX with an Informix database and an OSF/Motif interface, that same program should run *without modification* on a Windows NT machine with an Oracle database and a Windows 95 interface. Or, it could run on an AS/400 with a DB2 database using OS/2 as the front-end.

SAP also provides a suite of tools for administering the Basis system. These tools perform tasks such as system performance monitoring, configuration, and system maintenance. To access the Basis administration tools from the main menu, choose the path Tools->Administration.

Here are some examples of Basis administration tools:

- To see a list of the servers currently running in your R/3 system, choose the menu path Tools->Administration, Monitoring->System Monitoring->Servers.
- To view the current system log, choose Tools->Administration, Monitoring->System Log.

- To see system performance statistics, run transaction st03 (enter **/nst03** in the Command Field), choose This Application Server, Last Minute Load, and analyze the last 15 minutes. Press the Dialog button at the bottom of the screen, and you will see the average user response time for the last 15 minutes (look at Av. Response Time).

Basis is designed to run in a client/server configuration.

Understanding Client/Server

NEW TERM *Client/server* is two programs talking to each other (see Figure 1.15).

FIGURE 1.15.

The essence of client/server.

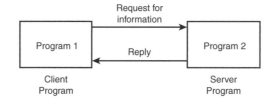

Here we see Program 1 asking Program 2 for some information. Program 1 is the *client* and Program 2 is the *server*. Program 2 *serves* Program 1 with the information it requested. This is different than a main program calling a subroutine and returning. A program that calls a subroutine transfers control to the subroutine and cannot perform any processing until the subroutine returns control.

With client/server, the client and server programs are independent processes. If the client sends a request to the server, it is free to perform other work while waiting for the response.

Figure 1.16 shows the three standard client/server configurations. R/3 can be tailored to run in any of these configurations.

When the client and server programs both run on the same computer, the configuration is referred to as *single-tier* client/server. (A *tier* is the boundary between two computers.) When they run on different computers, the configuration is referred to as *two-tier* client/server.

A program can function as both a client *and* a server if it both requests information and replies to requests. When you have three programs in communication, such as is shown in Figure 1.16, the configuration is called three-tier client/server.

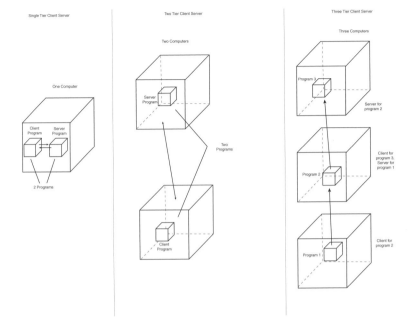

FIGURE 1.16.

One-, two-, and three-tiered client/server configurations.

The client/server configuration enables the R/3 system to spread its load across multiple computers. This provides the customer with the ability to scale the processing power of the system up or down by simply adding another computer to an existing configuration, instead of replacing a single computer that performs all of the processing, such as that which occurs in the mainframe world.

R/3 System Architecture

SAP based the architecture of R/3 on a three-tier client/server model. The R/3 system architecture appears in Figure 1.17.

Presentation Server

NEW TERM The *presentation server* is actually a program named `sapgui.exe`. It is usually installed on a user's workstation. To start it, the user double-clicks on an icon on the desktop or chooses a menu path. When started, the presentation server displays the R/3 menus within a window. This window is commonly known as the SAPGUI, or the user interface (or simply, *the interface*). The interface accepts input from the user in the form of keystrokes, mouse-clicks, and function keys, and sends these requests to the application server to be processed. The application server sends the results back to the SAPGUI which then formats the output for display to the user.

FIGURE 1.17.

*The R/3 system
architecture.*

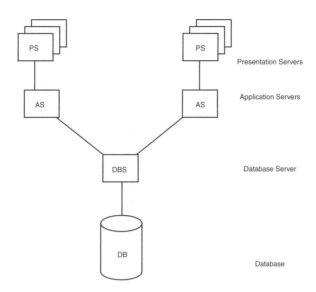

Presentation Servers

Application Servers

Database Server

Database

Application Server

NEW TERM An *application server* is a set of executables that collectively interpret the
ABAP/4 programs and manage the input and output for them. When an application server is started, these executables all start at the same time. When an application
server is stopped, they all shut down together. The number of processes that start up
when you bring up the application server is defined in a single configuration file called
the *application server profile*.

Each application server has a profile that specifies its characteristics when it starts up and
while it is running. For example, an application sever profile specifies:

- Number of processes and their types
- Amount of memory each process may use
- Length of time a user is inactive before being automatically logged off

The application server exists to interpret ABAP/4 programs, and they only run there—the
programs do not run on the presentation server. An ABAP/4 program can start an executable on the presentation server, but an ABAP/4 program cannot execute there.

If your ABAP/4 program requests information from the database, the application server will format the request and send it to the database server.

Discovering the Database Server

NEW TERM The *database server* is a set of executables that accept database requests from the application server. These requests are passed on to the RDBMS (Relation Database Management System). The RDBMS sends the data back to the database server, which then passes the information back to the application server. The application server in turn passes that information to your ABAP/4 program.

There is usually a separate computer dedicated to house the database server, and the RDBMS may run on that computer also, or may be installed on its own computer.

Configuring the Servers

During installation, the servers can be configured in four ways (see Figure 1.18).

FIGURE 1.18.

Possible R/3 system configurations.

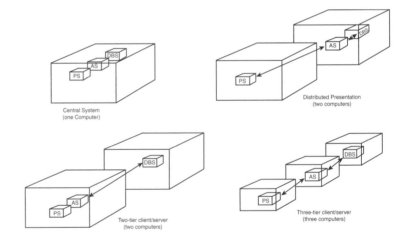

In a three-tier client/server configuration, the presentation servers, applications servers, and database server all run on separate machines. This is the most common configuration for large systems, and is common in production.

In the distribution presentation configuration, the application and database servers are combined on one computer and the presentation servers run separately. This is used for smaller systems, and is often seen on a development system.

In the two-tier client/server configuration, the presentation and application servers are combined and the database server is separate. This configuration is used in conjunction

1

with other application servers. It is used for a batch server when the batch is segregated from the online servers. A SAPGUI is installed on it to provide local control.

When all servers are combined onto a single machine, you have a *central* configuration. This is rarely seen because it describes a standalone R/3 system with only a single user.

Defining an R/3 System

The simplest definition of an R/3 system is "*one database.*" In one R/3 system, there is only one database. To expand the definition, R/3 is considered to be all of the components attached to that one database. One R/3 system is composed of one database server accessing a single database, one or more application servers, and one or more presentation servers. By definition, it is all of the components attached to one database. If you have one database, you have one system. If you have one system, you have one database. During an implementation, there is usually one system (or one database) assigned to development, one or more systems designated for testing, and one assigned to production.

NEW TERM   The term *R/3 system landscape* denotes a description of the number of systems within an SAP installation and how they are designated, such as development, test, or production.

Defining an R/3 Instance

NEW TERM   When you hear someone say the word *instance*, most of the time, that person will be referring to an application server. The term instance is synonymous with *application server*.

The term *central instance* refers to the database server. If an application server and database server both reside on the same machine, the term *central instance* refers to the computer on which both reside.

In the most general terms, an *instance* is a *server*. It is a set of R/3 processes providing services to the R/3 system.

Application Server Architecture

The components of an application server are shown in Figure 1.19. It consists of a dispatcher and multiple work processes.

All requests that come in from presentation servers are directed first to the dispatcher. The dispatcher writes them first to the dispatcher queue. The dispatcher pulls the requests from the queue on a first-in, first-out basis. Each request is then allocated to the first available work process. A work process handles one request at a time.

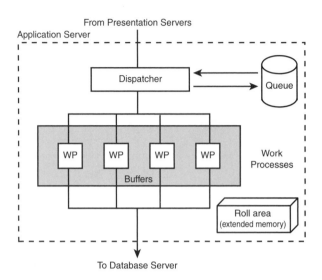

FIGURE 1.19.

Application server architecture.

To perform any processing for a user's request, a work process needs to address two special memory areas: the user context and the program roll area. The user context is a memory area that contains information about the user, and the roll area is a memory area that contains information about the programs execution.

Understanding a User Context

NEW TERM A *user context* is memory that is allocated to contain the characteristics of a user that is logged on the R/3 system. It holds information needed by R/3 about the user, such as:

- The user's current settings
- The user's authorizations
- The names of the programs the user is currently running

When a user logs on, a user context is allocated for that logon. When they log off, it is freed. It is used during program processing, and its importance is described further in the following sections.

Understanding a Roll Area

NEW TERM A *roll area* is memory that is allocated by a work process for an instance of a program. It holds information needed by R/3 about the program's execution, such as:

- The values of the variables

- The dynamic memory allocations
- The current program pointer

Each time a user starts a program, a roll area is created for that instance of the program. If two users run the same program at the same time, two roll areas will exist—one for each user. The roll area is freed when the program ends.

Note

> When speaking to a Basis consultant, you might hear the term roll area used to refer to all roll areas for one user or even all roll areas on one application server. You usually can determine the intended meaning from the context in which it is used.

Both the roll area and the user context play an important part in dialog step processing.

Understanding a Dialog Step

NEW TERM A *dialog step* is any screen change (see Figure 1.20).

FIGURE 1.20.

Changing from the Initial Screen to the Address Screen can be considered a dialog step.

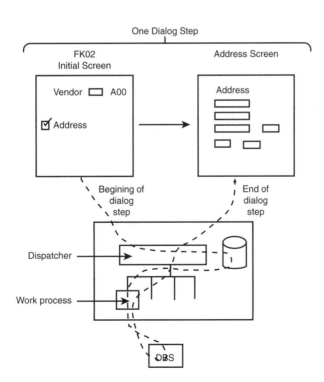

Note	A dialog step is used by Basis consultants as the unit of measure for system response time.

A dialog step is the processing needed to get from one screen to the next. It includes all processing that occurs after the user issues a request, up to and including the processing needed to display the next screen. For example, when the user clicks the Enter key on the Change Vendor: Initial Screen, he initiates a dialog step and the hourglass appears, preventing further input. The sapmf02k program retrieves the vendor information and displays it on the Change Vendor: Address screen, and the hourglass disappears. This marks the end of the dialog step and the user is now able to make another request.

There are four ways the user can initiate a dialog step. From the SAPGUI:

- Press Enter.
- Press a function key.
- Click on a button on the screen.
- Choose a menu item.

It is important for an ABAP/4 programmer to know about dialog steps because they form a discrete unit of processing for an ABAP/4 program.

Understanding Roll-In/Roll-Out Processing

NEW TERM An ABAP/4 program only occupies a work process for one dialog step. At the beginning of the dialog step, the roll area and user context are *rolled in* to the work process. At the end of the dialog step, they are *rolled out*. This is illustrated in Figure 1.21.

FIGURE 1.21.

Roll-in/roll-out processing.

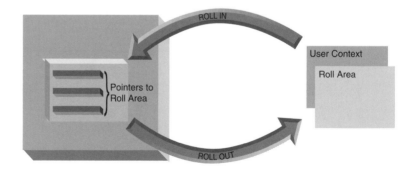

During the roll-in, pointers to the roll area and user context are populated in the work process. This enables the work process to access the data in those areas and so perform processing for that user and that program. Processing continues until the program sends a screen to the user. At that time, both areas are rolled out. Roll-out invalidates the pointers and disassociates these areas from the work process. That work process is now free to perform processing for other requests. The program is now only occupying memory, and not consuming any CPU. The user is looking at the screen that was sent, and will soon send another request.

When the next request is sent from the user to continue processing, the dispatcher allocates that request to the first available work process. It can be the same or a different work process. The user context and roll area for that program are again rolled in to the work process, and processing resumes from the point at which it was left off. Processing continues until the next screen is shown, or until the program terminates. If another screen is sent, the areas are again rolled out. When the program terminates, the roll area is freed. The user context remains allocated until the user logs off.

In a system with many users running many programs, only a few of those programs will be active in work processes at any one time. When they are not occupying a work process, they are rolled out to extended memory and only occupy RAM. This conserves CPU and enables the R/3 system to achieve high transaction throughput.

Note

ABAP/4 programs do not have the capability to intercept many common Windows events. The events that generate a lot of messages such as key presses, focus changes, and mouse movements are not passed to ABAP/4 programs. As a result, there is no way of performing some of the functions that are found in other Windows programs. For example, in ABAP/4, you cannot validate the contents of a field when the user presses the Tab key. You must instead wait until the user initiates a dialog step.

Discovering How the Data Is Sent to the Presentation Server

The messages exchanged between the presentation server and the application server are in an SAP proprietary format. The SAPGUI accepts the screen information sent from the application server and formats it appropriately for the platform it is running on. This enables different end-user hardware platforms to connect to a single application server. For example, an OS/2 PC and a Windows PC can both connect to the same application server at the same time.

Understanding the Components of a Work Process

Each work process has four components (see Figure 1.22).

FIGURE 1.22.

The components of a work process.

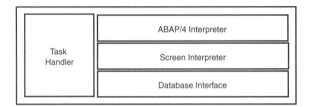

Each work process is composed of the following:

- A task handler
- An ABAP/4 interpreter
- A screen interpreter
- A database interface

All requests pass through the task handler, which then funnels the request to the appropriate part of the work process.

The interpreters interpret the ABAP/4 code. Notice that there are two interpreters: the ABAP/4 interpreter and the screen interpreter. There are actually two dialects of ABAP/4. One is the full-blown ABAP/4 data processing language and the other is a very specialized screen processing language. Each is processed by its own interpreter.

The database interface handles the job of communicating with the database.

Understanding the Types of Work Processes

There are seven types of work processes. Each handles a specific type of request. The type of work processes and the types of requests that they handle are shown in Table 1.2.

TABLE 1.2   TYPES OF WORK PROCESSES AND THE TYPES OF REQUESTS THEY HANDLE

WP Type	Request Type
D (Dialog)	Dialog requests
V (Update)	Requests to update data in the database
B (Background)	Background jobs
S (Spool)	Print spool requests
E (Enqueue)	Logical lock requests
M (Message)	Routes messages between application servers within an R/3 system
G (Gateway)	Funnels messages into and out of the R/3 system

Understanding the Logon Client

The term *logon client* has nothing to do with Client/Server—it is completely different. The *logon client* refers to the number that the user types in the Client field on the logon screen (see Figure 1.23).

FIGURE 1.23.

The user enters the logon client on the logon screen in the Client field.

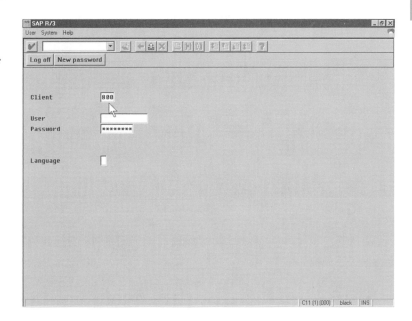

The number entered here by the user corresponds to a set of rows within each client-dependent table within the database.

Understanding Client-Dependent and Client-Independent Tables

There are two types of tables in an R/3 database: *client-dependent* and *client-independent*. A table is client-dependent if the first field is of type CLNT. The length will always be 3, and by convention, this field is always named mandt. If the first field is not of type CLNT, the table is client-independent. An example of a client-dependent table is shown in Figure 1.24. Figure 1.25 is an example of a client-independent table.

FIGURE 1.24.

This table is client-dependent because the first field is of type CLNT.

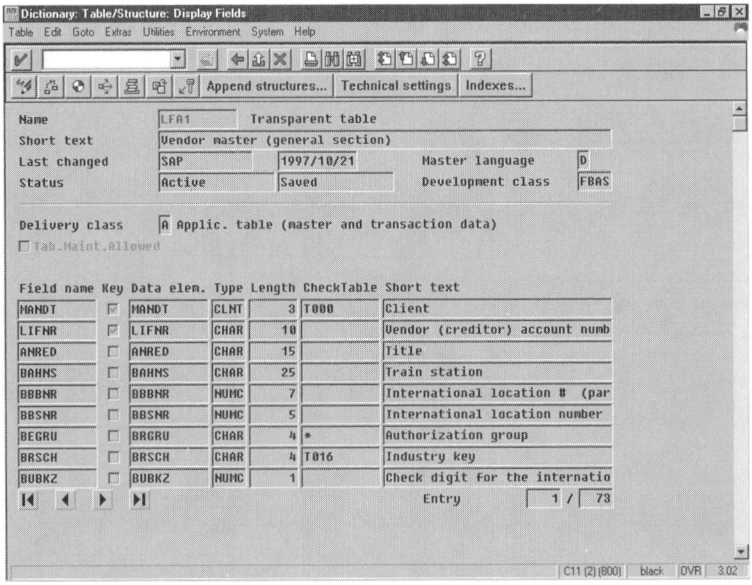

FIGURE 1.25.

This table is client-independent, because the first field is not type CLNT.

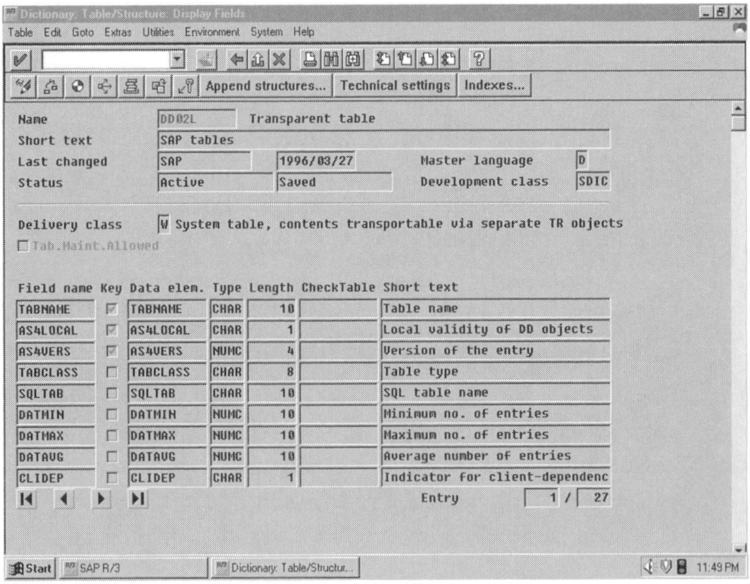

Figure 1.26 shows how this field affects the user.

In Figure 1.26, the user logs on to client 800 and runs the program shown. This program selects rows from table lfa1 and writes out lfa1-lifnr. When this program is run, only two rows are selected: only those where mandt equals 800. This happens automatically because the first field in the table is of type CLNT. There are five rows in the table, but the program writes out only those rows where mandt equals 800. If the user were to log on to client 700 and run the same program, three rows of data would be found and written out. If the user were to log on to client 900, only one row of data would be found.

FIGURE 1.26.

The effect of client-dependence.

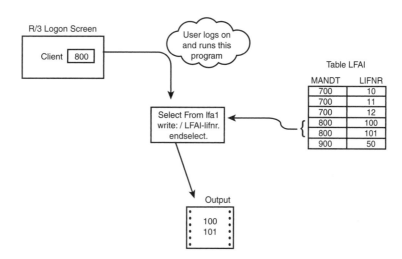

The logon client mechanism divides the rows within a client-dependant table into distinct groups. To access a different set of data, the user logs on and specifies a different client number.

 Note   The user master records (containing R/3 user IDs) are client-dependent. Therefore, to gain access to a client, the security administrator must create a new user ID for you within that client.

Developers and testers use the logon client mechanism to create and access multiple, independent sets of data within a single table.

For example, assume two typical, asocial programmers are working on an enhancement to the billing system. Jim is modifying the update transaction and Jane is creating a new report to go with Jim's modifications.

Jane sets up data for her test run, executes her report and obtains output. Jim works in the next cubicle, but due to his antisocial tendencies is blissfully unaware that his transaction uses the same tables as Jane's report. He runs his transaction and updates the data. Jim got what he wanted, but Jane then modifies her code and runs her program again. Her output differs from the last run, and the differences many not result from her changes, but rather they may result from Jim's changes. What we have here is a failure to communicate.

If the tables used by Jim and Jane's programs were client-dependent, they could each log in to separate clients, set up independent sets of data, and test their programs without ever talking to each other. They could perform all of their testing in the comfort of their cubicles and in isolation from their coworkers.

To make their tables client-dependant, they only need mandt as the first field and the R/3 system will take care of the rest. When records are added to the table, the system automatically moves the current logon client into the mandt field when the record is send to the database. Their Open SQL select statements will only return rows where the client number in the table is equal to the their current logon client number. The Open SQL database statements insert, update, modify, and delete also provide automatic client handling.

If the tables involved are all client-dependent, there can be more than one group of testers working at a time in one test system. Two teams of testers can test divergent functionality in the same set of programs at the same time provided they log on to different logon clients. The updates done by one team will not change the data belonging to the other team.

A training client could also exist on the test system. The students could log on to one client and the testers could log on to another. Both would run the same set of programs, but the programs would access independent sets of data.

 Note

> The average R/3 installation has three systems: development, test, and production. By default, each system comes with three clients installed: 000, 001, and 066. It is common to have from three to six clients in the development and test systems, but rarely will you see more than one client in production.

Using SAP's Open SQL

ABAP/4 code is portable between databases. To access the database in an ABAP/4 program you will code SAP's *Open SQL*. Open SQL is a subset and variation of ANSI SQL. The ABAP/4 interpreter passes all Open SQL statements to the database interface part of the work process (see Figure 1.27). There, they are converted to SQL that is native to the installed RDMS. For example, if you were running an Oracle database, your ABAP/4 Open SQL would be converted by the database interface to Oracle SQL statements.

FIGURE 1.27.

The database interface component of the work process.

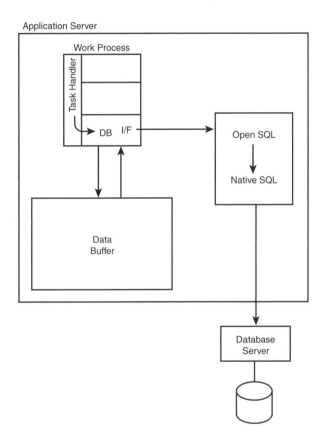

If you use Open SQL, your SQL statements will be passed to the database interface. Using Open SQL has three main advantages. All of these advantages are implemented via the database interface.

Portability

The first advantage is the fact that your SQL statements will be portable between databases. For example, if for some reason your company wanted to switch from an Oracle to an Informix database, it could change the database, and your ABAP/4 code would continue to run without modification.

Buffering Data on the Application Server

Secondly, the database interface buffers information from the database on the application server. When data is read from the database, it can be stored in buffers on the application server. If a request is then made to access the same records, they would already be on the application server, and the request is satisfied from the buffer without having to go to the database. This buffering technique reduces the load on the database server and on the network link between the database and application servers, and can speed up database access times by a factor of 10 to 100 times.

Automatic Client Handling

The third advantage of using Open SQL is *automatic client handling*. With Open SQL, the client field is automatically populated by the database interface. This gives your development and testing teams many advantages, such as the ability to perform multiple simultaneous testing and training on a single database without interference from each other.

Summary

- R/3 supports multiple hardware platforms, operating systems, and databases.
- In addition to allowing native SQL, ABAP/4 provides Open SQL. Using Open SQL makes your code portable, faster, and provides automatic client handling.
- The logon client enables multiple independent groups of data to be stored in the same table. The data you access depends on the client number you entered when you logged on.

Q&A

Q Can I copy an existing client to a new client?

A The Basis consultant can do this for you using a client copy utility. Each development system normally has at least a reference client and a working client. Your "good" data is kept in the reference client. It is copied to create the working client. If you corrupt the working client, the Basis consultant can restore it to its original state by copying the reference client again.

Q Can I write a program that reads data from a client other than the client I am currently logged on to?

A Yes. You can add the keywords *client specified* to any Open SQL statement. For example, to read data in client 900, you could code:

```
select * from tbl client specified where mandt = '900'.
```

However, you should realize that this should only be done if you are writing a system program. It is never done in an application program; they should always be client-independent. If you need to transmit data between two production clients, you should implement the data transfer via ALE.

Workshop

The Workshop provides you two ways for you to affirm what you've learned in this chapter. The Quiz section poses questions to help you solidify your understanding of the material covered and the Exercise section provides you with experience in using what you have learned. You can find answers to the quiz questions and exercises in Appendix B, "Answers to Quiz Questions and Exercises."

Quiz

1. Choose the menu path Tools->Administration, Monitoring->System monitoring->User overview. What is the transaction code for this transaction?

2. What is the transaction code for the R/3 main menu? (The main menu is the first menu displayed after logon.)

3. What is the transaction code for the menu path Tools->Development Workbench?

4. If there are three R/3 systems in your current system landscape, how many databases are there?

5. If an R/3 system has two application servers, how many instances does it have?

6. What is Open SQL?

7. What advantages does Open SQL offer over native SQL?

8. Which part of the work process is used to implement Open SQL?

9. When is a roll area allocated, when is it de-allocated, and what does it contain?

10. When is a user context allocated, when is it de-allocated, and what does it contain?

11. When does the roll-out occur, and why does it occur?

Exercise 1

Are the tables in Figures 1.28 through 1.31 client-dependent or client-independent?

FIGURE 1.28.

Is this table client-dependent or client-independent?

```
Dictionary: Table/Structure: Display Fields                              _ B X
Table  Edit  Goto  Extras  Utilities  Environment  System  Help

Name              TOBJ        Transparent table
Short text        Objects
Last changed      SAP              1995/08/23    Master language      D
Status            Act.             Saved         Development class     SUSR

Delivery class    W System table, contents transportable via separate TR objects
  Tab.Maint.Allowed

Field name  Key  Data elem.  Type  Length  CheckTable  Short text
OBJCT        ☑   XUOBJECT    CHAR      10               User master maintenance: Auth.
FIEL1            XUFIELD     CHAR      10               Field name for authorizations
FIEL2            XUFIELD     CHAR      10               Field name for authorizations
FIEL3            XUFIELD     CHAR      10               Field name for authorizations
FIEL4            XUFIELD     CHAR      10               Field name for authorizations
FIEL5            XUFIELD     CHAR      10               Field name for authorizations
FIEL6            XUFIELD     CHAR      10               Field name for authorizations
FIEL7            XUFIELD     CHAR      10               Field name for authorizations
FIEL8            XUFIELD     CHAR      10               Field name for authorizations
                                                        Entry        1 /  14
```

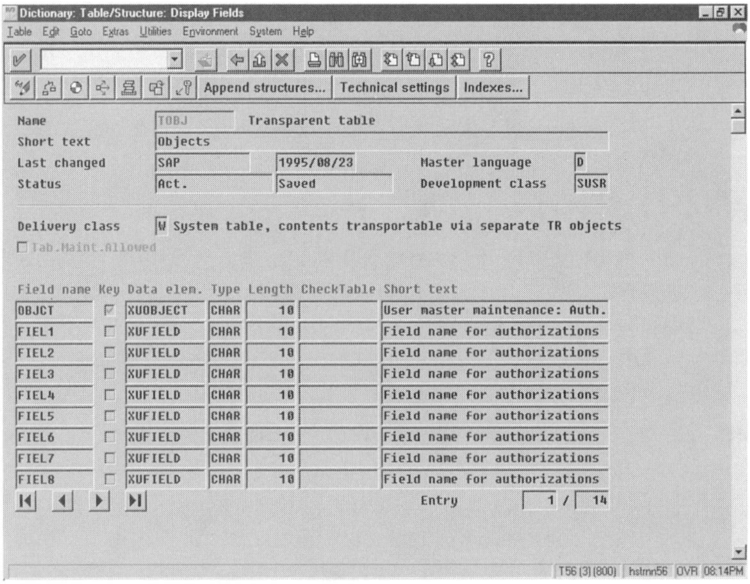

FIGURE 1.29.

Is this table client-dependent or client-independent?

```
Dictionary: Table/Structure: Display Fields                              _ B X
Table  Edit  Goto  Extras  Utilities  Environment  System  Help

Name              KNA1        Transparent table
Short text        General Data in Customer Master
Last changed      SAP              1996/07/22    Master language      D
Status            Act.             Saved         Development class     US

Delivery class    A Applic. table (master and transaction data)
  Tab.Maint.Allowed

Field name  Key  Data elem.  Type  Length  CheckTable  Short text
MANDT        ☑   MANDT       CLNT       3    T000       Client
KUNNR        ☑   KUNNR       CHAR      10               Customer number
ADRNR            ADRNR       CHAR      10    *          Address
ANRED            ANRED       CHAR      15               Form of address
AUFSD            AUFSD_X     CHAR       2    TVAST      Central order block for custom
BAHNE            BAHNE       CHAR      25               Express train station
BAHNS            BAHNS       CHAR      25               Train station
BBBNR            BBBNR       NUMC       7               International location number
BBSNR            BBSNR       NUMC       5               International location number
                                                        Entry        1 /  114
```

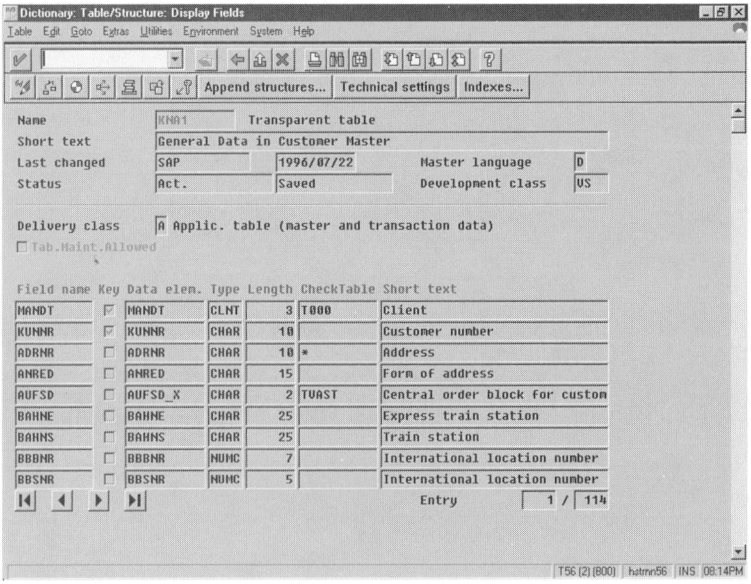

FIGURE 1.30.

Is this table client-dependent or client-independent?

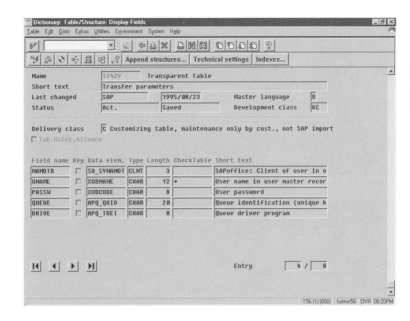

FIGURE 1.31.

Is this table client-dependent or client-independent?

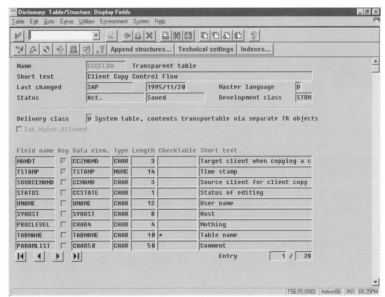

DAY **2**

Your First ABAP/4 Program

After you complete this chapter, you should be able to:

- Create and modify simple ABAP/4 programs.
- Use standard functions in the ABAP/4 editor.
- Use F1 and R/3 Library help functions.
- Find your programs using the Object Browser and the editor.
- Display a table and its contents using the Data Dictionary.
- Use the `tables` and `select` statements.
- Chain statements together using the chain operator.
- Add comments and documentation to your programs.

Before Proceeding

Before proceeding, you should:

- Be comfortable with a programming language such as C, COBOL, or Visual Basic. To obtain the full benefit from this and all following chapters, you should also have two or more years of previous development experience.
- Set up your interface as recommended in Day 1 in the section "The Interface Menu," if you have not done so already.
- Perform the install procedure for the ScreenCams on the CD-ROM. The install procedure is described in the readme.txt file found in the root directory of the CD-ROM.

NEW TERM Many of the procedures in this book are demonstrated using *ScreenCams*. ScreenCams are like movies; they show a series of screens, including keystrokes and mouse movements, with a descriptive voiceover. They can be found on the CD-ROM that comes with this book. See the readme.txt file found in the root directory of the CD-ROM for more information.

Exploring the Development Environment

NEW TERM A *development object* is anything created by a developer. Examples of development objects are programs, screens, tables, views, structures, data models, messages, and includes.

NEW TERM The R/3 system contains tools for creating and testing development objects. These tools are located in the *R/3 Development Workbench*. To access any development tool, you go to the workbench.

The workbench contains these tools to help you create development objects:

- The ABAP/4 program editor where you can create and modify ABAP/4 source code and other program components
- The Data Dictionary where you can create tables, structures, and views
- The Data modeler where you can document the relationships between tables
- The Function library where you can create global ABAP/4 function modules
- The screen and menu painters where you can create a user interface for your programs

The following testing and search tools are also available:

- the ABAP/4 Debugger
- the SQL trace tool used to tune SQL statements
- the runtime analyzer for optimizing your program's performance
- a where-used tool for impact analysis
- a computer-aided test tool for regression testing
- a repository search tool for finding development objects
- the Workbench Organizer for recording changes to objects and promoting them into production

All development objects are portable, meaning that you can copy them from one R/3 system to another. This is usually done to move your development objects from the development system to the production system. If the source and target systems are on different operating systems or use different database systems, your development objects will run as-is and without any modification. This is true for all platforms supported by R/3. (For a list of supported hardware and operating systems, refer to Table 1.1.)

Discovering Program Types

There are two main types of ABAP/4 programs:

- reports
- dialog programs

Defining Reports

The purpose of a report is to read data from the database and write it out. It consists of only two screens (see Figure 2.1).

New Term The first screen is called the *selection screen*. It contains input fields allowing the user to enter criteria for the report. For example, the report may produce a list of sales for a given date range, so the date range input fields would appear on the report's selection screen.

New Term The second screen is the output screen. It contains the *list*. The list is the output from the report, and usually does not have any input fields. In our example, it would contain a list of the sales that occurred within the specified date range.

The selection screen is optional. Not all reports have one. However, all reports generate a list.

In this book, you will learn how to create report programs.

FIGURE 2.1.

The selection screen and the output screen.

Defining Dialog Programs

Dialog programs are more flexible than reports, and so are more complex at the program level. They can contain any number of screens, and the screen sequence can be changed dynamically at run time. On each screen, you can have input fields, output fields, push-buttons, and more than one scrollable area.

Discovering Report Components

ABAP/4 reports consist of five components (shown in Figure 2.2):

- Source code
- Attributes
- Text elements
- Documentation
- Variants

FIGURE 2.2.

The components of an ABAP/4 program.

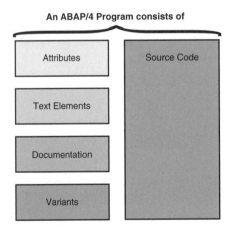

Only the source code and program attribute components are required. The rest of the components are optional.

All development objects and their components are stored in the R/3 database. For example, the source code for a report is stored in database table dd010s.

Discovering the Program Runtime Object

NEW TERM ABAP/4 programs are interpreted; they are not compiled. The first time you execute a program, the system automatically generates a *runtime object*. The runtime object is a pre-processed form of the source code. However, it is not an executable that you can run at the operating system level. Instead, it requires the R/3 system to interpret it. The runtime object is also known as the *generated form* of the program.

If you change the source code, the runtime object is automatically regenerated the next time you execute the program.

Introducing Program Naming Conventions

NEW TERM The company you work for is a customer of SAP. Therefore, programs that you create at your company are called *customer programs*.

NEW TERM Customer development objects must follow naming conventions that are predefined by SAP. These conventions are called the *customer name range*. For programs, the customer name range is two to eight characters long and the program name must start with the letter y or z. SAP reserves the letters a through x for their own programs.

NEW TERM Please take a moment now to choose a unique 3-character identifier for your programs. Within this book, I'll refer to this identifier as your *handle*. It must begin with a y or z. For example, you might use the letter z followed by your two initials. The notation ••• will indicate where you should use your handle. For example, if you chose zkg and you see the direction "Enter a program name of •••abc," you would enter zkgabc. I recommend that as you go through this book, you should use your handle as the first three characters of all development objects you create. If you do, they will be easy to recognize later, and easy to find.

The program naming conventions adopted for this book are as follows:

- Sample programs from the text of chapters follow the convention ztx*ccnn*, where *cc* is the chapter number and *nn* is a sequential number from 01 to 99.

- Program names used in exercises follow the convention zty*ccnn*, where *cc* is the chapter number and *nn* is a sequential number. The program name for the solution will be ztz*ccnn*.

- Utility programs provided on the CD-ROM follow the naming convention y-*xxxxxx*, where *xxxxxx* is the name of the utility.

The setup program that creates development objects and loads them with data for the exercises is called y-setup. If necessary, it can be re-run at any time to restore the exercise data to its original condition. To remove all the development objects and data created by the setup program from the system, run y-uninst. See the readme.txt file on the CD-ROM for more information.

Creating Your First Program

What follows is a description of the process you will follow to create a program.

When you sign on to R/3 to create your first ABAP/4 program, the first screen you see will be the SAP main menu. From there, you will go to the Development Workbench, and then to the editor. You will enter a program name, and create the program. The first screen you will see will be the Program Attributes screen. There, you must enter the program attributes and save them. You will then be allowed to proceed to the source code editor. In the source code editor, you'll enter source code, save it, and then execute the program.

SCREENCAM Start the ScreenCam "How to Create Your First Program" now.

Follow this procedure to create your first program. Help with common problems is given in the Troubleshooter that follows it. If you have trouble with any one of the steps, don't forget to consult the Troubleshooter.

1. From the R/3 main menu, select the menu path Tools->ABAP/4 Workbench. A screen with the title ABAP/4 Development Workbench is displayed.

2. Press the ABAP/4 Editor button on the application toolbar. The ABAP/4 Editor: Initial Screen is displayed.

3. In the Program field, type the program name •••0201.

4. Press the Create button. The ABAP/4: Program Attributes screen is displayed. The fields containing question marks are required.

5. Type My First ABAP/4 Program in the Title field. By default, the contents of this field will appear at the top of the list.

6. Type 1 in the Type field. A 1 indicates the program is a report.

7. Type an asterisk (*) in the Application field. The value in the Application field indicates to which application area this program belongs. The complete list of values can be obtained by positioning your cursor on this field and then clicking on the down-arrow to the right of it. For example, if this program belongs to Inventory management, you would put an L in the Application field. Since this is a simple test program, I have used an asterisk to indicate that this program does not belong to any particular application area.

8. Tickmark the Editor Lock check box. Enabling Editor lock will prevent changes to the program by anyone other than the creator. For your exercises, tickmark this box to safeguard your programs from accidental modification by others. However, you should *not* use this to lock actual development programs. It will prevent other programmers from maintaining them later.

9. To save the program attributes, press the Save button on the Standard toolbar. The Create Object Catalog Entry screen is displayed.

10. Press the Local Object button. The program attributes screen is redisplayed. In the status bar at the bottom of the screen, the message "Attributes for program saved" appears. (Note: the message you see will contain the program name too, but since this name will vary for each user, it is left out of the text in the book. This convention of leaving the development object name out of the message will be carried throughout the book.)

11. Press the Source Code button on the application toolbar. The ABAP/4 Editor: Edit Program screen is displayed.

12. Choose the menu path Settings->Editor Mode. The Editor: Settings screen is displayed.

13. Choose the radio button PC Mode With Line Numbering.

14. Choose the radio button Lower Case.

15. Press the Copy button (the green check mark). You have now saved your editor settings. (Editor settings only need to be set once.)

16. Look at line 1. If it does not contain the statement `report ···0201.`, type it now, as shown in Listing 2.1.

17. On line 2, type `write 'Hello SAP world'.` Use single quotes and put a period at the end of the line.

18. Press the Save button on the Standard toolbar.

19. To execute your program, choose the menu path Program->Execute. A screen with the title My First ABAP/4 Program is displayed, and the words `Hello SAP world` are written below it. This is the output of the report, also known as the *list*.

INPUT   **LISTING 2.1**   YOUR FIRST ABAP/4 PROGRAM

```
1 report ztx0201.
2 write 'Hello SAP World'.
```

The code in Listing 2.1 produces this output:

OUTPUT   `Hello SAP World`

Congratulations, you have just written your first ABAP/4 program! To return to the editor, press the green arrow button on the standard toolbar (or the F3 key).

THESE ARE THE COMMON PROBLEMS ENCOUNTERED WHILE CREATING A PROGRAM AND THEIR SOLUTIONS

Trouble	Solution
When you press the Create button, you get a dialog box saying Do Not Create Objects in the SAP Name Range.	You have entered the wrong program name. Your program names must start with y or z. Press the Cancel button (the red X) to return and enter a new program name.
When you press the Create button, you get a dialog box with an input field asking for a key.	You have entered the wrong program name. Your program names must start with y or z. Press the Cancel button (the red X) to return and enter a new program name.
You are getting a Change Request Query screen asking for a Request Number.	On the Create Object Catalog Entry screen, do not enter a value in the Development class field. Press the Local Object button instead.

▲

Exploring the Source Code Editor

In this section you will learn how to harness the power of the ABAP/4 editor. You will learn to use two screens in this section:

- ABAP/4 Editor: Initial Screen
- ABAP/4 Editor: Edit Program screen

Using the Editor: Initial Screen

The ABAP/4 Editor: Initial Screen is shown in Figure 2.3. From there, you can display or change all program components. For example, to change the source code component, choose the Source Code radio button and then press the Change button. Or, to display the attributes component, choose the Attributes radio button and then press the Display button.

NEW TERM   Pressing the Change button displays the selected component in *change mode*, which enables you to change the component.

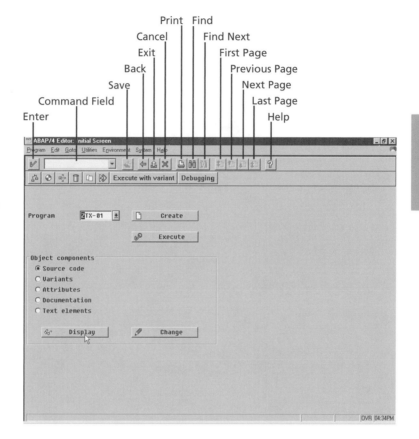

FIGURE 2.3.

From the ABAP/4 Editor: Initial Screen you can display or change program components.

 Tip

In Figure 2.3, notice that the Object Components group box encloses radio buttons, the Display button, and the Change button. When you see a group box enclosing both radio buttons and pushbuttons, the radio buttons determine the component acted upon by the enclosed pushbuttons. The effect of the radio buttons is limited by the group box; they have no effect on pushbuttons outside the box.

Exploring the Functionality of the Source Code Editor

From the ABAP/4 Editor: Initial Screen, choose the Source Code radio button and press the Change button. The ABAP/4 Editor: Edit Program screen is shown, as in Figure 2.4.

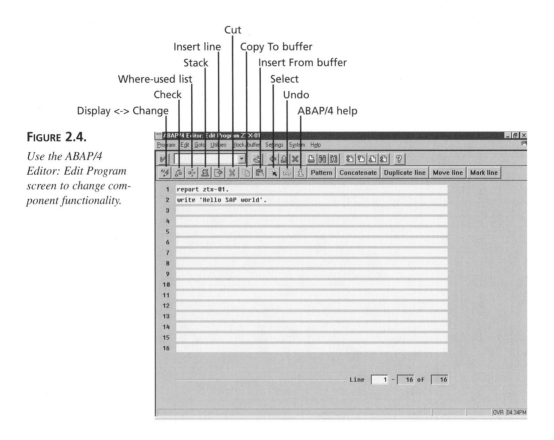

FIGURE 2.4.

Use the ABAP/4 Editor: Edit Program screen to change component functionality.

| Tip | Many developers find the R/3 user interface complex and therefore difficult to learn. I suggest that you adopt a methodical approach that enables you to become comfortable with each new screen. Whenever you come across a new screen, slowly scan the menu items and buttons. Begin at the top left corner of the screen and work down and to the right. Hold your cursor over each item long enough to read it and its accompanying ToolTip. Taking a few minutes on each new screen will help you become familiar with the functions available. |

Exploring the Standard Toolbar

SCREENCAM   Start the ScreenCam "Exploring the Standard Toolbar" now.

The Standard toolbar controls are shown in Figure 2.5.

FIGURE 2.5.

These are the controls on the Standard tool-bar within the ABAP/4 editor.

Standard toolbar controls

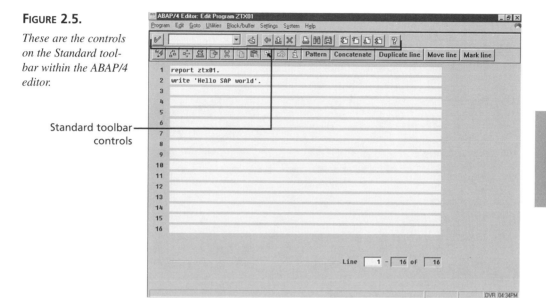

The Standard toolbar controls (refer to Figure 2.3), in order, are:

- Enter: Pressing the Enter button has the same effect as pressing the Enter key. It is also the split line function. To split a line of code, position the cursor at the point where you want to split the line and press Enter.

- Command Field: This accepts transaction codes and various other commands.

- Back and Exit: Both return you to the ABAP/4 Editor: Initial Screen. If you have unsaved changes, you will be prompted to save them.

- Cancel: Returns you to the ABAP/4 Editor: Initial Screen without saving your changes. If you have unsaved changes, you will be prompted to save them.

- Print: This will print the source code of your program. When you press it, the Print Parameters screen is displayed. To receive your output, be sure that the Print Immed. check box is checked.

- Find: Provides search and replace functionality. When you press it, the Search/Replace screen is shown. A more detailed explanation follows below.

- Find Next: This is a handy shortcut for finding the next occurrence of a string.

- First Page, Previous Page, Next Page, and Last Page: These enable you to page up and down through the source code.

• Help: Displays a dialog box from which you can obtain help about the editor and ABAP/4 syntax, among other things. Position your cursor on an ABAP/4 keyword or a blank line before pressing the Help button. For more information, see the section titled "Getting Help" later in this chapter.

Do	**Don't**
DO save your program before entering a /n command in the command field. Otherwise, you will lose your changes.	**DON'T** close the editor window by pressing the X button in the top right-hand corner of the window. You will lose unsaved changes.

Using Find and Replace

ScreenCam Start the ScreenCam "Using Find and Replace" now.

Press the Find button on the Standard toolbar and the system will display the Search/Replace screen (see Figure 2.6). Enter the string you want to find into the Find field.

Figure 2.6.

This is the Search/Replace screen. It enables you to find and change character strings in your program.

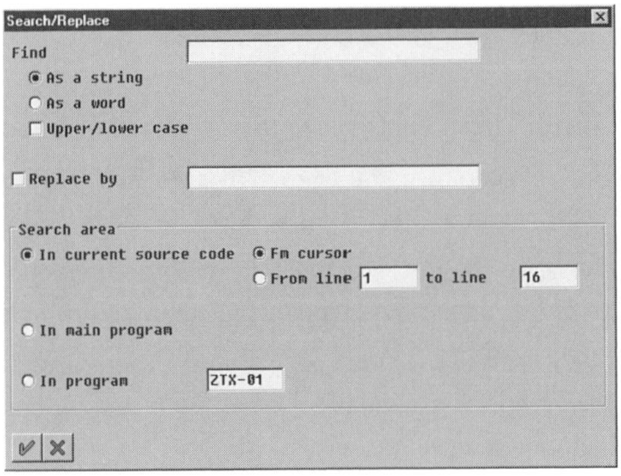

There are several options on this screen to control the find process:

• As a String will cause your string to be found anywhere in the program.

• As a Word will find it only if blanks or punctuation surround it on either side within the source code.

• Upper/Lower Case will make the search case-sensitive.

The Find field has some unusual qualities:

- To search for a string that contains embedded blanks, simply type the string along with the blanks into the Find field. Do not enclose the string in quotes. If you do, the quotes will be considered part of the search string.

- To perform a wildcard search, use the characters + and *. + will match any single character, and * will match any string of characters. However, * can only be used as a wildcard at the beginning or end of a string; within the body of a string it does not act as a wild card. For example, the search string wo+d will find word or wood; the string j++n will match john or joan, but not jan. *an will find ian, joan, or even an. Since * embedded within a string doesn't act as a wildcard, to find the string select * from, type exactly select * from. Notice that a string having * at the beginning or end produces the same results as the same string without the *; the * wildcard therefore is not particularly useful.

- - . , : ; are special characters. If your string *starts* with any of these characters, you must enclose it within delimiters. You can choose any of these same characters for a delimiter as long as it does not appear within your search string. For example, :hh begins with a special character. To find this string, enter -:hh- or .:hh. or ,:hh, or ;:hh;.

- The character # is also special. To find a string containing # anywhere within it, you must substitute ## for each # that occurs in the string. For example, to find the string a#b, use the search string a##b.

SCREENCAM Start the ScreenCam "Setting the Scope of a Search or Replace Function" now.

To set the scope for a search or replace function, follow these steps:

1. On the Search/Replace screen, type the string you want to find in the Find field.
2. Choose the In Current Source Code radio button.
3. Choose the Fm Cursor radio button to begin the search at the current cursor location. Alternatively, you can choose the From Line radio button and enter starting and ending line numbers for the search.
4. Press the Continue button. The cursor is placed to the left of the first matching string.
5. Press the Find next button to locate the next matching string.

SCREENCAM Start the ScreenCam "How to Find All Occurrences of a String" now.

To find all occurrences of a string:

1. On the Search/Replace screen, type the string you want to find in the Find field.
2. Choose the In Program radio button.
3. Press the Continue button. A summary of the occurrences found is displayed on the Global Search In Programs screen.
4. Double-click on a line to see it in the context of the source code.
5. Press the Back button to return to the Global Search In Programs screen.
6. Press the Back button once more to return to the source code editor.

ScreenCam Start the ScreenCam "How to Search and Replace in the Source Code" now.

To search and replace in the source code:

1. On the Search/Replace screen, type the string you want to find in the Find field.
2. Tickmark Replace By and enter a replacement string in the Replace by field.
3. Press the Continue button. The ABAP/4 Editor: Edit Program screen is displayed with the cursor positioned to the left of the next matching string.
4. To replace it, press the Replace button. The string at the cursor location is replaced and the cursor is positioned at the next matching string.
5. To go to the next position without replacing, press the Next Hit button. The cursor is positioned at the next matching string.
6. To replace all remaining matches from the current cursor position to the end of the source code, press the No Confirmation button.

ScreenCam Start the ScreenCam "How to Search and Replace Via a Summary Screen" now.

To search and replace via a summary screen:

1. On the Search/Replace screen, type the string you want to find in the Find field.
2. Tickmark Replace By and enter a replacement string in the Replace by field.
3. Choose the In Program radio button.
4. Press the Continue button. The Global Replace In Programs screen is displayed with the cursor positioned on the first matching string. All lines containing matching strings are displayed and the matching strings are highlighted.
5. To replace the string at the cursor position, press the Replace button. The string at the cursor location is replaced and the cursor is positioned at the next matching string.

6. To go to the next position without replacing, press the Next Hit button. The cursor is positioned at the next matching string.

7. To replace all remaining matches from the current cursor position to the end of the source code, press the No Confirmation button.

If you replaced any strings, you must save your changes before returning to the source code editor. To do so, press the Save button in the Standard toolbar, and then press the Back button. If you want to cancel your changes, press the Cancel button instead of the Save button.

Exploring the Application Toolbar

 Start the ScreenCam "Exploring the Application Toolbar of the ABAP/4 Editor" now.

Before proceeding, maximize your window (if it is not already). You may not see the buttons at the far right of the Application toolbar if your window is smaller than the maximum size.

The Application toolbar controls are shown in Figure 2.7.

FIGURE 2.7.

The Application toolbar controls.

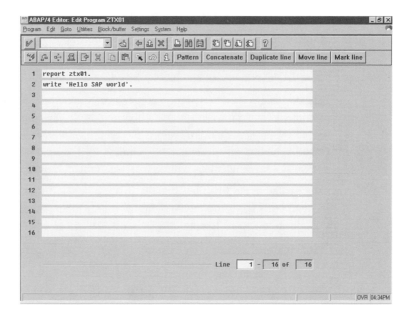

The Application toolbar controls, in the order they appear on the toolbar, are as follows:

- Display <-> Change: Changes the screen from display mode to change mode. Press it again to change it back to display mode.
- Check: Checks the syntax of the current program.
- Where-Used List: When you press this button while your cursor is on any variable name, it will display all the lines of code that use it.
- Stack: Displays the contents of the current navigation stack.
- Cut: Deletes the line containing the cursor and places it in the buffer.
- Copy To Buffer: Copies the contents of the line containing the cursor to the buffer.
- Insert From Buffer: Inserts the contents of the buffer to a new line above the current cursor position.
- Insert Line: Inserts a blank line above the current cursor position.
- Select: Selects a single line or a block of lines for moving, cutting, and pasting. Place your cursor on the first line of the block and press Select. Place your cursor on the last line of the block and press Select again. The lines contained in the block will turn red. You can now cut, copy, or duplicate the block of code the same way you did for a single line. To deselect the selected lines, choose the menu path Edit->Deselect.
- Undo: Reverses your last change. Only one level of undo is available.
- ABAP/4 Help: Provides help about the editor and about ABAP/4 in general.
- Pattern: Enables you to insert an automatically generated ABAP/4 statement. For example, to insert a write statement that writes out the contents of a variable named v1, press the Pattern button, choose the Write radio button, press the Continue button, enter the variable name in the Fld field, and then press the Copy button. A write statement will be inserted at the current cursor position.
- Concatenate: Joins two lines together. To use it, place your cursor at the end of a line and press the Concatenate button to concatenate the next one to it. To split a line, position your cursor where you want the split to occur and press the Enter key.

- Duplicate Line: Duplicates a single line or an entire block of code if one is selected (refer to the Select button, above).

- Move Line: Moves lines left and right. To move a line, put your cursor at the target position and press the Move Line button. To move a whole block of code, mark the block and place your cursor on the first line of the block at the position to which it should be moved, and then press the Move Line button. To move it to the left, place your cursor to the left of the beginning of the line and press the Move Line button.

- Mark Line: Places a bookmark on a line. You can display all marked lines with the menu path Goto -> Markers.

Tip

To bring a line to the top of the editor window, double-click between words or at the end of the line. Don't double-click on a word though; that won't work. An alternative method is to place your cursor at the end of a line and press the F2 key.

Using Cut and Paste

In most Windows applications, there is one Clipboard for cut and paste operations. In R/3, there are five clipboards. Table 2.1 describes them all.

TABLE 2.1 CUT AND PASTE BUFFERS

Called	Used for	How to Copy to It	How to Paste from It
The Buffer	Cut and paste within a program	Press the Cut or Copy buttons in the editor	Press the Insert From Buffer button
The X,Y,Z Buffers	Cut and paste between two programs	Menu path: Block/ Buffer->Copy to X Buffer	Menu path: Block/Buffer->Insert X Buffer
The Clip-board	Cut and paste between: – two R/3 sessions	Menu path: Block/Buffer-> Copy to Clipboard	Menu path: Block/Buffer->Insert from Clipboard to insert the Clipboard contents as new lines into the

continues

TABLE 2.1   CONTINUED

Called	Used for	How to Copy to It	How to Paste from It
	- R/3 and other Windows apps (e.g. Notepad)		program at the cursor position. Or Ctrl+V to paste over top of the existing lines. With Ctrl+V, data will be truncated if it won't all fit on the current screen.
	– copy code from F1 help to the editor editor – copy more than one line of code	1- Click once 2- Ctrl+Y 3- Drag and mark 4- Ctrl+C	

In the first row of Table 2.2 is program-specific buffer, simply called *the buffer*. It lets you copy within a program. To use it, place your cursor on a line or mark a block and press the Cut, Copy, or Insert From Buffer buttons. The buffer's contents are lost when you leave the editor.

The X, Y, and Z buffers are used to copy code from one program to another. Use the Block/Buffer menu to access them. Although they are three separate buffers, they are all used in the same way. Their contents are retained after you leave the editor, but they are lost when you log off.

The Clipboard is the same as the Windows Clipboard. Use it to cut and paste into other Windows applications such as MSWord or Notepad. It is also used to copy text from F1 help screens (see the following section titled "Getting Help").

In addition to the buttons on the Application toolbar and the menus, you can use standard Windows functions to perform cut and paste operations. To highlight a word or line, drag your cursor across it, or hold down the Shift key and tap the left or right arrow keys (you can only highlight one line at a time using this method). To highlight multiple lines, click once on the screen with the mouse and then press Ctrl+Y. The pointer will change to crosshairs. Drag the crosshairs to highlight the section you want to copy. Press Ctrl+C to copy the highlighted text to the Clipboard, or press Ctrl+X to cut. Paste from the Clipboard using Ctrl+V.

Using Other Convenient Editor Functions

Table 2.2 contains a summary of commonly used editor functions. All functions are accessed from the ABAP/4 Editor: Edit Program screen unless otherwise noted.

TABLE 2.2 OTHER CONVENIENT PROGRAM AND EDITOR FUNCTIONS

To...	Do...
Get help on the editor	Choose the menu path Help->Extended Help.
Get help on any ABAP/4 keyword	Put your cursor on a keyword within the code and press F1.
Save your program	Press F11.
Execute your program	Press F8.
Display function keys	Right-click anywhere in the screen area of a window.
Move the cursor to the command field	Press Ctrl+Tab.
Bring any line to the top of the screen	Double-click on whitespace (at the end of the line), or place your cursor on whitespace and press F2.
Insert a line	Press the Enter key with your cursor at the beginning or end of a line.
Delete a line	Put your cursor on the line and press the Cut button.
Mark a block of code	Place your cursor on the first line of the block and press F9 (select). Then place it on the last line of the block and press F9 again.
Delete a block of lines	Select the block and press the Cut button.
Repeat a line or block	Press the Duplicate Line button.
Split a line	Position your cursor at the split point and press the Enter key.
Join two lines together	Position your cursor at the end of the line and press the Concatenate button.
Copy lines within the current program	Mark a block. Press the Copy To Buffer button. Then position your cursor at the point where the code should be inserted, and press the Insert From Buffer button.
Copy lines to another program	Mark a block. Choose the menu path Block/Buffer->Copy to X buffer. Open a new program and choose the menu path Block/Buffer ->Insert X buffer. (You can also use the Y and Z buffers the same way.)
Copy to or from the Windows Clipboard	Mark a block. Choose the menu path Block/Buffer->Copy to clipboard. Then choose the menu path Block/Buffer->Insert clipboard.
Comment out a block of lines	Mark a block, and choose the menu path Block/Buffer->Insert comment.

continues

TABLE 2.2   CONTINUED

To...	Do...
Uncomment a block of lines	Mark a block, and choose the menu path Block/Buffer->Delete comment.
Print your program	Press the Print button.
Print your program's output	While viewing the output, choose the menu path System->List ->Print.
Find and repeat find	Press the Find and Find Next buttons.
Shift code left and right	Put your cursor on the line to be moved, in the column you want to move it to. Then press the Move Line button (F6). To move a block, position your cursor on the first line and then press the Move Line button.
Undo the last change	Press the Undo button. There is only one level of undo.
Automatically format source code	Choose the menu path Program >Pretty Printer.
Download a program to a file on your PC	Choose the menu path Utilities->Download.
Upload a program from a file on your PC	Choose the menu path Utilities->Upload.
Save a temporary copy of your program	Choose the menu path Program->Save Temp. Version. The temporary copy is deleted when you save the program.
Retrieve the temporary copy of your program	Choose the menu path Program->Get Temp. Version. You can retrieve the saved copy any number of times until you save the program.
Jump directly to the editor	From any screen, type /nse38 in the command field and press Enter.
Copy a program	From the ABAP/4 Editor: Initial Screen, choose the menu path Program->Copy.
Rename a program	From the ABAP/4 Editor: Initial Screen, choose the menu path Program->Rename.
Delete a program	From the ABAP/4 Editor: Initial Screen, choose the menu path Program->Delete.
Save your changes under a new program name	While editing a program, choose the menu path Program->Save As.
Display two programs at the same time	Starting on any screen, open a new window using the menu path System->Create new session. In the new window, go to the ABAP/4 Editor: Initial Screen, enter the second program name, and press the Display or Change button.

To...	Do...
Compare two programs for differences	From the ABAP/4 Editor: Initial Screen, choose the menu path Utilities->Splitscreen editor. Enter two program names and press the Display button. To display the first difference, press the Next Difference button. To align both programs at the next identical line, press the Align button.
Compare two programs on different systems	From the ABAP/4 Editor: InitialScreen, choose the menu path Utilities->Splitscreen editor. Press the Compare Diff. Systems button. Enter two program names and a system id and press the Display button.
Save a version of a program	From inside the editor, choose the menu path Program->Generate version. The current program is saved in the version database.
Retrieve a program version	From the Editor Initial screen, choose the menu path Utilities ->Version management. The Versions Of Object Of Type REPS screen is displayed. Deselect the active version and tickmark the version to restore. Press the Retrieve button and then press the Back button. Press the Yes button and the current version becomes the –1 generation, and a copy of the selected version becomes the current version.
Compare program versions	From the Editor Initial screen, choose the menu path Utilities ->Version management. The Versions Of Object Of Type REPS screen is displayed. Tickmark the versions you want to compare and press the Compare button. The Compare Programs: All screen is displayed. Scroll down to view the differences.
Print your program	Choose the menu path Program->Print. On the next screen, specify a printer and tickmark the Print Immed. check box.

Getting Help

 Start the ScreenCam "Getting Help" now.

For a complete tutorial on the editor:

1. Go to the ABAP/4 Editor: Edit Program screen.

2. Choose the menu path Help->Extended Help. The SAP R/3 Help screen is displayed.

3. Click on the text ABAP/4 Editor. The BC ABAP/4 Development Workbench Tools screen is displayed.

4. Click on any underlined text for help on that topic.

NEW TERM There are two basic types of help in the editor, *F1 help* and *R/3 Library help*. F1 help is also known as the *ABAP/4 keyword documentation*.

F1 help describes the syntax of ABAP/4 keywords and gives examples of their use. It is text-based and resides in tables within the R/3 database.

R/3 Library help is far more extensive and contains overviews of and procedures for creating development objects. It is Windows-based help and resides outside of the R/3 database, usually on a CD-ROM.

Obtaining F1 Help

F1 help is useful for looking up syntax and often contains useful code samples.

To obtain F1 help:

1. Go to the ABAP/4 Editor: Edit Program screen.
2. Place your cursor on the ABAP/4 keyword you want help for.
3. Press F1. The Display Hypertext screen is displayed.

Within F1 help, highlighted words are hypertext links. Clicking on them takes you to more information.

Tip You can use the *FindIt* utility on the CD-ROM to find even more code samples.

Within the help there are often code samples. To cut and paste them into your program, press Ctrl+Y, and then mark a block of code by dragging your cursor across it from the top left-hand corner to the bottom right-hand corner. Let go of the mouse and press Ctrl+C. Press the Back button to return to the ABAP/4 Editor: Edit Program screen and paste into your program using Block/Buffer->Insert Clipboard. Or you can paste *over top of your code* using Ctrl+V. (Ctrl+V doesn't paste *into* the source, it pastes *onto* the screen, so it won't paste past the bottom of the visible page.)

Obtaining R3 Library Help

R/3 Library help is stored in Windows help files. To view it:

1. From any screen, choose the menu path Help->R/3 Library. The R/3 System Online Help screen is displayed.

2. For help on ABAP/4, click on the text Basis Components. The Basis screen is displayed.

3. Click on the text ABAP/4 Development Workbench. The ABAP/4 Development Workbench screen is displayed.

4. From here you can get detailed help on almost any aspect of programming in ABAP/4. Click on the topic that you want help for.

Additionally, help can be obtained from the ABAP/4 Editor: Initial Screen. To view it:

1. Go to the ABAP/4 Editor: Initial Screen.

2. Choose the menu path Utilities->ABAP/4 key word doc. The Display Structure: ABAP/4—SAP's 4GL Program Language screen is displayed.

3. Press the Find button on the Application toolbar. The Search Chapter Titles screen is displayed.

4. Type the text you want to find in the Find field.

5. Press the Continue button. The first line containing that text is highlighted.

6. Double-click on the highlighted line to display more information, or press the Continue Search button on the Standard toolbar to locate the next occurrence.

Help can also be obtained from within the editor while you are editing the source code. Choose the menu path Utilities->Help on. Here, you can get the following types of help:

- Editor help
- ABAP/4 overview
- ABAP/4 keyword
- New features of the ABAP/4 language
- Display function modules
- Display table structures
- Display logical databases
- Display authorization objects
- Display infotypes

Finding Your Development Objects

SCREENCAM Start the ScreenCam "Finding Your Development Objects" now.

To display all of the development objects you have created in the R/3 system:

1. From the ABAP/4 Development Workbench screen, press the Object Browser button. The Object Browser: Initial Screen is displayed.

2. Choose the radio button Local Priv. Objects.

3. Press the Display pushbutton. The Object Browser: Development Class $TMP screen is displayed. Here you will see a list of development object categories. To the left of each category is a plus sign.

4. Click once on a plus sign to expand the node.

5. Double-click on an object name to display it. If the object you double-clicked on was a program, a tree view of the program and its components is displayed.

6. To display the program source code, double-click on the name of the program at the top of the tree. The ABAP/4 Editor: Display Program screen is displayed.

You are now in display mode on the selected object. You can press the Display <-> Change button to switch into edit mode.

Note

This method only works for objects that have been saved as *local* objects. They will be displayed here only if you pressed the Local Object button on the Create Object Catalog Entry screen when you created the object.

If you are looking for a program and you know the first few characters of its name, you can find it from the ABAP/4 Editor: Initial Screen. To do this:

1. Go to the ABAP/4 Editor: Initial Screen.

2. In the Program field, type the first few characters of your program name followed by an asterisk. For example, to display all programs beginning with ztx, type ztx*.

3. Click on the down-arrow to the right of the Program field. The Programs screen is displayed. A list of matching program names appears on this screen. To the right of each program name is the Short description from the program attributes.

4. Double-click on the program name you want to edit. The ABAP/4 Editor: Initial Screen is displayed, and the program name you double-clicked on appears in the Program field.

Introducing the R/3 Data Dictionary

NEW TERM The *R/3 Data Dictionary* (or *DDIC* for short) is a utility for defining data objects. Using the DDIC, you can create and store objects such as tables, structures, and views. To invoke the Data Dictionary, perform these steps:

1. Go to the ABAP/4 Development Workbench screen.

2. Press the ABAP/4 Dictionary button in the Standard toolbar. The Dictionary: Initial Screen is displayed, as shown in Figure 2.8.

2

FIGURE 2.8.

The Dictionary: Initial Screen.

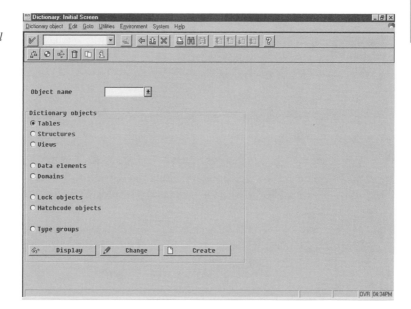

NEW TERM The DDIC is within the R/3 system. You can think of it as sitting on top of a database such as Oracle or Informix and acting like a remote control, generating and sending SQL statements to it. For example, you might create a table definition in the DDIC. When you *activate* the table definition, SQL statements are generated and sent to the RDBMS, causing it to create the actual table in the database. When you want to modify the table, you must modify the table definition in the DDIC. When you activate the table again, more SQL is generated causing the RDBMS to modify the table.

Do	Don't
DO use the DDIC to create and modify all database objects.	**DON'T** modify a table or anything else at the RDBMS level. The Data Dictionary definition cannot update itself and it will be out of sync with the database. This can cause application errors and even lead to a loss of data integrity.

Exploring Tables and Structures

NEW TERM   In R/3 a *table* is a collection of rows. Each row contains fields, also called *columns*. Normally, within a table, each row has the same number of columns as the other rows of the table.

A table holds persistent data. In other words, if you put data into a table, it remains there after your program ends. It will remain there until it is changed or deleted by your program or another program. The name of a table is unique within the entire R/3 system.

When you look at a table in the DDIC, you are looking at the description of a table in the underlying database. You are not looking directly at the database table itself. Figure 2.9 shows how a table definition appears in the R/3 DDIC.

FIGURE 2.9.

The DDIC definition for table lfa1.

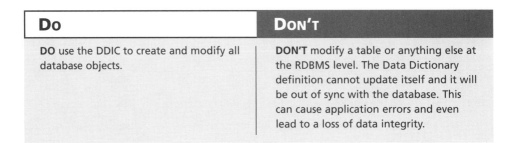

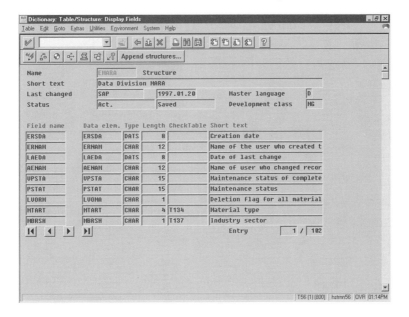

NEW TERM In R/3 a *structure* is a description of a group of fields. It describes the field names, their sequence, and their data types and lengths. Each structure has a name that is unique within the entire R/3 system. A structure cannot have the same name as a table.

A structure name can be used in two ways:

- In a program, a structure name can be used to allocate memory for a group of fields.
- In a table, a structure name can be used to describe a set of fields.

Strictly speaking, a structure is something that only exists within the R/3 Data Dictionary. If you see the word *structure*, you should immediately think "DDIC structure." However, some SAP documentation uses the word structure to also refer to a group of variables within a program. The structure emara is shown in Figure 2.10 as an example of how a structure appears in the DDIC.

FIGURE 2.10.

The DDIC definition for structure emara.

In R/3, tables and structures are both defined in the DDIC. You will notice however, when viewing them, there is very little difference between them. That is because in R/3, a table is just a *description* of an actual database table. It is the *structure of the table in the database*. So, both tables and structures within the DDIC define a layout—a series of fields. The major difference between the two is that a table has an underlying database table associated with it. A structure does not.

Some people find the R/3 documentation confusing at times, since SAP occasionally uses these two terms interchangeably.

Displaying a Table or Structure Definition

To display a table or structure definition in the DDIC:

1. Go to the Dictionary: Initial Screen.
2. Enter the table or structure name in the Object Name field.
3. Click the Tables or Structures radio button.
4. Click the Display button. The Dictionary: Table/Structure: Display Fields screen is displayed, as shown in Figures 2.9 and 2.10.

What you see in Figure 2.9 is the *structure* of table lfa1 in the R/3 Data Dictionary, not the actual database table. In R/3, only a table's structure can be defined, along with some attributes such as the primary key fields.

Displaying Data in the Table

R/3 also provides a utility to enable you to display data that exists within a table. To use it:

1. Go to the Dictionary: Table/Structure: Display Fields screen.
2. Choose the menu path Utilities->Table contents. The Data Browser: Table: Selection Screen is displayed.
3. To display *all* of the rows in the table, press the Execute button without entering any search criteria. The Data Browser: Table Select Entries screen is displayed (see Figure 2.11).

The number of records displayed is limited by the value in the Maximum No. Of Hits field on the Data Browser: Table: Selection Screen.

Caution   Don't blank out the Maximum No. Of Hits field to display all records unless you actually intend to look through the entire list. For large tables, this can consume a lot of CPU on both the database and application servers and also significantly increase network traffic, thereby slowing down the system. If such a large report is needed, it should usually be run in batch. The preferred approach is to narrow down your search by entering values into the fields on the Data Browser: Table: Selection Screen. This will be covered in detail in a later chapter.

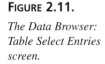

FIGURE 2.11.

The Data Browser:
Table Select Entries
screen.

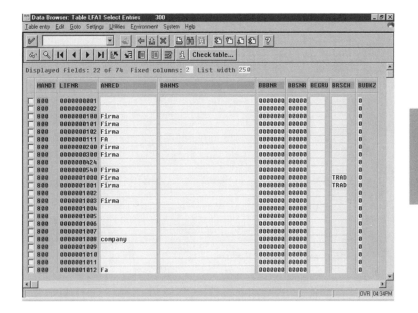

Determining Displayed Fields

You can control which fields are displayed on the Data Browser: Table: Selection Screen.
To do so:

1. Go to the Data Browser: Table: Selection Screen.
2. Choose the menu path Settings->Fields for selection. The Choose Fields For
   Selection screen is displayed.
3. Tickmark the fields you want included on the Data Browser: Table: Selection
   Screen. Uncheck any that you don't want to appear.
4. Press the Execute button. The Data Browser: Table: Selection Screen is displayed
   and contains the fields you selected.

Understanding ABAP/4 Syntax

Before continuing, you should now run the exercise setup utility supplied on the
CD-ROM. It will create the tables and data needed for the exercises in this book. For
instructions, see the `readme.txt` file located in the root directory of the CD-ROM.

Introducing the `select` Statement

The `select` statement retrieves records from the database.

Syntax for the `select` Statement

▼ SYNTAX

The following code shows simplified syntax for the `select` statement:

```
select * from t1 [into wa] [where f1 op v1 and/or f2 op v2 ...][order by
f1].
    (other abap/4 statements)
    endselect.
```

where:

* indicates that all fields in the table should be retrieved.

t1 is the name of a table previously defined on a `tables` statement.

wa is the name of work area that matches the structure of the table.

f1 is the name of a field in table *t1*.

op is one of the following logical operators: = <> > >= < <=.

v1 is a literal or variable.

and/or is either the word and or the word or.

Create a new program and name it •••0202. Enter the code as shown in Listing 2.2.

INPUT   **LISTING 2.2**   YOUR SECOND PROGRAM

```
1 report ztx0202.
2 tables ztxlfa1.
3 select * from ztxlfa1 into ztxlfa1 order by lifnr.
4     write / ztxlfa1-lifnr.
5     endselect.
```

The code in Listing 2.2 should produce this output:

OUTPUT
```
1000
1010
1020
1030
1040
1050
1060
1070
1080
1090
2000
V1
V10
```

```
V11
V12
V2
V3
V4
V5
V6
V7
V8
V9
```

Note

> Lfa1 is the vendor master table in R/3. Ztxlfa1 was created by the CD-ROM setup routine and is similar to lfa1, but is used for the exercises in this book. The field lifnr is the vendor number field.

ANALYSIS This program reads all the records from table ztxlfa1 and writes out the contents of the field lifnr (the vendor number) in ascending order.

- On line 1, the report statement is required as the first line of a report.

- On line 2, the tables statement does two things. First, it allocates a memory area (called a work area) named ztxlfa1. The work area has the same layout as the DDIC definition of table ztxlfa1. Secondly, it gives the program access to the database table ztxlfa1.

- On line 3, the select statement begins a loop. The endselect on line 5 marks the end of the loop. The lines of code between select and endselect are executed once for each row returned from the database.

- On line 4, the write statement is executed once for each row that is read from the table. The / (slash) after write begins a new line.

Notice that in your program, you have *two* things named ztxlfa1: a work area and a table. Both have the same name—ztxlfa1. The position of the name ztxlfa1 within a statement determines to which one you refer. On line 3, the first occurrence of ztxlfa1 refers to the database table. The second occurrence refers to the work area.

AVI Start the "AVI Select Statement Processing" now.

Processing proceeds as follows (see Figure 2.12):

1. Pressing F8 to execute the program causes a request to be sent from the SAPGUI to the dispatcher on the application server to execute program ztx0202.

2. The request is dispatched to the first available work process.

3. The user context is rolled into the work process.

4. The program is retrieved from the database.

5. The work process allocates a roll area to hold the program's variables, current program pointer, and private memory allocations.

6. The program is interpreted by the work process on the application server and begins executing on line 3. (Lines 1 and 2 are declarations, not executable code.)

7. Line 3 causes a row to be read from database table ztxlfa1 and placed into the work area named ztxlfa1.

8. The first time line 4 is executed, a virtual page is allocated for the list.

9. Line 4 causes the field lifnr to be written from the work area ztxlfa1 to the virtual page.

10. Line 5 loops back to line 3.

11. The next row is read from table ztxlfa1 and is placed into the work area ztxlfa1, overwriting the previous row.

12. The field lifnr is written to the next line of the virtual page.

13. Steps 9 through 11 are repeated for all rows in table ztxlfa1.

14. The loop ends automatically when the last row is read from ztxlfa1.

15. The program ends, but the roll area (containing the virtual page) remains allocated.

16. The work process determines the number of lines that the user's screen is capable of displaying, and sends that many lines from the virtual page as the first page of the list to the presentation server.

17. The user context and roll area are rolled out of the work process.

If the user then presses Page Down, processing proceeds as follows (see Figure 2.13):

1. Pressing Page Down causes a request to be sent from the SAPGUI to the dispatcher on the application server to get the next page of output from ztx0202.

2. The request is dispatched to the first available work process.

3. The user context and roll area for ztx0202 are rolled into the work process.

4. The work process sends the next page to the presentation server.

5. The roll area and user context are rolled out of the work process.

FIGURE 2.12.

This is how the select *statement works.*

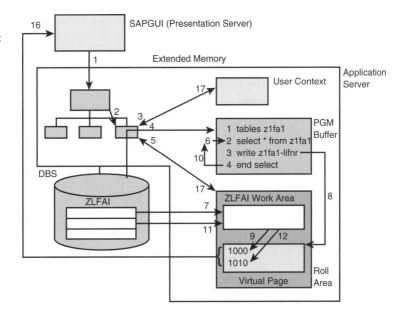

FIGURE 2.13.

This is the sequence of events triggered when the user presses page down.

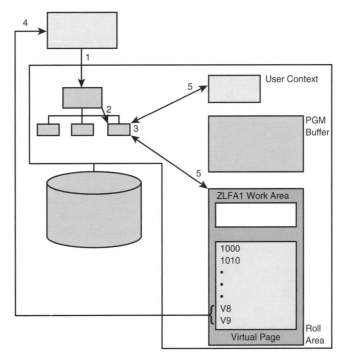

If the user then presses Back, processing proceeds as follows:

1. Pressing Back causes a request to be sent from the SAPGUI to the dispatcher on the application server to end program ztx0202.

2. The request is dispatched to the first available work process.

3. The user context and roll area for ztx0202 are rolled into the work process.

4. The system frees the roll area for the program.

5. The user context is rolled out.

> **Tip**
> To open a new R/3 window (called a *session*), from any screen choose the menu path System->Create New Session. You can open a maximum of six sessions. If you want to open more than six, simply log on a second time.

Understanding Table Work Areas

NEW TERM On line 3 of Listing 2.2, the words into ztxlfa1 are optional. If you leave them off, the work area of the same name as the table is used. In other words, the current row automatically goes into the ztxlfa1 work area. For this reason, it is known as the *default table work area*. In this case, the work area ztxlfa1 is the default work area for table ztxlfa1. Hence, the code in Listing 2.2 can be simplified to that shown in Listing 2.3.

INPUT **LISTING 2.3** YOUR SECOND PROGRAM SIMPLIFIED

```
1 report ztx0203.
2 tables ztxlfa1.
3 select * from ztxlfa1 order by lifnr.
4    write / ztxlfa1-lifnr.
5    endselect.
```

Compared to Listing 2.2, only line 3 has changed. This program works in exactly the same way and produces the same output as the previous one. Since no into clause is specified on the select statement, the system uses the default table work area ztxlfa1.

> **Tip**
> To copy a program, choose the menu path Program->Copy from the editor initial screen. Alternatively, while editing a program, you can choose the menu path Program->Save As.

Using An Explicit Work Area

The `tables` statement always creates a default table work area, so you usually do not have to define your own. In some cases however, you might want to define an additional table work area. For example, if you wanted to keep the original version of a row and have a modified version too, you would need two work areas.

You can define additional table work areas using the `data` statement.

Simplified Syntax for the `data` Statement

▼ SYNTAX

Below is the simplified syntax for the `data` statement.

```
data wa like t1.
```

where:

- *wa* is the name of a table work area you want to define

▲

- *t1* is the name of a table you want to pattern your work area after

Listing 2.4 shows how to use the `data` statement to create a new work area.

INPUT **LISTING 2.4** USING YOUR OWN TABLE WORK AREA

```
1 report ztx0204.
2 tables ztxlfa1.
3 data wa like ztxlfa1.
4 select * from ztxlfa1 into wa order by lifnr.
5     write / wa-lifnr.
6     endselect.
```

The code in Listing 2.4 should produce the same output as the previous two listings (see the output from Listing 2.3). Please note that in this example it is not necessary to define a new work area—one is used only to illustrate the concept.

ANALYSIS

- Line 3 defines a new work area named wa like the DDIC structure `ztxlfa1`.
- Line 4 reads one row at a time from table `ztxlfa1` into work area wa *instead* of the default table work area.
- Line 5 writes the row out from wa instead of `ztxlfa1`.

NEW TERM

When you explicitly name a work area on the `select` statement (such as `into` wa on line 5), that work area is called an *explicit work area*.

Introducing the where Clause

To restrict the number of rows returned from the database, a where clause can be added to the select statement. For example, to retrieve vendors that have vendor numbers less than 2000, use the code in Listing 2.5.

INPUT   **LISTING 2.5**   RESTRICTING THE VENDORS SELECTED

```
1 report ztx0205.
2 tables ztxlfa1.
3 select * from ztxlfa1 where lifnr < '0000002000' order by lifnr.
4     write / ztxlfa1-lifnr.
5     endselect.
```

The code in Listing 2.5 should produce this output:

OUTPUT
```
1000
1010
1020
1030
1040
1050
1060
1070
1080
1090
```

ANALYSIS This program reads all of the records from table ztxlfa1 where the vendor number is less than 2000, and writes out the contents of the field lifnr (the vendor number). In the database, lifnr is a character field containing numeric values that are right justified and padded on the left with zeros. Therefore, the value to be compared with lifnr should have the same format and data type to avoid data conversion and ensure the intended results are obtained.

Note that to code a character literal in ABAP/4 (such as '0000002000' on line 3), you must enclose the character string within *single* quotes.

Working with System Variables

NEW TERM The R/3 system makes *system variables* available within your program. You don't have to define anything to access them, they are always available, and are automatically updated by the system as your program's environment changes. All system variables begin with the prefix sy-. For example, the current system date is available in the system field sy-datum, and the current time in sy-uzeit. They are usually called *sy* fields (pronounced *sigh fields*) for short.

All system variables are defined in the DDIC structure syst. Do not define syst in your program though; its fields are automatically available within every program.

> **Note**
>
> System variable names can be coded using either the prefix sy- or syst-. For example, sy-datum can also be coded as syst-datum; they are functionally equivalent. Sy- is the preferred form, although you will occasionally see syst- in older programs. Syst is the *only* structure that has a duality of prefixes. For all others, you must use the full structure name as the prefix.

Two system variables are very useful to know when coding the select statement:

- sy-subrc
- sy-dbcnt

Discovering sy-subrc

NEW TERM To determine if the select statement returned any rows, test the value of the system variable *sy-subrc* (pronounced *sigh-sub-are-see*) after the endselect statement. If rows were found, the value of sy-subrc will be 0. If no rows were found, the value will be 4. (See Listing 2.6.)

INPUT **LISTING 2.6** USING sy-subrc TO DETERMINE IF ANY ROWS WERE SELECTED

```
1 report ztx0206.
2 tables ztxlfa1.
3 select * from ztxlfa1 where lifnr > 'Z'.
4     write / ztxlfa1-lifnr.
5     endselect.
6 if sy-subrc <> 0.
7     write / 'No records found'.
8     endif.
```

The code in Listing 2.6 produces this output:

OUTPUT
```
No records found
```

ANALYSIS The select statement on line 3 is restricted by a where clause. In this case, no rows match the criteria in the where clause, so after the endselect, the value of sy-subrc is set to 4.

> Many keywords assign values to sy-subrc. Some keywords do not set it at all. If a keyword sets sy-subrc, the values that it can have are documented in the F1 help for that keyword.

If you have coded a select and want to test the value of sy-subrc, your test must come *after* the endselect. Why? The answer lies in the fact that the code between the select and endselect is executed once for each row returned from the database.

If zero rows are returned from the database, the code between select and endselect is never executed. Therefore, you must code the test for sy-subrc *after* the endselect.

> Sy-subrc is *not* automatically initialized to zero when your program starts. However, this should never be a concern, because you should not check it until after a statement that sets it has executed.

Discovering sy-dbcnt

To determine the number of rows returned by a select statement, test the value of *sy-dbcnt* after the endselect. You can also use it as a loop counter; between the select and endselect it contains a count of the current iteration. For the first row, sy-dbcnt will be 1, for the second it will be 2, and so on. After the endselect, it will retain its value and so it will contain the number of rows selected. For example, to print sequential numbers beside each vendor and to print a total of the number of rows selected at the bottom of the report, use the code in Listing 2.7.

LISTING 2.7 USING sy-dbcnt TO COUNT ROWS RETURNED FROM THE select STATEMENT

```
1 report ztx0207.
2 tables ztxlfa1.
3 select * from ztxlfa1 order by lifnr.
4    write / sy-dbcnt.
5    write ztxlfa1-lifnr.
6    endselect.
7 write / sy-dbcnt.
8 write 'records found'.
```

The code in Listing 2.7 produces this output:

OUTPUT		
	1	1000
	2	1010
	3	1020
	4	1030
	5	1040
	6	1050
	7	1060
	8	1070
	9	1080
	10	1090
	11	2000
	12	V1
	13	V10
	14	V11
	15	V12
	16	V2
	17	V3
	18	V4
	19	V5
	20	V6
	21	V7
	22	V8
	23	V9
	23	records found

ANALYSIS

- Line 4 writes the value of sy-dbcnt for each row that is returned by the select. The slash (/) begins a new line, so each sy-dbcnt begins on a new line.

- Line 5 writes the value of ztxlfa1-lifnr on the same line as sy-dbcnt.

Displaying the syst Structure

There are two ways to display the components of structure syst:

- From the ABAP/4 Editor: Edit Program screen, double-click on the name of any sy field within your code

- Go to the Data Dictionary, enter syst, select the radio button Structure, and press the Display button

To find fields within the structure, press the Find button on the Standard toolbar, and enter the field name you want to find.

If you don't know the name of the field you want to find, but rather wish to find one by description, you can search the descriptions also.

SCREENCAM Start the ScreenCam "How to Search Through Field Descriptions" now.

To search through field descriptions, use this procedure:

1. Begin at the Dictionary: Table/Structure: Display fields screen.

2. Choose the menu path Table->Print. A dialog box will appear asking you which components you wish to print.

3. Tickmark all check boxes and press the Continue button. A dialog box will appear asking you for print parameters.

4. Press the Print Preview button. The dialog box will close and a list having a small font will appear.

5. Choose the menu path Goto->List Display. The list will change into a larger, fixed-space font.

6. In the command field, type %sc and press the Enter key. The Find dialog box will appear.

7. Type the text you want to find and press the Enter key. A list of matches will appear, and each match will be highlighted.

8. Click once on a highlighted word to jump immediately to that line in the list. If you wish to find another occurrence of the text, go to step 6 of this procedure.

Using the Chain Operator

NEW TERM The colon (:) is called the *chain operator*. Use it to combine lines of code that begin with the same word or sequence of words. Place the common part at the beginning of the statement followed by a colon. Then place the ending parts of the statements after it, each separated by a comma.

For example, to define two tables, you could code this:

```
tables ztxlfa1.
tables ztxlfb1.
```

Or, you could use the chain operator, like this:

```
tables: ztxlfa1, ztxlfb1.
```

Functionally, the two preceding code segments are identical, and at runtime there is no difference in performance. During code generation, the second code segment is expanded into two statements, so from a functional standpoint the two programs are identical.

Chain operators should be used to improve the readability of your program. Use of the chain operator is illustrated in Listing 2.8.

LISTING 2.8   USING THE CHAIN OPERATOR TO REDUCE REDUNDANCY IN THE
write STATEMENT

```
1 report ztx0208.
2 tables ztxlfa1.
3 select * from ztxlfa1 order by lifnr.
4     write: / sy-dbcnt, ztxlfa1-lifnr.
5     endselect.
6 write: / sy-dbcnt, 'records found'.
```

The code in Listing 2.8 produces the same output as the previous program (see the output from Listing 2.7).

- Line 4 combines lines 4 and 5 from Listing 2.7 into a single line using the chain operator.
- Line 6 combines lines 7 and 8 from Listing 2.7 into a single line using the chain operator.

Using the `select single` Statement

The `select single` statement retrieves one record from the database. If you know the entire primary key of the record you wish to retrieve, `select single` is much faster and more efficient than `select/endselect`.

Syntax for the `select single` Statement

Below is the simplified syntax for the `select single` statement.

```
select * from t1 [into wa] [where f1 op v1 and/or f2 op v2 ...].
```

where:

* indicates that all fields in the table should be retrieved.

t1 is the name of a table previously defined on a `tables` statement.

wa is the name of the work area that matches the structure of the table.

f1 is the name of a field in table *t1*.

op is one of the following logical operators: = <> > >= < <=.

v1 is a literal or variable.

and/or is either the word and or the word or.

The following points apply:

- `select single` does not begin a loop because it only returns one row. Therefore, do not code an `endselect` statement. If you do, you will get a syntax error.

- To ensure that one unique row is returned, you should specify all primary key fields in the `where` clause. If you don't, your program will run, but you will get a warning. (To display the warnings, choose the menu path Program->Check ->Display Warnings.

Listing 2.9 illustrates the `select single` statement. For practice, create a new program and enter the code as shown in Listing 2.9.

INPUT   **LISTING 2.9**   THE `select single` STATEMENT

```
1 report ztx0209.
2 tables ztxlfa1.
3 select single * from ztxlfa1 where lifnr = 'V1'.
4 if sy-subrc = 0.
5    write: / ztxlfa1-lifnr, ztxlfa1-name1.
6 else.
7    write 'record not found'.
8    endif.
```

The code in Listing 2.9 produces this output:

```
    V1        Quantity First Ltd.
```

  Line 3 finds vendor V1 in table ztxlfa1. Because only one row is returned, `order by` is not needed, and neither is `endselect`.

Commenting Code and Formal Documentation

There are two ways to put comments into your code:

- An * (asterisk) in column one indicates that the entire line is a comment. It will turn red within the editor to indicate that it is a full-line comment.

- " (double quotes) anywhere on a line indicates that the remainder of the line is a comment. The comment will not turn red as it does for a full-line comment.

For example:

```
* This is a comment
tables ztxlfa1.    " This is also a comment
```

There is no end-comment character. In other words, when you begin a comment, the remainder of the line will be a comment only. No more code can follow on that line. The comment ends at the end of the current line.

Aside from comments, you can formally document your code in the documentation component of the program. To do so, go to the Editor Initial screen, click on the Documentation radio button, and press Change. Type in your documentation and press Save.

2

Summary

- ABAP/4 programs are composed of components. The components are attributes, source code, variants, text elements and documentation. As a minimum, a program must have attributes and source code.

- ABAP/4 reports must begin with the report statement.

- The tables statement allocates a default table work area and also gives the program access to the database table of the same name.

- The select statement retrieves rows from a database table. Use select single to retrieve one row. Use select/endselect to retrieve multiple rows.

- select/endselect forms a loop. The code in the loop is executed once for each table row that satisfies the where clause. The loop ends automatically when all rows have been processed. If you don't specify an into clause, each row is placed into the default table work area and it overwrites the previous row. sy-subrc is set to 0 if any rows were selected, and set to 4 if no rows were selected. sy-dbcnt is incremented by 1 each time through the loop, and after the endselect it contains the number of rows retrieved.

- The chain operator is a colon (:). It is used to reduce redundancy where two or more statements begin with the same word or sequence of words.

Q&A

Q If I'm editing a program, what happens to my changes if I get disconnected from R/3; for example, if my PC freezes and I have to reboot? Will I lose my changes?

A If you log on again within 5 or 10 minutes, you can reconnect to your session. When you log on again, enter your user ID and password but *don't press the Enter key on the logon screen;* instead, choose the menu path User->Copy Session. You will be reconnected to your previous session and everything will be restored to the way it was when you lost your connection.

Q Is there an AutoSave feature in the editor like the one in MSWord?

A No. But when you want to save you can just press the F11 key.

Q Sometimes when I edit a program, I get a dialog box with the message "Program was temporarily buffered (possibly due to a system error/failure) Choose one of the following options." Why do I see it, and what should I do?

A It means that there are two copies of your program in the system: the "real" one and a temporary one. The temporary one is created when you execute your program without first saving it. It is normally deleted when you return to the editor and save your changes, but if you abnormally exit from the editor, it will remain. For example, you could modify your program, and then execute it right away without saving it. If your program produced a short dump, you would then need to press the Exit button and you would be returned to the Workbench. Your editor session would be gone. There are now two versions of your program in the database: the changed version (the one you just executed) and the original. (The changed version is stored under a temporary name consisting of ! and the last seven characters of your program name.) If you now return to the editor and attempt to edit your program again, the system will detect the presence of both versions in the database and display a dialog box asking you which version you want to edit, the saved one or the temporary one. To display the temporary copy (the one you executed) simply press the Continue button.

Q When I copy an entire program, the `report` statement still has the old report name on it. But if I run it, it runs without error. Shouldn't it give me an error?

A The program name on the `report` statement is required, but it doesn't have to match the actual program name. It's for documentation only.

Q Every time I log off R/3 I get a message box that says "Unsaved data will be lost"—even after I've saved everything. Why?

A Despite its wording, this message doesn't mean that there is unsaved data that will be lost. It means "If you haven't saved your data, it will be lost." The best thing to do is just ignore it. Everyone else does.

Q Can I nest `select` statements inside each other?

A Yes, you can, but most of the time you shouldn't because it can be extremely inefficient. A better alternative is to use a database *view*.

Workshop

The following exercises will give you practice using the editor and writing simple programs using the `tables`, `select`, and `write` statements. The answers are in Appendix B, "Answers to Quiz Questions and Exercises."

Quiz

1. What two things does the `tables` statement do?
2. To what does the term *default table work area* refer?
3. If the `select` statement is missing an `into` clause, where do the rows go?
4. If a `write` statement does not contain a slash, is the output written to the same line as the output for the previous write statement or is it written to a new line?
5. What is the name of the system variable that indicates whether any rows were found by the `select` statement?
6. What is the name of the system variable that indicates how many rows were found by the `select` statement?
7. Refer to Listing 2.6. If there are 30 rows in table `ztxlfa1`, how many times is line 4 executed?
8. Refer to Listing 2.6. If table `ztxlfa1` is empty (if it contains 0 rows), how many times is line 4 executed?

Editor Exercises

In the following exercise, you will copy a program, correct errors in the code, merge new code into it, execute it, print it, download it, upload it, create a version, and compare versions. Refer to Table 2.3 when necessary.

1. Copy program `zty0200a` to program ●●●`0200a`. To perform the copy, use the Copy button found on the Application toolbar of the ABAP/4 Editor: Initial Screen.

```
report zty0200a.
select * from ztxlfa1.
    write / ztxlfa1-lifnr.
    endselect.
    endselect.    " intentional duplicate line

report zty0200b.
    if sy-subrc <> 0.
        write: / 'no records found'.
        endif.
```

2. Edit program ●●●`0200a`. Correct the report name on the `report` statement.

3. Insert a new line after line 1. Type the appropriate `tables` statement on that line.

4. Get help for the `tables` statement. (Put your cursor on the `tables` statement and press F1.)

5. Return from help back to your program. (Press the Back button in the Application toolbar.)

6. Display the function key assignments. (Right-click anywhere in the screen area of the window.)

7. Bring line 3 to the top of the screen. (Double-click on whitespace on line 3, not on a word.)

8. Delete line 6. (Place your cursor on line 6 and press the Cut button on the Application toolbar.)

9. Open a new session and display program `zty0200b`. (Choose the menu path System->Create session. A new SAP R/3 window is displayed. Choose the menu path Tools->ABAP/4 Workbench. The ABAP/4 Development Workbench screen is displayed. Press the ABAP/4 Editor button on the Application toolbar. In the Program Name field, type **zty0200b**. Press the Display button.)

10. Mark lines 2 through 4 using the Select button. (Place your cursor on line 2. Press the Select button in the Application toolbar. Line 2 turns blue. Place your cursor on line 4. Press the Select button again. Lines 2 through 4 are marked in blue.)

11. Copy the marked block to the X buffer. (Choose the menu path Block/Buffer ->Copy to X Buffer.)

12. Switch back to the window in which program •••0200a is displayed.

13. Paste the lines from the X buffer after line 5. (Place your cursor on line 6. Choose the menu path Block/Buffer->Insert X Buffer.)

14. Mark the block of lines 6 through 8. (Place your cursor on line 6. Press the Select button on the Application toolbar. Place your cursor on line 8. Press the Select button again.)

15. Move the block four spaces to the left, aligning the `if` statement with the `select` statement. (Place your cursor on line 6 in column 1. Press the Move Line button on the Application toolbar.)

16. Choose the menu path Program->Save As and save your modified program as •••0200b.

17. Display program •••0200b using the menu path Program->Other Program.

18. Correct the program name in the `report` statement. (Change •••0200a to •••0200b on line 1.)

19. Select lines 3 through 5. (Place your cursor on line 3. Press the Select button on the Application toolbar. Place your cursor on line 5. Press the Select button again.)

20. Copy the selected block to the program-internal buffer. (Press the Copy To Buffer button on the Application toolbar.)

21. Paste the block you just copied at the end of your program. (Place your cursor on line 9 and press the Insert From Buffer button on the Application toolbar.)

22. Paste the same block again at the end of your program. (Place your cursor on line 12 and press the Insert From Buffer button on the Application toolbar.)

23. Undo the last paste. (Press the Undo button on the Application toolbar.)

24. Type the following code on lines 12 through 14. Begin each line in column 1.
```
if sy-dbcnt > 0.
write: / sy-dbcnt, 'records found'.
endif.
```

25. Automatically fix the indentation by choosing the menu path Program->Pretty Printer.

26. Save your program. (Press the Save button.)

27. Return to the ABAP/4 Editor: Initial Screen and document your program. (Press the Back button on the Standard toolbar. Choose the Documentation radio button. Press the Change button.)

28. Save your documentation and return to editing the source code. (Press the Save button. Press the Back button. Choose the Source Code radio button. Type •••0200b in the Program field. Press the Change pushbutton.)

29. Display the components of the SYST structure by double-clicking on a sy field. (Double-click on the word sy-subrc on line 6. The SYST structure is displayed.)

30. Return to editing your program. (Press the Back button.)

31. Find the first occurrence of the string ztxlfa1 in your program. (Press the Find button. The Search/Replace screen is displayed. Type **ztxlfa1** in the Find field. Press the From Line radio button. Press the Continue button.)

32. Repeat the find, finding each successive occurrence until you find them all. (Press the Find Next button repeatedly until the message "String *write* not found" displays in the status bar at the bottom of the window.)

33. Add the table name ztxlfa1 to the tables statement. (Change the tables statement so that it reads tables: ztxlfa1, ztxlfb1.)

34. Replace all occurrences of the string ztxlfa1 on lines 10 and 11 with the string ztxlfb1 using the Search/Replace function. (Put your cursor on line 10. Press the

Select button. Put your cursor on line 11. Press the Select button. Lines 10 and 11 are now marked as a block in red. Press the Find button. The Search/Replace screen is displayed. Type `ztxlfa1` in the Find field. Tickmark the Replace By check box. Type `ztxlfb1` in the Replace By field. Press the Continue button. The ABAP/4 Editor: Edit Program screen is displayed. Press the No Confirmation button. All occurrences of the string within the marked block are replaced.)

35. Use a function key to save your program, and another function key to execute it. (Press F11. Press F8.)

36. Save the list output to a file on your hard drive by choosing the menu path List ->Save->File. Use unconverted format.

37. Display your downloaded output using Notepad.

38. Return to editing your code. (Press the Back button.)

39. Download your program to the file `c:\temp\•••0200b.txt`. (Choose the menu path Utilities->Download. The Transfer to a Local File screen is displayed. Type `c:\temp\•••0200b.txt` in the File Name field. Press the OK button. The message "277 bytes transferred" appears in the status bar at the bottom of the window.)

40. Edit your downloaded program using Notepad. Add a full-line comment after the report statement with your name on it. (Insert a new line after the `report` statement: `*Created by Your Name`.)

41. Type the following comment at the end of the first `select` statement: `" read all records from table ztxlfa1`.

42. In Notepad, save your modified program to disk.

43. Upload it, replacing program •••0200b. (Switch to your ABAP/4 Editor: Edit Program •••0200b screen. Choose the menu path Utilities->Upload. The Import from a Local File screen is displayed. In the File Name field, type `c:\temp\•••0200b.txt`. Press the OK button.)

44. Save the uploaded program. (Press the Save button.)

45. Print your program. (Press the Print button on the Standard toolbar. The Print Parameters screen is displayed. Ensure the Print Immed. check box is checked. Press the Print button. Your output is sent to the printer, and you are returned to the ABAP/4 Editor: Edit Program screen.)

46. Run your program and print the output. (Choose the menu path Program->Execute. The list output is displayed. Press the Print button on the Standard toolbar. The Print Screen List screen is displayed. Ensure the Print Immed. check box is checked. Press the Print button. You are returned to the list output.)

47. Return to editing program •••0200b and save a version of it in the Versions database. (Press the Back button to return to the ABAP/4 Editor: Edit Program screen. Choose the menu path Program->Generate Version.)

48. Replace all occurrences of ztxlfb1 with ztxlfc3. (Press the Find button. The Search/Replace screen is displayed. Type ztxlfb1 in the Find field. Tickmark the Replace By check box. Type ztxlfc3 in the Replace By field. Press the In Program radio button. Press the Continue button. The Global Replace In Programs screen is displayed. Press the No Confirmation button. All occurrences of the string are replaced. Press the Save button. Press the Back button. You are returned to the ABAP/4 Editor: Edit Program screen.)

49. Save your changes. (Press the Save button.)

50. Return to the editor initial screen and compare the two versions. (Press the Back button. The ABAP/4 Editor: Initial Screen is displayed. Choose the menu path Utilities->Version management. The Versions Of Object •••0200b Of Type REPS screen is displayed. Tickmark the Version 00001 check box. Press the Compare button in the Application toolbar. The Compare Programs: All screen is displayed. Scroll down to view the differences.)

51. Retrieve the original version. (Press the Back button. The Versions Of Object •••0200b Of Type REPS screen is displayed. Remove the tickmark from the Act. check box. Press the Retrieve button on the Application toolbar (the system does not provide a response). Press the Back button. The Restore Version screen is displayed. Press the Yes button. The Versions Of Object •••0200b Of Type REPS screen is displayed. Press the Back button. The ABAP/4 Editor: Initial Screen is displayed.)

52. Edit your program and mark the last three lines as a block. (Press the Change button. The ABAP/4 Editor: Edit Program screen is displayed. Place your cursor on line 13. Press the Select button. Line 13 turns red. Place your cursor on line 15. Press the Select button. The block is marked in red.)

53. Comment out the block using the menu path Block/Buffer->Insert Comment *.

54. Mark the last three lines as a block (see step 51).

55. Remove the comments using the menu path Block/Buffer->Delete Comment *.

Programming Exercises

1. Write a program that retrieves all rows from table ztxlfb1 where the company code is equal to or greater than 3000. On each line of output should be a company code and a vendor number, with the company code first. The output should be sorted

first by company code in ascending order, then by vendor number in descending order. (Use F1 help to find the correct syntax.) Name your program •••e0201. A sample of how your output should appear follows.

```
1000 V9
1000 V8
1000 V6
2000 V9
```

2. Copy program zty0202 to •••e0202 (the listing appears below). It does not produce any output. Find the bug in it and correct it. When fixed, the correct output should be no records found.

```
1   report zty0202.
2   tables ztxlfa1.
3   select * from ztxlfa1 where lifnr like 'W%'.
4       if sy-subrc <> 0.
5           write / 'no records found'.
6           endif.
7       write / ztxlfa1-lifnr.
8       endselect.
```

3. Copy program zty0203 to •••e0203 (the listing appears below). It has a syntax error and a bug in it. Fix both the syntax error and the bug. When fixed, it should display vendor numbers greater than 1050 from table ztxlfa1.

```
1   report zty0203.
2   tables ztxlfa1
3   select * from ztxlfa1 where lifnr > '1050'.
4       write / ztxlfa1-lifnr.
5       endselect.
```

4. Copy program zty0204 to •••e0204 (the listing appears below). The output is incorrect. Look at the output, discover what is wrong, and fix the program.

```
1   report zty0204.
2   tables ztxlfa1.
3   select * from ztxlfa1 where lifnr > '0000001050'.
4       write / ztxlfa1-lifnr.
5       endselect.
6   if sy-dbcnt <> 0.
7       write / 'no records found'.
8       endif.
```

5. Copy program zty0205 to •••e0205 (the listing appears below). The output is incorrect. Look at the output, discover what is wrong, and fix the program.

```
1   report zty0205.
2   tables ztxlfa1.
3   select * from ztxlfa1 where lifnr > '0000001050'.
4   endselect.
5   write / ztxlfa1-lifnr.
```

```
6  if sy-subrc <> 0.
7      write / 'no records found'.
8      endif.
```

6. Copy program zty0206 to •••e0206 (the listing appears below). Simplify the program by remove unnecessary code and unneeded words.

```
1   report zty0206.
2   tables: ztxlfa1, ztxlfb1, ztxlfc3.
3   data wa like ztxlfb1.
4   select * from ztxlfa1 into ztxlfa1.
5       write / ztxlfa1-lifnr.
6       write   ztxlfa1-name1.
7       endselect.
8   if sy-subrc <> 0 or sy-dbcnt = 0.
9       write / 'no records found in ztxlfa1'.
10      endif.
11  uline.
12  select * from ztxlfb1 into wa.
13      write / wa-lifnr.
14      write   wa-bukrs.
15      endselect.
16  if sy-subrc <> 0.
17      write / 'no records found'.
18      endif.
```

7. Copy program zty0207 to •••e0207 (the listing appears below). It has both a syntax error and a programming error in it. Discover what is wrong and fix the program. The output should display a single record (vendor 1000) using the most efficient programming construct.

```
1   report zty0207.
2   tables ztxlfa1.
3   select single * from ztxlfa1 where lifnr > '0000001000'.
4       write / ztxlfa1-lifnr.
5       endselect.
6   if sy-subrc <> 0.
7       write / 'no records found'.
8       endif.
```

DAY **3**

The Data Dictionary, Part 1

Chapter Objectives

After you complete this chapter, you should be able to:

- Describe the differences between transparent, pooled, and cluster tables
- Create domains, data elements, and transparent tables in the Data Dictionary
- Create F1 help for the fields of a table, and create hypertext links within the F1 help
- Use the four SAP-supplied data browsers to view and modify data within tables

Discovering R/3 Release Levels

NEW TERM   There are many versions—also called *release levels*—of the R/3 system in use today. Release 3.0 was the first version, but since its introduction, SAP has also released versions 3.0a through 3.0f, 3.1g, 3.1h, and 4.0a through 4.0c. You can determine the release level of your system using the menu path System->Status.

This book was tested on a 3.0f system. Your system may be on another release level. Although most of the differences should be minor with regard to the topics covered here, some differences may cause confusion or cause the information in this book to appear incorrect. For example, menu paths can change between release levels. Wherever possible, differences that may cause confusion have been noted in this text. However, if the functionality in your system appears to differ from that described here, you can consult the R/3 release notes, available online, to determine if the difference can be attributed to the release level. To access the release notes, use the following procedure:

ScreenCam Start the ScreenCam "How to Display R/3 Release Notes" now.

To display the R/3 release notes:

1. Go to the main menu and choose the menu path Tools->Find->Search Interface. The Search Interface: Request screen appears.

2. Choose the radio button RELN.

3. Press the Choose button on the Application toolbar. The Find Release Notes screen is displayed.

4. Press the Complete List button. The Display Structure: Complete List of Release Notes screen is displayed.

5. Click on any + (plus sign) to expand the node. Modifications To ABAP will appear under the Basis node, under the sub-node ABAP/4 Development Workbench.

Delving Deeper into the R/3 Data Dictionary

As a review, please take a few minutes and re-read the section in Day 2 titled "Introducing the R/3 Data Dictionary" at this time.

Data Dictionary objects are used in most ABAP/4 programs. The interlocking nature of ABAP/4 programs and DDIC objects makes in-depth knowledge of the R/3 Data Dictionary an essential programming skill. Therefore, beginning with this chapter, you will learn how to create DDIC objects such as tables, data elements, and domains.

Note Many development objects used as examples throughout this book (such as tables, domains, and data elements) are based on actual development objects in the R/3 system. The example objects will have the same name as the actual R/3 objects, but they will be prefixed with ztx. For example, lfa1 is a real table in R/3, and the example table in this book is ztxlfa1.

Exploring the Types of Tables in R/3

In R/3 there are three table types: transparent tables, pooled tables, and cluster tables. They are shown in Figure 3.1.

FIGURE 3.1.

The three table types in the R/3 Data Dictionary.

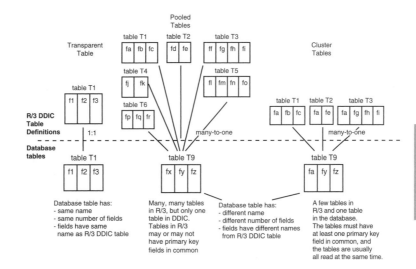

Transparent Tables

NEW TERM A transparent table in the dictionary has a one-to-one relationship with a table in the database. Its structure in R/3 Data Dictionary corresponds to a single database table. For each transparent table definition in the dictionary, there is one associated table in the database. The database table has the same name, the same number of fields, and the fields have the same names as the R/3 table definition. When looking at the definition of an R/3 transparent table, it might seem like you are looking at the database table itself.

NEW TERM Transparent tables are much more common than pooled or cluster tables. They are used to hold *application data*. Application data is the master data or transaction data used by an application. An example of master data is the table of vendors (called vendor master data), or the table of customers (called customer master data). An example of transaction data is the orders placed by the customers, or the orders sent to the vendors.

Transparent tables are probably the only type of table you will ever create. Pooled and cluster tables are not usually used to hold application data but instead hold system data, such as system configuration information, or historical and statistical data.

Both pooled and cluster tables have many-to-one relationships with database tables. Both can appear as many tables in R/3, but they are stored as a single table in the database. The database table has a different name, different number of fields, and different field names than the R/3 table. The difference between the two types lies in the characteristics of the data they hold, and will be explained in the following sections.

Table Pools and Pooled Tables

NEW TERM A *pooled table* in R/3 has a many-to-one relationship with a table in the database (see Figures 3.1 and 3.2). For one table in the database, there are many tables in the R/3 Data Dictionary. The table in the database has a different name than the tables in the DDIC, it has a different number of fields, and the fields have different names as well. Pooled tables are an SAP proprietary construct.

NEW TERM When you look at a pooled table in R/3, you see a description of a table. However, in the database, it is stored along with other pooled tables in a single table called a *table pool*. A table pool is a database table with a special structure that enables the data of many R/3 tables to be stored within it. It can only hold pooled tables.

R/3 uses table pools to hold a large number (tens to thousands) of very small tables (about 10 to 100 rows each). Table pools reduce the amount of database resources needed when many small tables have to be open at the same time. SAP uses them for system data. You might create a table pool if you need to create hundreds of small tables that each hold only a few rows of data. To implement these small tables as pooled tables, you first create the definition of a table pool in R/3 to hold them all. When activated, an associated single table (the table pool) will be created in the database. You can then define pooled tables within R/3 and assign them all to your table pool (see Figure 3.2).

Pooled tables are primarily used by SAP to hold customizing data.

NEW TERM When a corporation installs any large system, the system is usually customized in some way to meet the unique needs of the corporation. In R/3, such customization is done via *customizing tables*. Customizing tables contain codes, field validations, number ranges, and parameters that change the way the R/3 applications behave.

Some examples of data contained in customizing tables are country codes, region (state or province) codes, reconciliation account numbers, exchange rates, depreciation methods, and pricing conditions. Even screen flows, field validations, and individual field attributes are sometimes table-driven via settings in customizing tables.

FIGURE 3.2.

Pooled tables have a many-to-one relationship with table pools.

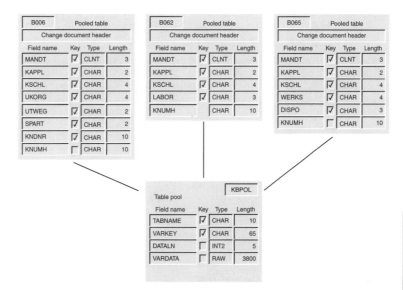

During the initial implementation of the system the data in the customizing tables is set up by a functional analyst. He or she will usually have experience relating to the business area being implemented and extensive training in the configuration of an R/3 system.

Table Clusters and Cluster Tables

NEW TERM A *cluster table* is similar to a pooled table. It has a many-to-one relationship with a table in the database. Many cluster tables are stored in a single table in the database called a *table cluster*.

NEW TERM A *table cluster* is similar to a table pool. It holds many tables within it. The tables it holds are all cluster tables.

Like pooled tables, cluster tables are another proprietary SAP construct. They are used to hold data from a few (approximately 2 to 10) very large tables. They would be used when these tables have a part of their primary keys in common, and if the data in these tables are all accessed simultaneously. The data is stored logically as shown in Figure 3.3.

Table clusters contain fewer tables than table pools and, unlike table pools, the primary key of each table within the table cluster begins with the same field or fields. Rows from the cluster tables are combined into a single row in the table cluster. The rows are combined based on the part of the primary key they have in common. Thus, when a row is read from any one of the tables in the cluster, all related rows in all cluster tables are also retrieved, but only a single I/O is needed.

A cluster is advantageous in the case where data is accessed from multiple tables simultaneously and those tables have at least one of their primary key fields in common. Cluster tables reduce the number of database reads and thereby improve performance.

FIGURE 3.3.

Table clusters store data from several tables based on the primary key fields that they have in common.

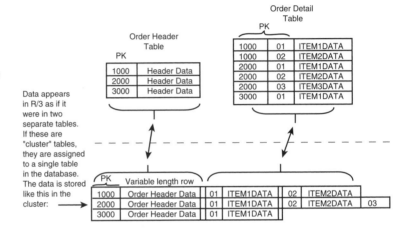

For example, as shown in Figure 3.4, the first four primary key fields in `cdhdr` and `cdpos` are identical. They become the primary key for the table cluster with the addition of a standard system field `pageno` to ensure that each row is unique.

As another example, assume the data from order header and order item tables is always needed at the same time and both have a primary key that begins with the order number. Both the header and items could be stored in a single cluster table because the first field of their primary keys is the same. When implemented as a cluster, if a header row is read, all item rows for it are also read because they are all stored in a single row in the table cluster. If a single item is read, the header and all items will also be read because they are stored in a single row.

FIGURE 3.4.

The cdhdr *and* cdpos
*tables have the first
four primary key fields
in common and are
always accessed
together and so are
stored in the table
cluster* cdcls.

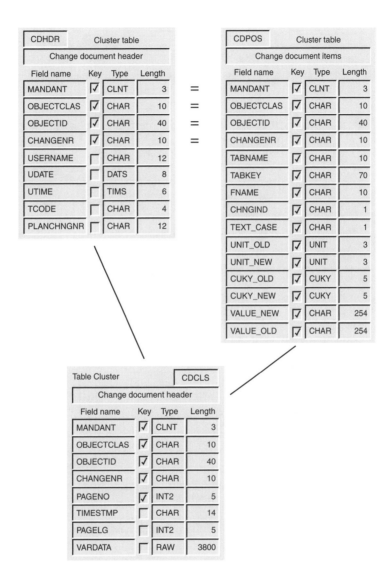

3

Restrictions on Pooled and Cluster Tables

Pooled and cluster tables are usually used only by SAP and not used by customers, probably because of the proprietary format of these tables within the database and because of
technical restrictions placed upon their use within ABAP/4 programs. On a pooled or cluster table:

- Secondary indexes cannot be created.

- You cannot use the ABAP/4 constructs select distinct or group by.

- You cannot use native SQL.
- You cannot specify field names after the order by clause. order by primary key is the only permitted variation.

  The use of pooled and cluster tables can prevent your company from using third-party reporting tools to their fullest extent if they directly read database tables because pooled and cluster tables have an SAP proprietary format. If your company wants to use such third-party tools, you may want to seek alternatives before creating pooled or cluster tables.

Because of these restrictions on pooled and cluster tables and because of their limited usefulness, this book concentrates on the creation and use of transparent tables. The creation of pooled and cluster tables is not covered.

Exploring Table Components

You now know what transparent tables are, and the differences between transparent, pooled, and cluster tables. You will now learn the components that are needed to create tables.

New Term A table is composed of fields. To create a field you need a *data element*. The data element contains the field labels and online documentation (also called *F1 help*) for the field. It is purely descriptive; it contains the semantic characteristics for the field, also known as the "business context." The labels you provide within a data element will be displayed on the screen beside an input field. The data element also contains documentation that is displayed when the user asks for help on that field by pressing the F1 key.

New Term A data element's definition requires a *domain* (see Figure 3.5). The domain contains the technical characteristics of a field, such as the field length and data type.

Domains and data elements are reusable. A domain can be used in more than one data element, and a data element can be used in more than one field and in more than one table.

For example, assume you need to design a customer information table called zcust that must contain work, fax, and home telephone numbers (see Figure 3.6).

FIGURE 3.5.

Tables are composed of fields that are composed of data elements, which, in turn, are composed of domains.

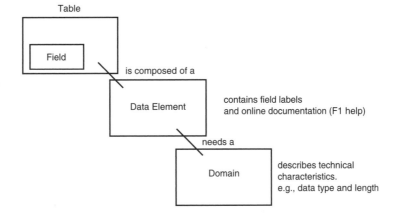

FIGURE 3.6.

A design example using tables, data elements, and domains.

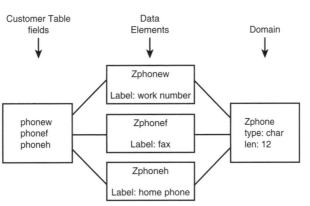

To create a field, you usually start by creating a domain for it. In this case, you might create a generic telephone number domain, name it zphone and give it a data type of CHAR and a length of 12. This would be a generic telephone number domain; most types of telephone numbers could be stored using this domain. As such, it can be used to define specific types of telephone numbers, such as fax or home telephone numbers.

After creating the domain to hold the purely technical description of a field, you then create a data element to hold the descriptive attributes of the field. In the data element you must enter the name of a domain to give it technical characteristics. Then, you enter the labels and documentation (F1 help) to describe the data you will store. In this example, you would probably create three data elements, one for each of the home, work, and fax telephone numbers. In each data element, you would enter field labels describing the type of telephone number you will store with it, and the F1 help for the end-user.

Having created the data elements, you can now create the table. You could create three phone number fields in the table (home, work, and fax) and assign the corresponding data element to each field. A data element is assigned to each field. This gives the field descriptive information from the data element and technical information from the domain that it references. When the field is used on a screen, it obtains a label and F1 help documentation from the data element, and its length and data type form the domain within the data element.

In another example, you might need to store a person's name in three different tables: customer, vendor, and employee tables. In the customer table you want to store a customer name, in the vendor table a vendor name, and in the employee table an employee name. Because it is a good idea to give the same data type and length to all person-name fields, you can create a single generic person-name domain, for example zpersname. Then you can create a data element for each business usage of a person's name: for the customer name, the vendor name, and the employee name. Within each data element you refer to your zpersname domain to give them all the same characteristics. You could then use these data elements to create fields within each table.

Maintaining Technical Characteristics of Fields

If you need to change the length of the field after you have created a table, you only need to change it in the domain. If the domain is used in more than one table, the change is automatically propagated to all fields that use that domain.

For example, if the business analysts requested that you increase the length of your person name field from 12 to 15 characters, you would change the length in the zpersname domain. When you activate your change, the lengths of all name fields based upon this domain (in the customer, vendor, and employee tables) will also change.

Determining When to Create or Reuse Domains and Data Elements

Each R/3 system comes with more than 13,000 preexisting domains created by SAP. When you create a new field, you must decide whether to create a new domain or reuse an existing one. To make this decision, determine whether the data type or length of your field should be dependent on an existing SAP field. If your field should be independent, create a new domain. If your field should be dependent, reuse an existing SAP domain. Similarly, you should reuse data elements if your field labels and documentation should change when SAP changes theirs.

For example, assume you wish to create a new table to contain additional vendor information. When you design the table, you must associate the vendors in your table to those in the SAP table.

In your table, create a primary key containing the vendor number. Use the existing data element to create your field. Both tables are now keyed on the SAP vendor number field using the same data elements and domains. If SAP changes the data type or length of their field, yours will change automatically.

Naming Conventions for Tables and Their Components

Tables, data elements, and domains created at the customer site must follow SAP naming conventions for customer objects. These are outlined in Table 3.1.

TABLE 3.1 NAMING CONVENTIONS FOR TABLES, FIELDS, DATA ELEMENTS, AND DOMAINS CREATED BY THE CUSTOMER

Object Type	Max Name Length	Allowed First Character
Table	10	y, z
Data element	10	y, z
Domain	10	y, z
Field	10	Any character

All names are a maximum of 10 characters long.

The names of all tables, domains, and data elements you create must start with the character y or z. You cannot use any other character at the beginning; all others are reserved by SAP. The R/3 system enforces this convention; you will get an error message if you try to create an object having a name that doesn't conform to these conventions.

Field names can begin with any character. However, certain words are reserved and cannot be used as field names. The DDIC table trese contains the complete list of reserved words. The contents of trese can be displayed using the Day 2 procedure in the section titled "Displaying Data in the Table."

Creating a Transparent Table and Its Components

In the following sections, you will create domains, data elements, and finally, your first transparent table—it will be a scaled-down version of the SAP-supplied vendor master table named lfa1.

3

Note   For the purposes of this book, please assume that the R/3 system doesn't already store any vendor master information. Assume that table lfa1 does not exist, nor do its data elements or its domains. Therefore, in these exercises we will create them.

To store vendor master information you will create table •••lfa1. It will contain fields for a vendor number, a name, a region code, and a country code. The field names and technical characteristics you will use are shown in Table 3.2. An x in the PK column indicates fields that form the primary key. (The install procedure created a table named ztxlfa1 in your R/3 system. It is very similar to the •••lfa1 table. Use it as a reference while reading this chapter.)

TABLE 3.2   FIELDS AND THEIR CHARACTERISTICS FOR TABLE •••lfa1

Field Name	PK	DE Name	DM Name	Data Type	Length
mandt	x	mandt			
lifnr	x	•••lifnr	•••lifnr	CHAR	10
name1		•••name1	•••name	CHAR	35
regio		•••regio	•••regio	CHAR	3
land1		•••land1	•••land1	CHAR	3

These field names and their technical characteristics are based on actual fields of table lfa1.

 Note   Don't change the names shown above. The exercises later in this book rely on these field names as shown. If you don't use these exact names, subsequent exercises may not work.

Since this table contains application data, it should be client-dependent. Therefore, the first field must be mandt. (See Chapter 1 if you need to review client dependent tables.)

Approaches for Creating Tables

There are two approaches you can use when creating tables:

- bottom-up
- top-down

In the bottom-up approach, you create the domains first, then the data elements, and then the table.

In the top-down approach, you create the table first, and then create the data elements and domains as you go along.

The bottom-up approach is more intuitive for the first-time student, but it quickly becomes cumbersome. The top-down approach is much easier to use after you become somewhat familiar with the table creation process. For these reasons, I will demonstrate both techniques, starting with bottom-up.

3

As you read the following sections you will first learn about an object—such as a domain—and then you will create one. The objects you will create are described in Table 3.2.

Remember, when creating any of the objects in this book, use your handle (•••) as the first three characters of the object name. (The characters ••• represent your handle. The handle was described in Chapter 2 in the section titled "Introducing Program Naming Conventions.")

Do *not* use ztx as the first three characters. If you use ztx, it will be very difficult to determine which objects are yours.

Activation of DDIC Objects

 Before learning about DDIC objects in depth, you should know about object activation. Activation applies to all dictionary objects.

After creating a Data Dictionary object, you will *activate* it. Activating an object is simple—you will simply press the Activate button. This changes the status of the object to Active.

An object must be Active before it can be used. For example, if you try to use an inactive data element when creating a field, you will get a message saying that the data element does not exist or is not active. Your response would be to activate the data element.

If you change an object, you must activate it again for the changes to take effect. If you save the changes but do not activate it, the objects that refer to it will not "know about" the change.

Discovering Domains

Before actually creating a domain, I will describe the screen you will use to create it.

In Figure 3.7 is the screen you will use to create a domain—the Dictionary: Maintain Domain screen. On this screen you specify short text, the data type, a field length, and optionally an output length. These items are explained in the following sections.

FIGURE 3.7.

The Dictionary: Maintain Domain screen is used to create a domain.

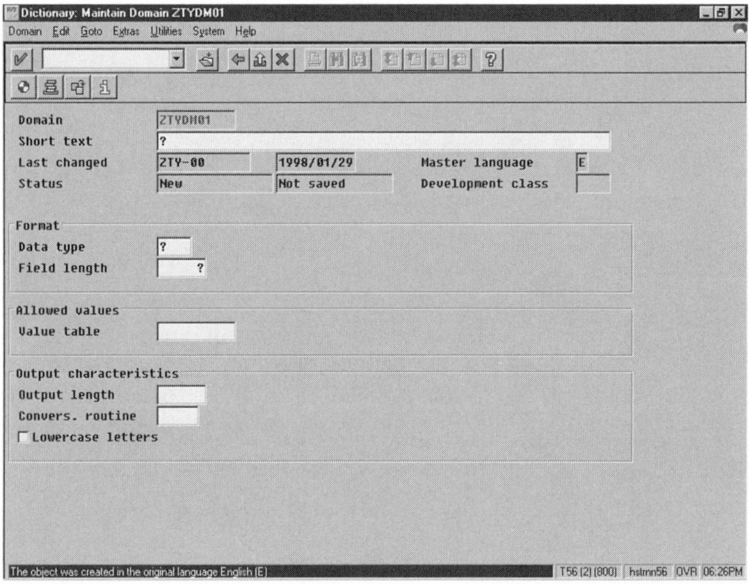

Short Text Field

The Short Text field will contain a description of the domain. The end user never sees it; it is only displayed to developers. You will see it when you bring up a list of domains, such as when you search for one.

In this field, you will describe the type of data the domain is intended to contain. For example, the description of a reusable telephone number domain might read "Generic telephone number" or "General telephone number."

Note   Adding the word "domain" to the end of the short text description is redundant and should be avoided. For example, the short text "Generic telephone number domain" should be avoided. Instead, type "Generic telephone number."

Data Type Field

The Data Type field specifies the representation used internally by the database to store the value for that field. For some data types, it also determines the input format validation and output format of the field. For example, fields of data type DATS (date) and TIMS (time) are automatically formatted with separators when output to a list or displayed onscreen. On input, they must also be in date or time format, or an error message is issued to the user.

The most commonly used data types are listed in Table 3.3.

TABLE 3.3   COMMONLY USED DATA TYPES

Type	Description
CHAR	Character strings (maximum 255 characters)
DEC	Decimal values (maximum length 31)
DATS	Date field
TIMS	Time field
INT1, INT2, INT4	Integer values
NUMC	Character field that can contain only numerics

Tip   You should always press the Enter key after you fill in the data type field. Pressing Enter causes the screen to change based on the data type you specified. If the data type is a signed numeric type, a Sign check box will appear. For fields that allow decimals, a Decimal Places field will appear. For character fields, a Lowercase Letters check box will appear.

Output Length, Decimal Places, and Lowercase Letters Fields

The Output Length field indicates the number of bytes needed to output the field to a list or a screen, including commas, decimal point, sign, and any other formatting characters. For example, on output, date and time fields are automatically formatted with separators. Internally, a date is stored as eight characters (always YYYYMMDD), but the output length in the domain should be specified as 10 to enable two separators to be inserted. If the Output Length field is left blank, its value is automatically calculated by the system when you press Enter.

For decimal fields, you can specify the number of decimal places in the Decimal Places field.

Character fields are usually converted to uppercase before they are stored in the database. You can turn this conversion off by tickmarking the Lowercase Letters check box.

Most developers do not have problems understanding the internal representation of character or integer fields. However, the location of the decimal point in decimal fields is often a point of confusion, so it is described here.

For type DEC fields, the decimal point is not stored in the database. Only the numeric portion is stored, not the decimal. On output, the position of the decimal is determined by the value you put in the Decimal Places field of the domain.

In order for the field to be properly displayed, you must specify an output length that includes one byte for the decimal point and one byte for each thousands separator that can be displayed. However, the system will calculate the output length for you if you simply blank out the Output Length field and press Enter.

Creating a Domain

In this section, you will learn the bottom-up approach to creating a domain.

ScreenCam Start the ScreenCam "How to Create a Domain" now.

Perform this procedure twice to create the ●●●lifnr and ●●●name1 domains. Help with common problems is given in the Troubleshooter that follows it. If you have trouble with any one of the steps, don't forget to consult the Troubleshooter.

1. Begin at the Dictionary: Initial Screen. (To get there from the SAP main menu, choose the menu path Tools->ABAP/4 Workbench, Development->ABAP/4 Dictionary.)

2. Enter the domain name in the Object Name field.

3. Choose the Domains radio button.

4. Press the Create pushbutton. You then see the Dictionary: Maintain Domain screen. The fields containing question marks are required fields.

5. Type a description of the domain in the Short Text field.

6. Fill in the Data Type field. You can put your cursor in this field and press the down arrow to display a list of allowed data types. Pick one from the list or type one in.

7. Enter a field length.

8. Press the Activate button on the Application toolbar to both save and activate the domain. The Create Object Catalog Entry screen is displayed.

9. Press the Local Object button. You are returned to the Dictionary: Maintain Domain screen.

10. Press the Back button on the Standard toolbar. This returns you to where you began this procedure, the Dictionary: Initial Screen.

Trouble	Possible Symptoms	Solution
Can't create domain	When you press the Create button, nothing happens.	Look at the status bar in the bottom of the window and press the button again. It is likely that you will see a message there.
	When you press the Create button, you see the message "System change option does not allow changes to SAP objects."	Change the domain name to start with y or z.
	When you press the Create button, you see the message "Enter access key."	Change the domain name to start with y or z.
	When you press the Create button, you see the message "You are not authorized to make changes."	Request development authorization from your security administrator.
	When you press the Create button, you see the message "already exists."	The name you entered already exists in the Data Dictionary. Choose a different domain name.
Getting message	"W: (calculated output length is smaller than specified)."	Blank out the Output Length field and press Enter and then Activate.
	"E: Value table does not exist."	Blank out the Value Table field and press Enter and then activate.

Obtaining SAP Documentation on Domains

There are many places to obtain SAP documentation on the features of domains.

If you wish to see documentation describing all data types and their uses, put your cursor on the Data Type field and press F1. You will see a dialog box containing highlighted fields. Click on these highlighted fields for more details.

You can also consult the R/3 library help for additional documentation on data types and other properties of the domain. To view this documentation, from any screen choose the menu path Help->R/3 Library. You will see the main menu of the R/3 library. From there, click on the following tabs: Basis Components->ABAP/4 Development Workbench->ABAP/4 Dictionary->New Developments In The ABAP/4 Dictionary In Release 3.0.

For still more documentation on the data types in the domain, from within the domain choose the menu path Help->Extended help. Then click on Creating Domains, and then click on External Data Type.

To obtain documentation that describes the mapping of domain data types to ABAP/4 data types, display F1 help for the "tables" keyword. (To do so, within the ABAP/4 editor, put your cursor on the word tables and press F1.)

Discovering Data Elements

Before actually creating a data element, I will describe the screen you will use to create it.

Figure 3.8 shows the screen used to create a data element. Here you specify the short text, domain name, labels, and a header, which are explained in the following sections. Documentation can also be created after the data element has been saved.

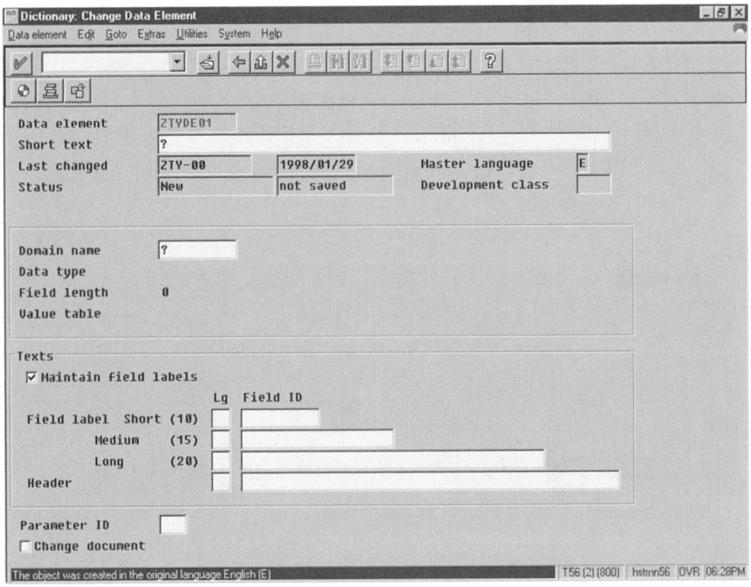

FIGURE 3.8.

The Dictionary: Change Data Element screen.

Short Text Field

The Short Text field describes a business context for a domain. For example, a "customer telephone number" is a specific business context for a "generic telephone number" domain, so it would be an appropriate description for a data element. The end user will see this description if they request F1 help for a field that was created using this data element.

Field Label and Header Fields

At the bottom of the screen shown in Figure 3.8 are four text fields. The first three are field labels. When any field appears on a screen (such as an input field on an input screen), one of the short, medium, or long fields will appear to the left of it as a field label. The programmer chooses one of these field labels when he creates a screen. The contents of the Header field will appear as a column header at the top of lists.

If the fields that you create with this data element will not appear on any screens, uncheck the Maintain Field Labels check box and press the Enter key. You will no longer see the Field Label and Header fields. You will have to press Enter twice to cause the fields to disappear if these fields contain values.

Data Element Documentation

After you save the data element, a Documentation button appears on the Application toolbar so that you can store free-form text. The user sees this text when he requests F1 help. In other words, when a table field that uses this data element is displayed on a screen, the user can place his cursor into that field and press F1 to display the documentation you entered here.

When you see the Documentation screen, the first line will contain the characters &DEFINITION&. This is a heading; do not change this line. Type your documentation beginning on line two.

Data element documentation is often very useful to the programmer. By reading this F1 help, the programmer can determine the business usage of the data. Therefore, you should always create F1 help for the user via the Documentation button.

Creating a Data Element

In this section, you learn the bottom-up approach to creating a data element.

 Start the ScreenCam "How to Create a Data Element" now.

Perform this procedure twice to create the ●●lifnr and ●●●name1 data elements. Help with common problems is given in the Troubleshooter that follows it. If you have trouble with any one of the steps, don't forget to consult the Troubleshooter.

1. Begin at the Dictionary: Initial Screen. (To get there from the SAP main menu, follow the menu path Tools->ABAP/4 Workbench, Development->ABAP/4 Dictionary.)

2. Type the data element name in the Object Name field.

3. Choose the Data Elements radio button.

4. Press the Create button. The Dictionary: Change Data Element screen appears.

5. Type short text for the data element.

6. Type a domain name and press the Enter key. If the domain exists and is active, its data type and length will appear. If you don't see a data type and length after pressing Enter, verify the name of the Data Element. If the name is correct, verify that it is active by opening a new session (use menu path System->Create Session) and displaying it in the Data Dictionary.

7. Enter field labels in the Field Label Short, Medium, Long, and Header fields. The value in the Short field should be a maximum of 10 characters, Medium should be a maximum of 15, and Long should be a maximum of 20. The value in the Header field should be the same length or shorter than the output length in the domain.

8. Press the Save button on the Standard toolbar. The Create Object Catalog Entry screen is displayed.

9. Press the Local Object button. You are returned to the Dictionary: Change Data Element screen. The Status fields contain the values New and Saved and the message "Saved without check" appears at the bottom of the window in the status bar. The Documentation button (among others) appears on the Application toolbar.

10. Press the Documentation button. The Change Data Element: Language E screen is displayed. Here you can type end user documentation. This documentation is displayed when the user requests F1 help for fields created using this data element. The first line contains the characters &DEFINITION&. This is a heading; do not change this line. Type your documentation beginning on line two. Press the Enter key to begin each new paragraph.

11. Press the Save Active button on the Application toolbar to save your text. The message "Document was saved in active status" appears in the status bar.

12. Press the Back button on the Standard toolbar. You are returned to the Dictionary: Change Data Element screen.

13. Press the Activate button on the Application toolbar. The value in the Status field changes to `Act.` and the message "was activated" appears in the status bar.

14. Press the Back button. You are returned to the Dictionary: Initial Screen.

Trouble	Possible Symptoms	Solution
Can't create data element	When you press the Create button, nothing happens.	Look at the status bar in the bottom of the window and press the button again. It is likely that you will see a message there.
	When you press the Create button, you see the message "System change option does not allow changes to SAP objects."	Change the data element name to start with y or z.
	When you press the Create button, you see the message "Enter access key."	Change the data element name to start with y or z.
	When you press the Create button, you see the message "You are not authorized to make changes."	Request development authorization from your security administrator.
	When you press the Create button, you see the message "already exists."	The name you entered already exists in the Data Dictionary. Choose a different domain name.
Can't activate data element	Seeing message "No active domain exists with name."	Go to the Dictionary: Change Data Element screen and double-click on the domain name.
	Either the domain name you entered on the previous screen does not exist or is not active.	You will then see either a dialog box or the Dictionary: Display Domain screen.
		If you see a dialog box with the title Create Domain, the domain does not exist. Check the name carefully. Did you enter the wrong name? It might be a good idea to open a new session and display the objects you created so far using the Object Browser. (In Day 2, see the section "Finding Your Development Objects.")

continues

3

Trouble	Possible Symptoms	Solution
		If, after double-clicking, you see the Dictionary: Display Domain screen, look at the Status field on that screen. Is the status New? If so, the domain needs to be activated. Press the Activate button and then press the Back button to return to the data element and try again to activate it.
Getting message	"Maintain field label."	Enter short, medium, and long field labels and then activate.
	"W: Length was increased to the actual text length."	The header text you entered was longer than the field length. This is not a serious error. To bypass it, just press Enter and then activate.
Can't enter field labels.	Input fields are missing from the screen.	Tickmark the Maintain Field Labels check box and press Enter.

Discovering Transparent Tables

Figure 3.9 shows the screen used to create a transparent table. Here you specify the short text, delivery class, field names, a data element name for each field, and select the primary key fields. The following sections explain these items in more detail.

FIGURE 3.9.

The Dictionary: Table/ Structure: Change Fields screen enables short text, attributes, and field names to be entered.

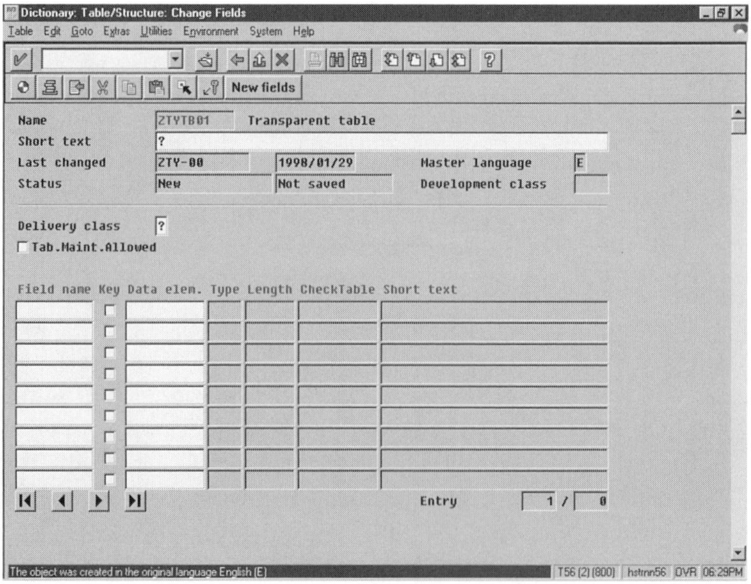

Short Text Field

The Short Text field is used for the same purposes as the domain Short Text fields. The end user will not see this description anywhere, but the developer will see it when bringing up a list of tables.

Delivery Class Field

The value in the Delivery Class field identifies the "owner" of the data in this table. The owner is responsible for maintaining the table contents. In customer tables, you always enter an A here, which indicates that the table contains application data owned by the customer only. Other values entered in the field are useful only to SAP, and indicate that either SAP owns the data or both SAP and the customer jointly own the data.

> **Tip** For a complete list of valid values and their meanings, put your cursor on the Delivery Class field and press F1.

3

Tab.Maint.Allowed Field

Tickmarking the Tab.Maint.Allowed check box causes the menu path Utilities->Create Entries to be enabled. After activating the table and choosing this menu path, the Table Insert screen is displayed, enabling you to enter data into your table. It is useful for testing and for manual entry of small amounts of data. If the Tab.Maint.Allowed check box is blank, the menu path Utilities->Create Entries will be grayed out.

Field Name Column

In the lower half of the screen you can enter field names in the Field Name column. The primary key fields must appear first in this list and must be indicated by a tickmark in the Key column. A data element name must be entered to the right of each field name. After filling in the field names, press the Next page button on the Standard toolbar if you want to enter additional fields.

Creating a Transparent Table Using Preexisting Domains and Data Elements

In this section, you learn the bottom-up approach to creating a transparent table.

 Start the ScreenCam "How to Create a Transparent Table Using Preexisting Domains and Data Elements" now.

Perform this procedure to create the •••lfa1 table. In this procedure, we will create the table, but will only include the first three fields (mandt, •••lifnr and •••name1) in it. Later on, we will add the remaining fields using the top-down approach.

Help with common problems is given in the Troubleshooter that follows this procedure. If you have trouble with any one of the steps, don't forget to consult the Troubleshooter.

1. Begin at the Dictionary: Initial Screen (To get there from the SAP main menu, use the menu path Tools->ABAP/4 Workbench, Development->ABAP/4 Dictionary).

2. Type the table name •••lfa1 in the Object Name field.

3. Choose the Tables radio button.

4. Press the Create pushbutton. This takes you to the Dictionary: Table/Structure: Change Fields screen.

5. Enter short text describing the table.

6. Type an A in the Delivery Class field.

7. Tickmark the Tab.Maint.Allowed. check box.

8. In the Field Name column, enter the name of the first field of the table.

9. Tickmark the Key column if it forms part of the primary key.

10. Enter the name of a data element in the Data Elem. column.

11. Press the Enter key.

12. Look at the status bar. If you see the message "Data element is not active," the data element either does not exist or has not been activated. These are the possible reasons why you might see this message:

    • It has not been created.

    • A misspelling occurred when you created the data element.

    • The data element name is misspelled on the current screen.

    • The data element exists and the name is spelled correctly, but it is not active.

    Check the name carefully. If the spelling is correct, double-click on it. If a data element of that name doesn't exist, you will see a dialog box titled Create Data Element. If the data element does exist, the data element itself will be displayed.

    If you are now looking at the data element, notice the value in the Status field. The Status field must contain Act. to indicate that it is active. If it does not, press the Activate button and verify the status is now Act. (If it will not activate, turn to the Troubleshooter associated with the procedure for creating data elements.) Once the data element has been activated, press the Back button to return to the Dictionary: Table/Structure: Change Fields screen.

13. Repeat steps 8 though 12 for each of the remaining fields in the table (•••lifnr and •••name1).

14. Press the Save button on the Standard toolbar. You will then see the Create Object Catalog Entry screen.

15. Press the Local Object button. You are then returned to the Dictionary: Table/Structure: Change Fields screen.

16. Press the Technical Settings button on the Application toolbar. The ABAP/4 Dictionary: Maintain Technical Settings screen is displayed.

17. In the Data Class field, enter **APPL0** (APPL0 with a *zero*, not with the letter *O*).

18. Enter **0** (zero) in the Size Category field.

19. Press the Save button.

20. Press the Back button. You are returned to the Dictionary: Table/Structure: Change Fields screen.

21. Press the Activate button on the Application toolbar. If the activation was successful, the message "was activated" appears in the status bar and the Status field contains the value Act.

22. Press the Back button to return to the Dictionary: Initial Screen.

Trouble	Possible Symptoms	Solution
Can't create table	When you press the Create button, nothing happens.	Look at the status bar in the bottom of the window and press the button again. It is likely that you will see a message there.
	When you press the Create button, you see the message "Enter access key."	Change the table name to start with *y* or *z*.
	When you press the Create button, you see the message "System change option does not allow changes to SAP objects."	Change the table name to start with *y* or *z*.
	When you press the Create button, you see the message "You are not authorized to make changes."	Request development authorization from your security administrator.
	When you press the Create button, you see the message "already exists."	The name you entered already exists in the Data Dictionary. Choose a different domain name.

continues

Trouble	Possible Symptoms	Solution
Can't activate table	Seeing message "E-Field (Data element or domain is not active or does not exist)."	Go back one screen to the Dictionary: Table/Structure: Change Fields screen. Double-click on the data element name. You will see either a dialog box or the data element itself.
		If you see a dialog box with the title Create Data Element, the data element does not exist. Check the name carefully. Did you enter the wrong name? It might be a good idea to open a new session and display the objects you have created so far using the Object Browser. (In Day 2, see the section "Finding Your Development Objects.")
		If you can display the data element, look at the Status field. Is the status New? If not, the data element needs to be activated. Press the Activate button and then press the Back button to return to the table.
Seeing screen ABAP/4 Dictionary: Maintain Technical Settings		The technical attributes were either not entered or not saved. Enter the technical attributes now, press the Save button, and then press Back.
Messages displayed in red	"E- Field (Data element or domain is not active or does not exist)."	See Can't activate table, above.
	"E- Entry in table TAORA missing."	Look further down for a message (in red) about the Data Class or Size category.
	"E- Error in code generation for creating table in the DB" "E- Table (Statements could not be generated)."	Look further down for a message (in red) about the Data Class or Size category.

Trouble	Possible Symptoms	Solution
		Look further down for a message (in red) about the Data Class or Size category.
	"E- Field Size category (Value not permitted)."	You entered an invalid value in the Size Category field of the technical settings. Press Back and then press Technical Settings, and change the Size Category to 0 (zero).
	"E- Field Data class (Value not permitted)."	You entered an invalid value in the Data Class field of the technical settings. Press Back and then press Technical settings, and change the Data Class to APPL0 (use a zero at the end of APPL).
	"E- Key is already defined; field cannot be in the key."	The primary key fields are not adjacent to each other. Press Back and make sure your primary key fields are all at the beginning of the table with no intervening non-key fields. (All of the tickmarks in the Key column must be together at the beginning of the table.)
Seeing dialog box titled Adjust Table with the text Table must be adjusted in the database.	Table needs to be converted.	You changed the table and now a table conversion must be done to complete the activation. Choose a processing type of Online and press the Adjust button.
Seeing message at bottom of screen "Initial value not permitted as the field name" or: can't scroll up or: can't see fields you entered.		You tried to remove a field by blanking it out. You can't do that; you must delete fields using the Cut button on Application toolbar. Press Cut until you see the message "Selected entries were copied to the clipboard" at the bottom of the window in the status bar.

3

continues

Trouble	Possible Symptoms	Solution
Can't get past a message	A message beginning with the characters "W:" appears in the status bar and you can't get any further.	Press the Enter key in response to the message.

Creating a Transparent Table Without Preexisting Domains and Data Elements

In this section you will learn to add fields to a table using the top-down approach. You will add the remaining two fields (•••regio and •••land1) to your •••lfa1 table.

Using the top-down approach, you can add fields to a table before you create the data elements and domains. You can simply create data elements and domains as you go along.

To do so, you will enter a data element or domain name and then double-click on it. You will be taken to the Creation screen. From there you create the domain or data element, activate it, and then press the Back button to return to where you were.

What follows is the procedure for adding fields to a transparent table without first creating the domains and data elements.

 Start the ScreenCam "How to Create a Transparent Table Without Preexisting Domains and Data Elements" now.

1. Begin at the Dictionary: Initial Screen (To get there from the SAP main menu, use the menu path Tools->ABAP/4 Workbench, Development->ABAP/4 Dictionary).

2. Type the table name •••lfa1 in the Object Name field.

3. Choose the Tables radio button.

4. Press the Change pushbutton. This takes you to the Dictionary: Table/Structure: Change Fields screen.

5. Press the New Fields pushbutton. Blank lines appear at the bottom of the screen, and the existing table fields are scrolled upward.

6. In the Field Name column, enter the name of the field you wish to add.

7. Tickmark the Key column if it forms part of the primary key. (The •••regio and •••land1 fields do not, but this procedure is written generically so that it can be used in general situations.)

8. Enter the name of the associated data elements in the Data Elem. column.

9. Press the Enter key.

10. Look at the status bar. You should see the message "Data element is not active," because the data element does not exist.

11. Double-click on the data element name. The Create Data Element dialog box will be displayed. In the Data Element field will be the name of the data element to be created. This will of course be the data element you wish to create, so unless it is misspelled, do not change it here.

12. Press the Continue button. The Dictionary: Change Data Element screen appears.

13. Enter short text for the data element.

14. Enter a domain name.

15. Double-click on the domain name to create it. The Create Domain dialog box will be displayed. In the Domain Name field will be the name of the domain to be created. This will of course be the domain you wish to create, so unless it is misspelled, do not change it here.

16. Press the Continue button. The Dictionary: Maintain Domain screen is displayed.

17. Fill in the Short Text, Data Type, and Field Length fields.

18. Press the Activate button on the Application toolbar.

19. Press the Local Object button. You are returned to the Dictionary: Maintain Domain screen. The value in the Status field changes to Act. and the message "was activated" appears in the status bar.

20. Press the Back button on the Standard toolbar to return to the Dictionary: Change Data Element screen.

21. Enter the remaining fields for the data element (refer to step number 7 of the Data Element Creation Procedure in the "Creating a Data Element" section).

22. Press the Activate button on the Application toolbar. You will then see the Create Object Catalog Entry screen.

23. Press the Local Object button. You are returned to the Dictionary: Change Data Element screen. The value in the Status field changes to Act. and the message "was activated" appears in the status bar.

24. Press the Back button on the Standard toolbar. You are returned to the Dictionary: Table/Structure: Change Fields screen. There should be no messages in the status bar.

25. Repeat steps 5 through 23 for each new data element you want to create.

26. After you have created all domains and data elements, press the Activate button on the Application toolbar. If the activation was successful, the message "was activated" appears in the status bar and the Status field contains the value Act.

27. Press the Back button to return to the Dictionary: Initial Screen.

3

Modifying Tables

After you have created a table, you can:

- copy it
- delete it
- add more fields to it
- delete fields from it
- change the fields within it

This section describes how to perform these functions.

Copying a Table

If a table is active in the DDIC, you can copy it. You might want to do this if the table you want to create will be very similar to a table that already exists in the database. Or, you might want to experiment with some dictionary functionality that is unfamiliar to you, but you don't want to modify an existing table.

To copy a table, follow this procedure:

1. Go to the Dictionary: Initial Screen. (To get there from the SAP main menu, use the menu path Tools->ABAP/4 Workbench, Development->ABAP/4 Dictionary.)
2. Choose the Tables radio button.
3. Press the Copy button on the Application toolbar.
4. Enter the name of the From and To tables.
5. Press the Continue button. You are returned to the Dictionary: Initial Screen and the message ++ appears in the status bar at the bottom of the window.
6. Press the Activate button on the application toolbar to activate the new table.

This procedure copies the table structure only, not the data. To copy table data, write a small ABAP/4 program of your own.

Note

> Tables can't be renamed. To change the name of a table, you must copy it to a different table with the desired name and then delete the original table. If this has to be done, be sure to copy both the structure and the data.

Deleting a Table

You can delete existing DDIC tables. You might want to do this if an existing table is no longer needed, or if you created a table for the purposes of trying out dictionary functionality that is unfamiliar to you.

To delete a table, follow this procedure:

1. Go to the Dictionary: Initial Screen. (To get there from the SAP main menu, use the menu path Tools->ABAP/4 Workbench, Development->ABAP/4 Dictionary.)
2. Enter the table name in the Object Name field.
3. Choose the Tables radio button.
4. Press the Delete button on the Application toolbar. A pop-up will ask you for confirmation of the delete request.
5. Verify the table name you entered and press Yes if you wish to continue.

Adding Fields

There are two ways to add fields to an existing table:

- inserting
- appending

Inserting a field enables you to position a field before an existing field.

Appending a field enables you to add new fields at the end of the table, after all of the existing fields.

Inserting a Field

To insert a new field above an existing field, perform this procedure:

1. Begin at the Dictionary: Initial Screen. (To get there from the SAP main menu, use the menu path Tools->ABAP/4 Workbench, Development->ABAP/4 Dictionary.)
2. Type the table name in the Object Name field.
3. Choose the Tables radio button.
4. Press the Change pushbutton. This takes you to the Dictionary: Table/Structure: Change Fields screen.
5. Position your cursor on a field.
6. Press the Insert Field button on the Application toolbar. A new row will appear above the cursor position.
7. Create your new field on the row that you just inserted.

Appending a Field

To append a field to the end of a table, perform this procedure:

1. Begin at the Dictionary: Initial Screen. (To get there from the SAP main menu, use the menu path Tools->ABAP/4 Workbench, Development->ABAP/4 Dictionary.)

2. Type the table name in the Object Name field.

3. Choose the Tables radio button.

4. Press the Change pushbutton. This takes you to the Dictionary: Table/Structure: Change Fields screen.

6. Press the New Fields button on the Application toolbar. On the bottom half of the screen, the existing fields scroll up to enable you to enter additional fields at the end.

7. Create your new fields in the rows that you just inserted.

Deleting Fields

You can delete existing fields from a table. You may wish to do this if the field is no longer needed in the table, or if you created a field for the purposes of trying out dictionary functionality that is unfamiliar to you.

To delete a field from a table, complete the following steps:

1. Go to the Dictionary: Initial Screen. (To get there from the SAP main menu, use the menu path Tools->ABAP/4 Workbench, Development->ABAP/4 Dictionary.)

2. Enter the table name.

3. Choose the Tables radio button.

4. Press the Change button.

5. Place your cursor on the field to be deleted.

6. Press the Cut button on the Application toolbar, or choose the menu path Edit->Delete Field.

7. Activate the table. The Adjust Table screen is displayed. Press the Adjust button to convert the table in the database.

Caution

To delete a field from a table, *do not* blank out the field name. Instead, put your cursor on the field name and press the Cut button. If you simply blank out the name, the message "Initial value not permitted as field name" will appear at the bottom of your screen in the status bar, and you won't be allowed to continue until you delete the row that you blanked out.

Changing the Data Type or Length of a Field

You can change the data type and/or length of existing fields in a table. You may wish to do this if the field length needs to be increased to hold longer values, or if the field validation rules change and the data type is no longer suitable for new data that should be entered in the field.

Complete the following steps to change the data type or length of a field:

1. Go to the Dictionary: Initial Screen. (To get there from the SAP main menu, use the menu path Tools->ABAP/4 Workbench, Development->ABAP/4 Dictionary.)

2. Enter the table name.

3. Choose the Tables radio button.

4. Press the Display button.

5. Double-click on the data element corresponding to the field you want to change. The data element will be displayed.

6. Double-click on the domain name in the data element. The domain will be displayed.

7. Press the Display <-> Change button on the Application toolbar. You will now be able to change the attributes of the domain.

8. Blank out the Output Length field.

9. Change the data type and/or length.

10. Press the Activate button. The Please note! screen is displayed showing a list of all tables and structures that use this domain. They will all be affected. To continue, press the Continue button.

Note

Making changes to a domain affects all fields that use that domain.

Working with Data

If you have not already done so, create your table now and activate it before proceeding.

NEW TERM   Within R/3 are SAP-supplied utilities called *data browsers* that enable you to manipulate the data within tables. Although the word *browser* implies that you will only read the data, data browsers can be used for both reading and updating.

You can use the data browser utilities to display or modify data within tables in these ways:

- search for and display rows that meet specified criteria
- add new rows
- modify existing rows
- delete rows

This section describes how to use the data browsers to perform these functions.

Accessing Data Browser Functionality From Within the DDIC

As noted above, one of the functions of a data browser is to insert new rows into a table. A quick and easy way to access this functionality is from the Dictionary: Table/Structure screen (in either display or change mode), choose the menu path Utilities->Create Entries. Choosing this menu path is a shortcut—it will invoke a data browser but will bypass the initial screen and take you directly to the screen that will allow you to insert new rows into a table.

If this menu path is disabled, tickmark the Tab.Maint.Allowed field and reactivate your table. Please refer to the section earlier in this chapter titled "Tab.Maint.Allowed Field" for an explanation of this field.

Choosing this menu path automatically performs these tasks in order:

- Generates an ABAP/4 update program specific to your table that a data browser can call. (This ABAP/4 program is only generated the first time you access this menu path for a given table, and each time you access it after a change has been made to the table.)
- It calls the data browser which, in turn, calls the newly generated ABAP/4 program.
- It shows you a screen allowing you to create rows in the table.

SCREENCAM Start the ScreenCam "How to Add Data to a Table" now.

Perform this procedure to add data to your table. Help with common problems is given in the Troubleshooter that follows it. If you have trouble with any one of the steps, don't forget to consult the Troubleshooter.

1. Go to the Dictionary: Initial Screen.
2. Type the name of your table in the Object Name field.

3. Press the Display button. The Dictionary: Table/Structure: Display Fields screen is displayed.

4. Choose the menu path Utilities->Create Entries. Watch the status bar at the bottom of your screen when you choose the menu path; you might be able to see the message "Compiling. . .". This message indicates that the system is generating the update program. The Table Insert screen is displayed. On this screen is an entry field for each field in your table. To the left of each entry field is the field name. The primary key fields appear first, followed by a blank line, then the remaining fields of the table. To see the program that was generated, choose Utilities->Create Entries and then choose the menu path System->Status. The program name appears in the Program (Screen) field.

Tip

If you place your cursor on any field and press the F1 key, the Help — Table Insert screen is displayed. On this screen you will see the documentation you entered into the data element. To return to the Table Insert screen, press either the Continue or Cancel button.

5. Fill in the fields with the data you want to insert into your table.

6. Press the Save button on the Standard toolbar. You will see the message "Database record successfully created" in the status bar.

7. Repeat steps 5 and 6 for each row you want to enter.

8. Press the Back button to return to the Dictionary: Table/Structure: Display Fields screen.

9. Choose the menu path Utilities->Table Contents to display the rows you just created. The Data Browser: Table: Selection Screen is displayed.

10. To display all of the rows in the table press the Execute button without entering any search criteria. The Data Browser: Table Select Entries screen is displayed, and the new rows you entered will be shown in a list.

Trouble	Possible Symptoms	Solution
Can't add data	The menu item Create Entries is grayed out and nothing happens when you click on it.	The Tab.Maint.Allowed check box is not checked. Go to the Dictionary: Table/Structure: Change Fields screen (to get there display the table and click on the Display <-> Change button on the Application toolbar until the fields are modifiable). Add a tickmark to the Tab.Maint.Allowed check box. Press the Activate button.
	When you press the Save button, you see the message "A data record with the specified key already exists" at the bottom of the window.	The table already contains a record with the same primary key as the one you are trying to save. The primary key fields are the first group of fields that appear on the screen. There is a blank space on the screen under the last field in the primary key. Change a value in one of the fields above the space and try saving your record again.

General Data Browser Utilities

The functionality you accessed in the preceding section is just one function of a single data browser. In the R/3 system, there are four general data browser utilities: SE16, SE17, SM30, and SM31. They are similar to each other in some ways, and yet provide varying types of functionality.

Using SE16

SE16 is the most used general-purpose data browser utility program. With it, you can search tables for specific rows and display them, update them, delete them, copy them, add new rows, and more. It can be accessed in either of these two ways:

- From the Dictionary: Table/Structure: Change Fields screen, choose the menu path Utilities->Table Contents.
- Type /nse16 in the Command field.

ScreenCam Start the ScreenCam "How to Display Table Data Using the Data Browser" now.

1. Type **/nse16** in the Command field.

2. Press the Enter key. The Data Browser: Initial Screen appears.

3. Type your table name in the Table Name field.

4. Press the Table Contents button on the Application toolbar. If the table contains more than 40 fields, you will see the Choose Fields For Selection screen. If you see it, place a tickmark beside the fields for which you want to enter search criteria, and press the Execute button. The fields you tickmark will be shown on the next screen—the Data Browser: Table: Selection screen. This screen is usually simply called a *selection screen*. Here you can enter search criteria to find specific rows in the table. To display all rows, do not enter any search criteria. If there will be more than 500 rows that match your criteria and you want to display them all, blank out the value in the Maximum No. Of Hits field.

5. Press the Execute button on the Application toolbar. You will then see the Data Browser: Table Select Entries screen. All rows that match your criteria are displayed up to the maximum number of rows specified in the Maximum No. of Hits field.

Trouble	Solution
Nothing happens when you press the Execute button.	• You intentionally or accidentally typed something into a field on the selection screen and no rows match that search criteria. Blank out all of the fields on the selection screen and press Execute again. • There is no data in the table. • Did you press Save after every record? • Did you enter data into the table?
There are fewer records in the output list than you inserted into the table.	• Did you press Save after every record? • Did you enter unique primary key field values for each record? • You intentionally or accidentally typed something into a field on the selection screen and not all records match that search criteria. Return to the selection screen, blank out all of the fields, and press the Execute button again.

Note   Like the menu path Utilities->Create Entries, Utilities->Table Contents also generates a program, and it is regenerated if you change the table structure. To display the program that it generates, from the selection screen choose the menu path System->Status.

SCREENCAM Start the ScreenCam "Data Browser Functionality" now.

On the data browser screen you can do the following:

- Scroll up and down.
- Scroll left and right.
- Double-click on a row to see more fields at a time.
- Create a new row by choosing the menu path Table Entry->Create.
- Change an existing row by tickmarking it and then choosing the menu path Table Entry->Change.
- Change multiple rows by tickmarking them, choosing the menu path Table Entry->Change, and then pressing the Next Entry and Previous Entry buttons on the Application toolbar.
- Copy an existing row by tickmarking it and then choosing the menu path Table Entry->Create w/reference.
- Copy multiple rows by tickmarking them, choosing the menu path Table Entry->Change, and then pressing the Next Entry and Previous Entry buttons on the Application toolbar.
- Delete a row or rows by tickmarking them, choosing the menu path Table Entry->Create w/reference, and then pressing the Delete Entry button on the Application toolbar for each row you want to delete.
- Select all rows and deselect all rows by pressing the corresponding buttons on the Application toolbar.
- Print the list by pressing the Print button on the Standard toolbar.
- Sort the list by placing your cursor on a column to sort by and then pressing the Sort Ascending or Sort Descending buttons on the Application toolbar.
- Find a string by pressing the Find button on the Standard toolbar. Type the string, press Find, and then click on a highlighted area to bring that row into view.
- Download the list to a file on your hard drive by choosing the menu path Edit->Download. You can choose ASCII, spreadsheet format, or rich text format.
- Select the fields you want to see in the list by choosing the menu path Settings->List format->Choose fields.
- Set various other list parameters using the menu path Settings->User parameters. Here you can set the output width, the maximum number of rows that can be displayed, enable conversion exits, or display the actual number of rows that match the selection criteria. You can also change the column headings to use the labels from data elements instead of the field names from the tables.

Using SM31 and SM30

SM31 and SM30 can also be used to display and update table data. SM31 is an older version of SM30 that has less functionality. The input field on the first screen of SM30 is long enough to accommodate any table name; on SM31 it is only five characters long. Before you can use either one, a special program called a standard maintenance dialog must be generated for the table you want to display.

 NEW TERM A *standard maintenance dialog* is an ABAP/4 program that you generate. When you invoke SM31 or SM30, the data browser will automatically find and invoke that generated program. It provides a more complex interface and more functionality than SE16. For more information on maintenance dialogs and the procedure to create them, consult the R/3 Library help.

Tip

> To find information on maintenance dialogs in the R/3 Library, choose the menu path System->R/3 Library Help. From there, click on the following tabs: Basis Components->ABAP/4 Development Workbench->Extended Applications Function Library->Extended Table Maintenance.

Comparing SE17 with SE16

SE17 is very similar to SE16 in the fact that it can be used to search for specific rows within a table. However, SE17 cannot be used for updates. Using SE16, you can specify complex search criteria for a maximum of 40 fields at a time; with SE17, you can specify simple search criteria for any number of fields at once. SE16 only enables output to be sorted by a single column at a time; SE17 enables you to specify any sort sequence across multiple columns. SE16 will not work for a table that has a standard maintenance dialog, but SE17 will.

Summing Up the Data Browsers

In special cases, for display only where you need to specify multiple sort criteria, use SE17. However, for most day-to-day display/update activities, use SE16. However, you will not be able to use SE16 if the table has a standard maintenance dialog. In that case, use SM31.

The simplest way to tell if you should use SE16 or SM31 is to simply try one. If it doesn't work, then the other probably will. If neither one works, resort to SM30.

Displaying the Data Using Your Own ABAP/4 Program

Instead of using a data browser, it is quite easy to write a small ABAP/4 program to display the data in your table. Try creating one now. Design your program to write out a suitable message if no rows exist in the table.

A sample solution is shown in Listing 3.1. Try creating one on your own before looking at the solution.

LISTING 3.1 SIMPLE PROGRAM TO DISPLAY THE DATA IN THE `ztxlfa1` TABLE

```
1   report ztx0301.
2   tables ztxlfa1.
3   select * from ztxlfa1.
4       write: / ztxlfa1-lifnr,
5                 ztxlfa1-name1,
6                 ztxlfa1-regio,
7                 ztxlfa1-land1.
8       endselect.
9   if sy-subrc <> 0.
10      write 'Table is empty.'.
11      endif.
```

Utilizing F1 Help

F1 help is the documentation seen by the user for a field. To obtain it, the user places his cursor on the field and presses F1. The documentation is displayed in a dialog box. You will use the following procedure to modify the F1 help you created earlier for the `lifnr` field.

Start the ScreenCam "How to Create or Modify F1 Help" now.

Adding F1 Help to a Field

To add F1 help to a field:

1. Begin on the Dictionary: Table/Structure screen (either change or display mode).

2. Locate the field to which you want to add help and double-click on the data element name corresponding to that field. The Dictionary: Display Data Element screen will be displayed.

3. Press the Display <-> Change button on the Application toolbar. The screen switches to change mode.

4. Press the Documentation button on the Application toolbar. The Change Data Element: Language E screen is displayed.

5. Type the text the user should see when he or she requests help for this field. The first line contains the characters &DEFINITION&. This is a heading; do not change this line. Type your documentation beginning on line two. Press the Enter key to begin each new paragraph.

6. Press the Save Active button on the Application toolbar to save your changes. The message "Document was saved in active status" appears in the status bar.

7. Press the Back button on the Standard toolbar. You are returned to the Dictionary: Change Data Element screen.

8. Press the Back button once more to return to the Dictionary: Table/Structure screen.

Testing F1 Help

To test your F1 help:

1. Begin on the Dictionary: Table/Structure screen (either change or display mode).

2. Choose the menu path Utilities->Create entries.

3. Put your cursor on the field with the modified help text.

4. Press F1. The system will display your modified documentation.

Adding Hypertext Links to F1 Help

NEW TERM *Hypertext links* enable you to click on a highlighted word or phrase in F1 help and display additional help for that word or phrase. To add hypertext links, you first create a document you want to link to, and then insert a reference to that document in your help text. Document names must start with y or z. You can include hyperlinks in your new document also and link from there to another document, ad infinitum.

SCREENCAM Start the ScreenCam "How to Create a Hypertext Link in F1 Help" now.

1. Begin at the R/3 main menu and choose the menu path Tools->ABAP/4 Development Workbench. The ABAP/4 Development Workbench screen is displayed.

2. Choose the menu path Utilities->Documentation. The Document Maintenance: Initial Screen is displayed.

3. Click on the down-arrow of the Document Class field. A list of document classes is displayed.

4. Double-click on General Text. The Document Class field now contains the value General text, and a field named General Text is displayed at the top of the Document Maintenance screen. (The Documentation Type field should already contain the value Original user. If it doesn't, click on the down arrow at the end of the field and change it.)

5. In the General Text field, type the name of a document you want to create. The name must start with y or z. REMEMBER THIS NAME.

6. Press the Create button. The Change General Text: Language E screen is displayed.

7. Type your document here. Press the Enter key at the end of each paragraph.

8. Press the Save Active button. The Create Object Catalog Entry screen is displayed.

9. Press the Local Object button. You are returned to the Change General Text screen and the message "Document was saved in active status" appears in the status bar.

10. Press the Back button to return to the Document Maintenance: Initial screen.

11. Press the Back button again to return to the ABAP/4 Development Workbench screen.

12. Go into the Data Dictionary and display your data element.

13. Press the Display <-> Change button on the Application toolbar. Your screen switches to change mode.

14. Press the Documentation button on the Application toolbar. The Change Data Element: Language E screen is displayed.

15. Place your cursor in the position at which you want to insert a hyperlink.

16. Choose the menu path Include->Reference. The Insert Link screen is displayed.

17. Click on the down arrow at the end of the Selected Reference field. The Title screen is displayed; notice that it contains a list of document classes.

18. Double-click on General text. The Selected Reference field now contains the value General text, and a field named General Text is displayed at the top of the screen.

19. In the General Text field, type the name of the document you created in step 6.

20. In the Name In Document field, enter the hyperlink text. This is the text that will be highlighted and on which the user will be able to click to receive more help.

21. Press the Continue button. You are returned to the Change Data Element: Language E screen and a link appears at the cursor position.

22. Press the Save Active button on the Application toolbar.

23. You can try out your new hyperlink immediately by choosing the menu path Document->Screen Output. The Display Documentation screen is displayed, your help text appears, and your hyperlink should be highlighted.

24. Click on the hyperlink. The Display Hypertext: screen is displayed and your document should appear.

25. Press Back three times to return to the Dictionary: Table/Structure screen.

26. To test your hyperlink, display your table and choose the menu path Utilities->Create Entries. The Table Insert screen is shown.

27. Position your cursor in the field for which you created F1 help.

28. Press F1. Your help text with the hyperlink should be displayed.

29. Click on the hyperlink. Your new document should be displayed.

TROUBLESHOOTER

Trouble	Solution
Can't find General Text in the list of document classes.	• Scroll up.
Seeing message "Change relevant to translation?"	• Press the Save Active button on the Application toolbar, not the Save button on the Standard toolbar.
Seeing message "Data element is not used in an ABAP/4 Dictionary structure."	• Change the document class to General Text.
I'm pressing the Documentation button in the data element screen, but it doesn't do anything.	• Is the screen title Dictionary: Display Data Element? If so, you are in display mode. You need to be in change mode. Press the Display <-> Change button and then try again.

3

Summary

- The Data Dictionary is a tool used by ABAP/4 programs to create and maintain tables. There are three types of tables: transparent, pooled, and cluster. Transparent tables are the most common and are used to contain application data. Pooled and cluster tables are primarily used by SAP to contain system data.

- To create a table, you first need domains and data elements. Domains provide the technical characteristics of a field; data elements provide the field labels and F1 help. Both are reusable.

- Dictionary objects must be active before they can be used. If you make a change to a dictionary object, you must reactivate the object before the changes take effect.

- Data browsers enable you to display and modify the data within tables. SE16 is the most general data browser. SE17, SM30, and SM31 are the other browsers that offer varying capabilities.

- You can create F1 help within a data element by pressing the Documentation button. Within that F1 help, you can create hypertext links to other F1 help documents.

Q&A

Q **If I make the length of a field smaller by changing the domain, and if that field is used in a table that already contains data filling the entire length of the field, what happens?**

A When you activate the domain, the system will attempt to activate the tables that are dependent upon that domain. The activation of the tables that would have lost data will fail, and a list of those tables will be shown to you. If you then go and activate those tables, the system will automatically convert the data in them, and the data in the column referenced by the domain will be truncated.

Q **How do you find out what tables will be affected before you change a domain?**

A Do a Where-used list on the domain. To do this, display the domain, press the Where-Used List button on the Application toolbar, select Other Objects, and press Continue. A tree list will be displayed. Double-click on the line that reads Table. The list of table names is displayed. Double-click on any line to display the table.

Q **Is it possible to create a table field without using a data element or domain? It seems like such a lot of work to have to create these for every field.**

A Yes, it is possible to create a table field without using a data element or domain. Display the table in change mode and then choose the menu path Edit->Direct Type Entry. You can then enter the field length and data type directly. This method is *not* recommended for fields that will appear onscreen; it is only appropriate for fields that will never be seen onscreen and will not have any foreign key relationships to other tables (see the following chapter for an explanation of foreign keys). SAP uses this method of creating tables for tables that hold system information such as database cursor IDs. You might use it in a staging table that holds raw data in transit into or out of the R/3 system. There are two main drawbacks of this method. One, no data elements are used and so no field labels or F1 help will exist. Two, no domains are used and so foreign keys cannot be created.

Workshop

The following exercises will give you practice creating objects in the data dictionary and using those objects in simple programs with the `tables`, `select`, and `write` statements. The answers appear in the appendix.

Quiz

1. What is the purpose of the domain?
2. What does the data element contain?

3. To what does the term *application data* refer?

4. For fields of type DEC, is the decimal point stored with the value of the field?

5. What are the transaction codes of the four data browsers. Which one is most commonly used, and which one cannot be used to update data?

6. What is the difference between a transparent table and a pooled or cluster table?

Exercise 1

Add the fields shown in Table 3.4 to your ●●●lfa1 table. None of these fields will have an x in the Key column because they do not form part of the primary key. The purpose of these fields is to contain a second name for the vendor, the date and time the row was created, and the user ID of the user who created the record. Create a new data element for all fields. Reuse the domain from the name1 field for the name2 field. For the rest of the fields, use the existing R/3 domain names shown below. Document these fields using the Documentation button in the data element. After you have activated your changes, use a data browser to update the existing rows in your table and put data into the new fields. While you are updating the rows, test your F1 help.

TABLE 3.4 NEW FIELDS AND THEIR CHARACTERISTICS FOR TABLE ztxlfa1

Field Name	DE Name	DM Name
name2	●●●name2	●●●name
erdat	●●●●erdat	datum
ertim	●●●●ertim	time
ername	●●●●ernam	usnam

Exercise 2

Create a transparent table ●●●kna1 to contain customer master data, as shown in Table 3.5. Use a data browser to add data to the table. Create a new program ●●●e0302 that reads the data from this table and writes it to the list.

TABLE 3.5   FIELDS AND THEIR CHARACTERISTICS FOR TABLE •••kna1

Description					
Field Name	*PK*	*DE Name*	*DM Name*	*Type*	*Len*
Client					
mandt	x	mandt			
Customer Number					
kunnr	x	•••kunnr	•••kunnr	CHAR	10
Customer Name					
name1		•••kname1	•••name	CHAR	35
City					
cityc		•••cityc	•••cityc	CHAR	4
Region					
regio		•••regio	•••regio	CHAR	3
Country					
land1		•••land1	•••land1	CHAR	3

DAY 4

The Data Dictionary, Part 2

Chapter Objectives

After you complete this chapter, you will be able to:

- Create foreign keys.
- Use the Value Table field in the domain.
- Create and use text tables.
- Describe the difference between a structure and a table, and create structures in the R/3 Data Dictionary.
- Create tables and structures containing currency and quantity fields.
- Nest structures within other structures or tables.

Discovering Foreign Keys

NEW TERM   A *foreign key* is a field in a table that is connected to another table via a foreign key relationship. The purpose of the foreign key relationship is to validate the data being entered into one table by checking against a valid set of values in another table. The table that contains the foreign key is called the *foreign key table*. The table that contains the valid set of values is called the *check table* (see Figure 4.1). The field that is validated and on which the foreign key relationship is created is called the foreign key.

FIGURE 4.1.

The foreign key table and the check table.

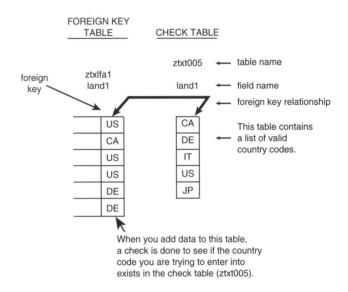

For example, your •••lfa1 table contains country codes in a field named land1. You can create a second table, for example •••t005, and fill it with a list of valid country codes. Then, if you create a foreign key like the one shown in Figure 4.1, a check will automatically be done against the check table for a valid value. With such a foreign key in place, the user cannot insert invalid country codes into table •••lfa1.

A foreign key gets its name from the fact that it must always check against a field in the primary key of another table.

Triggering the Foreign Key Check

Foreign key checking is performed by the R/3 user interface. When you type a value into a field and press the Enter key, behind the scenes the user interface formulates a select statement to validate the foreign key field and sends it to the database. If a matching row is not found in the check table, the user sees a standard message indicating that the value he entered is invalid. If a matching row exists in the check table, the values entered on the screen are allowed to pass to the underlying ABAP/4 program. Thus, the foreign keys are already checked before the program receives the values. In addition to the Enter key, foreign keys are also checked when a function key, a pushbutton, or a menu item is selected.

Foreign keys are checked by the user interface only. They *do not* exist in the database, and they are not checked if you merely issue a database update statement. No referential integrity constraints are kept in the database. Therefore, an incorrectly written ABAP/4 program can violate referential integrity; it can insert invalid values into database tables. For that reason, ABAP/4 programs that need to update the database with data that comes from a source other than the user interface usually pass that data through a user interface in order to validate it.

Note

> For more information on using the user interface to validate data, refer to the R/3 Library help for BDC (Batch Data Communication) programs. To view this documentation, from any screen choose the menu path Help->R/3 Library. You will see the main menu of the R/3 library. From there, click on the following tabs: Basis Components->ABAP/4 Development Workbench->Basis Programming Interfaces->Transferring Data With Batch Input.

Technical Requirements for Creating a Foreign Key

To create a foreign key:

- The check must occur against a field within the primary key of the check table.
- The domain names for the foreign key field and the check table field must be the same.

The second requirement exists to make sure that the fields being compared are compatible in data type and length (see Figure 4.2).

Note

> In Figure 4.2, both fields use the same data element as well as the same domain. Notice that it is not required that they both use the same data element—only the domains must be the same.

Because these fields share a common domain, the integrity of the comparison between the two fields is guaranteed because their data types and lengths will always match.

4

FIGURE 4.2.

This is a diagram of the foreign key field, check table field, and the common domain they share.

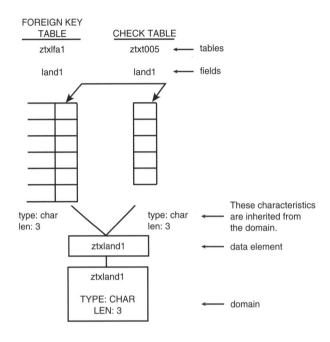

Creating a Foreign Key

Now it is time for you to create a simple foreign key. This example will enable you to become familiar with the screens involved in this process; all of the fields in those screens will be explained in detail later in this chapter. The following procedures demonstrate how create check table ztxt005, and then a foreign key on ztxlfa1-land1 by using ztxt005 as the check table. After viewing this procedure, you will be asked to create your own •••t005 table and then create a foreign key relationship from •••lfa1-land1 to check table •••t005.

Before you create a foreign key, you must first have a check table. Although there is already a country code table in R/3, for practice you will create and use your own. The check table will be named •••t005 and will contain the fields and use the data elements shown in Table 4.1. (An x in the PK column indicates fields that form the primary key.)

TABLE 4.1   THE FIELDS AND THEIR CHARACTERISTICS FOR TABLE •••t005

Field Name	PK	DE Name
mandt	x	mandt
land1	x	•••land1

Check Table Creation Procedure

Following is the creation procedure for check table •••t005. If you have trouble, refer to the troubleshooter for the transparent table creation procedure for pre-existing domains and data elements on Day 3.

SCREENCAM   Start the ScreenCam "How to Create Check Table •••t005" now.

To create your check table:

1. Begin at the Dictionary: Initial Screen.

2. Type the table name in the Object Name field.

3. Choose the Tables radio button.

4. Press the Create button. The Dictionary: Table/Structure: Change Fields screen is displayed.

5. Type a short text, choose delivery class A, and tickmark Tab. Maint. Allowed.

6. Type the field and data element names at the bottom of the screen.

7. Tickmark both fields to indicate that they both form the primary key.

8. Press the Save button on the Standard toolbar. The Create Object Catalog Entry screen appears.

9. Press the Local Object button. You are returned to the Dictionary: Table/Structure: Change Fields screen.

10. Press the Technical Settings button on the Application toolbar. The ABAP/4 Dictionary: Maintain Technical Settings screen is displayed.

11. In the Data Class field, enter **APPL0** (APPL0 with a *zero*, not APPLO with an alphabetic *O*).

12. Enter **0** (zero) in the Size Category field.

13. Press the Save button.

14. Press the Back button. You are returned to the Dictionary: Table/Structure: Change Fields screen.

15. Press the Activate button on the Application toolbar. The message "was activated" appears in the status bar and the Status field contains the value Act..

Choose the menu path Utilities->Create Entries to enter data into your newly created check table. Enter six rows with land1 values of US, CA, DE, IT, JP, and AU.

Foreign Key Creation Procedure

SCREENCAM Start the ScreenCam "How to Create a Foreign Key" now.

To create a foreign key:

1. Begin at the Dictionary: Initial Screen.
2. In the Object Name field, type the name of the table that is to contain the foreign key (•••lfa1).
3. Choose the Tables radio button.
4. Press the Change button. The Dictionary: Table/Structure: Change Fields screen is displayed.
5. Position your cursor on the field that is to become the foreign key (land1).
6. Press the Foreign Keys button on the Application toolbar. The Create Foreign Key screen will be displayed (see Figure 4.3).
7. Type a description of the foreign key in the Short Text field, for example, **Country Code validation**.
8. Type the name of the check table (•••t005) in the Check Table field, or click on the down-arrow and choose it from the list.
9. The Change Foreign Key pop-up appears. It states `Check table name was created or changed. Generate a proposal for field assignment?` Press the Yes button.
10. You are returned to the Create Foreign Key screen. The check table field names and the foreign key field names are displayed. (The check table field names are •••t005-mandt and •••t005-land1. The foreign key field names are •••lfa1-mandt and •••lfa1-land1).
11. Press the Copy button. You are returned to the Dictionary: Table/Structure: Change Fields screen and the message "Foreign key was transferred" appears in the status bar. The Status fields contain the values `Revised` and `Not saved`.
12. Press the Activate button on the Application toolbar. The message "was activated" appears in the status bar. The values in the Status fields are now `Act.` and `Saved`.

You have just created a foreign key relationship between the •••lfa1 and •••t005 tables. •••lfa1-land1 is the foreign key field, and •••t005 is the check table. The user interface will validate the value within the •••lfa1-land1 field against the values in the •••t005-land1 column.

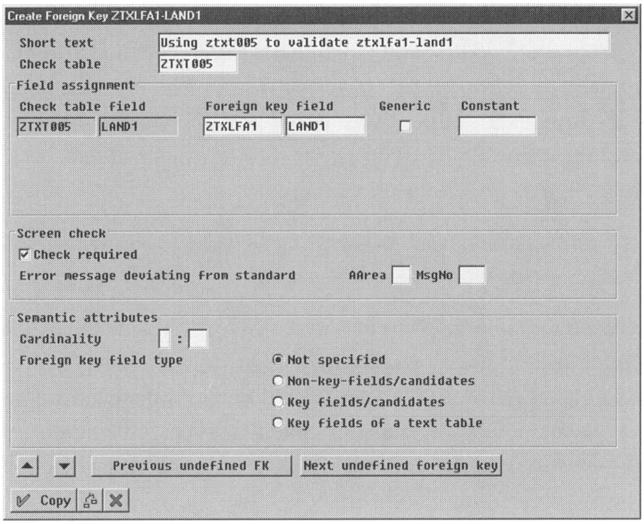

FIGURE 4.3.

The Create Foreign Key screen displays check table fields and their associated foreign key fields.

Testing the Foreign Key Relationship

If you encounter problems, the following procedure is described in more detail in the next section. To test your foreign key:

1. Begin on the Dictionary: Table/Structure screen (either change or display mode).

2. Choose the menu path Utilities->Create entries.

3. Type a value into the foreign key field (Country Code).

4. Press the Enter key. If the value is not found in the check table, the message "Entry does not exist (please check your entry)" is displayed.

Discovering the CheckTable Column

After you have created a foreign key, the name of the check table appears in the CheckTable column on the Dictionary: Table/Structure screen. If a field is a foreign key, the CheckTable column will contain the name of the check table for that field.

Look at your table now. You should see the name of your check table in the CheckTable column.

Automatic Determination of Foreign Key Fields

When you created the foreign key, you did not have to specify the fields that should participate in the foreign key relationship—the system determined it automatically. This section explains how the system determines these field names.

During the creation of a foreign key, you put your cursor on the foreign key field and pressed the foreign key button, and the system generated a foreign key proposal consisting of pairs of fields. In each pair, one field comes from the check table and the other from the foreign key table. The number of pairs is equal to the number of primary key fields of the check table. All of the primary key fields of the check table must be included in the foreign key relationship.

The system searches these primary key fields for the one that has the *same domain* as the foreign key field, and pairs it with your foreign key field.

If there are multiple fields in the primary key of the check table, it will try to find a match for each of the remaining fields. One by one, the system will try to find a field in the foreign key table that has the same domain as the check table field. Failing that, it will try to find a field that has the same data type and length. If it finds more than one match, the system picks one and warns you that the assignment is ambiguous. The process is repeated until all primary key fields from the check table have been paired with a field from the foreign key table.

Relating Foreign Keys to the Down-Arrow and F4 Help

NEW TERM   In addition to F1 help, you can also provide something called *F4 help* to the user. F4 help is a list of valid values that the user can enter into a field. In order to obtain F4 help, the user positions their cursor in a field and presses the F4 key. F4 help is also known as *possible entries help* because it is the list of possible entries allowed in the field. Both terms are used interchangeably by SAP.

When you create a foreign key, F4 help is automatically provided for that field.

SCREENCAM   Start the ScreenCam "Using a Foreign Key to Provide F4 Help" now.

On a screen, if you place your cursor within a foreign key field, a down-arrow will appear at the end of the input field. This is the F4 help. If you click the down-arrow or press the F4 key, a list of possible, valid entries is displayed. This list is the contents of the check table. In this list, the primary key columns of the check table are displayed, excluding mandt.

Note   The column heading and width in the possible entries list come from the Header field in the data element for the check table field displayed.

Follow this procedure to test the foreign key relationship you created on •••lfa1-land1. If your foreign key doesn't work, try this procedure using ztxlfa1, then compare ztxlfa1 with your table to determine the problem.

1. Begin on any screen.

2. In the Command field, type /nse16.

3. Press the Enter key. The Data Browser: Initial Screen is displayed.

4. Type •••lfa1 in the Table Name field.

5. Press the Create Entries button on the Application toolbar. The Table Insert screen is displayed.

6. Type any value in the vendor number field, for example, MY-V1.

7. Position your cursor on the Country Code field (land1). Although a down-arrow appears at the end of it, do not press it just yet.

8. Type the value XX in the Country Code field.

9. Press the Save button on the Standard toolbar. The message "Entry XX does not exist (please check your entry)" appears.

   Your cursor is positioned at the beginning of the field that contains the incorrect value. A down-arrow appears at the end of the field.

10. Click the down-arrow or press the F4 key. A pop-up containing the primary key columns of check table •••t005 appears.

11. Double-click US. The pop-up disappears and the value in the country code field changes to US.

12. Press the Save button on the Standard toolbar. The message "Database record successfully created" appears in the status bar.

The foreign key relationship provides a mechanism for validating data entered by the user on the screen. If the field is a foreign key field, the value is compared against the check table. If the value doesn't exist in the check table, a standard error message is issued.

Foreign Keys and Batch Programs

Batch programs that read sequential files or other sources of data other than the screen and update the database directly must validate the data. Such a program should be coded in one of three ways:

- It should pass the data through a user interface by calling a transaction containing screens. This is done entirely in the background. The data is automatically "keyed" into the screen fields to cause the foreign key check to be done. This technique is

called *BDC* (*Batch Data Communications*), and was mentioned earlier in the
"Forays into Foreign Keys" section. BDC is the standard technique used to import
data into the R/3 system.

- It can contain `select` statements that perform the foreign key checking. This technique is less reliable because the programs must be updated if new foreign keys are added or if existing ones change.

- It can pass the data to special function modules that perform both foreign key checking and database updates. SAP creates these function modules (called BAPIs, or Business APIs) and supplies them with the R/3 system.

Compound Foreign Keys

NEW TERM   A *compound foreign key* is a foreign key composed of two or more fields. In other words, a check is done to compare two fields in the foreign key table against two fields in the check table. The combination of values must exist in the check table before they can be inserted into the foreign key table. However only one field on the screen will trigger the compound foreign key check.

NEW TERM   When you create a compound foreign key, the field on which you actually define the foreign key is called the *check field*. Only a non-blank value in the check field triggers the check against the check table. A value in any of the other fields within the compound foreign key will not trigger the validation.

For example, the `regio` field in `ztxlfa1` should only contain valid state or province codes. The combination of `regio` and `land1` *together* must be valid. Therefore, a check table (`ztxt005s`) containing valid combinations of `regio` and `land1` is needed. After creating this check table, a compound foreign key is needed in `ztxlfa1` to validate the combination of `regio` and `land1` against the check table. Incidentally, `ztxt005s-land1` should also be validated against `ztxt005-land1` (see Figure 4.4).

FIGURE 4.4.

A compound foreign key validating the combination of region and country against the check table.

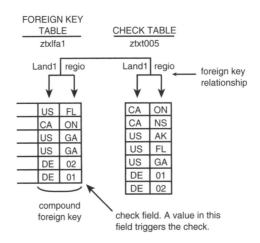

You create a compound foreign key almost exactly the same way as a foreign key containing a single field. You begin by positioning your cursor on a field, in this case ztxlfa1-regio, and then pressing the Foreign Keys button. Because your cursor is on regio, it becomes the *check field* of the compound foreign key. Although the foreign key is composed of multiple fields, only one of those fields will trigger a check against the database. Because regio is the check field, a value entered into it on the screen triggers a check. If the check field is non-blank when the user presses the Enter key, a check is carried out against the check table comparing all fields of the foreign key. If the check field is blank, no checking is done *even if the other fields contain values*.

Caution

As with the simple foreign key, the domain names of the check field and its associated field in the check table must match. However, when the foreign key is created, the rest of the domain names in the compound foreign key do not have to match; the foreign key can be created if only their data types and lengths match. Later, if the data type or length in one of these domains is changed, the fields will no longer match and the results of the foreign key check will be unpredictable. For this reason, although R/3 does not enforce that all domain names of a compound foreign key match, it is highly desirable.

As a rule of thumb, when changing the data type or length of field in a compound foreign key other than the check field, you must check to see whether the foreign key and check table fields are using the same domain. If they are not, you must update them both to have the same data type and length. Failure to do so will result in unpredictable operation of the foreign key.

4

If you create a foreign key relationship to a check table containing more than one field in the primary key, all of the primary key fields of the check table must be included in the foreign key. They do not all have to be checked (see the section "Generic Foreign Keys" that follows), but they all must be included.

Because most check tables contain the mandt field, it forms a part of most foreign keys (see Figures 4.5 and 4.6).

By including mandt in the check table, independent and valid sets of values can be defined for each logon client and can differ between clients. This capability is highly desirable to separate the data between clients and ensure that they are completely independent of each other.

F4 help is only available on the check field of a compound foreign key. When invoking F4 help, all of the primary key fields of the check table will be displayed. The column containing the check field will be highlighted in the list. The column widths and titles come from the Header field in the data elements.

FIGURE 4.5.

A compound foreign key involving the mandt *field.*

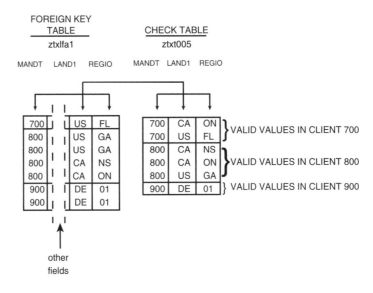

FIGURE 4.6.

The definition of the foreign key shown in Figure 4.5.

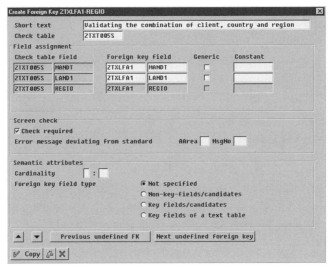

Understanding Cardinality

NEW TERM The *cardinality* of the foreign key relationship describes, for each value in the check table, *how many* rows of data are allowed to be in the foreign key table. It is entered on the Create Foreign Key screen (refer to Figure 4.3). Cardinality is described as X:Y, where X refers to the check table and Y refers to the foreign key table. X can only have the values 1 or C, and Y can be 1, C, N, or CN.

The values of X mean:

- 1: If the application program deletes a row from the check table it will also delete the corresponding rows from the foreign key table. For example, if the application program deletes the value US from the check table, it will delete all rows from the foreign key table where land1 = US. In other words, if there is a value in the foreign key table, there is always one and only one row having that value in the check table.
- C: Deletes are allowed from the check table without deleting the corresponding rows from the foreign key table. In other words, there can be values in the foreign key table without corresponding values in the check table.

The values of Y mean:

- 1: There is always one, and only one, row in the foreign key table for each row in the check table.
- C: There is, at the most, one row in the foreign key table for each row in the check table.
- N: There is always at least one row in the foreign key table for each row in the check table.
- CN: There might or might not be rows in the foreign key table for each row in the check table.

Cardinality is *not enforced* by the R/3 system. Specifying cardinality is optional, and the system will not check cardinality to determine whether that update should be allowed to take place if an ABAP/4 program updates a table. The only time cardinality is used is when you create an aggregate object in the DDIC.

NEW TERM An *aggregate object* is a DDIC object composed of more than one table. An example of an aggregate object is a view.

When you create a foreign key you should specify the cardinality. If you don't specify it, you will be unable to include the table in an aggregate object.

Foreign Key Field Type

The foreign key field type should also be specified on the same screen as the cardinality when you create the foreign key (refer to Figure 4.3). It can be one of the following values:

- Key fields/candidates
- Non-key fields/candidates
- Key fields of a text table

Key Fields

Choose Key Fields/Candidates if the foreign key field is one of the primary key fields of the foreign key table. Choose Non-Key Fields/Candidates if it is not. For example, assume table t1 is composed of fields f1 through f10, and its primary key fields are f1, f2, and f3. If you were to define a foreign key on field f3, Key Fields/Candidates would be the correct type because f3 is part of the primary key. If you were to define a foreign key on field f5, Non-key Fields/Candidates would be correct because f5 is not one of the primary key fields.

Key Candidates

NEW TERM   A *key candidate* is a field in a table that, by itself or in conjunction with another field that is not part of the primary key, could be used to uniquely identify a row in the table. To put it another way, if there is way to uniquely select a row from a table without using primary key fields, key candidates exist in that table. The key candidates are the fields *not* within the primary key that can be used to uniquely identify a row; in essence they can serve as an alternate primary key.

For example, ztxlfa1 has a single primary key field that contains a unique identifier for each row. If you assume that the combination of erdat and ertim (creation date and time) is also unique for every row, these date and time fields are key candidates. If either one appeared in a foreign key, the correct foreign key type would be key fields/candidates.

When creating a foreign key, you should choose key fields/candidates if the foreign key field is one of the primary key fields of the table or is a key candidate. Choose non-key fields/candidates if it is not.

Key Fields of a Text Table

The R/3 system supports multiple spoken languages, and thus enables users to sign on using the language of their choice. Because of this, descriptions in R/3 are stored in special language-dependent tables called text tables.

> **Tip**
>
> Users can set their own default logon language. This is done in the user profile by choosing the menu path System->User profile->User defaults. Changes to your user profile are not effective until you next log on.

NEW TERM   A *text table* is a table that contains spoken-language descriptions of values in a check table. These descriptions are stored in multiple languages. The primary key of the text table is the same as the primary key of the check table, with the addition of a spras (language) column.

For example, the ztxt005 table has country codes in it. Country names are stored in a separate table named ztxt005t (shown in Figure 4.7) because you actually need many names for one country code. Because it stores language-specific descriptions of a generalized code, ztxt005t is called a text table.

FIGURE 4.7.

The text table for ztxt005 is ztxt005t. It is composed of the fields mandt, spras, land1, landx, *and* natio.

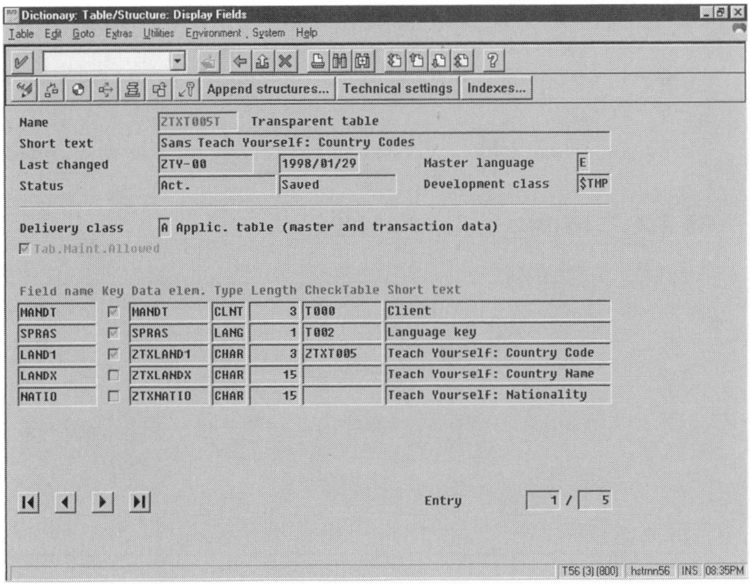

The primary key of ztxt005t contains the same fields as the primary key of ztxt005, with the addition of a spras (language) column. The spras field contains the language code and enables this table to contain a description for multiple logon languages.

The primary key of any text table is composed of the fields mandt and spras, followed by the validation field (or fields). One or more description fields follow this primary key.

A foreign key relationship is defined on ztxt005t-land1 to check table ztxt005. The foreign key field type should be *key fields of a text table*.

Relating Text Tables to F4 Help

NEW TERM The foreign key type "key fields of a text table" indicates to the R/3 system that the foreign key table is a text table. When you choose this type, the first description that follows the primary key is displayed in the F4 help, in the logon language of the user. Therefore, this key type has two special properties:

- When the rows of the check table are displayed in response to an F4 help request, the first description field from the text table will appear in the same list, as if it were a part of the check table.

- Only the rows from the text table having the same language code as the user's current logon language appear in the F4 help list.

For example, text table `ztxt005t` contains a foreign key relationship from `ztxt005t-land1` to check table `ztxt005`, and the type is "key fields of a text table". When you invoke F4 help on `ztxt005-land1`, the user sees the primary key columns of the check table `ztxt005`, *plus* the contents of the first column that follows the primary key of `ztxt005t`. Only the rows where `spras` is equal to the current logon language are displayed. The result is that the user sees descriptions in his logon language for the codes in `ztxlfa1`.

The contents of tables `ztxt005` and `ztxt005t` are shown in Tables 4.2 and 4.3.

TABLE 4.2 CONTENTS OF TABLE `ztx005`

land1
US
CA
DE
IT
JP
AQ
CC

TABLE 4.3 CONTENTS OF TABLE `ztxt005t`

spras	*land1*	*landx*
E	CA	Canada
D	CA	Kanada
E	DE	Germany
D	DE	Deutschland
E	US	United States
D	US	USA
E	IT	Italy
D	IT	Italien
E	JP	Japan
D	JP	Japan
E	AQ	Antarctica
D	AQ	Antarctica
E	CC	Coconut Islands
D	CC	Kobinseln

Start the ScreenCam "Text Table Demonstration: The Effect of the Logon Language" now.

1. Start transaction SE16 (type **/nse16** in the Command field and press the Enter key).

2. Enter the table name **ztxlfa1** in the Table Name field.

3. Press the Create Entries button on the Application toolbar.

4. Position your cursor on the Country Code field (**land1**).

5. Press the F4 key, or click the down-arrow at the end of the field. A pop-up appears displaying columns from both tables **ztxt005** and **ztxt005t**. Notice that the **land1** column from table **ztxt005** is displayed and the English-language descriptions from table **ztxt005t** are displayed.

6. Now log on again (you do not need to log off first). This time, enter **D** for Deutsche in the Language Field of the R/3 logon screen.

7. Repeat steps 1 through 5 in your new logon session.

8. Notice that this time the German descriptions from table **ztxt005t** are displayed.

Creating a Text Table and a Foreign Key for It

Now is a good time to try creating your own text table. Use **ztxt005t** as a model. Your text table will be named **•••t005t** and will contain the fields and use the data elements and domains shown in Table 4.4. You will also have to create the data element **•••landx**. Use the existing SAP domain **text15** for your new data element. An x in the PK column indicates fields that form the primary key.

TABLE 4.4   FIELDS AND THEIR CHARACTERISTICS FOR TABLE **•••t005t**

Field Name	PK	DE Name	DM Name
mandt	X	mandt	
spras	X	spras	
land1	X	•••land1	
landx		•••landx	text15

After activating **•••t005t**, enter data into it using SE16. Use the sample data shown in Table 4.3.

Now create a foreign key on **•••t005t-land1**. Follow the foreign key creation procedure previously given. Use **•••t005** as the check table. On the Create Foreign Key screen, specify a foreign key field type of Key fields of a text table. You might want to review the screencam "How to Create a Foreign Key" before beginning.

After creating your foreign key, follow the procedure for testing the foreign key relationship on •••lfa1-land1. In step 11, notice that the description from ztxt005t is also displayed. Also, log on again, this time specifying a logon language of D (German), and repeat the test. This time you should see the German descriptions in step 11.

Generic and Constant Foreign Keys

Recall that when you create a foreign key, all of the primary key fields of the check table must be included in the foreign key relationship. However at times, you may not want to perform a check against all of these fields. In other situations, you may wish to check against a constant value. In either of these cases, you can define either a generic or constant foreign key.

Generic Foreign Keys

NEW TERM A *generic foreign key* is a foreign key in which one of the primary key fields of the check table fields is marked as generic. When a primary key field is marked as generic, it doesn't have a counterpart in the foreign key table, and it does not participate in the check.

For example, within the Materials Management application, the mara table is the Material Master table. It contains the master list of materials used for manufacture and the attributes of each material.

The setup program for this book created a ztxmara table similar to mara. The fields of ztxmara are shown in Figure 4.8.

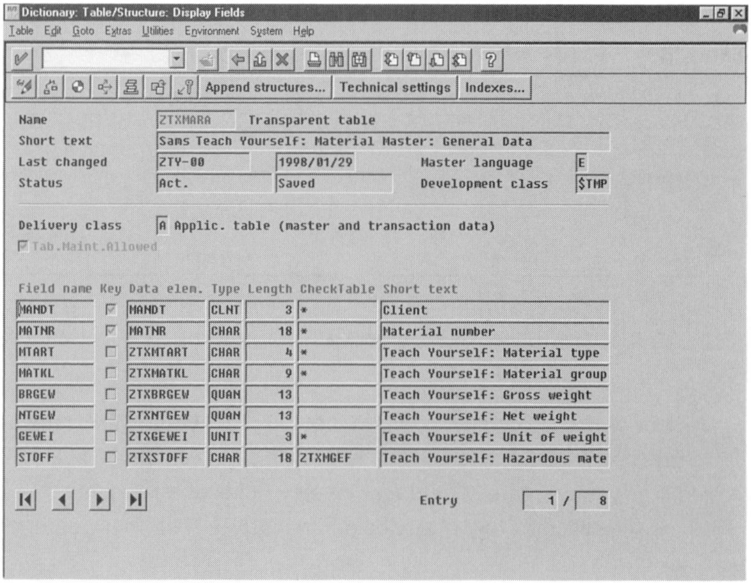

FIGURE 4.8.

Table ztxmara *is similar to the R/3 Material Master table* mara.

The ztxmara-stoff field contains a hazardous material number. If the field is non-blank, the material requires special handling; the stoff number indicates the type of handling required. The handling numbers are defined in table ztxmgef, which is illustrated in Figure 4.9. In our example, assume ztxmgef contains a row with stoff equal 1. That row indicates a handling procedure that requires gloves. Updating a material and placing a 1 in the ztxmara-stoff field for the material indicates that the material requires special handling with gloves.

FIGURE 4.9.

The ztxmara *and* ztxmgef *tables relate via the* stoff *field.*

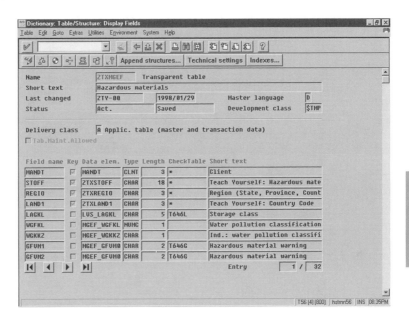

The check table for ztxmara-stoff is ztxmgef. The foreign key definition is shown in Figure 4.10.

This foreign key validates the values entered into ztxmara-stoff and ensures that only valid handling numbers exist in the ztxmara table. Unfortunately, handling regulations can vary with geographical regions. Therefore, the primary key of ztxmgef is composed of stoff, regio, and land1. However, ztxmara doesn't contain any geographical information — that information is contained in plant tables.

Remember, a foreign key must include all primary key fields from the check table. Therefore, regio and land1 from ztxmgef appear in the foreign key definition. However, for the purposes of ztxmara, validating ztxmara-stoff against ztxmgef-stoff is good enough; location information doesn't exist in ztxmara and doesn't matter for this validation. It is enough to know that the specified special handling number exists.

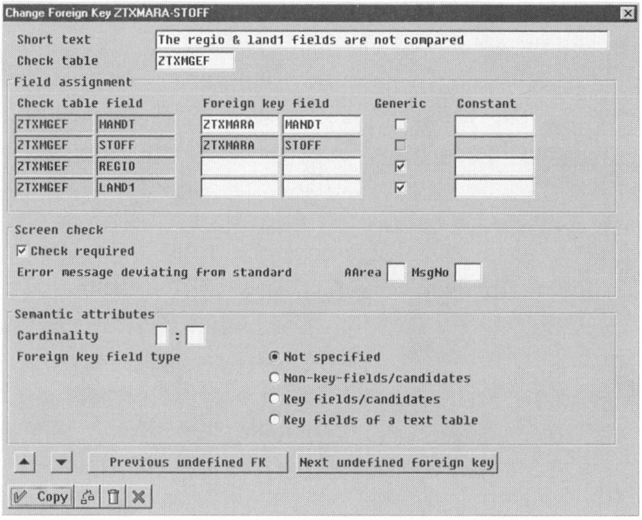

Figure 4.10.

A tickmark in the Generic *check box causes a field to be ignored during the foreign key check.*

In this foreign key relationship, the regio and land1 fields in the primary key of ztxmgef are be ignored. To cause these fields to be ignored during validation, they are defined in the foreign key relationship as *generic*. The tickmark in the Generic check box on the Create Foreign Key screen accomplishes this.

When this foreign key is checked, only the combination of mandt and stoff must exist in the check table. The regio and land1 fields are ignored.

Constant Foreign Keys

New Term *Constant foreign keys* are compound foreign keys where one of the check table field names is replaced by a constant value. This constant value is entered on the Create Foreign Key screen (see Figure 4.11).

For example, assume you need to create a new vendor table ztxlfa1us like ztxlfa1 containing U.S. vendors only, but for compatibility reasons, you want it to have exactly the same structure as ztxlfa1. The country code in this table would always be US. You could create a constant foreign key to restrict the values in table ztxlfa1us. An example of the definition is shown in Figure 4.11.

Adapted Foreign Keys

New Term Foreign key fields of a compound foreign key do not all have to reside in the same table. If they do not, this is known as an *adapted foreign key*. For example, assume that the country code for the vendor is not stored at all in ztxlfa1, but instead in ztxlfa1cc. When you create the foreign key on the region field, you would change the check table field for land1 to ztxlfa1cc-land1 (see Figure 4.12). The validation on the regio field would check to see whether the combination of mandt and regio existed in ztxt005s and whether land1 existed in any row of ztxt005cc.

FIGURE 4.11.

The country field as a constant foreign key.

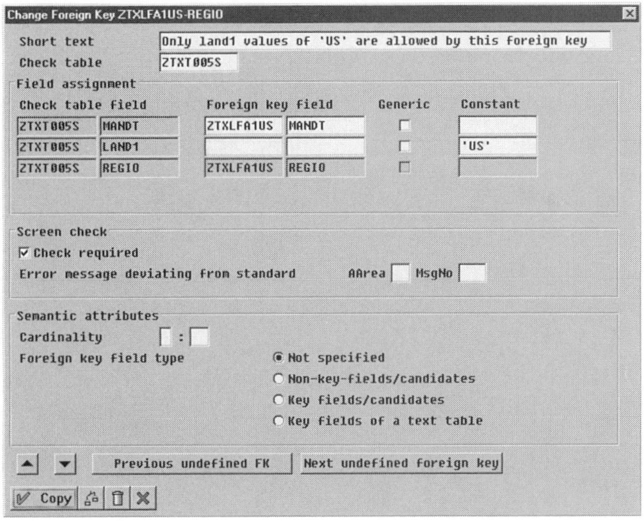

FIGURE 4.12.

An example of an adapted foreign key.

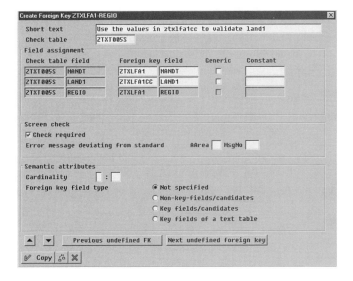

Defining a Value Table

NEW TERM   Within the domain is the *Value Table* field. The table named within this field provides the following functions to the domain:

- It is automatically proposed as the check table when creating a foreign key
- It provides a list of values for F4 (possible entries) help, but it does not provide validation

Whenever you create a foreign key relationship, the system looks in the value table field. If there is a table name there, it proposes that name as the check table.

Some readers will have difficulty with this concept, so I will explain it in depth in the following section.

Understanding the Value Table Field

In order to understand the purpose of the Value Table field, you should be familiar with the "bigger picture" of database design and development. I will begin by describing this bigger picture.

Before you create any tables in the DDIC, you usually do some database design. This design describes the tables that will be created, their relationships, and the type of data that each will contain. It will usually designate certain tables to be check tables for validating the data within other tables. For example, a country code check table may be needed to validate country codes for all of the tables where country codes will be stored. When you create a set of tables within R/3, you will usually create the check tables first.

When you create a check table, it exists for one primary purpose: to validate data. You can create multiple foreign key relationships linking many other tables to a single check table. The Value Table field in the domain exists to simplify the task of creating these relationships.

Before I continue, I want you to imagine that the Value Table field within the domain has a completely different name. Wipe the term "Value Table" from your mind, and imagine that field is called the "Default Check Table" field.

To simplify the example, our check table will have a single primary key field, illustrated in Figure 4.13. To illustrate this concept, I will describe the process you would go through to create this check table and use it in a foreign key relationship.

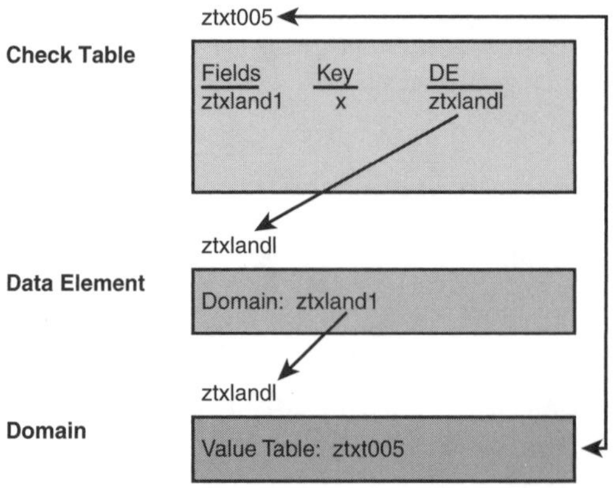

FIGURE 4.13.

The Value Table field within the domain contains the name of a check table.

When you create a check table, you must first create a domain. You would always create a new domain specifically for a check table. You would then create the data element, and then the table itself. You would then activate the table. You would then go back into the domain for the primary key field and put the name of the check table you just created in the Value Table field — but remember we call it the Default Check Table field.

Now, you would create another table, in our example it is ztxlfa1. You would create the land1 field and use the ztxland1 data element, and then both fields would use the same domain.

Now you would create the foreign key to validate land1. You would place your cursor on the ztxlfa1-land1 field and press the Foreign Key button. When you do this, the system will look in the domain at the Value Table field (remember we call it the Default Check Table field). If there were a table name there, the system would automatically propose that name as the name of the check table. In our case, the system would find ztxt005. Therefore, the system would propose ztxt005 as the check table—exactly what we would want. The foreign key proposal would be shown, and we could then save it.

In this example, the system automatically created the foreign key for us, because we put the name of the check table in the Value Table field. Using three mouse clicks, we created a foreign key! That, in essence, is the primary reason for the Value Table field. It exists to make the creation of foreign keys easier.

To summarize, the Value Table field is used in two ways by the system:

- The value table (remember to imagine Default Check Table) is automatically proposed as the check table when creating a foreign key.
- The value table provides a list of values for F4 help, but no validation is done on this list.

Value Table Field as the Check Table Proposal

In this section you will add a value table to a domain and observe its effect on the creation of a foreign key.

Edit domain •••land1 now and enter •••t005 in the Value Table field, then activate the domain.

Now you will delete the foreign key on the •••lfa1-land1 field and then create it again so that you can see the effect of the Value Table field on the foreign key creation process. To do so, follow the procedure below.

1. Begin at the Dictionary: Initial Screen.

2. In the Object Name field, type the name of the table (•••lfa1).

3. Choose the Tables radio button.

4. Press the Change button. The Dictionary: Table/Structure: Change Fields screen is displayed.

5. Position your cursor on the foreign key field (land1).

6. Press the Foreign Keys button on the Application toolbar. The Change Foreign Key screen is displayed.

7. Press the Delete button (the trashcan) at the bottom of the window.

8. You are returned to the Dictionary: Table/Structure: Change Fields screen. The message *Foreign key was deleted* appears in the status bar.

9. With your cursor still positioned on the foreign key field (land1), press the Foreign Keys button again. The Create Foreign Key screen is displayed. It reads *Foreign key does not exist. Generate proposal with value table as check table?* You see this message box because the system has looked in the domain and found a name in the Value Table field. It responds by issuing this message box.

10. Press the Yes button. The Create Foreign Key screen is displayed, and the Check Table field contains the value table from the domain. The Check Table fields and Foreign Key fields are filled in.

11. Press the Copy button. You are returned to the Dictionary: Table/Structure: Change Fields screen. The message *Foreign key was transferred* appears in the status bar. The Status fields read `Revised` and `Not saved`.

12. Press the Activate button. The message *was saved* appears in the status bar. The Status fields read `Act.` and `Saved`.

With a table name in the Value Table field in the domain you can quickly and reliably create foreign keys.

Rediscovering the CheckTable Column

The CheckTable column on the Dictionary: Table/Structure screen performs two functions:

- If a field is a foreign key, the CheckTable column will contain the name of the check table for that field.

- An asterisk (*) in this column means that a check table has not been defined for the field, but a value table exists in the domain.

There is an exception to the second point above. If you are currently displaying a value table, the asterisk will not appear in the field whose domain references the value table you are viewing.

Using the Value Table as a List of Possible Values

If a field contains a value table but is not a foreign key, when that field appears on a screen no validation is done on the field. The value table does not perform validation. Only a foreign key validates values.

With only a value table, a down-arrow will not appear at the end of the field as it does for a foreign key field. However, if you place your cursor in the field and press F4, the F4 key will still display a list of values from the value table. There is no indication on the screen that F4 functionality is available, and no checking is done if a value is entered in the field.

This functionality could be useful when you want to provide the user with a list of suggested values but want to allow other values to be typed into the field as well.

Special Table Fields

Two types of table fields need special treatment:

- currency fields
- quantity fields

Currency Fields

NEW TERM Assume you go to the bank and ask for 1000. The teller would probably ask you "1000 what?". You might reply "1000 dollars." Or you might be even more specific and ask for "1000 U.S. dollars." Monetary amounts in R/3 are stored in two fields: one to hold the actual numeric amount (1000) and one to hold the currency (USD). The numeric amount field is called the *currency field* and the other field is called the *currency key field*.

> **Tip**
>
> What many people refer to as currency is actually a currency code (USD for U.S. dollar, CAD for Canadian dollar, and so on). SAP uses the word "key" as a synonym for "code," so it calls the field containing the currency code the "currency key." This applies to most code fields in R/3; the country code is called the country key, the region code is the region key, and so on.

Currency fields have these requirements:

- The data type in the domain must be CURR.
- It must be linked to a field of type CUKY containing the currency key, such as USD (US dollars), CAD (Canadian dollars), ITL (Italian lira), and so on.

The currency key is known as the *reference field.* It is another field in the same or another table. It must have the type CUKY (currency key) in the domain. It indicates the currency key for the currency field that it references.

For example, assume you create a table containing a list of payments made to vendors. You would need a payment amount field (field name wrbtr) and a currency key field (usually waers) to completely indicate the amount and currency key used for that payment. To link the two fields together, you would double-click on the currency *field name* in the table and then enter the currency key table and field name in the fields Reference Table and Reference Field (see Figure 4.14).

FIGURE 4.14.

The reference fields on the Display Field screen.

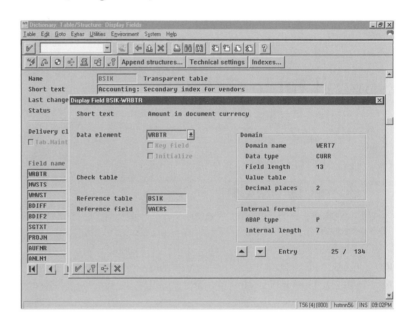

Quantity Fields

A *quantity field* is a field that contains a numeric measurement. For example, such a field might contain a measure of weight, length, temperature, or electricity. To be meaningful, a unit of measure such as pounds, inches, Fahrenheit, or kilovolts must accompany it. Quantity fields have these requirements:

- The data type in the domain must be QUAN.
- It must be linked to a field of type UNIT.

The UNIT field is the reference field for the QUAN field. The UNIT field can be in the same table or in another table. The UNIT field contains the measurement unit for the measurement in the quantity field.

For example, in table ztxmara, the ntgew field contains the net weight of a material and the gewei field contains the units, such as pounds or kilograms (see Figure 4.15). The ntgew field has a data type of QUAN and the data type of gewei is UNIT. If you double-click on ntgew, you will see that the reference table is ztxmara and the reference field is gewei (see Figure 4.16).

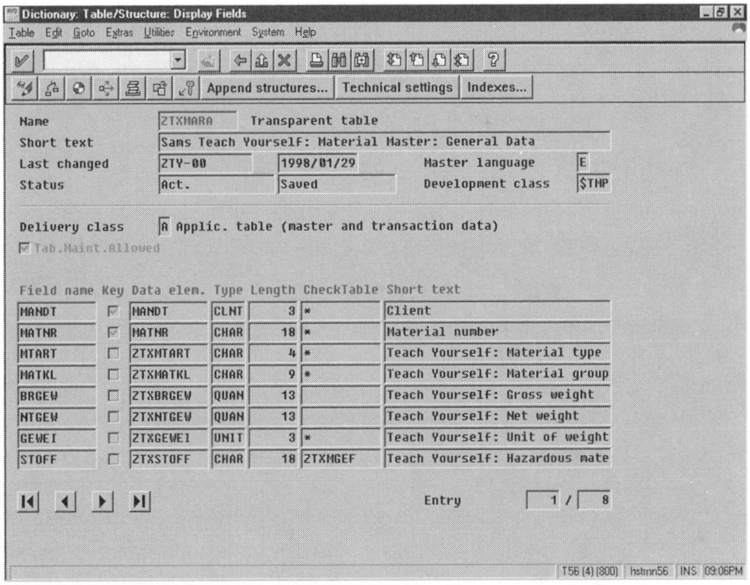

FIGURE 4.15.

This is the structure of the ztxmara table showing the ntgew and gewei fields.

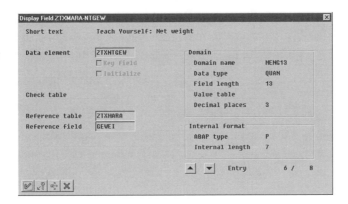

FIGURE 4.16.

These are the field attributes for the ntgew field. Notice that the two fields Reference Table and Reference Field provide the link to the UNIT field.

4

Structures in the Data Dictionary

NEW TERM In addition to tables, *structures* can also be defined in the Data Dictionary. As you might expect, a structure is a series of fields grouped together under a common name. It is very similar to a table. Like a table, it can be used within a program on the `tables` statement to define a work area.

The differences between a structure and a table are as follows:

- A structure doesn't have an associated database table.
- A structure doesn't have a primary key.
- A structure doesn't have technical attributes.

Structures follow the same naming conventions as transparent tables, and you cannot have a table and structure of the same name.

You would create a structure in the DDIC if you wanted to define the same work area in multiple programs. For example, if you wanted to write records to a sequential file using one ABAP/4 program and then read them in using another, both programs need to know the layout of those records. You would create a structure in the DDIC that defines the record layout, and then name that structure on the `tables` statement in both programs. This would create an identical work area in both programs.

The procedure for creating a structure is almost the same as for creating a transparent table. (Please refer to the procedures for creating a transparent table.) The only differences are the following:

- Instead of the Tables radio button, choose the Structures radio button.
- The Delivery Class and Tab.Maint.Allowed fields do not appear.
- Structures do not have a primary key.
- No technical attributes can be specified, such as data class, size category, or buffering.

Understanding Includes

A structure can contain another structure. In other words, you can nest structures one within another. This can be used to reduce maintenance by grouping fields together into a structure and then including that structure within another structure, or even within a table.

For example, a person's address is composed of a set of fields such as street, city, region, country, and postal code. You might need to keep such an address in multiple tables. Within the vendor table you might want to keep the vendor's address, in the customer master the customer's address, and in the employee table the employee's address. If you create a structure to group the fields that form the address together, you could then include that structure into the table definitions. When the table is activated, the fields of the structure are added to and exist in the database table as if they were defined within it. They will have the same name as the name in the structure. To include a structure within a table, (or within another structure), type **.INCLUDE** in the field name column, and enter the structure name in the data element column.

In Figure 4.17, the table ztxempl (employee table) includes structure ztxaddr (see Figure 4.18), which consists of address fields stras (street), ort01 (city), regio, and land1. Table ztxempl therefore contains these fields: ztxempl-stras, ztxempl-ort01, ztxempl-regio, and ztxempl-land1.

FIGURE 4.17.

The ztxempl *table contains an* .INCLUDE *to cause the fields of* ztxaddr *to be added to it.*

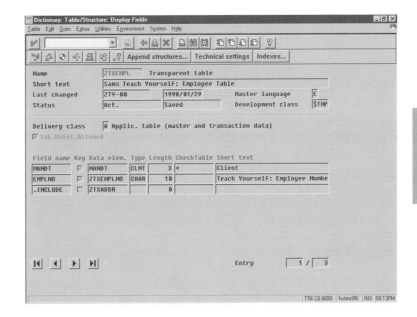

4

To view the expanded includes within the definition of the table itself, choose the menu path Extras->Substructures->Expand All Substr.. All the field names from an included structure will appear below the .INCLUDE, as shown in Figure 4.19.

NEW TERM The chain of structures created by including one structure within another is called an *include chain*. The maximum nesting depth is nine, and only one table can be included in an include chain. In other words, you cannot include a table within a table.

FIGURE 4.18.

The structure ztxaddr *contains the address fields that are included in table* ztxempl.

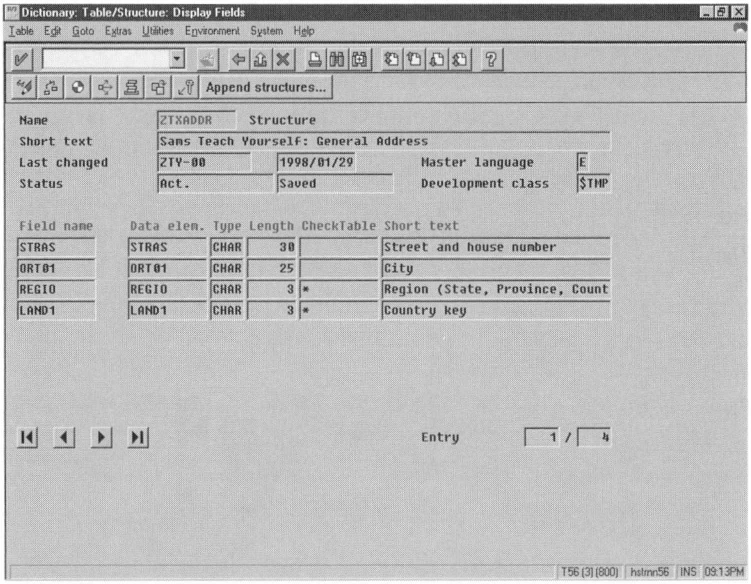

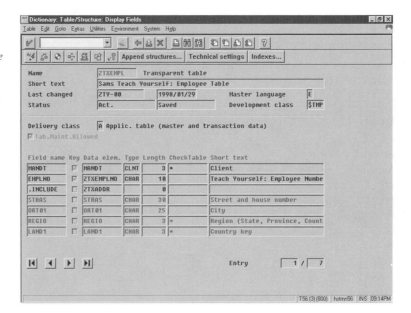

FIGURE 4.19.

The ztxempl *table* .INCLU-XXX *form of the* include *statement so that* ztxaddr *can be included twice without duplicating field names.*

Including the Same Structure Multiple Times

You can include the same structure multiple times within a table if, instead of .INCLUDE, you use .INCLU-XXX. The XXX represents your choice of any three characters. These three characters will be appended to each field name that is included to make it unique.

For example, assume you need to store two addresses in ztxempl: a home address and a mailing address. As shown in Figure 4.20, ztxempl2 includes structure ztxaddr twice. The first include, .INCLU-01, causes "01" to be appended to each of the field names of the structure. The second, .INCLU-02, appends "02" to each. The result, shown in Figure 4.21, can be seen by choosing the menu path Extras->Substructures->Expand All Substr.

FIGURE 4.20.

The ztxempl2 *table uses the* .INCLU-XXX *form of the* include *statement so that* ztxaddr *can be included twice without duplicating field names.*

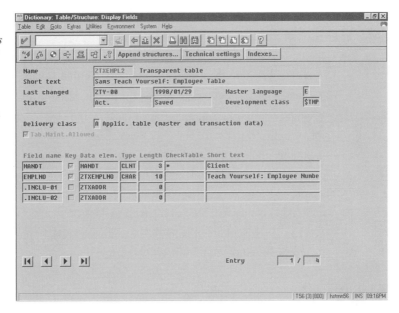

FIGURE 4.21.

Choosing the menu path Extras->Substructures->Expand all substr. causes fields from the structures appear in the list.

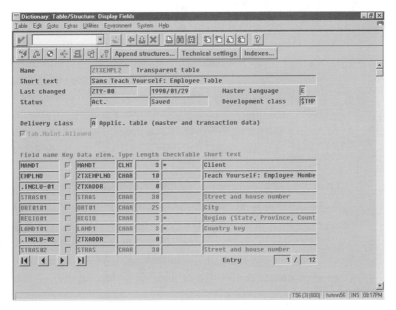

Tip

Structures and tables in R/3 are so similar that when looking at the Data Dictionary definition of each, they are difficult to tell apart. To determine which one you are looking at, look to the right of the name field. There you will see either Transparent table or Structure.

Summary

- Foreign keys ensure the integrity of data by performing onscreen validations, and provide F4 help to the user with list of permissible values.
- The value table provides a proposal for the check table and provides F4 help.
- Text tables provide multiple-language support for descriptions in R/3 and especially for F4 help.
- Within a table, each currency field must be linked to a currency key field, and each quantity field must be linked to a field containing the units of measurement.
- Tables and structures are very similar. The main difference is that a table has an underlying database table and a structure doesn't.
- You can use structures to define identical work areas in multiple programs. You can include a structure within other structures and tables.

Q&A

Q Can an ABAP/4 program ignore foreign key relationships and insert rows that violate referential integrity?

A Yes. However, most of the time the data comes to your program via a user interface. The user interface validates the information before you insert it into the database, so the foreign keys have already been checked. Even when importing data from external systems, you should use BDC to update the tables. This also enforces referential integrity by simulating user sessions and passing the data to the program via the interface. However, if you update the database without passing the data through the user interface, your ABAP/4 program must be written carefully so that it doesn't violate referential integrity.

Q If I want to guarantee the referential integrity of my database, could I go to the DBMS level and create integrity constraints? How would it affect R/3?

A No, never update the RDBMS definitions directly. You should only use the R/3 DDIC to change the definitions within the database. If you update the database manually, the database definitions and the R/3 DDIC definitions will be inconsistent, and the results will be unpredictable.

Q **If I delete a row from a check table, can I cause rows having the same value to be automatically deleted from the foreign key table also?**

A No. This feature is usually termed "cascade on delete", and it is not available in R/3.

Q **The foreign key type Key Fields Of A Text Table causes the system to behave differently. Do the other foreign key field types have any functionality behind them?**

A No. Only Key Fields Of A Text Table employs system functionality. The others do not cause anything to happen — they are mostly for documentation.

Q **Can structures have foreign key definitions?**

A Yes. This is commonly done because a table that includes a structure can inherit foreign key definitions from it. You can turn off this inheritance when you include the structure if you so desire.

Workshop

The following exercises will give you practice creating foreign keys, special fields, and structures.

Quiz

1. For a foreign key to be created, what must the foreign key field and the check table field have in common?

2. What is the syntax for including structure zs1 within table zt1?

3. What is the purpose of a text table?

4. Assume that check table zc exists and has a primary key consisting of mandt, f1, and f2. What should the primary key fields of a text table for zc be?

5. If you create a currency field, what type of field must it reference?

Exercise 1

Create a country code check table named •••t005. It will be used to validate all country codes entered into your tables. The specifications appear in Table 4.5.

TABLE 4.5   FIELDS AND THEIR CHARACTERISTICS FOR TABLE •••t005

Description		
Field Name	PK	DE Name
Client		
mandt	x	mandt
Country Key		
land1	x	•••land1

After you have activated this table, go into the •••land1 domain and type •••t005 in the Value Table field, then activate it. Use SE16 to add country codes to your table.

Exercise 2

Create a country code check table named •••t005s. It will be used to validate all region codes entered into your tables. The specifications appear in Table 4.6.

TABLE 4.6   FIELDS AND THEIR CHARACTERISTICS FOR TABLE •••t005s

Description			
Field Name	PK	DE Name	CheckTable
Client			
mandt	x	mandt	
Country Key			
land1	x	•••land1	•••t005
Region Code			
regio	x	•••regio	

After you have activated this table, go into the •••regio domain and type •••t005s in the Value Table field, then activate it. Use SE16 to add region codes to your table. Test your foreign key on land1 by trying to enter an invalid country code.

Exercise 3

Add appropriate foreign key relationships to the land1 and regio fields in your •••lfa1 table. Use SE16 to update the existing rows within •••lfa1 and enter valid country and region codes.

Exercise 4

Create a check table for field `cityc` in the customer master table •••`kna1` that you created on Day 3. Name this table •••`t005g`. It should contain a list of valid city codes. The specifications for it appear in Table 4.7.

TABLE 4.7 FIELDS AND THEIR CHARACTERISTICS FOR TABLE •••t005g

Description						
Field Name	*PK*	*DE Name*	*DM Name*	*Type*	*Len*	*CheckTable*
Client						
mandt	X	mandt				
Country Key						
land1	X	•••land1				•••t005
Region Code						
regio	X	•••regio				•••t005s
City Code						
cityc	X	•••cityc	•••cityc	CHAR	4	

Don't forget to create the foreign key relationships on the `land1` and `regio` fields.

Exercise 5

After you have activated you table, go into the •••`cityc` domain and put •••`t005g` in the Value Table field, then activate. Use SE16 to add city codes to table •••`t005g`, and test the foreign keys by trying to enter invalid country and region codes. Then create the foreign key within the •••`kna1` table on the `cityc` field, and use SE16 to add customers to •••`kna1`. Test the foreign key relationship by attempting to enter invalid city codes. Create a text table for •••`t005g`. Name it •••`t005h`; the specifications are shown in Table 4.8.

TABLE 4.8 FIELDS AND THEIR CHARACTERISTICS FOR TABLE •••t005h

Description						
Field Name	*PK*	*DE Name*	*DM Name*	*Type*	*Len*	*CheckTable*
Client						
mandt	X	mandt				
Language Key						
spras	X	spras			t002	

continues

TABLE 4.8   CONTINUED

Description						
Field Name	*PK*	*DE Name*	*DM Name*	*Type*	*Len*	*CheckTable*
Country Key						
land1	x	•••land1				•••t005
Region Code						
regio	x	•••regio				•••t005s
City Code						
cityc	x	•••cityc				•••t005g
Description						
bezei		•••bezei20	text20	CHAR	20	

The foreign key relationship on the `cityc` field should have the Foreign Key Field Type "Key Fields Of A Text Table". Use SE16 to create descriptions for each city code. Create these descriptions in two languages: E (English) and D (Deutsche). Test your text table by creating a new entry in •••kna1 and pressing F4 in the `cityc` field. The descriptions for each city code should appear in the list, but only in your current logon language. Sign on in German and retest to see the German descriptions.

Exercise 6

Create a structure named •••tel. The specifications appear in Table 4.9.

TABLE 4.9   FIELDS AND THEIR CHARACTERISTICS FOR STRUCTURE •••tel

Description	
Field Name	*DE Name*
First Telephone Number	
telf1	telf1
Second Telephone Number	
telf2	telf2
Fax Number	
telfx	telfx
Telex Number	
telx1	telx1

Include this structure at the end of your •••kna1 and •••lfa1 tables. Use SE16 to update some of your existing records and add telephone numbers to them.

Exercise 7

Add two more fields to the •••kna1 table. The specifications are shown in Table 4.10.

TABLE 4.10 ADDITIONAL FIELDS AND THEIR CHARACTERISTICS FOR TABLE •••kna1

Description						
Field Name	DE Name	DM Name	Type	Len	Decimals	ChkTbl
Credit Limit						
creditl	•••creditl	•••creditl	CURR	12	2	
Currency Key						
waers	waers					tcurc

The creditl field will contain the customer's credit limit. The waers field will contain the currency key for which the credit limit is valid. Don't forget to add the foreign key relationship to check table tcurc. Create F1 help for the creditl field by pressing the documentation button in the data element.

After adding these two fields, double-click creditl, in the Reference Table field type •••kna1, and in the Reference Field type creditl. Then activate your table. Use SE16 to update customer records and add a credit limit to each. View the F1 help you created.

4

DAY 5

The Data Dictionary, Part 3

Chapter Objectives

After you complete this chapter, you should be able to:

- Create and use secondary indexes appropriately
- Set up the technical attributes for transparent tables
- Set up buffering for tables

Understanding Table Indexes

An *index* is an efficiency mechanism for quickly finding rows within a table. It is needed because data is stored in a table in the order in which it was added (the *order of arrival*).

Picture yourself ripping all the pages out of this book and then throwing them into the air and mixing them all up. You then gather them into a stack without regard to any sort of order. If you were to look for a single page number within that stack, how would you do it?

Some people might just hunt and peck though the stack hoping to find it. I'm sure that most would soon give up and then turn the pages one by one. Obviously, this job would be easier if the pages were all back in order. With the pages in order, you could start somewhere in the middle and knowing which way to turn, you could quickly zero in on the page you want.

Imagine that you have now put the pages back in order. Picking up the newly ordered book, perhaps you begin to look for the page that describes SE16. Where do you look? You don't know the page number, so you look in the index. The index contains the most important words sorted in alphabetical order. You quickly locate SE16 in the index and obtain a page number. Using that, search through the book to find that page.

To create an index, the publisher duplicates important information and then sorts it, placing it at the end of the book apart from the rest. When you look at it, are you looking at the original information? No, of course not. You are looking at a copy of the original information; it has been duplicated. The book takes up a little more space on your bookshelf because of the index, it adds a little to the price of the book because of the time and effort required to create it, but no one complains because it saves so much time when you want to find something.

A table in the database is a lot like this book. Each row is given a sequential number when it is added to a table, much like a page number. The important columns are copied to an index and sorted, much like the index at the back of the book. To find any piece of data, the system searches the index first to find the row number and then quickly finds the row.

Each R/3 table has a primary index built on the primary key of the table. This index is needed because the data in the table is stored in the order it was added to the table. When a row is added, the key information is sorted and copied to the index, along with a pointer to the original row. Figure 5.1 shows an example using table ztxlfa1. The data from the lifnr field in ztxlfa1 is copied to the index, sorted alphabetically, and stored along with the row number of the original row. (The mandt field has been left out to simplify the example.)

Note

The row number is internally assigned by the database; you never see it in the DDIC. It is used by the index to point back to the original row from which the data came.

FIGURE 5.1.

A table index is a copy of one or more columns stored in sorted order with pointers to the original rows.

Primary Index for ztxlfa1

lifnr	row#
v1	4
v2	3
v3	1
v4	7
v5	6
v6	2
v7	5

Table ztxlfa1

row#	lifnr
1	v3
2	v6
3	v2
4	v1
5	v7
6	v5
7	v4

When the statement `select * from ztxlfa1 where lifnr = '0000001050'` is executed, the system recognizes that it has `lifnr` already sorted in an index, and thus uses it automatically. It finds `1050` in the index and obtains row number `2`. It then looks in the table for row number `2`.

Now suppose the statement `select * from ztxlfa1 where land1 = 'US'` is executed. The index is sorted by `lifnr`, not `land1`. The `land1` column is not in any particular order in the table. The system will have to scan the table from the beginning to the end looking for all rows where `land1 = 'US'`. The table in Figure 5.1 is very small, but this is a very time-consuming process on a larger table.

Now think back to the book example. Sometimes a book has more than one index. For example, a book on the medicinal uses of herbs might have the usual index, plus an index only for common plant names, another only for botanical names, and a third only for medicinal effects. To create these indexes, information has to be sorted and duplicated in three more places at the back of the book. Then, there are four ways to find a page number quickly: via the commonly used index or any of the three additional indexes.

NEW TERM The commonly used index is analogous to the primary index of a table. The additional indexes are analogous to *secondary indexes*. To support a `where` clause on a non-primary key field, a secondary index can be defined. A table can have multiple secondary indexes.

Figure 5.2 illustrates a secondary index on `ztxlfa1-land1`.

An index increases performance tremendously. In a table containing a million rows, a `select` on a column containing unique values that is not supported by an index would read, on average, 500,000 records to find the matching one, with a worst-case scenario of one million compares.

5

FIGURE 5.2.

A secondary index enables you to search quickly on columns other than those in the primary key.

Primary Index

lifnr	row#
v1	4
v2	3
v3	1
v4	7
v5	6
v6	2
v7	5

Table ztxlfa1

row#	lifnr	land1
1	v3	US
2	v6	CA
3	v2	US
4	v1	DE
5	v7	DE
6	v5	CA
7	v4	US

Secondary Index on land1

land1	row#
CA	2
CA	6
DE	4
DE	5
US	1
US	3
US	7

If you add an index, the system can use a binary search algorithm to find the record after comparing an average of only 10 records, with a worst-case scenario of 20 records! That's 50,000 times faster. For this reason, *you should ensure that fields in a* where *clause are always supported by an index.* This can be done either by displaying existing indexes and then organizing your logic to use these fields, or by creating a secondary index.

Displaying Indexes

Each index in R/3 has a unique one to three character identifier, or *id.* The primary index always has an id of 0 (zero). A secondary index id can be any other number or an alphabetic character.

SCREENCAM Start the ScreenCam "How to Display Secondary Indexes" now.

To display the existing secondary indexes on a database table, follow this procedure:

1. Display the table.
2. Press the Indexes. . . button on the Application toolbar. If you do not see this button, your window might be too narrow. Widen it or choose the menu path Goto->Indexes. . ..
3. If secondary indexes exist, a list of them will be displayed in a dialog box. If none exist, a message will be displayed.
4. To display one of them, double-click on it. The index is displayed in the ABAP/4 Dictionary: Table: Display Index screen, as shown in Figure 5.3.

The status of the index is displayed in the Status field. Whether the index exists in the database is indicated by a message appearing below the Status field. In the DB Index Name field is the name of the index as it is known in the database. The index name in the database is formed from the table name, followed by underscores, and then the index id. In the lower part of the window are the fields that comprise the index. The index sort order is the same as the field order.

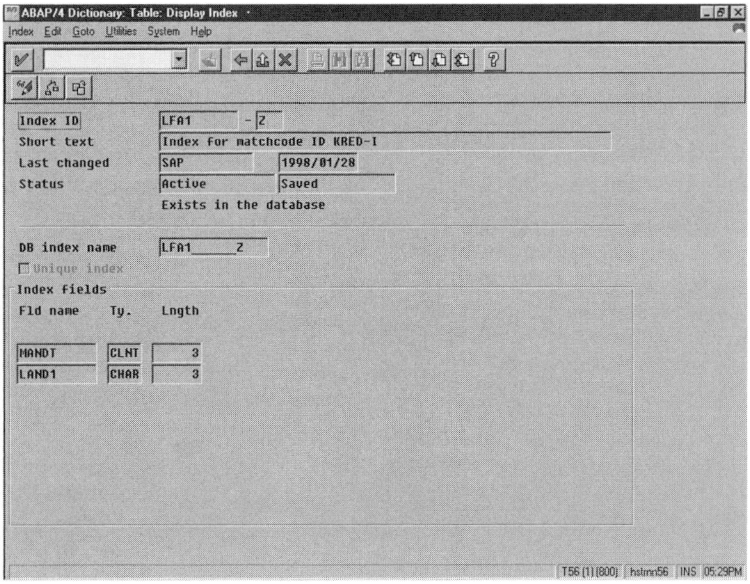

FIGURE 5.3.

The secondary index z
in table ztxlfa1 *is
composed of the fields*
mandt *and* land1.

The preceding procedure will only show secondary indexes. The index on the primary key (index 0) does not appear in this list.

SCREENCAM Start the ScreenCam "How to Display All Indexes" now.

To display all indexes, including the primary index, follow these steps:

1. Display the table.
2. Choose the menu path Utilities->Database Utility. The ABAP/4 Dictionary: Utility for Database Tables screen is displayed.
3. Choose the menu path Extras->Database Object->Display. A list of all fields in the table is displayed, and beneath it is a list of all indexes with their fields, including index 0.

Considerations When Creating an Index

NEW TERM An index can consist of more than one field. For example, building a secondary index on land1 and regio enables select * from ztxlfa1 where land1 = 'US' and regio = 'MA' to quickly find matching rows. When multiple indexes exist (a primary and one or more secondary indexes), the RDBMS uses an *optimizer* to pick the best one. To choose an index, the optimizer looks at the field names in the where clause and then it looks for an index having the same field names in the same order as they were specified in the `where` clause. Therefore, to ensure the system chooses the index you intend, *specify the fields in the where clause in the same order as they appear in the index.*

Indexes and `MANDT`

If a table begins with the `mandt` field, so should its indexes. If a table begins with `mandt` and an index doesn't, the optimizer might not use the index.

Remember, if you will, Open SQL's automatic client handling feature. When `select * from ztxlfa1 where land1 = 'US'` is executed, the actual SQL sent to the database is `select * from ztxlfa1 where mandt = sy-mandt and land1 = 'US'`. Sy-mandt contains the current logon client. When you select rows from a table using Open SQL, the system automatically adds `sy-mandt` to the `where` clause, which causes only those rows pertaining to the current logon client to be found.

When you create an index on a table containing `mandt`, therefore, you should also include `mandt` in the index. It should come first in the index, because it will always appear first in the generated SQL.

For the rest of this discussion, please assume that `mandt` is included in all indexes.

Code a `Select` to Use a Given Index

NEW TERM   If you code `select * from ztxlfa1 where regio = 'MA'`, there needs to be an index starting with `mandt` and `regio` to ensure that the optimizer uses it. If you code `select * from ztxlfa1 where land1 = 'US' and regio = 'MA'`, there should be an index containing `mandt`, `land1`, and `regio`. The ideal index would also have them in that order. If there wasn't an index in that order, but there was an index starting with `mandt` and `land1`, the optimizer would use it to match the first two fields of the `where` clause, and then perform an *index range scan* to find a match on `regio`. An index range scan is a sequential scan through a portion of an index.

Selective Indexes and Index Effectiveness

If the `where` clause contains more fields than the index, the system uses the index to narrow down the search. It then reads records from the table and scans them to find matches. For example, if an index is composed of fields `F1` and `F2`, and you code `where F1 = 1 and F2 = 2 and F3 = 3`, the system can only use the index to locate records where F1=1 and F2=2. It will read those records from the table to find out which ones have F3=3. Therefore, the index is only partially effective. It would be more effective if it contained all fields: `F1`, `F2`, and `F3`.

NEW TERM   How much more effective is the index with `F3`? It depends on the way the data is distributed in the table. If the combination of `F1` and `F2` is very specific (or *selective*) and results in only a few matching rows, the index is already very effective. Adding F3 to the index in this case might not be worthwhile because of the overhead of maintaining the index during table updates. If the combination of F1 and F2 results in a large number of the rows from the table being selected, the index is *not* very selective and adding F3 will probably increase performance and reduce resource consumption.

When creating or modifying indexes, try not to use a field that is already in an index. There is a chance, when a preexisting program is run, that the optimizer will choose the new index, and a preexisting program might run slower.

Guidelines for Creating an Index

As a rule of thumb, follow these guidelines when you create an index:

- Try not to add unnecessary indexes. Ask yourself, "Can I code this to use an existing index?"
- Try to avoid overlapping indexes; in other words, avoid including the same field in multiple indexes.
- Try to make indexes very selective, but don't include fields that increase selectiveness by only a little.

 Note | There is a maximum of 15 secondary indexes per table allowed by R/3.

Creating a Secondary Index

ScreenCam Start the ScreenCam "How to Create a Secondary Index" now.

To create a secondary index:

1. Display the table. You should begin on the Dictionary: Table/Structure: Display Fields screen.

2. Press the Indexes. . . button on the Application toolbar (or choose the menu path Goto->Indexes. . .).

3. If secondary indexes already exist, a list of them will be displayed in a dialog box named Indexes for Table xxxxx. To create an index, press the Create button. The Create Index dialog box will be displayed.

4. If no secondary indexes exist, you will not see a list of indexes. Instead, you will see the Create Index dialog box immediately.

5. Enter an index id in the Index ID field. Customer indexes should begin with *Y* or *Z*, although the system does not enforce this.

6. Press the Continue button. The ABAP/4 Dictionary: Table: Maintain Index screen is displayed.

7. In the Short Text field, type a description of the index.

8. In the Fld Name column, type the fields that should comprise the index in the order that they should be sorted.

9. If the values in these fields when taken together must always be unique, tickmark the Unique Index check box.

10. Press the Save button on the Application toolbar. The values in the Status fields are now New and Saved, and directly below them the message Does not exist in the database appears. Also, the message Index xxx to table xxxxx was saved appears at the bottom of the window in the status bar.

11. Press the Activate button on the Application toolbar. The system generates SQL and sends it to the RDBMS, creating the index in the database. If successful, the Status fields read Active and Saved, and below the status fields the message Exists in the database appears. The DB Index Name field will contain the name of the index in the database. Also, in the status bar, the message Index xxxxx was successfully activated. is displayed.

12. Press Back. The Indexes for Table xxxxx screen is displayed.

13. Press Cancel to return to the Dictionary: Table/Structure: Display Fields screen.

You have learned how to create a secondary index. Indexes improve the efficiency of the select statement.

Note If you tickmark the Unique Index check box, the combination of fields in the index is guaranteed to be unique; this is enforced by the RDBMS. An insert or modify statement will fail if the combination of values in index fields is already present in the table.

Deleting a Secondary Index

SCREENCAM Start the ScreenCam "How to Delete a Secondary Index" now.

To delete a secondary index:

1. Display the table. You should begin on the Dictionary: Table/Structure: Display Fields screen.

2. Press the Indexes. . . button on the Application toolbar (or choose the menu path Goto->Indexes. . .). If you see the Create Index dialog box, no secondary indexes exist for the table, so you cannot delete one. If secondary indexes already exist, a list of them will be displayed in a dialog box named Indexes for Table xxxxx.

3. Double-click on the index you want to delete. The ABAP/4 Dictionary: Table: Display Index screen is shown.

4. Press the Display <-> Change button on the Application toolbar. The screen switches to change mode, and the title of the screen reads ABAP/4 Dictionary: Table: Maintain Index.

5. Choose the menu path Index->Delete. The Delete Index Definition dialog box appears asking you to confirm the delete request.

6. Press the Yes button to delete the index. You are returned to the Dictionary: Table/Structure: Display Fields screen. The message `Index xxxxx deleted` appears in the status bar.

In step six, pressing the Yes button causes the index to be deleted from the database. When you return to the Dictionary: Table/Structure: Display Fields screen, you do not need to save the table. Also note that you cannot undo the delete by pressing the Cancel button on the table display screen.

Determining Which Index Is Used

When a `select` statement is executed, the optimizer attempts to choose the most appropriate index to speed up data retrieval. If you have several indexes on a table, how can you tell which index is actually being used, or even if it is using any at all?

To do this you can use the SQL trace tool.

 Caution Only one person can perform an SQL trace at a time. Remember to turn off the trace when you are finished. SQL trace slows the system down.

 Start the ScreenCam "How to Use SQL Trace to Determine the Index Used" now.

To determine which index is being used for a `select` statement:

1. Create a small ABAP/4 program that contains only the `select` statement. Before proceeding, test it to ensure that it works.

2. Open that program in the editor so that it is ready and waiting to execute.

3. Open a new session using the menu path System->Create session.

4. Run transaction ST05 (enter **/nst05**—zero-five, not oh-five—in the Command field, or choose the menu path System->Utilities->SQL Trace). The Trace SQL Database Requests screen is displayed.

5. If the Trace SQL Status Information box reads `Trace SQL is switched off`, go to step 7.

6. At this point, the Trace SQL Status Information box contains `Trace SQL switched on by`, followed by the user id who turned on the trace and the date and time it was started. You must switch it off before you can proceed. If the trace was started within the past hour, it is possible that it is still being used. Contact the indicated user or try again later. If the trace was started hours or days ago, the user probably left it on by mistake and it can be safely turned off. To turn off the trace, press the Trace Off pushbutton. The message in the Trace SQL Status Information box should now read `Trace SQL is switched off`.

7. Press the Trace On pushbutton. The Trace SQL Database Requests dialog box is displayed. The DB-Trace for User field should contain your user ID. If your user ID is not in this field, enter it now.

8. Press the OK button. You are returned to the Trace SQL Database Requests screen and the status information reads `Trace SQL switched on by`, indicating that you turned on the trace.

9. Switch back to the window containing your editor session (the one with your program waiting to execute).

10. Press F8 to run your program. (Only press F8, do not do anything else, do not even press the Back button.)

11. When your program has run and the hourglass is no longer displayed, switch back to the trace window.

12. Press the Trace Off pushbutton. The status information reads `Trace SQL is switched off`.

13. Press the List Trace pushbutton. The Trace SQL Database Requests dialog box is displayed. The fields on this screen will already contain values.

14. Press the OK button. You might need to wait a little while, at most a couple of minutes. The Trace SQL: List Database Requests screen is displayed.

15. Type **%sc** in the Command field and press the Enter key. The Find dialog box is displayed.

16. Type the name of the table you are tracing in the Search For field. (This is the table named in the `select` statement in your ABAP/4 program.)

17. Press the Find button. A search results list should be displayed with your table name highlighted.

18. Click on the first highlighted table name. You are returned to the Trace SQL: List Database Requests screen. Your cursor is positioned on the first line containing your table name. To the right of it, in the Operation column, should be the word PREPARE, OPEN, or REOPEN.

19. Press the Explain SQL button on the Application toolbar. The Show Execution Plan for SQL Statement screen is displayed.

20. Scroll down to the execution plan. The index used will be displayed in blue.

You have learned how to execute a SQL trace. This will help you determine what index is being used.

Displaying Technical Settings

To display the technical settings for a table, display the table and press the Technical Settings button on the Application toolbar. (If the button is not there, your window might be too narrow. Try widening your window or use the menu path Goto->Technical Settings.) To modify these settings, press the Display <-> Change button on the Application toolbar. The ABAP/4 Dictionary: Maintain Technical Settings screen is displayed, as shown in Figure 5.4.

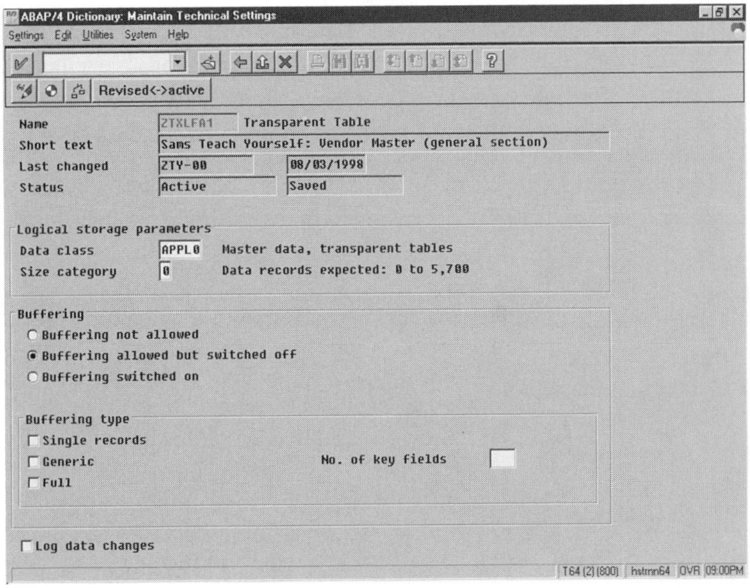

FIGURE 5.4.

On the ABAP/4 Dictionary: Maintain Technical Settings screen, you can set the data class, size category, and buffering options.

Data Class

NEW TERM The *data class* determines the tablespace that the table is assigned to. (The term
"tablespace" applies to Oracle databases. For Informix, substitute the term "DB
space.") A *tablespace* is a physical file on disk that is used to hold tables. Every table is
assigned to one tablespace. Tables with similar characteristics are usually grouped into
one tablespace, so tablespaces are the administrative units used by the DBA to manage
the database. For example, tables that grow quickly will be grouped together in a tablespace on a disk with a lot of free space.

Each data class has an associated tablespace. When you activate a table, it is created in
the tablespace associated with that data class. If you change the data class when the table
is active, nothing happens; it doesn't move to another tablespace.

The important data classes are:

- *APPL0 or master data.* By choosing APPL0 (master data), you signify that the table
  is not updated often and grows slowly. It will be placed in a tablespace with similar
  tables. Vendor master and customer master tables are good examples of master
  data.

- *APPL1 or transaction data.* By choosing APPL1 (transaction data), you signify that
  the table is expected to be updated often and to grow quickly. Orders placed with
  vendors and orders received from customers are good examples of transaction data.
  Tables containing these orders will have a data class of APPL1.

- *APPL2 or customizing data.* By choosing APPL2 (customizing data), you signify
  that the table's contents are determined before implementation and do not change
  often after that. Check tables and their associated text tables, such as ztxt005 and
  ztxt005t, are good examples of tables that should have a data class of APPL2.

In addition to these categories, there might be USER data classes as well. These are created
by your DBA, who will direct you in choosing them at the appropriate times.

Note Other data classes can be displayed by pressing the down arrow at the end
of the Data Class field and then pressing the System Data Types button.
These classes should only be used by SAP; they are for R/3 system tables that
hold, for example, Data Dictionary information and program source code.

Size Category

The Size Category field enables you to specify the maximum number of records you
expect this table to hold. You are setting the size of the initial extent and next extents, as

well as the maximum number of extents allowed for this table. An *extent* is the amount of space allocated for a table. The initial extent is the amount of space allocated for a table when it is created. If a table uses up that space, another extent will be allocated, causing the table's space to be extended.

The size categories are always 0 through 4, but the number of expected records in each size category will change with every table based on the length of a row. Choose an appropriate category based on the maximum number of records you expect that table to hold.

Caution

When choosing a size category, be generous. In R/3 it is much better to over-estimate than underestimate this parameter. If the size category is too small and the table grows larger than the initial allocation, the RDBMS allocates another extent. Secondary extents reduce performance and require a table-space reorganization to remove. Reorganizations can be very difficult to perform on a large database, especially one that requires high availability. It is much easier to reduce an overly generous size category than it is to increase an underestimated one.

Displaying the Number of Extents Allocated to a Table

You can display the number of extents allocated for a table by using the following procedure.

 Start the ScreenCam "How to Display the Number of Extents Used by a Table" now.

To display the number of extents for a table:

1. Run transaction DB02. (Type **/ndb02** in the Command field and press the Enter key.) The Database Performance: Tables and Indexes screen is displayed.

2. Press the Detailed analysis pushbutton. A Memory Management: Tables and Indexes dialog box is displayed.

3. Type the name of the table in the Tables field and press the OK button. A Memory Management: Tables and Indexes screen is displayed. The table name appears in the list.

4. Double-click on the table name. A Memory Management: Tables and Indexes dialog box is displayed.

5. Choose the Extents radio button.

5

6. Press the OK button. A Memory Management: Tables and Indexes screen is displayed, containing the list of extents, their tablespace names, extent numbers, physical file number, block size, extent size, and number of blocks in the extent. There is one line in this list for each extent.

You have learned how to look at the number of extents allocated in a table. This will give information about whether the table will need to be reorganized or not.

Buffering a Table

As mentioned on Day 1, data can be buffered in RAM on the application server. This is controlled on a per-table basis, and is specified in the technical settings for each table (refer to Figure 5.4).

Whenever an Open SQL statement is used to read a record, the data buffer is checked first to see whether it is there. If not, the data is read from the database. If the table's attributes indicate that the data should be buffered, the record is saved in RAM on the application server in data buffers. Later, if that record is read again, it is read from the buffer instead of the database. This process is diagrammed in Figure 5.5.

FIGURE 5.5.

Data can be buffered in RAM on the application sever.

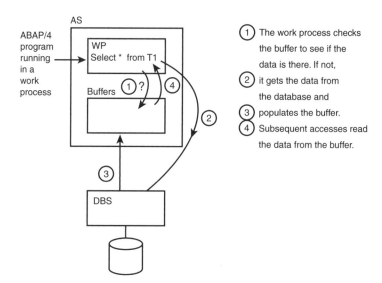

By buffering data, you increase performance in two important ways:

• The programs using the buffered data run faster because they don't have to wait for it to come from the database. This reduces delays waiting for the database and the network that connects it.

- The other programs that need to access the database run faster because there is less load on the database and less traffic on the network.

Buffering a table can cause a `select` to run 10 to 100 times faster or more. At first thought, it might seem like a good idea to buffer every table in the system. However, buffers are stored entirely in RAM, so space is limited by the amount of RAM available. In fact, there is so much more data than there is RAM that tables must be buffered judiciously to prevent overruns. If a buffer overruns, it might swap to disk, which can obliterate any performance gained by buffering.

Tables containing a numeric data type in the primary key cannot be buffered. The DDIC numeric data types are `CURR`, `DEC`, `FLTP`, `INT1`, `INT2`, `INT4`, `PREC`, and `QUAN`.

Tip

> Transaction ST02 displays buffers and usage statistics. On the Tune Summary screen, the data buffers are named Generic Key and Single Record. A double-click on each of these lines will display a detailed analysis. From there, the objects in the buffer can be displayed by pressing the Buffered Objects button on the Application toolbar.

The Basis consultant is responsible for monitoring the buffers and preventing buffer shortages from slowing the system down. Before buffering a table, it is a good idea to talk to your Basis consultant.

Buffer Synchronization

NEW TERM   If you have two application servers, the same record can be buffered on each server. This would not be a problem if it were not for the fact that data can be updated. If a buffered record is updated, the changes must be communicated to the other application server. This is done in a process known as *buffer synchronization,* which occurs at 1- to 4-minute intervals depending on your system configuration.

For example, as shown in Figure 5.6, suppose user 1 is logged on to application server 1 and user 2 is logged on to application server 2. User 1 reads record 1. Record 1 is buffered on application server 1.

In Figure 5.7, user 2 reads record 1. The same record is now in the buffers of both application servers.

In Figure 5.8, user 1 updates record 1. The update is reflected in both the database and the buffers on server 1, but the old record is still on server 2. An entry is made in the *synchronization log* on the database server indicating that record 1 has been updated.

5

FIGURE 5.6.

*Step A: User 1 reads
record 1, causing it
to be buffered on
application server 1.*

Legend:
AS = Application Server
DBS = Database Server
SP = Synchronization Process

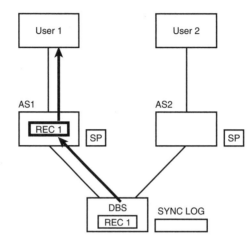

FIGURE 5.7.

*Step B: User 2 also
reads record 1, causing
it to be buffered on
application server 2.*

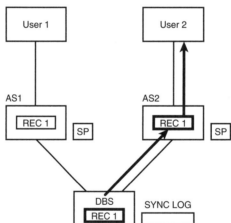

In Figure 5.9, user 2 reads record 1. The old version of record 1 is found in the buffer, so user 2 sees old data. User 2 will not see the new version of record 1 until a buffer synchronization occurs.

In Figure 5.10, the buffer synchronization process detects that the synchronization interval has expired and begins synchronization. It reads the synchronization log on the database server and determines that record 1 is out of sync. It then marks that record as invalid in the buffer. It does *not* yet refresh the record in the buffer from the database.

FIGURE 5.8.

Step C: User 1 updates record 1, causing it to be updated in the database and in the buffer on application server 1.

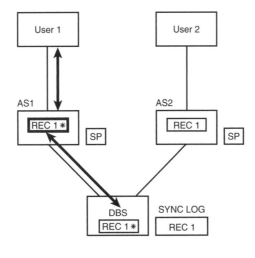

FIGURE 5.9.

Step D: User 2 reads record 1 and gets stale data.

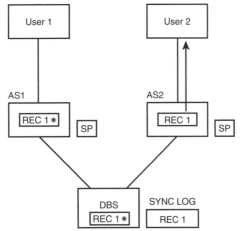

5

In Figure 5.11, user 2 reads record 1 again. This time, record 1 has been marked invalid in the buffer, so it is fetched from the database, thereby refreshing the buffer on application server 2.

As shown in Figures 5.6 through 5.11, buffer synchronization uses a synchronization process on each application server and a synchronization log on the database server. At a predefined interval, each synchronization process checks the log to see whether any buffered data has been modified. Data that has been modified is marked invalid in the buffer. The next time that data is read, it is refreshed from the database.

The Basis consultant sets the length of the buffer synchronization interval using the `rdisp/bufreftime` parameter.

FIGURE 5.10.

Step E: The buffer synchronization process invalidates record 1 in the buffer on application server 2.

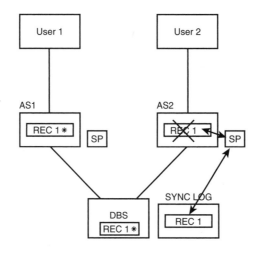

FIGURE 5.11.

Step F: User 2 tries to re-read record 1 but it is marked invalid in the buffer. It is refreshed from the database.

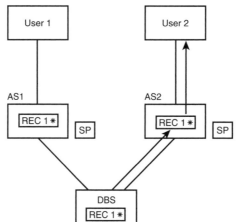

To display it, use transaction RZ10 as follows:

- Start transaction RZ10 (type **/nrz10** in the Command field and press the Enter key). The Edit Profiles screen is displayed.

- Choose the menu path Goto->Profile Values->Of a Server. The Active Application Servers screen is displayed.

- Double-click on an application server. You will see a list of all the profile parameter values for that server.

- Type **%sc** in the Command field and press the Enter key. The Find dialog box is displayed.

- Type **rdisp/buf** in the Search For field and press the Enter key. The buffer parameters are displayed and highlighted.
- Click on the highlighted word `rdisp/bufreftime`.
- The refresh time (in seconds) is displayed on the right side of the list.

Updating Buffered Tables

If you code a transaction that updates a buffered table, you must always be sure to go to the database and get the most up-to-date information before allowing a user to change it. The following example illustrates this point. Record locking is mentioned in the following paragraph for the sake of completeness.

Suppose record 1 contains fields F1 and F2. This time, user 2 reads it first, causing it to be buffered on server 2 (see Figure 5.12).

FIGURE 5.12.

Step A: User 2 reads record 1, causing it to be buffered on application server 2.

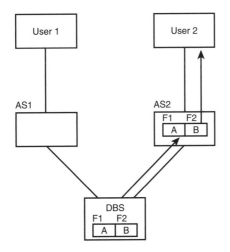

User 1, now wanting to update record 1, locks it and reads it (see Figure 5.13).

User 1 changes F1, writes it to the database (see Figure 5.14), and unlocks it.

At this point, the buffer on application server 2 still has the original copy of record 1 with the original contents of F1. If user 2 locks record 1 and reads it (from the buffer), changes F2 (see Figure 5.15), and then saves it to the database, the changes made by user 1 will be lost (see Figure 5.16).

FIGURE 5.13.

Step B: User 1 locks and reads record one, causing it to be buffered on application server 1.

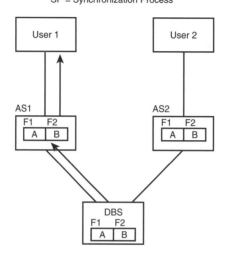

Legend:
AS = Application Server
DBS = Database Server
SP = Synchronization Process

FIGURE 5.14.

Step C: User 1 updates record 1, causing it to be updated in the database and in the buffer on application server 1. The lock is removed.

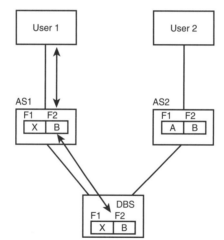

NEW TERM Use `bypassing buffer` on the `select` statement when you need the most up-to-date information, for example, `select * from ztxtlfa1 bypassing buffer`. Doing so causes the buffer to be ignored and the data to be read directly from the database. You should use this whenever you are *reading for update*, that is, reading a record that will be updated and written back to the database.

FIGURE 5.15.

Step D: User 2 reads the old record 1 and locks it.

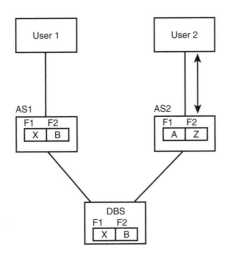

FIGURE 5.16.

Step E: User 2 saves record 1 to the database, overwriting user 1's change.

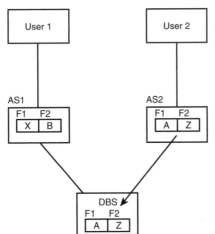

5

For example, in step D, if user 2 used bypassing buffer to read the record, the most up-to-date version of the record would have been read and user 1's changes would not have been lost.

Tip

Bypassing the buffer for updates provides the best balance between safety and speed. However, if you can be sure that all updates are done from a single application server, you don't need to code bypassing buffer. Bypassing the buffer does slow the update process a little because a database access is

> required. If you need the maximum amount of speed for updates, and if you
> can be *sure* that only one application server will be used, this alternative
> might work for you. Talk to your Basis consultant to find out whether it can
> be arranged.

Summarizing the Approaches for Buffering with Updates

You can take one of three buffering approaches for tables that can be updated. In order of best to worst performance, they are as follows:

- Buffer the table, do not use `bypassing buffer`, and ensure that all updates are done from a single application server.
- Buffer the table and use `bypassing buffer`.
- Do not buffer the table.

If a table is updated often, do not use the `bypassing buffer` approach. Each update will cause the buffers on all other application servers to be reloaded at the next synchronization. In this case, buffering could actually increase the total network traffic instead of decreasing it.

Buffering Techniques

The lower half of the Technical Settings screen (shown previously in Figure 5.4) contains the controls for buffer settings. If you create a table, you have complete control over these settings. To change these settings on a SAP table, you need to obtain a modification key from SAP.

You can set the buffering for a table when you create it, or you can change it later. Changing the buffer settings on SAP tables requires a modification key, which you can obtain from SAP.

These three radio buttons switch buffering off and on:

- Buffering Not Allowed
- Buffering Allowed But Switched Off
- Buffering Switched On

Choose Buffering Not Allowed if the table should never be buffered, which occurs in the following cases:

- Users must always have 100 percent up-to-the-second accurate information for both reads and writes. This might be the case for very sensitive queries such as stock market quotations or for real-time control systems such as goods movements on warehouse floors.

- Records from the table are updated as often as they are read, causing buffering to be unsuitable (see below).

Choose either Buffering Allowed But Turned Off or Buffering Turned On if the users of this data can tolerate a 1-to-4 minute buffer latency. Don't forget this latency will not exist when updating data because you will code `bypassing buffer` to get the latest information.

> **Caution**
>
> Buffering Not Allowed on a SAP table means you should *not* turn buffering on for this table. Doing so can cause unreliable operation of R/3 applications and possible loss or corruption of data.

Buffering Type

As shown on the Technical Settings screen in Figure 5.4, three types of buffering are possible:

- Full buffering
- Generic buffering
- Single-record buffering

Although you use a check box to indicate the buffering type, only one type can be selected at a time. If you choose more than one, an error message will be displayed.

There are two data buffers on each application server, and the buffering type chosen determines which buffer is used. On an application sever there are:

- The generic record buffer
- The single-record buffer

The generic record buffer is called TABL (short for "table"). The single-record buffer is TABLP ("P"' stands for "partial").

Full Buffering

To activate the full buffering type, tickmark the Full check box. When an attempt is made to read data from a fully buffered table, the system looks in the TABL buffer for it. If it is not found there, *all rows* are loaded from the database into TABL (see Figure 5.17). This happens whenever a `select` statement for it is executed, no matter how many records match the `where` clause. Even if no records match, all are loaded into the buffer if the table is not already there or if it has been invalidated due to buffer synchronization.

FIGURE 5.17.

All rows of a fully buffered table are loaded into TABL.

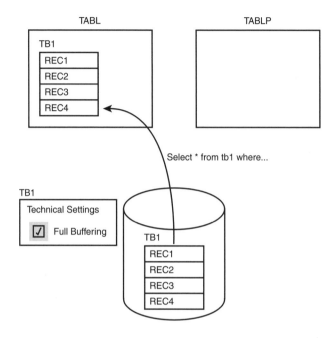

Loading of TABL does not occur with select single statements; only select/endselect does this. If the table is fully buffered and a select single statement is executed, no records are loaded into TABL. However, if the table is already loaded into TABL, select single will read records from it.

During buffer synchronization, the entire table is invalidated if any record within it changes. The next time data is read the entire table is reloaded.

Full buffering is appropriate for small tables that seldom change. Check tables and their text tables, such as ztxt005, ztxt005t, ztxt005s, and ztxt005u, should be fully buffered. They are set up with an initial set of valid values and descriptions and modified infrequently thereafter.

Tip

If a select statement is executed but quite often does *not* find data in the table, full buffering can still make the table accesses more efficient. Because the entire table is in the buffer, the system can determine whether the records exist before going to the database, thus avoiding a database access to find out.

Generic Buffering

With generic buffering, a *group* of records is loaded into TABL instead of the entire table. To activate this type of buffering, tickmark the Generic check box and put a number *n* in the No. of Key Fields so that the *n* left-most fields of the primary key will group records. When a record is read and *n* is 1, all records having the same value in the *first* field of the primary key are loaded into the buffer. When a record is read and *n* is 2, all records having the same value in the *first two* fields of the primary key are loaded into the buffer. This is illustrated in Figure 5.18.

FIGURE 5.18.

Generic buffering. n must be less than the number of fields in the primary key.

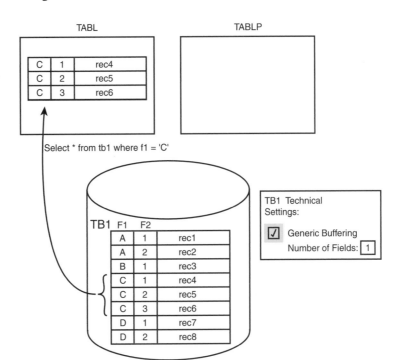

In another example, suppose you choose generic buffering for table ztxlfa1 and set the No. of Key Fields to 1. Because the first field is mandt, all records for a client are loaded into the buffer at one time.

Note

If you specify full buffering for a *client-dependent* table (having mandt in the first column), the system automatically buffers it generically with *n* equal to 1. That is, when a record is read, only records having the same client number are loaded into the buffer. You cannot see this reflected in the technical settings; they continue to indicate full buffering. It just happens "under the covers."

5

Generic buffering is suitable for tables in which records are usually accessed in sets or groups. It is suitable if, when one record of the group is accessed, more accesses will usually occur for records from the same group. For example, if a user logs on in English, it is highly probable that only English descriptions will be read by that user and by other users on the same application server. Text tables, where descriptions are stored, always have mandt and spras (the language code) as the first two fields. Therefore, generic buffering with n equal to 2 is appropriate.

Caution

> Each record group in the buffer requires administrative overhead. Try to have a relatively large number of records per group. With generic buffering, if you end up loading most of the rows of a table and they are loaded into many small groups, a fully buffered table will be more efficient.

During buffer synchronization, if a table is buffered generically and a record is invalidated in the buffer, all records in the group are invalidated. The next read of any record in that group will cause the entire group to be reloaded.

Single Record Buffering

Tickmarking the Single Records check box turns on single-record buffering. With this type of buffering, select single picks one record into the single record buffer TABLP, as shown in Figure 5.19. With this buffering type, records are only buffered when the select single statement is executed. Select/endselect does not load or read TABLP.

FIGURE 5.19.

With single-record buffering enabled, select single *loads records one at a time into the* TABLP *buffer.*

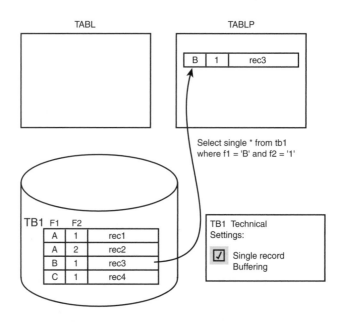

For example, if table `ztxlfa1` has a buffering type of single records, select *single* `*` `from ztxlfa1 where lifnr = 'V1'` causes the `TABLP` buffer to be searched for record `V1`. If it is found there, that copy is used. If it is not found, it is loaded into `TABLP` from the database.

Even if a record is *not* found, an entry is *still* made into the single record buffer. The entry indicates that record does not exist in the database. The next time that record is requested, the buffer can be used to resolve the request and a database access is not necessary.

For example, suppose vendor `X1` does not exist in the database. Executing select `single * from ztxlfa1 where lifnr = 'X1'` would cause an entry to be created in the single record buffer to indicate that record X1 does not exist in the database. The next time vendor `X1` is requested, the system looks in the buffer and discovers that it does not exist and does not need to go to the database.

Single-record buffering is appropriate for very large tables in which a small percentage of the records are read often. For single-record buffering to work, records must be read using the `select single` statement.

Buffering Types Summarized

In summary, there are two buffers: `TABL` (the generic record buffer) and `TABLP` (the single record buffer). There are also two varieties of the `select` statement: `select` and `select single`. The `select` statement loads `TABL` and the `select single` statement loads `TABLP`.

When reading, `select` only reads `TABL`; it ignores `TABLP`. `select single` reads both buffers. This behavior is summarized in Figure 5.20. Remember that a record can only be in one buffer at a time because a table can only have one buffering type.

FIGURE 5.20.

How the select state-
ments interact with the
buffers.

	generic record buffer	single record buffer
Select Single	READS ONLY	LOADS AND READS
Select	LOADS AND READS	DOES NOT LOAD OR READ

5

Tip

To clear the contents of both TABL and TABLP, type **/$tab** in the Command field and press the Enter key. You can use this method after you turn off buffering to clear the buffers before testing the difference in a program's performance. Note that this can slow system performance in general for up to a couple of hours until the buffers are again repopulated.

Buffer Displacement

If TABLP is full and a new record needs to be loaded, the oldest ones are thrown away to make room for it. The *oldest ones* are the ones that have been sitting there the longest without being accessed.

In TABL, old records are not discarded when new ones are loaded. Instead, entire tables are periodically unloaded from the buffer. The length of time between unloads and which tables are unloaded is determined by a caching algorithm within R/3. This complex algorithm is based on the amount of space used by a table in the buffer versus the number of read accesses on it in the previous period, and also on the amount of free space available in the buffer and the current access quality of the buffer.

Deciding Whether to Buffer

The goal in buffering is to reduce the number of database reads and the amount of network traffic from the database to the application servers. The following sections will list scenarios with buffering tables that are not updated, along with buffering and indexing.

Buffering Tables That Are not Updated

If a table is frequently accessed without being updated often, it should be buffered. You will need to consult your Basis administrator to find out if there is enough room in the buffer to add your table. If there is not, and your table will be accessed often, it might be possible to increase the amount of RAM allocated to the buffers. Alternatively, another table accessed less frequently than yours could be changed so that it is no longer buffered.

Buffering and Indexes

Records in a buffer have their own primary index built in RAM. When records are needed, the index is used to locate them in the buffer the same way the primary index in the database is used to locate records in a table. However, *secondary* indexes are *not* created in the buffer, nor are the database secondary indexes used to access buffered data. Therefore, when coding a select. . .where statement on a buffered table, use primary key fields in the where clause beginning with the first field of the primary key and using as many in sequence from the primary key as you can. If the first field of the primary key is missing from the where clause (not counting mandt), a full scan of the table in the buffer will be performed. For example, if table ztxlfa1 has been fully buffered, select * from ztxlfa1 where lifnr = 'V1' will be supported by the buffer's primary index. Select * from ztxlfa1 where land1 = 'CA' will cause a full table scan in the buffer to occur.

Being unable to use secondary indexes causes a peculiar catch-22 effect if you fully buffer large tables that have secondary indexes. Buffering such a table will cause selects on the primary index to speed up, but it will possibly slow selects on secondary indexes down. A select statement on a large table (size category 1 or greater) that is fully supported by a secondary index in the database could run slower against the buffer because a secondary index is not available there. How much slower (if at all) will depend on the amount of data in the table. To compensate for this problem, avoid the buffer and use the secondary indexes by adding bypassing buffer to the select statement where a secondary index should be used.

For example, table TSTC contains over 12,000 rows, is size category 1, is fully buffered, and has a secondary index on its pgmna field. Measurements show that select * from tstc *bypassing buffer* where pgmna = 'ZTXTEST' ran 18 times faster on average than select * from tstc where pgmna = 'ZTXTEST', *even though the table is fully buffered*. The first select was resolved in the database using a secondary index on the pgmna field; the second performed a full table scan in the buffer.

Caution

Be *very* careful when using bypassing buffer on buffered tables that are also updated. If you use it on *one* select statement, you should use it on *all* select statements for that table and all related tables within a single transaction. If you don't, you will in effect be mixing buffered and unbuffered data. This can cause data inconsistencies in your program and possibly in the database if your program also does updates.

5

Buffering Summarized

The following are points to remember about buffering tables and indexing:

- Buffering tables can make your programs run much faster. However, if carelessly used, buffering can have the opposite effect.
- Buffers sit in RAM on the application server, therefore space in the buffer is limited. A table that is not accessed often should not be buffered to conserve buffer space and prevent buffer overflow.
- Tables that are small (size category 0), accessed often, and rarely updated should be fully buffered.

- Tables that are large (size category > 0) and accessed often using `select single` should use single-record buffering.
- A table where records from a group are accessed together should use generic buffering. A partial primary key must identify the group.
- Tables that are updated often should not be buffered if your configuration has multiple application servers. Doing so increases network traffic because the data must be reloaded into the buffers on the other application servers each time it changes.
- If the table is buffered, use `bypassing buffer` to obtain the most recent data before allowing it to be updated.
- If possible, use the fields of the primary index in a `where` clause on buffered tables. If this is not possible, and the table is large (size category > 0), add `bypassing buffer` and use fields supported by a secondary index in the database.

Summary

- An index is a copy of specific columns of a table sorted in ascending order.
- Indexes speed up `select` statements. A `select` should always be supported by an index.
- You can create secondary indexes on a table. Create one when you cannot use the fields of an existing index in your `where` clause.
- The fields in a `where` clause should be listed in your program in the same order as they appear in the index.
- Transaction `ST05` can be used to show which index, if any, was used by a given `select` statement.
- A table's technical settings can be used to control the data class, size category, buffering type, and whether logging is enabled.
- The data class determines which tablespace the table will be created in. The most important data classes are APPL0 (master data) and APPL1 (transaction data).
- The size category determines the size of the table's initial and next extents and the maximum number of extents allowed. It should be chosen so that the initial extent is big enough to hold the entire table. Secondary extents slow system performance down and make reorganization necessary.
- Buffering speeds up data access by caching most-often-used data in RAM on the application server. Buffer space is limited, so tables should be buffered judiciously.

Do	Don't
DO place the fields in the `where` clause in the same order as they appear in the index.	**DON'T** code a `select` that is unsupported by an index.
DO be generous when choosing a size category.	**DON'T** choose a size category that will cause a table to require a secondary extent.
DO use `bypassing buffer` when reading a record for update from a buffered table.	

Q&A

Q **I can't display some of the screens that you mentioned. I get the error message `You are not authorized to use transaction XXXX`. How can I see these screens?**

A Ask your security administrator for authorization.

Q **When I display the data buffers using ST02, I see a lot of other buffers there, too. What are they all for?**

A Data buffers are only two of the many buffers kept on an application server. The nametabs (table runtime objects) are all buffered, as well as all programs, menus, and toolbars (a.k.a. CUA or GUI status), screens, and calendars. These buffers are all listed here.

Workshop

The Workshop provides you two ways for you to affirm what you've learned in this chapter. The Quiz section poses questions to help you solidify your understanding of the material covered and the Exercise section provides you with experience in using what you have learned. You can find answers to the quiz questions and exercises in Appendix B, "Answers to Quiz Questions and Exercises."

Quiz

1. Can I specify somewhere the exact index I want a `select` statement to use?

2. Can I create secondary indexes on SAP tables or buffer them?

3. Can I tell how much faster my program runs with buffered tables than without?

Exercise 1

What is the data class for tables: MARA, LFA1, and KNA1? What is the size category for MARA, LFA1, and KNA1?

DAY 6

The Data Dictionary, Part 4

Chapter Objectives

After you complete this chapter, you should be able to:

- Display and compare active and revised versions of DDIC objects
- Use the database utility to perform consistency checks, display database-specific table information, and drop and re-create tables in the database

Automatic Table History and Change Documents

NEW TERM Changes to data within a table can be automatically logged. Such automatic logging of changes is called *automatic table history*. To turn on logging, tickmark the Log Data Changes check box on the Technical Settings screen (refer to Figure 5.4). If not already done, the Basis consultant must also specify the client number(s) for which logging is to take on the system profile parameter rec/client.

> **Tip**
>
> To display the `rec/client` setting in your system, follow the procedure used to display `rdisp/bufreftime` in the section titled "Buffer Synchronization" in Day 5.

Change Documents

NEW TERM For each insert, update, or delete to a table enabled for automatic table history, a record is created in table `dbtabprt`. Each record is called a *change document*. Each change document contains the date and time of the change, the userid of the user who made the change, the transaction code and program name used to make the change, and the type of change performed. The type of change will be INS if the record was inserted, UPD if the record was updated, or DEL if the record was deleted.

Using transaction code SCU3 or OY18 (see Figure 6.1), you can display the change documents and compare them to current values in the table. There is no difference between these two transaction codes; they both run the same program.

FIGURE 6.1.

The Table History transaction displays change documents from tables with automatic table history enabled.

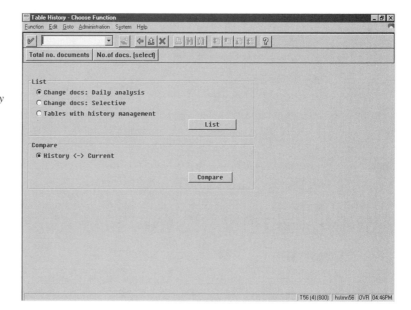

From the Table History – Choose Function screen, you can perform the following functions:

- To display the current day's change documents, choose the Change Docs: Daily Analysis radio button and press the List pushbutton. A list is displayed containing all changes for the current day.

- To search for change documents by date range or table name, choose the Change Docs: Selective radio button and press the List pushbutton. The Analysis of Table Log Database screen is displayed. Type your search criteria and press the Execute button. A list of change documents for the specified criterion is displayed. At the top of the list is a summary of information about the list, then a Notes section, and then the analysis. For each table, the fields of it are displayed first (see Figure 6.2) and the change documents for it follow (see Figure 6.3).

- To display a count of the number of change documents that exist for a given date range or table range, press the No.of Docs. (Select) pushbutton.

- To display the list of tables for which automatic history is kept, choose the Tables With History Management radio button and press the List pushbutton. This list shows all tables that have a tickmark in the Log Data Changes check box.

- To display the total number of change documents in table dbtabprt, press the Total No. Documents pushbutton on the Application toolbar.

- To compare field values in change documents with current field values in a table, choose the History <-> Current radio button and press the Compare pushbutton. The Table History screen is displayed. Enter search criteria for change documents and press the Compare pushbutton. The Table History – Comparison With Current State screen is displayed. The primary key of each record appears on the left and differences appear on the right (see Figure 6.4).

FIGURE 6.2.

The fields of table
HPR1007 *appear before
the change documents,
showing the field names,
primary key indicator,
data type, length,
column name, and
description.*

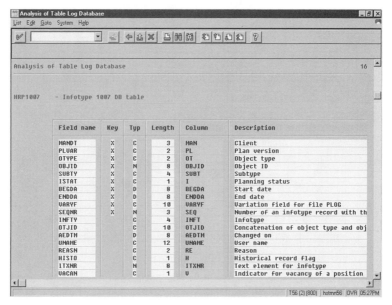

6

FIGURE 6.3.

The change documents of table HPR1007 *appear after the field list. The primary key of each record appears first (in turquoise) followed by the data (in white).*

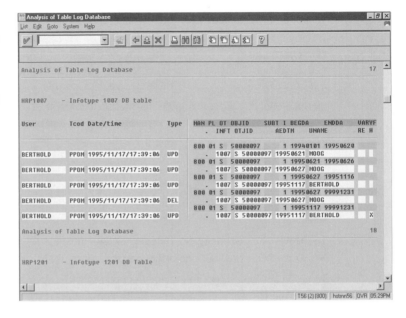

FIGURE 6.4.

Here, the data in dbtabprt *is compared to the current contents of each record.*

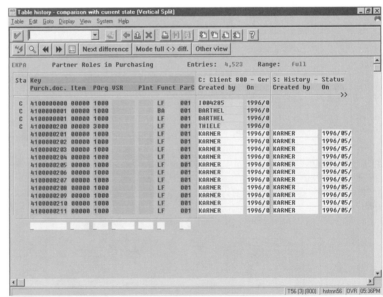

The primary key appears in turquoise on the left half of the screen. The right half of the screen is divided into current values and history values. Gray lines indicate that a difference exists. To display the meaning of the codes in the left-most column, place your cursor there and press F1. This report shows that four records exist in table EKPA but no history records exist for them.

Knowing When to Use Automatic Table History

Automatic table history should be used for tables that contain critical information and when every change must be tracked without fail, regardless of the update program used. Unfortunately, updates to the table are slowed down because a record is written to dbtabprt for each record changed. In most cases when table history is needed, Change Document Objects provides a faster and more efficient alternative, and so should instead be used. For more information on Change Document Objects, see the R/3 Library (Menu path Help->R/3 Library, Basis Components, ABAP/4 Development Workbench, Extended Applications Function Library, Change Documents.)

Caution

If the primary key of your table is longer than 86 bytes, or if the remainder of the row is longer than 500 bytes, you cannot use automatic table history. You will get an error when you try to activate the table and changes will not be logged. The reason for these restrictions lies in table dbtabprt. The vkey field contains the key of the record that was changed and is 86 bytes long. The vdata field contains the remainder of the record and is 500 bytes long.

Summarizing the Technical Settings

The following summarizes the technical settings for buffering, table extents, and the automatic logging of updated information:

- The data class determines the tablespace in which a table is created. The database administrator uses tablespaces to organize and maintain the database. Choosing the proper tablespace makes database administration easier, increases system performance, and to some extent even increases system availability because the database is usually taken offline for reorganizations.

- The size category determines the size of the initial extent and next extents, as well as the number of possible next extents. Choosing too low a number will cause one or more additional extents to be allocated. A table that spans multiple extents decreases system performance, increases database maintenance, and lowers system availability, again because the database is usually taken offline for reorganizations.

- Buffering increases system performance by caching data locally on the application server. When done properly, fewer database accesses are required because the data that is most often read is stored in RAM on the application server. Good candidates for buffering are tables that are seldom updated and often read.

6

- Activating the automatic logging feature on a table will cause a change document to be created each time the table is changed. This feature slows table updates, and so is only used for tables containing critical data. For non-critical tables, change document objects should be used.

Revised and Active Versions

NEW TERM   Two versions of a table can exist (or any DDIC object): the *Revised version* and the *Active version*. If you change a table and press the Save button without pressing Activate, you have created a Revised version of the table that contains your changes. The Active version still exists; it is the last version that was activated. ABAP/4 programs only use Active versions. The presence of Revised versions does not affect them.

The Revised version exists to enable you to prepare a change before it is needed and then activate it when it is required. It also enables you to change many objects and then activate them all simultaneously. When you activate them, the currently Active versions are discarded and your Revised versions become active and replace them.

The Revised version is displayed, if it exists, when you display a table (the Status field will contain `Revised`). The Application toolbar will have an Active Version button (see Figure 6.5). If you press it, the Active version will be displayed and the button on the toolbar will change to Revised Version, enabling you to press the button again and return to the previous display.

FIGURE 6.5.

When a table that has a Revised version is displayed, you see the Revised version by default.

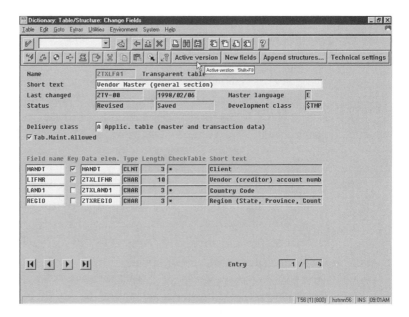

SCREENCAM Start the ScreenCam "How to Compare Revised and Active Versions" now.

To compare the Revised and Active versions:

1. From the Dictionary: Table/Structure: Display Fields screen, choose the menu path Utilities->Version management. The Versions of Object screen is displayed. The first line contains the word mod.. This is the Revised version. The next line contains act.. This is the Active version.

2. To compare the two versions, tickmark them both and press the Compare pushbutton. The Version Comparison for Tables screen is displayed. The changed lines are indicated in the right margin. <- only activ means that line only exists in the Active version. <- only modif means that line only exists in the Revised version.

3. To see a summary of changes, press the Delta display button on the Application toolbar. The list is updated to contain only the differences between the two versions.

Additional Versions

Aside from the Active and Revised versions, you can also create temporary versions of a table. To do this, choose the menu path Table->Generate version. The message Temporary version of active object stored. appears at the bottom of the window. This temporary version is kept until the table is transported into production To view the new version, choose the menu path Utilities->Version Management. The version with the highest number is the one you just created.

Discarding a Revised Version

To discard a Revised version without activating it, you must first generate a temporary version from the Active version and then restore it, as shown in the following procedure.

SCREENCAM Start the ScreenCam "How to Discard a Revised Version" now.

To discard a Revised version and restore the Active version:

1. From the Dictionary: Table/Structure: Change Fields screen, choose the menu path Table->Generate Version. A dialog box appears containing the message Version of >> active << object stored.

2. Press the Continue button. You are returned to the Dictionary: Table/Structure: Change Fields screen, and the message Temporary version of activate object stored is displayed at the bottom of the window.

3. Choose the menu path Utilities->Version management. The Versions Of Object screen is displayed. There will be a tickmark beside the word act..

6

4. Remove the tickmark beside the word `act.`.

5. Place a tickmark beneath the Version(s) In The Version Database: line beside the highest version number.

6. Press the Retrieve button on the Application toolbar. A dialog box appears containing the message `Version nnnnn is now new revised (non-active) version. Proceed?`.

7. Press the Yes button. You are returned to the Versions Of Object screen, and the message `Restored version must be activated!` appears at the bottom of the window. There will be a tickmark beside the word `act.`. The Revised version is now the same as the Active button.

8. To verify that the Revised version matches the Active version, place a tickmark beside the word `mod.`. Both the `act.` and `mod.` lines should now be tickmarked.

9. Press the Compare button on the Application toolbar. The Version Comparison For Tables screen is displayed.

10. Press the Delta Display button on the Application toolbar. The list should contain a line reading `General attributes: Unchanged` and another line that reads `Fields: Unchanged`. You have now confirmed that the Active and Revised versions match.

11. Press the Back button on the Standard toolbar. You are returned to the Versions of Object screen.

12. Press the Back button on the Standard toolbar. You are returned to the Dictionary: Table/Structure: Change Fields screen.

13. Press the Activate button on the Application toolbar. The Status field contains `Act.` and the message `xxxxx was activated` appears at the bottom of the window.

All DDIC objects, such as domains and data elements, have Revised and Active versions. They can all be displayed and compared the same way. Objects can use only Active versions. For example, if you modify a domain and create a Revised version, data elements using it continue to use the Active version until you activate the domain.

Using the Database Utility

 Within the DDIC lies a *database utility* tool. Using it, you can examine and modify tables at the database level.

SCREENCAM Start the ScreenCam "How to Access the Database Utility" now.

To access the database utility:

1. Begin at the Dictionary: Initial Screen.

2. Enter a table name in the Object Name field.

3. Press the Display pushbutton.

4. Select the menu path Utilities->Database Utility. The ABAP/4 Dictionary: Utility for Database Tables screen is displayed, as shown in Figure 6.6.

FIGURE 6.6.

Using the ABAP/4 Dictionary: Utility for Database Tables screen, you can communicate directly with the database to display or change a table.

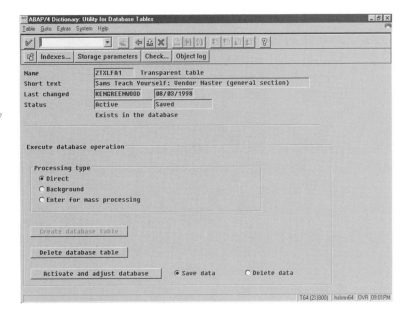

From here you can:

- Check the consistency of the R/3 DDIC definitions against the database.
- View the activation log to see the actual SQL statements sent to the database.
- Display and modify database storage parameters.
- Delete a table by dropping it in the database, or empty it by dropping and re-creating it in the database.

Consistency Checks

The definition of a transparent table exists in two places: the R/3 data dictionary and the database. To check for consistency between the two, from within the database utility choose the menu path Extras->Database Object->Check. The Active version of the table is compared to the database table. The Table xxxxx: Check Database Object screen will be displayed, and a message at the top of the list will indicate whether the database object is consistent (see Figure 6.7).

6

FIGURE 6.7.

A consistency check against the database confirms that the R/3 DDIC definition of table ztxlfa1 *and the database definition are identical.*

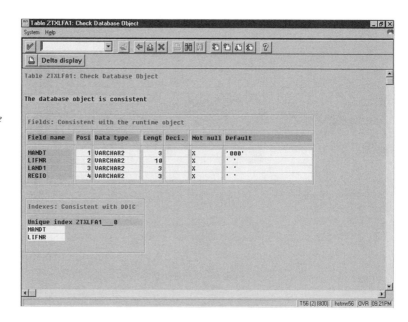

Inconsistencies can arise if:

- The definition of the table was altered at the database level. This can happen if someone manually alters the database definition, or if an ABAP/4 program alters it using native SQL.

- The database becomes corrupt.

You might do a consistency check if, when testing a program, you get an unusual SQL error, or if you get incorrect results from code that should work fine but inexplicably does not. Finding an inconsistency indicates that the source of the problem might lie outside of your program.

NEW TERM An R/3 table is in some ways like a traditional program. It exists in two forms: the "source" that you can display and modify, and the *compiled* form that is used at runtime, called the *runtime object*. The runtime object is created when you activate the table, and is also known as the *nametab*.

When a consistency check is performed, the nametab is compared against the database.

You can display the nametab from the database utility by choosing the menu path Extras->Runtime object->Display. The Object xxxxx: Display Active Runtime Object screen is displayed (see Figure 6.8). At the top is the time stamp of the nametab followed by the header information. It contains the table type (T for transparent), the table form in the database (again, T for transparent), the number of fields in the table, the length in bytes of the record, the number of key fields, the length of the key fields in bytes, buffering information, and more. (For detailed information on the header fields and their values, display the structure X030L.) Below the header is a list of the fields, their position in the table, the data type, length, number of decimal places, offset from the beginning of the record, external length the reference table, the check table, and more. The technical attributes of the table are completely described by the nametab.

FIGURE 6.8.

The nametab is the runtime object for a table. It contains all the table's technical characteristics such as field names, data types, and lengths.

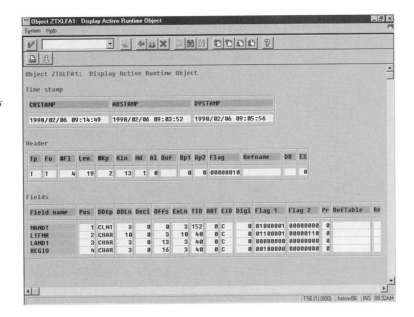

Role of the Nametab in ABAP/4 Programs

As you learned on Day 2, when you create an ABAP/4 program that selects data from a table, you must code a `tables` statement. The `tables` statement makes the structure of the table known to the program. However, when you generate the runtime object for the program, the definition of the table is not embedded into it. Instead, when the program's runtime object is executed, it makes a call to the nametab to determine the table's structure at runtime. This enables you to change a table (or structure) without having to regenerate all the ABAP/4 programs that use it. They dynamically determine the table characteristics at runtime by calling the nametab.

Although you do not have to regenerate all programs every time a change is made to a table, certain changes (such as renaming or deleting a field) will require you to make changes to the ABAP/4 code. In these cases, you will need to find all programs that use it.

6

SCREENCAM Start the ScreenCam "How to Perform a Where-Used List on a Table" now.

To find all programs that use a given table:

1. Begin at the Dictionary: Initial Screen.

2. Enter the table name in the Object Name field.

3. Press the Where-Used List button on the Application toolbar. A Where-Used List dialog box appears.

4. Choose the Programs radio button.

5. Press the Continue button. The Table xxxxx in Programs screen is displayed. A list of all programs using the table appears.

6. Double-click on a program name to display all lines of code in which the table is used.

7. Double-click on a line to display the code starting from that line.

Checking the Consistency of the Nametab

The nametab obtains its characteristics from the data elements and domains that make up the table. It is possible for the definition of the nametab to be out of sync with the data elements and domains. For example, when you activate a change to a domain, the tables containing it must also be reactivated to pick up those changes. Although this happens automatically, in certain situations a reactivation can fail because of a database restriction or because the table contains data and must be converted. This situation can be detected by performing a consistency check on the runtime object.

To check for consistency between the nametab and the Data Dictionary objects, from within the database utility choose the menu path Extras->Runtime Object->Check. The runtime object is compared to the DDIC source objects. The Object xxxxx: Check Active Runtime Object screen will be displayed, and a message at the top of the list will indicate whether the database object is consistent. Figures 6.9 and 6.10 show an example of an inconsistency in the nametab for table ztxlfa1.

If a domain is changed and the table reactivation fails, an inconsistency can exist between the nametab and the domain.

In the case of Figure 6.10, the check found that the data type of field lifnr is char 10 in the nametab and int4 in the domain.

ABAP/4 programs only use the nametab. Therefore, they will not know about inconsistencies, and thus are unaffected by them in the Development system. Transporting the DDIC objects before correcting inconsistencies can cause problems during import to Q/A or production, or even cause ABAP/4 programs in these environments to produce incorrect results. The reason lies in the fact that the changes have not affected the ABAP/4 programs, and thus have not yet been tested.

FIGURE 6.9.

In this screen, a consistency check indicates an error message that the record length, key length, and table alignment are inconsistent.

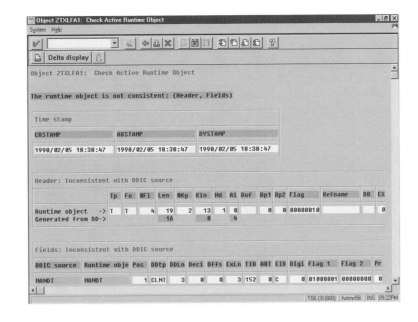

FIGURE 6.10.

Scrolling down in the list shows the fields of the nametab and the reason for the inconsistency.

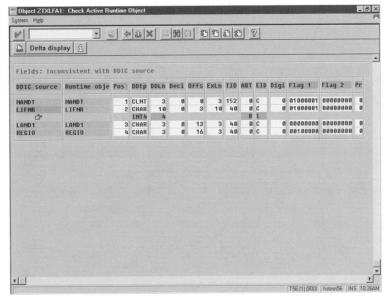

6

Displaying the Activation Log

From within the database utility, you can display the activation log by pressing the Object Log button on the Application toolbar. This log is only generated if the activation causes SQL to be generated. (In some cases, a table change can be activated without affecting the database, for example, a change to the short text.) The log contains the sequence of steps performed and all SQL statements sent to the database during the last activation (see Figures 6.11 and 6.12).

FIGURE 6.11.

The activation log displays the sequence of steps performed during activation and the SQL that was generated. This log shows that during the activation, the table was dropped in the database and re-created.

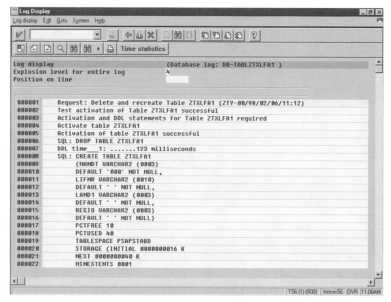

FIGURE 6.12.

This is the remainder of the activation log shown in Figure 6.11.

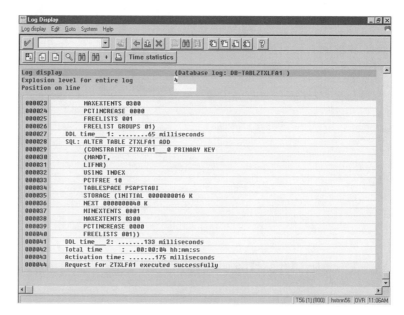

To display detail information describing any message in the log, position your cursor on the message and press the F1 key.

Displaying and Modifying Storage Parameters

Pressing the Storage Parameters button from within the database utility (refer to Figure 6.1) displays the DB Utility: Transparent Tables – Database Parameters screen. Figure 6.13 shows how this screen looks when an Oracle database is installed. This screen is primarily for use by the DBA to alter the storage parameters from within R/3 after a table has been activated. It is presented here for the sake of completeness.

FIGURE 6.13.

Database-specific parameters are shown on the DB Utility: Transparent Tables – Database Parameters screen. This screen shows that storage parameters for table ztxlfa1 *have been altered after activation because the DBS and CMP lines do not match.*

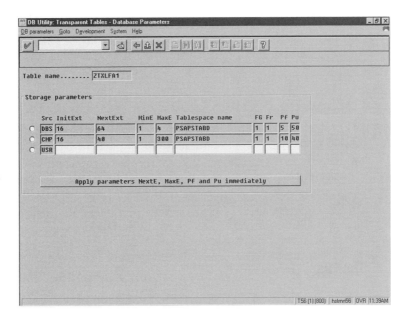

Database-specific information about the table's storage parameters is displayed here. The Src column indicates the source of the values. DBS means these values are the actual values in the database. CMP means these values are computed from the size category and data class. The USR line enables you to enter values for NextE, MaxE, Pf, and Pu and apply them immediately by pressing the Apply Parameters NextE, MaxE, Pf, and Pu Immediately pushbutton. Most of the time, the DBS and CMP lines will be the same, unless the storage parameters for the database table were altered manually after the table was activated.

The InitExt and NextExt columns contain the sizes (in blocks) of the initial and next extents. The MinE and MaxE columns contain the minimum and maximum number of extents allowed. The tablespace name is next, followed by the FG and Fr columns, which contain the number of freelist groups and the number of freelists in a group. (These two columns are only used if Oracle is being used in parallel processing mode.) The Pf and Pu columns contain the percentage of free space and percentage of space used in the data blocks. For more information on any column, position your cursor on it and press F1.

Although the only parameters that can be changed are NextExt, MaxE, Pf, and Pu, you must completely fill the line before pressing the Apply pushbutton. For example, to change the size of the next extent to 64 and to set the maximum number of extents to 4, first select the USR radio button. Then type **64** in the NextExt column, type **4** in the MaxE column, copy the rest of the values from the DBS line, and then press the Apply pushbutton.

Your changes are immediately applied in the database when you press the Apply pushbutton. To view the results, press the Back button to return to the ABAP/4 Dictionary: Utility for Database Tables screen, and then press the Storage Parameters button on the Application toolbar. The line having DBS in the Src column will contain the updated values.

Dropping and Re-Creating Tables in the Database

The fastest way to delete the data from a table is to "drop" it and then re-create it. To drop a table, from within the database utility press the Delete Database Table pushbutton. A dialog box will be displayed to confirm your request. The table and its contents will be deleted from the database. To create it again, press the Create Database Table pushbutton. The table will be re-created using the Active version of the table. You can use the database utility to do this instead of writing an ABAP/4 program to delete all rows.

Caution

Dropping a table causes all data within it to be permanently lost. It is a good idea to make a backup copy of the table before you delete it. If you copy the table manually, remember to copy both the table definition and the data.

Tip

If the table has more than one extent, dropping and re-creating a table is a fast and easy way to reorganize it. You will need to save the data to another table temporarily before dropping it, and then copy it back.

Summary

- Changes to critical data can be automatically logged in change documents. For non-critical data, change document objects should be used instead.

- A Revised version of a table is created when you modify without activating it. Only the Active version of an object can be used.

- Using the database utility, you can examine the nametab and compare its consistency to the Data Dictionary and to the database.

- The database utility also enables you to view the activation log for a table, the storage parameters, and to drop and re-create a table in the database.

Q&A

Q Where would a DBA go to alter the storage parameter of an activated table from within the SAP R/3 system?

A Go to the database utility and press the Storage parameters pushbutton.

Workshop

The Workshop provides two ways for you to affirm what you've learned in this chapter. The Quiz section poses questions to help you solidify your understanding of the material covered and the Exercise section provides you with experience in using what you have learned. You can find answers to the quiz questions and exercises in Appendix B, "Answers to Quiz Questions and Exercises."

Quiz

1. Is it possible that the definition of the table and the data elements and domains can be out of sync?

Exercise 1

1. What is the fastest way to delete the data from a table?

6

DAY 7

Defining Data in ABAP/4, Part 1

Chapter Objectives

After you complete this chapter, you should be able to

- Explain the program's roll area and its contents.
- Understand the elements of ABAP/4 syntax.
- Describe the concept of data objects and their visibility.
- Use literals and understand how to code each type.
- Define and use constants.
- Use the data statement to define variables and field strings.
- Understand ABAP/4 data types, and be able to identify the character and numeric data types.
- Understand the ABAP/4 definition of common DDIC data types.

Before proceeding, please turn to Day 2 and take a few minutes to re-read the analysis in the section "Understanding Code Syntax" now.

Program Buffer and the Roll Area

Programs are buffered on the application server in a *program buffer*. When a user makes a request to run a program, a search is done in the program buffer for it. If it is found, and if it has not been modified in the database, the buffered copy is used. If not, or if the copy in the database is newer, the program is reloaded.

A separate copy of the program is not made in memory for each user who executes it. Instead, all users execute the same copy of the program. The differentiating factor is a separate memory allocation called a *roll area*. One roll area is allocated per execution per user per program. The system uses the roll area to hold all information about the current execution of the program and all memory allocations. Information such as the variables and their values, the current program pointer, and the list output are all kept in the roll area. For example, suppose a user executes a program and a roll area is allocated. If, without waiting for it to finish, the user switches to another session and starts up the same program again, another roll area is allocated for the second execution of that program. The user has two roll areas, one for each execution of the program. If the user had instead run a different program, he would still have two roll areas, one for each program.

Elements of ABAP/4 Syntax

NEW TERM   Each ABAP/4 program is composed of one or more statements. Each statement contains one or more words separated by at least one space. The first word of a statement is the keyword. A statement can include one or more *additions*, and always ends with a period.

In Listing 7.1, the keywords are select, write, and endselect. Two additions appear on the select statement: where and order by. What is normally called a *clause* in other languages is called an *addition* in ABAP/4: It is any word or group of words after the keyword that modifies the behavior of the statement.

INPUT   **LISTING 7.1**   ILLUSTRATION OF BASIC ABAP/4 SYNTAX

```
1 select * from ztxlfa1 where lifnr > '0000001050' order by lifnr.
2    write: \ ztxlfa1-lifnr, ztxlfa1-name1, ztxlfa1-land1.
3    endselect.
```

A statement can begin in any column and can span any number of lines. To continue a statement on another line, break the statement between any two words. A continuation character is not needed. For example, the code in Listing 7.1 can be reformatted as shown in Listing 7.2.

LISTING 7.2   THIS CODE IS THE SAME AS LISTING 7.1, ONLY IT HAS BEEN
INPUT   FORMATTED DIFFERENTLY

```
1 select * from ztxlfa1
2    where lifnr > '0000001050'
3    order by lifnr.
4    write: \ ztxlfa1-lifnr,
5             ztxlfa1-name1,
6             ztxlfa1-land1. endselect.
```

ABAP/4 code is not case sensitive.

Defining Data Objects

NEW TERM   *Data objects* are memory locations that you use to hold data while the program is
running. There are two types of data objects: modifiable and non-modifiable. The
types of non-modifiable data objects are literals and constants. The modifiable data objects
are variables, field strings, and internal tables. A field string is the ABAP/4 equivalent of
a structure. An internal table is the ABAP/4 equivalent of an array.

When the program starts, the memory allocation for each data object occurs in the roll
area of the program. While the program is running, you can read the contents of a non-
modifiable data object or put data into a modifiable data object and then retrieve it. When
the program ends, the system frees the memory for all data objects and their contents are
lost.

NEW TERM   Data objects have three levels of *visibility:* local, global, and external. The visibility of a data object indicates from where in the program the data object is
accessible.

Locally visible data objects are accessible only from inside the subroutine in which they
are defined. Globally visible objects can be accessed from anywhere within the program.
Externally visible objects are accessible from outside of the program by another program. Figure 7.1 displays these three levels of visibility pictorially.

In Figure 7.1, the local data objects in subroutine 1A are visible only from within that
subroutine. Any statement outside of it cannot access them. Similarly, the local data
objects in subroutines 1B and 2A are not accessible from anywhere but within those subroutines.

Any statement in program 1, regardless of where the statement appears, can access the
global data objects in program 1. Similarly, any statement in program 2 can access
the global data objects in program 2.

7

FIGURE 7.1.

The visibility of a data object indicates its accessibility. If it is locally visible, it is only accessible from within a subroutine. If it is globally visible, it is accessible from anywhere within a program. If it is externally visible, it is accessible from outside of the program by another program.

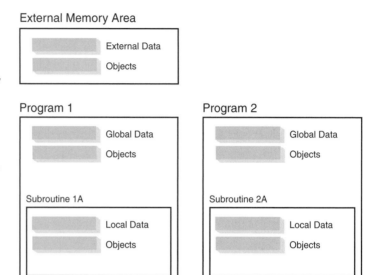

The external data objects could be accessed from any statement in program 1 or program 2. In actuality, whether they can be or not depends on the type of external memory area used and the relationship between the two programs. The details of this are described in the sections on SPA/GPA memory and on ABAP/4 memory.

Defining Literals

A *literal* is a non-modifiable data object. Literals can appear anywhere in a program, and they are defined merely by typing them where needed. There are four types: character string, numeric, floating-point, and hexadecimal.

Character String Literals

Character string literals are case-sensitive character strings of any length enclosed within single quotes. For example, `'JACK'` is a character string literal containing only uppercase characters. `'Caesar the cat'` is a character string literal containing a mixture of upper- and lowercase characters. Your first program used the character string literal `'Hello SAP world'`.

Because a character string literal is enclosed by quotes, you cannot use a single quote by itself in the value of the literal. To represent a single quote, you must use two consecutive single quotes. For example, the statement write 'Caesar''s tail'. will write Caesar's tail, but the statement write 'Caesar's tail' will cause a syntax error because it contains a single quote by itself. The statement write ''''. will cause a single quote to be written to the output page because the two consecutive quotes within quotes are translated to a single quote. Lastly, write: '''', 'Hello Caesar', ''''. will write ' **Hello Caesar** '.

Here are some examples of invalid character string literals and the correct way to code them. "Samantha" is incorrect; it should be enclosed in single quotes, not double quotes, and thus should be coded 'Samantha'. In 'Never ending, the trailing quote is missing and thus should be coded 'Never ending'. 'Don't bite' should contain two consecutive single quotes; it should be coded 'Don''t bite'.

Caution

When a literal is involved in a comparison, as a rule of thumb you should always use uppercase between quotes. Comparisons with character string literals are always case sensitive, so it is necessary to ensure you use the correct case to get the intended result. If the case doesn't match, usually the program will still run, but you will get either incorrect output or no output at all. 99.99 percent of the time, the values your character string literal will be compared with will be in uppercase. Therefore, always type the value for a character string literal in uppercase unless you *know* that it should be otherwise. For example, select single * from ztxlfa1 where lifnr = 'v1' will not find a record, but select single * from ztxlfa1 where lifnr = 'V1' will find a record. Did you notice the lowercase v?

Numeric Literals

Numeric literals are hard-coded numeric values with an optional leading sign. They are not usually enclosed in quotes. However, if a numeric literal contains a decimal, it must be coded as a character string enclosed within single quotes. If it is not, the syntax error Statement x is not defined. Please check your spelling. will occur. Table 7.1 shows the right and wrong ways to code literals.

For example, 256 is a numeric literal, as is -99. '10.5' is a numeric literal that contains a decimal point, so it is enclosed by single quotes. A literal can be used as the default value for a variable, or it can be used to supply a value in a statement. Examples of invalid literals are: 99- (trailing minus sign), "Confirm" (enclosed in double quotes), and 2.2 (contains a decimal but is not enclosed in quotes).

7

Floating-Point Literals

Floating-point literals are specified within single quotes as '<mantissa>E<exponent>'. The mantissa can be specified with a leading sign and with or without decimal places, and the exponent can be signed or unsigned, with or without leading zeros. For example, '9.99E9', '-10E-32', and '+1E09' are valid floating-point literals.

Hexadecimal Literals

A *hexadecimal literal* is specified within single quotes as if it were a character string. The permissible values are 0–9 and A–F. There must be an even number of characters in the string, and all characters *must be in uppercase*.

> If you specify a hexadecimal literal using lowercase characters, you will not receive any warnings or errors. However, when your program runs, the value of the literal will be wrong.

Examples of valid hexadecimal literals are '00', 'A2E5', and 'F1F0FF'. Examples of invalid hexadecimal literals are 'a2e5' (contains lowercase characters), '0' (contains an uneven number of characters), "FF" (enclosed in double quotes), and x'00' (should not have a preceding x).

> Hexadecimal values are rarely used in ABAP/4, because they are usually machine-dependent. The use of a hexadecimal value that creates machine dependence should be avoided.

Table 7.1 covers the right and wrong way of coding numeric and hexadecimal literals.

TABLE 7.1 RIGHT AND WRONG WAYS TO CODE LITERALS

Right	Wrong	Explanation
-99	99-	Trailing sign not permitted on a numeric unless it's within quotes.
'-12'		Numerics within quotes can have leading '12-' or trailing sign.
'12.3'	12.3	Numerics containing a decimal point must be enclosed in single quotes.
'Hi'	"Hi"	Double quotes are not permitted.

Right	Wrong	Explanation
`'Can''t'`	`'Can't'`	To represent a single quote, use two consecutive single quotes.
`'Hi'`	`'Hi`	Trailing quote is missing.
`'7E1'`	`7E1`	Floating-point values must be enclosed within quotes.
`'7e1'`		Lowercase e is allowed for floating-point literals.
`'0A00'`	`'0a00'`	Lowercase in hexadecimal literals gives incorrect results.
`'0A00'`	`'A00'`	An uneven number of hexadecimal digits gives incorrect results.
`'0A00'`	`X'0A00'`	A preceding or following character is not permitted for hexadecimal literals.

Defining Variables

Two statements are commonly used to define variables in an ABAP/4 program:

- `data`
- `parameters`

Using the `data` Statement to Define Variables

Using `data` statement, variables can be declared for the program. Variables defined in the data statement are assigned to a data type and can also have defaults.

Syntax for the `data` Statement

The following is the syntax for defining a variable using the `data` statement:

```
data v1[(l)] [type t] [decimals d] [value 'xxx'].
```

or

```
data v1 like v2 [value 'xxx'].
```

where:

- *v1* is the variable name.
- *v2* is the name of a variable previously defined in the program, or is the name of a field that belongs to a table or structure in the Data Dictionary.
- *(l)* is the internal length specification.
- *t* is the data type.
- *d* is the number of decimal places (used only with type p).
- *'xxx'* is a literal that supplies a default value.

▼ SYNTAX

▲

7

Listing 7.3 shows examples of variables defined with the data statement.

INPUT   **LISTING 7.3**   EXAMPLES OF VARIABLES DEFINED WITH THE data STATEMENT

```
1 data f1(2) type c.
2 data f2 like f1.
3 data max_value type i value 100.
4 data cur_date type d value '19980211'.
```

Variable names can be 1 to 30 characters long. They can contain any characters except
( ) + . , : and must contain at least one alphabetic character.

SAP recommends that variable names should always begin with a character and they
should not contain a dash. A dash has special meaning (see field strings below). Instead
of a dash, you should use an underscore (_).

Tip

> Do not use USING or CHANGING as variable names. Although they are syntacti-
> cally correct, they can cause problems if you try to pass them to subroutines.

The following points also apply to the data statement:

- The default length depends on the data type. (Default lengths are listed in Table 7.2.)
- The default data type is c (character).
- The default initial value is 0, except for data type c, which is blank.
- The value addition only accepts a literal or constant (see below); you cannot use a variable to supply a default value.
- When using the like addition, the variable being defined obtains its length and data type from the referenced variable. You cannot specify them on the same statement with like.
- When using the like addition, the value is *not* obtained from the referenced variable. You can specify the value addition to give the variable a default value. If you do not, it is assigned a default initial value of 0 (or blank for a character data type).

The data statement can appear anywhere in a program. The definition for a variable must
physically come before the statements that access it. If you place a data statement after
executable code, the statements above it cannot access the variables it defines. For an
example, see Listing 7.4.

INPUT　**LISTING 7.4** EXAMPLE OF A VARIABLE THAT IS INCORRECTLY ACCESSED BEFORE IT IS DEFINED

```
1 report ztx0704.
2 data f1(2) value 'Hi'.
3 write: f1, f2.
4 data f2(5) value 'there'.
```

ANALYSIS　The variable F2 is defined on line 4, and the write statement on line 3 is trying to access it. This will generate a syntax error. The data statement on line four should be moved before line 3.

Tip　It is good programming practice to place all data definitions together at the top of your program before the first executable statement.

ABAP/4 Data Types

There are two main categories of data in ABAP/4: character and numeric. Variables receive special treatment by the ABAP/4 processor based on their category that goes beyond the usual treatment given by other languages. Therefore, it is especially important for you to be able to recognize and distinguish between the character and numeric data types.

Character Data Types

The character data types are shown in Table 7.2. Notice that they include type n. Internal lengths are given in bytes. A dash in the Max length column appears for fixed length data types.

TABLE 7.2　LIST OF CHARACTER DATA TYPES

Data Type	Internal Description	Default Internal Length	Max Internal Length	Valid Values	Default Initial Value
c	character	1	65535	Any char	Blank
n	numeric text	1	65535	0-9	0
d	date	8 (fixed)	-	0-9	00000000
t	time	6 (fixed)	-	0-9	000000
x	hexadecimal	1	65535	Any	

7

The Default Initial Value column indicates the value given to the variable by default if you do not specify one using the `value` addition.

Internal Representation of Variables

Numeric text variables are called numeric character variables and hold unsigned positive integers. Each digit occupies one byte, and internally each is stored as a character. This is a character data type. It can only contain the characters 0–9.

Use numeric text to hold numbers that are used as unique identifiers, such as document numbers, account numbers, and order numbers. Also, use it for variables that hold a numeric extracted from a character data type. For example, if you were to extract the two-character month from a date field and needed a variable to store it, you should use a type n field.

Date and time are fixed length data types. You should not specify a length on the `data` statement for them. Values for date and time variables are always stored internally as YYYYMMDD and HHMMSS, respectively. The current date is available in the system field `sy-datum` and the current time in `sy-uzeit`.

Note

> The values of `sy-datum` and `sy-uzeit` are set at the beginning of program execution and do not change until the program ends. If you need access to the most current date and time during execution of a long-running program, use the statement `get time`. It updates the values of `sy-datum` and `sy-uzeit` to reflect the current date and time.

Absolute time values that have millisecond precision are not used in R/3. However, *relative* time values are available to millisecond precision. To obtain these, use the `get run time` statement and store them using data type i. See the chapter on runtime analysis for more details.

Numeric Data Types

The numeric data types are shown in Table 7.3. A dash in the Max Length column indicates the length cannot be changed. An asterisk indicates the attribute is machine-dependent.

TABLE 7.3 NUMERIC DATA TYPES

Data Type	Description	Default Internal Length	Max Length	Max Decimals	Valid Values	Default Initial Value
i	integer	4(fixed)	-	0	-2^{31} to $+2^{31}$	0
p	packed decimal	8	16	14	0-9 .	0
f	floating-point	8	8	15*	$-1E^{-307}$ to $1E^{308}$	0.0

All of the variables in Table 7.3 are signed. In floating-point variables, the exponent is also signed.

Use integers for variables that will be involved in simple computations or when no decimal points are required. Variables such as counters, indexes, positions, or offsets are good examples.

A decimal variable stores `(L*2)-1` digits, where L is the length of the variable in bytes. Decimal values are stored two digits per byte, except the end byte, which contains a single digit and a sign. The decimal point itself is not stored; it is an attribute of the definition. For example, `data f1(4) type p` defines a variable f1 that is four bytes long and can hold seven digits (plus a sign), as shown in Figure 7.2. `data f2(3) type p decimals 2` defines a variable f2 that is three bytes long and can hold five digits (plus a sign). The definition `data f3 type p` defines a variable f3 capable of holding 15 digits because the default length for type p is 8.

FIGURE 7.2.

Packed decimal values are stored two digits per byte. The end byte is an exception; it stores a single digit and the sign. The decimal point is not stored and so does not take up any space in the field; it is part of the definition.

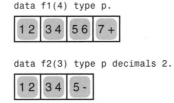

```
data f1(4) type p.
```
```
12 34 56 7+
```

```
data f2(3) type p decimals 2.
```
```
12 34 5-
```

7

Floating-point variables are always approximate. They can be used for calculations requiring very large values or many decimal places. Precision up to 15 decimal places is possible, but this is hardware-dependent.

Caution Be careful when you specify initial values on the data statement using the value addition. These values are not validated to see whether they are compatible with the data type. Using the value addition, you can assign invalid values to integers, date and time variables, numeric text, packed decimal variables, or floating-point variables, either accidentally or intentionally. The results of this assignment are machine-dependent and are undefined.

Mapping DDIC Data Types to ABAP/4 Data Types

Data types in the Data Dictionary are built from the ABAP/4 data types. Table 7.4 shows common Data Dictionary data types and their corresponding ABAP/4 data definitions. L is the length specified in the domain. For a complete list, view the F1 help for the tables statement.

TABLE 7.4 DATA DICTIONARY DATA TYPES AND THEIR CORRESPONDING ABAP/4 DATA TYPES

DDIC Data Type	Description	ABAP/4 Data Definition
char	Character	c(L)
clnt	Client	c(3)
dats	Date	d
tims	Time	t
cuky	Currency key	c(5)
curr	Currency	p((L+2)/2)
dec	Decimal	p((L+2)/2)
fltp	Floating-point	f
int1	1-byte integer	(none)
int2	2-byte integer	(none)
int4	4-byte integer	i
lang	Language	c(1)
numc	Numeric text	n(L)
prec	Precision	x(2)
quan	Quantity	p((L+2)/2)
unit	Units	c(L)

Using the `parameters` Statement to Define Variables

NEW TERM   A parameter is a special type of variable that is defined using the `parameters` statement. `parameters` is a lot like the `data` statement, but when you run the program, the system will display the parameters as input fields on a *selection screen* before the program actually begins to execute. The user can enter or modify their values and then press the Execute button to begin program execution. You can use both `parameters` and `data` in the same program. The rules for parameter names are the same as for variable names, except for the following:

- The maximum length is 8 characters instead of 30.
- In addition to literals and constants, you can also use a variable to supply default a default value.

Syntax for the `parameters` Statement

The following code is the syntax for defining a variable using the `parameters` statement.

```
parameters p1[(l)] [type t] [decimals d] ...
```

or

```
parameters p1 like v1 ...
... [default 'xxx'] [obligatory] [lower case] [as checkbox] [radiobutton
➥group g].
```

where:

- *p1* is the parameter name.
- *v1* is the name of a previously defined variable or parameter, or is the name of a field that belongs to a table or structure in the Data Dictionary.
- *(l)* is the internal length specification.
- *t* is the data type.
- *d* is the number of decimal places (used only with type p).
- *'xxx'* is a literal or previously defined variable that supplies a default value.

Listing 7.5 shows examples of parameters defined with the `parameters` statement.

LISTING 7.5   EXAMPLES OF PARAMETERS DEFINED USING THE `parameters`
INPUT   STATEMENT

```
1 parameters p1(2) type c.
2 parameters p2 like p1.
3 parameters max_value type i default 100.
4 parameters cur_date type d default '19980211' obligatory.
5 parameters cur_date like sy-datum default sy-datum obligatory.
```

7

Note

> There are two variations of the parameters statement: parameter and parameters. Operationally, there is no difference between the two; they are completely interchangeable. However, if you attempt to obtain F1 help on the parameter statement, none will be found. For this reason, I recommend that you use only the parameters statement.

A sample program using parameters is given in Listing 7.6, and the input screen it generates appears in Figure 7.3. Please run this report now.

INPUT

LISTING 7.6 EXAMPLE OF A PROGRAM THAT ACCEPTS INPUT PARAMETERS USING THE parameters STATEMENT

```
1   report ztx0706.
2   parameters: p1(15) type c,
3               p2  like p1 obligatory lower case,
4               p3  like sy-datum default sy-datum,
5               cb1 as checkbox,
6               cb2 as checkbox,
7               rb1 radiobutton group g1 default 'X',
8               rb2 radiobutton group g1,
9               rb3 radiobutton group g1.
10  write: / 'You entered:',
11         / '  p1 =', p1,
12         / '  p2 =', p2,
13         / '  p3 =', p3,
14         / '  cb1=', cb1,
15         / '  cb2=', cb2,
16         / '  rb1=', rb1,
17         / '  rb2=', rb2,
18         / '  rb3=', rb3.
```

The additions to the parameters statement are described in Table 7.5.

TABLE 7.5   ADDITIONS TO THE parameters STATEMENT AND THEIR USES

Addition	Use
type	Same as the data statement.
decimals	Same as the data statement.
like	Same as the data statement.
default	Same as the value addition on the data statement.
obligatory	The user must enter a value into the field before the program will execute.

Addition	Use
lower case	Prevents values from being translated into uppercase.
as checkbox	Displays the input field as a check box.
radiobutton group *g*	Displays the input field as a radio button belonging to group *g*.

FIGURE 7.3.

When you run report
ztx0706, *the parameters first appear on a selection screen. Obligatory parameters are indicated with question marks. To begin processing, the user must press the Execute button on the Application toolbar.*

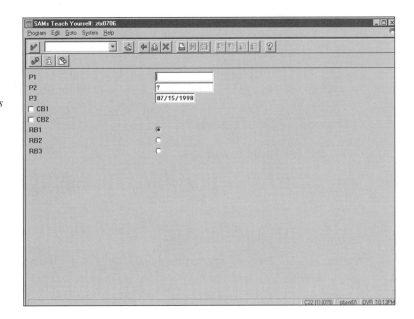

The following points also apply to the parameters statement:

- When the selection screen is shown, obligatory fields contain a question mark. These indicate to the user which fields must be filled in before continuing.

- The default data type is c (character).

- The default value is 0, except for data type c, which is blank.

- The value addition accepts a literal, a sy variable, or a variable previously defined in the program.

- When using the like addition, the parameter being defined obtains its length and data type from the referenced variable. You cannot specify them on the same statement with like.

- When using the like addition, the value is *not* obtained from the referenced variable. You can specify the value addition to give the parameter a default value. If you do not, it is assigned a default initial value of 0 (or blank for a character data type).

7

- Like data, the parameters statement can appear anywhere in a program, but the definition must physically come before the statements that access it.
- Parameters appear on a selection screen in the same order that they are defined in the program.
- All parameters statements, no matter where they appear in the program, are collected together by the ABAP/4 interpreter and displayed on the selection screen at the same time. Even if you put a parameter statement in the middle of the program, that parameter will still be displayed on the selection screen before the program executes.
- The parameters are displayed in an SAP standard format. To modify their appearance, for example, to move the input field left or move the label right, use the selection-screen statement, described in Day 21.

Using the Addition: lower case

All values entered into a parameter are translated into uppercase by default. To turn off this translation, use the addition lower case. This addition only applies to character fields.

Using the Addition: as checkbox

A check box has only two states: ticked and clear. You use them when you want to present the user with an on/off or true/false type of choice. You can use more than one check box on a screen. If you have multiple check boxes on a screen, they operate completely independently from each another.

To display a parameter as a check box, use the addition as checkbox. You cannot specify a data type or length; it will default to type c and length 1. The parameter will contain a capital X if the check box is ticked; it will contain a blank if the check box is clear. If the check box should initially contain a tickmark, use a default value of capital X. Run program ztx506 to see the check box.

Space and capital X are the only valid values. No other values are valid for a check box.

Using the Addition: radiobutton group *g*

Like check boxes, a radio button also has two states: selected and not selected. Unlike check boxes, radio buttons never operate alone, they operate only in groups. You can have any number of radio buttons in a group, but only one can be selected at a time. They are used when you need to present the user with a list of alternatives in which only one option can be chosen.

To display a parameter as a radio button, use the addition radiobutton group *g*. You cannot specify a data type or length; it will default to type c and length 1. *g* is an arbitrary group name one to four characters long. You can have more than one group in a program.

The parameter will contain a capital X if the radio button is selected; it will contain a blank if it is not selected. To be initially selected, the radio button should contain a default value of capital X. No other values are valid for a radio button. Try it by running program ztx006.

Parameter Input Field Labels

On the selection screen to the left of each parameter's input field is a label. By default, the label is the same as the name of the parameter. You can set these labels manually. For parameters defined like Data Dictionary fields, you can retrieve the label automatically from the data element.

Changing Parameter Labels

SCREENCAM   Start the ScreenCam "How to Change Input Field Labels" now.

To change a parameter's input field label:

1. Begin at the ABAP/4 Editor: Edit Program screen.

2. Choose the menu path Goto->Text Elements. The ABAP/4 Text Elements screen is displayed. In the Program Field is your current program name.

3. Select the Selection Texts radio button.

4. Press the Change button. The ABAP/4 Text Elements: Change PARAMETERS/SELECT-OPTIONS screen is displayed. Here, you can manually enter labels in the Text column.

5. Type field labels in the Text column.

6. For a parameter defined like a DDIC field, you can retrieve labels from the data element. To retrieve a label from the data element for a single field, position your cursor on the field and choose the menu path Utilities->Copy DD Text. The medium-length field label from the data element appears, the Text field is protected, and the Type field changes to contain the characters DDIC. At the bottom of the window the message Dictionary texts transferred for selection xxx appears.

7. To remove protection from a single field, position your cursor on the field and choose the menu path Utilities->No DD Text. The Text field becomes unprotected and the characters DDIC disappear from the Type field. At the bottom of the window the message Text for xxx no longer transferred from Dictionary. appears.

7

8. To retrieve field labels for all parameters that are defined like DDIC fields, choose the menu path Utilities->Copy DD Texts. Field labels for all DDIC fields are retrieved and protected. Any existing values in the Text column are overwritten. At the bottom of the window the message `All selection texts transferred from Dictionary` appears.

9. Press the Save button on the Application toolbar. At the bottom of the window, the message `Text elements for program xxxxx in language E accepted` appears.

10. Press the Back button on the Application toolbar twice to return to your program.

If you want to override the DDIC label for some fields but not others, type your labels in the Text column and then choose the menu path Utilities->Supplement DD Texts. All blank Text fields will be filled from the Data Dictionary, leaving the values you entered alone.

If the label changes in the DDIC, the label onscreen is *not* automatically updated. To update it, you must go to the ABAP/4 Text Elements: Change PARAMETERS/SELECT-OPTIONS screen and choose either menu path Utilities->Copy DD Text or Utilities->Copy DD Texts.

> **Caution**
>
> The `value` addition on the `parameters` statement, as with `data`, is not validated for compatibility with the data type.
>
> Giving a check box or a radio button a default value other than space or capital `x` is invalid. Although a cursory evaluation might not disclose problems, in-depth testing has uncovered unpredictable behavior in test programs.

Effect of Parameter Definitions: type Versus like

Always use the `like` addition to define a parameter. When you use it, the parameter acquires the following attributes from the Data Dictionary:

- F1 help is acquired from the Documentation button in the data element.
- F4 help is acquired if your parameter is like one that has a check table.
- A field label is acquired from the data element.

In addition to the advantages provided by the above,

- A field label obtained from the Data Dictionary is guaranteed to be consistent with the field label presented by other programs for the same field (provided they also obtain them from the DDIC). This eliminates the confusion of having two fields that are labeled differently refer to the same data.

- Modifications to the data type or length in the DDIC are automatically reflected by your program.

In view of all of these advantages, you should always use the `like` addition to define a parameter. This applies even to check boxes and radio buttons. If necessary, you should create a structure in the DDIC so that you can use `like` and at a minimum, provide F1 help. Note that F1 help is available even for radio buttons and check boxes.

Effect of a Check Table on a Parameter

If you define a parameter using `like st-f1`, and `st-f1` has a check table, a down arrow appears at the end of the input field when you run the program. You can press the down arrow to obtain a list of valid values for that field. However, the value entered into a parameter input field is not validated against the check table. Validation only occurs for dialog screens such as those you have seen in transaction `se16`. The user can type any value into the input field and it will be passed to the program when he presses the Execute button.

Note

You can perform your own selection-screen validations. They are detailed on Day 21, "Selection Screens."

Summary

- Programs are buffered in a program buffer on the application server. There is only one copy, so a roll area is necessary for each execution. The roll area contains the values of program variables and the current program pointer.

- An ABAP/4 program is composed of statements, each of which begins with a keyword and ends with a period. Statements can begin in any column and can span several lines.

- A data object is a memory location that contains data during the runtime of the program. The non-modifiable data objects are literals and constants. The modifiable data objects are variables, field strings, and internal tables. Data objects are allocated in the roll area of the program and are freed when the program ends.

- Data objects have three levels of visibility: local, global, and external. The visibility of a data object indicates from where the data object is accessible.

- Literals are data that is hard-coded in your program. Constants can be used to replace literals, thereby making the program easier to maintain.

- Data types are segregated into two broad categories: character and numeric. The character data types are c, n, d, t, and x; the numeric data types are i, p, and f.

- Variables can be defined using the data and parameters statements. The difference is that when the program is executed, the system displays an input field for each parameter on a selection screen. The user can enter values or change default values.
- Values entered into parameter input fields are by default converted to uppercase. To stop the conversion, use the addition lower case.
- You can change the parameter input field labels via the menu path Goto->Text Elements.

Do	**Don't**
DO use an underscore to make your variable names easier to read.	**DON'T** use a dash in a variable name; a dash delimits the components of a field string.

Q&A

Q Why do I need to code uppercase between quotes? How will I know if I need to code lowercase?

A Most of the time, the system automatically converts data to upper case before it is stored in the database. This conversion is performed by the domain. You can determine if the data is converted by looking at the domain. If the data type of the field is CHAR, and if the Lower Case checkbox is tickmarked, only then does the field contains mixed case.

Q Can I define a parameter that accepts multiple values from the user?

A Yes, the select-options statement enables the user to enter multiple values and complex criteria.

Workshop

The Workshop provides you two ways for you to affirm what you've learned in this chapter. The Quiz section poses questions to help you solidify your understanding of the material covered and the Exercise section provides you with experience in using what you have learned. You can find answers to the quiz questions and exercises in Appendix B, "Answers to Quiz Questions and Exercises."

Quiz

What is wrong with these literals, if anything? (There can be more than one error in each, and some do not have errors.) Write the correct definitions.

1. Character string literal: `"Don't bite."`

2. Floating-point literal: `'+2.2F03.3'`

3. Numeric literal: `-99`

4. Hexadecimal literal: `x'0000f'`

5. Numeric literal: `9.9-`

6. Floating-point literal: `'1.1E308'`

7. Hexadecimal literal: `'HA'`

8. Character string literal: `''''`

9. Character string literal: `'''"'''`

What is wrong with these data definitions? (There can be more than one error in each, and some do not have errors.) Write the correct definitions.

1. `data first-name(5) type c.`

2. `data f1 type character.`

3. `data f1 (20) type c.`

4. `data 1a(5) type i.`

5. `data per-cent type p value 55.5.`

6. `data f1(2) type p decimals 2 value '12.3'.`

Exercise 1

Write a program using parameters for Figure 7.4.

7

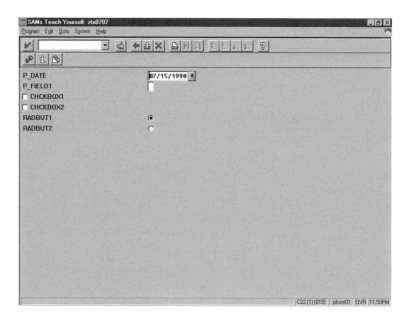

WEEK 1

In Review

In the past week, you have accomplished the following tasks:

- learned about the R/3 environment including Basis, logon clients, the ABAP/4 Development Workbench, and the Data Dictionary
- written simple ABAP/4 programs and become familiar with the ABAP/4 Editor
- created transparent tables, data elements, and domains
- created foreign keys to provide F4 help to the user
- documented data elements in order to provide F1 help
- created secondary indexes and buffers to speed up data access

1

2

3

4

5

6

7

WEEK 2

At a Glance

In Week 2, you create fixed and variable data objects using both predefined and user-defined data types. You learn the rules of ABAP/ 4 syntax, and the statements for controlling program flow, assignment statements, and conversion rules. You also define internal tables, fill them using implicit and explicit work areas, perform control break processing, and optimize `select` statements to directly and efficiently fill internal tables. Finally, you use the formatting options of the `write` statement, experience the effects of data type on the output, employ conversion exits, and detect their presence within domains.

- In Day 8, "Defining Data in ABAP/4, Part 2," you use the `tables` statement to define field strings, understand the `types` statement, and use it to define your own data types.

- Day 9, "Assignments, Conversions, and Calculations," teaches you to use common system variables and be able to display or find any system variable, predict and perform data conversions using assignment statements, and code mathematical expressions.

- In Day 10, "Common Control Statements," you learn to code the common control statements `if`, `case`, `do`, and `while`; control program sequence using `exit`, `continue`, and `check`; and code simple position and length specifications on the `write` statement.

- In Day 11, "Internal Tables," you learn to define an internal table with or without a header line, fill an internal table using `append` via a header line or an explicit work area, and sort internal tables and use the `as text` addition.

- During Day 12, "Advanced Internal Tables, Part 1," you learn to recognize the table body operator and use it to test for the existence of data in an internal table, and to compare the contents of two internal tables for equality.
- Day 13, "Advanced Internal Tables, Part 2," teaches you to fill an internal table from a database table using the most efficient constructs; perform control break processing on internal tables using at and on change of.
- During Day 14, "The Write Statement," you learn to understand the effect of data types on output, use the formatting options of the write statement, use conversion exits, and detect their presence within domains.

DAY **8**

Defining Data in ABAP/4, Part 2

Chapter Objectives

After you complete this chapter, you should be able to:

- Use the `tables` statement to define field strings and understand the difference between field strings defined using `data` and those defined using `tables`
- Understand the `types` statement and use it to define your own data types

Defining Constants

A constant is almost identical to a variable except that its value cannot be changed. To define one, you use the `constants` statement.

Use a constant when you need to include the same literal multiple times in a program. You can define a constant with the same value as the literal and use the constant in the body of the program in place of the literal. Later, if you need to change the value of the literal, you can simply change the value of the constant, causing its value to be updated wherever it is used in the program.

ABAP/4 has one pre-defined constant: SPACE. It is a constant having a value equal to spaces. You can use it in place of the literal ' '.

Syntax for the CONSTANTS Statement

The following code demonstrates the syntax for defining a constant. It is similar to the data statement; however, the addition value is required. In all other ways, constants conform to the same rules as variables defined using the data statement. See Listing 8.1 for examples of constant definitions.

```
constants c1[(l)] [type t] [decimals d] value 'xxx'.
```

or

```
constants c1 like cv value 'xxx'.
```

where:

- *c1* is the name of the constant.
- *cv* is the name of a previously defined constant or variable, or is the name of a field that belongs to a table or structure in the Data Dictionary.
- *(l)* is the internal length specification.
- *t* is the data type.
- *d* is the number of decimal places (used only with type p).
- *'xxx'* is a literal that supplies the value of the constant.

INPUT **LISTING 8.1** DEFINITIONS OF CONSTANTS

```
1 constants c1(2) type c value 'AA'.
2 constants c2 like c1 value 'BB'.
3 constants error_threshold type i value 5.
4 constants amalgamation_date like sy-datum value '19970305'.
```

Tip

Constants can be defined in a *type pool*. When they are, they can be shared by multiple programs. For more information, see the section called "Type Pools" at the end of this chapter.

Defining Field Strings

NEW TERM A *field string* is a type of variable, and is the equivalent of a structure in the DDIC but is defined within an ABAP/4 program. Like a structure, a field string is a series of fields grouped together under a common name. The difference lies mainly in where the definition resides. The term structure in R/3 applies only to a Data Dictionary object containing a collection of fields. The term field string applies to a collection of fields defined in an ABAP/4 program.

Two statements are usually used to define field strings in an ABAP/4 program:

- data
- tables

Using the DATA Statement to Define a Field String

A field string defined using the data statement is a modifiable data object. It can have global or local visibility.

Syntax for Defining a Field String Using the DATA Statement

The following is the syntax for defining a field string using the data statement.

SYNTAX ▼

```
data: begin of fs1,
        f1[(l)] [type t] [decimals d] [value 'xxx'],
        f2[(l)] [type t] [decimals d] [value 'xxx'],
        ...
        end of fs1.
```

or

```
data begin of fs1.
data f1[(l)] [type t] [decimals d] [value 'xxx'].
data f2[(l)] [type t] [decimals d] [value 'xxx'].
        ...
[include structure st1.]
data end of fs1.
```

or

```
data fs1 like fs2.
```

where:

- *fs1* is the field string name.
- *f1* and *f2* are the fields (also called components) of the field string.
- *fs2* is the name of a previously defined field string, or is the name of a table or structure in the Data Dictionary.

▼

▼   • (1) is the internal length specification.

      • t is the data type.

      • d is the number of decimal places (used only with type p).

      • 'xxx' is a literal that supplies a default value.

▲   • st1 is the name of a structure or table in the Data Dictionary.

Field strings follow the same rules as variables defined using the data statement. To refer to an individual component, its name must be prefixed by the name of the field string and a dash (-). For example, to write the number component of the cust_info field string, you would use the statement write cust_info-number.

The include statement is not part of the data statement; it is a separate statement. Therefore, it cannot be chained to a data statement. The statement before it must be concluded with a period.

Examples of programs that define and use field strings are shown in Listings 8.2 through 8.6.

LISTING 8.2   A SIMPLE EXAMPLE OF A FIELD STRING DEFINED USING THE
INPUT   data STATEMENT

```
 1 report ztx0802.
 2 data: begin of totals_1,
 3         region(7)    value 'unknown',
 4         debits(15)   type p,
 5         count        type i,
 6         end of totals_1,
 7       totals_2 like totals_1.
 8
 9 totals_1-debits = 100.
10 totals_1-count  = 10.
11 totals_2-debits = 200.
12
13 write: / totals_1-region, totals_1-debits, totals_1-count,
14        / totals_2-region, totals_2-debits, totals_2-count.
```

ANALYSIS   Line 2 begins the definition of field string totals_1. It contains three fields, the first of which is initialized with the value 'unknown'. On line 7, field string totals_2 is defined exactly like totals_1. The value of totals_1-region is *not* propagated to totals_2-region. On lines 9 through 11 values are assigned to components of the field strings, and on lines 13 and 14, the values of all components are written out.

8

LISTING 8.3 A FIELD STRING CAN CONTAIN ANOTHER FIELD STRING

```
 1 report ztx0803.
 2 data: begin of names,
 3         name1        like ztxkna1-name1,
 4         name2        like ztxkna1-name2,
 5       end of names.
 6 data: begin of cust_info,
 7         number(10)   type n,
 8         nm           like names,          "like a field string
 9       end of cust_info.
10
11 cust_info-number    = 15.
12 cust_info-nm-name1 = 'Jack'.
13 cust_info-nm-name2 = 'Gordon'.
14
15 write: / cust_info-number,
16          cust_info-nm-name1,
17          cust_info-nm-name2.
```

ANALYSIS Line 2 begins the definition of field string names. It contains two fields that are defined like fields of table ztxkna1 in the Data Dictionary. They are not given any initial values. On line 8, component cust_info-name is defined like field string names. When it is used on lines 12 and 13, nm is included in the component name.

LISTING 8.4 A FIELD STRING CAN BE DEFINED EXACTLY LIKE A DDIC TABLE OR
INPUT STRUCTURE

```
 1 report ztx0804.
 2 data: my_lfa1 like ztxlfa1,      "like a table in the DDIC
 3       my_addr like ztxaddr.      "like a structure in the DDIC
 4
 5 my_lfa1-name1 = 'Andrea Miller'.
 6 my_lfa1-telf1 = '1-243-2746'.
 7 my_addr-land1 = 'CA'.
 8
 9 write: / my_lfa1-name1,
10          my_lfa1-name2,
11          my_addr-land1.
```

ANALYSIS On line 2, my_lfa1 is defined exactly like the DDIC table ztxlfa1, and my_addr is defined like the DDIC structure ztxaddr.

Tip

> To view the DDIC definition of table ztxlfa1, double-click on its name in your source code.

LISTING 8.5   DDIC TABLES AND STRUCTURES CAN ALSO BE INCLUDED IN A
INPUT   FIELD STRING

```
 1 report ztx0805.
 2 data     begin of fs1.
 3 include   structure ztxlfa1.
 4 data:     extra_field(3) type c,
 5           end of fs1.
 6
 7 fs1-lifnr      = 12.
 8 fs1-extra_field = 'xyz'.
 9
10 write: / fs1-lifnr,
11           fs1-extra_field.
```

ANALYSIS   Line 2 begins the definition of field string fs1. The statement ends with a period because include structure is not part of the data statement; it is a separate statement. On line 3, the structure of table ztxlfa1 is included into the field string. On line 4, another field is included in the field string after the fields of table ztxlfa1. Any number of fields could be included, more structures could be included here as well, or any combination thereof.

LISTING 8.6   IF YOU USE like INSTEAD OF Include, YOU GET A DIFFERENT
RESULT. THE NAMES OF THE INCLUDED FIELDS ARE PREFIXED BY AN INTERMEDIATE
INPUT   COMPONENT NAME.

```
 1 report ztx0806.
 2 data: begin of fs1,
 3         mylfa1 like ztxlfa1,
 4         extra_field(3) type c,
 5         end of fs1.
 6
 7 fs1-mylfa1-lifnr  = 12.
 8 fs1-extra_field    = 'xyz'.
 9
10 write: / fs1-mylfa1-lifnr,
11           fs1-extra_field.
```

ANALYSIS   Line 2 begins the definition of field string lfa1_with_extra_field. The statement ends with a period because include structure is not part of the data statement; it is a separate statement. On line 3, the structure of table ztxlfa1 is included into the field string. On line 4, another field is included in the field string after the fields of table ztxlfa1. Any number of fields could be included, more structures could be included here as well, or any combination thereof.

Using a Field String as a Variable of Type `char`

Not only can you address the individual components of a field string, you can also address all components at once as if they were a single variable of type `char`. Listing 8.7 illustrates this concept.

INPUT

LISTING 8.7 AN EXAMPLE OF USING A FIELD STRING AS BOTH MULTIPLE VARIABLES AND AS A SINGLE VARIABLE OF TYPE `char`

```
 1 report ztx0807.
 2 data: begin of fs1,
 3          c1 value 'A',
 4          c2 value 'B',
 5          c3 value 'C',
 6          end of fs1.
 7
 8 write: / fs1-c1, fs1-c2, fs1-c3,
 9         / fs1.
10
11 fs1 = 'XYZ'.
12
13 write: / fs1-c1, fs1-c2, fs1-c3,
14         / fs1.
```

The code in Listing 8.7 should produce this output:

```
A B C
ABC
X Y Z
XYZ
```

ANALYSIS Lines 2 through 6 define field string `fs1`. It has three components, each with a default value. On line 8, each component is written out individually. On line 9, the field string is written out as if it were a single variable. Consequently, the output shows the contents of `fs1` as if it were a single variable defined as `char` 3. On line 11, the value `'XYZ'` is assigned to the field string, again treating it as a `char` variable. The resulting output shows that the individual components reflect the change because they are accessing the same storage.

One field string can be assigned to another, if they have the same structure, as shown in Listing 8.8.

INPUT   **LISTING 8.8**   AN EXAMPLE OF ASSIGNMENT INVOLVING TWO FIELD STRINGS

```
 1 report ztx0808.
 2 data: begin of fs1,
 3         c1 value 'A',
 4         c2 value 'B',
 5         c3 value 'C',
 6        end of fs1,
 7       fs2 like fs1.
 8
 9 fs2 = fs1.
10 write: / fs2-c1, fs2-c2, fs2-c3.
```

The code in Listing 8.8 should produce this output:

OUTPUT   A B C

ANALYSIS   Lines 2 through 6 define field string fs1. Line 7 defines field string fs2 exactly like fs1. On line 9, fs1 is moved to fs2, just as if it were a single variable of type char. On line 10, the components of fs2 are written out.

> **Note**
>
> A field string containing numeric data types needs special consideration during assignments. These considerations are covered on Day 9, in the "Assignments" section.

Using the TABLES Statement to Define a Field String

A field string defined using the tables statement is a modifiable data object. Field strings defined using the tables statement follow the same rules as field strings defined using the data statement. An example of a program using a tables field string appears in Listing 8.9.

Syntax for Defining a Field String Using the TABLES Statement

The following is the syntax for defining a field string using the tables statement.

```
tables fs1.
```

where:

- fs1 is the field string name. A table or structure of the same name must exist in the Data Dictionary.

INPUT **LISTING 8.9** SIMPLE EXAMPLE OF A FIELD STRING DEFINED USING THE `tables` STATEMENT

```
1 report ztx0809.
2 tables ztxlfa1.
3
4 ztxlfa1-name1 = 'Bugsy'.
5 ztxlfa1-land1 = 'US'.
6
7 write: / ztxlfa1-name1, ztxlfa1-land1.
```

ANALYSIS Line 2 defines field string `ztxlfa1`. Its definition is exactly like the Data Dictionary table of the same name. On lines 4 and 5, values are given to two of its components, which are written out on line 7.

Field String Defined Using TABLES Interacting with SELECT

The `tables` statement does more than just define a field string. It does two things:

- It defines a field string.

- It gives the program access to a database table of the same name, if one exists.

Your first `select` statement example is reproduced in Listing 8.10. You can now analyze it from a new perspective.

INPUT **LISTING 8.10** YOUR SECOND PROGRAM, REVISITED

```
1 report ztx0810.
2 tables ztxlfa1.
3 select * from ztxlfa1 into z lfa1 order by lifnr.
4     write / z lfa1-lifnr.
5     endselect.
```

ANALYSIS Line 2 defines field string `ztxlfa1`. Its definition is exactly like the Data Dictionary table of the same name. There is also a database table of the same name, so the program is given access to that table, meaning that it can now be used in a `select` statement. Each time line 3 is executed, a record is read from the database table `ztxlfa1` into field string `ztxlfa1`. For each record, the value of component `ztxlfa1-lifnr` is written out (line 4).

Visibility of a Field String Defined Using TABLES

A field string defined using `tables` *always has both global and external visibility no matter where it is defined in the program.* This means that if you place a `tables` statement in a subroutine, the definition is global and you cannot have another definition for the same field string anywhere in that program.

The field string is also externally visible. This means that if, in a calling and called program, the same `tables` statement appears, those field strings will share the same memory. This concept is illustrated in Figure 8.1. When the called program executes, it will "see" the value in `ztxlfa1` from the first program. If it changes `ztxlfa1`, the calling program "sees" the changes when it regains control.

FIGURE 8.1.

Identical tables *definitions in a calling and called program causes the memory for those field strings to be shared.*

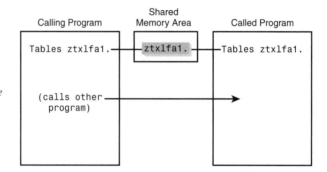

Defining Types

You can define your own data types using the `types` statement and base them on existing data types.

Syntax for the TYPES Statement

▼ SYNTAX

The following is the syntax for defining a type using the `types` statement.

```
types t1[(l)] [type t] [decimals d].
```

or

```
types t1 like v1.
```

where:

- *t1* is the type name.
- *v1* is the name of a variable previously defined in the program, or is the name of a field that belongs to a table or structure in the Data Dictionary.
- *(l)* is the internal length specification.
- *t* is the data type.
- ▲ *d* is the number of decimal places (used only with type p).

Listings 8.11 and 8.12 show examples of programs that define and use their own data types.

INPUT   **LISTING 8.11**   SIMPLE EXAMPLE OF A USER-DEFINED DATA TYPE char2

```
1 report ztx0811.
2 types char2(2) type c.
3 data: v1 type char2 value 'AB',
4       v2 type char2 value 'CD'.
5
6 write: v1, v2.
```

The code in Listing 8.11 produces this output:

OUTPUT   AB CD

ANALYSIS   Line 2 defines a data type named char2. It is a two-byte char field. On lines 3 and 4, variables v1 and v2 are defined as two-byte char fields using the data type char2. They are given default values and, on line 6, they are written out.

LISTING 8.12   USING TYPES CAN MAKE YOUR CODE CLEARER AND
INPUT   EASIER TO READ

```
1   report ztx0812.
2   types: dollars(16) type p decimals 2,
3          lira(16)    type p decimals 0.      "italian lira have no
➥decimals
4
5   data: begin of american_sums,
6           petty_cash type dollars,
7           pay_outs   type dollars,
8           lump_sums  type dollars,
9           end of american_sums,
10        begin of italian_sums,
11          petty_cash  type lira,
12          pay_outs    type lira,
13          lump_sums   type lira,
14          end of italian_sums.
15
16  american_sums-pay_outs = '9500.03'.      "need quotes when literal
➥contains a decimal
17  italian_sums-lump_sums = 5141.
18
19  write: / american_sums-pay_outs,
20         / italian_sums-lump_sums.
```

The code in Listing 8.12 produces this output:

OUTPUT
```
9,500.00
   5,141
```

ANALYSIS Line 2 defines a data type named `dollars` as a 16-byte packed decimal field with two decimal places. Line 3 defines a similar data type named `lira` with 0 decimal places. On lines 5 through 14, two field strings are defined using the new data types. One component of each is assigned a value on lines 16 and 17, and on lines 19 and 20 they are written out.

Think of a user-defined type as a variable, but one that you can't use to store data. It can only be used to create other variables. The same rules apply to types as apply to variables and field strings. Type names, like variable names, are one to 30 characters long, but unlike variables, their names cannot include the characters - < >.

Structured Types

NEW TERM A user-defined type can be based on the definition of a field string. This is known as a *structured type*. Listing 8.13 shows how you can shorten a program using a structured type.

INPUT **LISTING 8.13** USING STRUCTURED TYPES CAN REDUCE REDUNDANCY AND MAKE MAINTENANCE EASIER

```
 1 report ztx0813.
 2 types: begin of address,
 3             street(25),
 4             city(20),
 5             region(7),
 6             country(15),
 7             postal_code(9),
 8             end of address.
 9
10  data: customer_addr type address,
11        vendor_addr   type address,
12        employee_addr type address,
13        shipto_addr   type address.
14
15 customer_addr-street  = '101 Memory Lane'.
16 employee_addr-country = 'Transylvania'.
17
18 write: / customer_addr-street,
19           employee_addr-country.
```

ANALYSIS Lines 2 through 8 define a data type named `address` that contains five fields. On lines 10 through 13, four field strings are defined using the new type. Without the new type, these definitions would have used an additional 24 lines of code. Maintenance is also made easier: If a change to the definitions of the address field strings is needed, only the definition of the type needs to be changed.

Type Groups

NEW TERM A `types` statement can be stored in a *type group*. A type group (also known as a *type pool*) is a Data Dictionary object that exists merely to contain one or more `types` or `constants` statements. Using the `type-pools` statement in your program, you access types or constants from a type group and use them in your program. Multiple programs can share a type group, giving you the ability to create centralized definitions. Figure 8.2 illustrates this concept. Listing 8.14 contains an example of a type group, and Listing 8.15 presents an example of a program using `types` and `constants` from it.

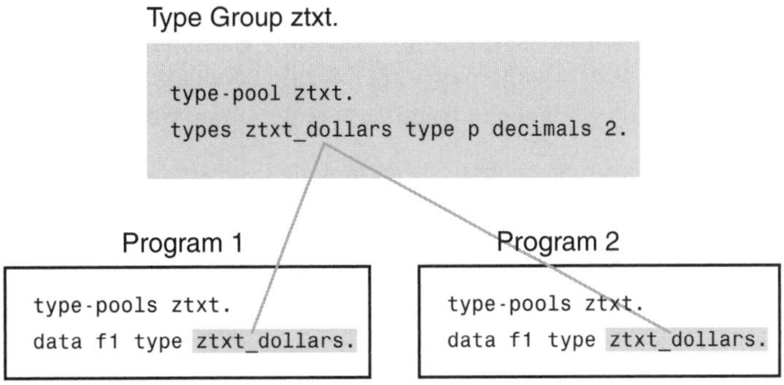

FIGURE 8.2.

A type group is a container for types *and* constants *statements. It can be shared among programs.*

Type Group ztxt.

```
type-pool ztxt.
types ztxt_dollars type p decimals 2.
```

Program 1

```
type-pools ztxt.
data f1 type ztxt_dollars.
```

Program 2

```
type-pools ztxt.
data f1 type ztxt_dollars.
```

INPUT **LISTING 8.14** AN EXAMPLE TYPE-POOL STATEMENT CONTAINING TYPES AND CONSTANTS

```
1 type-pool ztx1.
2 types:    ztx1_dollars(16)          type p decimals 2,
3           ztx1_lira(16)             type p decimals 0.
4 constants: ztx1_warning_threshold   type i value 5000,
5            ztx1_amalgamation_date   like sy-datum value '19970305'.
```

ANALYSIS Line 1 indicates the beginning of the type group and gives it a name. Lines 2 through 5 define `types` and `constants` that can be used in any program.

INPUT

LISTING 8.15 USING TYPE GROUP REDUCES DUPLICATION OF CODE FOR EASIER MAINTENANCE

```
 1 report ztx0815.
 2 type-pools ztx1.
 3 data: begin of american_sums,
 4          petty_cash type ztx1_dollars,
 5          pay_outs   type ztx1_dollars,
 6          lump_sums  type ztx1_dollars,
 7          end of american_sums.
 8
 9 american_sums-pay_outs = '9500.03'.
10
11 if american_sums-pay_outs > ztx1_warning_threshold.
12     write: / 'Warning', american_sums-pay_outs,
13              'exceeds threshold', ztx1_warning_threshold.
14     endif.
```

ANALYSIS Line 2 includes the definitions from type group ztx1 in the program. Lines 3 through 7 define a field string using type ztx1_dollars from the type group. Line 9 assigns a value to pay_outs, and it is compared with constant ztx1_warning_threshold from the type group on line 11.

If the type group has already been included, subsequent attempts to include it are ignored and they do not cause an error.

Type group names can be one to five characters long, and must begin with *y* or *z*. Types and constants included in a program using the type-pools statement always have global visibility.

Creating a Type Group

To create a type group in the Data Dictionary, use the following procedure.

SCREENCAM Start the ScreenCam "How to Create a Type Group" now.

To create a type group:

1. Begin at the Dictionary: Initial Screen (menu path Tools->ABAP/4 Workbench, Development->ABAP/4 Dictionary).
2. Type the name of your type group in the Object Name field.
3. Select the Type Groups radio button.
4. Press the Create pushbutton. The Type Group *xxxx*: Create Text screen is displayed.
5. Type a description of your type group in the Short Text field.

6. Press the Save button. The Create Object Catalog Entry screen is displayed.

7. Press the Local Object button. The ABAP/4 Editor: Edit Type Group screen is displayed. On the first line, the statement type-pool *t*. appears, where *t* is the name of your type group. If it does not appear, you should type it now.

8. On subsequent lines, type **constants** and **types** statements. All names must begin with *t*_, where *t* is the name of your type pool.

9. Press the Save button on the Application toolbar. At the bottom of the window, the message Type group saved is displayed.

10. Press the Back button on the Application toolbar to return to the Dictionary: Initial Screen.

To delete a type group, follow steps 1 through 3 of the preceding procedure and then press the Delete button on the Application toolbar.

Summary

- Field strings are like structures that are defined within your program. You can define them using either data or tables. Field strings defined using tables have both global and external visibility.

- You can define your own data types, even structured types, using the types statement. User-defined types reduce redundancy and make maintenance easier.

- You can define a type group in the Data Dictionary to make your user-defined types and constants reusable.

Do	Don't
DO use an underscore to make your variable names easier to read.	**DON'T** use a dash in a variable name; a dash delimits the components of a field string.

Q&A

Q Why do I need to create field strings? Why can't I use just simple variables?

A Field strings give you a way of organizing your variables into groups. When you have hundreds of variables in a program, organizing them into field strings makes the relationships between the variables clearer. Using field strings to group fields together also enables you to perform an operation on a group of variables as if they were a single variable. So, for example, if you need to move 100 variables, you can usually code a single statement to perform the move from one field string to another, instead of coding 100 assignment statements for individual variables. Moving a single field string is also more efficient than 100 move statements, so your program runs faster. You will see in the coming chapters that many statements can use a field string as an operand. If you can use field strings, you can take advantage of them, and they will save you a lot of coding and debugging time.

Q   Why would I use my own structured type instead of a DDIC structure? Can't I create field strings with both?

A   Yes, you can. The functionality of DDIC structures far outweighs that provided by structured types because they can provide labels, F1, and F4 help. However, types can be used to define nested structured types that contain internal tables. DDIC structures can't. This will be demonstrated in Chapter 12 in the section on internal tables.

Workshop

The Workshop provides you two ways for you to affirm what you've learned in this chapter. The Quiz section poses questions to help you solidify your understanding of the material covered and the Exercise section provides you with experience in using what you have learned. You can find answers to the quiz questions and exercises in Appendix B, "Answers to Quiz Questions and Exercises."

Quiz

1. What is the one pre-defined constant that can be used in an ABAP program. What is its equivalent using a literal?

2. What types of type statement can be used and what type can be defined in the Data Dictionary?

Exercise 1

What is another way to declare the variable below using a "type" declaration?

```
data: begin of usd_amount,
         hotel      type p decimals 2,
         rent_car   type p decimals 2,
         plane      type p decimals 2,
         food       type p decimals 2,
         end of usd_amount,
      begin of amex_pt,
         hotel      type p decimals 2,
         rent_car   type p decimals 0,
         plane      type p decimals 0,
         food       type p decimals 0,
         end of amex_pt.
```

Exercise 2

What is the outcome of this program?

```
report ztx0816.

data: begin of fld_stg1,
        var1 value '1',
        var2 value '3',
        var3 value '5',
        var4 value '7',
        var5 value '9',
        var6 value '4',
        var7 value '8',
        var8 value '6',
        end of fld_stg1,
      fld_stg2 like fld_stg1.

fld_stg2 = fld_stg1.

write: / fld_stg2-var1, fld_stg1-var2, fld_stg2-var6, fld_stg1-var3.
write: / fld_stg1-var5, fld_stg2-var7, fld_stg2-var4, fld_stg1-var8.
```

8

WEEK 2

DAY 9

Assignments, Conversions, and Calculations

Chapter Objectives

After you complete this chapter, you will be able to:

- Use common system variables and be able to display or find any system variable
- Use the clear statement and understand its effect on variables and field strings
- Perform assignments using the move and move-corresponding statements
- Predict and perform data conversions using assignment statements
- Code mathematical expressions

Before Proceeding

Programs in this and the following chapters use input and output formats that are set in the user defaults and can be different for each user. Before proceeding, it is a good idea to set your user defaults to match those in this book so that your output matches the output listings in this book.

Please set your user defaults now by following this procedure:

1. If you are currently in the R/3 system, save all your work now.
2. From any screen, choose the menu path System->User Profile->User Defaults. The Maintain User: Defaults screen is displayed.
3. In the Date Format group box, choose the YYYY/MM/DD radio button.
4. In the Decimal Notation group box, choose the Period radio button.
5. Press the Save button on the Application toolbar. At the bottom of the window, the message Values for user xxxxx saved is displayed. Changes to your user profile are not effective until the next time you log on.
6. Choose the menu path System->Log Off. The Log Off dialog box is displayed.
7. Press the Yes button. You are logged off of the system.

Your new user defaults will be in effect the next time you log on.

Working with System Variables

 There are 176 *system variables* available within every ABAP/4 program. You do not have to define them; they are automatically defined and are always available.

To display a list of system variables, display the DDIC structure syst. You can display it by using the Dictionary: Initial Screen, or by double-clicking on the name of any system variable in your program. The first page of syst is shown in Figure 9.1.

In Figure 9.1, the field names appear in the first column and the descriptions are on the right in the Short Text column. To view the entire description, scroll to the right by clicking on the Column Right; Next . . . button at the bottom of the screen.

To find a field by name, press the Find button on the Standard toolbar. The Find Field screen will appear, asking for the name of the field that you want to find.

The alias for syst is sy (pronounced *sigh*). In your code, you can use either name. For example, you can code either sy-datum or syst-datum; they are exactly equivalent. Most programmers use sy. Table 9.1 contains a short list of commonly used system variables. Additional variables are introduced throughout the book.

FIGURE 9.1.

This is the structure syst. It contains the definitions for all system variables. The Column Right; Next . . . button scrolls right one column at a time, causing the entire length of the Short Text to scroll into view.

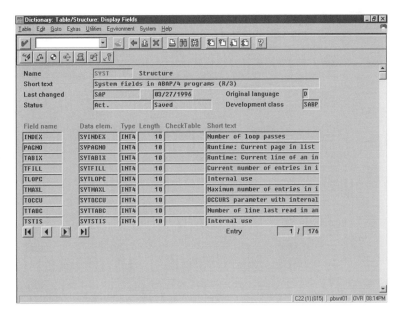

TABLE 9.1 COMMONLY USED SYSTEM VARIABLES

Name	Description
sy-datum	Current date
sy-uzeit	Current time
sy-uname	Current user id
sy-subrc	Last return code
sy-mandt	Logon client
sy-pagno	Current output page number
sy-colno	Current output column number
sy-linno	Current output list line number
sy-vline	Vertical line
sy-uline	Horizontal line
sy-repid	Current report name
sy-cprog	Main program name
sy-tcode	Current transaction code
sy-dbcnt	Within a select, contains the current iteration counter. After the endselect, contains number of rows that match the where clause.

Listing 9.1 shows a sample program that uses system variables.

INPUT   **LISTING 9.1**   USING BASIC SYSTEM VARIABLES

```
 1 report ztx0901.
 2 tables ztxlfa1.
 3 parameters `land1 like ztxlfa1-land1 obligatory default 'US'.
 4 write: / 'Current date:', sy-datum,
 5        / 'Current time:', sy-uzeit,
 6        / 'Current user:', sy-uname,
 7        / 'Vendors having country code', `land1,
 8        /.
 9 select * from ztxlfa1
10     where land1 = `land1
11     order by lifnr.
12     write: / sy-dbcnt, ztxlfa1-lifnr.
13     endselect.
14 write: / sy-dbcnt, 'records found'.
15 if sy-subrc <> 0.
16     write: / 'No vendors exist for country', `land1.
17     endif.
```

The code in Listing 9.1 produces this output:

OUTPUT
```
Current date: 1998/02/22
Current time: 14:38:24
Current user: KENGREENWOOD
Vendors having country code US

          1   1040
          2   1080
          3   1090
          4   2000
          5   V1
          6   V2
          7   V3
          8   V4
          9   V5
         10   V7
         10   records found
```

ANALYSIS

- Line 2 defines a field string ztxlfa1 exactly like the table of the same name.

- Line 3 defines a single input parameter `land1.

- On lines 4 through 6, the current date, time, and user id are written out from system variables sy-datum, sy-uzeit, and sy-uname.

- Line 7 writes out the country code that was entered in the parameter input field `land1 on the selection screen.

- Line 8 writes out a blank line.

- Line 9 selects records from table `ztxlfa1` and places them one at a time into field string `ztxlfa1`.

- Line 10 restricts the selection of records to only those having a country code equal to the one entered on the selection screen.

- Line 11 causes the records to be sorted in ascending order by `lifnr` (vendor number).

- Line 12 writes out the current iteration number from system variable `sy-dbcnt` and a vendor number from each record.

- Line 13 marks the end of the `select/endselect` loop.

- Line 14 writes out the total number of iterations of the `select` loop. This is the same as the number of records that matched the `where` clause using system variable `sy-dbcnt`.

- On line 15, the return code from the `select`, contained in system variable `sy-subrc`, is tested. If it is zero, records were found. If it is non-zero, no records were found and a message is written out on line 16.

Finding System Variables

Suppose you need to write a program that, given a country code as an input parameter, writes out the country description from table `ztxt005t` in the user's current logon language. As you might recall, `ztxt005t` is a text table containing country code descriptions in multiple languages. The primary key is `mandt`, `spras` (language), and `land1`. A sample solution is shown in Listing 9.2, but it is missing one crucial piece of information on line 5: the value of the current logon language.

Listing 9.2 is missing a variable at the position indicated by the question mark. When working with ABAP/4, you are often faced with the challenge of finding variables containing the information you need.

INPUT   **LISTING 9.2**   A SAMPLE PROGRAM WITH A SY VARIABLE MISSING

```
1 report ztx0902.
2 tables ztxt005t.
3 parameters `land1 like ztxlfa1-land1 obligatory default 'US'.
4 select single * from ztxt005t
5     where spras = ?               "current logon language
6     and   land1 = `land1.
7 if sy-subrc = 0.
8     write: 'Description:', ztxt005t-landx.
9 else.
10     write: 'No description exists for', `land1.
11     endif.
```

ANALYSIS

- Line 2 defines a field string `ztxt005t` exactly like the table of the same name.
- Line 3 defines a single input parameter `land1`.
- Lines 4 through 6 select a single record from table `ztxt005t` into field string `ztxt005t` using the current logon language from a yet-unknown source and the country code from parameter `land1`. There is no `endselect` because this is a `select single` statement. It only returns a single record; no loop is created.
- Line 7 checks the return code from the `select` and, if a record was found, writes out the description on line 8. If a record was not found, line 10 writes out an appropriate message.

The current logon language is available from a system variable. Unfortunately, to use the Find button on the Application toolbar you need to know the name of the field. You do not know the name of the field, so the Find button is of little use. Instead, use the following procedure to search the *descriptions* of the `syst` structure.

Tip

This procedure is very handy because it can be used to search the descriptions of any structure or table.

SCREENCAM Start the ScreenCam "How to Search the Descriptions of a Structure or Table" now.

To search the descriptions of a structure or table:

1. Begin at the Dictionary: Table/Structure: Display Fields screen.
2. Choose the menu path Table->Print. The Print Table Manual screen is displayed. Here you specify which details you want to see.
3. Tickmark all fields and press the Continue button. The Print: screen is displayed.
4. If the Output Device field is blank, position your cursor in the field, press the down arrow, and choose any output device. (It doesn't matter which device you choose; it won't be used.)
5. Press the Print Preview button at the bottom of the screen. The Print Preview for *xxxx* Page 00001 of *nnnnn* screen is displayed.
6. Choose the menu path Goto->List Display. The Print Preview for *xxxx* screen is displayed.
7. Type **%sc** in the Command field on the Standard toolbar.

8. Press the Enter key. The Find screen is displayed.

9. In the Search For field, type a character string to be found. If you are searching for the current logon language, you might type `language`. Wildcard characters are not permitted.

10. Press the Find button. A second Find screen appears showing the lines that contain the text you typed. Matches are highlighted.

11. To select a match, click once on a highlighted word. You are returned to the Print Preview for *xxxx* screen; the list is scrolled to the line you selected and the cursor is positioned on that line.

12. To search again, press the down arrow at the end of the Command field on the Standard toolbar. A drop-down box appears containing the most recently entered commands.

13. Scroll, if necessary, to the `%sc` command and click on it. `%sc` appears in the command field.

14. Press the Enter key. The Find screen is redisplayed.

15. Press the Find button. The search is performed starting at the current line. The second Find screen is redisplayed and the matches are shown.

16. Click once on any highlighted word to display it.

Tip

For future reference, you can save the list on the Print Preview for *xxxx* to a text file on your hard drive. To do this, from the Print Preview for *xxxx* screen, choose the menu path System->List->Save->Local File. On the Save List in File. . . screen, choose the Unconverted radio button and press the Continue button. On the Transfer List to a Local File screen, type the name of a text file, for example, `c:\temp\syst.txt`, and then press the OK button. This creates the file on your hard drive. You can open and search through it using WordPad at any time, without having to use the "How to Search the Descriptions of a Structure or Table" procedure shown above.

By following the preceding procedure, you have found that the current logon language is stored in `sy-langu`. The completed program appears in Listing 9.3.

INPUT   **LISTING 9.3**   LISTING 9.2 WITH THE MISSING sy VARIABLE ADDED ON LINE 5

```
1 report ztx0903.
2 tables ztxt005t.
3 parameters `land1 like ztxlfa1-land1 obligatory default 'US'.
4 select single * from ztxt005t
```

continues

LISTING 9.3 CONTINUED

```
5    where spras = sy-langu              "current logon language
6    and   land1 = `land1.
7 if sy-subrc = 0.
8    write: 'Description:', ztxt005t-landx.
9 else.
10   write: 'No description exists for', `land1.
11   endif.
```

The code in Listing 9.3 produces this output:

OUTPUT Description: United States

ANALYSIS Line 5 limits the select to return only records from ztxt005t that have a language code equal to the current logon language. Because mandt is automatically added at the beginning of every where, the primary key is now fully specified and a single, unique record is returned. Notice that the primary index supports this select, so the fields of the where clause have been specified in the same order as they appear in the primary index.

Assignment Statements

NEW TERM An *assignment statement* assigns a value to a variable or field string. Three assignment statements are commonly used:

- clear
- move
- move-corresponding

Using the clear Statement

NEW TERM The clear statement sets the value of a variable or a field string to zeros. If the data type is c, the value is instead set to blanks. Blanks and zeros are known as *default initial values*. It is often said that clear assigns default initial values to variables.

Syntax for the clear Statement

SYNTAX

The following is the syntax for the clear statement.

```
clear v1 [with v2 ¦ with 'A' ¦ with NULL]
```

where:

- v1 and v2 are variable or field string names.
- 'A' is a literal of any length.

The following points apply:

- If *v1* is a variable of type c without any additions, it is filled with blanks. If *v1* is any other data type, it is filled with zeros. If *v1* is a field string, its individual components are set to blanks or zeros depending on their individual data types.
- Using the addition with *v2*, the first byte from *v2* is used to fill the entire length of *v1*. If *v1* is a field string, it is treated as a variable of type c.
- Using the addition with 'A', the entire length of *v1* is filled using the first byte from literal 'A'.
- Using the addition with NULL, the entire length of *v1* is filled with hexadecimal zeros.

Listing 9.4 shows a sample program that clears variables and field strings.

 Note | Listing 9.4 uses a new addition called no-gap on the write statement. No-gap causes the next output value to be written immediately after the current one without an intervening space.

INPUT **LISTING 9.4** VARIABLES SET TO BLANKS OR ZEROS BY THE clear STATEMENT

```
 1 report ztx0904.
 2 tables ztxlfa1.
 3 data: f1(2) type c value 'AB',
 4       f2    type i value 12345,
 5       f3    type p value 12345,
 6       f4    type f value '1E1',
 7       f5(3) type n value '789',
 8       f6    type d value '19980101',
 9       f7    type t value '1201',
10       f8    type x value 'AA',
11       begin of s1,
12         f1(3) type c value 'XYZ',
13         f2    type i value 123456,
14       end of s1.
15 ztxlfa1-lifnr = 'XXX'.
16 ztxlfa1-land1 = 'CA'.
17 write: / 'f1=''' no-gap, f1 no-gap, '''',
18        / 'f2=''' no-gap, f2 no-gap, '''',
19        / 'f3=''' no-gap, f3 no-gap, '''',
20        / 'f4=''' no-gap, f4 no-gap, '''',
21        / 'f5=''' no-gap, f5 no-gap, '''',
22        / 'f6=''' no-gap, f6 no-gap, '''',
23        / 'f7=''' no-gap, f7 no-gap, '''',
24        / 'f8=''' no-gap, f8 no-gap, '''',
```

continues

LISTING 9.4   CONTINUED

```
25          / 's1-f1=''' no-gap, s1-f1 no-gap, '''',
26          / 's1-f2=''' no-gap, s1-f2 no-gap, '''',
27          / 'ztxlfa1-lifnr=''' no-gap, ztxlfa1-lifnr no-gap, '''',
28          / 'ztxlfa1-land1=''' no-gap, ztxlfa1-land1 no-gap, ''''.
29 clear: f1, f2, f3, f4, f5, f6, f7, f8, s1, ztxlfa1.
30 write: / 'f1=''' no-gap, f1 no-gap, '''',
31          / 'f2=''' no-gap, f2 no-gap, '''',
32          / 'f3=''' no-gap, f3 no-gap, '''',
33          / 'f4=''' no-gap, f4 no-gap, '''',
34          / 'f5=''' no-gap, f5 no-gap, '''',
35          / 'f6=''' no-gap, f6 no-gap, '''',
36          / 'f7=''' no-gap, f7 no-gap, '''',
37          / 'f8=''' no-gap, f8 no-gap, '''',
38          / 's1-f1=''' no-gap, s1-f1 no-gap, '''',
39          / 's1-f2=''' no-gap, s1-f2 no-gap, '''',
40          / 'ztxlfa1-lifnr=''' no-gap, ztxlfa1-lifnr no-gap, '''',
41          / 'ztxlfa1-land1=''' no-gap, ztxlfa1-land1 no-gap, ''''.
```

The code in Listing 9.4 produces this output:

OUTPUT

```
f1='AB'
f2='     12,345 '
f3='          12,345 '
f4=' 1.000000000000000E+01'
f5='789'
f6='19980101'
f7='120100'
f8='AA'
s1-f1='XYZ'
s1-f2='    123,456 '
ztxlfa1-lifnr='XXX        '
ztxlfa1-land1='CA '
f1='  '
f2='          0 '
f3='                0 '
f4=' 0.000000000000000E+00'
f5='000'
f6='00000000'
f7='000000'
f8='00'
s1-f1='   '
s1-f2='          0 '
ztxlfa1-lifnr='          '
ztxlfa1-land1='   '
```

ANALYSIS

- Line 2 defines field string ztxlfa1.
- Lines 4 through 10 define variables of every type and give them default values.

- Another field string, s1, is defined on line 11, with default values for each component.

- Values are assigned to two of the components for field string ztxlfa1 on lines 15 and 16.

- All variables and components of field strings are set to zeros and blanks by the clear statement on line 29. It can also be said that all variables and components are set to *default initial values*.

- The write statements beginning on line 30 write out the cleared variables and components surrounded by single quotes and without intervening spaces between the quotes and the values they surround.

Listing 9.5 shows a sample program that fills variables and components of field strings with values other than spaces or zeros.

LISTING 9.5 VARIABLES FILLED WITH CHARACTERS OTHER THAN BLANKS OR ZEROS USING THE with ADDITION OF THE clear STATEMENT

```
 1 report ztx0905.
 2 tables ztxlfa1.
 3 data: f1(2) type c value 'AB',
 4       f2(2) type c,
 5       f3    type i value 12345,
 6       begin of s1,
 7           f1(3) type c value 'XYZ',
 8           f2    type i value 123456,
 9           end of s1.
10 write: / 'f1=''' no-gap, f1 no-gap, '''',
11        / 'f2=''' no-gap, f2 no-gap, '''',
12        / 'f3=''' no-gap, f3 no-gap, '''',
13        / 's1-f1=''' no-gap, s1-f1 no-gap, '''',
14        / 's1-f2=''' no-gap, s1-f2 no-gap, '''',
15        / 'ztxlfa1-lifnr=''' no-gap, ztxlfa1-lifnr no-gap, '''',
16        / 'ztxlfa1-land1=''' no-gap, ztxlfa1-land1 no-gap, '''',
17        /.
18 clear: f1 with 'X',
19        f2 with f1,
20        f3 with 3,
21        s1 with 'X',
22        ztxlfa1 with 0.
23 write: / 'f1=''' no-gap, f1 no-gap, '''',
24        / 'f2=''' no-gap, f2 no-gap, '''',
25        / 'f3=''' no-gap, f3 no-gap, '''',
26        / 's1-f1=''' no-gap, s1-f1 no-gap, '''',
27        / 's1-f2=''' no-gap, s1-f2 no-gap, '''',
28        / 'ztxlfa1-lifnr=''' no-gap, ztxlfa1-lifnr no-gap, '''',
29        / 'ztxlfa1-land1=''' no-gap, ztxlfa1-land1 no-gap, '''.
```

The code in Listing 9.5 produces this output:

OUTPUT

```
f1='AB'
f2='  '
f3='    12,345 '
s1-f1='XYZ'
s1-f2='   123,456 '
ztxlfa1-lifnr='           '
ztxlfa1-land1='    '

f1='XX'
f2='XX'
f3='50,529,027 '
s1-f1='XXX'
s1-f2='1482184792 '
ztxlfa1-lifnr='##########'
ztxlfa1-land1='###'
```

ANALYSIS

- Line 18 fills f1 with the letter X.

- Line 19 fills f2 with the first byte of f1, also an X.

- Line 20 fills f3 with the first byte of the literal 3. A numeric literal up to nine digits long is stored as a four-byte integer (see the following section "Data Conversion"). f3 is filled with the first byte of this four-byte integer, essentially assigning garbage to f3.

- Line 21 treats s1 as a type c variable and fills it with X. Component f1 is type c, so it receives valid values. Component f2 is type i and so receives invalid values.

- Field string ztxlfa1 is filled with the first byte from the four-byte integer value 0, filling it with garbage. Garbage, in this case, is displayed as hash marks (#).

Using the move Statement

To move a value from one field to another, use the move statement. The entire contents or a portion thereof can be moved. Instead of move, you can use the assignment operator =, as shown below. They are both referred to as a move statement.

Syntax for the move Statement

SYNTAX

The following is the syntax for the move statement. Operators and operands must be separated by spaces. Multiple assignment occurs from right to left.

```
move v1 to v2.
```

▼ or

```
v2 = v1.
```

▼ or

▼   *v2 = v1 = vm = vn . . ..*

or

move *v1*[*+N*(*L*)] to *v2*[*+N*(*L*)].

or

v2[*+N*(*L*)] = *v1*[*+N*(*L*)].

where:

- *v1* is the sending variable or field string.
- *v2* is the receiving variable or field string.
- *N* is an offset from the beginning of the variable or field string.

▲   - *L* is the number of bytes to move.

These are two examples in Table 9.2 of the right and wrong ways to code assignment statements. Incorrect coding results in a syntax error.

TABLE 9.2   RIGHT AND WRONG CODING OF ASSIGNMENT

Right	Wrong
f1 = f2.	f1=f2.
f1 = f2 = f3.	f1=f2=f3.

Data Conversions

NEW TERM   If two variables have different data types or lengths, the data is converted when it is moved. This is called an *automatic adjustment*. If the lengths of the sending and receiving variables do not match, an automatic *length* adjustment is performed. If the data types do not match, an automatic *type* adjustment is performed.

If the data types of the sending and receiving fields are the same but the lengths differ, a length adjustment is performed as shown in Table 9.3. In this table, the sending field is the "From" field.

TABLE 9.3   EFFECT OF LENGTH ADJUSTMENT VARIES WITH THE DATA TYPE

Type	When assigning to a longer field, the 'from' value is:	When assigning to a shorter field, the 'from' value is:
c	Right-padded with blanks	Right-truncated
x	Right-padded with zeros	Right-truncated

continues

TABLE 9.3 CONTINUED

Type	When assigning to a longer field, the 'from' value is:	When assigning to a shorter field, the 'from' value is:
n	Left-padded with zeros	Left-truncated
p	Left-padded with zeros	Assigned if the numeric value will fit in the 'to' field.
		If the numeric value is too large for the receiving field, a short dump occurs.

The remaining data types (f, i, d, and t) are all of a fixed length, so the sending and receiving fields will always be the same length if they are of the same data type.

Rules for type adjustments are provided in Table 9.4. The conversion rules for type i are the same as for type p. Included are conversions with unusual behaviors. Points to notice are:

- The peculiar compression performed for type c to n.
- The capability to assign invalid values to types d and t.
- The odd treatment of invalid characters during conversion of type c to x.
- The unexpected usage of the reserved sign byte in p to c conversions.
- The use of * to indicate overflow in p to c conversions.
- An entirely blank c field is converted to a p field having a zero value.

TABLE 9.4 RULES FOR TYPE ADJUSTMENTS

From Type	To Type	Conversion Rules
c	p	The sending field can only contain numbers, a single decimal point, and an optional sign. The sign can be leading or trailing. Blanks can appear on either side of the value. It is right-justified and padded on the left with zeros. An entirely blank sending field is converted to zero.
c	d	The sending field should contain only a valid date in the format YYYYMMDD. If it does not, an error does not occur; instead, an invalid value is assigned to the receiving field. The results of using this value are undefined.
c	t	The sending field should only have a valid time in the format HHMMSS. If it does not, an error does not occur; instead, an invalid value is assigned to the receiving field. The results of using this value are undefined.
c	n	The sending field is scanned from left to right and only the digits 0–9 are transferred to the receiving field (right-justified) and padded on the left with zeros. All other characters are simply ignored.

From Type	To Type	Conversion Rules
c	x	Valid values for the sending field are 0–9 and capital letters A–F. The value is left-justified and padded on the right with zeros or truncated on the right. All characters after the first invalid value in the sending field are ignored.
p	c	The value is right-justified in the receiving field with the right-most byte reserved for a trailing sign. The sign is only displayed if the number is negative; therefore, positive numbers will be right-justified with a single trailing blank. In the event you try to move a positive value that contains as many digits as the receiving field is long, the system will use the entire length of the receiving field to contain the value without reserving the right-most byte for the sign. After considering the above, if the value in the sending field will not fit the receiving field, the number is truncated on the left. If truncation has occurred, the system indicates this by replacing the left-most digit with an asterisk (*). If the value does fit in the receiving field, leading zeros are suppressed. If the sending field is equal to zero, the receiving field receives a single zero.
p	d	The number is interpreted as the number of days since 0001/01/01, converted to a date, and stored internally in YYYYMMDD format.
p	t	The number is interpreted as the number of seconds since midnight, converted to 24-hour clock time, and stored internally in HHMMSS format.
d	p	The date is converted to a number representing the number of days since 0001/01/01.
t	p	The time is converted to a number representing the number of seconds since midnight.

For a complete list of conversion rules, consult the ABAP/4 keyword documentation for the move statement. The procedure for displaying it follows in the next section.

Listing 9.6 contains a demonstration program that performs sample data conversions.

INPUT **LISTING 9.6** SAMPLE DATA CONVERSIONS

```
1 report ztx0906.
2 constants >(3) value '==>'.      "defines a constant named '>'
3 data: fc(10)  type c value '-A1B2C3.4',
4       fn(10)  type n,
5       fp       type p,
6       fd       type d,
```

continues

LISTING 9.6   CONTINUED

```
 7          ft        type t,
 8          fx(4)     type x,
 9          fc1(5)    type c value '-1234',
10          fc2(5)    type c value '1234-',
11          fp1       type p value 123456789,
12          fp2       type p value '123456789-',
13          fp3       type p value 1234567899,
14          fp4       type p value 12345678901,
15          fp5       type p value 12345,
16          fp6       type p value 0.
17
18 fn = fc.      write: / fc, >, fn, 'non-numeric chars are ignored'.
19 fd = 'ABCDE'. write: / fd, 'date and time fields are invalid'.
20 ft = 'ABCDE'. write: / ft, '  when you load them with junk'.
21 fp = sy-datum. write: / sy-datum, >, fp, 'd->p: days since 0001/01/01'.
22 fp = sy-uzeit. write: / sy-uzeit, >, fp, 'd->t: secs since midnight'.
23 fx = 'A4 B4'. write: / 'A4 B4', >, fx, 'ignore all after invalid char'.
24 fp = fc1.     write: / fc1, >, fp, 'allows leading sign'.
25 fp = fc2.     write: / fc2, >, fp, 'also allows trailing sign'.
26 fc = fp1.     write: / fp1, >, fc, 'rightmost byte reserved for sign'.
27 fc = fp2.     write: / fp2, >, fc, 'only negative numbers use it, but'.
28 fc = fp3.     write: / fp3, >, fc, '+ve nums that need it use it too'.
29 fc = fp4.     write: / fp4, >, fc, 'overflow indicated by leading *'.
30 fc = fp5.     write: / fp5, >, fc, 'leading zeros are suppressed'.
31 fc = fp6.     write: / fp6, >, fc, 'zero in = zero out'.
32 fp = ' '.     write: / ' ', >, fp, 'blanks in = zero out'.
```

The code in Listing 9.6 produces the following output:

OUTPUT

```
-A1B2C3.4  ==> 0000001234 non-numeric chars are ignored
E    ABCD date and time fields are invalid
ABCDE0    when you load them with junk
1998/02/22 ==>           729,443 d->p: days since 0001/01/01
14:57:05 ==>              53,825 d->t: secs since midnight
A4 B4 ==> A4000000 ignore all after invalid char
-1234 ==>             1,234- allows leading sign
1234- ==>             1,234- also allows trailing sign
       123,456,789  ==> 123456789  rightmost byte reserved for sign
       123,456,789- ==> 123456789- only negative numbers use it, but
     1,234,567,899  ==> 1234567899 +ve nums that need it use it too
    12,345,678,901  ==> *345678901 overflow indicated by leading *
            12,345  ==>      12345  leading zeros are suppressed
                 0  ==>          0  zero in = zero out
                   ==>          0  blanks in = zero out
```

Start the ScreenCam "How to Display the Conversion Rules in the ABAP/4 Keyword Documentation" now.

To display the conversion rules in the ABAP/4 keyword documentation:

1. Begin at the ABAP/4 Editor: Initial Screen.

2. Choose the menu path Utilities->ABAP/4 Key Word doc. The Display Structure: ABAP/4 SAP's 4GL Programming Language screen is displayed.

3. Press the Find button on the Application toolbar. The Search Chapter Titles dialog box is displayed.

4. In the Find field, type `move`.

5. In the Type of Search group box, choose the From Struct. Start radio button.

6. Press the Continue button. The dialog box disappears and the `move` line is highlighted.

7. Double-click on the highlighted line. The Display Hypertext: screen is displayed.

8. Press the Page Down key twice. The beginning of the conversion table is displayed.

Subfields

NEW TERM   The portion of a field referenced by the specification of an offset and/or length is called a *subfield*.

Syntax for a Subfield

```
v1[+o][(L)] = v2[+o][(L)].
```

where:

- *v1* and *v2* are variable or field string names.
- *o* is a zero-based offset from the beginning of the field.
- *L* is a length in bytes.

The following points apply:

- A subfield can be specified for either the sending or receiving fields or both.
- Either the offset or length is optional. Both can be present.
- If the offset is not specified, the subfield starts at the beginning of the field.
- If the length is not specified, the subfield extends to the end of the field.
- No spaces can be used within the specification of the subfield.
- The offset, when present, is always preceded by a plus (+) sign.
- The length, when present, is always surrounded by parentheses.

Listing 9.7 shows a sample program that performs assignments and uses subfields.

INPUT   **LISTING 9.7**   MOVING A PORTION OF A FIELD USING A SUBFIELD ASSIGNMENT

```
 1 report ztx0907.
 2 data: f1(7),
 3        f2(7).
 4 f1      = 'BOY'.     "same as: move 'BOY' to f1.
 5 f2      = 'BIG'.     "same as: move 'BIG' to f2.
 6 f1+0(1) = 'T'.       "f1 now contains 'TOY    '.

 7 write / f1.
 8 f1(1)   = 'J'.       "same as: f1+0(1) = 'J'.
 9 write / f1.          "f1 now contains 'JOY    '.
10 f1(1)   = f2.        "same as: f1(1) = f2(1).
11 write / f1.          "f1 now contains 'BOY    '.
12 f1+4    = f1.        "same as: f1+4(3) = f1(3).
13 write / f1.          "f1 now contains 'BOY BOY'.
14 f1(3)   = f2(3).     "same as: f1+0(3) = f2+0(3).
15 write / f1.          "f1 now contains 'BIG BOY'.
```

The code in Listing 9.7 produces this output:

OUTPUT
```
TOY
JOY
BOY
BOY BOY
BIG BOY
```

ANALYSIS
- On line 6, an offset of 0 and a length of 1 is used to specify a subfield consisting of only the first byte of f1. Assigning the letter 'T' therefore fills only the first byte of f1.

- On line 8, the offset of 0 is left out. 0 is the default, so the subfield is the same as the one on line 6.

- On line 10, the same subfield is used, but this time the assignment is from f2. Only the first byte is transferred from f2 because the receiving subfield is only a single byte long.

- On line 12, an offset of 4 specifies that the subfield in f1 begins at the fifth byte and continues to the end of f1, making it three bytes long. The sending field is f1, causing the first three bytes of f1 to be duplicated in positions 4 through 6.

- On line 14, the first three bytes of f2 replace the first three bytes of f1.

Using move with Field Strings

With move, a field string name specified without a component name is treated as if it were a variable of type c. Figure 9.2 and Listing 9.8 illustrate this point.

FIGURE 9.2.

Using move *on a field string without using a component name causes it to be treated as a variable of type* c.

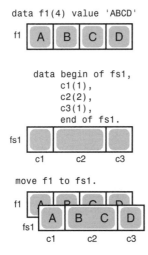

LISTING 9.8 THE move STATEMENT TREATS A FIELD STRING NAME WITHOUT A COMPONENT NAME LIKE A VARIABLE OF TYPE c

INPUT

```
 1 report ztx0908.
 2 data: f1(4) value 'ABCD',
 3       begin of s1,
 4           c1(1),
 5           c2(2),
 6           c3(1),
 7       end of s1.
 8 s1 = f1.                    "s1 is treated as a char 4 variable
 9 write: / s1,                "writes ABCD
10          / s1-c1, s1-c2, s1-c3.    "writes A BC D
```

The code in Listing 9.8 produces this output:

OUTPUT
```
ABCD
A BC D
```

ANALYSIS

- Line 2 defines f1 as a four-byte variable of type c.

- Lines 3 through 7 define s1 as a field string having three components: f1, f2, and f3. The total length of s1 is calculated by totaling the lengths of its components: 1+2+1=4.

- Line 8 moves the value from f1 to s1 byte by byte, as if they were both variables of type c.

- Line 9 writes s1 out as a four-character variable.

- Line 10 writes out the contents of the components of s1.

Field String Moves Involving Numeric Fields

If the sending field is category character (types c, n, d, t, or x) and the target is a field string containing a numeric field (types i, p, or f), *no data conversion is performed*. The move proceeds as if both were purely character. The reverse is also true. No conversions are performed when moving a numeric to a field string containing a character field. In both cases, the results are invalid and are undefined.

Listing 9.9 shows a sample program that make an invalid conversion of a numeric field to a character field string.

INPUT   **LISTING 9.9**   MOVING A NUMERIC FIELD TO A CHARACTER FIELD STRING IS INVALID

```
 1 report ztx0909.
 2 data: fc(5) type c,
 3       begin of s,
 4             fi type i,
 5             end of s.
 6
 7 fc = '1234'.
 8 s = fc.          "c<-c, no conversion performed
 9 write s-fi.      "writes junk
10
11 s-fi = 1234.     "assign a valid value
12 fc = s.          "c<-c, no conversion performed
13 write / fc.      "writes junk
14
15 s-fi = 1234.     "assign a valid value
16 fc = s-fi.       "c<-i conversion performed
17 write / fc.      "writes 1234
```

On my machine, the code in Listing 9.9 produces the following output. Your results might vary for the first two lines of output due to the invalid assignments performed.

OUTPUT
```
875770,417
Ò###
1234
```

ANALYSIS
- On line 2, f1 is defined as an integer having a value of 1234.
- On lines 3 through 5, s1 is defined as a single component c1 type c length 12.
- On line 6, f1 is moved to s1. No conversion is performed because s1 is a field string, so it is treated like type c.
- On line 7, s1-c1 is written out and the results are garbage.
- On line 8, s1-c1 is assigned a valid character string '1234'.
- On line 9, s1 is moved to f1. No conversion is performed.

- Line 10 writes out f1, and again, the results are garbage.

- On Line 11, f1 is assigned a valid value of 1234.

- On line 12, f1 is assigned to s1-c1. Because the assignment is to the component and not to the field string, conversion is performed and line 13 writes out a valid value.

Caution

> You should not move a type c variable to or from a field string containing a numeric type. The results are machine-dependent and therefore undefined.

Moving from One Field String to Another Using Character Data Types

You can use the move statement on two field strings if both strings contain components of only character data types (c, n, d, t, and x). Listing 9.10 illustrates this concept.

LISTING 9.10 USING move WITH TWO FIELD STRINGS COMPOSED ENTIRELY OF VALID CHARACTER DATA TYPES

INPUT

```
 1 report ztx0910.
 2 data: begin of s1,
 3          d1      type d value '19980217',   "8 bytes
 4          n1(4)   type n value '1234',       "4 bytes
 5          c1              value 'A',          "1 byte
 6          c2              value 'B',          "1 byte
 7          end of s1,
 8       begin of s2,
 9          y1(4)   type n,                     "4 bytes
10          m1(2)   type c,                     "2 bytes
11          d1(2)   type n,                     "2 bytes
12          n1(2)   type c,                     "2 bytes
13          c1(4)   type c,                     "4 bytes
14          end of s2.
15    s2 = s1.
16    write: / s1,
17           / s2,
18           / s1-d1, s1-n1, s1-c1, s1-c2,
19           / s2-y1, s2-m1, s2-d1, s2-n1, s2-c1.
```

The code in Listing 9.10 produces this output:

OUTPUT

```
199802171234AB
199802171234AB
19980217 1234 A B
1998 02 17 12 34AB
```

- Lines 2 through 14 define two field strings composed entirely of character type fields. Each field string is 14 bytes long in total.

- On line 15, s1 is moved to s2, treating each field string as if it is a single type c field 14 bytes long.

- On lines 16 and 17, both are written out as character fields.

- On lines 18 and 19, the components of each field string are written out. s1-d1 has been split across s2-y1, m1, and d1. The first two bytes of s1-n1 went into s2-n1. The remaining bytes from s1 went to s2-c1.

Moving from One Field String to Another with Numeric Data Types

NEW TERM Most operating systems require the machine address of numeric fields to conform to specific rules. For example, the address of a four-byte integer might be required to be divisible by two. That rule is often stated as "a four-byte integer must be aligned on an even byte boundary." Thus, the rule to which the address of a field conforms is called the *alignment*.

NEW TERM In order to satisfy alignment requirements, a typical compiler will insert *padding bytes* before a field that requires alignment. For example, if your four-byte integer begins at offset 0003 from the beginning of a program, a padding byte is necessary to align it on a two-byte boundary. The compiler will place an unused byte at offset 0003 so that the integer begins at offset 0004, causing it to be properly aligned. Padding bytes are invisible to the programmer, but their effects can be seen at times.

If you create a field string having a mixture of character and numeric fields, padding bytes are sometimes inserted by the system to bring numeric fields into alignment. If you attempt to use a move statement on such a field string to move its contents to another, these padding bytes can cause unexpected results.

Therefore, you can only use move if one of the following is true:

- Both field strings consist entirely of character fields (types c, n, d, t, and x).

- The data types, lengths, and position of all components in both field strings match exactly (the names of the components do not have to match).

If both the sending and receiving fields are entirely composed of character fields, no padding bytes will exist and the result of using move is predictable. If there is a mixture of character and numeric types, padding bytes might exist and the result of using move can be unexpected. An example is shown in Listing 9.11.

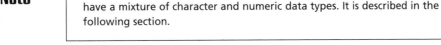

> **Note**
> The move-corresponding statement can be used to move field strings that
> have a mixture of character and numeric data types. It is described in the
> following section.

INPUT

LISTING 9.11 PADDING BYTES CAN CAUSE UNEXPECTED RESULTS WHEN MOVING
DATA BETWEEN FIELD STRINGS

9

```
 1 report ztx0911.
 2 data: begin of s1,
 3             c1 value 'A',           "one byte

 4             c2 type i value 1234,   "four bytes, usually needs padding
 5             c3 value 'B',           "one byte
 6             end of s1,

 7        begin of s2,
 8             c1,                      "one byte
 9             c2(4),                   "four bytes, no padding
10             c3,                      "one byte
11             end of s2,
12        begin of s3,                  "s3 matches s1 exactly:
13             x1,                      "- data types the same
14             x2 type i,               "- number of fields the same
15             x3,                      "- fields in the same order
16             end of s3.               "(names don't have to match)
17 s2 = s1.
18 write: / s2-c1, s2-c2, s2-c3.
19 s3 = s1.
20 write: / s3-x1, s3-x2, s3-x3.
```

On my system, the code in Listing 9.11 produces the following output. In your system,
results might vary for fields with invalid assignments.

OUTPUT

```
A ###Ò #
A      1,234  B
```

s1-c1 is only one byte long, so c2 has an uneven offset from the beginning of the field
string and requires padding on most systems, which makes s1 longer than s2. When s1 is
assigned to s2, c3 does not line up and some of s1-c2 ends up at the beginning of s2-c3.
However, s3 matches s1 exactly, so the move on line 14 works perfectly.

This example shows that you can't ignore the effects of having numeric fields within a
structure. The fact that each receiving field has the same number of bytes as each sending field is not enough to guarantee that the components will line up.

Alignment rules vary with the operating system, so the number of padding bytes and their positions vary. The results of a move on one operating system might be different on another. Therefore, to ensure that your programs are portable, never rely on padding bytes and don't consider them during moves. Each field string must be composed entirely of character data types or all components of each field string must match exactly (except for the name).

Using the `move-corresponding` Statement

To perform a move from one field string to another where the data types and/or lengths do not match, use the `move-corresponding` statement. It generates individual move statements for components with matching names. Components in the receiving field string that do not have a matching name in the sending field string are not changed. Listing 9.12 illustrates.

Syntax for the `move-corresponding` Statement

▼ SYNTAX

The following is the syntax for the move statement. Operators and operands must be separated by spaces. Multiple assignment occurs from right to left.

```
move-corresponding v1 to v2.
```

where:

- *v1* is the sending variable or field string.

▲
- *v2* is the receiving variable or field string.

LISTING 9.12   THE `move-corresponding` STATEMENT GENERATES INDIVIDUAL

INPUT   `move` STATEMENTS AND THUS PERFORMS DATA CONVERSION

```
 1 report ztx0912.
 2 data: begin of s1,
 3          c1     type p decimals 2 value '1234.56',
 4          c2(3)                     value 'ABC',
 5          c3(4)                     value '1234',
 6          end of s1,
 7        begin of s2,
 8          c1(8),
 9          x2(3)                     value 'XYZ',
10          c3     type i,
11          end of s2.
12 write: / 's1                            :', s1-c1, s1-c2, s1-c3.
13 write: / 's2 before move-corresponding:', s2-c1, s2-x2, s2-c3.
14 move-corresponding s1 to s2. "same as coding the following two statements
15 * move s1-c1 to s2-c1.        "performs conversion
16 * move s1-c3 to s2-c3.        "performs conversion
17 write: / 's2 after  move-corresponding:', s2-c1, s2-x2, s2-c3.
```

The code in Listing 9.12 produces this output:

OUTPUT

```
s1                            :        1,234.56  ABC 1234
s2 before move-corresponding:              XYZ         0
s2 after  move-corresponding: 1234.56    XYZ     1,234
```

ANALYSIS Line 14 generates two move statements; for sake of clarity, they are shown within comments on lines 15 and 16. Normally, you cannot see these move statements; the system generates and executes them automatically "behind the scenes." One move is generated for each component of the receiving field string that has the same name as a component in the sending field string. In this case, c1 and c3 have the same names, so two moves are generated. Data conversions are performed as they would be if you had coded these statements yourself. The contents of c2 are unchanged after the move-corresponding completes.

Tip

> If two field strings match exactly, don't use move-corresponding to move the data from one to another. Use move, it's more efficient.

Performing Calculations

You can perform calculations using the following statements:

- compute
- add or add-corresponding
- subtract or subtract-corresponding
- multiply or multiply-corresponding
- divide or divide-corresponding

Using the compute Statement

Compute is the statement most commonly used to perform calculations.

Syntax for the compute Statement

▼ SYNTAX

The following is the syntax for the compute statement. Operators and operands must be separated by spaces. More than one operator per statement is permitted.

```
compute v3 = v1 op v2 [op vn ...].
```

or

```
v3 = v2 op v2 [op vn ...].
```

where:

▼   • *v3* is the receiving variable for the result of the computation.

▲
- *v1*, *v2*, and *vn* are the operands.
- *op* is a mathematical operator.

Table 9.5 contains a list of the valid operators.

TABLE 9.5   Valid Operators for the compute Statement

Operator	Operation
+	Addition
-	Subtraction
*	Multiplication
/	Division
**	Exponentiation
DIV	Integer division
MOD	Remainder of integer division

There are also built-in functions. For a list, obtain F1 help for the keyword compute.

Operator precedence is as follows:

- Built-in functions are evaluated,
- then exponentiation,
- then *, /, DIV, and MOD, in the order they appear in the expression,
- then + and - in the order they appear in the expression.

Division by zero results in a short dump unless the operands are both zero. In that case, the result is zero. Values are converted when necessary during computation. The rules for data conversion and the order of data type precedence (described below with the if statement) determine how the conversion is performed.

Mathematical expressions can contain any number of parentheses. Each must be preceded and followed by at least one space. However, there is one exception to this rule. There cannot be a space after a built-in function name; the opening parenthesis must follow it immediately. Table 9.6 shows the right and wrong ways to code mathematical expressions.

TABLE 9.6   Right and Wrong Ways to Code Mathematical Statements

Right	Wrong
f1 = f2 + f3.	f1 = f2+f3.
f1 = (f2 + f3) * f4.	f1 = (f2 + f3) * f4.
f1 = sqrt(f2).	f1 = sqrt (f2).
	f1 = sqrt(f2).

The check box Fixed Point Arithmetic in the Program Attributes screen controls how decimal calculations are performed and should always be checked. If it is, intermediate results are calculated to 31 decimal places and then rounded off when assigned to the result variable. If it is not, intermediate results do not have any decimal places, which causes the loss of all decimal precision. For example, if Fixed Point Arithmetic is not checked, the calculation 1 / 3 * 3 will give a result of zero because the intermediate result of 0.333333 is rounded off to zero before being multiplied by 3. When it is checked, the result is 1.

Using the `add` and `add-corresponding` Statements

Use the `add` statement to add one number to another. Field strings with components having the same name can be added together with `add-corresponding`.

Syntax for the `add` Statement

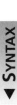

Following is the syntax for the `add` statement. Conversions are performed as necessary in the same way as the `compute` statement.

add *v1* to *v2*.

where:

- *v2* is the variable being added to.
- *v1* is the variable added to *v2*.

The syntax for the `subtract`, `multiply`, and `divide` is similar.

Syntax for the `add-corresponding` Statement

Below is the syntax for the `add-corresponding` statement.

add-corresponding *s1* to *s2*.

where:

- *s2* is the field string being added to.
- *s1* is the field string added to *s2*.

An `add` statement is generated for each pair of components having the same name in *s1* and *s2*. Data conversions are performed in the same way as for the `add` statement. `Subtract-corresponding`, `multiply-corresponding`, and `divide-corresponding` operate in a similar fashion.

Examples are given in Listing 9.13.

LISTING 9.13 USING add, subtract, multiply, divide, AND corresponding STATEMENTS

```
 1 report ztx0913.
 2 data: f1 type i value 2,
 3        f2 type i value 3,
 4        begin of s1,
 5            c1 type i value 10,
 6            c2 type i value 20,
 7            c3 type i value 30,
 8            end of s1,
 9        begin of s2,
10            c1 type i value 100,
11            x2 type i value 200,
12            c3 type i value 300,
13            end of s2.
14 add                      f1  to    f2.   write  / f2.    "f1 is unchanged
15 subtract                 f1  from  f2.   write  / f2.
16 multiply                 f2  by    f1.   write  / f2.
17 divide                   f2  by    f1.   write  / f2.
18 add-corresponding        s1  to    s2.   write: / s2-c1, s2-x2, s2-c3.
19 subtract-corresponding   s1  from  s2.   write: / s2-c1, s2-x2, s2-c3.
20 multiply-corresponding   s2  by    s1.   write: / s2-c1, s2-x2, s2-c3.
21 divide-corresponding     s2  by    s1.   write: / s2-c1, s2-x2, s2-c3.
```

The code in Listing 9.13 produces this output:

```
        5
        3
        6
        3
      110        200         330
      100        200         300
    1,000        200       9,000
      100        200         300
```

Date Calculations

A date variable (type d) can be used within mathematical expressions. Assigning the result of a date computation to a packed variable will give the difference in days. An example is given Listing 9.14.

LISTING 9.14 DATE CALCULATIONS USING THE DATE VARIABLE WITHIN A COMPUTATION

```
1 report ztx0914.
2 type-pools ztx1.                "contains ztx1_amalgamation_date
3 data: d1        like sy-datum,
```

```
 4         d2       like d1,
 5         num_days type p.
 6 d1 = d2 = sy-datum.
 7
 8 subtract 1 from d1.   write / d1.   "yesterday's date
 9 d2+6 = '01'.          write / d2.   "first day of current month
10 subtract 1 from d2.   write / d2.   "last day of previous month
11
12 num_days = sy-datum - ztx1_amalgamation_date.
13 write / num_days.                   "number of days since amalgamation
```

9

On February 22, 1998, the code in Listing 9.14 produced this output:

OUTPUT

```
1998/02/21
1998/02/01
1998/01/31
            354
```

ANALYSIS

- On line 2, the `type-pools` statement causes the constant `ztx1_amalgamation_date` to be included in the program.

- On line 6, the current date is assigned to d1 and d2.

- On line 8, yesterday's date is calculated by subtracting 1 from the current date.

- On line 9, a subfield in d2 at offset 6 with a length of 2 (length obtained from sending field) is set to `'01'`. Because dates are always stored using the internal format YYYYMMDD, the day value of the date in d2 is set to `'01'`. The result is that d2 contains a date equal to the first day of the current month.

- On line 10, 1 is subtracted from d2, giving the date of the last day in the previous month.

- On line 12, the difference in days between the current date and the amalgamation date is calculated. The result is assigned to the packed field num_days and written out on line 13.

Dynamic Assignment

 NEW TERM A *field-symbol* is a pointer you can dynamically assign to a field. After assignment, you can use the field-symbol anywhere in your program in place of the actual field name. Use the `field-symbol` statement to define a field-symbol, and use `assign` to assign a field to it. The field-symbol name must begin and end with angle brackets. Listing 9.15 contains a simple example.

LISTING 9.15   A FIELD-SYMBOL IS A REFERENCE TO ANOTHER FIELD

```
1  report ztx0915.
2  data f1(3) value 'ABC'.
3  field-symbols <f>.
4  assign f1 to <f>.    "<f> can now be used in place of f1
5  write <f>.           "writes the contents of f1
6  <f> = 'XYZ'.         "assigns a new value to f1
7  write / f1.
```

The code in Listing 9.15 produces this output:

 OUTPUT
```
ABC
XYZ
```

ANALYSIS
- Line 3 defines a field-symbol named `<f>`.
- Line 4 assigns the field `f1` to the field-symbol `<f>`. `<f>` now points to the storage for variable `f1`, and can be used in place of `f1` anywhere in the program.
- Line 5 writes out `<f>`, causing the contents of `f1` to be written.
- Line 6 modifies the contents of `<f>`, but actually modifies `f1`.
- Line 7 writes out the modified contents of `f1`.

You can use field-symbols to create very generic programs. Suppose, for example, that you want to create a program that accepts a table name as an input parameter and displays the contents. You could not hard-code the field names on the `write` statement because the names are different in every table. You could instead use a field-symbol on the `write` statement to refer to the field of a table.

Summary

- System variables are stored in the structure `syst`. You can search the descriptions of the fields and their data elements to find the field you are looking for. This procedure can be used to search through the fields of any table.
- The assignment statements are `clear`, `move`, and `move-corresponding`.
- `Clear` assigns default initial values to a variable or field string. You can also use it to fill a field with any character, or with `NULLs`.
- The `move` statement can also be written as `=`. Multiple assignments in a single line are possible, such as `v1 = v2 = v3`. Conversions are automatically performed when necessary. A field string name without a component name is treated as a variable of type `c`.

- To move data between field strings that match exactly in number of components, the data type, and length of each component, use move. To move data between field strings with components having (at least one component with) the same name but of different data types or lengths, use move-corresponding.

- To access the individual bytes of a field's value, use a subfield. A subfield can be used as either sending or receiving field, or both.

- You can perform calculations using compute, add, subtract, multiply, divide, add-corresponding, subtract-corresponding, multiply-corresponding, and divide-corresponding.

9

Do	Don't
DO use fields of the same data type when possible to avoid conversions.	**DON'T** move invalid values into fields.
DO use move-corresponding to move fields from one field string to another when the components have the same name but the data types and lengths do not match.	
DO use the clear statement to assign default initial values to a variable or field string.	

Q&A

Q I can use the clear statement to set a value to blanks or zeros, but is there a statement that can set a variable back to the value I specified using the value addition on the data statement?

A No, unfortunately there isn't.

Q Can I use the move statement with field strings of differing lengths?

A Yes, you can. They will both be treated as variables of type c. The sending value will be truncated or padded on the end with blanks as needed before assignment to the receiving field string.

Q Why do I need to know about padding bytes? Doesn't the system take care of that if I just follow all the rules?

A Technically, yes, it will. However, as you code more programs, occasionally you will inadvertently assign a field string incorrectly using move. If you understand padding bytes and how they affect your output, hopefully you will be able to recognize the cause of your problems, and won't resort to a "hack" to make the program work.

Q **It seems strange that I can assign invalid values to variables. What happens if I use one of these variables with an invalid value in it?**

A Anything can happen. I wouldn't write a program that intentionally relies on invalid values. For example, don't be tempted to use a special date value of all x to indicate something special like a missing date. The behavior of your program becomes unpredictable when you go outside the allowable boundaries of the language.

Q **The syntax messages often don't indicate what is truly wrong with my program. Is it me or is the syntax checker way out in left field sometimes?**

A Let's just say...it isn't you. My favorite of all time is the message *xxxx is expected.* It really means "xxxx is *not* expected." So when you see that message, insert the word *not*, and it will be correct.

Workshop

The Workshop provides two ways for you to affirm what you've learned in this chapter. The Quiz section poses questions to help you solidify your understanding of the material covered and the Exercise section provides you with experience in using what you have learned. You can find answers to the quiz questions and exercises in Appendix B, "Answers to Quiz Questions and Exercises."

Quiz

1. What is another way to move a value from one variable to another?
2. What must separate operands and operators in order for the computation to work?

Exercise 1

Using the procedure called "How to Search the Descriptions of a Structure or Table" to find the following:

1. The name of the Payment block field in the lfa1 table.
2. The name of the Group key field in the kna1 table.
3. The name of the system field that contains the location of a string.
4. The name of the system field that contains the message ID.
5. The name of the material group field in the mara table.

Two things are wrong with the program in Listing 9.16. What are they?

INPUT   **LISTING 9.16**   THIS CODE ILLUSTRATES THE USE OF SOME BASIC SYSTEM VARIABLES

```
report zty0916.
tables ztxlfa1.
parameters land1 like ztxlfa1-land1 obligatory default 'US'.
select * from ztxt005t
    where land1 = land1
    and   spras = sy-langu.
    write: / 'Description:', ztxt005t-landx.
    endselect.
if sy-subrc <> 0.
    write: / 'No descriptions exist for country', land1.
    endif.
```

9

DAY 10

Common Control Statements

Chapter Objectives

After you complete this chapter, you should be able to:

- Code the common control statements `if`, `case`, `do`, and `while`
- Control program sequence using `exit`, `continue`, and `check`
- Code simple position and length specifications on the `write` statement

Using the `if` Statement

The `if` statement in ABAP/4 has relational operators for equality and inequality and special relational operators for string comparisons and for bit masks.

Note   Bit comparisons are not often used in ABAP/4 and so they are not presented here. They are, however, detailed in the ABAP/4 keyword documentation under the heading "Relational Operators for Bit Masks."

Syntax for the `if` Statement

The following is the syntax for the `if` statement.

```
if [not] exp [ and [not] exp ] [ or [not] exp ].
    ---
[elseif exp.
    ---]
[else.
    ---]
    endif.
```

where:

- *exp* is a logical expression that evaluates to a true or false condition.
- `---` represents any number of lines of code. Even zero lines are allowed.

The following points apply:

- Every `if` must have a matching `endif`.
- `else` and `elseif` are optional.
- Parentheses can be used. Each parentheses must be separated by a space. For example, `if ( f1 = f2 ) or ( f1 = f3 )` is correct, and `if (f1 = f2) or (f1 = f3)` is incorrect.
- Variables can be compared with blanks or zeros using the addition `is initial`. For example, `if f1 is initial` will be true if `f1` is type `c` and is blank. If `f1` is any other data type, the statement is true if `f1` contains zeros.
- To accomplish negation, `not` must *precede* the logical expression. For example, `if not f1 is initial` is correct. `if f1 is not initial` is incorrect.
- Variables can be compared with nulls using the addition `is null`. For example, `if f1 is null`.

The logical operators for operands of any type are listed in Table 10.1.

TABLE 10.1 COMMON COMPARISONS AND THEIR ALTERNATE FORMS

Comparison	Alternate Forms	True When
v1 = *v2*	EQ	*v1* equals *v2*
v1 <> *v2*	NE, ><	*v1* does not equal *v2*

Comparison	Alternate Forms	True When
v1 > v2	GT	v1 is greater than v2
v1 < v2	LT	v1 is less than v2
v1 >= v2	GE, =>	v1 is greater than or equal to v2
v1 <= v2	LE, =<	v1 is less than or equal to v2
v1 between v2 and v3		v1 lies between v2 and v3 (inclusive)
not v1 between v2 and v3		v1 lies outside of the range v2 to v3 (inclusive)

In Table 10.1, *v1* and *v2* can be variables, literals, or field strings. In the case of variables or literals, automatic conversion is performed if the data type or length does not match. Field strings are treated as type c variables.

Comparing two values that do not have the same data type will result in an internal automatic type adjustment of one or both of the values. One type will take precedence and will dictate what type of conversion is performed. The order of precedence is:

- If one field is type f, the other is converted to type f.
- If one field is type p, the other is converted to type p.
- If one field is type i, the other is converted to type i.
- If one field is type d, the other is converted to type d. Types c and n, however, are not converted. They are compared directly.
- If one field is type t, the other is converted to type t. Types c and n, however, are not converted. They are compared directly.
- If one field is type n, *both* are converted to type p (at this point, the other field can only be type c or x).
- At this point, one field will be type c and the other will be type x. x is converted to type c.

Conversions follow the same rules as those performed by the move statement. Type conversions are fully detailed in the ABAP/4 keyword documentation under the heading "Relational Operators for All Data Types."

Data Conversion of Literals During Comparisons

Literals are stored internally with data types, as shown in Table 10.2.

TABLE 10.2   DATA TYPES OF LITERALS

Description	Data Type
Numbers one to nine digits long	i
Numbers 10 or more digits long	p
All others	c

Type conversions for literals follow the same order of precedence and the same conversion rules apply.

Listing 10.1 shows a sample program using the common comparison operators. A surprising conversion is also demonstrated.

INPUT   **LISTING 10.1**   AN EXAMPLE OF USING if IN THE PROGRAM

```
1   report ztx1001.
2   data: begin of s1,
3            x value 'X',
4            y value 'Y',
5            z value 'Z',
6           end of s1,
7         begin of s2,
8            x value 'X',
9            z value 'Z',
10          end of s2.
11
12 if s1-x = s2-x.
13     write: / s1-x, '=', s2-x.
14 else.
15     write: / s1-x, '<>', s2-x.
16     endif.
17
18 if s1-x between s2-x and s2-z.
19     write: / s1-X, 'is between', s2-x, 'and', s2-z.
20 else.
21     write: / s1-X, 'is not between', s2-x, 'and', s2-z.
22     endif.
23
24 if s1 = s2.        "comparing field strings byte by byte
25     write: / 's1 = s2'.
26 else.
27     write: / 's1 <> s2'.
28     endif.
29
30 if 0 = ' '.        "Watch out for this one
31     write: / '0 = '' '''.
32 else.
33     write: / '0 <> '' '''.
34     endif.
```

The code in Listing 10.1 produces this output:

OUTPUT

```
X = X
X is between X and Z
s1 <> s2
0 = ' '
```

ANALYSIS

- On line 12, s1-x is compared with s2-x. Both are type c, length 1. No conversion is performed and they are equal.

- Line 18 is similar, but uses the between operator. The value X lies in the range X to Z, and so the test proves true.

- Line 24 compares field strings s1 and s2 as if they were type c variables. The value of s1 is therefore XYZ, and the value of s2 is XZ. They are not equal.

- On line 30, the literal 0 is compared with a space. The zero is stored internally as type i, the other as type c. According to the order of precedence, type c is converted to type i. Converting a blank to an integer results in a zero value, and the comparison proves to be unexpectedly true.

Displaying Conversions

NEW TERM By performing a *program analysis,* you can determine where conversions occur within a program. To perform a program analysis, use the following procedure.

SCREENCAM Start the ScreenCam "How to Perform a Program Analysis" now.

1. Start at the ABAP/4 Editor: Initial Screen.

2. Type the program name to be analyzed in the Program field.

3. Choose the menu path Utilities->Program Analysis. The Conversions: *xxxxx* screen is displayed.

4. Press the Conversions pushbutton. The Conversions: *xxxxx* screen is displayed. All conversions are summarized on this screen. The first column contains field types compared.

5. Double-click on any line to view it within the program.

Note

> The first column on the Conversions: *xxxxx* screen does *not* show which conversion is performed. It merely shows the data types involved in the conversion.

Using `elseif`

You use `elseif` to avoid nesting `if`s. Nesting `if`s can be difficult to read and maintain. (see Listing 10.2).

LISTING 10.2   USING `elseif` IS CLEARER THAN USING NESTED `if`s

```
1   report ztx1002.
2   parameters: f1 default 'A',
3               f2 default 'B',
4               f3 default 'C'.
5
6   if      f1 = f2.   write: / f1, '=', f2.
7   elseif  f1 = f3.   write: / f1, '=', f3.
8   elseif  f2 = f3.   write: / f2, '=', f3.
9   else.              write: / 'all fields are different'.
10     endif.
11
12  *lines 5-9 do the same as lines 14-26
13
14  if f1 = f2.
15     write: / f1, '=', f2.
16  else.
17     if  f1 = f3.
18         write: / f1, '=', f3.
19     else.
20         if  f2 = f3.
21             write: / f2, '=', f3.
22         else.
23             write: / 'all fields are different'.
24             endif.
25         endif.
26     endif.
```

The code in Listing 10.2 produces this output:

```
all fields are different
all fields are different
```

- If f1 = f2, line 6 is true.

- If f1 = f3, line 7 is true.

- If f2 = f3, line 8 is true.

- If none of the above are true, line 9 is true.

- Lines 14 through 26 do the same as lines 6 through 10. They have been included so that you can see the two techniques side by side.

Using Character String Operators

Special operators for character strings are shown in Table 10.3.

TABLE 10.3 SPECIAL OPERATORS FOR CHARACTER STRINGS

Operator	Means	True When	Case Sensitive?	Trailing Blanks Ignored?
v1 CO v2	Contains Only	v1 is composed solely of characters in v2	Yes	No
v1 CN v2	not v1 CO v2	v1 contains characters that are not in v2	Yes	No
v1 CA v2	Contains Any	v1 contains at least one character in v2	Yes	No
v1 NA v2	not v1 CA v2	v1 does not contain any character in v2	Yes	No
v1 CS v2	Contains String	v1 contains the character string v2	No	Yes
v1 NS v2	not v1 CS v2	v1 does not contain the character string v2	No	Yes
v1 CP v2	Contains Pattern	v1 contains the pattern in v2	No	Yes
v1 NP v2	not v1 CP v2	v1 does not contain the pattern in v2	No	Yes

These operators can be used in any comparison expression. The CS, NS, CP, and NP operators ignore trailing blanks and are not case sensitive.

Although you can use variables, constants, or literals with relational operators for character strings, for clarity Listing 10.3 only uses literals. Also for clarity, the if statements here occupy a single line each.

INPUT   **LISTING 10.3** A SAMPLE PROGRAM EXERCISING CO, CN, CA, AND NA

```
1   report ztx1003.
2   * operator: co
3   write / '''AABB'' co ''AB'''.
4   if 'AABB' co 'AB'.          write 'True'. else. write 'False'. endif.
```

continues

LISTING 10.3 CONTINUED

```
 5  write / '''ABCD'' co ''ABC'''.
 6  if 'ABCD' co 'ABC'.           write 'True'. else. write 'False'. endif.
 7
 8  * operator: cn
 9  write / '''AABB'' cn ''AB'''.
10  if 'AABB' cn 'AB'.            write 'True'. else. write 'False'. endif.
11  write / '''ABCD'' cn ''ABC'''.
12  if 'ABCD' cn 'ABC'.           write 'True'. else. write 'False'. endif.
13
14  * operator: ca
15  write / '''AXCZ'' ca ''AB'''.
16  if 'AXCZ' ca 'AB'.            write 'True'. else. write 'False'. endif.
17  write / '''ABCD'' ca ''XYZ'''.
18  if 'ABCD' ca 'XYZ'.           write 'True'. else. write 'False'. endif.
19
20  * operator: na
21  write / '''AXCZ'' na ''ABC'''.
22  if 'AXCZ' na 'ABC'.           write 'True'. else. write 'False'. endif.
23  write / '''ABCD'' na ''XYZ'''.
24  if 'ABCD' na 'XYZ'.           write 'True'. else. write 'False'. endif.
```

The code in Listing 10.3 produces this output:

OUTPUT

```
'AABB' co 'AB' True
'ABCD' co 'ABC' False
'AABB' cn 'AB' False
'ABCD' cn 'ABC' True
'AXCZ' ca 'AB' True
'ABCD' ca 'XYZ' False
'AXCZ' na 'ABC' False
'ABCD' na 'XYZ' True
```

ANALYSIS

- co is the contains only operator. Line 4 is true because 'AABB' contains only characters from 'AB'.

- Line 6 is false because 'ABCD' contains a D, which is not in 'ABC'.

- Lines 10 and 12 are the opposites of lines 4 and 6 because cn is the same as not v1 co v2. Therefore, the results are inverted. Line 10 is false and line 12 is true.

- ca is the contains any operator and line 16 is true if 'AXCZ' contains any characters from 'AB'. It is true because it contains A.

- Line 18 is false because 'ABCD' does not contain any of the characters 'XYZ'.

- na is equivalent to not v1 ca v2. Therefore, lines 22 and 24 are the logical negation of lines 16 and 18.

Referring back to Table 10.3, the CP (contains pattern) and NP (no pattern) operators perform a string search that allows pattern-matching characters. The expression *v1* CP *v2* is true when *v1* contains a string that matches the pattern in *v2*. The expression *v1* NP *v2* is true when *v1* does not contain a string that matches the pattern in *v2*. It is equivalent to not v1 cp v2. The pattern matching characters allowed in *v2* are given in Table 10.4.

TABLE 10.4 CP AND NP OPERATORS

Character	Used to
*	Match any sequence of characters.
+	Match any single character.
#	Interpret the next character literally.

is the escape character. A single character following it is interpreted exactly. Special meaning, if it exists, is lost. You can also use # to make a search case sensitive or to search for the *, +, or # characters. Table 10.5 shows examples of how you might use these characters. The escape character is needed when you want to perform a case-sensitive search using CS, NS, CP, or NP. You also need it if you want to perform a pattern search (CP or NP) for a string containing *, +, or #.

TABLE 10.5 USING CHARACTERS

Statement	True When
v1 CP 'A+C'	*v1* contains "a" in the first position and "c" in the third. Either character can be in upper- or lowercase. Any character can appear in the second position.
v1 CP '*Ab*'	The string "ab" occurs anywhere within *v1*. Either character can be in upper- or in lowercase.
v1 CP '*#A#b*'	*v1* contains a capital A followed by lowercase b.
v1 CP '*##*'	*v1* contains a #.

Use of these operators always sets the system variable sy-fdpos. If the result of the comparison is true, sy-fdpos contains the zero-based offset of the first matching or nonmatching character. Otherwise, sy-fdpos contains the length of *v1*. The value assigned to sy-fdpos by each operator is described in Table 10.6.

After a comparison, sy-fdpos will contain either a 1st character offset or the length of v1. In this table, "1st char(v1)" means "the offset of the first character of (the string or pattern) v1 that is." So, for example, where you see "1st char(v1) in v2," read that as "the zero-based offset of the first character of v1 that is also in v2." Length(v1) means "the length of v1." Note that only the first column contains ABAP/4 statements.

TABLE 10.6   VALUE ASSIGNED TO `sy-fdpos` BY EACH OPERATOR

Comparison	if TRUE sy-fdpos =	if FALSE sy-fdpos =
v1 CO *v2*	length (*v1*)	1stchar (*v1*) not in *v2*
v1 CN *v2*	1stchar (*v1*) in *v2*	length (*v1*)
v1 CA *v2*	1stchar (*v1*) in *v2*	length (*v1*)
v1 NA *v2*	length (*v1*)	1stchar (*v1*) in *v2*
v1 CS *v2*	1stchar (*v2*) in *v1*	length (*v1*)
v1 NS *v2*	length (*v1*)	1stchar (*v1*) in *v2*
v1 CP *v2*	1stchar (*v2*) in *v1*	length (*v1*)

Listing 10.4 is similar to Listing 10.3, but lines have been added to display the value of `sy-fdpos` after each comparison.

INPUT

LISTING 10.4   USING `sy-fdpos` TO SEE THE OFFSET OF THE FIRST MATCHING OR NON-MATCHING CHARACTER

```
 1   report ztx1004.
 2   * operator: co
 3   write / '''AABB'' co ''AB'''.
 4   if 'AABB' co 'AB'.          write 'True'. else. write 'False'. endif.
 5                               write: 'sy-fdpos=', sy-fdpos.
 6   write / '''ABCD'' co ''ABC'''.
 7   if 'ABCD' co 'ABC'.         write 'True'. else. write 'False'. endif.
 8                               write: 'sy-fdpos=', sy-fdpos.
 9
10   * operator: cn
11   write / '''AABB'' cn ''AB'''.
12   if 'AABB' cn 'AB'.          write 'True'. else. write 'False'. endif.
13                               write: 'sy-fdpos=', sy-fdpos.
14   write / '''ABCD'' cn ''ABC'''.
15   if 'ABCD' cn 'ABC'.         write 'True'. else. write 'False'. endif.
16                               write: 'sy-fdpos=', sy-fdpos.
17
18   * operator: ca
19   write / '''AXCZ'' ca ''AB'''.
20   if 'AXCZ' ca 'AB'.          write 'True'. else. write 'False'. endif.
21                               write: 'sy-fdpos=', sy-fdpos.
22
23   write / '''ABCD'' ca ''XYZ'''.
24   if 'ABCD' ca 'XYZ'.         write 'True'. else. write 'False'. endif.
25                               write: 'sy-fdpos=', sy-fdpos.
26
27
28   * operator: na
```

```
29 write / '''AXCZ'' na ''ABC'''.
30 if 'AXCZ' na 'ABC'.              write 'True'. else. write 'False'. endif.
31                                  write: 'sy-fdpos=', sy-fdpos.
32
33 write / '''ABCD'' na ''XYZ'''.
34 if 'ABCD' na 'XYZ'.              write 'True'. else. write 'False'. endif.
35                                  write: 'sy-fdpos=', sy-fdpos.
```

The code in Listing 10.4 produces this output:

OUTPUT

```
'AABB' co 'AB'  True sy-fdpos=      4
'ABCD' co 'ABC' False sy-fdpos=     3
'AABB' cn 'AB'  False sy-fdpos=     4
'ABCD' cn 'ABC' True sy-fdpos=      3
'AXCZ' ca 'AB'  True sy-fdpos=      0
'ABCD' ca 'XYZ' False sy-fdpos=     4
'AXCZ' na 'ABC' False sy-fdpos=     0
'ABCD' na 'XYZ' True sy-fdpos=      4
```

ANALYSIS

- Line 4, a co comparison, is true. Therefore, sy-fdpos contains 4, the length of the first operand.

- Line 7, also a co, is false because *v1* contains values not in *v2*. Sy-fdpos contains 3, the zero-based offset of the first character in *v1* that is not in *v2*.

- Although lines 12 and 15 are the logical opposites of lines 4 and 7, the values of sy-fdpos do not change.

- Line 20, a ca comparison, is true because *v1* contains a character from *v2*. Sy-fdpos contains 0: the zero-based offset of the first character in *v1* that is also in *v2*.

- On line 24, *v1* does not contain any of the characters in *v2*, therefore sy-fdpos contains 4: the length of *v1*.

- Line 30 is the logical negation of a ca test. 'AXCZ' does contain a value from 'ABC' and so a ca test would be true. Negating this result gives false. Sy-fdpos is set to the zero-based offset of the first character in 'AXCZ' that is also in 'ABC'.

- Line 34 is, again, a logical negation of a ca test. 'ABCD' does not contain a value from 'XYZ' and so a ca test would be false. Negating this result yields true. Sy-fdpos is set to the length of 'ABCD'.

Using the case Statement

The case statement performs a series of comparisons.

Syntax for the case Statement

The following is the syntax for the case statement.

```
case v1.
    when v2 [ or vn ... ].
        ---
    when v3 [ or vn ... ].
        ---
    [ when others.
        --- ]
    endcase.
```

where:

▲

- v1 or v2 can be a variable, literal, constant, or field string.
- --- represents any number of lines of code. Even zero lines are allowed.

The following points apply:

- Only statements following the first matching when are executed.
- when others matches if none of the preceding whens match.
- If when others is not coded and none of the whens match, processing continues with the first statement following endcase.
- Expressions are not allowed.
- Field strings are treated as type c variables.

Case is very similar to if/elseif. The only difference is that on each if/elseif, you can specify a complex expression. With case, you can specify only a single value to be compared, and values are always compared for equality. An example is given in Listing 10.5.

INPUT **LISTING 10.5** THE case STATEMENT PERFORMS A SERIES OF COMPARISONS

```
1  report ztx1005.
2  parameters f1 type i default 2.
3
4  case f1.
5      when 1.        write / 'f1 = 1'.
6      when 2.        write / 'f1 = 2'.
7      when 3.        write / 'f1 = 3'.
8      when others.   write / 'f1 is not 1, 2, or 3'.
9      endcase.
10
11 * The following code is equivalent to the above case statement
12 if         f1 = 1.  write / 'f1 = 1'.
13     elseif f1 = 2.  write / 'f1 = 2'.
14     elseif f1 = 3.  write / 'f1 = 3'.
15     else.           write / 'f1 is not 1, 2, or 3'.
16     endif.
```

The code in Listing 10.5 produces this output:

OUTPUT
```
f1 = 2
f1 = 2
```

ANALYSIS
- Line 2 defines f1 as a single character parameter having a default value 2.
- On line 4, the case statement begins and f1 is compared with 1, 2, and 3, in sequence.
- Line 6 matches and executes the write statement that immediately follows it. The remaining when statements are ignored.
- The next line executed is line 12.

Using the exit Statement

The exit statement prevents further processing from occurring.

SYNTAX

Syntax for the exit Statement

```
exit.
```

Listing 10.6 shows a sample program using exit.

INPUT   LISTING 10.6   USING exit TO STOP PROGRAM PROCESSING DEAD IN ITS TRACKS

```
1   report ztx1006.
2   write: / 'Hi'.
3   exit.
4   write: / 'There'.
```

The code in Listing 10.6 produces this output:

OUTPUT   Hi

ANALYSIS   Exit prevents further processing, so the exit on line 3 prevents line 4 from being executed.

exit can be used in many situations. It can have varying effects depending on where it appears in the code. However, it always prevents further processing. Within loop structures, it leaves loop processing introduced by statements such as loop, select, do, and while. Within subroutines, it leaves subroutines introduced by FORM. Its effects in other situations will be fully explored as they arise.

10

Using the do Statement

The do statement is a basic loop mechanism.

Syntax for the do Statement

▼ SYNTAX

The following is the syntax for the do statement.

```
do [ v1 times ] [ varying f1 from s-c1 next s-c2 [ varying f2 from s2-c1
next s2-c2 ... ] ].
    ---
    [exit.]
    ---
    enddo.
```

where:

- *v1* is a variable, literal, or constant.
- *s* is a field string having the components *c1* and *c2*.
- *f1* is a variable. The components of *s* must be able to be converted to the data type and length of *f1*.
- ... represents any number of complete varying clauses.
- --- represents any number of lines of code.

▲

The following points apply:

- do loops can be nested an unlimited number of times.
- exit prevents further *loop* processing and exits immediately out of the current loop. It does not terminate the program when inside of a do loop. Processing continues at the next executable statement after the enddo.
- You can create an infinite loop by coding do without any additions. In that situation, use exit within the loop to terminate loop processing.
- Modifying the value of *v1* within the loop does not affect loop processing.

Within the loop, sy-index contains the current iteration number. For example, the first time through the loop, sy-index will be 1. The second time through, sy-index will be 2, and so on. After enddo, sy-index contains the value it had before entering the loop. With nested do loops, sy-index contains the iteration number of the loop in which it is used (see Listing 10.7).

INPUT   **LISTING 10.7**   Sy-index CONTAINS THE CURRENT ITERATION NUMBER

```
1  report ztx1007.
2  sy-index = 99.
3  write: / 'before  loop, sy-index =', sy-index, / ''.
4  do 5 times.
5      write sy-index.
6      enddo.
7  write: / 'after   loop, sy-index =', sy-index, / ''.
8
9  do 4 times.
10     write: / 'outer   loop, sy-index =', sy-index.
11     do 3 times.
12         write: / '  inner loop, sy-index =', sy-index.
13         enddo.
14     enddo.
15
16 write: / ''.                   "new line
17 do 10 times.
18     write sy-index.
19     if sy-index = 3.
20         exit.
21         endif.
22     enddo.
```

The code in Listing 10.7 produces this output:

```
OUTPUT    before  loop, sy-index =       99
                  1           2           3           4           5
          after   loop, sy-index =       99
          outer   loop, sy-index =        1
            inner loop, sy-index =        1
            inner loop, sy-index =        2
            inner loop, sy-index =        3
          outer   loop, sy-index =        2
            inner loop, sy-index =        1
            inner loop, sy-index =        2
            inner loop, sy-index =        3
          outer   loop, sy-index =        3
            inner loop, sy-index =        1
            inner loop, sy-index =        2
            inner loop, sy-index =        3
          outer   loop, sy-index =        4
            inner loop, sy-index =        1
            inner loop, sy-index =        2
            inner loop, sy-index =        3
                  1           2           3
```

10

> **Tip**
>
> On rare occasions the need arises to "kill time" in a program. You should not use an empty loop to accomplish this; you will burn up CPU needlessly if you do. Instead, you should call the function module `rzl_sleep`.

Changes made to the value of sy-index do not affect loop control. For example, if you code do 10 times and during the very first loop pass set the value of sy-index to 11, it will maintain that value until the enddo statement is executed. At that point, the value will be reset to 1, then incremented to 2, and the loop will continue processing as if you had not changed it at all.

Terminating an Endless Loop

There will be occasions when a program you run will loop endlessly. Listing 10.8 shows such a program.

INPUT

LISTING 10.8 AN ENDLESS LOOP CAN BE FRUSTRATING IF YOU DON'T KNOW HOW TO BREAK OUT

```
1   report ztx1008.
2   do.
3       write sy-index.
4       if sy-index = 0.
5           exit.
6           endif.
7       enddo.
```

If you run this program, it will loop infinitely and that session will be clocked. Ending the SAPGUI task or even rebooting will not interrupt the program because it runs in a work process on the application server, not on your PC. If you reboot and then log on again, you will find that (if you were in the editor when you rebooted) you will not be able to even edit that program. Your logon session is still "out there" on the application server and it will still have the lock on your source code. After about five or ten minutes, your logon session will time out, and you will be able to edit your source code once again. However, the program could still be running in the work process, which slows the system down. Eventually, your program will consume the maximum amount of CPU allowed in your configuration and the work process will restart itself.

To terminate an endless loop, you must have at least two sessions open created via the menu path System->Create Session. You must start them *before* running your program. If you are in an infinite loop and do not have another session running, it is too late. Sessions created by logging on again will not work.

SCREENCAM Start the ScreenCam "How to Terminate an Endless Loop" now.

To terminate an endless loop:

1. When you first log on, chose the menu path System->Create Session.
2. Minimize your new session and leave it in the background until you need it. You can now test programs with impunity.
3. Now run a program that contains an endless loop, such as ztx1008. You see an hourglass when your pointer is over the window. Notice your session number in the status bar at the bottom of the window.
4. Hold down the Alt key and press Tab successive times until the focus rests on the R3 icon representing your other session.
5. Let go of the Alt key.
6. Type **/o** in the Command field on the Standard toolbar.
7. Press the Enter key. The Overview Of Sessions dialog box appears. It contains a list of your sessions. To the left of each is the associated session number.
8. Find the session numer of the looping session, and click once on that line.
9. Press the Debugging button.
10. Switch back to the looping session using Alt+Tab. That session will now be stopped in the debugger. You can debug from here, or press the Exit button on the Application toolbar to end the program.

If the debugger did not show up and the session is still looping, you can end the entire session by repeating the procedure from step 6. Then, in step 9, instead of pressing the Debugging button, press the End Session button. This terminates the program *and* the session containing it. You will need to open another session to replace the one you terminated.

Using the `varying` Addition

Use the addition `varying` to obtain components of a field string in sequence. `next` establishes a distance (in bytes) between two components per iteration. The receiving component establishes the number of bytes to read from each component. This is best explained by example, as shown in Listing 10.9.

LISTING 10.9   THE ADDITION varying RETURNS THE COMPONENTS OF A FIELD
INPUT   STRING IN SEQUENCE

```
1   report ztx1009.
2   data: f1,
3         begin of s,
4             c1 value 'A',
5             c2 value 'B',
6             c3 value 'C',
7             c4 value 'D',
8             c5 value 'E',
9             c6 value 'F',
10            end of s.
11
12  write / ''.
13  do 6 times varying f1 from s-c1 next s-c2.
14      write f1.
15      enddo.
16
17  write / ''.
18  do 3 times varying f1 from s-c1 next s-c3.
19      write f1.
20      enddo.
```

The code in Listing 10.9 produces this output:

OUTPUT
```
A B C D E F
A C E
```

ANALYSIS   On line 13, next establishes a distance per iteration equal to the distance between c1 and c2. The length of f1 determines the number of bytes to read from each component. Do then begins at s-c1, and assigns its value to f1. On successive loop passes, the previously established distance is added to the address of the current component, causing successive values to be assigned from s to f1.

All components of s accessed by the do loop must be separated by exactly the same number of bytes. Data conversion is not performed on assignment to f1.

Caution   It is possible to read past the end of the structure, but doing so can result in unpredictable behavior and even in program termination. You must either specify the addition times to limit the number of loop passes or use an exit statement to leave the loop before reading past the end of the field string.

Some tables in R/3 are not completely normalized. Instead of having multiple records, a single record might contain a series of fields repeated in succession. You can use varying to retrieve these values in sequence.

For example, table lfc1 contains Vendor Master transaction figures. Fields umNNs, umNNh, and umNNu contain the total debit and credit postings for a month and the sales in the posting period. This group of fields is repeated 16 times for each record in this table (NN is a sequential number from 01 to 16). Table knc1 contains a similar sequence of fields. In another example, table mvke contains, within include envke, 10 fields for product attributes: prat1 through prata. They are side by side, making them an equal distance apart, and thus able to be accessed with varying.

A more complex example of the use of varying is shown in Listing 10.10.

10

INPUT

LISTING 10.10 THE ADDITION varying CAN APPEAR MORE THAN ONCE ON THE do STATEMENT

```
1  report ztx1010.
2  data: f1    type i,
3        f2    type i,
4        tot1  type i,
5        tot2  type i,
6        begin of s,
7            c1 type i value 1,
8            c2 type i value 2,
9            c3 type i value 3,
10           c4 type i value 4,
11           c5 type i value 5,
12           c6 type i value 6,
13           end of s.
14
15 do 3 times varying f1 from s-c1 next s-c3
16            varying f2 from s-c2 next s-c4.
17    write: / f1, f2.
18    add: f1 TO tot1,
19         f2 to tot2.
20    enddo.
21 write: / '---------- -----------',
22        / tot1, tot2.
```

The code in Listing 10.10 produces this output:

OUTPUT

```
           1              2
           3              4
           5              6
---------- -----------
           9             12
```

ANALYSIS F1 is assigned every other component from s beginning with s-c1, and f2 is assigned every other component beginning with s-c2.

Modifying Values within do ... varying/enddo

You can modify the value of either *f1* or *s* within the do ... varying/enddo loop. When the enddo statement is executed, *the current value of f1 value is copied back to the component it came from, whether it was modified or not.* In Listing 10.11, report ztx1011 illustrates this functionality.

INPUT **LISTING 10.11** THE CURRENT VALUE OF f1 IS WRITTEN BACK TO THE SENDING COMPONENT WHEN enddo IS EXECUTED

```
1   report ztx1011.
2   data: f1 type i,
3         begin of s,
4             c1 type i value 1,
5             c2 type i value 2,
6             c3 type i value 3,
7             c4 type i value 4,
8             c5 type i value 5,
9             c6 type i value 6,
10            end of s.
11  field-symbols <f>.
12
13  write / ''.
14  do 6 times varying f1 from s-c1 next s-c2.
15      if sy-index = 6.
16          s-c6 = 99.
17      else.
18          f1 = f1 * 2.
19          endif.
20      assign component sy-index of structure s to <f>. "<f> now points to
21      write <f>.                                       "a component of s
22      enddo.
23
24  write / ''.
25  do 6 times varying f1 from s-c1 next s-c2.
26      write f1.
27      enddo.
```

The code in Listing 10.11 produces this output:

OUTPUT

1	2	3	4	5	99
2	4	6	8	10	6

ANALYSIS • On line 14, values are read from the components of field string s into f1 one at a time.

- Line 18 modifies the value of each f1, multiplying it by 2. The last value of f1 is not modified. Instead, the sending component is assigned the value 99.
- Line 20 assigns a component of s to field-symbol <f>. The first time through the loop, component 1 (c1) is assigned to <f>. The second time through, component 2 (c2) is assigned, and so on. Line 21 writes out the contents of the component that sent its value to f1. In the output listing, you can see the contents of each component of s before enddo is executed.
- When the enddo statement is executed on line 22, the contents of f1 replace the contents of the sending component.
- Varying through the loop again (lines 25 through 27) displays the new contents of s. This shows that the value of f1 within the loop always overwrites the contents of the sending component.

An exit statement within the loop will *not* prevent the modified contents of f1 from being written back to the sending field. The only way to leave the loop without the contents of f1 overwriting the sending field is by executing a stop statement or an error message statement within the loop (both covered in later chapters).

Using the while Statement

The while statement is a looping mechanism similar to do.

Syntax for the while Statement

▼ SYNTAX

The following is the syntax for the while statement.

```
while exp [ vary f1 from s-c1 next s-c2 [ vary f2 from s2-c1 next s2-c2 ... ]
    ---
    [ exit. ]
    ---
    endwhile.
```

where:

- exp is a logical expression.
- s is a field string having the components c1 and c2.
- f1 is a variable. The components of s must be able to be converted to the data type and length of f1.
- ... represents any number of complete vary clauses.
- --- represents any number of lines of code.

The following points apply:

- `while` loops can be nested an infinite number of times and also be nested within any other type of loop.

- `exit` prevents further loop processing and exits immediately out of the current loop. Processing continues at the next executable statement after `endwhile`.

- Within the loop, `sy-index` contains the current iteration number. After `endwhile`, `sy-index` contains the value it had before entering the loop. With nested `while` loops, `sy-index` contains the iteration number of the loop in which it is used.

- `endwhile` always copies the value of `f1` back into the sending component.

- On a `while` statement containing a logical expression and a `varying` addition, the logical expression is evaluated first.

`while` is very similar to `do`. Here, it is used to place an equal number of dashes on either side of a string.

INPUT   **LISTING 10.12**   AN EXAMPLE OF THE USE OF THE `while` STATEMENT

```
1  report ztx1012.
2  data: l,                      "leading  characters
3        t,                      "trailing characters
4        done.                   "done flag
5  parameters p(25) default '    Vendor Number'.
6  while done = ' '              "the expression is evaluated first
7      vary l from p+0  next p+1  "then vary assignments are performed
8      vary t from p+24 next p+23.
9      if l = ' ' and t = ' '.
10         l = t = '-'.
11     else.
12         done = 'X'.
13         endif.
14     endwhile.
15 write: / p.
```

The code in Listing 10.12 produces this output:

OUTPUT   `----Vendor Number     ----`

ANALYSIS
- Lines 2 and 3 define two single character variables `l` and `t`. Line 3 defines a flag to indicate when processing is complete.

- Line 5 defines `p` as character `25` with a default value.

- On line 6, the expression on the while statement is first evaluated. It proves true the first time through the loop. The assignments on lines 7 and 8 are then performed. Line 7 assigns the first character from p to l and line 8 assigns the last character to t.

- If l and t are both blank, line 10 assigns a dash to both. If they are not, line 12 assigns an 'X' to the done flag.

- On line 14, endwhile copies the values from l and t back to p.

- The while loop repeats again from line 6 as long as the done flag is blank.

Using the `continue` statement

The continue statement is coded within a loop. It acts like a goto, passing control immediately to the terminating statement of the loop and beginning a new loop pass. In effect, it causes the statements below it within the loop to be ignored and a new loop pass to begin. The effect of the continue statement is shown in Figure 10.1.

FIGURE 10.1.

The continue *statement jumps to the end of the loop, ignoring all statements after it for the current loop pass.*

```
do 10 times.
    if sy-index between 3 and 8.
      continue.
     endif.
    write sy-index.
    enddo.
```

The code in Figure 10.1 produces this output:

OUTPUT   1 2 9 10

Syntax for the `continue` Statement

The following is the syntax for the continue statement. It can be used within a do, while, select, or loop. (The loop statement is covered in the next chapter.)

```
[do/while/select/loop]
    ---
    continue.
    ---
    [enddo/endwhile/endselect/endloop]
```

where:

- --- represents any number of lines of code.

The following points apply:

- continue can only be coded within a loop.

- continue has no additions.

Listing 10.13 is like a goto statement. It causes a jump to the end of the current loop. This program removes duplicate colon and backslash characters from an input string.

INPUT **LISTING 10.13** AN EXAMPLE OF THE USE OF THE continue STATEMENT

```
 1   report ztx1013.
 2   parameters p(20) default 'c::\\\xxx\\yyy'.
 3   data: c,                  "current character
 4         n.                  "next    character
 5
 6   do 19 times varying c from p+0 next p+1
 7                varying n from p+1 next p+2.
 8     if c na ':\'.
 9         continue.
10         endif.
11     if c = n.
12         write: / 'duplicate', c, 'found', 'at position', sy-index.
13         endif.
14     enddo.
```

The code in Listing 10.13 produces this output:

OUTPUT
```
duplicate : found at position        2
duplicate \ found at position        4
duplicate \ found at position        5
duplicate \ found at position       10
```

ANALYSIS

- Line 2 defines a character length 20 input parameter p and assigns it a default value.

- Line 6 starts a loop. At the first loop pass, the first character of p is assigned to c and the character following it is assigned to n.

- Line 8 is true when c contains a character other than : or /.

- Line 9 jumps directly to line 14, causing the loop to repeat using the next character.

- If line 8 is not true, line 11 is executed and is true if the next character is the same as the current character.

- The enddo copies the values from c and n back into p and the loop repeats 19 times altogether.

Using the check statement

The check statement is coded within a loop. It can act very much like continue, passing control immediately to the terminating statement of the loop and bypassing the statements between. Unlike continue, it accepts a logical expression. If the expression is true, it does nothing. If it is false, it jumps to the end of the loop. The effect of the check statement is shown in Figure 10.2.

FIGURE 10.2.

The check *statement is a conditional* continue *statement. It jumps to the end of the loop if the logical expression is false.*

```
do 10 times.
    check not sy-index between 3 and 8.
    write sy-index.
enddo.
```

The code in Figure 10.2 produces the same output as that in Figure 10.1:

OUTPUT   1 2 9 10

Syntax for the check Statement

▼ **SYNTAX**

The following is the syntax for the check statement. It can be used within a do, while, select, or loop. (The loop statement is covered in the next chapter.)

```
[do/while/select/loop]
    ---
    check exp.
    ---
    [enddo/endwhile/endselect/endloop]
```

where:

- *exp* is a logical expression.

▲   - --- represents any number of lines of code.

In listing 10.14, check behaves like a continue statement when the logical expression is false. When it is true, it does nothing.

LISTING 10.14   LISTING 10.3 WAS RE-CODED TO USE THE check STATEMENT

INPUT   INSTEAD OF continue

```
1  report ztx1014.
2  parameters p(20) default 'c::\\\xxx\\yyy'.
3  data: c,                    "current character
```

continues

LISTING 10.14 CONTINUED

```
4      n.                     "next    character
5
6  do 19 times varying c from p+0 next p+1
7             varying n from p+1 next p+2.
8    check c ca ':\'.
9    if c = n.
10      write: / 'duplicate', c, 'found', 'at position', sy-index.
11      endif.
12    enddo.
```

The code in Listing 10.14 produces this output:

OUTPUT

```
duplicate : found at position      2
duplicate \ found at position      4
duplicate \ found at position      5
duplicate \ found at position     10
```

ANALYSIS Lines 8 through 10 in Listing 10.13 were replaced by line 8 in Listing 10.14. The program works in exactly the same way.

Tip   Using check or continue within a select loop can be very inefficient. You should, whenever possible, modify the where clause to select fewer records instead.

Comparing the exit, continue, and check Statements

In Table 10.7, the exit, continue, and check statements are compared.

TABLE 10.7 COMPARING exit, continue, AND check

Statement	Effect
exit	Leaves the current loop.
continue	Unconditional jump to the end of the loop.
check exp	Jumps to the end of the loop if exp is false.

Simple Position and Length Specifications for the `write` Statement

The `write` statement permits specification of an output position and length.

Although the `write` statement permits many complex specifications, elementary position and length specifications are presented here to enable you to create basic reports in this and in the following chapter. A detailed treatment of the `write` statement appears later in chapter 14.

Syntax for Simple Position and Length Specifications on the `write` Statement

▼ SYNTAX

The following is the syntax for simple position and length specifications on the `write` statement.

```
write [/][P][(L)] v1.
```

where:

- *v1* is a variable, literal, or constant.
- *P* is a number indicating a position on the current line of output.

▲
- *L* is a number indicating the number of bytes allocated in the list for outputting *v1*.

The following points apply:

- / begins a new line.
- /, *P*, and *L* must be coded without any intervening spaces.

Table 10.8 shows the right and wrong ways to code position and length specifications on the `write` statement.

TABLE 10.8 RIGHT AND WRONG WAYS TO CODE POSITION AND LENGTH SPECIFICATIONS ON THE `write` STATEMENT

Right	Wrong
write /10(2) 'Hi'.	write / 10(2) 'Hi'.
	write / 10 (2) 'Hi'.
	write /10 (2) 'Hi'.
	write /10(2) 'Hi'.
	write /10(2) 'Hi'.

continues

TABLE 10.8 CONTINUED

Right	Wrong
write (2) 'Hi'.	write (2) 'Hi'.
	write 'Hi'(2).
write 10 'Hi'.	write 10'Hi'.
	write 'Hi' 10.

> **Tip**
>
> If you leave a space between a / and the position or length specification, the syntax checker can automatically correct it for you. Simply press the Correct button at the bottom of the message window when it appears.

Listing 10.15 illustrates the use of simple position and length specifications on the write statement. It also shows some of the pitfalls. Line 3 writes out a ruler so that you can see column numbers on the output.

LISTING 10.15 USE OF SIMPLE POSITION AND LENGTH SPECIFICATIONS ON THE
INPUT write STATEMENT

```
1   report ztx1015.
2   data: f1 type p value 123,
3         f2 type p value -123.
4   write: / '....+....1....+....2....+....3....+....4',
5          /1    'Hi', 4       'There',
6          /1    'Hi', 3       'There',
7          /1    'Hi', 2       'There',
8          /1    'Hi', 1       'There',
9          /2    'Hi',         'There',
10         /2(1) 'Hi',         'There',
11         /2(3) 'Hi',         'There',
12         /2    'Hi', 10(3)   'There',
13         /     f1,           f2,
14         /     f1,   4       f2,
15         /(3)  f1,
16         /(2)  f1.
```

The code in Listing 10.15 produces this output:

OUTPUT

```
....+....1....+....2....+....3....+....4
Hi There
HiThere
HThere
There
 Hi There
 H There
 Hi   There
 Hi        The
          123                    123-
               123-
123
*3
```

ANALYSIS

- Line 4 writes out a ruler so that you can clearly see the columns in the output list.

- Line 5 writes Hi beginning at position 1 and There beginning at position 4.

- Line 6 writes Hi beginning at position 1 and There beginning at position 3.

- Line 7 writes Hi beginning at position 1 and There beginning at position 2. There overwrites the last position of Hi.

- Line 8 writes Hi beginning at position 1 and There also beginning at position 1. There completely overwrites Hi, and you cannot tell if Hi was even written to the list.

- Line 9 writes Hi beginning at position 2 and There following it. Write leaves a space between values if you do not specify an output position.

- Line 10 writes Hi beginning at position 2 for a length of 1. This writes out only the first character: H.

- Line 11 writes Hi beginning at position 2 for a length of 3. An intervening space follows, making for two, and then There follows.

- Line 12 writes Hi beginning at position 2 and There at position 10 for a length of 3, causing The to appear in the list.

- Line 13 writes the packed decimal fields f1 and f2, in succession.

- Line 14 also writes f1 and f2. This time, f2 is written beginning at position 4. The leading spaces beginning at position 4 overwrite the value from f1, causing only f2 to appear in the output.

- Line 15 writes f1 and allocates only three bytes in the output list for the value. f1 appears in the list beginning at position 1; it fills the output field entirely.

- Line 16 writes f1 and allocates only 2 bytes in the output list for the value. The value of f1 cannot be displayed in three bytes, so an asterisk (*) appears in the first column to indicate overflow.

10

Summary

- The comparison statements are if and case.
- case provides a capability similar to if/elseif, but compares two values only and only for equality.
- Conversions occur when comparing differing data types. The program analysis tool will pinpoint conversions wherever they occur.
- Special operators are available for string comparisons. Use CP and NP to match strings against patterns. Sy-fdpos is set after each comparison.
- The loop statements are do and while.
- sy-index always contains the counter for the current loop pass. After the loop is finished, its value is reset to the value it had when the loop began. Although you can change sy-index, its value is reset with the next pass of the loop.
- Use varying to assign the next value of a series to a variable. If you modify that variable, enddo or endwhile copies the modified value back to where it came from.
- Use another session and the /o command to terminate an endless loop.
- Use the exit, continue, and check statements to modify loop processing.
- exit terminates loop processing and continues execution at the first statement following the loop.
- continue jumps to the end of the loop immediately.
- check exp jumps to the end of the loop if exp is false. When exp is true, check does nothing.
- On the write statement, position and length can be specified immediately before the output value. No intervening spaces should appear between each specification.

Do	Don't
DO open two sessions whenever you log on so that you can terminate an infinite loop.	**DON'T** use check or continue within a select loop to filter out records. Instead, use the where clause to filter them out.
DO use varying to read a series of equidistant fields from a field string.	**DON'T** read past the end of a variable or field string with the varying addition. Protection exceptions and unpredictable behavior can result.

Q&A

Q **Why aren't bit operations used much in ABAP/4? What does it use instead?**

A The use of a bit operation creates an operating system dependency. This reduces portability, so they are not used unless necessary. Instead, a single character variable is used to hold a single on/off value. Most commonly, "X" represents an "on" value and space represents an "off" value.

Q **Why do they use X and space to represent the binary values of on and off? I should think they would use 1/0, T/F, or Y/N, as is common in the industry.**

A This convention is for compatibility with character-based user interfaces. Written out, the X value indicates a present selection, and space indicates not present.

Q **You recommend opening multiple sessions whenever I log on. Isn't this a waste of resources? If everyone did that, wouldn't it slow the application server down?**

A The most precious resource is CPU. It is true that a small amount of additional memory is required on the application server to accommodate each new session. However, no CPU is used by the idle session, so it does not slow the server down. If you write a program that begins looping, it will waste a tremendous amount of resources, primarily CPU, and will without a doubt degrade the server while it is running. If you are unable to stop it, you will be unable to mitigate the waste of resources. Unchecked, the program will run, possibly for five or ten minutes, until it exceeds its allotment of CPU and then it will be terminated. The next time you run it, it might do the same again. In short, opening another session is choosing the lesser of two evils.

Q **How do padding bytes affect the use of `varying`? Do I have to watch out for anything as I do when moving from and to field strings?**

A The easiest way to ensure that `varying` will work is to make sure the exact sequence of fields repeats. If the same sequence of fields is repeated, the same number of bytes will always separate them. As long as you follow this rule, there is no need to think about padding bytes.

Q **Can I use a variable to indicate position and/or length on a `write` statement?**

A Yes. The `write` statement is presented in detail in chapter 14 and variable specifications are covered there.

Workshop

The Workshop provides two ways for you to affirm what you've learned in this chapter. The Quiz section poses questions to help you solidify your understanding of the material covered and the Exercise section provides you with experience in using what you have learned. You can find answers to the quiz questions and exercises in Appendix B, "Answers to Quiz Questions and Exercises."

Quiz

1. In the following section of code, change the `if` statements into a `case` statement.

```
if v1 eq 5.
write 'The number is five.'.
endif.
if v1 eq 10.
write 'The number is ten.'.
endif.
if v1 <> 5 and v1 <> 10.
write 'The number is not five or ten.'.
endif.
```

2. Which string comparison operators use the three characters *, +, and #?

3. What are the three program control statements discussed in this chapter? What are the differences between them?

Exercise 1

Write a program that produces the output in the Figure.

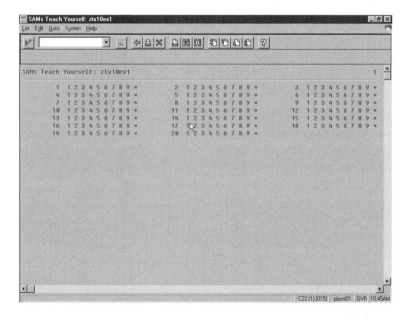

Do not hardcode as strings. Instead, compute the numbers and either write them out a single byte at a time or use the syst table.

DAY 11

Internal Tables

Chapter Objectives

After you complete this chapter, you should be able to:

- Define an internal table with or without a header line using the `data` and `include structure` statements.
- Fill an internal table by using `append` via a header line or an explicit work area.
- Use `loop at` and `loop at...where` to read the contents of an internal table, and use `sy-tabix` to determine the current row index.
- Locate a single row in an internal table by using `read table` and its variations.
- Sort internal tables and use the `as text` addition.

Internal Table Basics

NEW TERM   An *internal table* is a temporary table stored in RAM on the application server. It is created and filled by a program during execution and is discarded when the program ends. Like a database table, an internal table consists of one or more rows with an identical structure, but unlike a database table, it cannot hold data after the program ends. Use it as temporary storage for manipulating data or as a temporary private buffer.

Definition of an Internal Table

An internal table consists of a body and an optional header line (see Figure 11.1).

 The *body* holds the rows of the internal table. All rows within it have the same structure. The term "internal table" itself usually refers to the body of the internal table.

 The *header line* is a field string with the same structure as a row of the body, but it can only hold a single row. It is a buffer used to hold each record before it is added or each record as it is retrieved from the internal table.

Figure 11.1 shows the definition of an internal table named it.

> **Note**
>
> In this book, a naming convention is used for internal tables. For simple programs with only a single internal table, the internal table name will usually be it (for internal table). If multiple internal tables exist, the name of each will usually begin with it.

FIGURE 11.1.

The definition of an internal table named it *is shown at the top of this figure. The header line and body are also shown.*

```
data: begin of it occurs 3,
        f1(1),
        f2(2),
      end of it.
```

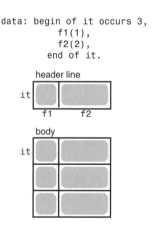

To define an internal table body, use occurs *n* on the definition of any field string except tables. occurs creates the body of the internal table. The memory for the body is not allocated until the first row is added to it. Without occurs, you only have a field string.

To define an internal table with a header line, you must include either begin of or with header line in the definition. A header line is automatically created if begin of appears in the definition. If you use `like` instead of `begin of`, the internal table will not have a header line unless you add `with header line` after the `occurs` clause. This is illustrated in lines 2 through 10 of Listing 11.1.

The only time you would create an internal table without a header line is in the case of a nested internal table. A nested internal table cannot have a header line.

INPUT

LISTING 11.1   BASIC WAYS OF DEFINING INTERNAL TABLES WITH AND WITHOUT A HEADER LINE

```
 1 report ztx1101.
 2 data: begin of it1 occurs 10,         "has a header line
 3           f1,
 4           f2,
 5           f3,
 6           end of it1.
 7
 8 data it2 like ztxlfa1 occurs 100.      "doesn't have a header line
 9
10 data it3 like ztxlfa1 occurs 100 with header line. "it does now
```

The code in Listing 11.1 does not produce any output.

ANALYSIS

- Line 2 begins the definition of an internal table named `it1`. It is an internal table because of the presence of the `occurs` clause. It has three components: `f1`, `f2`, and `f3`. Each is type c, length 1. This internal table has a header line because the definition contains the words `begin of`.

- Line 8 defines internal table `it2`. It has the same components as the DDIC structure `ztxlfa1`. It does not have a header because neither `begin of` nor `with header line` appear in the definition.

- The definition of `it3` on line 10 is almost the same as the one for `it2` on line 8. The only difference is the addition `with header line`. This, of course, causes `it3` to have a header line.

Clearing Up the Main Source of Confusion Surrounding Internal Tables

Figure 11.1 contains a typical internal table definition. It defines *two* things: the body of an internal table and a header line. Confusion arises because both the body and the header line are named `it`. `it` is the name of the body, and `it` is also the name of the header line. Where you place the name `it` in your code determines to what you are referring.

When used in an assignment statement, `it` always refers to the header line. For example, `it-f1 = 'A'` refers to component `f1` of the header line named `it`. Or in `f3 = it-f1`, the header line `it` is also referred to.

11

Examples of Internal Table Definitions

To define internal tables with and without header lines, use the forms recommended in Listing 11.2.

INPUT **LISTING 11.2** THESE DEFINITIONS CREATE INTERNAL TABLES WITH AND WITHOUT A HEADER LINE

```
 1 report ztx1102.
 2 data: begin of it1 occurs 10,        "has a header line
 3         f1,
 4         f2,
 5         f3,
 6         end of it1.
 7
 8 data it2 like ztxlfa1 occurs 100.       "doesn't have a header line
 9
10 data it3 like ztxlfa1 occurs 100 with header line. "it does now
11
12 data it4 like it3 occurs 100.        "doesn't have a header line
13
14 data     begin of it5 occurs 100.      "has a header line
15 include      structure ztxlfa1.
16 data         end of it5.
17
18 data     begin of it6 occurs 100.      "this is why you might use
19 include      structure ztxlfa1.      "the include statement
20 data:        delflag,
21              rowtotal,
22              end of it6.
23
24 data: begin of it7 occurs 100,       "don't do it this way
25         s like ztxlfa1,             "component names will be
26         end of it7.                 "prefixed with it7-s-
27
28 data it8 like sy-index occurs 10
29    with header line.
30
31 data: begin of it9 occurs 10,
32         f1 like sy-index,
33         end of it9.
```

The code in Listing 11.2 does not produce any output.

ANALYSIS • Lines 2 through 10 are the same as those in Listing 11.1; they are included here for your review.

- On line 12, `it4` is defined like the field string named `it3`, *not* like the internal table `it3`. Thus, an `occurs` addition is required to make it an internal table; this one does not have a header line because there is no `begin of` or `with header line`.

- Lines 14 through 16 show the old way of defining an internal table. `It5` is the same as `it3` defined on line 10. The `like` addition was only introduced in release 3.0; prior programs use definitions like this one. `Include structure` is not used now except for cases such as the following definition of `it6`. (At this time, you might want to review the `include structure` statement covered on Day 5, "The Data Dictionary, Part 3.")

- This is the only practical reason you would use the `include` statement now (after release 3). It enables you to create a field string having all components from a DDIC structure plus some additional ones. The definition of `it6` contains the components of `ztxlfa1` and two additional fields `delflag` and `row-total`. This internal table has a header line because you see `begin of` in the definition.

- Lines 24 through 26 show the wrong way to use `like`. The components of this internal table all begin with `it7-s`, for example, `it7-s-lifnr` and `it7-s-land1`. Although it is workable, it is probably not what was intended, and introduces an unnecessary level into the component names.

- When defining an internal table that has a single component, you can use either the declaration on line 28 or on line 31.

Adding Data to an Internal Table Using the append Statement

To add a single row to a internal table, you can use the `append` statement. `append` copies a single row from any work area and places it in the body at the end of the existing rows. The work area can be the header line, or it can be any other field string having the same structure as a row in the body.

Syntax for the append Statement

▼ SYNTAX
▲

The following is the syntax for the `append` statement.

```
append [wa to] [initial line to] it.
```

where:

- *wa* is the name of a work area.

- *it* is the name of a previously defined internal table.

The following points apply:

- *wa* must have the same structure as a row of the body.
- *wa* can be the header line or it can be any field string having the same structure as a row in the body.
- If you do not specify a work area, by default the system uses the header line. In effect, the header line is the default work area.
- After append, sy-tabix is set to the relative row number of the row just appended. For example, after appending the first row, sy-tabix will be set to 1. After appending the second row, sy-tabix will be 2, and so on.

The statement append it to it appends the header line named it to the body named it. The statement append it does the same thing, because the default work area is the header line. Being more succinct, the latter is usually used.

NEW TERM A work area mentioned explicitly in the append statement is known as an *explicit work area*. Any field string having the same structure as a row of the internal table can be used as an explicit work area. If a work area is not mentioned, the *implicit work area* (the header line) is used.

The statement append initial line to it appends a row containing initial values (blanks and zeros) to the internal table. It is the same as executing the following two statements in succession: clear it and append it.

Listing 11.3 shows a sample program that appends three rows to an internal table.

LISTING **11.3** THIS PROGRAM ADDS THREE ROWS TO INTERNAL TABLE it FROM
INPUT THE HEADER LINE

```
1 report ztx1103.
2 data: begin of it occurs 3,
3          f1(1),
4          f2(2),
5          end of it.
6 it-f1 = 'A'.
7 it-f2 = 'XX'.
8 append it to it.    "appends header line IT to body IT
9 write: / 'sy-tabix =', sy-tabix.
10 it-f1 = 'B'.
11 it-f2 = 'YY'.
12 append it.          "same as line 8
13 write: / 'sy-tabix =', sy-tabix.
14 it-f1 = 'C'.
15 append it.          "the internal table now contains three rows.
16 write: / 'sy-tabix =', sy-tabix.
```

The code in Listing 11.3 produces this output:

```
sy-tabix =            1
sy-tabix =            2
sy-tabix =            3
```

ANALYSIS

- Line 2 defines an internal table named it and a header line named it. Both have two components: f1 and f2.

- Lines 6 and 7 set the contents of header line fields f1 and f2 (shown in Figure 11.2). Here, it refers to the header line.

FIGURE 11.2.

These are assignment statements, so it refers to the header line.

```
it-f1 = 'A'.
it-f2 = 'XX'.
```

- Line 8 copies the contents of the header line named it to the body named it (shown in Figure 11.3).

FIGURE 11.3.

Append it to it *copies the contents of the header line it to the body it.*

```
append it to it.
```

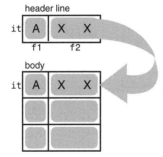

- Lines 10 and 11 assign new contents to the components of the header line, overwriting the existing contents (shown in Figure 11.4).

FIGURE 11.4.

These assignment statements overwrite the existing contents of the header line it.

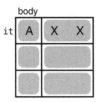

- Line 12 appends the new contents of the header line to the body (see Figure 11.5). This statement is functionally equivalent to the one on line 8. Because a work area is not named, the default work area—the header line—is used.

FIGURE 11.5.

The default work area is the header line. Here, it is implicitly appended to the body.

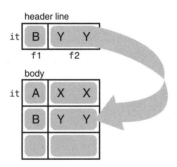

- Line 14 changes the value of it-f1 and leaves the in it-f2 alone (see Figure 11.6).

FIGURE 11.6.

The value of header line component it-f1 is overwritten. The value of it-f2 is left alone.

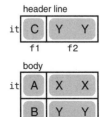

- Line 15 appends a third row from the header line it to the body it (see Figure 11.7).

FIGURE 11.7.

Here, the contents of the implicit work area are appended to the body.

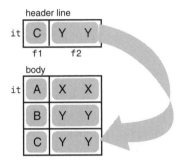

Using the occurs Addition

occurs does not limit the number of rows that can be added to the internal table. For example, if you specify occurs 10, you can put more than 10 rows into the internal table. The number of rows you can put into an internal table is theoretically only limited by the amount of virtual memory available on the application server.

Note

In actuality, your Basis consultant sets a limit on the maximum amount of extended memory an internal table can allocate. If you exceed that amount, your program will allocate private memory from the work process and it will no longer be able to roll your program out. This makes the work process unavailable for use by other programs until your program has completely finished processing. To avoid this problem, you should use an extract instead.

The system uses the occurs clause only as a guideline to determine how much memory to allocate. The first time a row is added to the internal table, enough memory is allocated to hold the number of rows specified on the occurs clause. If you use that memory up, more is allocated as needed.

Alternatively, you can specify occurs 0. If you do this, the system allocates 8KB pages of memory at a time. However, there are no advantages to using occurs 0 other than the fact it is only a little easier to code occurs 0 than it is to estimate the size of the internal table.

For peak performance and minimum wasted memory, choose an occurs value equal to the average maximum number of rows in the table. For example, if most of the time the internal table is filled with a maximum of 100 rows, but every once in a while it is filled with a maximum of 1,000 rows, set the occurs value to 100.

> **Note**
>
> Don't use occurs 0 if you expect to store less than 8KB in an internal table. If you do, the system will allocate 8KB from the paging area. Memory will be wasted and paging could increase, resulting in poorer performance.

Depending on the occurs clause and the size of the internal table, the system will allocate memory from either the program roll area or the system paging area, or both. Memory accesses in the roll area can be slightly faster than accesses in the paging area. Allocations in the paging area are always one page in size (usually 8KB, or 8,192 bytes).

There are two methods that the system uses to perform allocations. In the first, occurs is non-zero, and the size of the internal table (calculated from occurs * number of bytes per row) is less than or equal to 8KB. (The number of bytes per row can be obtained using the describe table statement detailed in the next chapter, or via the Field view in the debugger.) When the first row is added to the internal table, memory is allocated from the program roll area. The amount allocated is equal to the calculated size of the internal table. If this amount is exceeded, an equal amount is allocated and the process is repeated until the total exceeds 8KB. When this happens, subsequent allocations obtain 8KB pages from the paging area.

If you specify occurs 0, all allocations are done in the paging area, causing one 8KB page to be allocated at a time. If the calculated size of the internal table is greater than 8KB, the system changes the occurs value to zero when the first allocation is done and all allocations are satisfied from the paging area. You can see the change to occurs by using the describe table statement after the first allocation and displaying the value of sy-toccu. This statement is described on Day 9, "Assignments, Conversions, and Calculations."

Reading Data from an Internal Table

Two statements are commonly used to read the data from an internal table:

- loop at
- read table

Use `loop at` to read multiple rows from the internal table. Use `read table` to read a single row.

Reading Multiple Rows Using the `loop at` Statement

To read some or all rows from an internal table, you can use the `loop at` statement. `Loop at` reads the contents of the internal table, placing them one at a time into a work area.

Syntax for the `loop at` Statement

The following is the syntax for the `loop at` statement.

```
loop at it [into wa] [from m] [to n] [where exp].
    ---
    endloop.
```

SYNTAX ▼

▲

where:

- *it* is the name of an internal table.

- *wa* is the name of a work area.

- *m* and *n* are integer literals, constants, or variables representing a relative row number. For example, 1 means the first row in the table, 2 means the second, and so on.

- *exp* is a logical expression restricting the rows that are read.

- `---` represents any number of lines of code. These lines are executed once for each row retrieved from the internal table.

The rows are read from the internal table one at a time and placed in succession into the work area. The lines of code between the `loop at` and `endloop` are executed for each row retrieved. The loop finishes automatically when the last row has been read, and the statement following the `endloop` is then executed.

The following points apply:

- *wa* must have the same structure as a row of the body.

- *wa* can be the header line or it can be any field string having the same structure as a row in the body.

- If you do not specify a work area, by default the system uses the header line. For example, `loop at it into it` reads rows from the internal table `it`, placing them one at a time into the header line `it`. An equivalent statement is `loop at it`.

- If `from` is not specified, the default is to begin reading from the first row.

- If `to` is not specified, the default is to read to the last row.

- Components of *it* specified in the logical expression should not be preceded by the internal table name. For example, `where f1 = 'X'` is correct, but `where it-f1 = 'X'` will cause a syntax error.

11

- *exp* can be any logical expression. However, the first operand of each comparison must be a component of the internal table. For example, if *it* contains a component f1, then where f1 = 'X' would be correct; where 'X' = f1 would be incorrect and causes a syntax error.

- The from, to, and where additions can be mixed at will.

Within the loop, sy-tabix contains the relative row number of the current record. For example, while processing the first record in the internal table, the value of sy-tabix will be 1. While processing the second, sy-tabix will be 2. Upon exiting the loop, the value of sy-tabix is reset to the value it had when the loop began. If loops are nested, the value in sy-tabix relates to the current loop.

After endloop, sy-subrc will be zero if any rows were read. It will be non-zero if no rows were read from the internal table.

Listing 11.4 expands on Listing 11.3, looping at and writing out the rows of the internal table.

LISTING 11.4 THIS PROGRAM ADDS 3 ROWS TO INTERNAL TABLE it FROM THE
INPUT HEADER LINE, AND THEN WRITES THEM BACK OUT AGAIN

```
 1 report ztx1104.
 2 data: begin of it occurs 3,
 3            f1(1),
 4            f2(2),
 5           end of it.
 6 it-f1 = 'A'.
 7 it-f2 = 'XX'.
 8 append it to it.     "appends header line IT to body IT
 9 it-f1 = 'B'.
10 it-f2 = 'YY'.
11 append it.          "same as line 8
12 it-f1 = 'C'.
13 append it.          "the internal table now contains three rows.
14 sy-tabix = sy-subrc = 99.
15 loop at it.         "same as: loop at it into it
16     write: / sy-tabix, it-f1, it-f2.
17     endloop.
18 write: / 'done. sy-tabix =', sy-tabix,
19          / '        sy-subrc =', sy-subrc.
```

The code in Listing 11.4 produces this output:

OUTPUT
```
             1  A XX
             2  B YY
             3  C YY
   done. sy-tabix =          99
         sy-subrc =        0
```

11

ANALYSIS

- Lines 2 through 13 are the same as those in Listing 11.3. They add three rows to the internal table.

- Line 14 sets `sy-tabix` and `sy-subrc` to an arbitrary value.

- Line 15 begins a loop that reads the first row from the internal table named `it`, placing it into the header line `it`.

- Line 16 writes out the value of `sy-tabix` and values in the components of the header line.

- Line 17 marks the end of the loop. It returns to line 15.

- Line 15 is re-executed. This time, the second row from the internal table is placed into the header line, overwriting the previous contents.

- Line 16 is executed, again writing out values from the header line.

- On line 17, the loop repeats until all rows have been retrieved from the internal table. When the last row has been read, it stops looping.

- On line 18, `sy-tabix` has been restored to the value it had before the loop was executed. `Sy-subrc` contains zero, indicating that rows were retrieved from the internal table by the `loop at` statement.

Restricting the Rows Read from the Internal Table

Using the `from`, `to`, and `where` additions, you can restrict the number of rows read from the internal table. Listing 11.5 expands on Listing 11.4, looping at the internal table four times. Each time it writes out only certain rows.

LISTING 11.5 THIS PROGRAM IS LIKE LISTING 11.4, BUT ONLY SOME OF THE

INPUT ROWS ARE READ

```
 1 report ztx1105.
 2 data: begin of it occurs 3,
 3          f1(1),
 4          f2(2),
 5          end of it.
 6 it-f1 = 'A'.
 7 it-f2 = 'XX'.
 8 append it.
 9 it-f1 = 'B'.
10 it-f2 = 'YY'.
11 append it.
12 it-f1 = 'C'.
13 append it.                "it now contains three rows
14
15 loop at it where f2 = 'YY'. "f2 is right, it-f2 would be wrong here
16     write: / sy-tabix, it-f1, it-f2.
```

continues

LISTING 11.5 CONTINUED

```
17     endloop.
18 skip.
19
20 loop at it to 2.               "same as: loop at it from 1 to 2.
21     write: / sy-tabix, it-f1, it-f2.
22     endloop.
23 skip.
24
25 loop at it from 2.             "same as: loop at it from 2 to 3.
26     write: / sy-tabix, it-f1, it-f2.
27     endloop.
28 skip.
29
30 loop at it from 2 where f1 = 'C'.
31     write: / sy-tabix, it-f1, it-f2.
32     endloop.
```

The code in Listing 11.5 produces this output:

OUTPUT

```
2  B YY
3  C YY

1  A XX
2  B YY

2  B YY
3  C YY

3  C YY
```

ANALYSIS

- Lines 2 through 13 add three rows to the internal table.

- Lines 15 through 17 read only those rows from the internal table where f2 has a value equal to 'YY'. Only rows 2 and 3 satisfy the criteria.

- Line 18 skips a line in the output, in effect writing a blank line.

- Lines 20 through 22 read only rows 1 and 2 from the internal table.

- Lines 25 through 27 read only rows 2 and 3 from the internal table.

- Line 30 reads beginning from row 2, looking for all rows having an f1 value of 'C'. Row 3 is the only matching row in this range.

If you make sure the data type and length of the field in *exp* matches the internal table field exactly, no conversions will be performed. This causes your loop to run more quickly. If conversion is required, it is performed on every loop pass and this can slow processing down considerably. Use like or constants to avoid conversion.

Although the where returns a subset of the table contents, a full table scan
is always performed.

Using exit, continue, stop, and check

Table 11.1 illustrates the effects of exit, continue, and check when used within a loop
at/endloop construct.

TABLE 11.1 STATEMENTS THAT CAN ALTER LOOP PROCESSING FOR INTERNAL TABLES

Statement	Effect
exit	Terminates the loop immediately. Processing continues at the statement immediately following endloop.
continue	Goes immediately to the endloop statement, bypassing all following statements within the loop. The next row is returned from the internal table and processing continues from the top of the loop. If there are no more rows to retrieve, processing continues at the first statement following endloop.
check exp	If exp is true, processing continues as if this statement had not been executed. If exp is false, its effect is the same as continue.

Reading a Single Row Using the read table Statement

To locate and read a single row from an internal table, use read table. It reads a single
row that matches specific criteria and places it in a work area.

Syntax for the read table Statement

▼ SYNTAX

The following is the syntax for the read table statement.

```
read table it [into wa] [index i ¦ with key keyexp [binary search] ]
[comparing cmpexp] [transporting texp].
```

where:

- *it* is the name of an internal table.
- *wa* is the name of a work area.
- *i* is an integer literal, constant, or variable representing a relative row number. For example, 1 means the first row in the table, 2 means the second, and so on.
- *keyexp* is an expression representing a value to be found.
- *cmpexp* is a comparison expression representing a test to be performed on the found row.

▼

▼ • *texp* is an expression representing the fields to be transported to the work area after a row has been found.

▲ • If both `comparing` and `transporting` are specified, `comparing` must come first.

The following points apply:

- *wa* must have the same structure as a row of the body.

- *wa* can be the header line, or it can be any field string having the same structure as a row in the body.

- If you do not specify a work area, by default the system uses the header line. For example, `read table it into it` reads one row from the internal table *it*, placing it into the header line *it*. An equivalent statement is `read table it`.

Using the `index` Addition

NEW TERM An internal table row's *index* is its relative row number. For example, the first row in the table is index 1, the second is index 2, and so on. On the `read table` statement, if `index` *i* is specified, the system retrieves the *i*th row from the internal table and places it into the work area. For example, `read table it index 7` reads the seventh row from the internal table and places it in the header line.

If the read was successful (that is, if the *i*th row exists), `sy-subrc` is set to zero and `sy-tabix` is set to *i* (see Listing 11.6).

LISTING 11.6 THE `index` ADDITION ON THE `read table` STATEMENT LOCATES

INPUT A SINGLE ROW BY ITS RELATIVE ROW NUMBER

```
 1 report ztx1106.
 2 data: begin of it occurs 3,
 3           f1(2) type n,
 4           f2    type i,
 5           f3(2) type c,
 6           f4    type p,
 7         end of it,
 8       wa like it.
 9
10 it-f1 = '10'. it-f3 = 'AA'. it-f2 = it-f4 = 1. append it.
11 it-f1 = '20'. it-f3 = 'BB'. it-f2 = it-f4 = 2. append it.
12 it-f1 = '30'. it-f3 = 'CC'. it-f2 = it-f4 = 3. append it.
13
14 read table it index 2.
15 write: / 'sy-subrc =', sy-subrc,
16        / 'sy-tabix =', sy-tabix,
17        / it-f1, it-f2, it-f3, it-f4.
18
19 read table it into wa index 1.
```

```
20 write: /,
21          / 'sy-subrc =', sy-subrc,
22          / 'sy-tabix =', sy-tabix,
23          / it-f1, it-f2, it-f3, it-f4,
24          / wa-f1, wa-f2, wa-f3, wa-f4.
25
26 read table it index 4.
27 write: /,
28          / 'sy-subrc =', sy-subrc,
29          / 'sy-tabix =', sy-tabix,
30          / it-f1, it-f2, it-f3, it-f4,
31          / wa-f1, wa-f2, wa-f3, wa-f4.
```

The code in Listing 11.6 produces this output:

OUTPUT

```
sy-subrc =       0
sy-tabix =               2
20             2   BB                    2

sy-subrc =       0
sy-tabix =               1
20             2   BB                    2
10             1   AA                    1

sy-subrc =       4
sy-tabix =               0
20             2   BB                    2
10             1   AA                    1
```

11

ANALYSIS

- Lines 2 through 7 define an internal table with a header line.

- Line 8 defines a work area wa like the header line of it.

- Lines 10 through 12 append three rows to the internal table.

- Line 14 reads the second row. Because no work area is specified, the contents are placed in the header line. After the read, sy-subrc is set to zero. This indicates the row existed and that sy-tabix is set to the row number.

- Line 19 reads row 1 into the work area wa. The contents of the header line are unchanged after the read.

- Line 26 attempts to read row 4 into the header line. There is no row 4, so sy-subrc is set to 4, sy-tabix is 0, and the header line and work area wa are unchanged.

Using the with key Addition

If with key *keyexp* is specified, the system finds a row that matches the key expression and places it in the header line. Table 11.2 describes key expressions and their effects. Using a key expression, you can specify a single row to be retrieved. If more than one row matches the expression, the first one found (the one with the lowest index) is returned.

TABLE 11.2 KEY EXPRESSIONS AND THEIR EFFECTS

Key Expression	Effect
c1 = v1 c2 = v2 ...	Locates the first row in the internal table where component c1 has the value v1 and component c2 has the value v2, and so on. v1 is a literal, constant, or variable.
(f1) = v1 (f2) = v2 ...	Same as above, but f1 is a variable that contains the name of the component to be compared. The value in f1 must be in uppercase. If f1 is blank, the comparison is ignored.
= wa	wa is a work area identical in structure to an internal table row. This key expression locates the first row in the internal table that is exactly equal to the contents of wa. Blanks are treated as values to be found; they do not match any value other than blanks.
wa	wa is a work area identical to or shorter than the structure of the internal table. If wa has *n* fields, the fields of wa match the first *n* fields of an internal table row. This key expression locates the first row in the internal table whose first *n* fields match the contents of wa. Blanks are treated as values to be found; they do not match any value other than blanks.

Note

In release 4, conversions necessary for the first three key expressions in Table 11.2 are performed with the same order of precedence as that used for logical expressions. In systems prior, conversions were performed by converting from the value on the right to the data type and length of the component on the left.

Table 11.3 describes the values of sy-subrc and sy-tabix after a read table it with key... has executed.

TABLE 11.3 VALUES ASSIGNED TO sy-subrc AND sy-tabix

Result	sy-subrc	sy-tabix
Read was successful (a matching row was found)	0	index of matching row
Read unsuccessful, but a row with a key greater than the one requested exists	4	index of row with next higher key

Result	sy-subrc	sy-tabix
Read unsuccessful, and no rows found having a higher key	8	number of rows in *it* + 1

Listing 11.7 illustrates the use of key expressions.

INPUT **LISTING 11.7**   USING A KEY EXPRESSION, YOU CAN SEARCH FOR A ROW BY SPECIFYING A VALUE INSTEAD OF AN INDEX

```
 1 report ztx1107.
 2 data: begin of it occurs 3,
 3            f1(2) type n,
 4            f2    type i,
 5            f3(2) type c,
 6            f4    type p,
 7            end of it,
 8         begin of w1,
 9            f1 like it-f1,
10            f2 like it-f2,
11            end of w1,
12         w2 like it,
13         f(8).
14
15 it-f1 = '10'. it-f3 = 'AA'. it-f2 = it-f4 = 1. append it.
16 it-f1 = '20'. it-f3 = 'BB'. it-f2 = it-f4 = 2. append it.
17 it-f1 = '30'. it-f3 = 'CC'. it-f2 = it-f4 = 3. append it.
18
19 read table it with key f1 = '30' f2 = 3.
20 write: / 'sy-subrc =', sy-subrc,
21         / 'sy-tabix =', sy-tabix,
22         / it-f1, it-f2, it-f3, it-f4.
23
24 f = 'F2'.                             "must be in uppercase
25 read table it into w2 with key (f) = 2.
26 write: /,
27         / 'sy-subrc =', sy-subrc,
28         / 'sy-tabix =', sy-tabix,
29         / it-f1, it-f2, it-f3, it-f4,
30         / w2-f1, w2-f2, w2-f3, w2-f4.
31
32 clear w2.
33 w2-f1 = '10'. w2-f3 = 'AA'. w2-f2 = w2-f4 = 1.
34 read table it with key = w2.
35 write: /,
36         / 'sy-subrc =', sy-subrc,
37         / 'sy-tabix =', sy-tabix,
38         / it-f1, it-f2, it-f3, it-f4.
39
```

11

continues

LISTING 11.7 CONTINUED

```
40 w1-f1 = '20'. w1-f2 = 2.
41 read table it into w2 with key w1.
42 write: /,
43        / 'sy-subrc =', sy-subrc,
44        / 'sy-tabix =', sy-tabix,
45        / it-f1, it-f2, it-f3, it-f4.
```

The code in Listing 11.7 produces this output:

OUTPUT

```
sy-subrc =      0
sy-tabix =            3
30           3  CC                 3

sy-subrc =      0
sy-tabix =            2
30           3  CC                 3
20           2  BB                 2

sy-subrc =      0
sy-tabix =            1
10           1  AA                 1

sy-subrc =      0
sy-tabix =            2
10           1  AA                 1
```

ANALYSIS

- Lines 2 through 7 define an internal table with a header line.

- Line 8 defines a work area w1 like the first two fields of header line it.

- Line 9 defines a work area w2 like the entire length of header line it.

- Lines 15 through 17 append three rows to the internal table.

- Line 19 reads a row that has value '30' in f1 and 3 in f2. Sy-subrc is set to zero to indicate a matching row was found and sy-tabix is set to the row number. Because no work area is specified, the contents are placed in the header line.

- Line 25 searches for a row having a value of 2 in the f2 column. It is found and placed into work area w2. The contents of the header line are unchanged after the read.

- Line 34 searches for a row having the values specified in all fields of w2. With this syntax, w2 must match the entire structure of it. The contents of the matching row are placed in the header line. Fields containing blanks are searched for in the table; they do not match all values as they do when searching using the default key (see the next section).

- Line 41 searches for a row having the values specified in all fields of w1. With this syntax, w1 can be shorter than it. The contents of the matching row are placed in the header line. As before, blank values are treated as values to be found and match only themselves.

Using the `binary search` Addition

Whenever you use the `with key` addition, you should also use the `binary search` addition, which causes the row to be located using a binary search algorithm instead of a linear table scan. This results in the same performance gains as those achieved when searching a database table via an index. Beforehand, the table must be sorted in ascending order by the components specified in the key expression (see the following section on sorting).

No Additions

NEW TERM If neither an `index` nor a key expression are specified, the table is scanned from the beginning for a row that matches the *default key* contained in the header line. The default key is an imaginary key composed of all character fields in the header line (types c, d, t, n, and x). A blank value in a default key column causes all values in that column to match. Afterward, the values of sy-subrc and sy-tabix are set they same way as they are after a `read table` using a key expression.

> **Caution**
>
> Only blanks in a default key field will match all values. This means that you cannot clear types d, t, n, and x and obtain a match—clearing will set them to zeros, not blanks. You must force blanks into these fields for them to match. You can do this using a field string (see the following example), using a subfield, or using a field symbol (see the previous section on field symbols for more information).

Listing 11.8 provides an example.

 LISTING 11.8 THIS PROGRAM FINDS A ROW HAVING THE SAME VALUES AS THE DEFAULT KEY FIELDS IN THE HEADER LINE. BLANKS IN A DEFAULT KEY FIELD CAUSE A COLUMN TO BE IGNORED.

```
1 report ztx1108.
2 data: begin of it occurs 3,
3          f1(2) type n,   "character field -     part of default key
4          f2    type i,   "numeric  field - not part of default key
5          f3(2) type c,   "character field -     part of default key
6          f4    type p,   "numeric  field - not part of default key
```

continues

LISTING **11.8**   CONTINUED

```
 7              end of it.
 8
 9 it-f1 = '10'. it-f3 = 'AA'. it-f2 = it-f4 = 1. append it.
10 it-f1 = '20'. it-f3 = 'BB'. it-f2 = it-f4 = 2. append it.
11 it-f1 = '30'. it-f3 = 'CC'. it-f2 = it-f4 = 3. append it.
12
13 sort it by f1 f3.
14 clear it.
15 it(2) = ' '. it-f3 = 'BB'.
16 read table it binary search.
17 write: / 'sy-subrc =', sy-subrc,
18         / 'sy-tabix =', sy-tabix,
19         / 'f1=', it-f1, 'f2=', it-f2, 'f3=', it-f3, 'f4=', it-f4.
20
21 clear it.
22 it-f1 = '30'. it-f3 = 'AA'.
23 read table it binary search.
24 write: / 'sy-subrc =', sy-subrc,
25         / 'sy-tabix =', sy-tabix,
26         / 'f1=', it-f1, 'f2=', it-f2, 'f3=', it-f3, 'f4=', it-f4.
```

The code in Listing 11.8 produces this output:

OUTPUT

```
sy-subrc =      0
sy-tabix =          2
f1= 20 f2=          2  f3= BB f4=              2
sy-subrc =      4
sy-tabix =          3
f1= 30 f2=          0  f3= AA f4=              0
```

ANALYSIS

- Lines 2 through 7 define an internal table with a header line. F1 and f3 are the character data types and thus form the default key.

- Lines 9 through 11 append three rows to the internal table.

- Line 13 sorts it by f1 and f3 in ascending order.

- Line 14 clears the contents of the header line, setting all components to blanks and zeros. f1 is type n, and so is set to zeros.

- Using a subfield, line 15 forces blanks into the f1 field so that it will match all values. The other default key field (f3) is set to 'BB'.

- Line 16 performs a binary search for a row containing 'BB' in component f3.

- After the search, the output shows that sy-subrc is set to zero, indicating that a row was found matching the criteria. Sy-tabix contains 2, the relative row number of the matching row. The header line has been populated with the contents of the matching row and is written out.

- Line 21 clears the header line.
- Line 22 places a `'30'` and `'AA'` in the default key fields `f1` and `f3`.
- Line 23 performs a binary search for `f1 = '30'` and `f3 = 'AA'`. The return value of `sy-subrc` is 4. This indicates that a matching row did not exist, and `sy-tabix` contains 3—the number of rows in the table. The contents of the header line are unchanged from what it was on line 22.

In this example, the internal table only contains a few rows, so `binary search` would not produce a measurable improvement in performance. It is only included to illustrate how it should be used.

 Note | The `read table` statement can only be used to read internal tables. It doesn't work with database tables. Use `select single` instead.

Using the `comparing` Addition

`comparing` detects differences between the contents of the work area and a row that was found before it is placed in the work area. Use it in conjunction with `index` or `with key`. If, after a row has been found, the work area contents are the same as the found row, `sy-subrc` will be 0. If the contents are different, `sy-subrc` will be 2 and the contents will be overwritten by the found row. If the row is not found, `sy-subrc` will be > 2 and the contents will remain unchanged.

Table 11.4 describes the values for the comparison expression (*cmpexp* in the syntax for `read table`).

TABLE 11.4 FORMS FOR THE COMPARISON EXPRESSION IN THE READ TABLE STATEMENT

Cmpexp	Description
`f1 f2 ...`	After a row is found, the value of `f1` in the found row is compared with the value of `f1` in the work area. Then the value of `f2` is compared with the value of `f2` in the work area, and so on. If they are all equal, `sy-subrc` is set to 0. If any are different, `sy-subrc` is set to 2.
`all fields`	All fields are compared, as described for `f1 f2...`.
`no fields`	No fields are compared. This is the default.

Listing 11.9 provides examples.

LISTING 11.9 THE comparing ADDITION SETS THE VALUE OF sy-subrc TO 2
WHENEVER FIELDS DIFFER

INPUT

```
 1 report ztx1109.
 2 data: begin of it occurs 3,
 3           f1(2) type n,
 4           f2    type i,
 5           f3(2) type c,
 6           f4    type p,
 7           end of it,
 8        wa like it.
 9
10 it-f1 = '10'. it-f3 = 'AA'. it-f2 = it-f4 = 1. append it.
11 it-f1 = '20'. it-f3 = 'BB'. it-f2 = it-f4 = 2. append it.
12 it-f1 = '30'. it-f3 = 'CC'. it-f2 = it-f4 = 3. append it.
13
14 read table it index 2 comparing f1.
15 write: / 'sy-subrc =', sy-subrc,
16        / 'sy-tabix =', sy-tabix,
17        / it-f1, it-f2, it-f3, it-f4.
18
19 read table it into wa index 1 comparing f2 f4.
20 write: /,
21        / 'sy-subrc =', sy-subrc,
22        / 'sy-tabix =', sy-tabix,
23        / it-f1, it-f2, it-f3, it-f4,
24        / wa-f1, wa-f2, wa-f3, wa-f4.
25
26 it = wa.
27 read table it with key f3 = 'AA' comparing all fields.
28 write: /,
29        / 'sy-subrc =', sy-subrc,
30        / 'sy-tabix =', sy-tabix,
31        / it-f1, it-f2, it-f3, it-f4,
32        / wa-f1, wa-f2, wa-f3, wa-f4.
```

The code in Listing 11.9 produces this output:

OUTPUT

```
sy-subrc =      2
sy-tabix =             2
20           2  BB                 2

sy-subrc =      2
sy-tabix =             1
20           2  BB                 2
10           1  AA                 1

sy-subrc =      0
sy-tabix =             1
10           1  AA                 1
10           1  AA                 1
```

ANALYSIS

- On line 14, `index 2` locates row 2 in `it`. Before the row is copied to the header line, the value of `f1` in the body is compared with the value of `f1` in the header line. In this case, the header line still contains 3 (unchanged after appending the last row) and the found row contains a 2. They are different, so `sy-subrc` is set to 2. The contents of the internal table row are then copied into the header line and it overlays the existing contents.

- On line 19, row 1 is located. The values of `f2` and `f4` in row 1 of the body are compared with header line components of the same name. The header line contains row 2 (retrieved by statement 14), and so they are different. As a result, `sy-subrc` is set to 2.

- Line 26 transfers the contents of `wa` to the header line.

- On line 27, a row having `f3 = 'AA'` is searched for. Row 1 matches, as shown by the values of `sy-subrc` and `sy-tabix` in the output. Row 1 is already in the header line, therefore all fields match in value and `sy-subrc` to be set to 0.

Using the `transporting` Addition

`transporting` affects how fields are moved from the found row to the work area. If it is specified, only the values of the specified components are moved to the work area. If a row is not found, `transporting` does nothing.

Table 11.5 describes the values for the transporting expression (*texp* in the syntax for `read table`).

TABLE 11.5 FORMS FOR THE TRANSPORTING EXPRESSION IN THE read table STATEMENT

Cmpexp	Description
`f1 f2 ...`	After a row is found, the value of `f1` in the found row overlays the value of `f1` in the work area. Then the value of `f2` overlays the value of `f2` in the work area, and so on. Only the components named after `transporting` are moved. All other components remain unchanged.
`all fields`	All fields are transported. This is the default, and has the same effect as leaving off the `transporting` addition.
`no fields`	No fields are transported. None of the fields in the work area are changed.

This addition is useful if you only want to test for the existence of a row in an internal table without disturbing the contents of the header line. For example, before appending a row, you might want to determine whether the row already exists in the internal table. Listing 11.10 provides an example.

11

LISTING 11.10 THE MOST EFFICIENT WAY TO INSERT ROWS INTO A SORTED
INTERNAL TABLE WHILE MAINTAINING THE SORT ORDER.

> **INPUT**

```
 1 report ztx1110.
 2 data: begin of it occurs 3,
 3             f1(2) type n,
 4             f2    type i,
 5             f3(2) type c,
 6             f4    type p,
 7           end of it.
 8
 9 it-f1 = '40'. it-f3 = 'DD'. it-f2 = it-f4 = 4. append it.
10 it-f1 = '20'. it-f3 = 'BB'. it-f2 = it-f4 = 2. append it.
11
12 sort it by f1.
13 do 5 times.
14     it-f1 = sy-index * 10.
15     it-f3 = 'XX'.
16     it-f2 = it-f4 = sy-index.
17     read table it
18         with key f1 = it-f1
19         binary search
20         transporting no fields.
21     if sy-subrc <> 0.
22         insert it index sy-tabix.
23       endif.
24     enddo.
25
26 loop at it.
27     write: / it-f1, it-f2, it-f3, it-f4.
28     endloop.
```

The code in Listing 11.10 produces this output:

> **OUTPUT**

```
10        1  XX        1
20        2  BB        2
30        3  XX        3
40        4  DD        4
50        5  XX        5
```

> **ANALYSIS**

- Lines 9 and 10 add two rows to it. (They are purposely out of order for sake of example.)

- Line 12 sorts it by f1 ascending so that the following read table can use the binary search addition.

- Line 13 loops five times. Each time through the loop it creates a new row for it and places it in the header line (lines 14, 15, and 16).

- Lines 17 and 21 determine whether a row already exists that has the same f1 value as that in the header line. If that row is not found, sy-subrc is set to non-zero and sy-tabix is set to the index of the row with the next higher value, or to the number of rows in the internal table plus 1.

- Line 22 inserts the new row before the row pointed to by sy-tabix. This maintains the current sort order.

Sorting the Contents of an Internal Table

To sort the contents of an internal table, use the sort statement. Rows can be sorted by one or more columns in ascending or descending order. The sort sequence itself can also be modified.

Syntax for the sort Statement

The following is the syntax for the sort statement.

```
sort it [descending] [as text] [by f1 [ascending¦descending] [as text]
➥f2 ...].
```

where:

- *it* is the name of an internal table.

- *f1* and *f2* are components of *it*.

- ... represents any number of field names optionally followed by ascending, descending, and/or as text.

The following points apply:

- ascending is the default sort order.

- If descending appears after sort and before any component names, it becomes the default and applies to all components. This default can be overridden on an individual component by specifying ascending after the component name.

- If no additions are specified, the internal table is sorted by the default key fields (all fields of type c, n, p, d, and t) in ascending order.

The sort order for rows that have the same value is not predictable. Rows having the same value in a sorted column can appear in any order after the sort. Listing 11.11 shows examples of the sort statement and also illustrates this point.

LISTING 11.11   USE THE sort STATEMENT TO REORDER THE ROWS OF AN INTERNAL TABLE

```
 1 report ztx1111.
 2 data: begin of it occurs 5,
 3            i like  sy-index,
 4            t,
 5            end of it,
 6        alpha(5) value 'CBABB'.
 7
 8 do 5 times varying it-t from alpha+0 next alpha+1.
 9     it-i = sy-index.
10     append it.
11     enddo.
12
13 loop at it.
14     write: / it-i, it-t.
15     endloop.
16
17 skip.
18 sort it by t.
19 loop at it.
20     write: / it-i, it-t.
21     endloop.
22
23 skip.
24 sort it by t.
25 loop at it.
26     write: / it-i, it-t.
27     endloop.
28
29 skip.
30 sort it by t i.
31 loop at it.
32     write: / it-i, it-t.
33     endloop.
34
35 skip.
36 sort it by t descending i.
37 *same as: sort it descending by t i ascending.
38 loop at it.
39     write: / it-i, it-t.
40     endloop.
41
42 skip.
43 sort it.
44 *same as: sort it by t.
45 loop at it.
46     write: / it-t.
47     endloop.
```

The code in Listing 11.11 produces this output:

OUTPUT

```
1   C
2   B
3   A
4   B
5   B

3   A
2   B
4   B
5   B
1   C

3   A
5   B
4   B
2   B
1   C

3   A
2   B
4   B
5   B
1   C

1   C
2   B
4   B
5   B
3   A

A
B
B
B
C
```

ANALYSIS

- Lines 2 through 5 define an internal table having two components: i and t. The occurs clause is 5 because the internal table will be filled with five rows.

- Line 6 defines alpha as a type c variable length 5 and gives it a default value.

- Lines 8 through 11 append five rows to the internal table. Each one contains a letter from alpha and the value of sy-index when the row is appended.

- Lines 13 through 15 write out the contents of the internal table. The row number from sy-tabix appears on the left of the output. The internal table rows are in their original order, so the values of sy-index and sy-tabix match.

11

- Line 18 reorders the rows so that the values of t are in ascending order.
- On line 24, the internal table is sorted again using the same statement. Notice that the relative order of the rows having a value of 'B' is not maintained. If you want the values in a column to be in a particular order, you must specify that on the sort statement. The order of rows containing identical values is not preserved during a sort.
- On line 30, the internal table is sorted by t in ascending order and then by i in ascending order.
- On line 36, the internal table is sorted by t in descending order and then by i in ascending order.
- Line 37 shows an alternate syntax that achieves the same effect as line 36. In this statement, placing descending after it causes it to become the default. Component t is therefore sorted descending, and on component i, the default is overridden with the ascending addition.
- Line 43 sorts the internal table by the default key fields (types c, n, d, t, and x). In this case, there is only one field in the default key, t, so the internal table sorts in ascending order by t only.

Sort Order and the as text Addition

NEW TERM Internally within the operating system, each character you see on the screen is represented by a numeric value. During a sort, the character's numeric value determines the resulting order. For example, when an ABAP/4 program runs on an ASCII platform, the letter o has an ASCII decimal value of 111, and p is 112. Therefore, p comes after o in the sort sequence. This sort sequence is called the *binary sort sequence*.

When a language contains accented characters, there is a numeric value assigned to represent each accented form of a character. For example, o and ö (o with an umlaut) are distinct and separate characters, each with an individual numeric value. (In ASCII, the value of ö is decimal 246.) When you sort data containing accented characters, the accented forms should be appear with the non-accented forms. For example, for example, o and ö should be together, and then p. However, the binary values of the accented and non-accented characters do not follow each other in numeric sequence. Therefore, a way is needed to change the sort order so that accented characters are sorted correctly.

The as text addition modifies the sort order so that accented characters are sorted correctly. With as text, the binary sort sequence is not used. Instead, the text environment determines the sort sequence.

NEW TERM The *text environment* is a set of characteristics associated with the user's logon language. It is determined by the language code you enter when you log on, and consists primarily of the language's character set and collating sequence. You can also change the text environment at runtime using the set locale statement. This statement sets the value of sy-langu, the current character set and collating sequence to the language specified.

The following points apply to the as text addition:

- It can only be used with type c fields.

- It can be specified after sort and before any component names. In this case, it applies to all type c components used by the sort.

- It can be specified after an individual component name. In this case it applies only to that component.

Listing 11.12 provides an example.

LISTING 11.12 SORTING ACCENTED CHARACTERS REQUIRES THE USE OF THE as text ADDITION

INPUT

```
 1 report ztx1112.
 2 data: begin of it occurs 4,
 3          t(30),
 4          end of it.
 5
 6 it-t = 'Higgle'.    append it.
 7 it-t = 'Hoffman'.   append it.
 8 it-t = 'Höllman'.   append it.
 9 it-t = 'Hubble'.    append it.
10
11 write: / 'sy-langu=', sy-langu.
12 sort it. "sorts by default key. t is type c, therefore sorts by t.
13 loop at it.
14     write: / it-t.
15     endloop.
16
17 skip.
18 set locale language 'D'. "Equivalent to signing on in German
19 write: / 'sy-langu=', sy-langu.
20 sort it as text.        "as text here applies to all type c components
21 *same as: sort it by t as text.
22 loop at it.
23     write: / it-t.
24     endloop.
```

11

The code in Listing 11.12 produces this output:

```
sy-langu= E
Higgle
Hoffman
Hubble
Höllman

sy-langu= D
Higgle
Hoffman
Höllman
Hubble
```

ANALYSIS

- Lines 6 through 9 add four rows to the internal table. The one on line 8 contains an ö (o umlaut.)

- Line 11 writes out the current logon language.

- Line 12 sorts *it* by the default key in binary sort sequence according to the current logon language. The output shows that ö comes last in the sort sequence.

- Set `locale` on line 18 changes the program's environment; it produces an effect similar to signing on in German. Sy-langu is set to D, and the German character set and collating sequences are used from that point forward in the program.

- Line 20 uses sort with the `as text` addition after the internal table name. This causes `as text` to apply to all type c components. In the output, o and ö appear together.

> **Caution**
>
> After sorting `as text`, do not use `read table` with the addition `binary search`. The rows will not be sorted in binary order, so a binary search will yield incorrect results. To use `binary search` successfully, see the ABAP/4 keyword documentation on the `convert into sortable code` statement.

Sort sequences vary with platforms. When transporting from one operating system to another, the only guaranteed sort sequences are A–Z, a–z, and 0–9, but not necessarily in that order.

> **Tip**
>
> After sorting, you can delete duplicates from an internal table using the `delete adjacent duplicates` statement, described in the ABAP/4 keyword documentation.

Summary

- An internal table is a collection of rows stored in RAM on the application server. It consists of a header line and a body. The header line is optional. The header line is the implicit work area for the internal table.

- The existence of the `occurs` clause creates an internal table. It is used as a guideline for the system to allocate memory. It does not limit the number of rows you can add to an internal table.

- Use the `loop at` statement to retrieve multiple rows from an internal table. Each row is placed into the header line or an explicit work area one at a time. Use `from`, `to`, and `where` to specify the rows to be returned. Inside of the loop, `sy-tabix` contains the 1-based relative row number. After `endloop`, `sy-subrc` will be zero if any rows were processed in the loop.

- Inside of a loop, the flow of processing can be altered by an `exit`, `continue`, or `check` statement. `Exit` terminates the loop and continues with the statement following the `endloop`. `Continue` bypasses the remaining statements of the loop and immediately begins the next iteration. `Check`, like `continue`, also begins a new iteration, but only does so when its logical expression is `false`.

- Use the `read table` statement to locate a single row in the internal table. Using the `index` addition, you can locate a single row by relative row number. This is the most efficient way to locate a row. Using the `with key` addition, you can locate a row by specifying a value to be found. `comparing` determines whether values in the work area differ from values in the found row. `transporting` avoids unnecessary or undesired assignments from the found row to the work area.

- The `sort` statement sorts an internal table by named components. If no components are named, the table is sorted by its default key fields (types c, n, d, t, and x).

Do	Don't
DO use the `binary search` addition on the `read table` statement. It will increase the performance of the search tremendously. **DO** use the `index` addition on the `read table` statement whenever possible. It is the fastest way to locate a single row.	**DON'T** use `occurs 0` for internal tables smaller than 8KB. This results in over-allocation of memory and slower performance.

11

Q&A

Q In some programs, I've seen a user-defined type that has an `occurs` clause. The type is then used to define an internal table type and subsequently an internal table, like that shown in Listing 11.13. Why do they do it this way? Can't you always define the internal table with the `data` statement? Why introduce the `types` statement?

INPUT   **LISTING 11.13**   DEFINING AN INTERNAL TABLE WITH A USER-DEFINED TYPE

```
1   report ztx1113.
2   types: begin of my_type,
3            f1,
4            f2,
5            end of my_type,
6          t_it type my_type occurs 10.
7   data it type t_it.
```

A There is no advantage to using internal table types in the way shown in Listing 11.13. Types are useful only if you use them to define more than one data object. In this listing, only one data object is defined of the type `t_it`. It would be simpler in this case to do away with the `types` statements and create the entire definition using `data`.

Theoretically, types are useful if you need to define multiple data objects that are the same. Listing 11.14 shows three ways of defining multiple internal tables: using data only, using `types`, and using a DDIC structure.

INPUT   **LISTING 11.14**   DEFINING MULTIPLE INTERNAL TABLES WITH `types` SIMPLIFIES THE DEFINITIONS

```
1 report ztx1113.
2
3 * Define 3 identical internal tables using DATA only
4 data: begin of it_1a occurs 10,
5          f1,
6          f2,
7          end of it_1a,
8        it_1b like it_1a occurs 10 with header line,
9        it_1c like it_1a occurs 10 with header line.
10
11 * Define 3 more identical internal tables using TYPES
12 types: begin of t_,
13          f1,
14          f2,
```

```
15              end of t_,
16        t_it type t_ occurs 10.
17 data: it_2a type t_it,
18        it_2b type t_it,
19        it_2c type t_it.
20
21 * Define 3 more using a DDIC structure
22 data: it_3a like ztx_it occurs 10 with header line,
23        it_3b like ztx_it occurs 10 with header line,
24        it_3c like ztx_it occurs 10 with header line.
```

ANALYSIS Of the first two methods, it is a matter of opinion which is clearer; neither one appears to have much of an advantage over the other. I believe the third method, however, to be the preferred one. It is clearer, and to see the definition, you can simply double-click the DDIC structure name. When viewing the structure, what you will see is much more meaningful than an ABAP/4 definition; there will be short text for each data element and one for the structure itself. These texts can also be translated. In addition, the structure is available for re-use within multiple programs. In my opinion, using a structure wins hands-down over the use of a types definition.

There is only one thing that a type can do that a structure can't: It can contain the definition for a nested internal table. Only in that case would I use a type. In all other cases, a data begin of or a like a structure in the DDIC is the way to go.

Workshop

The Workshop provides you two ways for you to affirm what you've learned in this chapter. The Quiz section poses questions to help you solidify your understanding of the material covered and the Exercise section provides you with experience in using what you have learned. You can find answers to the quiz questions and exercises in Appendix B, "Answers to Quiz Questions and Exercises."

Quiz Questions

1. Who sets a limit on the maximum amount of extended memory an internal table can allocate?

2. Why shouldn't you use occurs 0 if you expect to store less than 8KB in an internal table?

3. Can you use the read table statement to read database tables?

11

Exercise 1

Display and explain the conversions that occur in program ztx1110 (see Listing 11.15).

LISTING 11.15 CONVERSIONS (HINT: PROGRAM->ANALYSIS)

```
 1 report ztx1110.
 2 data: begin of it occurs 3,
 3           f1(2) type n,
 4           f2    type i,
 5           f3(2) type c,
 6           f4    type p,
 7         end of it.
 8
 9 it-f1 = '40'. it-f3 = 'DD'. it-f2 = it-f4 = 4. append it.
10 it-f1 = '20'. it-f3 = 'BB'. it-f2 = it-f4 = 2. append it.
11
12 sort it by f1.
13 do 5 times.
14     it-f1 = sy-index * 10.
15     it-f3 = 'XX'.
16     it-f2 = it-f4 = sy-index.
17     read table it
18         with key f1 = it-f1
19         binary search
20         transporting no fields.
21     if sy-subrc <> 0.
22         insert it index sy-tabix.
23         endif.
24     enddo.
25
26 loop at it.
27     write: / it-f1, it-f2, it-f3, it-f4.
28     endloop.
```

DAY **12**

Advanced Internal Tables, Part 1

Chapter Objectives

After you complete this chapter, you should be able to:

- Recognize the table body operator and use it to test for the existence of data in an internal table, and to compare the contents of two internal tables for equality
- Determine the number of rows in an internal table using `describe` and `sy-tfill`
- Copy the contents from one internal table to another using the table body operator and the `append lines` and `insert lines` statements
- View and modify internal tables using `editor-call`
- Use the `insert` and `modify` statements to change the internal table contents
- Delete rows from an internal table using `delete`, `delete ... where`, `clear`, `clear it[]`, `refresh`, and `free`
- Fill an internal table using `append sorted by` and `collect`

Testing and Modifying Internal Table Contents

Use the following constructs to test and modify the contents of internal tables:

- The table body operator
- `describe table`
- `append lines`
- `insert lines`
- `editor-call`
- `insert`
- `modify`
- `free`
- `delete`
- `clear`
- `refresh`
- `append sorted by`
- `collect`

The body of an internal table is represented by the syntax `it[]`, where `it` is the name of any internal table. `it[]` means "the body of the internal table `it`." There cannot be anything between the square brackets; they must be written precisely as shown. You can use this syntax to perform efficient table operations that do not require the use of a header line. These operations are described throughout this chapter.

If an internal table does not have a header line, the internal table name itself represents the body. For example, if internal table `it` does not have a header line, you can use either `it[]` or `it` to represent the body; they are equivalent.

Obtaining Information About an Internal Table

You can obtain the following commonly needed information about an internal table:

- Whether the internal table contains data
- How many rows it contains

Determining Whether an Internal Table Is Empty

If the body of an internal table contains only initial values (blanks and spaces), it is empty. Therefore, to determine whether an internal table contains any rows, test the body with the following statement:

```
if it[] is initial.
```

If the test is true, the internal table is empty. When false, it contains at least one row.

Determining the Number of Rows in an Internal Table

To determine the number of rows in an internal table, use the `sy-tfill` variable. It is set by the `describe table` statement.

Syntax for the `describe table` Statement

▼ SYNTAX

▲

The following is the syntax for the `describe table` statement.

```
describe table it [lines i] [occurs j].
```

where:

- *it* is the name of an internal table.
- *i* and *j* are numeric variables.

This statement fills the three system variables shown in Table 12.1.

TABLE 12.1   `describe table` STATEMENT FILLS THESE SYSTEM VARIABLES

Variable	Value
sy-tfill	Number of rows
sy-tleng	Length of a row in bytes
sy-toccu	Current value of the occurs clause

12

The following points apply:

- If the `lines` *i* addition is specified, the number of rows is placed in both `sy-tfill` and *i*.
- If the `occurs` *j* addition is specified, the size of the occurs clause is placed in both `sy-toccu` and *j*.

Note

There is only one instance where `sy-toccu` will differ from the occurs clause on the table definition. When `sy-tleng * sy-toccu > 8192`, and after one row has been added to the internal table, `sy-toccu` will be zero. This indicates that memory is being allocated in 8KB chunks for this internal table.

Sample Program that Obtains Information About an Internal Table

Listing 12.1 shows a sample program that obtains information about an internal table.

INPUT **LISTING 12.1** THE describe table STATEMENT USES SYSTEM VARIABLES TO QUANTIFY TABLE CONTENTS

```
 1  report ztx1201.
 2  data: begin of it occurs 3,
 3           f1 value 'X',
 4           end of it,
 5        n type i.
 6
 7  if it[] is initial.
 8      write: / 'it is empty'.
 9      endif.
10
11 append: it, it, it.     "same as writing 'append it' 3 times.
12
13 if not it[] is initial.
14     write: / 'it is not empty'.
15     endif.
16
17 write: / 'number of  rows from sy-tabix:', sy-tabix.
18 describe table it lines n.
19 write: / 'number of  rows from sy-tfill:', sy-tfill,
20         / 'length of a row from sy-tleng:', sy-tleng,
21         / 'occurs value    from sy-toccu:', sy-toccu.
```

The code in Listing 12.1 produces this output:

OUTPUT
```
it is empty
it is not empty
number of  rows from sy-tabix:       3
number of  rows from sy-tfill:       3
length of a row from sy-tleng:   1
occurs value    from sy-toccu:       3
```

ANALYSIS
- Line 7 compares the body of the internal table using the table body operator with initial values. The internal table does not yet contain any rows, so the test is true.

- Line 11 uses the chain operator (:) to append three identical rows to it.

- Line 13 tests the body again. This time, the test is preceded by a logical not. The internal table contains data, so this test is true.

- After each append statement, the value of sy-tabix is set to the number of rows in the internal table. Line 17 writes out its value.

- Line 18 uses the describe statement to obtain the number of rows and places it in sy-tfill. It also obtains the row length and size of the occurs clause and places them into sy-tleng and sy-toccu.

> **Tip**
>
> If you only need to know whether the table contains data and not how many rows it has, use the table body operator. It is more efficient than the describe table statement.

Copying Data from One Internal Table to Another

If two internal tables have the same structure, use the following statement to duplicate the contents of one internal table in another:

```
it2[] = it1[].
```

> **Note**
>
> Two internal tables have the same structure if 1) they both have the same number of components, and 2) the data type and length of each component is the same as the corresponding component of the other internal table. Only the component names do not have to match.

12

The preceding statement copies the contents of the body of it1 and places it in the body of it2. Any existing contents in it2 are overwritten. The contents of the header lines, if either internal table has one, remain unchanged. This is the most efficient way to copy the contents from one internal table to another.

Copying a Portion of an Internal Table

If you want to copy a portion of an internal table to another, or if you want to leave the contents of the target table in place, use the append lines and insert lines statements.

Using the append lines Statement

Use the append lines statement when you want to append rows to the end of the target table.

Syntax for the `append lines` Statement

▼ SYNTAX

The following is the syntax for the append lines statement.

append lines of *it1* [from *nf*] [to *nt*] to *it2*.

where:

▲

- *it1* and *it2* are internal tables with or without header lines.
- *nf* and *nt* are numeric variables, literals, or constants.

The following points apply:

- The structures of *it1* and *it2* must match.
- *nf* is the index of the first row to be copied from *it1*. If the from addition is not specified, copying begins from the first row of *it1*.
- *nt* is the index of the last row to be copied from *it1*. If the to addition is not specified, copying continues to the last row of *it1*.
- If neither from nor to are specified, the entire table is appended.
- After the append lines statement has executed, sy-tabix contains the number of rows in the table.

> **Tip**
>
> Using append lines is three to four times faster than using append to add the rows one at a time.

Using the `insert lines` Statement

Use the insert lines statement when you want to insert rows at a place other than the end into the target table.

Syntax for the `insert lines` Statement

▼ SYNTAX

The following is the syntax for the insert lines statement.

insert lines of *it1* [from *nf*] [to *nt*] into *it2* [index *nb*].

where:

▲

- *it1* and *it2* are internal tables with or without header lines.
- *nf*, *nt*, and *nb* are numeric variables, literals, or constants.

All of the points that apply to the append lines statement also apply here. The difference is that rows from *it1* are inserted into *it2* before row number *nb*. If the value of *nb* is the number of rows in *it2* plus 1, the row is appended to the end of *it2*. If *nb* is greater than that, the row is not appended and sy-subrc is set to 4. If *nb* is less than 1, a runtime error occurs.

You can use this statement inside or outside of loop at *it2*. If used outside, you must specify the index addition. Inside, index is optional. If it is not specified, the current row number in *it2* is assumed.

Sample Program that Copies Data Between Internal Tables

Listing 12.2 shows a sample program that copies data from one internal table to another.

LISTING 12.2 THIS PROGRAM COPIES THE DATA FROM ONE INTERNAL TABLE TO
INPUT ANOTHER USING THE append lines AND insert lines STATEMENTS

```
 1  report ztx1202.
 2  data: begin of it1 occurs 10,
 3          f1,
 4          end of it1,
 5        it2 like it1 occurs 10 with header line,
 6        alpha(10) value 'ABCDEFGHIJ'.
 7
 8  do 10 times varying it1-f1 from alpha+0 next alpha+1.
 9      append it1.
10      enddo.
11
12  append lines of it1 from 2 to 5 to it2.
13  loop at it2.
14      write it2-f1.
15      endloop.
16
17  insert lines of it1 from 8 into it2 index 2.
18  skip.
19  loop at it2.
20      write it2-f1.
21      endloop.
22
23  loop at it2.
24      if it2-f1 >= 'E'.
25          insert lines of it1 to 1 into it2.
26          endif.
27      endloop.
28
29  skip.
30  loop at it2.
31      write it2-f1.
32      endloop.
```

continues

LISTING **12.2**   CONTINUED

```
33
34 skip.
35 it2[] = it1[].
36 loop at it2.
37     write it2-f1.
38     endloop.
```

The code in Listing 12.2 produces this output:

OUTPUT

```
B C D E

B H I J C D E

B A H A I A J C D A E

A B C D E F G H I J
```

ANALYSIS

- Lines 8 through 10 fill it1 with 10 rows containing the first 10 letters of the alphabet.

- Line 12 appends rows 2 through 5 of it1 to it2. it2 now has four rows containing the letters B through E.

- On line 17, the to addition is not specified, so the end of it1 is assumed. This inserts rows 8, 9, and 10 from it1 into it2 before row 2.

- On line 24, if the letter in it2-f1 is greater than or equal to E, row 1 of it1 is inserted before the current row of it2. (The from addition is not specified, so the beginning of it1 is assumed.) This results in four rows being inserted. In the output, they are the 'A' values.

- Line 35 copies the contents of it1 to it2, completely overlaying the existing contents.

Comparing the Contents of Two Internal Tables

You can use the table body operator to compare the contents of two internal tables, as shown here:

```
if it1[] = it2[].
```

To use this construct, the internal tables must have the same structure. If they do not, you will have to compare them manually, row by row.

This statement is true when it1 and it2 contain the same number of rows and the contents of each row are the same.

Tip

> The If - Equal to statement is the most efficient way to compare the contents of two internal tables.

Using the `editor-call` Statement

The `editor-call` statement displays the contents of an internal table to the user in an editor similar to the ABAP/4 source code editor. It is useful for debugging and as a simple interface for allowing the user to enter and modify data in tabular form.

Syntax for the `editor-call` Statement

The following is the syntax for the `editor-call` statement.

```
editor-call for it [title t] [display mode]
```

where:

- *it* is the name of an internal table.
- *t* is a literal, constant, or variable.

The following points apply:

- *it* can only contain type c components.
- The maximum length for a row is 72 characters.
- *t* is the text displayed in the title bar of the editor window.
- The `display mode` addition causes the data to be displayed in the editor in display mode. The user will be able to search and scroll, but will not be able to change the contents.

After viewing or modifying the internal table contents via the editor, the user presses one of these buttons: Save, Back, Exit, or Cancel. Save saves the changes made to the internal table contents and returns to the program. Back, Exit, and Cancel leave the editor and return to the program. If changes have been made, the user is prompted to save or cancel the changes.

After the `editor-call` statement has executed, `sy-subrc` is set to the values shown in Table 12.2.

SYNTAX

12

TABLE 12.2 VALUES OF sy-subrc AFTER THE editor-call STATEMENT

sy-subrc	Meaning
0	A save was performed. The contents of the internal table might or might not be changed.
4	The user did not perform a save. The contents of the internal table are unchanged.

Listing 12.3 shows a sample program that uses the editor-call statement. In this example, the internal table is filled with five lines and displayed in the editor so that the user can modify the data. The contents are then written out, and a message is also written to indicate whether a change was performed.

LISTING 12.3 USE THE editor-call STATEMENT TO VIEW, EDIT, AND DEBUG

INPUT THE CONTENTS OF AN INTERNAL TABLE.

```
 1  report ztx1203.
 2  data: begin of it occurs 10,
 3            t(72),                   "text
 4            end of it,
 5          save_it like it occurs 10.  "will contain copy of the original
 6
 7  it-t = 'Name          :'. append it.
 8  it-t = 'Address       :'. append it.
 9  it-t = 'Phone         :'. append it.
10  it-t = 'Freeform Text '. append it.
11  clear it-t with '-'.      append it.
12
13  save_it = it[].                    "same as: save_it[] = it[].
14  editor-call for it title 'Freeform Entry'.
15  if sy-subrc = 4.                   "user did not perform a save
16      write: / 'Data was not changed'.
17  elseif save_it[] <> it[].          "user performed a save
18      write: / 'Data was changed'.
19  else.
20      write: / 'Data was not changed'.
21      endif.
22  write: / sy-uline(72).
23  loop at it.
24      write: / it-t.
25      endloop.
```

If no data is entered when the editor is displayed, the code in Listing 12.3 produces this output:

OUTPUT

```
Data was not changed
- - - - - - - - - - - - - - - - - - - - - - - - - - - - - - - - - - - - - - - - - - - - - - - - - - - - -
Name           :
Address        :
Phone          :
Freeform Text
- - - - - - - - - - - - - - - - - - - - - - - - - - - - - - - - - - - - - - - - - - - - - - - - - - - - -
```

ANALYSIS

- Lines 2 through 4 define an internal table having a single component t, character length 72.

- Line 5 defines a second internal table like the first. It will be used to hold a reference copy of the data in it. It does not have a header line. The header line has been left off because it is not needed in this program.

- Lines 7 through 11 append five lines to the internal table from the header line.

- Line 13 copies the body of it to the body of save_it. Because save_it does not have a header line, the left side of the assignment can be written with or without square brackets.

- Line 14 displays the contents of the internal table in the editor with the title Freeform Entry.

- Line 15 checks the value of sy-subrc to determine whether the user performed a save. If he did not, it is not possible that data was changed and a message is written out.

- Line 17 compares the new contents of it with the reference copy in save_it. If they are different, a message is written out. If they are the same, line 20 writes out a message to indicate this.

- Lines 22 writes out an underline 72 characters long.

- Lines 23 through 25 write out the new contents of the internal table, including any user modifications.

12

Inserting Rows Into an Internal Table

To insert a single row into an internal table, use the insert statement.

Syntax for the insert Statement

SYNTAX

The following is the syntax for the insert statement.

```
insert [wa into] it [index n]
```

where:

▲

- *wa* is a work area with the same structure as a row of internal table *it*.
- *n* is a numeric literal, variable, or constant.

The following points apply:

- If *wa* is specified, the contents of *wa* are inserted into *it*. *wa* must have the same structure as *it*.
- If *wa* is not specified, the contents of the header line are inserted into *it*. If *it* does not have a header line, *wa* must be specified.
- If index is specified, the new row is inserted before row *n*. Row *n* then becomes row *n*+1.
- The insert statement can be used inside or outside of loop at it. If it is outside, the index addition must be specified. If it is inside, index is optional. If it is not specified, the current row is assumed.

Listing 12.4 contains a sample program that uses the insert statement.

LISTING 12.4   USE THE insert STATEMENT TO INSERT A SINGLE ROW INTO AN INTERNAL TABLE

`INPUT`

```
1   report ztx1204.
2   data: begin of it occurs 5,
3              f1 like sy-index,
4              end of it.
5
6   do 5 times.
7       it-f1 = sy-index.
8       append it.
9       enddo.
10
11  it-f1 = -99.
12  insert it index 3.
13
14  loop at it.
15      write / it-f1.
16      endloop.
17
18  loop at it where f1 >= 4.
19      it-f1 = -88.
20      insert it.
21      endloop.
22
23  skip.
24  loop at it.
25      write / it-f1.
26      endloop.
```

The code in Listing 12.4 produces this output:

OUTPUT

```
1
2
99 -
3
4
5

1
2
99 -
3
88 -
4
88 -
5
```

ANALYSIS

- Lines 6 through 9 append five rows containing the numbers 1 through 5 to it.
- Line 11 assigns to the header line component it-f1 a value of -99.
- Line 12 inserts the header line of it as new row into the body of it before row 3. The existing row 3 becomes row 4 after the insert.
- Line 18 retrieves those rows from the internal table that have an f1 value greater than or equal to 4. Before each row, line 20 inserts a new row from the header line of it. Prior to the insert, line 19 changed the f1 component to contain -88.

Tip

After each insert statement is executed, the system re-indexes all rows below the one inserted. This introduces overhead when you insert rows near the top of a large internal table. If you need to insert a block of rows into a large internal table, prepare another table with the rows to be inserted and use insert lines instead. The rows in the target table will only be re-indexed once, after this statement has executed.

12

When inserting a new row into it inside of a loop at it, the insert does not affect the internal table immediately, but instead it becomes effective on the next loop pass. When inserting a row *after* the current row, the table is re-indexed at the endloop, sy-tabix is incremented, and the next loop pass processes the row pointed to by sy-tabix. For example, suppose you are in the third loop pass and you insert a record before row 4. When endloop is executed, the new row becomes row 4, the old row 4 becomes row 5, and so on. Sy-tabix is incremented by 1, and the next loop pass processes the newly inserted record.

If, inside of a loop, you insert a row *before* the current row, the table is again re-indexed at the endloop. This time, however, sy-tabix is incremented by 1 plus the number of rows inserted before the current row. The next time through the loop, the row following the current row is processed. Suppose, for example, in the third loop pass you insert a row before row 3. At the endloop, the new row becomes row 3, row 3 becomes row 4, and so on. The row you just processed now has an index of 4. sy-tabix is incremented by 2, which gives 5. Row 4 was re-indexed to 5, so it is processed on the next loop pass.

Modifying Rows in an Internal Table

To modify the contents of one or more rows of an internal table, use the modify statement.

Syntax for the modify Statement

The following is the syntax for the modify statement.

```
modify it [from wa] [index n] [transporting c1 c2 ... [where exp]]
```

where:

- *it* is the name of an internal table with or without a header line.
- *wa* is a work area with the same structure as a row in the body of *it*.
- *n* is a numeric literal, variable, or constant.
- *c1* and *c2* are components of *it*.
- *exp* is a logical expression involving components of *it*.

The following points apply:

- If from *wa* is specified, the row is overwritten with the contents of *wa*.
- If from *wa* is not specified, the row is overwritten with the contents of the header line.
- If index *n* is specified, *n* identifies the number of the row that is overwritten.
- modify it can be specified inside or outside of loop at it. If it is outside, index *n* must be specified. When inside, index *n* is optional. If it is not specified, the current row is modified.

transporting specifies which components are to be overwritten. Without it, all are over-written. With it, only the specified components are overwritten. The rest remain unchanged.

Specifying a where condition after transporting causes the specified components to be overwritten in all rows that satisfy the where clause. The left-hand side of each part of *exp* must specify a component of *it*. The same component can be specified both after transporting and in *exp*.

You can't use modify it with where:

- Inside of loop at it
- With the index addition

Listing 12.5 shows a sample program that modifies the contents of an internal table.

LISTING 12.5   USE modify TO OVERWRITE THE EXISTING CONTENTS OF ONE OR

INPUT   MORE ROWS OF AN INTERNAL TABLE

```
 1  report ztx1205.
 2  data: begin of it occurs 5,
 3            f1 like sy-index,
 4            f2,
 5            end of it,
 6         alpha(5) value 'ABCDE'.
 7
 8  do 5 times varying it-f2 from alpha+0 next alpha+1.
 9      it-f1 = sy-index.
10      append it.
11      enddo.
12
13 it-f2 = 'Z'.
14 modify it index 4.
15
16 loop at it.
17      write: / it-f1, it-f2.
18      endloop.
19
20 loop at it.
21      it-f1 = it-f1 * 2.
22      modify it.
23      endloop.
24
25 skip.
26 loop at it.
27      write: / it-f1, it-f2.
28      endloop.
29
30 it-f2 = 'X'.
31 modify it transporting f2 where f1 <> 10.
32
33 skip.
34 loop at it.
35      write: / it-f1, it-f2.
36      endloop.
```

12

The code in Listing 12.5 produces this output:

```
1    A
2    B
3    C
5    Z
5    E

2    A
4    B
6    C
10   Z
10   E

2    X
4    X
6    X
10   Z
10   E
```

- Lines 8 through 11 add five rows to it. Each row contains a sequential number and letter of the alphabet.

- Line 13 modifies the contents of it-f2, giving it a value of 'Z'. it-f1 is not modified, so it still contains the last value added to the table: 5.

- Line 14 overwrites row 4 with the contents of the header line, changing f1 to 5 and f2 to Z.

- Lines 20 through 23 loop through all rows of it, placing each row one at a time into the header line. Line 21 multiplies by 2 the contents of header line component f1. Line 22 copies the contents of the header line back into the current row in the body of it, overwriting it.

- Line 30 modifies the contents of the header line component f2, assigning it a value of 'X'.

- Line 31 modifies all rows in the body where f1 is not equal to 10. Only the value of f2 is copied from the header line and overwrites the f2 values in the body. f1 remains unchanged in the body and in the header line.

Deleting Internal Table Contents

To delete contents of an internal table, you can use the following statements:

- `free`

- `refresh`

- `clear`

- `delete`

Using `free` to Delete Internal Table Contents

Use the `free` statement to delete all rows from an internal table and free the associated memory.

Syntax for the `free` Statement

The following is the syntax for the `free` statement.

```
free it.
```

where:

- *it* is an internal table with or without a header line.

The following points apply:

- All rows are deleted and all memory used by the body of the internal table is freed.
- The header line, if it exists, remains unchanged.

Use `free` when you are finished using an internal table.

> **Tip**
>
> Although the memory for internal tables is automatically freed when your program ends, freeing it yourself is usually more efficient. The reason for this lies in the fact that when the output is displayed to the user, technically your program has not yet ended. All resources remain allocated and the program does not end until the user presses the Back button. This finally ends your program and frees all internal table contents. You can free the internal tables sooner by putting `free` statements at the end of your program. The internal table contents will be released before the user sees the list instead of after.

Listing 12.6 shows how to use the `free` statement.

LISTING 12.6   USE THE `free` STATEMENT TO DELETE ALL ROWS FROM AN
INPUT   INTERNAL TABLE AND FREE THE ASSOCIATED MEMORY

```
1   report ztx1206.
2   data: begin of it occurs 3,
3            f1 like sy-index,
4            end of it.
5
6   do 3 times.
7       it-f1 = sy-index.
8       append it.
```

continues

12

LISTING 12.6 CONTINUED

```
 9       enddo.
10
11 loop at it.
12     write it-f1.
13     endloop.
14
15 free it.
16 if it[] is initial.
17     write: / 'no rows exist in it after free'.
18     endif.
```

The code in Listing 12.6 produces this output:

```
             1          2          3
no rows exist in it after free
```

 ANALYSIS Line 15 deletes all rows from the internal table and frees the associated memory.

Using `refresh` to Delete Internal Table Contents

Use the `refresh` statement to delete all rows from an internal table but leave the memory allocated.

Syntax for the `refresh` Statement

The following is the syntax for the `refresh` statement.

```
refresh it.
```

where:

- *it* is an internal table with or without a header line.

The following points apply:

- All rows are deleted. All memory used by the body of the internal table remains allocated.
- The header line, if it exists, is unchanged.

Use `refresh` when you want to delete all rows but you intend to fill the internal table back up again. For example, if you are producing a sales report by department, you might fill the internal table with all sales for one department, process the data, and write it out. Then, after a `refresh`, you could fill the internal table with the data for the next department, write it out, and so on.

If you intend to refill a table immediately after clearing it, `refresh` is more efficient than `free` because it avoids unnecessary memory allocations.

Listing 12.7 shows how to use the `refresh` statement.

LISTING 12.7   USE THE `refresh` STATEMENT TO DELETE ALL ROWS FROM AN
INPUT   INTERNAL TABLE

```
 1  report ztx1207.
 2  data: begin of it occurs 3,
 3            f1 like sy-index,
 4          end of it,
 5        i like sy-index.
 6
 7  do 3 times.
 8      i = sy-index.
 9      do 3 times.
10        it-f1 = i * sy-index.
11        append it.
12      enddo.
13    write: / ''.
14    loop at it.
15        write it-f1.
16        endloop.
17    refresh it.
18    enddo.
19
20 free it.
```

The code in Listing 12.7 produces this output:

OUTPUT

```
1        2        3
2        4        6
3        6        9
```

ANALYSIS

- Line 7 begins a loop that is executed three times. It contains a nested inner loop.

- Line 8 stores the current value of `sy-index` from the outer loop.

- Line 9 begins the inner loop.

- On line 10, the number of the inner loop pass is multiplied by the number of the outer loop pass.

- Line 11 adds each row to the internal table.

- Line 13 begins a new line of output.

- Lines 14 through 16 write out the contents of the internal table.

- Line 17 deletes all rows from the internal table but does not free the memory. Refresh is used here instead of `free` because the outer loop repeats and refills the internal table again immediately.

12

- Line 20 deletes all rows and frees the memory for the internal table before the list is shown. This makes the program more efficient.

Using `clear` with an Internal Table

You can use the `clear` statement to do either of the following:

- Delete all rows from an internal table and leave the memory allocated.
- Clear the header line (set its components to blanks and zeros).

▼ SYNTAX

Syntax for the `clear` Statement When Used with an Internal Table

The following is the syntax for the `clear` statement when used with an internal table.

```
clear it ¦ clear it[]
```

where:

▲

- `it` is the name of an internal table.

The following points apply:

- If `it` has a header line, `clear it[]` deletes all rows. `clear it` clears the header line.
- If `it` does not have a header line, both forms delete all rows and leave the memory allocated.

The effect of `clear` on an internal table is summarized in Table 12.3. The effect of `clear` varies depending on whether the internal table has a header line or not.

TABLE 12.3   EFFECT OF `clear` ON AN INTERNAL TABLE

Statement	If it has a header line	If it doesn't have a header line
`clear it`	Clears the header line	Deletes all rows
`clear it[]`	Deletes all rows	Deletes all rows

The program in Listing 12.8 illustrates the use of the `clear` statement with an internal table.

INPUT

LISTING 12.8 THE clear STATEMENT CAN BE USED TO CLEAR THE HEADER LINE OR DELETE THE CONTENTS OF AN INTERNAL TABLE

```
 1  report ztx1208.
 2  data: begin of it occurs 3,
 3            f1,
 4            end of it.
 5
 6  it-f1 = 'X'.
 7  append: it, it.
 8
 9  clear it.          "it has a header line so clears the header line
10  write: 'f1=', it-f1.
11
12  write: / ''.
13  loop at it.
14      write it-f1.
15      endloop.
16
17  clear it[].        "same as: refresh it.
18  loop at it.
19      write it-f1.
20      endloop.
21  write: / 'sy-subrc=', sy-subrc.
```

The code in Listing 12.8 produces this output:

OUTPUT

```
f1=
   X X
sy-subrc=      4
```

ANALYSIS

- Line 6 places 'X' in the header line of it.

- Line 7 appends two rows to it; both have 'X' in f1.

- Line 9 clears the header line for it.

- Line 10 writes blanks, showing that the header line for it is clear.

- Lines 13 through 15 produce output to show that the internal table still contains two rows.

- Line 17 clears the body of it, effectively deleting all rows and leaving the memory allocated. The contents of the header line are unchanged.

- Lines 18 through 20 do not produce any output because the internal table is empty.

- Line 21 shows the return code after the loop. This again confirms that no rows exist in the internal table.

12

Using the `delete` Statement to Delete Rows from an Internal Table

Using the `delete` statement, you can delete one or more rows from an internal table.

Syntax for the `delete` Statement

▼ SYNTAX

The following is the syntax for the `delete` statement.

```
delete it  (a) [index n]
           (b) [from i] [to j]
           (c) [where exp]
```

where:

▲

- *n*, *fn*, and *tn* are numeric literals, variables, or constants.
- *exp* is a logical expression involving components of *it*.

The following points apply:

- The additions following *(a)*, *(b)*, and *(c)* are all optional.
- Only one of *(a)*, *(b)*, or *(c)* can be specified.
- `delete it` without any additions can only be used inside `loop at it`. In that case, it deletes the current row.
- If `index n` is specified, the *n*th row of *it* is deleted.
- If `from i` is specified, rows are deleted beginning with the *i*th row.
- If `to j` is specified, rows are deleted up to and including the *j*th row.
- If `from` is not specified with `to`, `from 1` is assumed.
- If `to` is not specified with `from`, to the last row in the table is assumed.
- The expression *exp* must have a component of *it* on the left side of each comparison. For example, if *it* has components *f1* and *f2*, *exp* could be `where f1 = 'A' and f2 = 'B'`.

Listing 12.9 shows a sample program that deletes data from an internal table using the `delete` statement.

INPUT

LISTING 12.9 DELETING ROWS FROM AN INTERNAL TABLE CAN ALSO BE DONE USING THE `delete` STATEMENT

```
1  report ztx1209.
2  data: begin of it occurs 12,
3          f1,
4          end of it,
```

```
 5            alpha(12) value 'ABCDEFGHIJKL'.
 6
 7  do 12 times varying it-f1 from alpha+0 next alpha+1.
 8      append it.
 9      enddo.
10
11 loop at it.
12     write: / sy-tabix, it-f1.
13     endloop.
14
15 delete it index 5.
16 skip.
17 loop at it.
18     write: / sy-tabix, it-f1.
19     endloop.
20
21 delete it from 6 to 8.
22 skip.
23 loop at it.
24     write: / sy-tabix, it-f1.
25     endloop.
26
27 delete it where f1 between 'B' and 'D'.
28 skip.
29 loop at it.
30     write: / sy-tabix, it-f1.
31     endloop.
32
33 loop at it where f1 between 'E' and 'J'.
34     delete it.
35     endloop.
36
37 skip.
38 loop at it.
39     write: / sy-tabix, it-f1.
40     endloop.
41
42 read table it with key f1 = 'K' binary search.
43 write: /, / 'sy-subrc=', sy-subrc, 'sy-tabix=', sy-tabix, / ''.
44 if sy-subrc = 0.
45     delete it index sy-tabix.
46     endif.
47
48 skip.
49 loop at it.
50     write: / sy-tabix, it-f1.
51     endloop.
52
53 free it.
```

12

The code in Listing 12.9 produces this output:

OUTPUT

```
 1   A
 2   B
 3   C
 4   D
 5   E
 6   F
 7   G
 8   H
 9   I
10   J
11   K
12   L

 1   A
 2   B
 3   C
 4   D
 5   F
 6   G
 7   H
 8   I
 9   J
10   K
11   L

 1   A
 2   B
 3   C
 4   D
 5   F
 6   J
 7   K
 8   L

 1   A
 2   F
 3   J
 4   K
 5   L

 1   A
 2   K
 3   L

sy-subrc=       0  sy-tabix=              2

 1   A
 2   L
```

ANALYSIS
- Lines 7 through 9 fill `it` with 12 rows containing the values `'A'` through `'L'`.
- Lines 11 through 13 write out the contents of the internal table.
- Line 15 deletes the fifth row, removing `'E'` from the table. The sixth row becomes the fifth, the seventh becomes the sixth, and so on.
- Line 21 deletes the sixth through eighth rows, removing G, H, and I from the table. The ninth row becomes the sixth, and so on.
- Line 27 deletes rows that have `f1` values between `'B'` and `'D'`, inclusive. This causes the second, third and fourth rows to be deleted.
- Line 33 retrieves rows having an `f1` value between `'E'` and `'J'`, inclusive. Rows 2 and 3 meet the criteria. The `delete` statement on line 34 doesn't have any additions, so it deletes the current row on each pass of the loop. This causes the second and third rows to be deleted.
- Line 42 locates the row having an `f1` value of `'K'`. Although `it` only contains three rows, `binary search` is included for the sake of good example. Row 2 matches, so `sy-subrc` is set to zero and `sy-tabix` is set to 2.
- Line 45 is executed because `sy-subrc` is zero. It deletes row 2, removing `'K'` from the internal table.

Like inserts, deletes inside of a `loop at it` do not affect the internal table immediately, but instead become effective on the next loop pass. When deleting a row *after* the current row, the table is re-indexed at the `endloop`, `sy-tabix` is incremented, and the next loop pass processes the row pointed to by `sy-tabix`. For example, suppose you are in the third loop pass and you delete row 4. When `endloop` is executed, the row is deleted, row 5 becomes row 4, and so on. `sy-tabix` is incremented by 1 and the next loop pass processes the next record.

If, when inside a loop, you delete a row *before* the current row, the table is again re-indexed at the `endloop`. This time, however, `sy-tabix` is incremented by 1 minus the number or rows deleted before the current row. The next time through the loop, the row following the current row is processed. Suppose, for example, in the third loop pass you delete row 3. At the `endloop`, row 4 becomes row 3, and so on. `sy-tabix` is incremented by 0, giving 3. Row 4 was re-indexed to 3, so it is processed on the next loop pass.

Creating Top 10 Lists Using `append sorted by`

Imagine that you are asked to create a report of the top 10 sales representatives in your company. Assuming you have a way of obtaining the total sales for each rep, you could do one of the following:

- Append all reps and their total sales into an internal table.

12

- Sort them descending by sales.
- Write out the first 10.

This seems like a logical way to proceed. However, using the append sorted by statement often can produce the same result and be twice as efficient.

Syntax for the append sorted by Statement

The following is the syntax for the append sorted by statement.

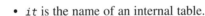

append [wa to] it sorted by c.

where:

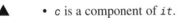

- it is the name of an internal table.
- wa is a work area having the same structure as a row of the internal table.
- c is a component of it.

The following points apply:

- If wa to is not specified, the row to be appended is taken from the header line.
- If wa to is specified, the row to be appended is taken from the work area wa.
- Only one component c can be specified.

The append sorted by statement takes a row from the work area and inserts it into the internal table at the point where it belongs in the sort order. It has two unusual properties:

- The number of rows that can be appended is limited by the value on the occurs clause. For example, if the occurs clause is 10, a maximum of 10 rows can be appended to the internal table. This is the only situation where occurs limits the number of rows that can be added to an internal table.
- It only sorts in descending order.

The net effect is a "top *n* list," where *n* is the number on the occurs clause.

With each append, the system searches the existing table contents to determine where the new row fits. The sort order is by c descending. If there are fewer rows in the internal table than specified by *n* on the occurs clause, the row is as per the sort order. If there are *n* rows in the internal table, the row is inserted as per the sort order and the last row is discarded. If the value in c already exists in the internal table, the new row is always appended after existing rows that have the same value. Therefore, if occurs is 3 and row 3 contains 'X' in c, a new row having 'X' in c will not be appended.

Listing 12.10 shows a sample program that creates a list of the top three sales reps.

INPUT   **LISTING 12.10**   USING append sorted by TO FIND THE TOP THREE SALES REPS

```
1  report ztx1210.
2  data: begin of it occurs 3,
3            sales type p decimals 2,
4            name(10),
5            end of it.
6
7  it-sales    = 100.
8  it-name     = 'Jack'.
9  append it sorted by sales.
10
11 it-sales    = 50.
12 it-name     = 'Jim'.
13 append it sorted by sales.
14
15 it-sales    = 150.
16 it-name     = 'Jane'.
17 append it sorted by sales.
18
19 it-sales    = 75.
20 it-name     = 'George'.
21 append it sorted by sales.
22
23 it-sales    = 200.
24 it-name     = 'Gina'.
25 append it sorted by sales.
26
27 it-sales    = 100.
28 it-name     = 'Jeff'.
29 append it sorted by sales.
30
31 loop at it.
32    write: / it-sales, it-name.
33    endloop.
```

The code in Listing 12.10 produces this output:

OUTPUT
```
200.00  Gina
150.00  Jane
100.00  Jack
```

ANALYSIS
- Lines 2 through 5 define an internal table with an occurs value of 3. If this internal table is filled using append sorted by, the maximum number of rows in this internal table will be limited to three.

- Lines 7 and 8 assign values to the header line.

- Line 9 searches it for the correct spot to insert the new row. The internal table is empty, so the row is simply appended (see Figure 12.1).

12

FIGURE 12.1.

No rows exist in the internal table, so the first row is simply appended.

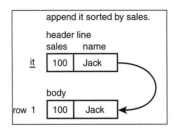

• 50 comes after 100 when sorting sales descending, so line 13 inserts the new row after the existing one (see Figure 12.2).

FIGURE 12.2.

The second row is inserted in the correct sort sequence so that it comes after the first row.

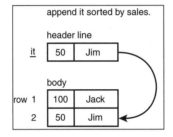

• 150 comes before 100, so line 15 inserts the new row before the first row. The internal table now contains the maximum number of rows: three rows (see Figure 12.3).

FIGURE 12.3.

This time the sort sequence dictates that the new row be inserted before the first.

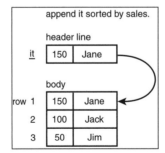

• 75 comes after 100, so line 21 inserts the new row after the second row, thereby making the new row the third row. The third row would become the fourth, but it can only hold three rows, so the fourth is discarded (see Figure 12.4).

• 200 comes before 150, so line 25 inserts it before the first row. The rest of the rows are pushed down and the last is discarded (see Figure 12.5).

FIGURE 12.4.

This row fits after the second, so it is inserted there. The internal table can hold a maximum of three rows, so the fourth row is discarded.

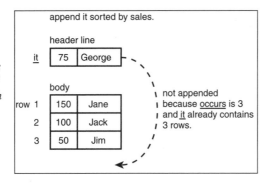

append it sorted by sales.

header line

it | 75 | George

body

row 1 | 150 | Jane
2 | 100 | Jack
3 | 50 | Jim

not appended because <u>occurs</u> is 3 and <u>it</u> already contains 3 rows.

FIGURE 12.5.

This time the new row should come first. The existing rows are pushed down and the last one is discarded.

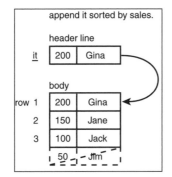

append it sorted by sales.

header line

it | 200 | Gina

body

row 1 | 200 | Gina
2 | 150 | Jane
3 | 100 | Jack
| 50 | Jim

- 100 comes after 150, but there is already a 100 there. Line 29 therefore tries to insert the new row after the existing value of 100. That would make it row 4, so the row is not inserted at all (see Figure 12.6).

12

FIGURE 12.6.

This new row will follow all existing rows that have the same value. That would make it row 4, so it is not inserted.

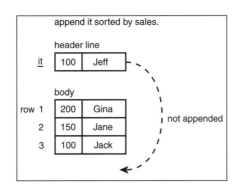

append it sorted by sales.

header line

it | 100 | Jeff

body

row 1 | 200 | Gina
2 | 150 | Jane
3 | 100 | Jack

not appended

Do not mix append sorted by with any other statements that add data to an internal table (such as insert or append). If you fill it with append sorted by, that should be the only statement you use. Mixing these statements will result in unpredictable behavior.

> **Tip**
>
> `append sorted by` is more efficient when you are appending one row at a time to an internal table. If you already have the data in a database table and merely want to find the top 10 values, it is more efficient to insert the rows using an array operation and then sort. (For information on array operations, see Day 13, "Advanced Internal Tables: Part 2.")

Filling an Internal Table Using `collect`

Using the `collect` statement, you can create totals within an internal table as you fill it.

Syntax for the `collect` Statement

The following is the syntax for the `collect` statement.

```
collect [wa into] it.
```

where:

- *it* is an internal table.
- *wa* is a work area that has the same structure as *it*.

The following points apply:

- If *wa* `into` is specified, the row to be collected is taken from the explicit work area *wa*. In this case, the header line of the internal table is ignored, if it has one.
- If *wa* `into` is not specified, the internal table must have a header line. The row to be collected is taken from the header line for *it*.

When `collect` is executed, the system forms a key from the default key fields in the work area. The default key fields are the character fields (types c, n, d, t, and x). Therefore the key is composed of the values from all fields of type c, n, d, t, and x. It doesn't matter if they are beside one another or separated from each other by other fields.

The system then searches the body of the internal table for a row that has the same key as the key in the work area. If it doesn't find one, the row is appended to the end of the table. If it does find one, the numeric fields (types i, p, and f) in the work area are added to the corresponding fields in the found row. Listing 12.11 illustrates this concept.

> **INPUT**
>
> **LISTING 12.11**   `collect` COMBINES ROWS AS THEY ARE ADDED TO AN INTERNAL TABLE

```
1   report ztx1211.
2   data: begin of it occurs 10,
3           date type d,                    "   part of default key
4           tot_sales type p decimals 2,    "not part of default key
```

```
 5              name(10),                  "   part of default key
 6              num_sales type i value 1,  "not part of default key
 7              end of it.
 8
 9  it-date     = '19980101'.
10 it-tot_sales = 100.
11 it-name      = 'Jack'.
12 collect it.
13
14 it-date      = '19980101'.
15 it-tot_sales = 200.
16 it-name      = 'Jim'.
17 collect it.
18
19 it-date      = '19980101'.
20 it-tot_sales = 300.
21 it-name      = 'Jack'.
22 collect it.
23
24 it-date      = '19980101'.
25 it-tot_sales = 400.
26 it-name      = 'Jack'.
27 collect it.
28
29 it-date      = '19980101'.
30 it-tot_sales = 500.
31 it-name      = 'Jim'.
32 collect it.
33
34 it-date      = '19980101'.
35 it-tot_sales = 600.
36 it-name      = 'Jane'.
37 collect it.
38
39 it-date      = '19980102'.
40 it-tot_sales = 700.
41 it-name      = 'Jack'.
42 collect it.
43
44 loop at it.
45    write: / it-date, it-tot_sales, it-name, it-num_sales.
46    endloop.
```

The code in Listing 12.11 produces this output:

OUTPUT
```
19980101          800.00  Jack          3
19980101          700.00  Jim           2
19980101          600.00  Jane          1
19980102          700.00  Jack          1
```

- Lines 2 through 7 define an internal table that has four components. Two are character types (date and name) and two are numeric types (tot_sales and num_sales). The default key is therefore composed of the components date and name.

- Lines 9 through 11 assign values to the header line components date, tot_sales, and name. num_sales still has a default value of 1, assigned on line 6.

- Line 12 searches the body of it for a row that has the same values in date and name (the default key fields) as those in the header line. The internal table is empty, so no rows match. The header line is therefore appended to the internal table (see Figure 12.7).

FIGURE 12.7.

If the default key is not found in the body, the row is appended. The default key is composed of all non-numeric fields, so in this diagram it is the combination of date (first field) and name (third field).

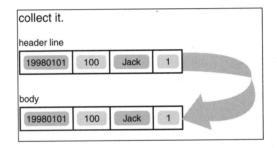

- Line 17 behaves like line 12. The internal table has one row, but the values in the date and name fields don't match, so the header line is appended to the internal table (see Figure 12.8).

FIGURE 12.8.

Again, the default key is not found in the table, so this row is also appended.

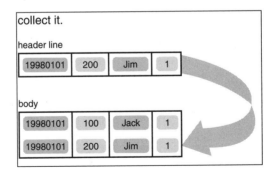

- Line 22 searches the internal table for a row that has '19980101' in the date field and 'Jack' in the name field. Row 1 matches, so the numeric fields are added together. The header line tot_sales field contains 200. This is added to the tot_sales field in row 1, yielding a total of 300. The value in the num_sales field in the header line is also added to the num_sales field in row 1, giving a value of 2. Row 1 is updated with these values. The contents of the header line are unchanged (see Figure 12.9).

FIGURE 12.9.

This time the default key matches the first row of the table. The numeric fields in the work area are added to the corresponding fields in the first row.

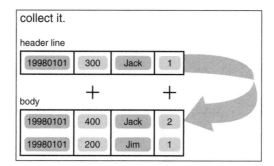

- Line 27 searches for a row with a date of '19980101' and a name of 'Jack'. Row 1 matches, so the contents of the numeric fields (tot_sales and num_sales) in the header line are added to the numeric fields in the found row (see Figure 12.10).

FIGURE 12.10.

Again, the default key matches the first row of the table. The numeric fields in the work area are added to the corresponding fields in the first row.

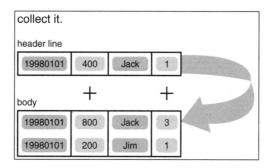

12

- Line 32 matches on row 2 and adds '500' to tot_sales and 1 to num_sales (see Figure 12.11).
- On line 37, the values in date and name (the default key fields) of the header line do not match any rows in it, so a new row is appended to the end of the table (see Figure 12.12).

FIGURE **12.11.**

FIGURE 12.11.

This time the default key matches the second row of the table. The numeric fields in the work area are added to the corresponding fields in the second row.

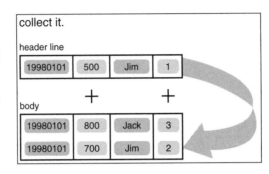

FIGURE 12.12.

The default key does not match any rows this time, so a new row is appended.

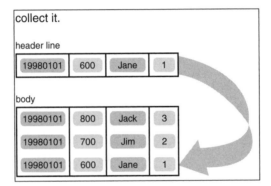

- Line 42 also causes a new row to be appended to the internal table because the values in date and name do not match in any rows of it (see Figure 12.13).

FIGURE 12.13.

The default keys again do not match any rows, so another row is appended.

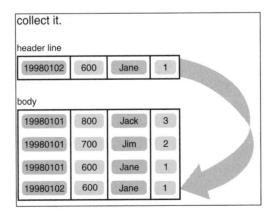

> If you use `collect` to add rows to an internal table, all rows should be added using `collect`. You should not combine `collect` with `append` or any other statement that adds data to an internal table. The results will be unpredictable. The only other statement that you can use to modify the contents of an internal table filled via `collect` is `modify ... transporting f1 f2 ...`, where `f1` and `f2` are numeric fields only (non-default key fields).

Summary

- The table body operator provides an efficient way to test for existence of data, to compare two internal tables for equality, or to duplicate an internal table.

- The `describe table` statement places the number of internal table rows into `sy-tfill`, the width of a row in bytes into `sy-tleng`, and the size of the `occurs` clause into `sy-toccu`.

- To copy a portion of an internal table from one to another, use `append lines of` or `insert lines of`.

- `editor-call` displays the contents of an internal table in an editor. It enables the user to modify the data, and is also a useful debugging tool.

- `insert` inserts a row at any position into an internal table. The position can be specified using an index or it can operate on the current row inside a loop.

- `modify` modifies the contents of one or more rows. The row can be specified using an index or it can operate on the current row inside a loop. Using the `where` clause, you can modify the contents of many rows.

- `delete` removes one or more rows. When used inside of a loop without additions, it deletes the current row. You can also specify a single index, an index range, or a `where` clause.

- `clear it` clears the header line of `it`. If there is no header line, all rows are deleted. `clear it[]` always deletes all rows from `it`. The internal table memory remains allocated.

- `refresh` always deletes all rows and leaves the memory allocated. It is exactly equivalent to `clear it[]`. It is used if the internal table will be refilled with data.

- `free it` deletes all rows from `it` and frees the memory. It should be placed in the program immediately after internal table processing is complete.

- Use `append sorted by` to create top 10 lists instead of appending row by row and then sorting.

- Use `collect` to accumulate counts and totals within an internal table as it is being filled. It can also be used to ensure that all entries are unique.

12

Do	Don't
DO use the `free` statement at the end of your program for all internal tables. This explicitly frees memory that will no longer be used while the user views the output. **DO** use the table body operator to test for the existence of data. **DO** use the `append sorted by` statement when creating top 10 lists, unless the list already exists and only needs to be sorted.	**DON'T** append or insert lines one at a time if they can processed as a group using `insert lines of` or `append lines of`.

Q&A

Q In this chapter you have covered so many ways to accomplish similar tasks. In ABAP/4 there always seems to be many ways to do the same thing. I'm just learning. I can only remember so many ways of doing something. Why not just show me the best way and forget the rest?

A I appreciate your concern. Wherever possible I leave out archaic, inefficient, rarely used, and duplicate methods. But there are two very good reasons for including the variations I have described here: 1) efficiency and 2) understanding of existing code. Due to the amount of data that resides in an R/3 system, efficiency is a primary concern in ABAP/4 programs. You should strive to use the most efficient form of each statement in a given situation. This can result in drastic performance improvements not only for your programs, but also for the entire system. It is common to have to rewrite code after it reaches production because it impacts system performance. As for the second point, programmers often spend more time reading existing code than creating new code, so you need to understand the subtle variations of these statements. They are used in abundance in SAP code. If you don't understand SAP's code, you won't be able to understand how the data got to its present state or how the output is arrived at.

Workshop

The Workshop provides you two ways for you to affirm what you've learned in this chapter. The Quiz section poses questions to help you solidify your understanding of the material covered and the Exercise section provides you with experience in using what you have learned. You can find answers to the quiz questions and exercises in Appendix B, "Answers to Quiz Questions and Exercises."

Quiz

1. If I modify the value of sy-tabix inside a loop, does this change the current row? For example, would the insert, modify, and delete statements operate on the row in the work area or the row indicated by sy-tabix?

2. When would I use the value of sy-toccu? Why would I need to know the value of the occurs clause at runtime?

Exercise 1

Read the contents of ztxlfa1 into an internal table (use select into table). Then modify the land1 column so that the third row contains 'US' (use modify transporting where). Also modify the regions, changing all MA to TX (use modify transporting where).

12

DAY 13

Advanced Internal Tables, Part 2

Chapter Objectives

After you complete this chapter, you will be able to:

- Fill an internal table from a database table using the most efficient constructs
- Perform control break processing on internal tables using `at` and `on change of`

Filling an Internal Table from a Database Table

Quite often in ABAP/4, the data you put into an internal table comes from one or more database tables. This section presents the best ways to do this.

The ways of filling an internal table from the database fall into two categories:

- Selecting multiple rows directly into the body of an internal table
- Selecting single rows into a work area and then appending

Selecting Multiple Rows Directly into an Internal Table

To select multiple rows directly into the body of an internal table, use the `into table` addition of the `select` statement. It takes the selected rows and places them into the body of an internal table in a single operation known as an array operation. No work areas are used or needed.

NEW TERM An *array operation* is any statement that performs an operation on multiple rows of an internal table, instead of a single row at a time. Array operations are always more efficient than single row operations.

> **Tip**
>
> `select into table` is the most efficient way to fill an internal table from the database.

Syntax for the `into table` Addition of the `select` Statement

The following is the syntax for the `into table` addition of the `select` statement.

```
(a) select *
(b) select f1 f2 . . .

            from dbtab into [corresponding fields of] table it.
```

where:

- *dbtab* is the name of a database table.
- *f1* and *f2* are fields within *dbtab*.
- *it* is the name of an internal table.

The following points apply:

- *it* can have a header line.
- Other additions, such as `where` and `order by`, can follow *it*.
- `endselect` is not used with `into table`. `select into table` does not start a loop, consequently no `endselect` is needed.

The `select into table` statement places all selected rows directly into the body of *it*. Existing internal table contents are first discarded. Listing 13.1 contains a sample program using `select into table`.

LISTING 13.1   THIS PROGRAM READS ROWS FROM A DATABASE TABLE DIRECTLY
INTO AN INTERNAL TABLE

```
1  report ztx1301.
2  tables ztxlfa1.
3  data it like ztxlfa1 occurs 23 with header line.
4
5  select * from ztxlfa1 into table it.    "don't code an endselect
6  loop at it.
7      write: / it-lifnr, it-name1.
8      endloop.
9
10 select * from ztxlfa1 into table it
11     where lifnr between 'V2' and 'V5'.
12 skip.
13 loop at it.
14     write: / it-lifnr, it-name1.
15     endloop.
16 free it.
```

The code in Listing 13.1 produces this output:

```
V9          Code Now, Specs Later Ltd.
1000        Parts Unlimited
1010        Industrial Pumps Inc.
1020        Chemical Nation Ltd.
1030        ChickenFeed Ltd.
1050        The Bit Bucket
1060        Memory Lane Ltd.
1070        Flip My Switch Inc.
V10         Duncan's Mouse Inc.
V6          Anna Banana Ltd.
V8          Smile When You Say That Ltd.
V11         Weiner Schnittsel Inc.
V12         Saurkrouten
1040        Motherboards Inc.
1080        Silicon Sandwich Ltd.
1090        Consume Inc.
2000        Monitors and More Ltd.
V1          Quantity First Ltd.
V2          OverPriced Goods Inc.
V3          Fluffy Bunnies Ltd.
V4          Moo like a Cow Inc.
V5          Wolfman Sport Accessories Inc.
V7          The Breakfast Club Inc.

V2          OverPriced Goods Inc.
V3          Fluffy Bunnies Ltd.
V4          Moo like a Cow Inc.
V5          Wolfman Sport Accessories Inc.
```

13

• Line 5 retrieves all rows from database table ztxlfa1 and places them directly into the body of the internal table it. The header line is not used and its contents are unchanged.

• Line 10 is like line 5, except that it only retrieves vendor numbers between V2 and V5. The existing contents of it are discarded before it is filled.

 Don't use an endselect with select into table. A syntax error will occur.

select into table and Sorting

Suppose your program already reads data into an internal table. If that data needs to be sorted, use the sort statement. Don't use order by on select even if those fields are supported by an index. On a quiet, standalone system, measurements reveal that the sort statement is a little faster. Even if they were at a par, sort would still be the preferred method because it offloads cycles from the database server to the application server.

 Don't use order by with select into table. Use sort on the internal table instead.

Fields You Select Must Fit into the Internal Table

Imagine this scenario:

• A row is retrieved from *dbtab*.

• A row is allocated in *it*.

• The row from *dbtab* is moved byte-by-byte into the new row in *it*.

Each row from *dbtab* is moved byte-by-byte into a new row of *it*, which is exactly like assigning one field string to another. There is only one difference between this and a field string assignment: *dbtab* can be shorter (in bytes) than *it*, but it cannot be longer than *it*. If it is longer, a short dump (error SAPSQL_SELECT_TAB_TOO_SMALL) occurs. The data types and lengths of each sending field in *dbtab* should match the receiving field in *it*. Any remaining fields in *it* are filled with initial values (blanks or zeros). Figures 13.1 through 13.4 illustrate this point.

FIGURE 13.1.

Database table
ztx1302 *contains three fields:* f1, f2, *and* f3.
f1 *is a single byte,* f2 *is two bytes long, and* f3 *is one byte.*

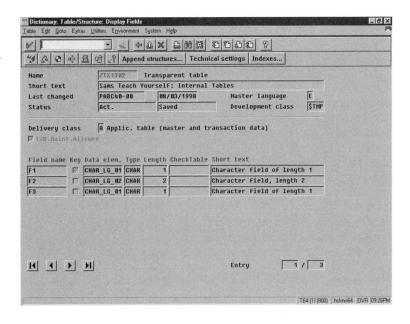

FIGURE 13.2.

*The * causes all fields to be selected, in order, from database table* ztx1302. *They fit exactly into each row of* it *because the structure of* it *matches that of the database table.*

```
tables ztx1302.
data it like ztx1302 occurs 5.

select  *  from ztx1302 into table it.
```

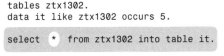

FIGURE 13.3.

In this example, only the first two fields are selected from database table ztx1302, *for a total of three bytes. They are placed byte-by-byte into the first three bytes of each row of* it.

```
tables ztx1302.
data it like ztx1302 occurs 5.

select f1 f2 from ztx1302 into table it.
```

13

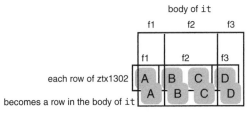

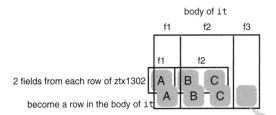

Figure 13.4.

Again, the first two fields are selected from database table ztx1302, *but this time in a different order than they appear in the internal table. This causes corrupt data when they are placed byte-by-byte into each row of* it. it-f1 *receives the first byte of* f2, *and* it-f2 *receives the last byte of* f2 *and one byte from* f1.

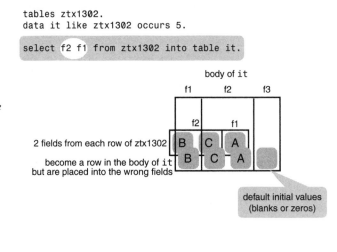

Table 13.1 summarizes the rules for using select with into table. Selected fields must fit into the internal table. This table describes the restrictions you will face.

Table 13.1 Rules for Using select with into table

Statement	Which Fields Are Selected?	Restrictions
Select *	All fields in the database table	The internal table must contain at least as many fields as the database table, and they must be like the database table fields.
Select f1	f1 from the database table	The internal table must begin with a field like f1, or have only one field and it must be like f1.

Listings 13.2 and 13.3 illustrate this concept.

Listing 13.2 What Happens if Table Structures Differ When Using the Select-into Statement

`INPUT`

```
1   report ztx1302.
2   tables ztxlfa1.
3   data            begin of it occurs 2.
4   include structure    ztxlfa1.
5   data:                invoice_amt type p,
```

```
6                           end of it.
7
8  select * from ztxlfa1 into table it where land1 = 'DE'.
9  loop at it.
10     write: / it-lifnr, it-land1, it-regio, it-invoice_amt.
11     endloop.
12
13 skip.
14 select lifnr land1 regio from ztxlfa1 into table it where land1 = 'DE'.
15 loop at it.
16     write: / it-mandt, it-lifnr, it-land1, it-regio.
17     endloop.
18 free it.
```

The code in Listing 13.2 produces this output:

OUTPUT

```
V11        DE  07              0
V12        DE  14              0
V8         DE  03              0

V11  DE         07
V12  DE         14
V8   DE         03
```

ANALYSIS

- Line 3 defines it as having all of the fields of DDIC structure ztxlfa1, plus an additional field.

- Line 8 selects all fields from ztxlfa1. They fill the beginning of each row in it. Invoice_amt is set to zero.

- Line 14 selects lifnr land1 and regio into the first part of each row of it. However, it begins with mandt, not lifnr, because the DDIC structure ztxlfa1 begins with mandt. The output shows that the first three bytes of lifnr end up in it-mandt, it-lifnr is shifted left three bytes and also contains land1, and regio is empty.

INPUT

LISTING 13.3 YOUR PROGRAM WILL PRODUCE A SHORT DUMP IF YOU TRY TO PUT MORE FIELDS INTO AN INTERNAL TABLE THAN EXIST IN THAT TABLE

13

```
1  report ztx1303.
2  tables ztxlfa1.
3  data: begin of it occurs 23,
4          lifnr like ztxlfa1-lifnr,    "this is a char 10 field
5          land1 like ztxlfa1-land1,    "this is a char  3 field
6          end of it.
7
8  *The next line causes a short dump. The internal table is too narrow.
9  select * from ztxlfa1 into table it.
```

The code in Listing 13.3 produces the output shown in Figure 13.5.

FIGURE 13.5.

This short dump occurs when you run report ztx1303. *It happens when you select more fields than will fit into the internal table.*

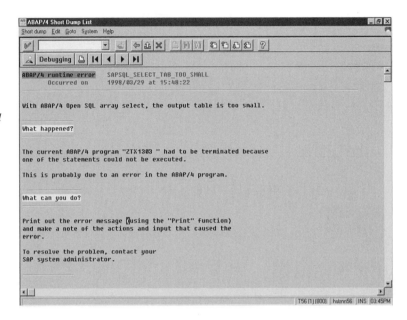

 ANALYSIS

- Line 3 defines an internal table that has two components. The total length of it is 13 bytes.
- Line 9 selects all fields from ztxlfa1 into it. The total length of all of these fields is more than 13 bytes. Consequently, a short dump occurs.

Using the `corresponding fields` Addition

If the components of the internal table aren't in the same order as those from the database, or if they don't have the same data type and length, you can use the `corresponding fields` addition. This addition has the same effect as the `move corresponding` statement does on a field string: It moves fields from the database table into fields *of the same name* in the internal table body.

> **Tip**
>
> `corresponding fields` performs one assignment per field instead of a single assignment for the entire row, so it adds overhead to the `select` statement. You should use it only when necessary.

The following points apply:

- The order of the sending and receiving fields does not matter.
- Sending fields that do not have a corresponding receiving field are discarded.

- Receiving fields that do not have a corresponding sending field are unchanged.

Listing 13.4 shows efficient and inefficient uses for this addition.

LISTING 13.4 USING THE corresponding fields ADDITION TO FILL
INTERNAL TABLES FROM THE DATABASE

`INPUT`

```
1  report ztx1304.
2  tables ztxlfa1.
3  data: begin of it1 occurs 23,
4          lifnr     like ztxlfa1-lifnr,
5          lifnr_ext like ztxlfa1-lifnr,
6          land1     like ztxlfa1-land1,
7          end of it1,
8        begin of it2 occurs 23,
9          lifnr     like ztxlfa1-lifnr,
10         land1     like ztxlfa1-land1,
11         end of it2.
12
13 * This is efficient usage:
14 select lifnr land1 from ztxlfa1
15     into corresponding fields of table it1
16     where lifnr between 'V10' and 'V12'.
17 loop at it1.
18     write: / it1-lifnr, it1-land1.
19     endloop.
20
21 * This is inefficient:
22 select * from ztxlfa1
23     into corresponding fields of table it2
24     where lifnr between 'V10' and 'V12'.
25 skip.
26 loop at it1.
27     write: / it1-lifnr, it1-land1.
28     endloop.
29
30 * Instead, write:
31 select lifnr land1 from ztxlfa1 into table it2
32     where lifnr between 'V10' and 'V12'.
33 skip.
34 loop at it2.
35     write: / it2-lifnr, it2-land1.
36     endloop.
37 free: it1, it2.
```

`13`

The code in Listing 13.4 produces this output:

`OUTPUT`

```
V10        CC
V11        DE
V12        DE
```

```
         V10        CC
         V11        DE
         V12        DE

         V10        CC
         V11        DE
         V12        DE
```

ANALYSIS
- Line 14 reads the lifnr and land1 fields from table ztxlfa1 into the lifnr and land1 fields of internal table it1. The internal table has field lifnr_ext between lifnr and land1, so you cannot use into table. If it1 requires the fields to be in this order, the usage of corresponding fields is appropriate here.

- Line 22 selects all fields from table ztxlfa1 into only two fields of table it2. This is inefficient. Instead, line 31 shows that by selecting only the needed fields in the correct order, you can use into table.

Adding Rows One by One Using select

Using select to add rows one at a time requires the use of a work area and a second statement such as append, insert, or collect. Omitting the table addition causes the row to be assigned to a work area. It is common to use the header line of an internal table as an explicit work area. Alternatively, you can use the default table work area (defined using tables).

Listing 13.5 shows some examples of using select to add rows one at a time to an internal table.

LISTING 13.5 USING select WITH THE append STATEMENT TO FILL
INPUT INTERNAL TABLES

```
1  report ztx1305.
2  tables ztxlfa1.
3  data it like ztxlfa1 occurs 2 with header line.
4
5  *Do it this way
6  select * from ztxlfa1 into it    "notice 'table' is omitted so the
7            where land1 = 'DE'.    "row goes into the header line of it
8      append it.
9      endselect.
10
11 loop at it.
12     write: / it-lifnr, it-land1, it-regio.
13     endloop.
14 refresh it.
15
```

```
16 *Or this way
17 select * from ztxlfa1            "no 'into' so the row goes into the
18         where land1 = 'DE'.      "default table work area
19     append ztxlfa1 to it.        "and then is appended to it
20     endselect.
21
22 skip.
23 loop at it.
24     write: / it-lifnr, it-land1, it-regio.
25     endloop.
26 refresh it.
27
28 *Not this way
29 select * from ztxlfa1            "row goes into default table work area
30         where land1 = 'DE'.
31     it = ztxlfa1.                "then is assigned to the header line
32     append it.
33     endselect.
34
35 skip.
36 loop at it.
37     write: / it-lifnr, it-land1, it-regio.
38     endloop.
39 free it.
```

The code in Listing 13.5 produces this output:

OUTPUT

```
V11        DE   07
V12        DE   14
V8         DE   03

V11        DE   07
V12        DE   14
V8         DE   03

V11        DE   07
V12        DE   14
V8         DE   03
```

ANALYSIS

- On line 6, table does not appear before it, so the fields from ztxlfa1 go into the header line for it. Line 8 appends the header line to it.

- On line 17, there is no into clause, so each row goes into the default table work area ztxlfa1. Line 19 appends work area ztxlfa1 to the internal table (the header line is not used).

- Line 29 places each row into work area ztxlfa1. Line 31 moves ztxlfa1 to the header line of it before appending. This is the least efficient method.

into corresponding fields can also be used to place data into a work area instead of into the body of the internal table. The effect is similar to that of the move-corresponding statement and is more efficient. Listing 13.6 shows how.

13

LISTING 13.6 HOW THE corresponding fields ADDITION TO THE select STATEMENT PRODUCES THE SAME EFFECT AS THE move-corresponding STATEMENT

INPUT

```
 1 report ztx1306.
 2 tables ztxlfa1.
 3 data: begin of it occurs 2,
 4          lifnr     like ztxlfa1-lifnr,
 5          row_id    like sy-index,
 6          land1     like ztxlfa1-land1,
 7          end of it.
 8
 9 *Do it this way:
10 select lifnr land1 from ztxlfa1
11      into corresponding fields of it   "notice 'table' is omitted
12      where land1 = 'DE'.
13    append it.
14    endselect.
15
16 loop at it.
17    write: / it-lifnr, it-row_id, it-land1.
18    endloop.
19 refresh it.
20
21 *Not this way:
22 select * from ztxlfa1
23      where land1 = 'DE'.
24    move-corresponding ztxlfa1 to it.
25    append it.
26    endselect.
27
28 skip.
29 loop at it.
30    write: / it-lifnr, it-row_id, it-land1.
31    endloop.
32 free it.
```

The code in Listing 13.6 produces this output:

OUTPUT

```
V11              0   DE
V12              0   DE
V8               0   DE

V11              0   DE
V12              0   DE
V8               0   DE
```

ANALYSIS

- On line 11, the `table` addition is omitted from before `it` so that the row goes into the header line. `lifnr` goes into `it-lifnr` and `land1` goes into `it-land1`. Line 7 appends the header line to `it`.

- Line 22 moves rows into work area `ztxlfa1`. Line 24 uses an additional statement—`move-corresponding`—to transfer the work area to the header line `it`. Line 25 then appends the header line to the body of `it`. This accomplishes the same result as the first `select`, but it involves an additional statement and so is less efficient.

Summing Up `select`, Internal Tables, and Efficiency

Table 13.2 contains a list of the various forms of `select` as it is used with internal tables and their relative efficiency. They are in descending order of most-to-least efficient.

TABLE 13.2   VARIOUS FORMS OF `select` WHEN FILLING AN INTERNAL TABLE

Statement(s)	Writes To
`select into table it`	Body
`select into corresponding fields of table it`	Body
`select into it`	Header line
`select into corresponding fields of it`	Header line

Using the `lfa1`, `lfb1`, `lfc1`, and `lfc3` Sample Tables

Before discussing the next topic, it will be helpful to become more acquainted with the sample tables `ztxlfa1`, `ztxlfb1`, `ztxlfc1`, and `ztxlfc3`; they will be frequently used in the examples and exercises that follow. These tables are based on the R/3 tables `lfa1`, `lfb1`, `lfc1`, and `lfc3`. Please review the structures of these tables within the DDIC as you read the descriptions below.

SAP designed R/3 to be usable by a conglomerate that consists of multiple companies. During initial R/3 configuration, a company code is assigned to each company in the conglomerate. The company code forms part of the primary key in many master data tables, which enables the conglomerate to keep the information for all of its companies in a single database. Management can run reports for an individual company code as well as consolidated reports spanning multiple companies.

Table `lfa1` contains vendor master information that is consistent across all companies. Ignoring `mandt`, its primary key consists only of `lifnr`, the vendor number. The fields of

13

lfa1, for example, are vendor name and address, telephone numbers, spoken language, and industry key (defined by the type of product the vendor produces, such as chemical, agricultural, and so on).

Table lfb1 contains vendor master information that is specific to a company. Its primary key consists of lifnr and bukrs: the company code field (see Figure 13.6). Stored within lfb1 are the company's account number with the vendor, reconciliation account number, withholding tax information, an interest calculation indicator, and so on.

FIGURE 13.6.

The relationship between the primary keys.

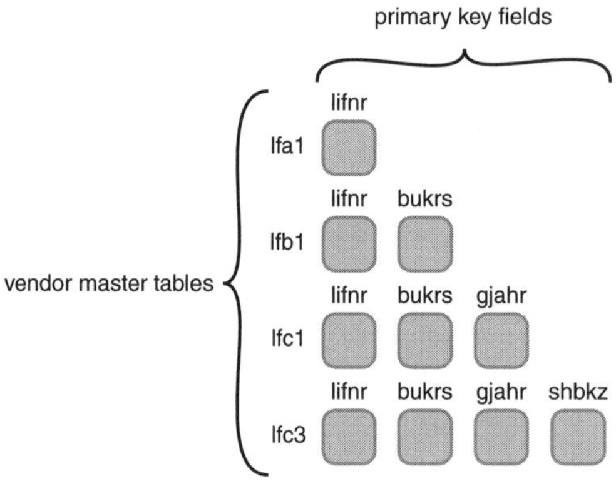

Figure 13.6 is the relationship between the primary keys of tables lfa1 through lfc3. They all begin with lifnr, and lfa1 uses it as the entire primary key. lfb1 uses the vendor number and company code. lfc1 uses vendor number, company code, and fiscal year. lfc3 uses those same fields plus a special G/L indicator.

Table lfc1 contains G/L (general ledger) transaction figures. Each row holds one fiscal year's worth of transaction figures for a vendor within a company. The primary key consists of lifnr, bukrs, and gjahr, the fiscal year.

The set of fields named umNNs, umNNh, and umNNu is repeated 16 times within an lfc1 row. Each of the first 12 sets contains the debit postings, credit postings, and sales for one posting period (usually a month) of the fiscal year. The last four sets are additional closing periods used to contain year-end accounting adjustments.

Note

There can be either 12 or 13 posting periods in a fiscal year. This is determined when the system is initially configured. If there are 13, then there are only three additional closing periods.

Table `lfc3` contains special G/L transaction figures. Special G/Ls use an alternative reconciliation account in the general ledger. Each row of `lfc3` holds a summary of the special G/Ls for an entire fiscal year in three fields: `saldv`, `soll1`, and `habn1`. These contain the balance carried forward and the total debit and credit posting for the fiscal year. The primary key is the same as `lfc1`, plus a special G/L indicator: `shbkz`. The value in this field indicates which alternative reconciliation account is used.

Most master data tables use a similar model for their primary key structures.

In this book, simplified versions of these tables are used: `ztxlfa1`, `ztxlfb1`, `ztxlfc1`, and `ztxlfc3`. These were created and populated by the setup routine.

Control Break Processing

After you fill an internal table with data, you often need to write the data out. This output will frequently contain summary information (such as totals) at the top or bottom of the report. There might also be interim summaries (such as subtotals) within the body of the report.

For example, suppose you need to write the G/L figures from `ztxlfc1` for each vendor, with subtotals by fiscal year and a grand total at the bottom of the report.

To do this, you can read the data into an internal table and then, within `loop at`, use the following statements:

- `at first` / `endat`
- `at last` / `endat`
- `at new` / `endat`
- `at end of` / `endat`
- `sum`
- `on change of` / `endon`

NEW TERM The first statement of each of these statement pairs—except for `sum`—controls when the code that lies between them is executed. This type of control is called a *control break*. Their purpose is to execute the code between them whenever a specific condition in the data is detected during the processing of the loop.

13

Using the `at first` and `at last` Statements

Use the `at first` and `at last` statements to perform processing during the first or last loop pass of an internal table.

Syntax for the `at first` and `at last` Statements

▼ SYNTAX

The following is the syntax for the `at first` and `at last` statements.

```
loop at it.
   ---
   at first.
       ---
       endat.
   ---
   at last.
       ---
       endat.
   ---
   endloop.
```

where:

▲

- *it* is an internal table.
- `---` represents any number of lines of code (even zero).

The following points apply:

- These statements can only be used within `loop at`; they cannot be used within `select`.
- `at first` does not have to come before `at last`. The order of these statements can be interchanged.
- These statements can appear multiple times within the same loop. For example, you could have two `at first` and three `at last` statements within one loop and they can appear in any order.
- These statements should not be nested inside of one another (that is, `at last` should not be placed inside of `at first` and `endat`).
- There are no additions to these statements.

The first time through the loop, the lines of code between `at first` and `endat` are executed. The last time through the loop, the lines of code between `at last` and `endat` are executed. If there are multiple occurrences of `at first`, they are all executed. `at last` behaves in a similar fashion.

Use `at first` for:

- Loop initialization processing
- Writing totals at the top of a report
- Writing headings

Use at last for:

- Loop termination processing
- Writing totals at the bottom of a report
- Writing footings

Listing 13.7 shows a sample program that uses these constructs.

LISTING 13.7 USING at first TO WRITE HEADINGS AND at last TO UNDERLINE THE LAST LINE

```
 1  report ztx1307.
 2  tables ztxlfc3.
 3  data it like ztxlfc3 occurs 25 with header line.
 4  select * from ztxlfc3 into table it where shbkz = 'Z'.
 5  loop at it.
 6      at first.
 7          write: /  'Vendor',
 8                 12 'Cpny',
 9                 17 'Year',
10                 22 'Bal C/F'.
11          uline.
12          endat.
13      write: /   it-lifnr,
14             12  it-bukrs,
15             17  it-gjahr,
16             22  it-saldv.
17      at last.
18          write: /  '----------',
19                 12 '----',
20                 17 '----',
21                 22 '------------------'.
22          endat.
23      endloop.
24 free it.
```

The code in Listing 13.7 produces this output:

Vendor	Cpny	Year	Bal C/F
1000	1000	1995	0.00
1000	1000	1996	5,000.00
1000	1000	1998	4,000.00
1040	4000	1997	0.00
1070	2000	1997	1,000.00
1090	2000	1997	250.50
V1	1000	1992	1,000.00
V1	3000	1990	1,000.00

13

```
V1        3000 1994        1,000.00
V4        4000 1997          100.00
V6        2000 1997        1,000.00
V6        4000 1997            0.00
--------- ---- ---- --------------------
```

ANALYSIS
- Lines 6 through 11 are only executed the first time through the loop. This example writes headings followed by an underline (line 11).
- Lines 13 through 16 write out the contents of a row. They are executed for every row.
- Lines 17 through 22 are only executed the last time through the loop. This example writes an underline at the bottom of each of the columns.

Using the Unexpected: Component Values Gone

Between the at first and endat, or between the at last and endat, the component values of the work area row will not contain any data. The default key fields are filled with * (asterisks) and the numeric fields are set to zeros. The endat restores the contents to the values they had prior to entering the at. Changes to the work area within at and endat are lost.

Listing 13.8 demonstrates that the components of the default key fields are filled with asterisks, and the non-key fields filled with zeros, inside an at or endat statement.

INPUT   **LISTING 13.8**   THE CONTENTS OF THE INTERNAL TABLE FIELDS BETWEEN at AND endat

```
1   report ztx1308.
2   tables ztxlfc3.
3   data it like ztxlfc3 occurs 1 with header line.
4   select * up to 1 rows from ztxlfc3 into table it.
5   loop at it.
6       write: / 'Before ''at first'':',
7              / it-lifnr, it-bukrs, it-gjahr, it-shbkz, it-saldv,
8                it-solll.
9       at first.
10          write: / 'Inside ''at first'':',
11                 / it-lifnr, it-bukrs, it-gjahr, it-shbkz, it-saldv,
12                   it-solll.
13          it-lifnr = 'XXXX'.
14      endat.
15      write: / 'Between ''at first'' and ''at last'':',
16             / it-lifnr, it-bukrs, it-gjahr, it-shbkz, it-saldv,
17               it-solll.
18      at last.
19          write: / 'Inside ''at last'':',
20                 / it-lifnr, it-bukrs, it-gjahr, it-shbkz, it-saldv,
21                   it-solll.
```

```
22           it-lifnr = 'XXXX'.
23         endat.
24    write: / 'After ''at last'':',
25              / it-lifnr, it-bukrs, it-gjahr, it-shbkz, it-saldv,
26                  it-solll.
27       endloop.
28 free it.
```

The code in Listing 13.8 produces this output:

OUTPUT
```
Before 'at first':
1000         1000 1990 A                1,000.00              500.00
Inside 'at first':
********** **** **** *                   0.00                0.00
Between 'at first' and 'at last':
1000         1000 1990 A                1,000.00              500.00
Inside 'at last':
********** **** **** *                   0.00                0.00
After 'at last':
1000         1000 1990 A                1,000.00              500.00
```

ANALYSIS

- Line 4 selects one record from `ztxlfc3` into `it`.

- Within the loop that begins on line 5, the contents of the row are written out first. They are then written again inside of an `at first` and `endat`. The output shows that the default key fields contain asterisks and the rest contain zeros.

- Line 13 assigns a new value to `it-lifnr`.

- After the `endat` on line 14, the output shows that all values have been restored to the work area. Changes to the header line made inside of the `at` / `endat` are lost.

- Line 18 shows that `at last` exhibits the same behavior.

- Line 27 exits the loop on the first pass to keep the output simple.

Using the `at new` and `at end of` Statements

Use the `at new` and `at end of` statements to detect a change in a column from one loop pass to the next. These statements enable you to execute code at the beginning and end of a group of records.

Syntax for the `at new` and `at end ff` Statements

The following is the syntax for the `at new` and `at end of` statements.

▼ SYNTAX

```
sort by c.
loop at it.
   ---
   at new c.
```

13

▼
```
       - - -
       endat.
   - - -
at end of c.
       - - -
       endat.
   - - -
   endloop.
```

where:

▲
- *it* is an internal table.
- *c* is a component of *it*.
- - - - represents any number of lines of code (even zero).

The following points apply:

- These statements can only be used within loop at; they cannot be used within select.
- at new does not have to come before at end of. These statements can appear in any order.
- These statements can appear multiple times within the same loop. For example, you could have two at new and three at end of statements within one loop and they can appear in any order.
- These statements should not be nested inside of one another (that is, at end of should not be placed inside of at new / endat).
- There are no additions to these statements.

Using at new

Each time the value of *c* changes, the lines of code between at new and endat are executed. This block is also executed during the first loop pass or if any fields to the left of *c* change. Between at and endat, the numeric fields to the right of *c* are set to zero. The non-numeric fields are filled with asterisks (*). If there are multiple occurrences of at new, they are all executed. at end of behaves in a similar fashion.

NEW TERM   A *control level* is the component named on a control break statement; it regulates the control break. For example, in the following code snippet, f2 is a control level because it appears on the at new statement.

```
loop at it.
    at new f2.
        "(some code here)
        endat.
    endloop.
```

It is said that a control break is triggered if the control level changes. This means that when the contents of the control level change, the code between the at and endat is executed.

A control break is also triggered if any of the fields prior to the control level in the structure change. Therefore, you should define the internal table structure to begin with the fields that form your control levels. You must also sort by all fields prior to and including c.

Between at and endat, numeric fields to the right of the control level will be zero and non-numeric fields will be filled with asterisks.

Figures 13.7 and 13.8 illustrate the use of at new.

FIGURE 13.7.

This figure shows that the control level is triggered when the value of f1 changes. It also shows that f2 contains an asterisk within the control break (between at and endat).

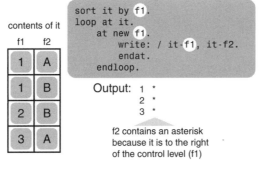

FIGURE 13.8.

This figure shows that the control level is triggered when f2 or f1 changes. This happens because f1 is prior to f2 in the structure of it.

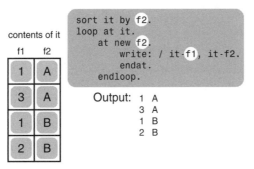

This program provides a working example of Figures 13.7 and 13.8. It illustrates the point that a control break is triggered whenever the control level changes or any field prior to the control level changes.

13

LISTING 13.9 THE CODE IN FIGURES 13.7 AND 13.8 IS REPRODUCED IN A
INPUT WORKING EXAMPLE

```
1 report ztx1309.
2 data: begin of it occurs 4,
3          f1,
```

continues

LISTING 13.9 CONTINUED

```
4             f2,
5             end of it.
6
7  it = '1A'. append it. "Fill it with data
8  it = '3A'. append it.
9  it = '1B'. append it.
10 it = '2B'. append it.
11
12 sort it by f1.      "it now looks like figure 13.7
13 loop at it.
14     at new f1.
15         write: / it-f1, it-f2.
16         endat.
17     endloop.
18 skip.
19 sort it by f2.      "it now looks like figure 13.8
20 loop at it.
21     at new f2.
22         write: / it-f1, it-f2.
23         endat.
24     endloop.
25 skip.
26 sort it by f1 f2.     "it now looks like figure 13.8
27 loop at it.
28     at new f1.
29         write: / it-f1.
30         endat.
31     at new f2.
32         write: /4 it-f2.
33         endat.
34     endloop.
35 free it.
```

The code in Listing 13.9 produces this output:

```
OUTPUT     1 *
           2 *
           3 *

           1 A
           3 A
           1 B
           2 B

           1
               A
               B
           2
               B
           3
               A
```

| ANALYSIS |

- Line 12 sorts it by f1. On line 14, at new is triggered the first time through the loop and each time f1 changes.

- Line 19 sorts it by f2. On line 20, at new is triggered the first time through or each time the value of f1 or f2 changes. This happens because a control level is triggered each time f2 changes or any field prior to f2 changes.

- Line 26 sorts it by both f1 and f2. On line 28, at new is triggered each time the value of f1 changes, and on line 31, at new is triggered each time f1 or f2 changes.

Using at end of

The lines of code between at end of and endat are executed:

- If the control level changes.

- If any field prior to the control level changes.

- If this is the last row of the table.

Listing 13.10 illustrates this statement.

| INPUT |

LISTING 13.10 HOW THE at new AND at end of ARE TRIGGERED BY THE FIELD CHANGES AND CONTROL LEVEL CHANGES

```
1   report ztx1310.
2   data: begin of it occurs 4,
3             f1,
4             f2,
5             end of it.
6
7   it = '1A'. append it. "Fill it with data
8   it = '3A'. append it.
9   it = '1B'. append it.
10  it = '2B'. append it.
11
12  sort it by f1.
13  loop at it.
14      at new f1.
15          write: / 'start of:', it-f1.
16          endat.
17      write: /4 it-f1.
18      at end of f1.
19          write: / 'end   of:', it-f1.
20          endat.
21      endloop.
22  free it.
```

13

The code in Listing 13.10 produces this output:

```
start of: 1
    1
    1
end    of: 1
start of: 2
    2
end    of: 2
start of: 3
    3
end    of: 3
```

- Line 12 sorts it by f1.
- On line 14, at new is triggered each time f1 changes.
- On line 18, at end of is triggered if the control level will change when the next row is read or if this is the last row.

Caution

> Do not use control break statements within a loop at *it* where . . . construct; the effects are unpredictable.

Using the sum Statement

Use the sum statement to calculate totals for the rows of a control level.

Syntax for the sum Statement

The following is the syntax for the sum statement.

```
at first/last/new/end of.
    - - -
    sum.
    - - -
    endat.
```

where:

▲

- - - - represents any number of lines of code.

Sum calculates a total for the current value of the control level that contains it. This is clearer if you imagine that it does the following:

- It finds all rows that have the same values within the control level field and all fields to the left of it.
- It sums each numeric column to the right of the control level.
- It places the totals in the corresponding fields of the work area.

Listing 13.11 illustrates this statement.

INPUT

LISTING 13.11 USING THE sum STATEMENT TO CALCULATE THE TOTALS OF A CONTROL LEVEL

```
 1  report ztx1311.
 2  data: begin of it occurs 4,
 3             f1,
 4             f2 type i,
 5             f3 type i,
 6             end of it.
 7
 8  it-f1 = 'A'. it-f2 = 1. it-f3 = 10. append it.
 9  it-f1 = 'B'. it-f2 = 3. it-f3 = 30. append it.
10  it-f1 = 'A'. it-f2 = 2. it-f3 = 20. append it.
11  it-f1 = 'B'. it-f2 = 4. it-f3 = 40. append it.
12
13  sort it by f1.        "it now looks like figure 13.9
14  loop at it.
15     at new f1.
16         sum.
17         write: / 'total:', it-f1, it-f2, it-f3.
18         endat.
19     write: /11 it-f2, it-f3.
20     endloop.
21  free it.
```

The code in Listing 13.11 produces this output:

OUTPUT

```
total: A        3       30
                1       10
                2       20
total: B        7       70
                3       30
                4       40
```

ANALYSIS

- Line 13 sorts it by f1 ascending. The contents after sorting appear as shown in Figure 13.9.

- The first time through the loop, the code between lines 15 and 18 is executed. The control level contains the value 'A'.

- Before line 16 is executed, the work area fields to the right of the control level contain zeros. The sum statement finds all adjacent rows that have an 'A' in f1. It sums the numeric columns to the right of the control level and places the results in the work area (see Figure 13.9).

- In the second iteration of the loop, at new is not triggered.

- In the third loop iteration, f1 contains 'B' and at new (line 15) is triggered.

13

- Before line 16 is executed, the work area fields to the right of the control level contain zeros. The sum statement finds all adjacent rows that have a 'B' in f1. It sums the numeric columns to the right of the control level and places the results in the work area (see Figure 13.10).

FIGURE 13.9.

This figure illustrates what occurs in Listing 13.11. The first time through the loop the control break is triggered and the sum statement is executed. All rows having the same value as the control level are found and the numeric fields to the right of the control level are summed up into the work area.

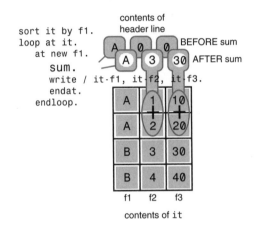

FIGURE 13.10.

This figure shows what transpires the second time the control break is triggered and the sum statement is executed.

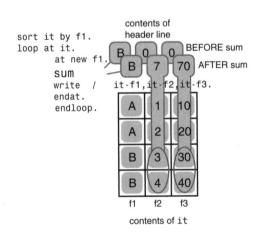

Tip

Summing can result in overflow because the total is placed into a field of the same length. Overflow causes a short dump with the error SUM_OVERFLOW. When using sum, avoid overflow by increasing the length of numeric fields before populating the internal table.

Using the `on change of` Statement

Another statement you can use to perform control break processing is `on change of`. It behaves in a manner similar to `at new`.

Syntax for the `on change of` Statement

▼ SYNTAX

The following is the syntax for the `on change of` statement.

```
on change of v1 [or v2 . . .].
    ---
[else.
    ---]
    endon.
```

where:

- *v1* and *v2* are variable or field string names.

- `. . .` indicates that any number of `or` conditions might follow.

▲

- `---` represents any number of lines of code.

The following points apply:

- If the value of any of the variables (*v1*, *v2*, and so on) changes from one test to the next, the statements following `on change of` are executed.

- If no change is detected and `else` is specified, the statements following `else` are executed.

`on change of` differs from `at new` in the following respects:

- It can be used in any loop construct, not just `loop at`. For example, it can be used within `select` and `endselect`, `do` and `enddo`, or `while` and `endwhile`, as well as inside `get` events.

- A single `on change of` can be triggered by a change within one or more fields named after `of` and separated by `or`. These fields can be elementary fields or field strings. If you are within a loop, these fields do not have to belong to the loop.

- When used within a loop, a change in a field to the left of the control level does not trigger a control break.

- When used within a loop, fields to the right still contain their original values; they are not changed to contain zeros or asterisks.

- You can use `else` between `on change of` and `endon`.

- You can use it with `loop at` *it* `where . . ..`

- You can use `sum` with `on change of`. It sums all numeric fields except the one(s) named after `of`.

13

- Any values changed within on change of remain changed after endon. The contents of the header line are not restored as they are for at and endat.

Behind the Scenes of on change of

When a loop begins execution, the system creates a global auxiliary field for each field named in an on change of statement contained by the loop. On creation, these fields are given default initial values (blanks or zeros). They are freed when the loop ends.

Note   Because global auxiliary fields do not exist outside a loop, you cannot use on change of outside of a loop.

Each time on change of is executed, the contents of its fields are compared with the contents of the global auxiliary fields. If they are different, the on change of is triggered and the auxiliary fields are updated with the new values. If they are the same, the code within on change of is not executed.

This concept is graphically illustrated in Figures 13.11 through 13.16.

FIGURE 13.11.

This is the first time though a loop using on change of.

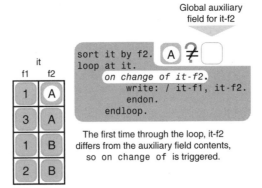

The first time through the loop, it-f2 differs from the auxiliary field contents, so on change of is triggered.

FIGURE 13.12.

When on change of *is triggered, the auxiliary field is updated.*

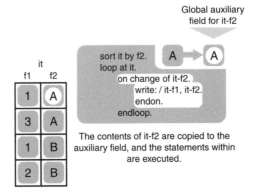

The contents of it-f2 are copied to the auxiliary field, and the statements within are executed.

FIGURE 13.13.

This is the second loop pass. The auxiliary field contents match and on change of *is not triggered.*

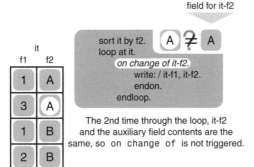

The 2nd time through the loop, it-f2 and the auxiliary field contents are the same, so on change of is not triggered.

FIGURE 13.14.

This is the third loop pass. on change of *is triggered.*

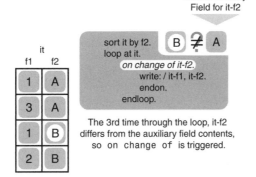

The 3rd time through the loop, it-f2 differs from the auxiliary field contents, so on change of is triggered.

FIGURE 13.15.

Here the auxiliary field is updated.

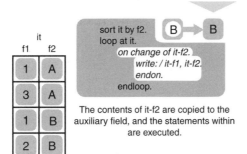

The contents of it-f2 are copied to the auxiliary field, and the statements within are executed.

13

FIGURE 13.16.

This is the fourth loop pass. on change of *is not triggered.*

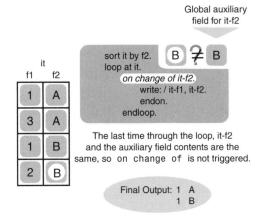

Global auxiliary
field for it-f2

it
f1   f2

```
sort it by f2.
loop at it.
   on change of it-f2.
      write: / it-f1, it-f2.
   endon.
endloop.
```

B ≠ B

The last time through the loop, it-f2
and the auxiliary field contents are the
same, so on change of is not triggered.

Final Output: 1   A
              1   B

Using on change of

Listing 13.12 illustrates the use of on change of.

LISTING 13.12 USING on change of IN TWO DIFFERENT WAYS: INSIDE OF

INPUT   loop at AND INSIDE OF select

```
1   report ztx1312.
2   tables ztxlfa1.
3   data: begin of it occurs 4,
4            f1 type i,
5            f2,
6            f3 type i,
7            f4,
8            end of it.
9
10  it-f1 = 1. it-f2 = 'A'. it-f3 = 11. it-f4 = 'W'. append it.
11  it-f1 = 3. it-f2 = 'A'. it-f3 = 22. it-f4 = 'X'. append it.
12  it-f1 = 1. it-f2 = 'A'. it-f3 = 33. it-f4 = 'Y'. append it.
13  it-f1 = 2. it-f2 = 'A'. it-f3 = 44. it-f4 = 'Z'. append it.
14
15  loop at it.
16      on change of it-f2.
17          write: / it-f1, it-f2, it-f3, it-f4.
18          endon.
19      endloop.
20  write: / 'End of loop'.
21
22  * executing the same code again - the aux field still contains 'A'
23  loop at it.
24      at first.
25          write: / 'Looping without a reset...'.
26          endat.
27      on change of it-f2.
```

```
28          write: / it-f1, it-f2, it-f3, it-f4.
29      else.
30          write: / 'on change of not triggered for row', sy-tabix.
31          endon.
32      endloop.
33 write: / 'End of loop'.
34
35 *reset the aux field to blanks
36 clear it-f2.
37 on change of it-f2.
38      endon.
39 loop at it.
40      at first.
41          write: / 'Looping after reset...'.
42          endat.
43      on change of it-f2.
44          write: / it-f1, it-f2, it-f3, it-f4.
45          endon.
46      endloop.
47 write: / 'End of loop'.
48 free it.
49
50 select * from ztxlfa1 where land1 = 'US'.
51      on change of ztxlfa1-land1.
52          write: / 'land1=', ztxlfa1-land1.
53          endon.
54      endselect.
55 write: / 'End of select'.
56
57 *executing the same select again without a reset works find
58 select * from ztxlfa1 where land1 = 'US'.
59      on change of ztxlfa1-land1.
60          write: / 'land1=', ztxlfa1-land1.
61          endon.
62      endselect.
63 write: / 'End of select'.
```

OUTPUT In a 3.0F environment and above, the code in Listing 13.12 produces this output:

```
        1 A          11 W
End of loop
Looping without a reset...
on change of not triggered for row        2
on change of not triggered for row        3
on change of not triggered for row        4
End of loop
Looping after reset...
        1 A          11 W
End of loop
land1= US
End of select
land1= US
End of select
```

13

ANALYSIS

- Lines 10 through 13 seed the internal table with data. it-f2 contains value 'A' in all four rows.

- Line 16 writes out each row as it is processed.

- Lines 17, 20, 23, and 26 are triggered the first time through the loop. This happens because the auxiliary fields contain zeros or blanks, so they differ from the values in the first row. The first row values are copied to the auxiliary fields and the values are written out by the write statements.

- Line 20 is not triggered again because on all subsequent loop passes, the value of it-f2 is 'A' and the global auxiliary field also contains 'A'. Notice that a change in the value to the left of f2 does not trigger on change of as it does with at new.

- The internal table is not used after line 31, so here it is freed. This deletes all rows and releases the memory.

- Line 33 selects all rows from ztxlfa1 in land1 order.

- Although this select returns 23 rows, as shown by the last line of output, only five unique values of land1 exist and are written out.

Using the Hidden Danger in on change of

The first time through a loop, the global auxiliary field is created with initial values (blanks or zeros). If the first value in a loop happens to be blank or zero, on change of will not be triggered. Listing 13.13 illustrates this problem and offers a solution.

INPUT **LISTING 13.13** THE FIRST ROW OF LOOP #1 DOES NOT TRIGGER on change of

```
1   report ztx1313.
2   data: begin of it occurs 4,
3             f1 type i,
4             end of it.
5
6   it-f1 = 0. append it.
7   it-f1 = 3. append it.
8   it-f1 = 1. append it.
9   it-f1 = 2. append it.
10
11  loop at it.                              "loop #1
12      write: / '==new row==', 12 it-f1.
13      on change of it-f1.
14          write: / 'f1 changed:', 12 it-f1.
15          endon.
16      endloop.
17
18  skip.
```

```
19 loop at it.                                    "loop #2
20    write: / '==new row==', 12 it-f1.
21    on change of it-f1.
22        write: / 'f1 changed:', 12 it-f1.
23    else.
24        if sy-tabix = 1.
25            write: / 'f1 changed:', 12 it-f1.
26        endif.
27    endon.
28    endloop.
29 free it.
```

The code in Listing 13.13 produces this output:

OUTPUT

```
==new row==        0
==new row==        3
f1 changed:        3
==new row==        1
f1 changed:        1
==new row==        2
f1 changed:        2

==new row==        0
f1 changed:        0
==new row==        3
f1 changed:        3
==new row==        1
f1 changed:        1
==new row==        2
f1 changed:        2
```

ANALYSIS

- Lines 6 though 9 fill the internal table with four rows. The value of it-f1 in the first row is zero.

- On line 13, the first loop pass does not trigger the on change of because the global auxiliary field contains zero.

- Lines 23 and 24 have been added to loop #2 to detect the error. Notice that at first cannot be used to detect this problem because all numeric fields in the work area will be set to zero inside of at first and endat.

13

Note

In versions prior to 3.0F, only select and get statements automatically reset the global auxiliary fields. However, if you reset them yourself, you can use on change of in any type of loop. Use this code to perform the reset: clear f1. on change of f1. endon. clear moves initial values to f1. on change of compares f1 to the global auxiliary field. If they differ, the empty on change of overwrites it with initial values. Use this to fill the auxiliary fields with any value from f1.

Summary

- An array operation is the most efficient way to fill an internal table from a database table. It reads rows from the database table directly into the body of the internal table without using any work areas. It is implemented via the `into table` addition on the `select` statement.

- The internal table must be wide enough to accommodate the columns you select from the database table. To be precise, the width of an internal table row in bytes must be greater than or equal to the total number of bytes from all columns selected from the database table into the internal table. If the internal table row is wider, the columns selected from the database table fill the left-most bytes of each internal table row. The remaining bytes will be set to default initial values.

- Use the `into corresponding fields` addition if the fields of the internal table are in a different order or are separated from each other by fields not selected from the database table.

- Use `at` and `endat` to trigger processing based on a change in the column of an internal table or any column to the left of it.

- Use `sum` within `at` and `endat` or on `change of` to calculate totals and subtotals.

- Use on `change of` within loops to trigger processing based on a change in one of the selected columns.

Note

> Don't use `select` and `append`. Whenever possible, use `select into table` instead.
>
> Don't use `order by` with `select into table`. Use `sort` on the internal table instead.

Q&A

Q **The first part of this chapter seems to place a lot of emphasis on efficiency. I'm just learning and I find all of these methods confusing. Does this really make that much of a difference, or are you splitting hairs?**

A Experience has taught me that students who learn correctly the first time are far better off. ABAP/4 programs often process gargantuan amounts of data, so unfortunately, "easy code" often translates into "overhead overhead overhead." If you only learn easy methods first, they become habits and are difficult to discard. Poor code affects the performance of your programs and of the system.

Workshop

The Workshop provides two ways for you to affirm what you've learned in this chapter. The Quiz section poses questions to help you solidify your understanding of the material covered and the Exercise section provides you with experience in using what you have learned. You can find answers to the quiz questions and exercises in Appendix B, "Answers to Quiz Questions and Exercises."

Quiz

1. What are the values of the fields to the right of the control level between the at and endat statements?

Exercise 1

Copy program ztx1110 to •••e1301. Change it so that if a row is found and the contents of any fields in the found row differ from what is in the header line, overwrite the found row with the current contents of the header line. The output should look like this:

```
10          1  XX          1
20          2  XX          2
30          3  XX          3
40          4  XX          4
50          5  XX          5
```

Hint: Use the comparing addition on the read table statement.

Exercise 2

The following program produces a short dump. Describe the problem, copy the program to •••e1302 and fix it.

```
report zty1302
tables: ztxlfa1.
data: begin of it occurs 10,
        lifnr like ztxlfa1-lifnr,
        land1 like ztxlfa1-land1,
        end of it.
select * from ztxlfa1 into table it.
loop at it.
    write: / it-lifnr,
             it-land1.
    endloop.
```

13

DAY 14

The write Statement

Chapter Objectives

After you complete this chapter, you will be able to:

- Understand the effect of data types on output
- Use the formatting options of the write statement
- Use conversion exits and detect their presence within domains

Default Lengths and Formatting

If you do not specify any length or formatting options when you use the write statement, the system uses a default format and length based on the data type of each variable written. The following sections describe these defaults.

Default Lengths

NEW TERM The *output length* of a field is the number of characters used to display the value of that field. Output length is used by the write statement to allocate space on the output list for a field. Fields defined within a program via the data statement have a default output length as shown in Table 14.1.

TABLE 14.1 ABAP/4 DATA TYPE DETERMINES THE DEFAULT OUTPUT FORMAT AND LENGTH

Data	Justification	Format	Sign	Dflt Output Type Length
i	Right	Zeros suppressed	Trailing	11
p	Right	Zeros suppressed	Trailing	2*fldlen or (2*fldlen)+1
f	None	Scientific notation	Leading	22
n	Right	Leading zeros shown	None	fldlen
c	Left	Leading blanks suppressed		fldlen
d	Left	Determined by user defaults		8
t	Left	HH:MM:SS		6
x	Left			2*fldlen

Fields from the Data Dictionary have DDIC data types such as DEC, CHAR, CURR, and so on. These are all based on ABAP/4 data types and they inherit default length and format from the ABAP/4 data type. To determine the ABAP/4 data type, and thus the default output format, look up the ABAP/4 keyword documentation for the tables statement. To do this, place your cursor on a tables statement within your code and press the F1 key.

In addition, DDIC fields have their output length and number of decimals defined in the domain. These fields override the default, and are shown in Figure 14.1.

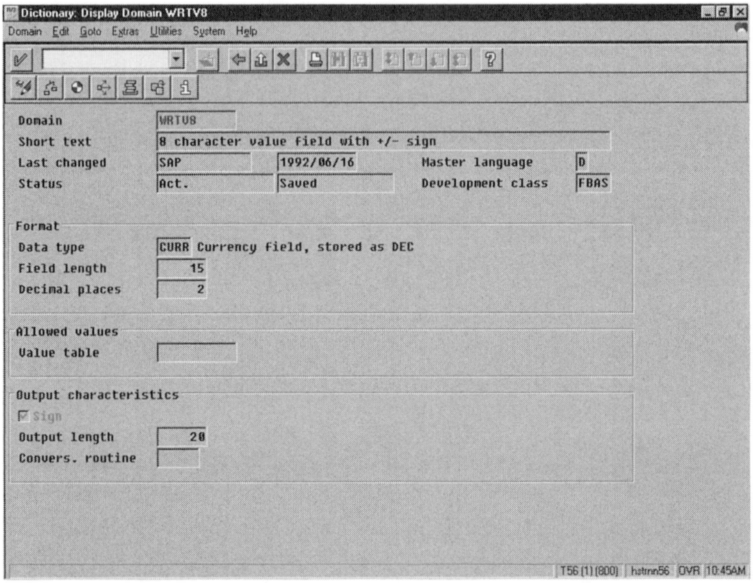

FIGURE 14.1.

The Output Length and Decimal Places fields override the defaults inherited from the ABAP/4 data types.

The output length and decimal places are inherited by all fields that are created from a domain. For example, in Figure 14.1, the field length is 15, indicating that 15 digits can be stored in any field that uses this domain. The output length is 20, so the output enables enough room for a decimal point, a sign, and three thousands separators.

Packed Fields

The default output length of a type p field is twice the defined field length. If decimal places are defined, the default output length is increased by 1 so that it is 2 * field length + 1. Table 14.2 shows sample default output lengths for type p fields.

TABLE 14.2 DEFAULT OUTPUT LENGTH FOR PACKED DECIMAL FIELDS

Data Definition	Default Output Length
data f1(4) type p.	8
data f2(4) type p decimals 2.	9
data f3(5) type p.	10
data f4(5) type p decimals 3.	11

Default Formatting

The default format is derived from the data type of the variable. Table 14.1 described how the output will be formatted for each ABAP/4 data type. The output of numeric fields (types p, i, and f) is right-justified with leading zeros suppressed and the rest are left-justified. Additional type-specific formatting also applies.

Default Date Formatting

Date values are output according to the Date Format setting in the User Defaults as long as the output length is 10 or greater. The default output length is 8, so you must increase it to at least 10 before the separators can be seen. Defining a variable using like (for example, like sy-datum) causes the output length to be taken from the domain.

Default Time Formatting

Time values are output in HH:MM:SS format as long as the output length is 8 or greater. The default output length is 6, so you must increase it to at least 8 before the separators can be seen. Defining a variable using like (for example, like sy-uzeit) causes the output length to be taken from the domain.

Default Numeric Formatting

The population of North America writes a number as 1,234.56. In other countries, such as those in Europe, the same number is written as 1.234,56—the use of the comma and

14

decimal are interchanged. R/3 enables each individual user to specify one of these formats via the user profile setting Decimal Notation (from any screen, choose the menu path System->User Profile->User Defaults).

| **Caution** | You must sign off and sign back on again to the R/3 system before changes to user defaults take effect. |

Table 14.3 shows the effect of the Decimal Notation setting on numeric output.

TABLE 14.3 DECIMAL NOTATION SETTING IN THE USER DEFAULTS AFFECTS NUMERIC
OUTPUT FORMATS

Setting	Sample Output
Comma	1,234.56
Period	1.234,56

The default output format for floating-point (type f) variables is via scientific notation. This can be modified by using an edit mask or conversion exit.

Overflow Formatting

When dealing with numbers that are too big for the output field, the system puts an asterisk in the first column of output to indicate overflow. However, before that occurs, the system tries to output all the digits, if possible. Thousands separators are only output if there is enough room in the output field. If there isn't, they are dropped one at a time beginning from the left of the field and working to the right. If the number is positive and will fit in the output by using the sign field, the system will use it.

Sample Program Demonstrating Default Formatting

Listing 14.1 illustrates default length and formatting. It also illustrates handling of numbers that are close to overflowing the output field.

INPUT **LISTING 14.1** DEFAULT FORMATTING AND LENGTHS

```
1   report ztx1401.
2   data: t1    type t          value '123456',
3         t2    like sy-uzeit   value '123456',
4         d1    type d          value '19980201',
5         d2    like sy-datum   value '19980201',
6         f1    type f          value '-1234',
```

```
7        i1    type i              value '12345678-',
8        i2    type i              value '123456789-',
9        i3    type i              value '1123456789-',
10       i4    type i              value '1123456789',
11       n1(5) type n              value 123,
12       p1(5) type p              value '123456789-',
13       c1(5) type c              value 'ABC',
14       x1(2) type x value 'A0B0'.
15
16 write: /     t1,   26 'type t: default output length = 6',
17         /(8)  t1,   26 'type t: increased output length to 8',
18         /(12) t1,   26 'type t: increased output length to 12',
19         /     t2,   26 'type t: default output length = 8 (from domain)',
20         /     d1,   26 'type d: default output length = 8',
21         /(10) d1,   26 'type d: increased output length to 10',
22         /     d2,   26 'type d: default output length = 10 (from domain)',
23         /     f1,   26 'type f: default output length = 22',
24         /     i1,   26 'type i: default output length = 11',
25         /     i2,   26 'type i: same output length, more digits',
26         /     i3,   26 'type i: same output length, even more digits',
27         /(10) i3,   26 'type i: smaller output length, negative number',
28         /(10) i4,   26 'type i: smaller output length, positive number',
29         /     n1,   26 'type n: default output length = field length',
30         /     p1,   26 'type p: default output length = 2 * length = 10',
31         /(12) p1,   26 'type p: output length increased to 12',
32         /(15) p1,   26 'type p: output length increased to 15',
33         /     c1,   26 'type c: output length = field length (left just)',
34         /     x1,   26 'type x: default output length = 2 * length = 4'.
```

The code in Listing 14.1 produces this output:

```
OUTPUT   123456                    type t: default output length = 6
         12:34:56                  type t: increased output length to 8
         12:34:56                  type t: increased output length to 12
         12:34:56                  type t: default output length = 8 (from
         ➥domain)
         19980201                  type d: default output length = 8
         1998/02/01                type d: increased output length to 10
         1998/02/01                type d: default output length = 10 (from
         ➥domain)
         -1.234000000000000E+03    type f: default output length = 22
         12,345,678-               type i: default output length = 11
         123456,789-               type i: same output length, more digits
         1123456789-               type i: same output length, even more
         ➥digits
         *23456789-                type i: smaller output length, negative
         ➥number
         1123456789                type i: smaller output length, positive
         ➥number
```

14

```
00123                        type n: default output length = field
➥length
123456789-                   type p: default output length = 2 * length
➥= 10
123,456,789-                 type p: output length increased to 12
    123,456,789-             type p: output length increased to 15
ABC                          type c: output length = field length (left
➥just)
A0B0                         type x: default output length = 2 *
➥length = 4
```

ANALYSIS

- Line 16 writes a type t variable using its default length of 6. There is no room for the separators, so they are not written.

- Line 17 writes the same variable using an output length of 8, which was specified on the write statement. This output length overrides the default output length and provides enough room in the output to include the separators.

- Line 18 shows that if the output field is larger than 8 characters, the time field is output left-justified within that field by default.

- Line 19 writes out a field defined like sy-uzeit. Within the domain for sy-uzeit, the Output Length field is set to 8. Therefore, the output length for field t2 is also 8, which provides enough room to write the separators as well.

- Line 20 writes out a type d field that has a default output length of 8. There is not enough room for separators, so the field does not contain separators. However, the year/month/day order is still determined from the user defaults.

- Line 21 writes out the same date field, this time increasing the output length to 10 to allow for separators.

- Line 22 writes out field d2. The length of d2 is obtained from the domain for sy-datum.

- Line 23 writes out a floating-point field showing scientific notation and a leading sign.

- Line 24 writes out an integer using the default length of 11.

- Line 25 writes out a bigger integer using the same length. The first thousands separator is dropped to enable the extra digit to be written.

- Line 26 increases the number again by one digit, causing the second separator to be dropped.

- Line 27 writes out the same number, this time decreasing the output length by 1, and the overflow indicator is seen in the first character of the output field.

- Line 28 writes the same number using the same length, but this time the number is positive. The system shifts the number right and uses the sign field to prevent overflow.

- Line 29 writes a numeric field showing that it is right-justified and padded on the left with leading zeros.

- Line 30 writes a packed decimal field showing the default output length and the dropping of separators.

- Lines 31 and 32 increase the output length to 12 and 15, showing the separators and right justification.

- Line 33 shows a character field left-justified in the output field.

- Line 34 shows the output from a hexadecimal field.

Additions to the write Statement

This section details some of the specific output specifications that can be used with the write statement.

Syntax for the write Statement

The following is the syntax for the write statement.

```
write [at] [/p(1)] v1[+o(sl)]
       (1)   under v2 ¦ no-gap
       (2)   using edit mask m ¦ using no edit mask
       (3)   mm/dd/yy      ¦ dd/mm/yy
       (4)   mm/dd/yyyy ¦ dd/mm/yyyy
       (5)   mmddyy        ¦ ddmmyy       ¦ yymmdd
       (6)   no-zero
       (7)   no-sign
       (8)   decimals n
       (9)   round n
       (10)  currency c ¦ unit u
       (11)  left-justified ¦ centered ¦ right-justified
```

where:

- *v1* is a literal, variable, or field string name.

- *p*, *1*, and *n* are numeric literals or variables.

- *p* is the position specification. It identifies the output column in which the output field should begin.

- *1* is the length specification. It identifies the length of the output field in which the value should be written.

▲ SYNTAX

▼

14

- *o* is a subfield offset specification that can contain numeric literals only.
- *s1* is a subfield length specification that can contain numeric literals only.
- *m* is an edit mask.
- *c* is a currency key (from table tcurc).
- *u* is a unit of measure (from table t006).
- *n* is a numeric literal or variable.

The following points apply:

- If either *p* or *1* is a variable, the word at is required.
- A slash (/) begins a new line before writing the variable value.

If no additions are specified and two write statements are executed (such as write: v1, v2.), the value of v2 appears on the same line as that of v1 separated from it by one space. If the value of v2 will not fit on the remainder of the current line, it appears on the next line. If the output length of v2 is greater than the line length, the output is truncated on the right. If the value is output right-justified (as with type p variables) before truncating it on the right, it will be shifted left as long as there are leading blanks to avoid truncating it. Separators are also removed, if necessary, to avoid truncation.

Note   A new line of output always begins at the start of a new event. Events are covered in Chapter 17, "Modularization: Events and Subroutines."

Understanding the Position Specification

Referring to the syntax given above, *p* specifies the output column. The output value can overwrite all or part of a preceding write. The program in Listing 14.2 illustrates the effect of a series of write statements. Table 14.4 shows the cumulative effect of each write, in sequence, to show how the output is arrived at.

LISTING 14.2   A SERIES OF write STATEMENTS TO ILLUSTRATE THE EFFECT OF THE
OUTPUT   OUTPUT COLUMN SPECIFICATION

```
1   report ztx1402.
2   data f1(4) type p value 1234.
3   write: / '----+----1----+--',
4          / '12345678901234567'.
5   skip.
6   write /1 'X'.
7   write    'YZ'.
```

```
 8  write  2 'YZ'.
 9  write  3 'ABC'.
10  write  4 f1.
11  write  7 f1.
12  write    'Z'.
```

The code in Listing 14.2 produces this output:

OUTPUT

```
----+----1----+--
12345678901234567

XYA  1  1,234  Z
```

ANALYSIS

- Lines 3 and 4 write out a ruler so that you can see the output columns.

- Line 6 writes an 'X' beginning in column 1.

- Line 7 writes 'YZ' beginning one space after the 'X'.

- Line 8 writes 'YZ' beginning in column 2. This overwrites the space and the 'Y' that was written previously.

- Line 9 writes 'ABC' beginning in column 3. This overwrites the two 'Z's, plus one space.

- Line 10 writes f1 beginning in column 4. The default output length of f1 is 8; the default format is right-justified with the last character reserved for the sign. The three leading blanks overwrite the existing output beginning in column 4.

- Line 11 writes f1 again, this time beginning in column 7.

- Line 12 writes 'Z' one space after f1. In the output, there appears to be two spaces. The first space after the 4 is the sign field for f1. Then one space is written, and then 'Z' in column 16.

TABLE 14.4 write STATEMENT EXAMPLES AND CORRESPONDING OUTPUT

Statements	Cumulative Output ----+----1----+-- 12345678901234567
write 1 'X'.	X
write 'YZ'.	X YZ
write 2 'YZ'.	XYZZ
write 3 'ABC'.	XYABC
write 4 f1.	XYA 1,234
write 7 f1.	XYA 1 1,234
write 'Z'.	XYA 1 1,234 Z

14

Understanding the Length Specification

In the syntax description for the write statement, o specifies the output length. This is the number of characters on the output line used to hold the output value.

Position and length specifications are always optional. They can be specified using either a literal or a variable. If either one is a variable, it must be preceded by the word at. at is optional if the position and length are both literals, but it is required if either is a variable.

If a slash (/) precedes a position or length specification, there cannot be an intervening space between them. Listing 14.3 provides examples.

INPUT

LISTING 14.3 ILLUSTRATING THE USE OF THE POSITION AND LENGTH SPECIFICATIONS

```
1  report ztx1403.
2  data: f1(4) type p value 1234,
3        p      type i value 5,
4        l      type i value 8.
5
6  write: / '----+----1----+--',
7         / '12345678901234567'.
8  skip.
9  write /(2) 'XYZ'.
10 write /(4) 'XYZ'.
11 write      'ABC'.
12 write /5(4) f1.
13 write at /p(l) f1.
```

The code in Listing 14.3 produces this output:

OUTPUT

```
----+----1----+--
12345678901234567

XY
XYZ  ABC
     1234
       1,234
```

ANALYSIS

- Line 6 writes the first two characters of 'XYZ'.

- Line 7 writes 'XYZ' using four characters of output. Default formatting is used, so the value is left-justified and padded on the right with blanks.

- Line 8 writes 'ABC' one space after the previous value. The previous value was padded on the right with one blank. Another blank is added, and then 'ABC' is written.

- Line 9 writes f1 in a field that is four characters long beginning in column 5. The system removes the separators to make the value fit into four characters.

- Line 10 writes f1 into a field that is eight characters long beginning in column 5. Variables are used, so the word at is required. Default formatting applies, so the value is right-justified with leading zeros suppressed and, because there is enough room, separators are also written.

Working with Subfields

You can specify a subfield in the write statement by using offset and length specifications immediately after the value without an intervening space. (If necessary, refer to the previous section on additions to the write statement.) You cannot use a subfield with a literal or a numeric field (types p, i, and f). Listing 14.4 provides examples.

INPUT   **LISTING 14.4**   USING SUBFIELDS

```
1   report ztx1404.
2   data f1(4) type c value 'ABCD'.
3
4   write: / '----+----1----+--',
5          / '12345678901234567'.
6   skip.
7   write  / f1(2).
8   write  / f1+1(2).
9   write: /(2) f1+2(1), f1.
```

The code in Listing 14.4 produces this output:

OUTPUT

```
----+----1----+--
12345678901234567

AB
BC
C   ABCD
```

ANALYSIS

- Line 7 writes the first and second characters of f1.

- Line 8 writes the second and third characters of f1.

- Line 9 writes the third character of f1 beginning on a new line in a field that is two characters long. It is left-justified in that field and padded on the right with blanks. It then writes out the entire contents of f1 with an intervening blank beforehand.

14

Using the under Addition

Using under causes the first character of the field to be positioned in the same column as the first character of a previously written field. You cannot use under with an explicit position specification. Listing 14.5 shows examples.

INPUT   **LISTING 14.5**   USING THE under ADDITION

```
1   report ztx1405.
2   tables: ztxlfa1.
3
4   select * up to 5 rows from ztxlfa1 order by lifnr.
5       write: /1  ztxlfa1-lifnr,
6               15 ztxlfa1-land1,
7               25 ztxlfa1-name1,
8              /   ztxlfa1-spras under ztxlfa1-land1,
9                  ztxlfa1-stras under ztxlfa1-name1.
10      skip.
11      endselect.
```

The code in Listing 14.5 produces this output:

OUTPUT

```
1000          CA          Parts Unlimited
              E           111 Queen St.

1010          CA          Industrial Pumps Inc.
              E           1520 Avenue Rd.

1020          CA          Chemical Nation Ltd.
              E           123 River Ave.

1030          CA          ChickenFeed Ltd.
              E           8718 Wishbone Lane

1040          US          Motherboards Inc.
              E           64 BitBus Blvd.
```

ANALYSIS

- Line 6 writes the land1 field beginning in column 15.

- Line 7 writes the name1 field beginning in column 25.

- Line 8 writes the spras field beginning in the same column as land1. It consequently is written beginning in column 15.

- Line 9 writes the stras field beginning in the same column as name1. It is therefore written beginning in column 25.

Using the no-gap Addition

Using no-gap suppresses the intervening gap automatically placed after a field if the following field has no column specification. Listing 14.6 illustrates the use of no-gap.

INPUT   **LISTING 14.6**   USING no-gap

```
1  report ztx1406.
2  data f1(4) value 'ABCD'.
3
4  write: / f1, f1,
5         / f1 no-gap, f1,
6         / '''', f1, '''',
7         / '''', 2 f1, 6 '''',
8         / '''' no-gap, f1 no-gap, ''''.
```

The code in Listing 14.6 produces this output:

OUTPUT
```
ABCD ABCD
ABCDABCD
' ABCD '
'ABCD'
'ABCD'
```

ANALYSIS
- Line 4 writes f1 twice on the same line. Because there is no position specification for the second f1, a single intervening space is written before it.

- Line 5 also writes f1 twice. Using no-gap after the first causes the two values to appear in the output without an intervening space.

- Line 6 writes f1 with a single quote on either side. Intervening spaces appear without the use of no-gap.

- Line 7 writes f1 enclosed by single quotes. Position specifications cause the quotes to appear without intervening spaces.

- Line 8 uses no-gap to achieve the same output.

Using Edit Masks

Edit masks enable you to:

- Insert characters into the output
- Move the sign to the beginning of a numeric field
- Artificially insert or move a decimal point
- Display a floating-point number without using scientific notation

14

Anywhere within an edit mask, the underscore character (_) has special meaning. At the beginning of an edit mask, V, LL, RR, and == have special meaning. All other characters are transferred without change to the output.

Underscores within an edit mask are replaced one-by-one with the characters from the source field (the field you are writing out). The number of characters taken from the source field will be equal to the number of underscores in the edit mask. For example, if there are three characters in the edit mask, at most three characters from the source field will be output. All other characters in the edit mask are inserted into the output. You also usually need to increase the length of the output field to accommodate the extra characters inserted by the mask.

For example, the statement `write (6) 'ABCD' using edit mask '_:__:_'` writes A:BC:D. Characters are taken from the source field one at a time, and characters from the edit mask are inserted at the points indicated by the mask. The statement `write 'ABCD' using edit mask '_:__:_'` only writes A:BC because the default output length is equal to the length of the source field (4).

If there are fewer underscores in the mask than there are in the source field, the default is to take the left-most n characters from the source field, where n equals the number of underscores in the edit mask. This can also be explicitly specified by preceding the edit mask with LL. For example, `write 'ABCD' using edit mask 'LL__:_'` takes the left-most three characters and writes out AB:C. Using RR instead takes the right-most three characters, so `write 'ABCD' using edit mask 'RR__:_'` will write out BC:D.

If there are more underscores than there are source field characters, the effect of LL is to left-justify the value in the output; RR right-justifies the value (see Listing 14.7 for an example).

An edit mask beginning with a V, when applied to a numeric field (types i, p, and f), causes the sign field to be displayed at the beginning. If applied to a character field, a V is actually output.

INPUT **LISTING 14.7** THE EFFECT OF VARIOUS EDIT MASKS

```
1   report ztx1407.
2   data: f1(4) value 'ABCD',
3         f2    type i value '1234-'.
4
5   write: / ' 5. ', f1,
6          / ' 6. ', (6) f1 using edit mask '_:__:_',
7          / ' 7. ', f1 using edit mask 'LL_:__',
8          / ' 8. ', f1 using edit mask 'RR_:__',
```

```
9       / ' 9. ', f2 using edit mask 'LLV_____',
10      / '10. ', f2 using edit mask 'RRV_____',
11      / '11. ', f2 using edit mask 'RRV___,___',
12      / '12. ', f2 using edit mask 'LLV___,___',
13      / '13. ', f1 using edit mask 'V___'.
```

The code in Listing 14.7 produces this output:

OUTPUT

```
5.   ABCD
6.   A:BC:D
7.   A:BC
8.   B:CD
9.   -1234
10.  -  1234
11.  -  1,234
12.  -123,4
13.  VABC
```

ANALYSIS

- Line 5 outputs f1 without any edit masks.

- Line 6 outputs all four characters of f1 using colons to separate them.

- There are three underscores in the edit mask on line 7, but four characters in f1. Therefore, the first three characters of f1 are used in the edit mask.

- Line 8 takes the last three characters of f1 and applies them to the edit mask.

- There are six underscores in the edit mask on line 9, more than the four characters from f1. The value of f1 is output left-justified with a leading sign.

- On line 10, the value of f1 is output right-justified with a leading sign.

- Lines 11 and 12 show the effect of combining inserted characters with justification. The inserted characters do not move relative to the output field.

- Line 13 shows the effect of using a V with a character field. The V itself is output.

Using Conversion Exits

NEW TERM A conversion exit is a called routine that formats the output. An edit mask that begins with == followed by a four-character ID calls a function module that formats the output. That four-character ID is known as a *conversion exit*, or *conversion routine*. (Function modules are covered in a subsequent chapter, but, for now, think of a function module as a subroutine within another program.) The name of the function module will be CONVERSION_EXIT_*XXXX*_OUTPUT, where *XXXX* is the four-character id that follows ==. For example, write '00001000' using edit mask '==ALPHA' calls the function module CONVERSION_EXIT_ALPHA_OUTPUT. The write statement passes the value first to the function module, which changes it in any desired way and then returns the

14

changed value, and that value is written out. This particular exit (ALPHA) examines the value to determine whether it consists entirely of numbers. If it does, leading zeros are stripped and the number is left-justified. Values containing non-numerics are not changed by ALPHA. SAP supplies about 60 conversion exits for various formatting tasks. After Chapter 19, "Modularization: Function Modules, Part 1," on function modules, you will know enough to be able to create your own conversion exits.

Conversion exits are particularly useful for complex formatting tasks that are needed in more than one program. To illustrate, the conversion exit CUNIT automatically converts the code representing a unit of measure into a description meaningful in the current logon language. For example, within R/3, the code for a crate of materials is KI. (KI is an abbreviation of *kiste*, the German word for "box.") However, CUNIT converts KI to the English mnemonic CR. Therefore, when logged on in English, write: '1', 'KI' using edit mask '==CUNIT'. writes 1 CR. For a user signed on in German, the output would be 1 KI. Using such a conversion exit enables a standard set of codes stored in the database to be automatically converted to be meaningful to the current logon language whenever output to a report.

Conversion Routines within a Domain

A conversion exit can also be placed into the Convers. Routine field in a domain. The exit is inherited by all fields that use that domain, and will be automatically applied when the value is written out. Figure 14.2 shows that domain ztxlifnr uses the conversion routine ALPHA.

FIGURE 14.2.

Notice the contents of the Convers. Routine field.

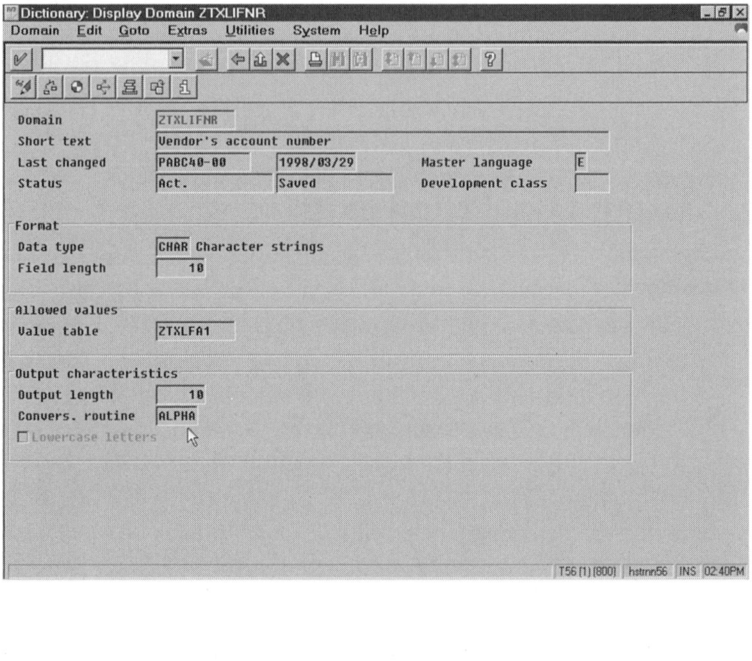

Therefore, whenever ztxlfa1-lifnr is written, the value first passes through the function module CONVERSION_EXIT_ALPHA_OUTPUT, which strips leading zeros from numeric values.

A conversion exit within a domain can be turned off by specifying using no edit mask on the write statement.

Listing 14.8 illustrates the use of conversion exits.

INPUT **LISTING 14.8** USING CONVERSION EXITS

```
1   report ztx1408.
2   tables: ztxlfa1, ztxmara.
3   data: f1(10) value '0000001000'.
4
5   write: / f1,
6           / f1 using edit mask '==ALPHA'.
7
8   skip.
9   select * from ztxlfa1 where lifnr = '00000010000'
10                          or lifnr = 'V1'
11                      order by lifnr.
12      write: / ztxlfa1-lifnr,      "domain contains convers. exit ALPHA
13             / ztxlfa1-lifnr using no edit mask.
14      endselect.
15
16  skip.
17  select single * from ztxmara where matnr = 'M103'.
18  write: /      ztxmara-matnr,
19         (10) ztxmara-brgew,
20              ztxmara-gewei.       "domain contains convers. exit CUNIT
21  set locale language 'D'.
22  write: /      ztxmara-matnr,
23         (10) ztxmara-brgew,
24              ztxmara-gewei.       "domain contains convers. exit CUNIT
```

The code in Listing 14.8 produces this output:

OUTPUT
```
0000001000
1000

1000
0000001000
V1
V1

M103                    50.000   CR
M103                    50.000   KI
```

14

ANALYSIS
- Line 5 writes the value from f1.
- Line 6 writes the same value but applies conversion exit ALPHA. Before being written, f1 is passed to the function module CONVERSION_EXIT_ALPHA_OUTPUT, which detects that the value is entirely numeric and strips off leading zeros and left-justifies it.
- Line 9 retrieves two records from ztxlfa1and and writes the lifnr field twice for each.
- The domain for ztxlfa1-lifnr contains the conversion exit ALPHA, so line 12 writes lifnr using that conversion exit.
- Line 13 writes lifnr out, but turns off the conversion exit. This causes the actual value in the table to be written out.
- Line 17 selects a single record from ztxmara.
- Line 20 writes gewei (unit of weight) using conversion exit CUNIT in the domain.
- Line 21 changes the text environment to German. This is equivalent to logging on in German.
- Line 24 writes the same gewei value, but this time CUNIT displays the German mnemonic.

Displaying Existing Conversion Exits

To display the existing conversion exits, use the following procedure.

SCREENCAM Start the ScreenCam "How to Display Existing Conversion Exits" now.

1. From the Development Workbench screen, choose the menu path Overview-> Repository Infosys. The ABAP/4 Repository Information System screen is displayed.
2. Click on the plus (+) beside Programming. The tree expands.
3. Click on the plus (+) beside Function Library. The tree expands.
4. Double-click on the line Function Modules. The ABAP/4 Repository Information System: Function Module screen is displayed.
5. In the Function Module field, enter **CONVERSION_EXIT_*_OUTPUT** (the field is scrollable; you can enter more characters into it than it can display).
6. Press the Execute button on the Application toolbar. The Function Modules screen is displayed. All of the conversion exits that can be used on the write statement will be listed here.

Working with Date Formatting

Date formatting specifications, for the most part, do *not* do what you think they will. Most pull their format from the Date Format specification in the user defaults (menu path System->User Profile->User Defaults).

Table 14.5 contains a description of the effect of each.

TABLE 14.5 EFFECTS OF THE DATE FORMAT SPECIFICATIONS

Format	Effect
mm/dd/yyyy dd/mm/yyyy	Writes out the date using the format specified in the user's profile. This is the default, so these formats do not actually do anything.
mm/dd/yy dd/mm/yy	Writes out the date with a two-character year using the format specified in the user's profile. They both do the same thing.
mmddyy ddmmyy	Writes out the date using a two-character year using the format specified in the user's profile, without separators. They both do the same thing.
yymmdd	Writes out the date in yymmdd format without separators.

Tip

Conversion exits IDATE and SDATE provide alternate date formats. Also, the function module RH_GET_DATE_DAYNAME returns the name of the day of the week for a given date and language. As an alternative, DATE_COMPUTE_DAY returns a number representing the day of the week.

Listing 14.9 illustrates the use of the date format specifications.

INPUT   **LISTING 14.9**   USING DATE FORMAT SPECIFICATIONS

```
1   report ztx1409.
2   data: f1 like sy-datum value '19981123',
3         begin of f2,
4             y(4),
5             m(2),
6             d(2),
7         end of f2,
8         begin of f3,
9             d(2),
10            m(2),
11            y(4),
```

continues

14

LISTING 14.9   CONTINUED

```
12              end of f3,
13          begin of f4,
14              m(2),
15              d(2),
16              y(4),
17              end of f4.
18
19 write: / f1,              "user profile sets format
20        / f1 mm/dd/yyyy,   "user profile sets format
21        / f1 dd/mm/yyyy,   "user profile sets format
22        / f1 mm/dd/yy,     "user profile fmt, display with 2-digit year
23        / f1 dd/mm/yy,     "user profile fmt, display with 2-digit year
24        / f1 mmddyy,       "user profile fmt, 2-digit year, no separators
25        / f1 ddmmyy,       "user profile fmt, 2-digit year, no separators
26        / f1 yymmdd,       "yymmdd format, no separators
27        / f1 using edit mask '==IDATE',
28        /(11) f1 using edit mask '==SDATE'.
29
30 f2 = f1.
31 move-corresponding f2 to: f3, f4.
32 write: /(10) f3 using edit mask '__/__/____', "dd/mm/yyyy format
33        /(10) f4 using edit mask '__/__/____'. "mm/dd/yyyy format
```

The code in Listing 14.9 produces this output:

OUTPUT
```
1998/11/23
1998/11/23
1998/11/23
98/11/23
98/11/23
981123
981123
981123
1998NOV23
1998/NOV/23
23/11/1998
11/23/1998
```

ANALYSIS

- Line 2 defines f1 like sy-datum. The output length in the domain for sy-datum is 10, so separators will be displayed when the value of f1 is written out.

- Lines 19, 20, and 21 all do the same thing: They write f1 using the format specified in the user's profile.

- Lines 22 and 23 both do the same thing: They write f1 using the format specified in the user's profile, but using a two-digit year.

- Lines 24 and 25 both do the same thing: They write f1 using the format specified in the user's profile using a two-digit year, but without separators.

- Line 27 formats the date using the conversion exit IDATE. The output of IDATE is yyyymmmdd format.

- Line 28 formats the date using the conversion exit SDATE. The output of SDATE is yyyy/mmm/dd format.

- Lines 30 through 33 show how to create your own output format. If you were to do this in real life, it would be better to put this code into a conversion exit and then name the conversion exit on the write statement. Not only would you be able to simplify your code, but it would also be available to you and all other programmers for instant application in any program.

Using the no-zero and no-sign Additions

The no-zero addition suppresses leading zeros when used with type c or type n variables. In the case of a zero value, the output is all blanks.

The no-sign addition, when used with variables of type i, p, or f, suppresses the output of the sign character. In other words, negative numbers will not have a sign and will appear as if they were positive.

Listing 14.10 illustrates the use of these two additions.

INPUT **LISTING 14.10** USING no-zero AND no-sign

```
1   report ztx1410.
2   data: c1(10) type c value '000123',
3         n1(10) type n value 123,
4         n2(10) type n value 0,
5         i1     type i value '123-',
6         i2     type i value 123.

7   write: / c1,          20 'type c',
8          / c1 no-zero, 20 'type c using no-zero',
9          / n1,          20 'type n',
10         / n1 no-zero, 20 'type n using no-zero',
11         / n2,          20 'type n: zero value',
12         / n2 no-zero, 20 'type n: zero value using no-zero',
13         / i1,          20 'type i',
14         / i2 no-sign, 20 'type i using no-sign'.
```

The code in Listing 14.10 produces this output:

OUTPUT

```
000123            type c
   123            type c using no-zero
0000000123        type n
       123        type n using no-zero
0000000000        type n: zero value
```

14

```
                          type n: zero value using no-zero
              123-        type i
              123         type i using no-sign
```

Specifying Decimals and Rounding

Two statements perform rounding:

- decimals
- round

Three statements are used to specify the number of decimal places in the output:

- decimals
- currency
- unit

Using the `decimals` and `round` Additions

The decimals *n* addition can be used to increase or decrease the number of decimal places displayed in the output list. If you decrease the number of decimal places, the value is rounded before being written to the list. The source variable value is not changed, only the output appears differently. If you increase the number of decimals, zeros are appended to the end of the value. Negative values of *n* move the decimal to the right, effectively multiplying the number by factors of 10 and then rounding before display.

The round *n* addition causes the output to be scaled by factors of 10 and then rounded before display. This has the same effect as multiplying by 10**n. Positive *n* values move the decimal to the left, and negative values move it to the right. This is useful, for example, when you want to output values to the nearest thousand.

The difference between decimals and round is that decimals changes the number of digits seen after the decimal point to *n* and then performs rounding. round moves the decimal point left or right by *n*, maintaining the number of digits after the decimal, and then performs rounding to the number of decimal digits displayed.

Listing 14.11 illustrates the use of decimals and round.

INPUT   **LISTING 14.11**   USING THE decimals AND round ADDITIONS

```
1  report ztx1411.
2  data f1 type p decimals 3 value '1575.456'.
3  write: / f1,               20 'as-is',
4          / f1 decimals 4,   20 'decimals 4',
5          / f1 decimals 3,   20 'decimals 3',
6          / f1 decimals 2,   20 'decimals 2',
7          / f1 decimals 1,   20 'decimals 1',
```

```
 8        / f1 decimals 0,        20 'decimals 0',
 9        / f1 decimals -1,       20 'decimals -1',
10        / f1 round 4,           20 'round 4',
11        / f1 round 3,           20 'round 3',
12        / f1 round 2,           20 'round 2',
13        / f1 round 1,           20 'round 1',
14        / f1 round 0,           20 'round 0',
15        / f1 round -1,          20 'round -1',
16        / f1 round -2,          20 'round -2',
17        / f1 round 3 decimals 1, 20 'round 3 decimals 1',
18        / f1 round 3 decimals 3, 20 'round 3 decimals 3'.
```

The code in Listing 14.11 produces this output:

OUTPUT

```
1,575.456   as-is
    1,575.4560   decimals 4
    1,575.456    decimals 3
    1,575.46     decimals 2
    1,575.5      decimals 1
    1,575        decimals 0
        158      decimals -1
      0.158      round 4
      1.575      round 3
     15.755      round 2
    157.546      round 1
  1,575.456      round 0
 15,754.560      round -1
157,545.600      round -2
        1.6      round 3 decimals 1
        1.575    round 3 decimals 3
```

ANALYSIS On line 8, the decimals 0 addition does not round up because the fractional part of the number is less than .5.

Note

The decimals addition overrides decimal places defined in the domain. Regardless of where the decimals specification comes from, it never indicates an actual decimal point in the number. The number is always stored as an integer value. The decimals statement is a format specification applied to the number before it is used anywhere, for example, on the write statement or in a calculation.

14

Using the currency and unit Additions

The additions currency and unit are an alternate way of indicating the position of the decimal point for a type p field. They cannot be used with the decimals addition.

Note	The DDIC types CURR and QUAN are based on the ABAP/4 data type p (packed decimal).

Using the currency Addition

When you write out a currency amount, you should also use the currency addition. Such amounts are usually retrieved from a type CURR field in a database table.

Use currency instead of decimals to specify the number of decimal places for currency amount fields. Unlike decimals, on which you specify the number of decimal places, you instead specify a currency code, such as USD (U.S. Dollars), ITL (Italian Lira), or JPY (Japanese Yen). The system then looks up that currency code in table TCURX to determine the number of decimal places that should be used to display the value. If the currency code is not found in TCURX, a default of two decimal places is used.

The currency code is usually also stored either in the same database table or another, related one. For example, the currency key for type CURR fields (saldv, solll, and habnl) in table ztxlfc3 is stored in the field ztxt001-waers. You can find this out by double-clicking on any of these fields. For example, if you double-click on ztxlfc3-saldv, you will see the Display Field ZTXLFC3-SALDV screen shown in Figure 14.3.

FIGURE 14.3.

A double-click on field saldv in table ztxlfc3 displays this screen.

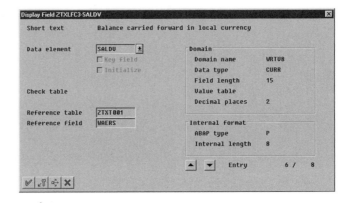

The reference table and reference field indicate that ztxt001-waers contains the currency key.

The table ztxt001 itself contains the attributes of all company codes; its primary key is bukrs. If you take the value from ztxlfc3-bukrs and look up the single row in ztxt001 that matches, waers will contain the currency key. Listing 14.12 illustrates.

INPUT   **LISTING 14.12**   USING THE currency ADDITION

```
1  report ztx1412.
2  tables: ztxlfc3.

3  data: f1 type p decimals 1 value '12345.6'.
4
5  write: / f1,
6          / f1 currency 'USD', 'USD',      "US Dollars
7          / f1 currency 'ITL', 'ITL'.      "Italian Lira
8
9  skip.
10 select * from ztxlfc3 where gjahr = '1997'
11                        and saldv >= 100
12                        order by bukrs.
13     on change of ztxlfc3-bukrs.
14       select single * from ztxt001 where bukrs = ztxlfc3-bukrs.
15       endon.
16     write: / ztxlfc3-saldv currency ztxt001-waers, ztxt001-waers.
17     endselect.
```

The code in Listing 14.12 produces this output:

OUTPUT
```
      123,456
    1,234.56  USD
      123,456  ITL

         100.00  USD
         100.00  USD
         100.00  USD
         100.00  USD
         100,000  ITL
          25,050  ITL
         100,000  ITL
         100,000  JPY
         300,000  JPY
          250.50  CAD
          200.00  CAD
        1,000.00  CAD
          100.00  CAD
```

ANALYSIS
- Line 5 writes the value of f1 as-is.

- Line 6 writes the same value, but first it looks up 'USD' in table TCURX to determine the number of decimal places. The value 'USD' is not in that table, so the output is formatted using the default (two decimal places).

- When line 7 is executed, table TCURX indicates that ITL has no decimal places and so formats the value without any decimals.

- Line 10 selects records from table ztxlfc3 in company code order (bukrs).

14

- Line 13 is triggered each time the company code changes.
- Line 14 looks up the company code in table ztxt001 to find the currency for that company. The currency key is available in field ztxt001-waers.
- Line 16 writes the balance carried forward using the number of decimal places indicated by the currency key in field ztxt001-waers.

Using the unit Addition

The unit addition is used to specify the number of decimals displayed for a quantity field. Units, such as cm (centimeters) or lb (pounds), determine the number of decimal places displayed. The code, such as '%' (percent) or 'KM' (kilometers) is specified after unit is looked up automatically in table t006. The fields decan and andec then determine how many decimal places are displayed. They both contain a numeric value.

decan specifies the number of zero-valued decimal values to truncate. It removes trailing zeros; it will never truncate nonzero decimal places. It also never increases the number of decimal places displayed. For example, if the value is 12.30 and decan is 1, the output will be 12.3. If the value is 12.34 and decan is 1, the output will be 12.34.

andec appends zeros after decan has been applied. The number of decimal digits displayed must be a multiple of andec. If necessary, andec will pad the value on the right with zeros. If andec is zero, no zeros are appended. For example, if the value is 12.34 after decan has been applied, and the value of andec is 3, there must be 0, 3, 6, or 9 (or any other multiple of 3) decimal digits. The output value will therefore be padded with zeros to become 12.340. If the value after decan is 12.3456, the output will be 12.345600. If the value after decan is 12.30 and andec is 2, the output will be 12.30.

Table 14.6 contains more examples of the effects of decan and andec on the output format.

TABLE 14.6 HOW THE decan AND andec FIELDS FROM TABLE t006 AFFECT THE OUTPUT FORMATTING OF A FIELD

Input	decan	andec	Result
30.1	1	0	30.1
30.1	1	2	30.10
30.1	1	3	30.100
30.1234	1	3	30.123400
30	1	3	30
30	2	0	30
30.1	2	0	30.1
30.11	2	0	30.11

Input	decan	andec	Result
30.11	2	2	30.11
30.11	2	4	30.1100

The unit addition is typically used with fields of type QUAN that are stored in the database. Each field must have a reference field of type UNIT. The unit of measurement for the value in the QUAN field is stored there. Figure 14.4 shows that the reference field for ztxmara-brgew is ztxmara-gewei.

FIGURE 14.4.

If you double-click on the ztxmara-brgew *field, you will see a screen indicating the reference table and field.*

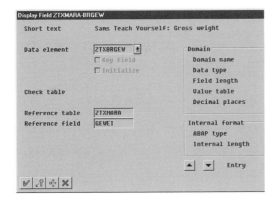

Listing 14.13 illustrates the use of this addition.

LISTING 14.13   USING THE unit ADDITION

```
1   report ztx1413.
2   tables: ztxmara, t006.
3   data: f1 type p decimals 4 value '99.0000',
4         f2 type p decimals 4 value '99.1234',
5         f3 type p decimals 4 value '99.1200',
6         f4 type p decimals 1 value '99.1'.
7
8   write: / f1,             'as-is',
9          / f1 unit 'ML', 'ml - milliliters decan 3 andec 3',
10         / f1 unit '%',  '% - percent      decan 2 andec 0',
11         / f1 unit '"',  '" - inches       decan 0 andec 3',
12         /,
13         / f2,             'as-is',
14         / f2 unit '%',  '%',
15         / f3,             'as-is',
16         / f3 unit '%',  '%',
```

continues

14

LISTING 14.13 CONTINUED

```
17          / f4,              'as-is',
18          / f4 unit '%',  '%'.
19
20 skip.
21 write: /12 'brgew as-is',
22         31 'with units',
23         48 'ntgew as-is',
24         67 'with units',
25         79 'units',
26         85 'decan',
27         91 'andec'.
28 uline.
29 select * from ztxmara.
30     select single * from t006 where msehi = ztxmara-gewei.
31     write: /(5) ztxmara-matnr,
32               ztxmara-brgew,
33               ztxmara-brgew unit ztxmara-gewei,
34               ztxmara-ntgew,
35               ztxmara-ntgew unit ztxmara-gewei,
36               ztxmara-gewei,
37            85 t006-decan,
38            91 t006-andec.
39     endselect.
```

The code in Listing 14.13 produces this output:

OUTPUT

```
99.0000  as-is
 99.000  ml - milliliters decan 3 andec 3
 99.00   %  - percent        decan 2 andec 0
    99   "  - inches         decan 0 andec 3

99.1234  as-is
99.1234  %
99.1200  as-is
 99.12   %
  99.1   as-is
  99.1   %


       brgew as-is    w/units    ntgew as-is   w/units   units decan
  ➥andec
------------------------------------------------------------------------
  M100      102.560    102.560      100.000       100   M3     0    3
  M101       10.100     10.100       10.000        10   PAL    0    0
  M102        1.000          1        0.000         0   ROL    0    0
  M103       50.000         50        0.000         0   CR     0    0
```

ANALYSIS

- Line 8 writes f1 without using the units addition.

- Line 9 uses the unit ML (milliliters). A lookup is automatically done in table t006 for ML. That row contains decan 3, and andec 3. decan 3 causes zeros after the third decimal place to be dropped. andec 3 causes the number of decimals to be a multiple of three. At this point, it already is, so the output is displayed using three decimals.

- Line 10 formats f1 using the unit % (percent), which has decan 2 and andec 0. decan 2 dictates that trailing zeros after the second decimal should be dropped. andec 0 indicates that there is no further modification, and so two decimal places are output.

- Line 11 uses the " unit (inches). decan 0 indicates that all decimal zeros should be truncated. andec 3 indicates that the number of decimals should be padded with zeros to three decimal places.

- Lines 13 through 18 format f2 through f4 using the unit %.

- On line 14, decan 2 indicates trailing zeros after the second decimal digit should be truncated. There aren't any, so nothing is truncated. andec 0 indicates no further padding, therefore the output is formatted using four decimal digits.

- On line 16, decan 2 truncates the trailing zeros.

- On line 18, decan 2 does not do anything because there are no trailing zeros to truncate. andec is 0, so no zeros are appended to the end.

- Line 29 selects all records from table ztxmara.

- For each, line 30 selects the record from t006 that contains the unit in ztxmara-gewei. Please note that this is not normally done. It is only done here to show you the values of decan and andec.

- On lines 32 through 35, the values gewei and ntgew are written out in two ways. First they are written out as-is, and then they are written using the unit addition to show the before-and-after.

- Lines 37 and 38 write out the decan and andec values that were used to format each row.

Shifting Justification

Using left-justified, centered, and right-justified, you can shift the output value within the space allotted for the output field. Listing 14.14 illustrates.

continues

INPUT   **LISTING 14.14**   USING THE JUSTIFICATION ADDITIONS TO THE write STATEMENT

14

```
1   report ztx1414.
2   data: f1(6) value 'AB'.
3   write: /      '....+....1',
4          /      '1234567890',
```

LISTING 14.14 CONTINUED

```
5              /      f1,
6              /      f1 left-justified,
7              /      f1 centered,
8              /      f1 right-justified,
9              /      '....+....1....+....2....+....3....+....4',
10             /      '12345678901234567890123456789012345678901234567890',
11             /(40)  f1 left-justified,
12             /(40)  f1 centered,
13             /(40)  f1 right-justified.
```

The code in Listing 14.14 produces this output:

OUTPUT

```
....+....1
1234567890
AB
AB
   AB
      AB
....+....1....+....2....+....3....+....4
12345678901234567890123456789012345678901234567890
AB
                       AB
                                        AB
```

ANALYSIS

- Lines 3, 4, 9, and 10 write out a ruler so that you can see the column numbers in the output.

- Line 5 writes f1 using default length and formatting. Default formatting for a type c variable dictates left-justification, so the output appears left-justified within its default output length (6).

- Line 6 produces the same output because it also specifies left-justification.

- Line 7 centers the value within the default output length of 6.

- Line 8 right-justifies the value within the default output length of 6.

- Lines 11, 12, and 13 specify an output length of 40. The value is then left-justified, centered, and right-justified within that length.

Summary

- If you do not specify any format or length specification on the write statement, the default format and length of the field are used. These defaults originate in the ABAP/4 data types. DDIC fields are based on ABAP/4 data types, and they thereby inherit the default format and length. In addition, format specifications such as number of decimal places and output length can also be specified in the domain; these override the inherited values.

- Date and time fields are displayed with separators if there is enough room in the output field for them. If there is not, the separators are completely dropped. In numeric field, thousands separators are dropped one at a time, beginning at the left of the field and moving right, in order to display more digits. Even the sign field is used if it is blank.

- For most date format specifications, user defaults define at least in part how date fields should be formatted. Of all of the date format specifications, only `yymmdd` completely overrides the user defaults.

- An edit mask can be used to insert characters into the output. It can also invoke a conversion exit that can format the value using ABAP/4 code. A conversion exit is like a reusable container that contains code to format a field.

- Use `no-zero` to suppress leading zeros in type n and type c fields.

- Use `no-sign` to remove the trailing sign field from the display.

- Use `decimals` to specify the number of decimal places that should be displayed.

- Use `round` to indicate the position of the decimal point in the value.

- Use `currency` to specify the number of decimal places for currency amount fields. It looks up the currency code in table `tcurx` to determine the number of decimals. If the code is not found, a default of two decimal places is used.

- Use `unit` to format quantity fields. The unit is looked up in table `t006`. `decan` determines the number of decimal zeros to remove, and `andec` determines the number of zeros to add. Non-zero decimal digits are never removed.

- Use `left-justified`, `centered`, and `right-justified` to justify the value within the length of the output field.

Do	Don't
DO enable users to specify their own date formats.	**DON'T** hard-code `decimals 2` for dollar amounts. Use the `currency` addition instead.
DO use conversion exits to perform repetitive formatting tasks, especially if they are complex.	**DON'T** hard-code two decimal places for % or any other unit of measure. Use the `unit` addition instead.

14

Q&A

Q I noticed that there are also function modules that have names like CONVERSION_EXIT_XXXXX_INPUT. What are these for?

A The INPUT function module is called whenever a value is entered into a field, provided the domain for that field specifies a conversion exit. The INPUT conversion exit converts the user's input into a new format before the program receives it. It is used to reduce the amount of repetitive code that is needed to reformat an input value so that the program that uses it doesn't have to.

Q How do I create a conversion exit?

A If you don't know how to create a function module, you'll need to read that chapter first. If you do know how to create one, create one with the name CONVERSION_EXIT_XXXXX_OUTPUT where XXXXX is a five-character name you make up. There must be one import parameter named INPUT and one export parameter named OUTPUT. The original value passed from the write statement is received via the INPUT parameter. You can reformat it, and at the end of the function module, assign the new value to the OUTPUT parameter. A good way to start is to copy an existing one.

Workshop

The Workshop provides two ways for you to affirm what you've learned in this chapter. The Quiz section poses questions to help you solidify your understanding of the material covered and the Exercise section provides you with experience in using what you have learned. You can find answers to the quiz questions and exercises in Appendix B, "Answers to Quiz Questions and Exercises."

Quiz

1. What do you have to do to make sure changes to user defaults take effect?

2. What happens when an edit mask beginning with a V is applied to a numeric field or character field?

3. What variable types can the no-sign addition be used with to make a negative number appear as if it were positive?

Exercise 1

Write a program that produces the following output:

```
....+....1....+....2....+....3....+....4
First                                 December
            January
                   First
```

WEEK 2

In Review

In the past week, you have accomplished the following tasks:

- created fixed and variable data objects using both pre-defined and user-defined data types
- learned the rules of ABAP/4 syntax and the statements for controlling program flow
- discovered assignment statements and conversion rules
- defined internal tables and filled them using implicit and explicit work areas
- optimized the `select` statement to directly and efficiently fill an internal table
- performed control break processing on internal tables
- used the formatting options of the `write` statement and experienced the effects of data type on the output
- employed conversion exits and detected their presence within the domain

8

9

10

11

12

13

14

WEEK 3

At a Glance

In Week 3, you produce reports that use graphical symbols and icons, attach headings and footings to lists, and send output to the print spool using the `new-page print` statement. Following that, you become familiar with the `initialization`, `start-of-selection`, `end-of-selection`, `top-of-page`, and `end-of-page` events. You also code internal and external subroutines and function modules, and pass typed and untyped parameters to them by value, by value and result, and by reference. Finally, you raise exceptions within function modules to set the return value of `sy-subrc`, and create selection screens using the `select-options` statement.

- In Day 15, "Formatting Techniques, Part 1," you use the graphical formatting options of the write statement (`as symbol`, `as icon`, `as line`), print list output, and manipulate the output on the spool.

- During Day 16, "Formatting Techniques, Part 2," you use the common formatting statements `new-line`, `new-page`, `skip`, `back`, `position`, and `set blank lines`; and send output to the spool using `new-page print`.

- Within Day 17, "Modularization: Events and Subroutines," you use the events `initialization`, `start-of-selection`, and `end-of-selection`; define internal and external subroutines; and define global, local, and static variables and table work areas.

- During Day 18, "Modularization: Passing Parameters to Subroutines," you pass typed and untyped parameters to subroutines; pass parameters three ways: by reference, by value, and by value and result; and pass field strings and internal tables to a subroutine.

- During Day 19, "Modularization: Function Modules, Part 1," you understand and use the `include` statement, create function groups and function modules, and define import, export, and changing parameters.
- Within Day 20, "Modularization: Function Modules, Part 2," you understand the components and structure of a function group, and define global data and subroutines within a function group.
- In Day 21, "Selection Screens," you code selection screens that interact with the user, use formatting elements to create efficient, well-designed selection screens, and use selection screens to maintain data integrity.

DAY 15

Formatting Techniques, Part 1

Chapter Objectives

After you have completed this chapter, you will be able to

- Use the graphical formatting options of the `write` statement (as symbols, icons, and lines).
- Print list output and manipulate the output on the spool.
- Create headers and footers (no `standard page heading`, `top-of-page`, `end-of-page`).
- Use the `reserve` statement to keep groups of lines together in the output list.

Graphical Formatting with the `write` Statement

To write simple graphics you can use the three additions shown in Table 15.1.

TABLE 15.1 GRAPHICAL FORMATTING ADDITIONS FOR THE `write` STATEMENT

Addition	Effect
`as symbol`	Displays a black-and-white symbol
`as icon`	Displays a color icon
`as line`	Displays a line-draw character

Syntax for the Graphical Additions to the `write` Statement

```
write n1 (a) as symbol.
        (b) as icon.
        (c) as line.
```

where:

- Additions `(a)`, `(b)`, and `(c)` are mutually exclusive.

- *n1* is the name of a symbol, icon, or `line-draw` character.

Using the `as symbol` Addition

NEW TERM   A *symbol* is a simple two-color picture of a common symbol such as a square, circle, folder, or document. Most symbols take the place of a single character in the output list, although some can take two spaces, for example, the symbol of a fist pointing left (sym_left_hand). A sample statement would be `write sym_left_hand as symbol`.

In order to write a symbol, you must include one of the two following statements at the top of your program:

```
include <symbol>.
```

or

```
include <list>.
```

All symbols are printable. This means that if you send your output to the printer, they will appear on paper exactly as you see them online.

NEW TERM The name between angle brackets is an *include program*. It contains a set of statements that define the names of the symbols you can use. The `<symbol>` include contains only the symbol definitions. The `<list>` include contains symbols, icons, line-draw characters, and color definitions. Listing 15.1 contains a sample program using symbols.

INPUT   **LISTING 15.1**   DISPLAY SYMBOLS

```
1   report ztx1501.
2   include <symbol>.
3   tables ztxlfa1.
4   write: /  sym_plus_box as symbol, 'Vendor Master Tables',
5          /4 sym_filled_circle as symbol, 'LFA1',
6          /4 sym_filled_circle as symbol, 'LFB1',
7          /4 sym_filled_circle as symbol, 'LFC1',
8          /  sym_plus_box as symbol, 'Customer Master Tables',
9          /4 sym_filled_square as symbol, 'KNA1',
10         /4 sym_filled_square as symbol, 'KNB1',
11         /4 sym_filled_square as symbol, 'KNC1'.
12  skip.
13  uline.
14  select * up to 5 rows from ztxlfa1.
15     write: / ztxlfa1-lifnr,
16              ztxlfa1-name1,
17              sym_phone as symbol,
18              ztxlfa1-telf1.
19     endselect.
```

OUTPUT   The code in Listing 15.1 produces the output shown in Figure 15.1.

ANALYSIS
• Lines 4 through 11 write out a list of hard-coded table names in bullet form.
• Lines 14 through 19 write out vendor numbers, names, and telephone numbers preceded by the telephone symbol.

Using the as `icon` Addition

NEW TERM An *icon* is similar to a symbol, but is a multi-colored picture that can appear in the output list. Most icons take two spaces in the output list, although a few take more. An example of a write statement that writes an icon would be `write icon_led_red as icon`.

To write an icon, you must include one of the two following statements at the top of your program:

```
include <icon>.
```

or

```
include <list>.
```

FIGURE 15.1.

*This is a sample of
list output containing
symbols.*

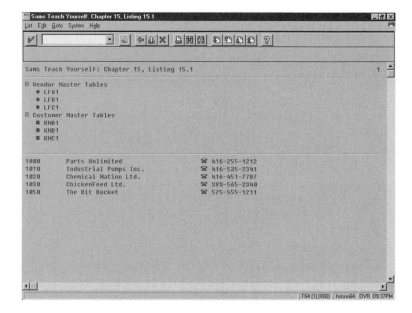

Not all icons are printable. The procedure to determine which ones can be printed follows later in this chapter.

Listing 15.2 writes out a few sample icons.

INPUT   **LISTING 15.2**   HOW TO WRITE ICONS TO THE LIST

```
 1  report ztx1502.
 2  include <icon>.
 3  tables: ztxmara, ztxmgef.
 4  data ico like icon_generate.
 5
 6  write: / 'checkmark',   15 icon_checked as icon,
 7         / 'red x',       15 icon_incomplete as icon,
 8         / 'overview',    15 icon_overview as icon,
 9         / 'time period', 15 icon_period as icon.
10  skip.
11  uline.
12  skip.
13  write: / 'List of Materials with Radioactive Indicators'.
14  uline.
15  select * from ztxmara.
```

```
16      clear ico.
17      if not ztxmara-stoff is initial.
18          select single * from ztxmgef where stoff = ztxmara-stoff.
19          if ztxmgef-lagkl = 7.
20              ico = icon_generate.
21              endif.
22          endif.
23      write: / ico as icon,
24              ztxmara-matnr,
25              ztxmara-mtart,
26              ztxmara-matkl,
27              ztxmara-brgew,
28              ztxmara-ntgew,
29              ztxmara-gewei.
30      endselect.
```

OUTPUT The code in Listing 15.2 produces the output shown in Figure 15.2.

FIGURE 15.2.

This is a sample of list output containing icons.

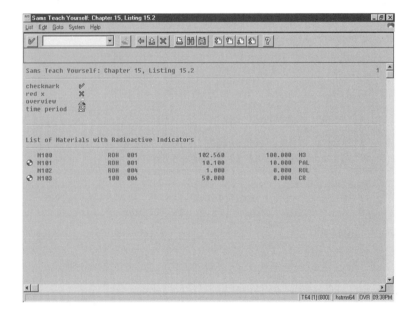

ANALYSIS

- Lines 6 through 9 write out a sample of four different icons.

- Line 4 defines a variable named `ico` to contain an icon to be written out. Any icon name can appear after `like`.

- Line 15 selects records from the materials table `ztxmara`.

- For each record, line 17 looks up the hazardous material number in `ztxmgef`.

- Line 19 determines if the material is radioactive. If so, the icon named
  `icon_generate` is assigned to variable `ico`.
- Line 23 writes the value of `ico` using as `icon` to cause the value to be interpreted as an icon. Additional fields from `ztxmara` are also written.

Using the as `line` Addition

NEW TERM   A *line-draw character* is a character that can be used to draw lines on a list. You
can use them to create horizontal or vertical lines, a box, a grid, or a tree-like
structure.

Typically, to create a horizontal line you would use `sy-uline`. Simply write it out and
specify the length needed. For example, to write a horizontal line beginning at position 5
for a length of 10, you would code `write 5(10) sy-uline`. To create a vertical line use
`sy-vline`; for example, `write: sy-vline, 'X', sy-vline` would write a vertical line
on either side of an X. If lines intersect in the output, the system will insert the appropriate connecting character. For example, where the edge of a horizontal line and vertical
line meet, a box corner will be drawn. To provide absolute control of the line drawing
there are additional `line-draw` characters available.

LISTING 15.3 SYMBOLS AND `line-draw` CHARACTERS

```
1   report ztx1503.
2   include <list>.
3   tables: ztxlfa1, ztxlfb1, ztxlfc3.
4   data: line1 like line_horizontal_line,
5         line2 like line_horizontal_line.
6
7   select * from ztxlfa1.
8       select single * from ztxlfb1 where lifnr = ztxlfa1-lifnr.
9       if sy-subrc = 0.
10          write: / sy-vline, sym_open_folder as symbol.
11      else.
12          write: / sy-vline, sym_folder as symbol.
13          endif.
14      write: ztxlfa1-lifnr, 30 sy-vline.
15      select * from ztxlfb1 where lifnr = ztxlfa1-lifnr.
16          select single lifnr from ztxlfb1 into (ztxlfb1-lifnr)
17                                    where lifnr = ztxlfb1-lifnr
18                                      and bukrs > ztxlfb1-bukrs.
19          if sy-subrc = 0.
20              line1 = line_left_middle_corner.
21              line2 = line_vertical_line.
22          else.
23              line1 = line_bottom_left_corner.
24              clear line2.
25              endif.
```

15

```
26        write: /   sy-vline,
27                 4 line1 as line,
28                   ztxlfb1-bukrs,
29               30 sy-vline.
30        select * from ztxlfc3 where lifnr = ztxlfb1-lifnr
31                              and bukrs = ztxlfb1-bukrs.
32          write: /   sy-vline,
33                 4 line2 as line,
34                 8 line_left_middle_corner as line,
35                   ztxlfc3-gjahr, ztxlfc3-shbkz,
36               30 sy-vline.
37          endselect.
38        if sy-subrc = 0.
39          write 8(2) line_bottom_left_corner as line.
40          endif.
41        endselect.
42        write: /(30) sy-uline.
43      endselect.
```

OUTPUT   The code in Listing 15.3 produces the output shown in Figure 15.3.

FIGURE 15.3.

This is a sample of list output containing line-draw characters.

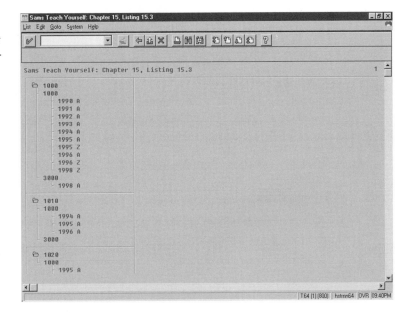

ANALYSIS
- Line 2 includes the definitions for all symbols and line-draw characters so they can be used in this program.
- Line 4 defines two variables that can hold line-draw characters.
- Line 7 reads all rows from ztxlfa1.

- Line 8 reads `ztxlfb1` to see if there are any child records for the current `ztxlfa1` record.
- If child records exist, line 10 writes a vertical line and an open folder symbol. If none are found, a vertical line and closed folder are written.
- Line 14 writes the vendor number on the same line, and then a vertical line at position 30.
- Line 15 reads the child records from `ztxlfb1`.
- Line 16 performs a look-ahead to determine if this is the last child record or if there are more.
- If there are more child records, line 19 sets the `line1` variable to hold a left middle corner line-draw character, and `line2` to hold a vertical line. `Sy-vline` could have been used here instead of `line_vertical_line`.
- Line 26 writes out the `line1` variable using the `as line` addition so that the value is interpreted as a line-draw character.
- Lines 30 through 37 write out the children of the current `ztxlfb1` record using appropriate line-draw characters.
- Line 42 writes an underline having a length of 30 characters.

Displaying the Available Symbols, Icons, and `line-draw` Characters

Use steps 1 through 8 of the following procedure to display the available symbols, icons, and line-draw characters. Following all steps causes a `write` statement to be generated that writes the selected item to the list.

1. Begin by editing any program in the ABAP/4 Editor. You should be on the ABAP/4 Editor: Edit Program XXXXX screen.
2. Place your cursor on a blank line.
3. Click the Pattern button, or choose the menu path Edit->Insert Statement. The system displays the Insert Statement screen.
4. Select the Write radio button.
5. Click the Continue button. The system displays the Assemble a Write Statement screen.
6. Choose Symbol, Icon, or Line.
7. Place your cursor in the input field to the right of the radio button you chose.
8. Press the F4 key. The system displays a list of the available items.
9. Double-click one to choose it. You are returned to the Assemble A Write Statement screen.

10. Click the Copy button. You are returned to the ABAP/4 Editor: Edit Program
    XXXXX screen, and a `write` statement is inserted that will write the item out.

 Caution | Not all icons can be printed. When you display them using the previous steps, you can see that the printable ones are flagged in the list.

INPUT   **LISTING 15.4**   SYMBOLS, ICONS, AND `line-draw` CHARACTERS

```
1   report ztx1504.
2   include <list>.              "definitions for icons, symbols + line-draw
3   tables: ztxlfa1, ztxlfc3.
4 data: it like ztxlfc3 occurs 100 with header line,
5       ico_l like icon_green_light.
6 select * from ztxlfc3 into table it.
7 sort it by lifnr bukrs gjahr shbkz.
8 loop at it.
9     if it-saldv < 1000.
10        ico_l = icon_green_light.
11    elseif it-saldv between 1000 and 3000.
12        ico_l = icon_yellow_light.
13    else.
14        ico_l = icon_red_light.
15        endif.
16    at new lifnr.
17        if sy-tabix > 1.
18            write: /5(82) sy-uline,
19                    19 line_bottom_middle_corner as line,
20                    21 line_bottom_middle_corner as line.
21            skip.
22            endif.
23        write: /5(15) sy-uline,
24                /5 sy-vline, sym_documents as symbol,
25                it-lifnr, 19 sy-vline,
26                /5(82) sy-uline,
27                19 line_cross as line,
28                21 line_top_middle_corner as line.
29        endat.
30    write: / ico_l as icon,
31            5 sy-vline, it-bukrs, sy-vline,
32            it-gjahr, line_left_middle_corner as line no-gap,
33            it-shbkz no-gap, line_right_middle_corner as line,
34            it-saldv,
35            it-solll,
36            it-habnl, sy-vline.
37    at last.
38        write /5(84) sy-uline.
39        endat.
40    endloop.
```

OUTPUT The code in Listing 15.4 produces the output shown in Figure 15.4.

FIGURE 15.4.

This is a sample of list output containing symbols, icons, and line-draw characters.

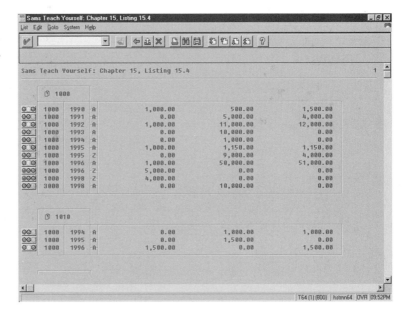

Report Formatting and Printing

This section covers the following report formatting techniques:

- Controlling page size
- Report titles, headers, and footers
- Common position and formatting statements

Controlling Page Size

To control the size of the output page, use the following additions on the `report` statement:

- `line-size`
- `line-count`

The `line-size` addition controls the width of the output list; `line-count` controls the number of lines per page.

Syntax for the `line-size` and `line-count` Additions to the `report` Statement

The syntax for the `line-size` and `line-count` additions to the `report` statement is as follows:

```
report line-size i line-count j(k).
```

where:

▲

- i, j, and k are numeric constants. Variables are not allowed.
- i specifies the width of the output list (in characters).
- j specifies the number of lines per page in the output list.
- k specifies the number of lines reserved for a footer at the bottom of each page.
- Do not enclose i, j, or k in quotes.

Using `line-size` and `line-count`

By default, the width of the output list is equal to the maximized window width. For example, if your window is maximized before you execute a report, the system will use that width as the output width of your program. If your window has been resized to be less than the maximum, the system will still use the maximized size. A scroll bar will appear at the bottom of the window to allow you to scroll right and see the rest of the report.

To override this behavior, specify the list output width by using `line-size`. Valid values are 2 through 255.

Tip

Most printers cannot print more than 132 characters on a line. If you think your users may want to print the output list, try not to exceed 132 characters per line.

The page number is printed in the top-right corner of the list. The default number of lines per page is 60,000—the maximum allowed. You can use `line-count` to override this number. For example, to specify 55 lines per page, enter `report line-count 55`. Specifying `line-count 0` means use the maximum (60,000).

The user can specify the number of lines per page that is appropriate for the printer when he or she prints the report.

Tip

You can also set the `line-count` in the middle of the report, so different pages can have different numbers of output lines. To do this, use the `new-page` statement (covered later). It can also be used to set the number of lines per-page before any output is generated.

`line-count` is not usually used with reports that are viewed online. For example, suppose R/3 incremented the page number each time you pressed the page down key. If the user generates a report, scrolls to page 3, and then resizes the window, will he still be on page 3? Obviously, the ability to resize the window makes it difficult to make rules about page numbers online. You could try making the page size equal to the window height when the report was run. But if the user resizes the window after the report has been generated, the page breaks will no longer match the window height. The user will see gaps in the output and the beginning of pages in the middle of the window. To avoid these problems in online reports, use the default value for `line-count`.

Listing 15.5 shows a sample program that illustrates the use of `line-count` and `line-size`.

INPUT   **LISTING 15.5**   `line-count` AND `line-size`

```
1    report ztx1505 line-size 132 line-count 55.
2    tables ztxlfc3.
3    select * from ztxlfc3 order by lifnr bukrs gjahr shbkz.
4        on change of ztxlfc3-lifnr.
5            write / ztxlfc3-lifnr.
6            endon.
7        on change of ztxlfc3-gjahr.
8            write /10 ztxlfc3-bukrs.
9            endon.
10       write: /20 ztxlfc3-gjahr,
11                   ztxlfc3-shbkz,
12                   ztxlfc3-saldv,
13                   ztxlfc3-solll,
14                   ztxlfc3-habnl.
15       endselect.
```

OUTPUT   The code in Listing 15.5 produces the output shown in Figure 15.5.

FIGURE 15.5.

This is the effect of the line-count *addition.*

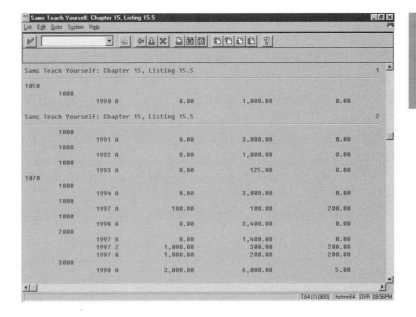

- On line 1, line-size sets the number of output columns to 132. This sets a fixed number of output columns independent of the output window width. The user can use the scroll bar at the bottom of the window to view the output off to the right.

- On line 1, line-count sets the number of lines per page to 55. This causes a problem when the user scrolls down. This would not occur if the default value for line-count had been used. Another problem can occur when the user prints the list. If the printer does not print exactly 55 lines per page, the page breaks will be incorrect in the printed output. Again, by using the default line-count this problem can be avoided, because the user specifies the number of lines per page when he or she selects a printer.

Printing List Output

Start the ScreenCam "How to Print List Output" now.

To print the output from Listing 15.5, first run the report, and then follow this procedure:

1. From the output list, click the Print button on the application toolbar. If it is not available, choose the menu path System->List->Print. The Print Screen List screen will be displayed.

2. In the Output Device field, type your printer ID. You can obtain a list of all printers defined to your system by placing your cursor in this field and then pressing F4.

3. Place a tickmark in the Print Immed check box.

4. Click the Print button on the application toolbar. You are returned to the list, and the message Spool request (number nnnnn) created appears at the bottom of the window.

> Your Basis Consultant can also define a fax machine as a print destination. To fax a report, specify Choose a Fax Machine ID instead of a Printer ID in the Output Device field.

Default printer settings are specified in your user profile. Use the menu path System-> User Profile->User Defaults to change them. These settings will be used each time you print a report.

> To send a report to multiple printers at the same time, ask your Basis Consultant to install a printer pool (he must run report RSP00051 first, and then define a printer of type P—pool—using transaction SPAD). Then, when you print, choose this printer pool from the list of printers. This functionality is available in release 3.0F and later.

Working with the Spool

When you click the Print button, your output is sent first to the R/3 spool, and then to the operating system's spool. If you didn't tickmark Print Immed, the list output is held in the R/3 spool—it is not sent to the operating system spool. It remains there until you delete it, or print it with the delete option turned on (the Delete After Print check box on the Print Screen List screen), or until it ages enough for a cleanup job to delete it. Cleanup jobs are scheduled by the Basis Consultant; they usually delete spool files older than 2 weeks. For the exact length of time in your shop, contact your Basis Consultant.

To view output on the spool, use the following procedure.

SCREENCAM Start the ScreenCam "Working with the Spool" now.

1. From any screen, choose the menu path System->Services->Print Requests. The Spool: Request Screen is displayed.

2. Enter criteria to find your output. Your user Id (entered in the User Name field), Client, and a From Date are usually sufficient.

3. Press Enter. The Spool: Requests screen is displayed. It contains a list of the matching entries on the spool.

4. To display the output for one entry, place a tickmark beside it, and then click the Display button.

5. To display the output for multiple entries, place tickmarks beside Multiple Entries or use the menu path Edit->Choose All. Then click the Display button. The first entry is displayed. To view the next entry, click the Next Spool Request button on the application toolbar. To view the preview entry, click the Prev. Spool Request button.

6. To print an entry, Click the Print button.

If you didn't tickmark Delete After Print on the Print Screen List screen, the output remains in the spool. This allows you to reprint it later. This is useful if your printer has a lot of personality.

Creating Page Headers and Footers

By default, the Title from the Program Attributes screen appears as the title at the top of your report. You can create your own titles by using one of two methods:

- Standard page headers
- The top-of-page event

Creating Standard Page Headers

Using standard page headers is the easiest way to create report headers. The following procedure describes the easiest way to create them.

> **Caution**
>
> This procedure won't work if you change your program and try this procedure without saving your changes first. When you choose the menu path to add the headers, you will instead see a dialog box indicating that you are not allowed to change an SAP program. This happens if you haven't saved your changes because then you are actually running a temporary copy of the original—one that contains your changes. The name of this copy doesn't start with Y or Z, so R/3 won't let you change it.

 Start the ScreenCam "How to Create Standard Report Headers from the List" now.

1. Start from the ABAP/4 Editor: Edit Program screen.

2. If you have made any changes, save your report. As mentioned in the last Caution, you *must* do this for the following steps to work.

3. Execute the report. You then see the list output.

4. Choose the menu path System->List->List Header. Input fields appear at the top of the report—one for the header and four for column headers.

5. Type a list and column headers in the white input fields.

6. Click the Save button on the application toolbar. The message `Changed texts active from next start of xxxxx in language E` appears. This means you will see the new headers the next time you run this program.

7. Click the Back button twice. You are returned to the ABAP/4 Editor: Edit Program screen.

8. Execute the report again. You will see your new headers at the top of the output.

You may be asking yourself, where are these headers stored? Then again, you may not be asking yourself this, but you're about to find out anyway.

NEW TERM The headers you just entered are stored with your program as *text elements*. A text element is any character string that is displayed in the list output. It might appear at the top as a header, in the middle (as a character string that does not come from the database), or at the bottom as a footer. SAP likes to provide multi-lingual capabilities in its programs, so anything that might need to be translated, for example report headers, are stored separately from the source code as text elements. These elements can be translated without changing the source code. In this section we deal specifically with text elements for the report and column headers, but there are others as well that will be dealt with later.

Since the standard headers are stored as text elements, you can see them and modify them by accessing the text elements of the program. These are contained in the ABAP/4 Text Elements: Change Title and Heading screen, shown in Figure 15.6.

Use the following procedure to view, change, or create standard headers.

SCREENCAM Start the ScreenCam "How to Create Standard Report Headers Via Text Elements" now.

1. From the ABAP/4 Editor: Edit Program screen, choose the menu path Goto->Text Elements. The ABAP/4 Text Elements screen is displayed.

2. Choose the Titles and Headers radio button.

3. Click the Change button. The ABAP/4 Text Elements: Change Title And Heading screen is displayed. The Title field contains the title text you entered in the

ABAP/4: Program xxxxx Attributes screen. If the List Header field is blank, the Title is displayed at the top of the list. The List Header field allows you to override the Title and specify a header that is different from the report title. Enter a List Header, and enter column headers at the bottom of the screen in the Column Header fields. Click the buttons at the bottom right of the screen to scroll left and right, to maximum of 255 characters.

4. Press the Save button to save your changes.

5. Press the Back button. The ABAP/4 Editor: Edit Program screen is displayed.

6. Execute your program. Your new title and headers appear at the top of your report.

FIGURE 15.6.

This screen contains the standard Titles and Headers text elements.

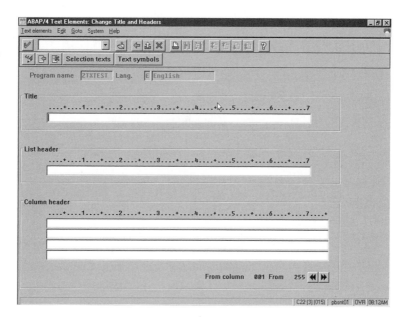

Text elements can also be accessed from the ABAP/4 Editor: Initial Screen by choosing the Text Elements button, and then clicking the Change button. You may find it useful to review the section on the components of an ABAP/4 program at this point (see Figure 2.1 in Chapter 2, "Your First ABAP/4 Program").

To review, on the ABAP/4 Text Elements: Change Title And Heading screen, if the List Header field is non-blank, it is used as the header. If it is blank, the Title field is used as the header.

> **Note** The SAP standard is to left-justify the header on the output list. As a result, the header *cannot* be centered. Even if you center it manually by putting leading spaces in front of it, it will appear left-justified in the output.

Translating Text Elements

Creating titles and headers as text elements allows them to be translated into foreign languages, usually by an someone who specializes in the translation of technical or industry-specific phrases. In this section you can try this yourself to get a feel for the process.

 Start the ScreenCam "Translating Titles and Headers" now.

1. From the ABAP/4 Text Elements: Change Title and Heading screen, choose the menu path Goto->Translation. The Target Language For Translation screen is shown.

2. In the Target Language field, choose the language into which you want to translate your text elements. The language you choose must have been previously installed on your system by the Basis Consultant. *Deutsch* (German) is installed on every system, because it is the master language for all R/3 systems. Therefore, choose D (*Deutsch*).

3. Click the Translate button. The Translate Title And Headers For Program xxxxx screen is displayed. On this screen is the name of the field, a Remark field into which the translator can enter comments, followed by the original text and an input field for the translation. When blank, this input field contains an underscore.

4. In the fields containing an underscore, type your German translations. If you don't know German, just substitute Ks for all of your Cs, and use lots of phrases ending with *schnitzel* or containing the name *Wolfgang*.

5. Click the Save button on the standard toolbar. If you have more translations to do, you will remain on the same screen. Click the Back button to see the next set. When there is no more text to be translated, you will be returned to the ABAP/4 Text Elements: Change Title and Heading screen.

6. Now log on again, but this time enter D in the Language field in the log on screen.

7. Run your program. The translated titles will appear. If you display the program attributes, you will see the translated title on the ABAP/4: Program attribute xxxxx screen.

All translations are stored in a proposal pool from which you can retrieve previous translations of a word or phrase. If you enter a translation that differs from those stored in the pool, the system will automatically prompt you with the previous translations. You must then either save the new one or select a previous one.

Note

> The employee who does the translation will usually use the SE63 transaction. It provides a set of programs that allow all texts in the system to be translated. For example, the descriptions of the data elements, indexes, selection texts in programs, and so on can be translated here. Beginning at the ABAP/4 Development Workbench screen, the menu path is Utilities-> Translation->Short/Long Texts.

Using Variables in Standard Page Headers

You can use up to 10 variables in the standard page headings for one program. In your program, assign values to the variables named sy-tvar0 through sy-tvar9. In your headings, use the variable names &0 through &9 to correspond to the sy variables within your program. For example, if in your program you code sy-tvar0 = 'AA' and sy-tvar1 = 'BB', &0 will be replaced by AA and &1 will be replaced by BB in the header.

Although each sy-tvar variable can hold a value up to 20 characters long, the variable output length is 2 by default. This means that for example, wherever &0 appears in the header, exactly two spaces are reserved for the value of sy-tvar0. If the value in sy-tvar0 is 'A', 'A' appears. If the value is 'AA', 'AA' appears. If the value is 'AAA', 'AA' appears.

The output length can be increased by appending periods to the end of the output variable. For example, to increase the output length of &0 from 2 to 4, code &0.. (two periods have been appended). To increase the output length to 7 append 5 periods (&0.....).

Listing 15.6 contains a program that uses standard page headings containing variables. Figure 15.7 shows how to code these variables on the ABAP/4 Text Elements: Change Title and Heading screen.

INPUT   **LISTING 15.6**   VARIABLES IN STANDARD PAGE HEADERS

```
1   report ztx1506.
2   tables ztxlfa1.
3   parameters: p_land1 like ztxlfa1-land1 default 'US'.
4   sy-tvar0 = sy-uname.
5   write: sy-datum to sy-tvar1,
6         sy-uzeit to sy-tvar2.
7   sy-tvar3 = p_land1.
8   select * from ztxlfa1 where land1 = p_land1.
9       write: / ztxlfa1-lifnr, ztxlfa1-name1.
10      endselect.
```

FIGURE 15.7.

The ABAP/4 Text Elements: Change Title And Heading screen for program ztx1506.

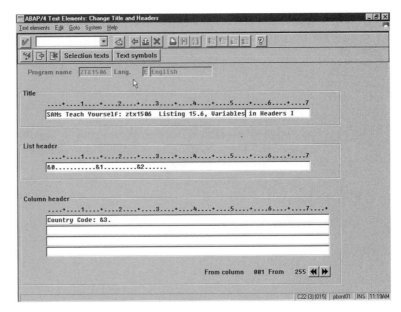

The code in Listing 15.6 produces this output:

OUTPUT

```
KENGREENWOOD    1998/05/05 19:40:38
------------------------------------------------
Country Code: US
------------------------------------------------
1040       Motherboards Inc.
1080       Silicon Sandwich Ltd.
1090       Consume Inc.
2000       Monitors and More Ltd.
V1         Quantity First Ltd.
V2         OverPriced Goods Inc.
V3         Fluffy Bunnies Ltd.
V4         Moo like a Cow Inc.
V5         Wolfman Sport Accessories Inc.
V7         The Breakfast Club Inc.
```

ANALYSIS

- Line 3 defines p_land1 and prompts the user for a value.

- Line 4 assigns the current user Id to sy-tvar0.

- The write statement on line 5 moves the value of sy-datum to sy-tvar1. An ordinary assignment statement (using =) would have moved the value without formatting it. Using write causes the field to be formatted with separators according to the user's profile.

- Line 6 formats the current time and moves it to sy-tvar2.

- Line 7 assigns the value that was entered by the user to sy-tvar3.

- Lines 8 through 10 write out a simple vendor report.

- In Figure 15.7, &0.......... indicates where the value of sy-tvar0 will appear. The periods increase the output length of the variable from 2 to 12. &1........ indicates where the value of sy-tvar1 will appear, &2...... indicates where the value of sy-tvar2 will appear, and &3. the value of sy-tvar3. The periods increase the output lengths to 10, 8, and 3, respectively.

Creating Manual Page Headers

Standard page headers are easy to create, but they have some limitations too. They are limited to one line for the page header and four lines for the column headers. A maximum of 10 variables can be used, each with a minimum length of two characters. The header is always left justified, and the colors are standard and cannot be changed. Manual headings, however, have no such limitations.

To create manual headings, you need to

- Turn off standard page headers.

- Use the top-of-page event to create custom headings.

To turn off the standard page headings, add no standard page heading to the end of the report statement.

NEW TERM An event in ABAP/4 is like a subroutine in other languages. It is an independent section of code; it performs a task and then returns to the point of invocation. However, unlike subroutines, *you* do not code the call to an event. Instead, the system triggers the event *for you* when a specific condition arises.

The top-of-page event is triggered when the first write statement is executed. Before any values are written to the list, the system branches to the code following top-of-page and executes it. It then returns to the write statement and writes out the values. Listing 15.7 and Figure 15.8 illustrate this process.

INPUT **LISTING 15.7** THE top-of-page EVENT

```
1   report ztx1507 no standard page heading.
2   data f1(5) value 'Init'.
3   f1 = 'Title'.
4   write: / 'Hi'.
5
6   top-of-page.
7     write: / 'My', f1.
8     uline.
```

OUTPUT Figure 15.8 shows the output for Listing 15.7.

FIGURE 15.8.

Output of Listing 15.7.

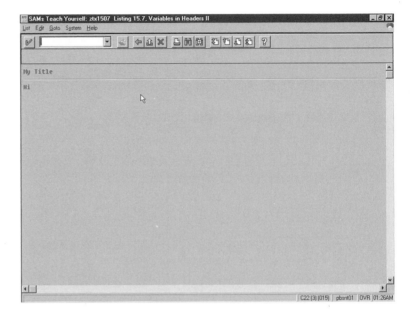

ANALYSIS

- On line 1, the report statement contains the no standard page heading addition, so standard headers are not written.
- Line 2 defines f1 as character length 5 and gives it an initial value of 'Init'.
- Line 3 assigns the value 'Title' to f1.
- The write statement on line 4 triggers the top-of-page event on line 6. Lines 7 and 8 are then executed, causing My Title to be written to the first line of the list, followed by an underline (written by the uline statement on line 8). Processing then returns to the write statement on line 4 and Hi is written to line 3 of the output list.
- After line 4 has been executed, the program ends and the output is shown.

Notice that the value of f1 written out at the top of the page is the value at the time the first write statement is issued, not the value at the beginning of the program.

Creating Page Footers

As discussed earlier, after an online report has been generated, the user can change his window size. To avoid mid-page breaks, online reports always consist of a single very long virtual page, so having footers doesn't make much sense because there would be only one.

Batch reports are usually printed, and thus will have a definite page size that doesn't change after the report is created, so they can have page footers.

To create page footers you need

- To reserve space for the footer at the bottom of the page using the `line-count` addition on the `report` statement.
- The `end-of-page` event.

To reserve space for your footer, you can code `line-count` $n(m)$ on the `report` statement, where n is the number of lines per page, and m is the number of lines to reserve for the footer. You don't want to hard-code n, because the user should be able to specify the number of lines per page when printing the report. Therefore simply leave it off, and enter `report zxx line-count` (m).

During report processing, `sy-pagno` contains the current page number and `sy-linno` contains the current line number being written to.

Code `end-of-page` at the bottom of your program, as shown in Listing 12.8. The statements following `end-of-page` are executed before each new page is begun. A new page is begun when a `write` statement is executed and if the output will not fit on the current page. For example, you may have coded `report zxx line-count (3)` leaving three rows for the footer, and the user may have specified 60 lines per page. The footer area is therefore contained within lines 58 through 60. If you have just written to the 57th line, the next `write` statement to a new line will trigger the `end-of-page` event, followed by a page break, the `top-of-page` event, and then write output to the next page.

 Note

> Technically, events can appear in any order or position within your program. For now code them as shown. A subsequent chapter will explain more about how to code events.

INPUT   **LISTING 15.8**   `top-of-page` AND `end-of-page` EVENTS

```
1   report ztx1508 line-count 20(3) no standard page heading.
2   do 80 times.
3       write: / 'Please kick me', sy-index, 'times'.
4       enddo.
5
6   top-of-page.
```

```
7    write: / 'CONFIDENTIAL',
8           / 'This page begins with number', sy-index.
9    uline.
10
11 end-of-page.
12   write: / sy-uline,
13          / 'The number of kicks at the top of the next page will be',
14              sy-index,
15          / 'Copyright 1998 by the ALA (Abuse Lovers Of America)'.
```

The first part of the output for Listing 15.8 appears as follows:

OUTPUT

```
CONFIDENTIAL
This page begins with number             1
-----------------------------------------------------------------
Please kick me          1   times
Please kick me          2   times
Please kick me          3   times
Please kick me          4   times
Please kick me          5   times
Please kick me          6   times
Please kick me          7   times
Please kick me          8   times
Please kick me          9   times
Please kick me         10   times
Please kick me         11   times
Please kick me         12   times
Please kick me         13   times
Please kick me         14   times

-----------------------------------------------------------------
The number of kicks at the top of the next page will be        15
Copyright 1998 by the ALA (Abuse Lovers Of America)
CONFIDENTIAL
This page begins with number            15
-----------------------------------------------------------------
Please kick me         15   times
Please kick me         16   times
Please kick me         17   times
Please kick me         18   times
```

- Line 1 suppresses the use of standard page headers because we only want the manual page headers to be shown. It also sets the number of lines in the footer area to 3. The number of lines per page is set to 20 so we can test the page footer code online. Normally an online report does not specify the number of lines per page.

ANALYSIS

- The first time through the loop, line 2 triggers the `top-of-page` event on line 6, causing lines 7 through 9 to write two header lines followed by an underline. Control returns to line 3 and the `write` statement writes to the fourth line in the output list.

- After looping 14 times, the 15th `write` statement triggers the `end-of-page` statement on line 11. Lines 12 through 15 are executed, writing out the footer. The `top-of-page` statement on line 6 is then executed, and lines 7 through 9 write the page heading at the top of the next page. Then control returns to line 3 and the `write` statement writes to the fourth line on page 2.

- No page footer is written at the bottom of the last page.

Using the `reserve` Statement

Sometimes you may need to write out information that belongs together, but spread over multiple lines. For example, you may write the vendor number and name on one line, followed by the address on the next line, and the telephone numbers on the line after that. It would make sense to keep these lines together as a group in the output, and prevent them from being spread across two pages.

Use the `reserve` statement to keep a group of lines together in the output list.

Syntax for the `reserve` Statement

SYNTAX

```
reserve n lines.
```

where:

- *n* is a numeric literal or variable.

When the `reserve` statement is executed, the system checks to see if there are *n* lines available on the current page. If there are fewer than *n* lines left on the current page, a page break is generated. This triggers the `end-of-page` event (if it exists), followed by the `top-of-page` event (if it exists). The next `write` statement begins at the top of the new page.

If at least *n* lines are available when the `reserve` statement is executed, it does nothing.

Listing 15.9 shows a sample program that uses the `reserve` statement.

INPUT   **LISTING 15.9**   THE `reserve` STATEMENT

```
1   report ztx1509 line-count 18(2) no standard page heading.
2   tables ztxlfa1.
3
4   select * from ztxlfa1.
```

```
 5       reserve 3 lines.
 6       write: / ztxlfa1-lifnr, ztxlfa1-name1,
 7               / ztxlfa1-stras, ztxlfa1-regio, ztxlfa1-land1,
 8               / ztxlfa1-telf1.
 9       skip.
10       endselect.
11
12 top-of-page.
13       write / 'Vendor Report'.
14       uline.
15
16 end-of-page.
17       uline.
18       write: / 'Report', sy-repid, ' Created by', sy-uname.
```

The code in Listing 15.9 produces the following output:

OUTPUT

```
Vendor Report
- - - - - - - - - - - - - - - - - - - - - - - - - - - - - - - - - - - - - - - -
1000         Parts Unlimited
111 Queen St.                        ON  CA
416-255-1212


1010         Industrial Pumps Inc.
1520 Avenue Rd.                      ON  CA
416-535-2341


1020         Chemical Nation Ltd.
123 River Ave.                       ON  CA
416-451-7787




- - - - - - - - - - - - - - - - - - - - - - - - - - - - - - - - - - - - - - -
Report ZTX1209   Created by KENGREENWOOD

Vendor Report
- - - - - - - - - - - - - - - - - - - - - - - - - - - - - - - - - - - - - - -
1030         ChickenFeed Ltd.
8718 Wishbone Lane                   AB  CA
393-565-2340


1040         Motherboards Inc.
64 BitBus Blvd.                      MA  US
617-535-0198
```

ANALYSIS Line 5 determines if there is space for three more lines on the current page. If there is, it does nothing and line 6 writes out vendor information over the next lines. If there isn't, it triggers the end-of-page event (lines 15 through 17), and then issues a page break. It then triggers the top-of-page event (lines 11 through 13). Then the write statement on line 6 is executed and the lines are written at the top of the new page.

Summary

- You can create simple graphical output in the list using the as symbol, as icon, and as line additions on the write statement. When using these additions, you must use the include statement to bring the symbol, icon and line-draw character definitions into your program.

- Use the line-size addition on the report statement to set the width of the output list. Use the line-count addition to set the number of lines per page in the output list. You can also use it to specify the number of lines reserved for the footer. You cannot use variables on the report statement, so use the new-page statement for these additions if you want to set these attributes at run time.

- To create page headers you can use either standard page headers or the top-of-page statement.

- Up to 10 variables can be used in standard page headers. Values assigned to sy-tvar0 through sy-tvar9 replace &0 through &9 in the list. Use periods to extend the output length of these replacement variables.

- To suppress output of the standard page header, use the no standard page heading addition on the report statement.

- If you include the top-of-page event in your program, it is triggered when the first write statement is executed. The statements following it are executed, then control returns to the write statement.

- Use the end-of-page event to create footers. You must also use line-count on the report or new-page statement to specify the number of lines per page and reserve space for the footer.

- Use the reserve statement to keep a group of lines together in the list.

Q&A

Q Which is the preferred method of creating customer titles—using `sy-tvar` variables or the `top-of-page` event?

A The `top-of-page` event is more flexible, so more programmers prefer to use that method. Provided you use text symbols for your text literals, both can be translated so there aren't any advantages to `sy-tvar` variables.

Workshop

The Workshop provides two ways for you to affirm what you've learned in this chapter. The Quiz section poses questions to help you solidify your understanding of the material covered and the Exercise section provides you with experience in using what you have learned. You can find answers to the quiz questions and exercises in Appendix B, "Answers to Quiz Questions and Exercises."

Quiz

1. What are the three graphical additions that are used with the write statement? What statement must also be included in order to write the graphical additions? Give an example of an include statement.

2. What are the two additions that are used with report statement to control size of the output page? Can the variable used for the two additions be variable?

Exercise 1

Write out a program that will display the following symbols: square, diamond, circle, glasses, pencil, phone, note, and folder.

DAY 16

Formatting Techniques, Part 2

Chapter Objectives

ANALYSIS After you have completed this chapter, you will be able to

- Use the formatting statements `new-line`, `new-page`, `skip`, `back`, `position` and `set blank lines`.
- Send output to the spool using `new-page print`.

List Formatting Statements

There are several statements commonly needed to format a list:

- `new-line`
- `new-page`
- `skip`

- back
- position
- set blank lines

Using the new-line Statement

Use the new-line statement to cause the output of the next write statement to begin on a new line. Unlike skip or write /, consecutive new-line statements do not cause a blank line to appear in the output list.

Syntax for the new-line Statement

SYNTAX

new-line [no-scrolling].

The no-scrolling addition locks the next line in place. Horizontal scrolling has no effect on lines that have been locked in this way.

Listing 16.1 illustrates the use of the new-line statement.

INPUT   **LISTING 16.1**   THE new-line STATEMENT

```
1    report ztx1601 line-size 255.
2    tables: ztxlfa1, ztxlfc3.
3    select * from ztxlfa1.
4        new-line no-scrolling.
5        write: ztxlfa1-lifnr, ztxlfa1-name1. "this line won't scroll right
6        select * from ztxlfc3 where lifnr = ztxlfa1-lifnr.
7            write: /14 ztxlfc3-bukrs, ztxlfc3-gjahr, ztxlfc3-shbkz,
8                    40 ztxlfc3-saldv, ztxlfc3-solll, ztxlfc3-habnl.
9            endselect.
10       endselect.
```

The code in Listing 16.1 produces the following output:

OUTPUT

```
1000        Parts Unlimited
            1000 1990 A              1,000.00            500.00
            1000 1991 A                  0.00          5,000.00
            1000 1992 A              1,000.00         11,000.00
            1000 1993 A                  0.00         10,000.00
            1000 1994 A                  0.00          1,000.00
            1000 1995 A              1,000.00          1,150.00
            1000 1995 Z                  0.00          9,000.00
            1000 1996 A              1,000.00         50,000.00
            1000 1996 Z              5,000.00              0.00
```

```
              1000 1998 Z                4,000.00            0.00
              3000 1998 A                    0.00       10,000.00
     1010     Industrial Pumps Inc.
              1000 1994 A                    0.00        1,000.00
              1000 1995 A                    0.00        1,500.00
              1000 1996 A                1,500.00            0.00
     1020     Chemical Nation Ltd.
              1000 1995 A                    0.00        2,000.00
              1000 1996 A                    0.00            0.00
     1030     ChickenFeed Ltd.
     1040     Motherboards Inc.
              1000 1990 A                  100.00        3,000.00
              1000 1997 A                  100.00        1,500.00
              2000 1997 A                    0.00          500.00
              2000 1998 A                1,000.00          300.00
              3000 1998 A                    0.00        2,400.00
```

ANALYSIS Lines 7 and 8 write vendor detail lines that are wider than the screen. Scrolling to the right allows you to see the right portion of the lines, but the vendor name and number stay within view. This happens because the `write` statement on line 5 is preceded by the `new-line no-scrolling` statement on line 4.

Using the `new-page` Statement

Use the `new-page` statement to

- Cause the output of the next `write` statement to begin on a new page. Consecutive `new-page` statements do not generate blank pages.
- Turn titles and headers on or off.
- Vary the line count or line size from one page to the next.
- Turn printing on and off.

Syntax for the `new-page` Statement

▼ SYNTAX

```
new-page [no-title ¦ with-title]
         [no-heading ¦ with-heading]
         [line-count n(m)]
         [line-size k]
         [print on ¦ print off]
```

where:

▲

- *n*, *m*, and *k* are numeric variables or literals.

The following points apply:

- `new-page` can be used anywhere in the program. You can use it even before the first `write` statement to set the characteristics of the list output. Because it accepts variables, it is more flexible than similar additions on the `report` statement.

- `no-title` turns off the standard title on the following pages. (The title is the first line of the standard page headers.) `with-title` turns it on.

- `no-heading` turns off the standard column headers for the following pages. `with-heading` turns it on.

- `line-count` sets the number of lines per page and the number of lines reserved at the bottom of each page for a footer. Either one of these values, or both, can be specified. This was covered earlier in this chapter.

- `line-size` sets the number of output columns for the following pages. The default is the current window width.

- `print-on` causes output from following `write` statements to be sent to the spool instead of the list. Users do not see this output unless they look in the spool. (View and printing spool output was covered earlier in this chapter.) `print-off` does the reverse.

- Consecutive `new-page` statements do not generate blank pages.

- `new-page` does not trigger the `end-of-page` event. Therefore, a footer will not be printed at the bottom of the current page if you issue the `new-page` statement.

Tip

> If you want to cause a page break and trigger the `end-of-page` event, code reserve sy-linct lines. `sy-linct` contains the current number of lines per page. The output from the next `write` will appear at the top of a new page, and the `end-of-page` event will be triggered beforehand causing a page footer to be created.

Using `new-page print`

At times there is a need for a report that both writes to the output list and sends output to the printer at the same time. For example, you may wish to write a report that shows a summary to the user online, and send a detail report to the printer at the same time. Use `new-page print on` to do this. The output from all `write` statements that follow `new-page print on` will not appear in the list. Instead, it will be sent to the spool. Issuing `new-page print off` reverses this effect. The output from all `write` statements that follow it will again be seen in the list.

Each time `new-page print on` is executed

- The system displays the Print Parameters screen to the user (shown in Figure 16.1). It prompts the user for parameters such as the printer ID and Output Format.

- If, on the Print Parameters screen, there is a tickmark in the New Spool Request field it creates a new spool request. A spool request is a separate list in the spool.

FIGURE 16.1.

The Print Parameters screen.

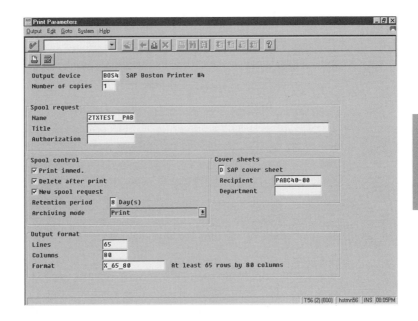

16

Syntax for the `new-page print on` Statement

▼ SYNTAX

```
new-page print on
    [no dialog]
    [new section]
    [immediately        immedflag]
    [destination        destid]
    [copies             numcopies]
    [layout             layoutid]
    [list name          listname]
    [sap cover page     coverpageflag]
    [cover text         title]
    [department         dept]
    [receiver           recievername]
    [keep in spool      keepflag]
    [dataset expiration numdays]
    [line-count         linesperpage]
    [line-size          numcolumns]
```

where:

▲   • Any of the italicized names in the proceeding code can be a literal or a variable.

The following points apply:

• Use `no dialog` to suppress the display of the Print Parameters screen that asks the user for print parameters. The user's defaults are used instead. If the user has not filled in a printer ID in his defaults, the Print Parameters screen will be shown even when you specify `no dialog`.

- Use new section to restart page numbering, beginning again at 1.
- Use immediately 'X' to cause the list to be printed immediately. The default is immediately ' ', which holds the list in the spool.
- Use destination to specify a printer ID.
- Use copies to specify the number of copies to print.
- Use layout to specify a printer layout. The printer layout determines printer characteristics such as the number of lines per page and the number of columns per line. You can see the printer layouts defined for your installation by printing something and looking at the Format field on the Print List Output screen.
- Use list name to specify a name for the list while in the spool. You can use this to search for it later in the spool. (Enter this value in the 3rd field beside Spool Request Name on the Spool: Request Screen)
- Use sap cover page to control the printing of a cover page with the output. A blank value suppresses the cover page, 'X' causes one to print, and 'D' indicates that the printer settings should determine whether a cover page is printed or not.
- Use cover text to specify the title to be printed on the cover page.
- Use department to specify a department ID to be printed on the cover page.
- Use receiver to specify the name of the person who should receive the report. It is printed on the cover page.
- Use keep in spool 'X' to cause the spool request to stay in the spool after the report has been printed. This allows the user to reprint the list without re-running the report.
- Use dataset expiration to specify how many days the spool request should stay on the spool. When the request expires, it is deleted from the spool.
- Use line-count and line-size to specify the number of lines per page and number of columns per line.

Additional parameters are documented in the ABAP/4 keyword documentation.

Note

When you send output directly to the spool using new-page print on, you can also use two additional statements. The set margins statement allows you to control the margins during printing. The print-control statement allows you to send printer control codes directly to the printer. By using print-control, you can control any printer characteristic, such as CPI (character per inch), LPI (lines per inch), or font. These statements have no effect on lists printed via the Print button or via the List Print menu option; they only affect lists printed via new-page print on. They do not affect the way the list is displayed on screen. See the ABAP/4 keyword documentation for more details.

Listing 16.2 illustrates the use of the new-page print statement.

INPUT   **LISTING 16.2**   THE new-page print STATEMENT

```
1  report ztx1602.
2  tables ztxlfa1.
3  parameters: prt_id like estwo-spooldest obligatory.
4
5  new-page print on
6      no dialog
7      immediately 'X'
8      destination prt_id.
9
10 select * from ztxlfa1.
11     write: / ztxlfa1-lifnr.
12     endselect.
13
14 new-page print off.
15 write: / sy-dbcnt, 'lines sent to printer', prt_id.
```

The code in Listing 16.2 produces the following output:

OUTPUT   23 lines sent to printer B0S4

ANALYSIS
- Line 3 prompts the user for a printer ID. The field estwo-spooldest has a foreign key relationship to the table that contains the printer IDs, so a down-arrow is displayed on the input field. It allows the user to display a list of the available printer IDs.

- Line 5 redirects the output for subsequent write statements. no dialog suppresses the display of the Print Parameters screen. Instead the parameters are taken from the user profile, and from the parameters specified on lines 6 through 8. immediately 'X' causes the output to be printed immediately. Line 8 passes the printer ID entered by the user on the selection screen.

- The output from lines 10 through 12 is sent directly to the printer. It is not seen in the output list.

- Line 14 removes the indirection and the output from subsequent write statements appear in the list.

Displaying the ABAP/4 Keyword Documentation for new-page Ppint

Normally, F1 help will not display the new-page print documentation. To display it, use the following procedure:

1. Begin at the ABAP/4 Editor: Initial Screen.

2. Choose the menu path Utilities-> ABAP/4 Key Word Doc. You then see the Display Structure: ABAP/4-SAP's 4GL Programming Language screen.

3. Click the Find button on the standard toolbar. The Search Chapter Titles screen is displayed.

4. In the Find field, type new-page print.

5. Click the Continue button. You are returned to the previous screen and your cursor is positioned on the new-page print line.

6. Double-click that line. The documentation for new-page print is displayed.

Using the skip Statement

The skip statement allows you to

- Generate blank lines.
- Move the current output position up or down within the current output page.

Syntax for the skip Statement

SYNTAX

```
skip [n ¦ to line n].
```

where:

- *n* is a numeric literal or variable.

Without any additions, skip generates a blank line. Skip *n* generates *n* blank lines. If *n* is less than 1, no blank lines are generated. skip at the end of the current page will cause a page break. skip will generate blank lines after any write statement, at the top of the first page, and at the top of any page begun by the new-page statement. It will not generate blank lines at the beginning of any other new page or at the end of the last page of the list. For example, if there is space for two more lines at the bottom of the current page, skip 5 will generate two blank lines at the bottom of the current page, but none at the top of the next page. This happens because the new page was not the first page and was not generated by a new-page statement.

> **Tip**
>
> If you want a footer on the last page of your report, code skip sy-linct as the last statement in your program. This statement will write footers. If you want to trigger a new page and you want a footer at the bottom the current page, code skip sy-linct instead of new-page.

skip to line *n* causes the current output position to be set to the beginning of line *n* of the current page. The output from the next write statement will begin at that position.

For example, `skip to line 3` causes the output from the next `write` statement to begin in column 1 of line 3. A `skip to line` statement that contains a line number greater than the current number of lines per page is ignored.

Listing 16.3 illustrates the use of the `skip` statement.

INPUT   **LISTING 16.3**   THE `skip` STATEMENT

16

```
1   report ztx1603.
2   tables ztxlfa1.
3   data n type i.
4   select * from ztxlfa1 order by land1.
5       on change of ztxlfa1-land1.
6           if sy-dbcnt > 1.
7               n = sy-linno - 1.
8               skip to line n.
9               write 35 '*** Last Vendor With This Country Code ***'.
10          endif.
11          write / ztxlfa1-land1.
12      endon.
13      write: /4 ztxlfa1-lifnr, ztxlfa1-name1.
14  endselect.
```

The code in Listing 16.3 produces the following output:

OUTPUT
```
CA
    1000        Parts Unlimited
    1010        Industrial Pumps Inc.
    1020        Chemical Nation Ltd.
    1030        ChickenFeed Ltd.
    1050        The Bit Bucket
    1060        Memory Lane Ltd.
    1070        Flip My Switch Inc. *** Last Vendor With This
➡Country Code ***
CC V9           Code Now, Specs Later Ltd.
    V10         Duncan's Mouse Inc. *** Last Vendor With This
➡Country Code ***
DE V6           Anna Banana Ltd.
    V11         Wiener Schnitzel Inc.
    V12         Sauerkraut AG       *** Last Vendor With This
➡Country Code ***
US V8           Smile When You Say That Ltd.
    1040        Motherboards Inc.
    1080        Silicon Sandwich Ltd.
    1090        Consume Ltd.
    2000        Monitors and More Ltd.
    V1          Quality First Ltd.
    V2          OverPriced Goods Inc.
```

```
V3          Fluffy Bunnies Ltd.
V4          Moo like a Cow Inc.
V5          Wolfman Sport Accessories Inc.
V7          The Breakfast Club Inc.
```

ANALYSIS Each time the value of `ztxlfa1-land1` changes

- Line 5 is triggered each time the value of `land1` changes.

- On line 6, `sy-dbcnt` is the current loop pass counter. When the first record is being processed it has a value of one, and so the code inside the `if` is not executed for the first record, but it is for every succeeding record.

- For succeeding records, on line 7 `sy-linno` contains the line number of the current list line. That is, it is the line number that the next `write` statement will write to. One is subtracted from it and this is assigned to n.

- Line 8 moves the output position to the beginning of line n, which is the previously written line.

- Line 9 writes on that line, flagging the last vendor of each group.

Using the back Statement

Use the `back` statement to return the current output position to

- The first line of the current page (the first line after `top-of-page` has been processed).

- The first line output after a `reserve` statement has been issued.

Syntax for the back Statement

▼ SYNTAX ▲

The following is the syntax for the **back** statement:

```
back.
```

where:

- `back` issued from within the `top-of-page` event returns to the first line written within `top-of-page`.

Explaining further, if you specified `no standard page heading` on the `report` statement, it returns to the first line of the page. If you have a standard page heading, the output position is set to line first line following the standard header.

A sample program is shown in Listing 16.4.

INPUT   **LISTING 16.4**   THE *back* STATEMENT

```
1  report ztx1604 no standard page heading.
2  data n type i.
3  do 4 times.
4     write: /(4) sy-index.
5     enddo.
6  back.
7  do 4 times.
8     n = sy-index * 10.
9     write: /10(4) n.
10    enddo.
11
12 top-of-page.
13    write: / 'This was my title'.
14    uline.
15    back.
16    write 6 'is '.
17    skip.
```

The code in Listing 16.4 produces the following output:

OUTPUT

```
This is  my title
- - - - - - - - - - - - - - - - - - - - - -
       1        10
       2        20
       3        30
       4        40
```

ANALYSIS

- The first execution of line 4 triggers line 12 (the top-of-page event).

- Line 13 writes a title, and line 14 underlines it.

- Line 15 sets the current output position to the first line in the output list.

- Line 16 overwrites 'was' with 'is '.

- Line 17 moves the current output position down one line. The second line of the output list is now the current output line.

- Control returns to line 4. It issues a new line character and the first value from this loop is output to the third line of output. The remaining values are output on succeeding lines.

- Line 6 returns the current output position to what it was for the first write after the top-of-page processing (output list line 2).

- The loop on lines 7 through 10 overwrites the output list beginning on line 3. This data is written to the right of the existing data, beginning in column 10.

Using the `position` Statement

Use the `position` statement to specify the next output column on the current line. For example, `skip to line 2. position 3. write 'Hi'.` would write `Hi` on line 2 beginning in column 3.

Syntax for the `position` Statement

`position` *v1*.

where:

▲   • *v1* is a numeric variable or literal.

Listing 16.5 illustrates the use of the `position` statement.

INPUT   **LISTING 16.5**   THE `position` STATEMENT

```
1   report ztx1605.
2   data n type i.
3   do 4 times.
4       do 4 times.
5           position sy-index.
6           write 'A'.
7           enddo.
8       new-line.
9       enddo.
10
11  skip.
12  do 4 times.
13      do 4 times.
14          position sy-index.
15          write 'A'.
16          enddo.
17      skip.
18      enddo.
```

The code in Listing 16.5 produces the following output:

```
AAAA
AAAA
AAAA
AAAA

AAAA

AAAA

AAAA

AAAA
```

- Line 3 begins a do loop.
- Line 4 begins a nested do loop. Each time through, line 5 sets the current output position equal to the current loop iteration. So, the first time through, the current output position is set to 1. The second time through it's set to 2, and so on. This causes line 6 to write the letter A 4 times, in columns 1 through 4.
- Line 8 moves the output position down one line. This results in the output being written on successive lines, beginning at the line following the standard headers.
- Line 11 outputs a blank line.
- Lines 12 through 18 are the same as lines 3 through 9, except instead of `new-line`, `skip` is used on line 17. This has the effect of inserting blank lines between successive output lines.

Note

> Using the `position` statement followed immediately by a `write` is equivalent to issuing a single `write` at statement (covered in the previous chapter).

Using the `set blank lines` Statement

Normally, if your program issues a `write` statement that results in a blank line being output, this blank line will be suppressed. For example, when writing out a variable that contains blanks, you will not see a blank line in the list. Use the `set blank lines` statement to change this behavior.

Syntax for the `set blank lines` Statement

SYNTAX

```
set blank lines on ¦ off.
```

The following points apply:

- The default setting is off.
- Blank lines generated by the `skip` statement are not suppressed.
- Blank lines generated by `write /` without a variable are not suppressed. For example, `write /.` will always generate a blank line. `Write / ' '.` will only generate a blank line if `set blank lines on` has been executed beforehand.

Listing 16.6 illustrates the `set blank lines` statement.

LISTING 16.6   THE set blank lines STATEMENT

```
1   report ztx1606.
2   data: f1, f2, f3.
3   write: / 'Text 1'.
4   write: / f1, / f2, / f3.
5   write: / 'Text 2'.
6   skip.
7
8   set blank lines on.
9   write: / 'Text 3'.
10  write: / f1, / f2, / f3.
11  write: / 'Text 4'.
12
13  set blank lines off.
14  skip.
15  write: / 'Text 5'.
16  write: / f1, / f2, / f3.
17  write: / 'Text 6'.
```

The code in Listing 16.6 produces the following output:

```
Text 1
Text 2


Text 3




Text 4

Text 5
Text 6
```

- Line 2 defines three variables. All are character length 1, and have a default initial value of blanks.

- By default, blank lines that would result from attempting to write blanks are suppressed. Therefore, the line 4 does not cause any blank lines to be written.

- The skip statement always writes blank lines, so line 6 generates a blank line.

- Line 8 allows the write statement to write entirely blank lines to the list.

- Line 10 writes three blank lines.

- Line 13 sets blank lines off again.

- Line 14 generates a blank line.

- Line 16 does not generate blank lines.

Summary

- Use `new-line` to begin a new line or to lock a specific line in place. It can prevent horizontal scrolling of any individual line.
- Use `new-page` to generate a page break, to turn titles and headers on or off, change the line count or line size between pages, or to send output to the spool.
- Use `skip` to generate blank lines in the output. `skip to line` sets the output position to a specific line.
- Use `back` to return to the top of a page, or to the beginning of a group of lines.
- Use `position` to specify the next output column.
- Use `set blank lines` to allow blank lines to be created by writing variables that contain blanks.

16

Do	Don't
DO use symbols and icons in your report to increase readability.	**DON'T** hard-code a page size. Allow the users to specify it when they print the report.
	DON'T create reports wider than 132 characters if the user may print it. Most printers cannot print pages wider than 132 characters.

Q&A

Q I don't really understand the difference between `skip` and `new-line`. Don't they both cause the next `write` to go to a new line?

A The purpose of `skip` is to generate a blank line in the output. `new-line` causes the next line of output to be written to a new line, and does not generate blank lines.

Workshop

The Workshop provides two ways for you to affirm what you've learned in this chapter. The Quiz section poses questions to help you solidify your understanding of the material covered and the Exercise section provides you with experience in using what you have learned. You can find answers to the quiz questions and exercises in Appendix B, "Answers to Quiz Questions and Exercises."

Quiz

1. What statement can you use to overwrite the same line?

2. When would you want to use `skip sy-linct` instead of `new-page` if you want a footer?

Exercise 1

Explain the flow of control in the following program, and how it works.

INPUT   **LISTING 16.7**   top-of-page, *position*, AND *skip*

```
report zty1607.
data n type i.
do 4 times.
    do 4 times.
        position sy-index.
        write 'A'.
        enddo.
    add 1 to n.
    skip to line n.
    enddo.

top-of-page.
    n = sy-linno.
```

The code in Listing 16.7 produces the following output:

```
AAAA
AAAA
AAAA
AAAA
```

DAY 17

Modularization: Events and Subroutines

After you have completed this chapter, you will be able to

- Know the types of modularization units available in ABAP/4
- Understand ABAP/4 events
- Use the `initialization`, `start-of-selection`, and `end-of-selection` events
- Define internal and external subroutines
- Define global, local, and static variables and table work areas
- Understand the effect of `exit`, `check`, and `stop` within events and subroutines

Modularization Units in ABAP/4

NEW TERM   A *modularization unit* is a like a shell into which you can put code. It allows you to segregate a group of lines of code from the rest, and then execute them at a specific time. The lines of code within a modularization unit act very much like a mini-program that can be called from another program.

ABAP/4 offers three types of modularization units:

- Events
- Subroutines
- Function modules

This chapter explains events and subroutines. The next chapter explains function modules.

Use modularization units to eliminate redundant code within your program and to make your program easier to read. For example, suppose you have a series of statements that format a mailing address, and you need to format mailing addresses at several different places in your program. Instead of duplicating the code within your program, it's a good idea to place that code into a modularization unit and call it whenever you need to format an address.

Events

Contrary to first appearances, ABAP/4 programs are event-driven. A good understanding of events are the key to a good understanding of ABAP/4.

Defining Events

NEW TERM An *event* is a tag that identifies a section of code. The section of code associated with an event begins with an event name and ends when the next event name is encountered. In Listing 17.1, the event names are `initialization`, `start-of-selection`, and `end-of-selection`. Event names are reserved words. You cannot create new events—you can only use existing ones.

INPUT **LISTING 17.1** THREE BASIC EVENTS

```
1  report ztx1701.
2  initialization.
3    write / '1'.
4
5  start-of-selection.
6    write / '2'.
7
8  end-of-selection.
9    write / '3'.
```

The code in Listing 17.1 produces the following output:

```
1
2
3
```

ANALYSIS

- Line 2 identifies the beginning of the `initialization` event.
- Line 3 is associated with the `initialization` event. If more lines of code followed this one, they would all belong to the `initialization` event.
- Line 4 marks the end of the code belonging to `initialization` and the beginning of the `start-of-selection` event.
- Line 6 belongs to the `start-of-selection` event.
- Line 8 marks the lower boundary of the code belonging to the `start-of-selection` event and the upper boundary of the `end-of-selection` event.
- Line 9 belongs to the `end-of-selection` event.
- The lower boundary of the code belonging to `end-of-selection` is marked by the end of the program.
- When you run this program, these events are triggered by a driver program. The following paragraphs explain this concept in detail.

NEW TERM A *driver program* is one program that controls another (driven) program. SAP supplies driver programs with the R/3 system. You supply the *driven* program. When you start your program, a driver program always starts first, and then it calls the events in your program. To reiterate, a driver program starts first and then controls when your program gets control. This has always been the case for all of the programs you have written so far; you just have not been aware of it until now. Please be sure you read this paragraph carefully. To repeat once more, when *you* start *your* program, a driver program starts first and controls your program by calling events within it.

The code associated with an event is triggered by a statement in a driver program. Events are triggered by the driver program in a predefined and predictable sequence. Figure 17.1 illustrates this point.

FIGURE 17.1.

The driver program and the events it can trigger.

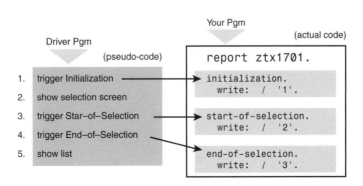

Figure 17.1 has pseudocode within the driver program. The code shown in the program on the right is actual code. When program ztx1701 is executed, the driver on the left starts first. The program then follows this sequence of steps:

- It triggers the initialization event, causing the code belonging to initialization to be executed. If you have not coded an initialization event in your program, the driver program skips this step.

- It shows the selection screen for your program. (A selection screen is the screen that contains the input fields for your parameter statements.) If your program doesn't have a selection screen, it skips this step.

- It triggers the start-of-selection event, causing the code belonging to that event to be executed. If you have not coded a start-of-selection event in your program, it skips this step.

- It triggers the end-of-selection event in your program, executing all of the code belonging to it. If you haven't coded an end-of-selection, it skips this step.

- It shows the output list to the user.

The order of execution for events is determined by the driver program, not by your program. Therefore, you can code the events in any order and the execution order will still be the same. The order of events in your program doesn't matter; they will always be triggered in the same sequence by the driver program. Listing 17.2 illustrates this point.

LISTING 17.2   EVENTS TRIGGERED IN THE ORDER DICTATED BY THE
INPUT   DRIVER PROGRAM

```
1  report ztx1702.
2  data f1 type i value 1.
3
4  end-of-selection.
5    write: / '3.  f1 =', f1.
6
7  start-of-selection.
8    write: / '2.  f1 =', f1.
9    f1 = 99.
10
11 initialization.
12   write: / '1.  f1 =', f1.
13   add 1 to f1.
```

The code in Listing 17.2 produces the following output:

```
1.  f1 =          1
2.  f1 =          2
3.  f1 =          99
```

ANALYSIS

- When you start ztx1702, the driver program starts first.
- It triggers the initialization event.
- The code associated with initialization is executed (lines 12 and 13). The value of f1 is written out and 1 is added to it. Control then returns to the driver program.
- The driver program looks for a selection screen. There isn't one for this program, so it looks for a start-of-selection event. It finds it on line 7, and so branches to ztx1702 beginning at line 8. Lines 8 and 9 are executed and control then returns to the driver.
- The driver program then looks for an end-of-selection event. Finding it on line 4, it transfers control ztx1702 beginning at line 5. Only line 5 belongs to the end-of-selection event, so it is executed and control then returns to the driver.
- The driver then displays the list to the user.

This example illustrates that you can put the events in a different order, but the execution sequence is not changed. The execution sequence is always initialization, start-of-selection, end-of-selection. There are other events as well; some occur after initialization and some occur between start-of-selection and end-of-selection.

Programmers usually position events in the order in which they are triggered to make their programs easier to understand.

There are eleven different events in ABAP/4, categorized in Table 17.1 according to how they are triggered.

TABLE 17.1 ABAP/4 EVENTS

Category	Events
Driver	initialization
	at selection-screen
	start-of-selection
	get
	end-of-selection

continues

TABLE 17.1 CONTINUED

Category	Events
User	at line-selection
	at pfn
	at user-command
Program	top-of-page
	end-of-page

Driver events are triggered by the driver program. User events are triggered by the user via the user interface. Program events are those triggered from within your program. This chapter details the use of `initialization`, `start-of-selection`, and `end-of-selection`. Note that some of these events occur between `start-of-selection` and `end-of-selection`.

In the previous chapter, "Formatting Techniques, Part 2," you learned about the `top-of-page` and `bottom-of-page` events. The information in this chapter also applies to them, but these are triggered by statements inside your program, not from the driver.

Special Considerations When Using `write` Within Events

Events have two unusual affects on the `write` statement:

- If a program has a selection screen and you issue a `write` statement in an event triggered before `start-of-selection`, you will not see the output from it. For example, if you have a `parameters` statement in your program, a selection screen is created for your program to allow the user to enter the parameter value. If in this program you issue a `write` in `initialization`, you will not see the output from the `write` statement.

- A new event always begins a new line in the output. For example, if you issue a `write` statement in `start-of-selection`, a `write` in `end-of-selection` will begin on a new line. You can use `skip to line` if it is necessary to continue writing on the same line.

Triggering `top-of-page`

This section describes when `top-of-page` is triggered in relation to driver program events. If your program doesn't have a selection screen, the first `write` statement executed triggers `top-of-page`. If your program does have a selection screen, is it possible for `top-of-page` to be triggered twice:

- By the first `write` statement executed before the selection screen is shown
- By the first `write` statement after the selection screen is shown

Only if you are doing something unusual in top-of-page, like opening files or initializing data, do you have to be wary of the double-trigger effect.

If top-of-page is triggered twice, you will only see the output from write statements within it the second time it is triggered. The output created by write statements during the first time it is triggered is discarded. This double-triggering doesn't usually cause any problems with your program or with your output because

- You can't see the output from writes issued before a selection is shown, so you usually don't code them there.
- The top-of-page event usually only contains write statements, and the output from the first triggering is discarded so no harm is done when it is triggered twice.

Note

The write to variation of the write statement doesn't trigger top-of-page.

17

Defaulting to start-of-selection

If the first executable statement in your program is not preceded by an event name, at runtime the system automatically inserts start-of-selection before the first line of executable code. Therefore, if you haven't coded any events, or you have put code at the top of the program without naming an event, start-of-selection is assumed. Listing 17.3 provides an example of this, in a program containing both a selection screen and events. It also contains a program-driven event—top-of-page.

INPUT

LISTING 17.3 start-of-selection AUTOMATICALLY INSERTED BEFORE THE FIRST LINE OF CODE

```
1   report ztx1703 no standard page heading.
2   parameters p1(8).
3
4   write: / 'p1 =', p1.
5
6   initialization.
7     p1 = 'Init'.
8
9   end-of-selection.
10    write: /(14) sy-uline,
11           / 'End of program'.
12
13  top-of-page.
14    write: / 'This is My Title'.
15    skip.
```

The code in Listing 17.3 produces the following output:

OUTPUT
```
This is My Title
p1 = INIT
--------------
End of program
```

ANALYSIS
- When you execute program ztx1703, a driver program starts up first. Since there is code at the beginning of the program that doesn't belong to any events, a start-of-selection is automatically inserted at line 3.

- The driver program triggers the initialization event. Line 7 executes and assigns the value 'Init' to p1. Control returns to the driver program.

- Since there is a selection screen for this program, the selection screen is now shown. It appears in Figure 17.2. The value assigned to p1 on line 7 appears in the input field.

- The user presses Execute on the selection screen. Control returns to the driver program, which then triggers the start-of-selection event.

- Since start-of-selection was inserted at line 3, control passes to ztx1703 starting at line 4.

- Line 4 is executed. Since this is the first write statement executed after start-of-selection it triggers the top-of-page event. Control transfers to line 14.

- Line 14 writes a title. Line 15 writes a blank line. Control returns to line 4.

- Line 4 writes the value of p1.

- The driver then triggers the end-of-selection event. Control passes to line 10.

- Line 10 writes a horizontal line for 14 bytes.

- Line 11 writes End of program. Control returns to the driver program.

- The driver displays the list to the user.

You cannot put a condition around an event or enclose an event in a loop. To do so will cause a syntax error. For example, the code in Listing 17.4 causes a syntax error.

INPUT   **LISTING 17.4**   DON'T ENCLOSE AN EVENT WITHIN A CONDITION OR A LOOP

```
1   report ztx1704.
2   data f1.
3
4   start-of-selection.
5     f1 = 'A'.
6
7   if f1 = 'A'.
8     end-of-selection.
9     write: / f1.
10    endif.
```

FIGURE 17.2.

The selection screen for the ztx1703 *program.*

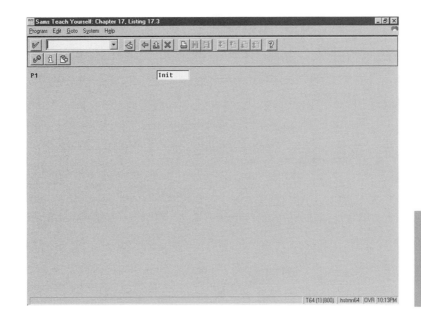

The code in Listing 17.4 produces this syntax error: Incorrect nesting: before the statement "END-OF-SELECTION", the structure introduced by "IF" must be concluded by "ENDIF".

Event names have higher priority than other ABAP/4 statements. The if statement on line 7 belongs to the start-of-selection event. The endif statement on line 10 belongs to the end-of-selection event. You close all open conditions and loops within the event to which they belong. Therefore, this program must have an endif before the end-of-selection event. Because there is also an endif within end-of-selection on line 10, that endif would have to be removed before the program would run.

You should not put data definitions within events. Although this doesn't cause a syntax error, it is poor programming style. All data definitions should be done at the top of the program.

Each event has a specific purpose and is needed to accomplish a specific programming task. As the need arises, I will refer to them in the material that follows. If you don't see any events in a program, always remember that one still exists—start-of-selection.

Leaving an Event

You can exit out of an event at any time using the following statements:

- `exit`
- `check`
- `stop`

At this time, please review the function of the `check` statement (presented in Chapter 10, "Common Control Statements").

The following paragraphs describe the effect of `check` and `exit` when they are coded outside a loop. The effect of `stop` is the same regardless of whether is it coded within a loop or not.

 Note
Although at this point only three events have been presented in detail, this section is written in a general sense so that it will apply equally well after you have learned to use all events.

In all events

- `check` immediately leaves the current event and processing continues with the next event (or action, such as displaying the selection screen or output list).
- `stop` immediately leaves the current event and goes directly to the `end-of-selection` event. Executing `stop` within `end-of-selection` leaves the event. It doesn't cause an infinite loop.

In events that occur before `start-of-selection`

- `exit` and `check` have the same behavior. They both leave the event immediately and processing continues with the next event (or action, such as display of the selection screen).

In `start-of-selection` and events that occur after it

- `exit` terminates the report and shows the output list. A single exception exists; within `top-of-page`, `exit` behaves like `check`.
- `check` leaves the event and processing continues with the next event (or action, such as display of the output list).

> **Caution**
>
> Don't use stop in the following events: initialization, at selection-screen output, top-of-page, and end-of-page. Technically, stop can work with top-of-page and end-of-page if you refrain from issuing write statements within end-of-selection afterward. In the case of top-of-page a write, can cause a short dump; in the case of end-of-page, you can lose output. It is safer to avoid it altogether within these events.

check, exit, and stop do *not* set the value of sy-subrc. If you want to set it, you can assign a numeric value to it before leaving.

The report shown in Listing 17.5 allows you to try the effects of these statements within various events. Copy it and remove comments one at a time to experiment with the possible variations.

17

INPUT   **LISTING 17.5**   EFFECTS OF exit, check, AND stop WITHIN EVENTS

```
 1  report ztx1705 no standard page heading line-count 6(2).
 2  *in events before start-of-selection:
 3  *    - exit and check have the same behavior. They both leave the event
 4  *      and processing continues with the next event or action.
 5  *    - stop goes directly to the end-of-selection event
 6  *      (don't use stop in initialization or at selection-screen output)
 7
 8  *in start-of-selection and subsequent events:
 9  *    - exit terminates the report and shows the output list
10  *      exception: top-of-page: exit leaves the event
11  *    - check leaves the event and processing continues with the next one.
12  *    - stop goes directly to the end-of-selection event
13
14                                      "execute an:
15  parameters: exit_sos radiobutton group g1, "exit in start-of-selection
16              exit_eos radiobutton group g1, "exit in end-of-selection
17              chck_sos radiobutton group g1, "check in start-of-selection
18              chck_eos radiobutton group g1, "check in end of selection
19              stop_sos radiobutton group g1, "stop in start-of-selection
20              stop_eos radiobutton group g1, "stop in end-of-selection
21              none     radiobutton group g1. "no stop, exit or check
22
23  initialization.
24  *    exit.                          "exits event
25  *    check 1 = 2.                   "exits event
26  *    stop.                          "don't do this
27       chck_sos = 'X'.
28
29  at selection-screen output.
```

continues

LISTING 17.5   CONTINUED

```
30 *    exit.                         "exits event
31 *    check 1 = 2.                  "exits event
32 *    stop.                         "don't do this
33      message s789(zk) with 'at selection-screen output'.
34
35 at selection-screen on radiobutton group g1.
36 *    exit.                         "exits event
37 *    check 1 = 2.                  "exits event
38 *    stop.                         "goes to end-of-selection
39      message i789(zk) with 'at selection-screen on rbg'.
40
41 at selection-screen.
42 *    exit.                         "exits event
43 *    check 1 = 2.                  "exits event
44 *    stop.                         "goes to end-of-selection
45      message i789(zk) with 'at selection-screen'.
46
47 start-of-selection.
48      write: / 'Top of SOS'.
49      if      exit_sos = 'X'.
50         exit.                      "exits report
51      elseif  chck_sos = 'X'.
52         check 1 = 2.               "exits event
53      elseif  stop_sos = 'X'.
54         stop.                      "goes to end-of-selection
55         endif.
56      write: / 'Bottom of SOS'.
57
58 end-of-selection.
59      write: / 'Top of EOS'.
60      if      exit_eos = 'X'.
61         exit.                      "exits report
62      elseif  chck_eos = 'X'.
63         check 1 = 2.               "exits report
64      elseif  stop_eos = 'X'.
65         stop.                      "exits report
66         endif.
67      write: / 'Bottom of EOS'.
68      write: / '1',
69             / '2',
70             / '3'.
71
72 top-of-page.
73      write: / 'Title'.
74 *    exit.                "exits event and returns to write statement
75 *    check 'X' = 'Y'.     "exits event and returns to write statement
76 *    stop.                "goto end-of-selection - don't write after it
77      uline.
```

```
78
79 end-of-page.
80     uline.
81 *   exit.                    "exits report
82 *   check 'X' = 'Y'.         "exits event and returns to write statement
83 *   stop.                    "goto end-of-selection - don't write after it
84     write: / 'Footer'.
```

ANALYSIS
- Line 15 defines a group of radio buttons. Choosing one will cause the statement mentioned in the comment to be executed as indicated. For example, choosing exit_sos causes the exit statement to be executed in the start-of-selection event.
- check 1 = 2 is hard-coded so it always returns a negative result.
- You may wish to increase the line count to make the output more readable. It is set so that the bottom-of-page event will be triggered.

Returning from the List

Let's look more closely at events in the context of a report that has a selection screen. (Recall that the parameters statement generates a selection screen.)

When the user executes the report, the driver triggers initialization and then shows the selection screen. After pressing the Execute button, the driver triggers the remaining events, the program ends and the user sees the list. The user presses the Back button to return. The driver then restarts processing beginning at the top of the event list. It triggers the initialization event, and then all subsequent events follow again in their normal sequence. The result is that the user sees the selection screen after pressing the Back button. There is, however, a difference in processing when a restart occurs.

The selection screen has its own copy of all variables that are displayed on it. The first time the report runs and the driver program regains control after the initialization event has finished, it copies values from program variables to the corresponding selection screen variables and displays them. The user can modify the input fields. When the user presses the Execute button, the driver stores the values from the selection screen into two data areas: one belonging to the selection screen and then into your program's variables.

However, this dual action only occurs the first time you run the program. When the user presses Back from the list, initialization is triggered again. When control returns to the driver, it doesn't copy your program variables into the screen data area. Instead, it shows the existing values from the screen data area; it still contains the values the user entered. The result is that the user sees the values that he last entered regardless of what has changed in your program. Then, after the user presses the Execute button, the values onscreen are copied to the screen's data area and then to your program, overwriting any differences. For example, if you set up values during initialization, those values will be seen on the selection screen when you start the program. When you press the Back button on the selection screen, initialization will execute but values set within it won't be shown. The user will instead see the values that he entered.

Subroutines

NEW TERM   A *subroutine* is a reusable section of code. It is like a mini-program that can be called from another point in your program. Within it you can define variables, execute statements, compute results, and write output. To define a subroutine, use the form statement to indicate the start of a subroutine, and use endform to indicate the end of the subroutine. The name of a subroutine cannot exceed 30 characters.

To call a subroutine, use the perform statement.

Listing 17.6 provides a sample program that defines and calls a subroutine.

INPUT   **LISTING 17.6**   DEFINING AND CALLING A SUBROUTINE

```
1   report ztx1706.
2
3   write: / 'Before call 1'.
4   perform sub1.
5   write: / 'Before call 2'.
6   perform sub1.
7   write: / 'After calls'.
8
9   form sub1.
10    write: / 'Inside sub1'.
11    endform.
```

The code in Listing 17.6 produces the following output:

OUTPUT
```
Before call 1
Inside sub1
Before call 2
Inside sub1
After calls
```

ANALYSIS
- Line 3 executes.
- Line 4 transfers control to line 9.
- Line 10 executes.
- Line 11 transfers control back to line 4.

- Line 5 executes.
- Line 6 transfers control to line 9.
- Line 10 executes.
- Line 11 returns control to line 6.
- Line 7 executes.

There are two types of subroutines:

- Internal subroutines
- External subroutines

Listing 17.6 illustrated a call to an internal subroutine.

Defining and Calling Internal Subroutines

Subroutine definitions are usually placed at the end of the program, after all events. The `form` statement defines the end of the preceding event, and the beginning of a subroutine. Subroutines cannot be nested inside of events.

Syntax for the `form` Statement

▼ SYNTAX

```
form s [tables t1 t2 ...]
       [using u1 value(u2) ...]
       [changing c1 value(c2) ...].
    ---
    endform.
```

where:

- s is the name of the subroutine.
- t1, t2, u1, u2, c1, and c2 are parameters.
- `tables` allows internal tables to be passed as parameters.
- The `value` addition cannot be used after `tables`.
- The `value` addition can be applied to any variables passed via `using` or `changing`.

▲
- --- represents any number of lines of code.

The following points apply:

- All additions are optional.
- When they are coded, additions must appear in the order shown here. If coded, `tables` must come first, then `using`, and then `changing`.
- Each addition can only be specified once. For example, the `tables` addition can only appear once. However, multiple tables can appear after it.

17

- Do not use commas to separate parameters.

- `tables` only allows internal tables to be passed—not database tables.

- A subroutine can call another subroutine.

- Recursion is supported. A subroutine can call itself or a subroutine that calls it.

- Subroutine definitions cannot be nested. (You cannot define a subroutine within another subroutine.)

Syntax for the `perform` Statement

▼ SYNTAX

```
perform a) s
        b) n of s1 s2 s3 ...
                           [tables t1 t2 ...]
                           [using u1 u2 ...]
                           [changing c1 c2 ...].
```

where:

- *s, s1, s2, s3,* are subroutine names.

- *n* is a numeric variable.

- a) and b) are mutually exclusive.

- `tables, using,` and `changing` can appear with either a) or b).

▲   - The addition `value()` cannot be used with `perform`.

Using syntax b) you can specify that one of a list of subroutines be performed. The *n*th subroutine in the list of subroutine names following `of` is performed. For example, if *n* is 2, the second subroutine in the list will be performed. Listing 17.7 illustrates this syntax.

INPUT   **LISTING 17.7** CALLING A SERIES OF SUBROUTINES

```
1   report ztx1707.
2   do 3 times.
3       perform sy-index of s1 s2 s3.
4       enddo.
5
6   form s1.
7       write: / 'Hi from s1'.
8       endform.
9
10  form s2.
11      write: / 'Hi from s2'.
12      endform.
13
14  form s3.
15      write: / 'Hi from s3'.
16      endform.
```

The code in Listing 17.7 produces the following output:

OUTPUT

```
Hi from s1
Hi from s2
Hi from s3
```

ANALYSIS

- Line 2 begins a loop that executes three times. Sy-index is the loop counter, and is incremented by one with each loop pass.
- The first time line 3 is executed, sy-index has a value of 1. Therefore, the first subroutine (s1) is performed.
- The second time line 3 is executed, sy-index has a value of 2. Therefore, the second subroutine (s2) is performed.
- The third time line 3 is executed, sy-index has a value of 3. Therefore, the third subroutine (s3) is performed.

Leaving a Subroutine

You can exit out of a subroutine at any time using the following statements:

- exit
- check
- stop

The following paragraphs describe the effect of check and exit when they are coded within a subroutine but outside of a loop. The effect of stop within a subroutine is the same, regardless of whether is it coded within a loop.

In subroutines

- check and exit immediately leave the subroutine and processing continues with the next executable statement following perform.
- stop immediately leaves the subroutine and goes directly to the end-of-selection event.

check, exit, and stop do not set the value of sy-subrc. If you want to set it, assign a numeric value to it before leaving.

Listing 17.8 illustrates the effects of these statements within subroutines.

INPUT **LISTING 17.8** EFFECTS OF exit, check, AND stop WITHIN A SUBROUTINE

```
1   report ztx1708.
2   data f1 value 'X'.
3
4   clear sy-subrc.
```

continues

LISTING 17.8 CONTINUED

```
5  perform s1. write: / 'sy-subrc =', sy-subrc.
6  perform s2. write: / 'sy-subrc =', sy-subrc.
7  perform s3. write: / 'sy-subrc =', sy-subrc.
8  perform s4. write: / 'sy-subrc =', sy-subrc.
9
10 end-of-selection.
11     write:  'Stopped, sy-subrc =', sy-subrc.
12     if sy-subrc = 7.
13         stop.
14         endif.
15     write: / 'After Stop'.
16
17 form s1.
18     do 4 times.
19         exit.
20         enddo.
21     write / 'In s1'.
22     exit.
23     write / 'After Exit'.
24     endform.
25
26 form s2.
27     do 4 times.
28         check f1 = 'Y'.
29         write / sy-index.
30         enddo.
31     write / 'In s2'.
32     check f1 = 'Y'.
33     write / 'After Check'.
34     endform.
35
36 form s3.
37     do 4 times.
38         sy-subrc = 7.
39         stop.
40         write / sy-index.
41         enddo.
42     endform.
43
44 form s4.
45     write: / 'In s4'.
46     endform.
```

The code in Listing 17.8 produces the following output:

OUTPUT
```
In s1
sy-subrc =      0
In s2
sy-subrc =      0

Stopped, sy-subrc =      7
```

ANALYSIS
- Line 5 transfers control to line 17.
- Line 18 begins a loop. Line 19 exits the loop, not the subroutine.
- Line 22 exits the subroutine. Control returns to line 6.
- Line 6 transfers control to line 26.
- Line 28 transfers control to line 27 4 times.
- Line 32 leaves the subroutine. Control return to line 7.
- Line 7 transfers control to line 36.
- Line 39 transfers control directly to line 10.
- The output from line 11 begins on a new line because a new event has begun.
- Line 13 exits the event and the list is shown.

Defining Global and Local Variables

NEW TERM A *global variable* is one that is defined outside of a subroutine by using the `tables` or `data` statement. It can be accessed from any point in the program, be it inside an event or inside a subroutine. It is good programming practice to place global variable definitions at the top of the program, somewhere before the first line of executable code.

NEW TERM A *local variable* is a variable that is defined inside a subroutine using the `local`, `data`, or `statics` statement. It is said to be local to the subroutine. Variables defined by using `local` are accessible from outside the subroutine; variables defined by using `data` or `statics` are not. Thus if the subroutine calls another subroutine, variables defined by using `local` are visible from within the called subroutine—variables defined by using `data` or `statics` are not.

For local variables defined by using `local` or `data`, memory is allocated each time the subroutine is called. That memory is freed when the subroutine ends, and so the values within it are lost. For `statics`, the memory is retained. These characteristics will be described in depth in this chapter.

Defining a `tables` Work Area

Variables defined by using the `tables` statement are always global. Placing the `tables` statement at the top of a program defines a global field string. Placing the same statement inside a subroutine also defines a `global` field string of that name. Therefore, you should not use the `tables` statement inside a subroutine since the definition is always global; global definitions should be placed at the top of your program.

To define a local table work area inside a subroutine, use `local` instead of the `tables` statement. The syntax is the same as `tables`, but it defines a local field string instead of a

global one. The variables defined by using local are visible from within the subroutine
and all subroutines it calls.

 Note

> To be precise, a variable is only known within a program after the point at
> which it is defined. For example, if you define a variable on line 10, you
> would be able to access it on lines 11 and later, but not on lines before line
> 10. In the case of a local definition, you can access the global version of the
> variable at any point before the local definition.

Listing 17.9 illustrates the local statement.

INPUT   **LISTING 17.9**   THE local STATEMENT

```
 1   report ztx1709.
 2   tables ztxlfa1.
 3
 4   select single * from ztxlfa1 where lifnr = 'V9'.
 5   write: / '*-----', ztxlfa1-lifnr.
 6   perform s1.
 7   write: / '*S1---', ztxlfa1-lifnr.
 8   perform s2.
 9   write: / '*S2---', ztxlfa1-lifnr.
10
11  form s1.
12     write: / ' S1-A', ztxlfa1-lifnr.
13     local ztxlfa1.
14     select single * from ztxlfa1 where lifnr = 'V1'.
15     write: / ' S1-B', ztxlfa1-lifnr.
16     perform s2.
17     write: / ' S1-C', ztxlfa1-lifnr.
18     endform.
19
20  form s2.
21     write: / '  S2-A', ztxlfa1-lifnr.
22     select single * from ztxlfa1 where lifnr = 'V2'.
23     write: / '  S2-B', ztxlfa1-lifnr.
24     endform.
```

The code in Listing 17.9 produces the following output:

OUTPUT

```
*  -  -  -  -  -V9
 S1-A V9
 S1-B V1
  S2-A V1
  S2-B V2
 S1-C V2
*S1 -  -  -V9
  S2-A V9
  S2-B V2
*S2 -  -  -V2
```

ANALYSIS

- Line 2 defines a global work area named ztxlfa1.
- Line 4 selects a single record from table ztxlfa1 and places it into the global work area ztxlfa1.
- Line 5 writes the value V9 from the global work area ztxlfa1.
- Line 6 passes control to line 11.
- Line 12 writes the value of lifnr from the global work area ztxlfa1.
- Line 13 defines a local field string ztxlfa1. (It is good programming practice to place this definition at the top of the subroutine. For the purposes of this example, it is placed after the write to completely demonstrate the effect of local.) A new memory location is allocated having the name ztxlfa1. References to ztxlfa1 after this point in the subroutine and in all called subroutines will refer to this local definition of ztxlfa1, not the global one. The global one is now inaccessible.
- Line 14 selects a single record and places it into the local work area ztxlfa1.
- Line 15 writes a value from the local work area. It is V1.
- Line 16 transfers control to line 20. The local memory remains allocated and will still be visible within s2.
- Line 21 writes from the local memory area defined in s1.
- Line 22 selects a new value into the local ztxlfa1.
- Line 23 writes from the local ztxlfa1.
- Line 24 returns control to line17. The local memory remains allocated and unchanged.
- Line 17 writes the value put into the local ztxlfa1 by s2.
- Line 18 returns control to line 6. The local memory is freed, and the value V2 is discarded.
- Line 7 writes the value of lifnr. It is now V9—the same value it had when s1 was called.

17

- Line 8 transfers control to line 20.
- Prior to executing line 21, a local definition of ztxlfa1 has not been created. Therefore, the global ztxlfa1-lifnr is written out.
- Line 22 selects a record into the global work area ztxlfa1.
- Line 23 writes V2 from the global work area.
- Line 24 returns control to line 8.
- Line 9 writes V2 from the global work area.

If you define a local variable having the same name as a global variable, the local variable will take precedence inside the subroutine. Consequently, you will not be able to access the global variable of the same name within that subroutine. All references will refer to the local variable.

Defining Data

Variables defined by the data statement at the top of the program are global. data definitions within a subroutine are local to the subroutine. Memory is allocated for these variables when the subroutine is called, and freed when it returns. Like variables defined by using local, the values in data variables will be lost when the subroutine returns.

Use the statics statement to create local variables that are not freed when the subroutine ends. The syntax for statics is the same as the syntax for the data statement. The memory for a static variable is allocated the first time the subroutine is called, and retained when the subroutine ends. However, a static variable is only visible from within the subroutine itself, not within subroutines that it calls. The next time the subroutine is called, the memory for that variable becomes visible again. The value within it will be what it was when you last returned from that subroutine.

The memory of a static variable belongs to the subroutine that allocated it; that variable is not visible from other subroutines. If you allocate a static variable of the same name in multiple subroutines, these are separate variables with their own memory and values.

Listing 17.10 illustrates variables defined by using data and statics.

INPUT   **LISTING 17.10**   data AND statics

```
1   report ztx1710.
2   data: f1 type i value 8,
3         f2 type i value 9.
4
5   write: / 'before s1:', f1, f2.
6   do 3 times.
7       perform s1.
```

```
8       enddo.
9  write: / 'after  s1:', f1, f2.
10
11 form s1.
12      data    f1 type i value 1.
13      statics f2 type i value 1.
14      write: / 'inside s1:', f1, f2.
15      perform s2.
16      f1 = f2 = f2 * 2.
17      endform.
18
19 form s2.
20      write: ' S2-', f1, f2.
21      endform.
```

The code in Listing 17.10 produces the following output:

17

OUTPUT

```
before s1:        8         9
inside s1:        1         1  S2-       8         9
inside s1:        1         2  S2-       8         9
inside s1:        1         4  S2-       8         9
after  s1:        8         9
```

- Lines 2 and 3 define global variables f1 and f2.

- Line 7 transfers control to line 11.

- Line 12 allocates new memory for local variable f1 and assigns it a value of 1.

- Line 13 allocates new memory for static variable f2 and assigns it a value of 1.

- Line 15 transfers control to line 19.

- Line 20 writes from the global variables f1 and f2.

- Line 21 returns control to line 15.

- Line 16 multiplies f2 by 2 and assigns the value to both f1 and f2.

- Line 17 returns control to line 6. The memory for f1 is freed, but the memory for f2 is retained. However, it will not be visible again until the next time the subroutine is called.

- The loop loops and line 7 again transfers control to line 11.

- Line 12 allocates new memory for f1 and assigns it a value of 1.

- Line 13 causes the previously allocated memory for f2 to again become visible with this subroutine. The value in f2 is 2, as it was when the subroutine ended last.

Summary

- ABAP/4 has three types of modularization units: events, subroutines, and function modules.

- Events exist in all programs. If none are coded, the default event `start-of-selection` is automatically inserted. `initialization` is often used to assign values to parameters that appear on a selection screen. `end-of-selection` is for program cleanup, summaries, or abnormal termination routines. Events are triggered by the driver program. The driver always starts before your program and controls when the events are executed. You cannot place a condition around an event name. All events are triggered again when the user returns from the list. However, the selection screen variables are not repopulated from the program's data area.

- Use `exit`, `check`, and `stop` to leave an event.

Q&A

Q What happens if I have two events of the same name within the same program?

A If you have coded two statements of the same name within the same program, when the event is triggered the system executes them both in the order in which they appear in your program.

Q How can I tell the difference between an event name and a statement?

A If you see a single word followed by a period, that is usually an event. Beyond that, events don't have any identifiable characteristics other than their names. They are simply reserved words and to recognize one you must memorize their names, just as you memorize the keywords in statements.

Q Can I see the driver program? Can I choose the driver? Can I create a driver? What are the differences between the driver programs available?

NEW TERM **A** The driver program is called a *logical database*. You can choose the driver program by filling in the logical database fields in the program attributes screen. If you don't specify one, a default is automatically assigned. The only time you would want to choose the driver is when you want it to read data from the database and supply it to your program automatically. The default logical databases do not read from the database—they only trigger events. Regardless of the driver you choose, the events are always triggered in the same relative order. Even if you create your own logical database program, you cannot change the relative sequence of events or their names, nor can you create new ones. To see a driver program, start from within the source code editor. Choose the menu path Utilities->Help On.

Choose the Logical Database radio button and type a logical database id (KDF, for example). You will then see the structure of the logical database. Choose the menu path Goto->Database Program to see the driver program. Remember, the code shown within the driver in this chapter was pseudocode, so you won't see statements like trigger initialization in there. Logical databases are a complex topic and require many chapters to fully describe.

Q **If I put a `write` statement in an event that comes before `start-of-selection`, it works but only when there isn't a selection screen. If there is a selection screen, I don't see the output. Why?**

A R/3 uses something called a *screen context* to accept input and to display output to you. You can think of the screen context as one screen. Each screen context is processed in two phases: the dialog phase and the list phase. The dialog phase always occurs first, followed by the list. The dialog phase is used to display input fields to the user, such as those generated by a parameters statement. The list phase is used to display the output of `write` statement to the user. Both phases use the same screen context, so they overwrite each other. The dialog phase, however, pauses for user input and so allows itself to be shown before the list is shown. So if you issue a `write` statement in the `initialization` event and if the selection screen is shown, the selection screen overwrites the output from the `write` and that output is lost. You then choose Execute on the selection screen, and, if `write` statements are then issued, the list overwrites the selection screen and you see the output. However, if you don't have a selection screen, the writes that occur in `initialization` can still be seen.

Workshop

The Workshop provides you two ways for you to affirm what you've learned in this chapter. The Quiz section poses questions to help you solidify your understanding of the material covered and the Exercise section provides you with experience in using what you have learned. You can find answers to the quiz questions and exercises in Appendix B, "Answers to Quiz Questions and Exercises."

Quiz

1. Does the `write to` variation of the `write` statement trigger `top-of-page`?

2. Which events should you not use `stop` in?

3. At what point is a variable known within a program?

Exercise 1

Create a report that accepts an input parameter named p_land1. Define it like ztxlfa1-land1. Fill this field with the default value US at runtime by using the Initialization event. Your main program should have a single statement to call a subroutine that selects records from ztxlfa1 where the land1 field equals the p_land1 parameter. Inside the select, call another subroutine to write the record out. Use the top-of-page event to create the report title. Write the value of the p_land1 field in the title.

Modularization: Passing Parameters to Subroutines

After you have completed this chapter, you will be able to

- Pass typed and untyped parameters to subroutines
- Pass parameters three ways: by reference, by value, and by value and result
- Pass field strings and internal tables to a subroutine
- Understand how variables are shared between internal and external subroutines

Passing Parameters

In addition to defining variables by using `tables`, `local`, `data`, and `statics`, variables can also be defined on the `form` statement itself. These are known as parameters. Parameters can be either local or references to global variables. The memory for local parameters is allocated when the subroutine is called and freed when it ends.

If you define variables on the form statement, the perform statement must pass a value to each of these variables.

NEW TERM Parameter names that appear on the form statement are called *formal parameters*. This term is easy to remember because "formal" starts with "form." For example, in the statement form s1 using p1 changing p2 p3, the parameters p1, p2, and p3 are called formal parameters.

NEW TERM Parameter names that appear on the perform statement are called *actual parameters*. For example, in the statement perform s1 using f1 changing f2 f3, the parameters f1, f2, and f3 are called actual parameters.

Defining variables as parameters is illustrated in Listing 18.1.

INPUT **LISTING 18.1** PASSING PARAMETERS TO A SUBROUTINE

```
1   report ztx1801.
2   data: f1 value 'A',
3         f2 value 'B',
4         f3 value 'C'.
5
6   perform: s1 using f1 f2 f3,
7            s2 using f1 f2 f3.
8
9   form s1 using p1 p2 p3.
10     write: / f1, f2, f3,
11            / p1, p2, p3.
12     endform.
13
14  form s2 using f1 f2 f3.
15     skip.
16     write: / f1, f2, f3.
17     endform.
```

The code in Listing 18.1 produces the following output:

OUTPUT
```
A B C
A B C

A B C
```

ANALYSIS
- Line 6 transfers control to line 9.
- Line 9 defines three variables: p1, p2, and p3. It assigns the value of f1 to p1, the value of f2 to p2, and the value of f3 to p3.
- Line 10 writes the values of the variables p1, p2, and p3 and the global variables f1, f2, and f3.

- Line 12 returns control to line 6.

- Line 7 transfers control to line 14.

- Line 14 defines three variables: f1, f2, and f3. It assigns the value of f1 to f1, the value of f2 to f2, and the value of f3 to f3.

- Line 16 writes the values of the variables defined on line 14 on the form statement: f1, f2, and f3.

- Line 17 returns control to line 7.

Please review the syntax for the form and perform statements before continuing. See the section "Defining and Calling Internal Subroutines" in Chapter 19.

Do	Don't
DO used typed formal parameters—they are more efficient than untyped parameters.	**DON'T** pass internal tables by value or by value and result unless you really need a new copy of the internal table. Pass parameters by reference whenever possible.

18

Creating Typed Parameters

NEW TERM Formal parameters can be either typed or untyped. A *typed parameter* is a formal parameter that has a data type following its name on the form statement. An *untyped parameter* is a formal parameter that doesn't have a data type following its definition on the form statement. In Listing 18.1, all parameters were untyped.

Untyped formal parameters allow you to pass a variable of any data type or length to it. The formal parameter uses the attributes of the actual parameter. For example, if you pass a four-byte integer to an untyped formal parameter p1, p1 becomes a four-byte integer. If you pass a character string length 3 to the same parameter, it will become character 3.

Syntax for Typed Parameters

▼ SYNTAX

```
form s1 using u1 type t value(u2) type t
        changing c1 type t value(c2) type t.
```

where:

- s1 is a subroutine name.

- u1, u2, c1, and c2 are formal parameters.

▲

- t is either an ABAP/4 data type or a user-defined data type.

The following points apply:

- Only a data type can be specified on the form statement. A length cannot be specified.

- If you define a formal parameter using a fixed-length data type (those are types d, t, i, and f), the length of the actual parameter must match the data type of the formal parameter. This is usually the case, since you will usually design your program such that the data types of the actual and formal parameters will match. You usually do not pass one data type to a different data type.

Passing a variable of the wrong data type or length to a typed parameter causes a syntax error. Listing 18.2 shows how to use typed parameters.

INPUT   **LISTING 18.2**   USING TYPED PARAMETERS

```
1   report ztx1802.
2   data: f1 value 'A',
3         f2 type i value 4,
4         f3 like sy-datum,
5         f4 like sy-uzeit.
6
7   f3 = sy-datum.
8   f4 = sy-uzeit.
9
10  perform s1 using f1 f2 f3 f4.
11
12  form s1 using p1 type c
13               p2 type i
14               p3 type d
15               p4 type t.
16      write: / p1,
17             / p2,
18             / p3,
19             / p4.
20      endform.
```

The code in Listing 18.2 produces the following output:

OUTPUT
```
AAA
         4
19980510
164836
```

ANALYSIS   • Lines 2 through 5 define four variables having various data types. F3 is type c length 8, with an output length of 10 (defined in the domain for syst-datum). F4 is type c length 6 with an output length of 8 (defined in the domain for sy-uzeit).

- Line 10 transfers control to line 12.
- On line 12, p1 accepts only actual parameters of type c. f1 is type c length 3, so a length of 3 is assigned to p1. If f1 had not been type c a syntax error would have occurred. p2 is a fixed-length data type; type i is always length 4; f2 is also, so the parameters match fully. p3 and p4 are also fixed-length data types, as are their actual parameters.
- Lines 16 through 19 write out the values of p1 through p4. Notice the output length is not passed from the actual to the formal parameter. The output length of the formal parameters is set to the default for each data type. This causes the date and time to be output without separators.

Typed parameters have three advantages:

- They are more efficient. Less CPU is needed to allocate memory for a typed parameter than an untyped one.
- They help prevent coding errors. Because you cannot pass a parameter of an incompatible type, the syntax checker will point out the error to you if you try to pass an incompatible parameter.
- They help prevent runtime errors. For example, if your program accepts an untyped variable and performs an arithmetic operation on it, it is possible to pass character data to that subroutine. If this happens at runtime, a short dump will result.

Passing Field Strings

You can pass a field string the same way as any other parameter. However, if you want to access the components of the field string within the subroutine, you must make the structure of the field string known to the subroutine via one of two additions to the form statement:

- like x
- structure x

Here, x can be a field string or a DDIC structure or table. For example, form s1 using fs1 structure ztxlfa1 defines fs1 as having the structure of DDIC table ztxlfa1.

Controlling How Parameters Are Passed

There are three ways of passing parameters to a subroutine:

- Pass by reference
- Pass by value
- Pass by value and result

The syntax on the form statement determines how variables are passed. The syntax on perform does not. What this means will be explained in the next section. The first thing needed is to learn how to code each method.

Table 18.2 shows the relationship between syntax and passing methods.

TABLE 18.2   form STATEMENT ADDITIONS AND THE RESULTING PARAMETER PASSING METHOD

Addition	Method
using v1	Pass by reference
changing v1	Pass by reference
using value(v1)	Pass by value
changing value(v1)	Pass by value and result

Although the syntax on form and perform can differ, for the sake of program clarity they should be the same.

Listing 18.3 illustrates how to code these additions.

INPUT   LISTING 18.3   HOW TO CODE PARAMETER ADDITIONS

```
1   report ztx1803.
2   data: f1 value 'A',
3         f2 value 'B',
4         f3 value 'C',
5         f4 value 'D',
6         f5 value 'E',
7         f6 value 'F'.
8
9   perform s1 using   f1 f2
10                changing  f3 f4.
11
12  perform s2 using   f1 f2 f3 f4
13                changing  f5 f6.
14
15  perform s3 using   f1 f2 f3.
16
17  form s1 using   p1 value(p2)
18          changing  p3 value(p4).
19     write: / p1, p2, p3, p4.
20     endform.
21
22  form s2 using   p1 value(p2) value(p3) p4
23          changing  value(p5) p6.
24     write: / p1, p2, p3, p4, p5, p6.
25     endform.
```

```
26
27 form s3 using  value(p1)
28         changing  p2 value(p3).
29    write: / p1, p2, p3.
30    endform.
```

The code in Listing 18.3 produces the following output:

```
A B C D
A B C D E F
A B C
```

ANALYSIS

- Line 9 passes four parameters to subroutine s1. The syntax on line 17 determines how they are passed. f1 and f3 are passed by reference; f2 is passed by value; f4 is passed by value and result.

- Line 9 passes six parameters to subroutine s2. f1, f4, and f6 are passed by reference; f2 and f3 are passed by value. f5 is passed by value and result.

- Line 12 passes three parameters to subroutine s2. f3 is passed by value, f3 is passed by reference, and f5 is passed by value and result. Although the perform statement only specifies using, the form statement is allowed to differ. It specifies both using and changing. The syntax on the form statement takes precedence and determines the method by which the parameters are passed.

Remember to keep the following things in mind:

- perform and form must contain the same number of parameters.
- The syntax on the perform and form statements can differ.
- The syntax on the form statement alone determines the method by which a parameter is passed.
- The value() addition cannot be used on the perform statement.
- using must come before changing.
- The addition using can only occur once in a statement. The same rule applies to changing.

Using the Methods by Which You Pass Parameters

Table 18.3 briefly describes the three methods of passing parameters.

TABLE 18.3 METHODS OF PASSING PARAMETERS

Method	Description	Advantages
By reference	Passes a pointer to the original memory location.	Very efficient
By value	Allocates a new memory location for use within the subroutine. The memory is freed when the subroutine ends.	Prevents changes to passed variable
By value and result	Similar to pass by value, but the contents of the new memory is copied back into the original memory before returning.	Allows changes and allows a rollback

Passing Parameters by Reference

When you pass a parameter by reference, new memory is not allocated for the value. Instead, a pointer to the original memory location is passed. All references to the parameter are references to the original memory location. Changes to the variable within the subroutine update the original memory location immediately. Figure 18.1 and Listing 18.4 illustrate how this works.

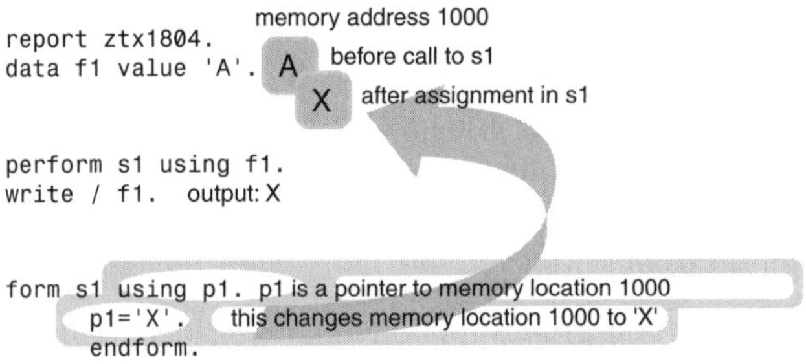

FIGURE 18.1.

How a parameter passed by reference affects the original memory location.

```
                             memory address 1000
report ztx1804.
data f1 value 'A'.    A    before call to s1
                      X    after assignment in s1

perform s1 using f1.
write / f1.   output: X


form s1 using p1.  p1 is a pointer to memory location 1000
    p1='X'.    this changes memory location 1000 to 'X'
    endform.
```

INPUT **LISTING 18.4** EFFECT OF PASS BY REFERENCE

```
1   report ztx1804.
2   data f1 value 'A'.
3
4   perform s1 using f1.
5   write / f1.
6
7   form s1 using p1.
8       p1 = 'X'.
9       endform.
```

The code in Listing 18.4 produces the following output:

OUTPUT X

ANALYSIS
- Line 2 allocates memory for variable f1. For the sake of this example, let's assume the memory location is 1000.
- Line 4 transfers control to line 7.
- Line 7 causes f1 to be passed by reference. Therefore, p1 is a pointer to memory location 1000.
- Line 8 modifies memory location 1000, causing the memory for f1 to change to X.
- Line 9 returns control to line 5.
- Line 5 writes out the value X.

With internal subroutines, there is little difference between passing parameters by reference and accessing global variables from within the subroutine. Both allow you to change the value of a global variable directly. In external subroutines and function modules (see Chapter 19, "Modularization: Function Modules, Part 1") the pass by reference is more useful. Even so, passing parameters to a subroutine—be it internal or external—is good programming style. It makes maintenance easier and improves the readability of your program.

The additions using f1 and changing f1 both pass f1 by reference—they are identical in function. The reason they both exist is that—used properly—they can document whether the subroutine will change a parameter or not.

Code changing with parameters, the subroutine changes. You should code using with parameters that are not changed by the subroutine. Listing 18.5 illustrates this point.

INPUT **LISTING 18.5** using AND changing ARE IDENTICAL IN FUNCTION

```
1   report ztx1805.
2   data: f1 value 'A',
3         f2 value 'B'.
4
5   write: / f1, f2.
6   perform s1 using f1
7            changing f2.
8   write: / f1, f2.
9
10  form s1 using p1
11           changing p2.
12      p1 = p2 = 'X'.
13      endform.
```

18

The code in Listing 18.5 produces the following output:

OUTPUT
A B
X X

ANALYSIS
f1 and f2 are both passed by reference to s1. Therefore, p1 and p2 are pointers to f1 and f2. Changes to p1 and p2 are immediately reflected in f1 and f2. This example only illustrates that it is possible to change any parameter that is passed by reference. You should code your parameters so that using and changing properly document your usage of those parameters.

Passing Parameters by Value

When you pass a parameter by value, new memory is allocated for the value. This memory is allocated when the subroutine is called and is freed when the subroutine returns. Therefore, references to the parameter are thus references to a unique memory area that is known only within the subroutine; the original memory location is separate. The original is unchanged if you change the value of the parameter. Figure 18.2 and Listing 18.6 illustrate how this works.

FIGURE 18.2.

How a parameter passed by value allocates a new storage location independent of the original.

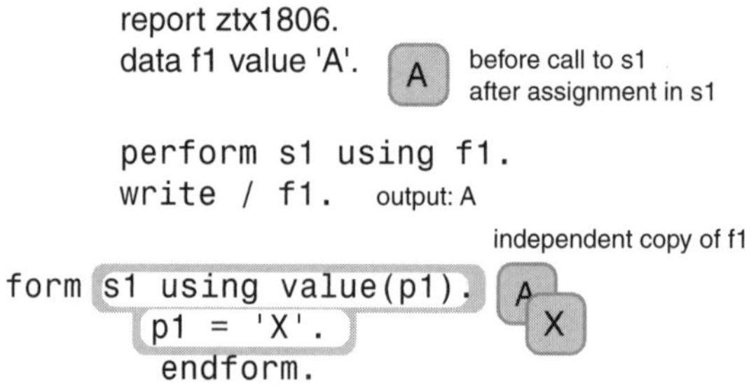

```
report ztx1806.
data f1 value 'A'.      A    before call to s1
                             after assignment in s1

perform s1 using f1.
write / f1.     output: A
                                    independent copy of f1

form s1 using value(p1).    A
     p1 = 'X'.                   X
     endform.
```

INPUT   **LISTING 18.6**   EFFECT OF PASS BY VALUE

```
1   report ztx1806.
2   data: f1 value 'A'.
3
4   perform s1 using f1.
5   write / f1.
6
7   form s1 using value(p1).
8       p1 = 'X'.
9       write / p1.
10      endform.
```

The code in Listing 18.6 produces the following output:

X
A

ANALYSIS

- Line 2 allocates memory for variable f1.
- Line 4 transfers control to line 7.
- Line 7 causes f1 to be passed by value. Therefore, p1 refers to a new memory location that is independent of f1. The value of f1 is automatically copied into the memory for p1.
- Line 8 modifies the memory for p1. f1 is unchanged.
- Line 9 writes out the value X.
- Line 10 returns control to line 5.
- Line 5 writes out the value A.

Use pass by value when you need a local copy of a variable that you can change without affecting the original. Pass by reference is more efficient than pass by value. Use pass by reference unless you need an independent local copy of the variable.

Passing Parameters by Value and Result

Pass by value and result is very similar to pass by value. Like pass by value, a new memory area is allocated and it holds an independent copy of the variable. It is freed when the subroutine ends, and that is also when the difference occurs.

When the endform statement executes, it copies the value of the local memory area back into the original memory area. Changes to the parameter within the subroutine are reflected in the original, but not until the subroutine returns.

This may seem like a small difference, but the difference become greater. You can change whether the copy takes place or not.

The copy always takes place unless you leave the subroutine by using one of two statements:

- stop
- message e*nnn*

The stop statement terminates the subroutine and goes directly to the end-of-selection event. If p1 was passed by value and result, changes to p1 are discarded before end-of-selection is triggered. In a sense, stop behaves like a mini-rollback for value and result parameters. When it is used inside of a subroutine, the stop statement is usually preceded by a test for an abnormal condition within the program. If the abnormal condition arises, `stop` is executed. It discards the changes to value and result variables, and triggers `end-of-selection`, where cleanup procedures are then executed.

Use pass by value and result for parameters you want to change, but there may be a possibility that you will want to discard the changes if an abnormal condition should arise in your subroutine.

> **Note**   The `message` statement and its affect on subroutines is covered in Chapter 21, "Selection Screens."

Figure 18.3 and Listing 18.7 illustrate parameters passed by value and result.

FIGURE 18.3.

How a parameter passed by value and result allocates a new storage location independent of the original and copies the value back in again.

```
report ztx1807.        memory address 1000
data f1 value 'A'.  A     before call to s1
                       X    after return from s1


perform s1 using f1.
write / f1.   output: X


form s1 changing value(p1).
     p1 = 'X'.       A    independent copy of f1
     endform.        X    value copied back at endform
```

INPUT   **LISTING 18.7**   EFFECT OF PASS BY VALUE AND RESULT

```
1    report ztx1807.
2    data: f1 value 'A'.
3
4    perform: s1 changing f1,
5            s2 changing f1.
6
7    end-of-selection.
8        write: / 'Stopped. f1 =', f1.
9
10   form s1 changing value(p1).
11       p1 = 'B'.
12       endform.
13
14   form s2 changing value(p1).
15       p1 = 'X'.
16       stop.
17       endform.
```

The code in Listing 18.7 produces the following output:

OUTPUT   `Stopped. f1 = B`

ANALYSIS

- Line 2 allocates memory for variable `f1`.
- Line 4 transfers control to line 9.
- Line 10 causes `f1` to be passed by value and result. Therefore, `p1` refers to a new memory location that is independent of `f1`. The value of `f1` is automatically copied into the memory for `p1`.
- Line 11 modifies the memory for `p1`. `f1` is unchanged.
- Line 12 copies the value of `p1` back into `f1`, frees `p1`, and transfers control to line 5.
- Line 5 passes control to line 14.
- Line 14 causes `f1` to be passed by value and result. A new memory area is allocated for `p1` and the value of `f1` is copied into it.
- Line 15 changes the value of `p1` to `B`.
- Line 16 issues the `stop` statement. It frees the memory for `p1`, and the changed value is lost. Control transfers to line 7.
- Line 8 writes out the value `B`.

Passing Internal Tables as Parameters

It may be a good idea to review internal tables now, especially the *it[]* syntax.

You can use one of two methods to pass an internal table to a subroutine:

1. Pass with header line
2. Pass body only

If the internal table has a header line, method 1 passes both the header line and the body to the subroutine. Method 2 passes only the body to the subroutine.

If the internal table doesn't have a header line, you can also use both methods. However, method 1 will behave a little differently—it will automatically create a header line for the internal table within the subroutine.

At this point, you may be asking yourself, "Why would I want to pass an internal table without a header line?" Most of the time, you wouldn't. However, if you have a special case that requires an internal table without a header line, you will need to pass it without a header line. You will need to do this if you use nested internal tables—a nested internal table cannot have a header line. Nested internal tables are used more often in release 4, so this technique will be needed more often on newer systems.

18

Table 18.4 summarizes the effect of each of these methods on internal tables with and without header lines.

TABLE 18.4 METHODS AND RESULTS OF PASSING AN INTERNAL TABLE TO A SUBROUTINE

Method	If Internal Table Has a Header Line	If Internal Table Doesn't Have a Header Line
With header line	Passes both	Creates a header line inside subroutine
Without header line	Passes body only	Passes body

Table 18.5 shows the syntax for each method of passing an internal table to a subroutine.

TABLE 18.5 SYNTAX FOR EACH METHOD OF PASSING AN INTERNAL TABLE TO A SUBROUTINE

Method	Syntax	How Passed
With header line	`form s1 tables it`	By reference
Body only	`form s1 using it[]`	By reference
	`form s1 changing it[]`	By reference
	`form s1 using value(it[])`	By value
	`form s1 changing value(it[])`	By value and result

If the internal table has a header line, the first method in Table 18.4 passes both the header and body to the subroutine. The rest of the methods pass the body only.

If the internal table doesn't have a header line, the first method in Table 18.4 passes the body and creates a header line within the subroutine. The rest pass the body only.

Making the Components of an Internal Table Known Within the Subroutine

Merely passing an internal table is usually not enough—you must also describe the structure of the internal table to the subroutine. If you don't describe the structure of the internal table on the `form` statement, the components of the internal table will be unknown within the subroutine. Accessing any component within the subroutine will then result in a syntax error.

The syntax you need depends on the method you use to pass the internal table. Table 18.6 shows the appropriate syntax for each method.

TABLE 18.6   SYNTAX FOR DESCRIBING THE INTERNAL TABLE TO THE SUBROUTINE

Method	Syntax	Valid Values for x
With header line	`tables it structure x`	A field string
		A DDIC structure
		A DDIC table
		An internal table with a header line
	`tables it like x`	An internal table without a header line
		An internal table body (`it[]`)
Without header line	`using it[] like x`	An internal table without header line
		An internal table body (`it[]`)

The `structure` addition expects a field string name after it. Here, code the name of any field string, DDIC structure or table, or the name of an internal table that has a header line.

The `like` addition expects a table body after it. Here, code a reference to the body of an internal table. If the internal table you wish to name here doesn't have a header line, either `it` or `it[]` refers to the body of `it`. If `it` has a header line, only the syntax `it[]` can be used to refer to the body of `it`.

If you pass the body only, you will usually need a work area within the subroutine to add records to and retrieve records from the internal table. To define it, you can use `local`, `data`, or `statics`. If a global work area is already available, you might use that one, although it is less desirable because accessing global variables from within a subroutine makes program maintenance more difficult. If you elect to use the `data` statement to define your work area, the `like line of` *itabbody* addition is available. It defines a field string using only the body of an internal table. The resulting field string is exactly like a line of the internal table body *itabbody*. For example, `data fs like line of it[]` defines a field string named `fs`. It has the same structure as a single row of `it`.

Passing an Internal Table with Header Line

If an internal table has a header line and you want to pass both the header line and the body to a subroutine, use the syntax shown in the first row of Table 18.5. This passes both the header line and the body, and they are both passed by reference. Therefore, changes made to either the header line or body of the internal table within the subroutine are immediately reflected in the original.

18

Listing 18.8 illustrates this syntax.

LISTING 18.8 How to Pass an Internal Table That Has a Header Line with
INPUT Its Header Line

```
1   report ztx1808.
2   * Here, IT is an internal table that has a header line
3   * This program shows how to pass both the header line and body.
4   tables ztxlfa1.
5   data it like ztxlfa1 occurs 5 with header line.
6
7   select * up to 5 rows from ztxlfa1 into table it order by lifnr.
8   perform s1 tables it.
9   loop at it.
10      write / it-lifnr.
11      endloop.
12
13  form s1 tables pt structure ztxlfa1. "uses the field string ztxlfa1
14                                        "here, you can use:
15                  "structure fs     "a field string
16                  "structure ddicst "a ddic structure or table
17                  "structure it     "any internal table with header line
18                  "like it.         "ok if itab doesn't have header line
19                  "like it[].       "any internal table
20      read table pt index 3.
21      pt-lifnr = 'XXX'.
22      modify pt index 3.
23      endform.
```

The code in Listing 18.8 produces the following output:

OUTPUT
```
1000
1010
XXX
1030
1040
```

ANALYSIS
- Line 4 defines a global work area ztxlfa1. This work area is a field string having the same structure as the DDIC table ztxlfa1.

- Line 5 defines internal table it with a header line.

- Line 7 populates the internal table with 5 rows from table ztxlfa1.

- Line 8 transfers control to line 13.

- Line 13 causes the internal table to be passed together with its header line. It is passed by reference, so pt is a pointer to the original. structure is needed to make the structure of the internal table known to the subroutine. Without it, any access to a component of the internal table would cause a syntax error.

- Lines 15 through 19 show the choices available for making the structure `it` known within the subroutine.

- Line 20 reads row 3 from `pt` and places it into the header line. Without the `structure` addition on line 13, this line would have caused a syntax error.

- Line 21 changes the value of `lifnr` in the header line. Since the internal table was passed with header line by reference, this modifies the contents of the original header line.

- Line 22 overwrites row 3 from the header line. Since the internal table was passed by reference, this modifies the contents of the original internal table.

- Line 23 returns control to line 8.

- Lines 9 through 11 write out the contents of the internal table. The output shows that the contents have changed.

If an internal table doesn't have a header line and you want to pass the body and create a header line in the subroutine, you can also use the syntax shown in the first row of Table 18.5. This passes the body by reference, and creates a header line locally in the subroutine. Changes made to the body of the internal table within the subroutine are immediately reflected in the original.

Listing 18.9 illustrates this syntax.

LISTING 18.9 HOW TO PASS AN INTERNAL TABLE WITHOUT A HEADER LINE TO A SUBROUTINE AND AUTOMATICALLY CREATE A HEADER LINE

INPUT

```
1   report ztx1809.
2   * Here, an internal table that doesn't have a header line
3   * is passed with header line
4   tables ztxlfa1.
5   data: it like ztxlfa1 occurs 5.      "doesn't have a header line
6
7   select * up to 5 rows from ztxlfa1 into table it order by lifnr.
8   perform s1 tables it.
9   loop at it into ztxlfa1.              "need to use a work area because it
10      write / ztxlfa1-lifnr.            "doesn't have a header line
11      endloop.
12
13  form s1 tables pt structure ztxlfa1. "or you can use:
14                                        "   like it
15                                        "   like it[]
16      read table pt index 3.
17      pt-lifnr = 'XXX'.
18      modify pt index 3.
19      endform.
```

The code in Listing 18.9 produces the following output:

```
1000
1010
XXX
1030
1040
```

ANALYSIS

- Line 4 defines a global work area ztxlfa1. This work area is a field string having the same structure as the DDIC table ztxlfa1.

- Line 5 defines internal table it without a header line.

- Line 7 populates the internal table with 5 rows from table ztxlfa1.

- Line 8 transfers control to line 13.

- Line 13 causes the body of the internal table to be passed and automatically creates a header line for it. The body is passed by reference, so pt is a pointer to the original body and to the local header line. structure is used to make the structure of the internal table known to the subroutine. Without it, any access to a component of the internal table would cause a syntax error.

- Lines 14 and 15 show the other choices available for making the structure it known within the subroutine.

- Line 16 reads row 3 from pt and places it into the local header line. Without the structure addition on line 13, this line would have caused a syntax error.

- Line 17 changes the value of lifnr in the header line. Because the original internal table doesn't have a header line, this doesn't modify anything outside of the subroutine.

- Line 18 overwrites row 3 from the local header line. Because the internal table was passed by reference, this modifies the contents of the original internal table.

- Line 19 returns control to line 8. The memory for the local header line is freed.

- Lines 9 through 11 write out the contents of the internal table. Because it doesn't have a header line, the field string ztxlfa1 is used as an explicit work area. The output shows that the contents have changed.

If an internal table doesn't have a header line and you want to pass the body without automatically creating a header line in the subroutine, you can use the syntax shown in rows two through five of Table 18.5. By using this syntax, you can pass the body by reference, by value, or by value and result. If you pass it by reference, changes made to the body of the internal table within the subroutine are immediately reflected in the original.

If you pass it by value, a local copy of it is created—changes are discarded at the end of the subroutine when the local memory for it is freed. If you pass it by value and result, changes are copied back into the original when endform is executed. A stop statement within the subroutine will discard all changes to it and transfer control directly to end-of-selection.

Listing 18.10 illustrates these methods.

LISTING 18.10 HOW TO PASS AN INTERNAL TABLE WITHOUT A HEADER LINE TO A SUBROUTINE

```
1   report ztx1810.
2   * Here, an internal table that doesn't have a header line
3   * is passed without creating a header line automatically
4   tables ztxlfa1.
5   data: it like ztxlfa1 occurs 5.          "doesn't have a header line
6
7   select * up to 5 rows from ztxlfa1 into table it order by lifnr.
8   perform: s1 using it,
9            s2 using it,
10           s3 using it,
11           writeitout tables it.
12
13  end-of-selection.
14    write: / 'In End-Of-Selection'.
15    perform writeitout tables it.
16
17  form s1 using value(pt) like it. "pass by value
18  *                     you can also use: like it[].
19     data wa like line of pt.
20  *    you can also use:
21  *       data wa like ztxlfa1.
22  *       data wa like line of pt[].
23  *       local ztxlfa1.            "if you use this, the work area name
24  *                                 "will be ztxlfa1, not wa
25     read table pt into wa index 1.
26     wa-lifnr = 'XXX'.
27     modify pt from wa index 1.
28     endform.
29
30  form s2 using pt like it. "pass by reference
31     data wa like line of pt.
32     read table pt into wa index 2.
33     wa-lifnr = 'YYY'.
34     modify pt from wa index 2.
35     endform.
36
```

18

continues

LISTING **18.10**   CONTINUED

```
37 form s3 changing value(pt) like it. "pass by value and result
38     data wa like line of pt.
39     read table pt into wa index 3.
40     wa-lifnr = 'ZZZ'.
41     modify pt from wa index 3.
42     stop.
43     endform.
44
45 form writeitout tables it structure ztxlfa1.
46     loop at it.
47         write / it-lifnr.
48         endloop.
49     endform.
```

The code in Listing 18.10 produces the following output:

OUTPUT

```
In End-Of-Selection
1000
YYY
1020
1030
1040
```

ANALYSIS
- Line 4 defines a global work area ztxlfa1. This work area is a field string having the same structure as the DDIC table ztxlfa1.

- Line 5 defines internal table it without a header line.

- Line 7 populates the internal table with 5 rows from table ztxlfa1.

- Line 8 transfers control to line 17.

- Line 17 causes the body of the internal table to be passed by value and does not create a header line for it. Pass by value causes a separate copy of the internal table to be created, so pt refers to a local copy of the internal table. like is needed to define pt as an internal table. Without like, pt would be a simple variable and a syntax error would occur.

- Line 18 shows the other choice available for defining pt as an internal table.

- Line 19 defines a local work area wa that has the same structure as a row of pt. Lines 20 through 24 show the other choices available for defining a local work area for pt.

- Line 25 reads row 1 from pt and places it into wa.

- Line 26 changes the value of lifnr in the work area wa.

- Line 27 overwrites row 1 from wa. Since the internal table was passed by value, this modifies the contents of the local copy. The original is unchanged.

- Line 28 returns control to line 8. The memory for pt is freed and the change is lost.

- Line 9 transfers control to line 30.

- Line 30 causes the body of the internal table to be passed by reference and does not create a header line for it. pt now refers to the original. like is needed to define pt as an internal table. Without like, pt would be a simple variable and a syntax error would occur.

- Line 31 defines a local work area wa that has the same structure as a row in pt.

- Line 32 reads row 2 from pt and places it into wa.

- Line 33 changes the value of lifnr in the work area wa.

- Line 34 overwrites row 2 from wa. Since the internal table was passed by reference, this modifies the contents of the original. The original is now changed.

- Line 35 returns control to line 9.

- Line 10 transfers control to line 37.

- Line 37 causes the body of the internal table to be passed by value and result and does not create a header line for it. pt now refers to a copy of the original. like is needed to define pt as an internal table. Without like, pt would be a simple variable, and a syntax error would occur.

- Line 38 defines a local work area wa that has the same structure as a row in pt.

- Line 39 reads row 3 from pt and places it into wa.

- Line 40 changes the value of lifnr in the work area wa.

- Line 41 overwrites row 3 from wa. Since the internal table was passed by value and result, this modifies the contents of the local copy. The original hasn't yet been changed.

- Line 42 bypasses the endform statement—it transfers control directly to line 13. This causes the local copy to be discarded. If the stop statement had not been executed, the endform would have caused the local copy to overwrite the original, and the change would have been kept.

- Line 15 transfers control to line 45.

- Line 45 causes the internal table to be passed by reference and a header line automatically created.

- Lines 46 through 48 write out the contents of the internal table. The only change is in row 2, and was performed in s2.

18

Defining and Calling External Subroutines

NEW TERM An *external subroutine* is one that resides in a different program than the `perform` statement that calls it. Figure 18.4 illustrates an external subroutine.

FIGURE 18.4.

An illustration of an external subroutine.

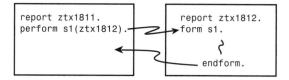

When a `perform` calls an external subroutine

- The external program containing the subroutine is loaded.
- The entire external program is checked for syntax.
- Control transfers to the `form` in the external program.
- The statements within the external subroutine are executed.
- The `endform` transfers control back to the statement following the `perform`.

The fact that the syntax check occurs at runtime is important, for the following two reasons:

- If the formal parameter is typed, a mismatched actual parameter causes a runtime error instead of a syntax error.
- A syntax error anywhere in the external program causes a runtime error, whether it is inside or outside the external subroutine.

External subroutines are very similar to internal subroutines:

- Both allow parameters to be passed.
- Both allow typed formal parameters.
- Both allow parameters to be passed by value, by value and result, and by reference.
- Both allow local variable definitions.

Figure 18.5 illustrates the differences between internal and external subroutines.

FIGURE 18.5.

The differences between internal and external subroutines.

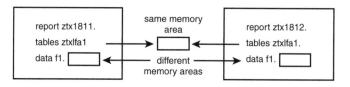

The following are differences between external and internal subroutines:

- A global variable defined by using data is known only within the program that defines it. For example, in Figure 18.5 the data f1 statement appears in both programs. This defines two memory areas named f1. The f1 defined within ztx1811 is only accessible from within ztx1811. The f1 defined within ztx1812 is only accessible from within ztx1812. All references to f1 within ztx1812 are references to the f1 defined within ztx1812.

- A global variable that has the same name in both programs and is defined using the tables statement in both programs is common to both programs. A change to this variable in one program affects the other. In Figure 18.5, the memory area named ztxlfa1 is shared between both programs. Any change to that work area is seen immediately by both programs.

Listings 18.11 and 18.12 illustrate a call to an external subroutine.

INPUT **LISTING 18.11** CALLING THE SUBROUTINE SHOWN IN LISTING 18.12

```
1   report ztx1811.
2   tables ztxlfa1.
3   data    f1(3) value 'AAA'.
4
5   ztxlfa1-lifnr = '1000'.
6   perform s1(ztx1812).
7   write: / 'f1 =', f1,
8          / 'lifnr =', ztxlfa1-lifnr.
```

INPUT **LISTING 18.12** SUBROUTINE CALLED FROM THE PROGRAM IN LISTING 18.11

```
1   report ztx1812.
2   tables ztxlfa1.
3   data    f1(3).
4
5   form s1.
6       f1 = 'ZZZ'.
7       ztxlfa1-lifnr = '9999'.
8       endform.
```

The code in Listing 18.11 produces the following output:

OUTPUT
```
f1 = AAA
lifnr = 9999
```

- In both programs, line 2 defines a global work area ztxlfa1. This work area is shared between both programs.
- In both programs, line 3 defines a global work variable f1. Two independent memory areas are defined, one for each program.
- In ztx1811, line 5 assigns a value of 1000 to ztxlfa1-lifnr.
- In ztx1811, line 6 passes control to line 5 in ztx1812.
- In ztx1812, line 6 assigns ZZZ to the global variable f1 for ztx1812. f1 in ztx1811 is unaffected.
- In ztx1812, line 7 assigns 9999 to ztxlfa1. This affects both programs.
- In ztx1812, line 8 returns control to line 6 in ztx1811.
- In ztx1811, lines 7 and 8 write out the values of f1 and ztxlfa1-lifnr. f1 is unchanged, and lifnr has been changed.

> **Tip**
>
> Use the local statement within external subroutines to avoid sharing tables work areas.

Summary

- Parameters can be passed in three ways: by value, by value and results, and by reference. The syntax on the form statement determines which method is used.
- The body of an internal table can be passed via using or changing. The body (and header line, if present) can be passed via tables. If the internal table doesn't have a header line, tables creates one inside the subroutine.
- To access the components of a field string or subroutine known within the subroutine, the structure must be declared on the form statement.
- External subroutines are very similar to internal subroutines. With external subroutines, variables defined by using data are known only within the program that defines them. Variables having the same name that are defined by using tables are common to both programs.

Q&A

Q **Why do I need to know all of the variations of passing an internal table with header line and without? Don't just a few of these variations cover all circumstances?**

A If you were merely creating programs in ABAP/4, you wouldn't need to know all of these variations. You could code most of your programs with just a few simple variations. However, the majority of an ABAP/4 programmer's time is not usually spent creating ABAP/4 code—it is spent reading it. Passing internal tables to subroutines is a sticky subject, and 80 percent of your time will be spent reading code that does these sticky things—less than 20 percent of your time will be spent creating your own code. This sad imbalance dictates that you must learn the variations used by SAP, so you can spend less time pulling your hair out while trying to understand the SAP code. This will leave you with more time for writing your own code, and more hair.

Workshop

The Workshop provides two ways for you to affirm what you've learned in this chapter. The Quiz section poses questions to help you solidify your understanding of the material covered and the Exercise section provides you with experience in using what you have learned. You can find answers to the quiz questions and exercises in Appendix B, "Answers to Quiz Questions and Exercises."

18

Quiz

1. What are parameters that appear on the `form` statement called?

2. What does passing a variable of the wrong data type or length to a typed parameter cause?

3. When you pass a parameter by reference, is new memory allocated for the value?

4. What effect do the additions `using f1` and `changing f1` have on the way parameters are passed?

Exercise 1

Run the program shown in Listing 18.13. Comment out the parameters statement and run it again. Describe the sequence of events that occur in each case.

LISTING 18.13 EXPLAIN THE SEQUENCE OF EVENTS THAT OCCURS IN THIS PROGRAM

```
report ztx1813 no standard page heading.
ztx1813 data: flag,
      ctr type i.

parameters p1.

initialization.
  flag = 'I'.
  write: / 'in Initialization'.

start-of-selection.
  flag = 'S'.
  write: / 'in Start-Of-Selection',
         / 'p1 =', p1.

top-of-page.
   add 1 to ctr.
   write: / 'Top of page, flag =', flag, 'ctr =', ctr.
   uline.
```

DAY **19**

Modularization: Function Modules, Part 1

After you complete this chapter, you will be able to:

- Understand and use the `include` statement
- Create function groups and function modules
- Define import, export, and changing parameters

Using the `include` Statement

NEW TERM   An *include program* is a program in which the contents are designed to be used by another program. It is not usually complete all by itself. Instead, other programs use the code the include program contains by copying the lines of code from the include program into themselves. The copy is performed at runtime via the `include` statement. An include program is also known as an *included program*.

| New Term | A program that includes another is known as an *including program*. |

Syntax for the `include` Statement

The following is the syntax for the `include` statement.

```
include ipgm.
```

where:

▲

- *ipgm* is a type i program.

The following points apply:

- An include program must be type i. You specify the program type in the Type field on the Program Attributes screen when you create the program.
- An include program can be included into one or more including programs.
- A type i program cannot contain partial or incomplete statements.

The `include` statement copies the contents of the include program into the including program. The code from the include program is copied as-is and replaces the `include` statement at the time of program generation. Figure 19.1 illustrates the `include` statement.

FIGURE 19.1.

An illustration of the `include` *statement.*

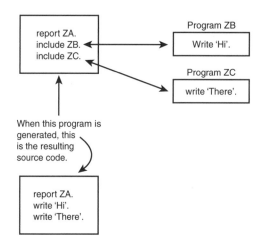

In Figure 19.1, za is the including program. The include programs are zb and zc. At the time za is generated, the source code for zb and zc is inserted into za, making the program shown at the bottom of the figure.

Listings 19.1 through 19.3 illustrate include programs.

INPUT   **LISTING 19.1**   AN INCLUDING PROGRAM

```
1  report ztx1901 no standard page heading.
2  tables: ztxlfa1, ztxlfb1.
3  parameters p_lifnr like ztxlfa1-lifnr obligatory default '1000'.
4
5  include: ztx1902,
6          ztx1903.
7
8  top-of-page.
9      write: / 'Company Codes for Vendor', p_lifnr.
10     uline.
```

INPUT   **LISTING 19.2**   THIS PROGRAM IS INCLUDED INTO ztx1901

```
1  ***INCLUDE ZTX1902.
2  select single * from ztxlfa1 where lifnr = p_lifnr.
```

INPUT   **LISTING 19.3**   THIS PROGRAM IS ALSO INCLUDED INTO ztx1901

```
1  ***INCLUDE ZTX1903.
2  select * from ztxlfb1 where lifnr = ztxlfa1-lifnr.
3      write: / ztxlfb1-bukrs.
4      endselect.
```

The code in Listings 19.1 through 19.3 produces this output:

OUTPUT
```
Company Codes for Vendor 1000
-------------------------------
1000
3000
```

19

ANALYSIS
- At generation time for ztx1901, line 5 copies the code from program ztx1902 into ztx1901. The inserted code replaces line 5.

- Still during program generation of ztx1901, line 6 copies the code from program ztx1903 into ztx1901. The inserted code replaces line 6.

- When the program runs, ztx1901 behaves like a single program, as if those lines of code from the included programs had been typed directly into ztx1901.

SAP uses includes to reduce code redundancy and to divide very large programs into smaller units.

Tip

> While viewing an including program, you can view the contents of an
> included program simply by double-clicking on its name. For example, while
> editing ztx1901 from the ABAP/4 Editor: Edit Program screen, double-click
> on the name ztx1902 or ztx1903. The included program will be displayed
> immediately.

Tip

> If you want to see the resulting code with all includes expanded in-line, run
> program RSINCL00. On the selection screen for RSINCL00, in the Program
> field, enter the name of a program that includes other programs. Place an X
> in the Program Source Code and Expand Include Lines fields and press
> Execute. A list of the resulting source code will be displayed on the next
> screen.

Introducing Function Modules

NEW TERM   A *function module* is the last of the four main ABAP/4 modularization units. It is
very similar to an external subroutine in these ways:

- Both exist within an external program.
- Both enable parameters to be passed and returned.
- Parameters can be passed by value, by value and result, or by reference.

The major differences between function modules and external subroutines are the following:

- Function modules have a special screen used for defining parameters—parameters
  are not defined via ABAP/4 statements.
- tables work areas are *not* shared between the function module and the calling program.
- Different syntax is used to call a function module than to call a subroutine.
- Leaving a function module is accomplished via the raise statement instead of
  check, exit, or stop.

A function module name has a practical minimum length of three characters and a maximum length of 30 characters. Customer function modules must begin with *Y_* or *Z_*. The
name of each function module is unique within the entire R/3 system.

Understanding Function Groups

As stated before, a function group is a program that contains function modules. With each R/3 system, SAP supplies more than 5,000 pre-existing function groups. In total, they contain more than 30,000 function modules. If the functionality you require is not already covered by these SAP-supplied function modules, you can also create your own function groups and function modules.

 Each function group is known by a four-character identifier called a *function group ID*. If you create your own function group, you must choose a function group ID that begins with *Y* or *Z*. The ID must be exactly four characters long and cannot contain blanks or special characters.

> **Caution**
>
> On releases prior to 3.0F, the R/3 system enables you to specify a function group ID of fewer than four characters or to use spaces within it. However, you should not do this because the tools that manipulate function modules will behave erratically with such a function group.

To illustrate function groups, I will briefly describe the process of creating a function group and a function module within it. Let's assume that neither the function group nor the function module yet exist.

You begin by creating a function module. When you create a function module, the system will first ask you for a function group ID. This ID tells the system where to store the function module.

When you supply the ID, and if it doesn't yet exist, the system creates:

- A main program
- A top `include`
- A UXX `include`
- A function module `include`

Collectively, these components are known as the function group. Their relationships are illustrated in Figure 19.2.

The name of the main program will be `saplfgid`, where `fgid` is your four-character function group ID. The system automatically places two `include` statements into it:

- `include lfgidtop.`
- `include lfgiduxx.`

FIGURE 19.2.

This is the hierarchical relationship of the components of a function group.

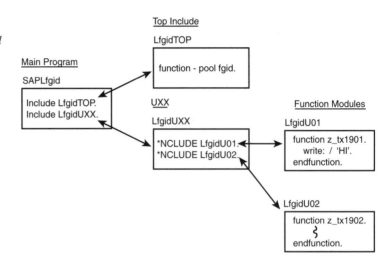

<image name="NEW TERM"></image> The first include program—lfgidtop—is known as the *top include*. Within it you can place global data definitions. These are data definitions that are global to all function modules within the group.

<image name="NEW TERM"></image> The second include program—lfgiduxx—is known as the *UXX*. You are not allowed to modify the UXX. The system will automatically place an include statement in the UXX for each function module you create in this function group. For the first function module, the statement include lfgidu01 will be inserted into the UXX. When you create a second function module in this group, the system will add a second statement: include lfgidu02. Each time you add a new function module to the group, the system will add a new include statement to the UXX. The number of the include will be 01 for the first function module created within the group, 02 for the second, 03 for the third, and so on.

Within each include mentioned in the UXX is the source code for a function module.

Accessing the Function Library

<image name="NEW TERM"></image> Function groups are stored in a group of tables within the database called the *function library*. By accessing the function library, you can also access the tools by which you manipulate function modules and groups. To access the function library from the Development Workbench, press the Function Library button on the Application toolbar. The transaction code is SE37.

Each of the components of a function group can be accessed from the Function Library Initial Screen shown in Figure 19.3.

FIGURE 19.3.

The Function Library Initial Screen.

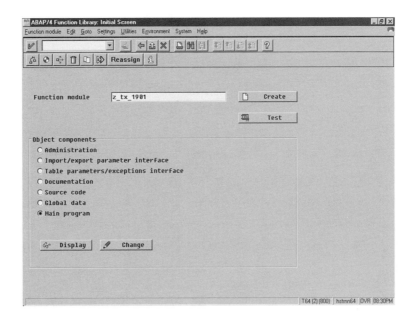

For example, to access the main program of the function group, choose the Main Program radio button and then press the Display pushbutton. The main program of function group ztxa is shown in Figure 19.4.

FIGURE 19.4.

The main program of function group ztxa.

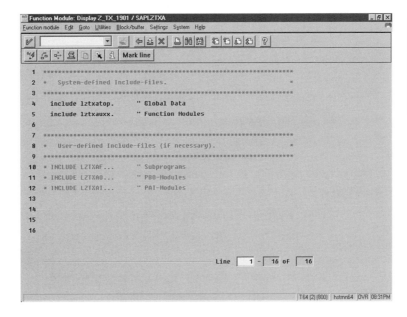

Figure 19.5 shows the UXX for function group ztxa.

FIGURE 19.5.

The UXX for function group ztxa.

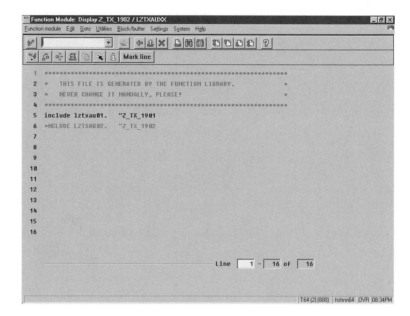

In Figure 19.5, you can see that function group ztxa contains two function modules: z_tx_1901 and z_tx_1902. The first one is active, the second is not (its name is commented out).

Activating a Function Module

A function module must be *activated* before it can be called. There is an Activate button on the Function Library Initial Screen. Pressing it activates the function module.

When the function module is first created, the include statement for it within the UXX is commented out. Activating the function module causes the system to remove the comment from the include statement. The function module is then available to be called from other programs. If you change the code within the function module, it doesn't need to be activated again. On the other hand, re-activating won't do any harm, either.

If you want, you can deactivate a function module. From the ABAP/4 Function Library: Initial Screen, choose the menu path Function Module->Deactivate. Choosing this menu path comments out the include statement for that function module within the UXX.

All the function modules that belong to a single group exist within the main program: sapl*fgid*. Because of that, a syntax error in any one of these function modules will cause the rest to become inoperative; executing any one of them will result in a syntax error. The Activate and Deactivate functions enable you to work on any single function module of a group without affecting the rest. You can deactivate a function module before you work on it, change the code, and then perform a syntax check on that single module before reactivating it. In that way, the rest of the function modules can still be called, even while you are working on one of them.

Defining Data within a Function Module

Data definitions within function modules are similar to those of subroutines.

Within a function module, use the `data` statement to define local variables that are reinitialized each time the function module is called. Use the `statics` statement to define local variables that are allocated the first time the function module is called. The value of a static variable is remembered between calls.

Define parameters within the function module interface to create local definitions of variables that are passed into the function module and returned from it (see the next section).

You cannot use the `local` statement within a function module. Instead, globalized interface parameters serve the same purpose. See the following section on defining global data to learn about local and global interface parameters.

Defining the Function Module Interface

NEW TERM To pass parameters to a function module, you must define a *function module interface*. The function module interface is the description of the parameters that are passed to and received from the function module. It is also simply known as the *interface*. In the remainder of this chapter, I will refer to the function module interface simply as the interface.

To define parameters, you must go to one of two parameter definition screens:

- Import/Export Parameter Interface
- Table Parameters/Exceptions Interface

The Import/Export Parameter Interface screen is shown in Figure 19.6. On this screen you can define the following:

- Import parameters
- Export parameters
- Changing parameters

19

FIGURE 19.6.

The Import/Export Parameter Interface screen.

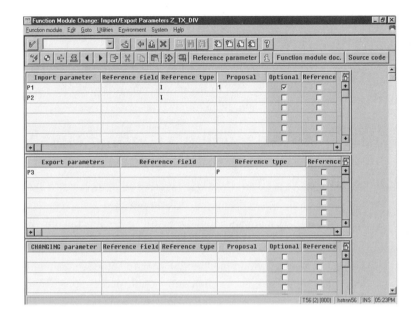

The Table Parameters/Exceptions Interface screen is shown in Figure 19.7. On this screen you can:

- Define internal table parameters
- Document exceptions

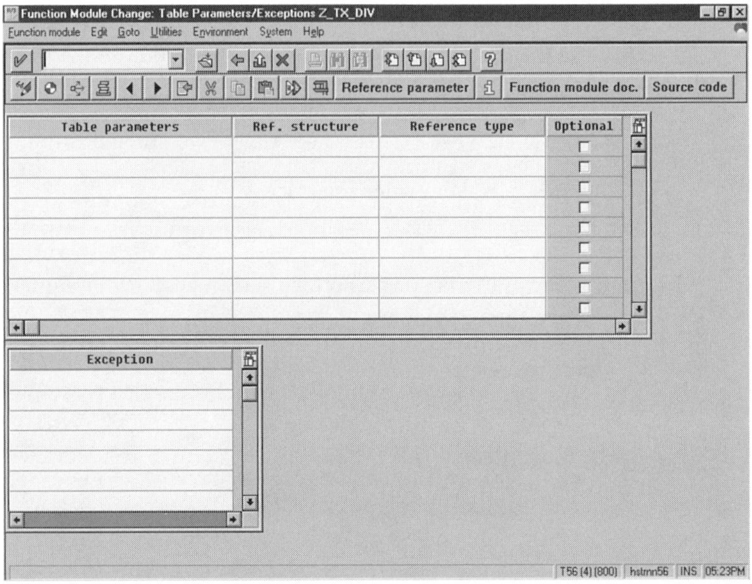

FIGURE 19.7.

The Table Parameters/Exceptions Interface screen.

You enter the name of the parameter in the first column and the attributes of the parameter in the remaining columns. Enter one parameter per row.

NEW TERM *Import parameters* are variables or field strings that contain values passed into the function module from the calling program. These values originate outside of the function module and they are imported into it.

NEW TERM *Export parameters* are variables or field strings that contain values returned from the function module. These values originate within the function module and they are exported out of it.

NEW TERM *Changing parameters* are variables or field strings that contain values that are passed into the function module, changed by the code within the function module, and then returned. These values originate outside the function module. They are passed into it, changed, and passed back.

NEW TERM *Table parameters* are internal tables that are passed to the function module, changed within it, and returned. The internal tables must be defined in the calling program.

NEW TERM An *exception* is a name for an error that occurs within a function module. Exceptions are described in detail in the following section.

Passing Parameters

The methods for passing parameters to function modules are very similar to those for passing parameters to external subroutines.

By default:

- Import and export parameters are passed by value.
- Changing parameters are passed by value and result.
- Internal tables are passed by reference.

You can cause import, export, and changing parameters to be passed by reference by placing a tickmark in the Reference check box on the Import/Export Parameters screen (refer to Figure 19.6).

19

Note The concept of an export parameter being passed by value is a little strange for most programmers. Think of it this way: When passed by value, the memory for an export parameter is defined within the function module. The endfunction statement copies the value of the export parameter from within the function module to the variable assigned to it in the calling program.

> If the endfunction statement is not executed (for example, if you leave the function module abnormally via the raise statement), the value is not copied and the caller's variable remains unchanged.

Using Typed and Untyped Parameters

Like subroutines, function module parameters can be typed or untyped. Typing works the same way for function modules as it does for subroutines. Untyped parameters adopt all of their technical characteristics from the passing parameter. For example, if the passed parameter is type c length 12 and the function module parameter is untyped, the function module parameter becomes type c length 12.

Typed parameters for function modules follow the same rules as typed parameters for subroutines. There are two ways of specifying typed parameters in the Import/Export Parameters screen:

- By specifying an ABAP/4 data type in the Reference Type column
- By specifying the name of a DDIC structure or component of a DDIC structure in the Reference Field column

You cannot use both of these methods at the same time for a single parameter. You must use either one or the other.

Using the first method, simply specify an ABAP/4 data type in the Reference Type column on the Import/Export Parameters screen. For example, in Figure 19.8, p1 and p2 are typed parameters that have an ABAP/4 data type of i (integer). P3 is also typed, having a data type of p. Type i is a fixed length data type and so has a length of 4. Type p is a variable length data type, and takes its length and number of decimal places from the parameter that is passed to it.

Using the second method, enter the name of a Data Dictionary structure in the Reference Field column. The parameters are defined as if you had used the like addition on the form statement in an external subroutine.

Parameters can also be made optional and given default values. To make an import parameter optional, place a tickmark in the Optional column (refer to Figure 19.7). If you make an import parameter optional, you do not have to name it on the call function statement when you call the function module. Export parameters are always optional. By that, I mean that you are not required to code any export parameters on the call function statement. For example, if function module z_xyz returns three export parameters, e1, e2, and e3, and you only want e2, then only code e2 on the call function statement. Simply omit the rest.

To give an import parameter a default value, enter a value in the Proposal column, making sure to enclose character values within single quotes. sy variable names are also allowed. If you specify a proposal, the system will automatically place a tickmark in the Optional column.

All parameters that you define in the interface also appear at the top of the source code within special comments. Each special comment line begins with the characters *". Each time you change the interface the system automatically updates these special comments to reflect your changes.

Caution

Don't change or delete these comments; they are generated by the system. If you change them, the function module might not work.

In Figure 19.8, you can see that p1, p2, and p3 are passed by value.

FIGURE 19.8.

The system-generated comments at the top of the source code.

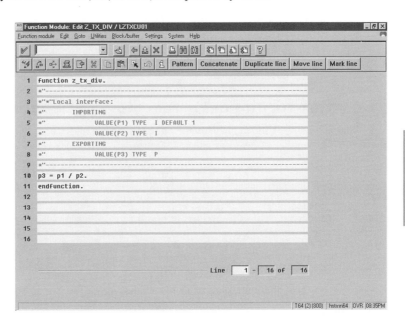

19

Calling Function Modules

To call a function module, you code the call function statement. The flow of control is within Listing 19.4.

LISTING 19.4   THIS PROGRAM PERFORMS A SIMPLE CALL TO A FUNCTION MODULE

```
1  report ztx1904.
2
3  write: / 'Before Call'.
4  call function 'Z_TX_1901'.
5  write: / 'After Call'.
```

The code in Listing 19.4 produces this output:

OUTPUT
```
Before Call
Hi from Z_TX_1901
After Call
```

ANALYSIS
- Line 4 transfers control to the beginning of function module z_tx_1901. In this example, the function module exists within the function group ztxa. saplztxa is the main program of this function group and acts as the container for z_tx_1901.

- The code within the function module executes.

- The last line of the function module returns control to the call function statement. Processing continues with the next statement after call function.

Syntax for the `call function` Statement

The following is the syntax for the call function statement.

```
call function 'F'
    [exporting   p1 = v1 ...  ]
    [importing   p2 = v2 ...  ]
    [changing    p3 = v3 ...  ]
    [tables      p4 = it ...  ]
    [exceptions  x1 = n [others = n]].
```

where:

- F is the function module name.
- *p1* through *p4* are parameter names defined in the function module interface.
- *v1* through *v3* are variable or field string names defined within the calling program.
- *it* is an internal table defined within the calling program.
- *n* is any integer literal; *n* cannot be a variable.
- *x1* is an exception name raised within the function module.

The following points apply:

- All additions are optional.
- `call function` is a single statement. Do not place periods or commas after parameters or exception names.
- The function module name must be coded in uppercase. If it is coded in lowercase, the function will not be found and a short dump will result.

Use the `call function` statement to transfer control to a function module and specify parameters. Figure 19.9 illustrates how parameters are passed to and received from the function module.

FIGURE 19.9.

This figure illustrates how parameters are passed to and received from the function module.

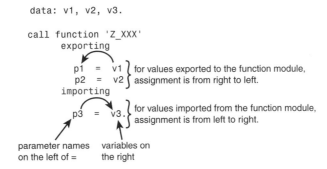

On the `call function` statement, exports and imports are from the point of view of the program. Values that are exported by `call function` are imported by the function module. Values exported from the function module are imported by the `call function` statement.

On the left of the assignment operator (=) is a list of the parameter names defined in the function module's interface. On the right are variables defined within the calling program. Assignments after `exporting` proceed from right-to-left. Assignments after `importing` proceed from left-to-right. Assignments after `changing` and `tables` are bidirectional. Before the call, the assignment is from right-to-left. On return, the return value is assigned from left-to-right.

Let's use Figure 19.9 as an example. When you call function module Z_XXX, the value of variable v1 is assigned to parameter p1 and the value of variable v2 is assigned to p2. Control then transfers to the function module. On return, the value of p3 is assigned to v3.

19

Note   In this book, the term "import parameters" by itself (without reference to whether it is from the point of view of the program or function module) refers to parameters imported into the function module. The term "export parameters" without a reference refers to parameters exported from the function module.

Running a Sample Function Module

In this section I will illustrate a call to a sample function module z_tx_div, which simply divides two numbers and returns the result of the division.

Listing 19.5 calls z_tx_div and passes parameters. Figure 19.7 shows the Import/Export Parameters screen for this function module, and Listing 19.6 shows the source code for it.

INPUT   **LISTING 19.5**   USING THE call function STATEMENT WITH PARAMETERS

```
1  report ztx1905.
2  parameters: op1 type i default 2,    "operand 1
3              op2 type i default 3.    "operand 2
4  data rslt type p decimals 2.         "result
5
6  call function 'Z_TX_DIV'
7        exporting
8             p1      = op1
9             p2      = op2
10       importing
11            p3      = rslt.
12
13 write: / op1, '/', op2, '=', rslt.
```

INPUT   **LISTING 19.6**   THE SOURCE CODE FOR THE z_tx_div FUNCTION MODULE

```
1  function z_tx_div.
2  *"----------------------------------------------------------
3  *"*"Local interface:
4  *"       IMPORTING
5  *"             VALUE(P1)  TYPE   I DEFAULT 1
6  *"             VALUE(P2)  TYPE   I
7  *"       EXPORTING
8  *"             VALUE(P3)  TYPE   P
9  *"----------------------------------------------------------
10 p3 = p1 / p2.
11 endfunction.
```

The code in Listing 19.6 is called from line 6 of Listing 19.5.

The code in Listing 19.5 produces this output:

OUTPUT

```
2  /          3  =              0.67
```

ANALYSIS

- In Listing 19.5, lines 2 and 3 define two variables, op1 and op2. Because these are defined using the `parameters` statement, the user is prompted for values for these variables when the program executes.

- Line 4 defines a variable named `rslt` type p with two decimal places.

- Line 6 transfers control to function module Z_TX_DIV. The value of variable op1 is assigned to import parameter p1 and the value of op2 is assigned to import parameter p2. In the Export/Import Parameters screen, a Reference Type is specified for these parameters, which makes them typed parameters. Because these parameters are typed, they do not obtain their technical attributes from p1 and p2. Instead, the data types of op1 and op2 must match the data types of p1 and p2. op1 and op2 are defined as integers, therefore the data types match. P3 is type p; it is a partially typed parameter. It obtains its length and number of decimals from `rslt`. The values of op1 and op2 are transferred to the function module and control transfers to line 1 of Listing 19.6.

- In Listing 19.6, line 10 performs a simple division.

- The function module returns control to line 6 of Listing 19.5. The value of p3 is assigned to variable `rslt`.

- Line 13 writes out the result of the division.

19

Tip

> Press the Pattern button on the ABAP/4 Editor: Edit Program screen to automatically insert the `call function` statement into your code. You will be asked for the function module name and it automatically codes the left-hand side of all interface parameter assignments for you.

Creating a Function Module

Use the following procedure to create a function module. For an exercise, follow this procedure and create a function module exactly like z_tx_div. Call yours z_••div, and put it in function group z••a (remember to replace the •• with the two characters that you are using to identify your programs).

SCREENCAM Start the ScreenCam "How to Create a Function Module" now.

1. From the ABAP/4 Development Workbench screen, press the Function Library button on the Application toolbar. The Function Library Initial Screen is shown (refer to Figure 19.3).

2. Type the name of your function module in the Function Module field. The name must begin with *Y_* or *Z_*.

3. Press the Create button. The Function Module Create: Administration screen is shown (see Figure 19.10).

4. Type the name of a function group in the Function Group field. The function group name must be four characters long and must begin with *Y* or *Z*.

5. Type an **S** in the Application field. This field is used to indicate which function area uses the function module. Our functionality is not used by any functional area, it is simply an example, so any choice will do. (S indicates that the function module contains functionality needed by Basis.)

6. Type a description of the function module in the Short Text field. The contents of this field are seen when displaying a list of function modules.

7. Press the Save button on the Application toolbar.

8. If the function group does not already exist, a pop-up informs you of that fact and asks you if you want to create it. Press the Yes button to create the function group. The Create Function Group dialog box appears. Type a description in the Short Text field and press the Save button. The Create Object Catalog Entry screen appears. Press the Local Object button. You are returned to the Function Module Change: Administration screen.

9. Press the Source Code button on the Application toolbar. The Function Module Edit screen is displayed (refer to Figure 19.8).

10. Type the source code for your function module. Do not change the system-generated comment lines under any circumstances! Your function module might fail to operate if you do.

11. Press the Save button on the Application toolbar. The message `Program xxxxx saved` appears in the status bar at the bottom of the window.

12. Press the Back button on the Application toolbar. You are returned to the Function Library Initial screen.

13. If you want to define import or export parameters, select the Import/Export Parameter Interface radio button. Press the Change pushbutton. You are shown the Import/Export Parameters screen (refer to Figure 19.6). Type the names of your

parameters in the first column and enter any other desired characteristics for each parameter. When you are finished, press the Save button and then the Back button.

14. Finally, to activate your function module, press the Activate button on the Application toolbar of the Function Library Initial Screen.

FIGURE 19.10.

This is the Function Module Create: Administration screen.

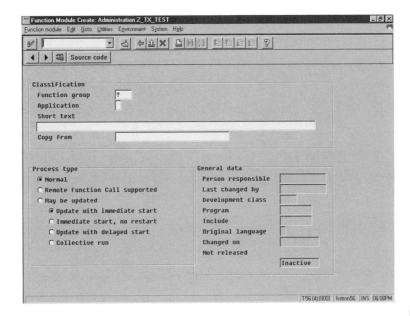

Now would be a good time to create an ABAP/4 program to call your function module and try it out. Create a program like the one shown in Listing 19.5. Within your program, be sure to code the function module name in uppercase. If you don't, you will get a short dump because the system won't be able to find the function module.

19

Tip

Use the Object Browser to list the function modules you have created. From the Object browser, choose Local Priv. Objects and press the Display pushbutton.

Summary

- You can use the `include` statement to segregate your code into smaller, more manageable chunks. Include programs have a program type of `i`. Their code is copied into the including program at the point of the `include` statement and completely replaces it.

- Function modules are modularization units with unique names that can be called from any program in the entire R/3 system. They hold code that is used by more than one program.

- A function group is a collection of programs and has a predefined structure. The names of all programs within the group all contain the four-character function group ID.

- The interface of a function module contains the definitions for importing, exporting, and changing parameters, as well as the documentation for exceptions raised within the function module.

- Typed and untyped parameters can be specified and they can be passed by reference, by value, or by value and result.

Do	Don't
DO use pass-by-reference for import parameters. It is more efficient. Be careful when using it with export parameters. The values of by-reference parameters are changed immediately in the caller. If you change export parameters before you issue the raise statement, you will return but the values will already be changed in the calling program. **DO** document all exceptions in the function module interface and document all parameters in the Documentation component of the function module. **DO** save your test data so that you can retest your function module after modifications using the same data.	**DON'T** change the system-generated comments at the top of the function module source code. **DON'T** import values that you don't need from a function module. Simply omit unneeded imports from the call function statement. **DON'T** use stop, exit, or check within a function module. (check and exit are okay if they are within a loop inside of the function module.)

Q&A

Q How do I decide whether to use an `include`, an internal subroutine, an external subroutine, or a function module to implement my code?

A If the code will not be used by any other programs, then use an internal subroutine. If the code might be useful to other programs, use a function module. You should not create external subroutines. They were only covered in the previous chapter so that you would know how to use them because there are still many in use in the

R/3 system. It's also easier to understand function modules if you know how external subroutines work. Instead of external subroutines, use function modules. `includes` should be used to simplify your program structure and group similar components together. They should not be used as containers for reusable code that is included into multiple programs. For example, you might put all of your data declarations into one `include`, your events into another, your subroutines into a third, and your calls to function modules into a fourth.

Q **How do I decide which function group to put a new function module into? When should I create a new one, and when should I reuse an existing one?**

A Put function modules that have similar functionality into the same function group. For example, you might put all of the function modules that calculate depreciation into one function group, all that perform calendar functions into another function group, and those that provide external communication interfaces into a third.

Workshop

The Workshop provides two ways for you to affirm what you've learned in this chapter. The Quiz section poses questions to help you solidify your understanding of the material covered and the Exercise section provides you with experience in using what you have learned. You can find answers to the quiz questions and exercises in Appendix B, "Answers to Quiz Questions and Exercises."

Quiz

1. True or False: An import parameter that has a proposal is always optional.
2. True or False: All export parameters are optional.

Exercise 1

Use the Test function within the Function Library to test the function module POPUP_WITH_TABLE_DISPLAY. After testing this function module, look at the following program and predict its behavior.

```
report ztx1910.
data: begin of it occurs 5,
        data(10),
      end of it,
      result(10).

perform: fill_table tables it,
         call_fm tables it changing result.
write: / 'Result=', result.
```

```
form fill_table tables it like it.
    move 'Select' to it-data. append it.
    move 'One'    to it-data. append it.
    move 'Option' to it-data. append it.
endform.

form call_fm tables it changing result.
    call function 'POPUP_WITH_TABLE_DISPLAY'
      importing
        endpos_col   = 30
        endpos_row   = 30
        startpos_col = 1
        startpos_row = 1
        titletext    = 'Look Ma, a Window'
      exporting
          choise     = result
      tables
          valuetab   = it.
endform.
```

DAY **20**

Modularization: Function Modules, Part 2

After you complete this chapter, you will be able to:

- Understand the components and structure of a function group
- Define global data and subroutines within a function group

Defining Global Data for Function Modules

NEW TERM Two types of *global data* can be defined for a function module:

- Data definitions placed in the top include are accessible from all function modules and subroutines within the group. This type of global data is persistent across function module calls.

- Data definitions within the interface are known only within the function module. If the interface is defined as a *global interface*, the parameter definitions are also known within all subroutines that the function module calls. This type of global data is not persistent across function module calls.

The global data defined within the top include is accessible from all function modules within the group. It is analogous to the global data definitions at the top of an ABAP/4 program.

The parameters defined within a *global interface* are accessible from all subroutines called from the function module. It is analogous to variables defined within a subroutine using the locals statement.

The parameters defined within a *local interface* are inaccessible from subroutines called from the function module. It is analogous to variables defined within a subroutine using the data statement. By default, interfaces are local.

To make an interface global, from the Function Module Change: Import/Export Parameters screen, choose the menu path Edit->Globalize Parameters. To make it local again, choose the menu path Edit->Localize Parameters.

Caution

If a parameter with the same name exists in two function modules within a group and both interfaces are global, the data definitions of both of these parameters must be identical.

Global data defined within the top include is allocated when a program makes its first call to any function module of a group. It remains allocated as long as the calling program remains active. Each subsequent call to a function module within the same group sees the previous values within the global data area. The values in the global data area persist until the calling program ends.

Global data defined by making the interface global is reinitialized each time the function module is called.

Listings 20.1 through 20.4 illustrate the persistence of global data defined within the top include.

INPUT   **LISTING 20.1**   THIS PROGRAM ILLUSTRATES THE PERSISTENCE OF GLOBAL DATA

```
1 report ztx2001.
2 parameters parm_in(10) default 'XYZ' obligatory.
3 data f1(10) value 'INIT'.
4
```

```
 5 perform: call_fm12,
 6           call_fm13.
 7 write: / 'f1 =', f1.
 8
 9 *_____
10 form call_fm12.
11   call function 'Z_TX_2002'
12        exporting
13             p_in    = parm_in
14        exceptions
15             others  = 1.
16   endform.
17
18 *_____
19 form call_fm13.
20   call function 'Z_TX_2003'
21        importing
22             p_out   = f1
23        exceptions
24             others  = 1.
25   endform.
```

INPUT **LISTING 20.2** THIS IS THE SOURCE CODE OF THE FIRST FUNCTION MODULE CALLED FROM LISTING 20.1

```
1  function z_tx_2002.
2  *"-----------------------------------------------------------
3  *"*"Local interface:
4  *"        IMPORTING
5  *"             VALUE(P_IN)
6  *"-----------------------------------------------------------
7  g1 = p_in.
8  endfunction.
```

INPUT **LISTING 20.3** THIS IS THE SOURCE CODE OF THE SECOND FUNCTION MODULE CALLED FROM LISTING 20.1

```
1  function z_tx_2003.
2  *"-----------------------------------------------------------
3  *"*"Local interface:
4  *"        EXPORTING
5  *"             VALUE(P_OUT)
6  *"-----------------------------------------------------------
7  p_out = g1.
8  endfunction.
```

20

INPUT

LISTING 20.4 THIS IS THE TOP include FOR THE FUNCTION GROUP ztxb—
ztxb CONTAINS THE FUNCTION MODULES SHOWN IN LISTINGS 20.2 AND 20.3

```
1  function-pool ztxb.
2  data g1(10).
```

The code in Listings 20.1 through 20.4 produce this output:

OUTPUT   f1 = XYZ

ANALYSIS
- In Listing 20.1, line 5 transfers control to line 10, and line 11 calls function module z_tx_2002, which exists in function group ztxb. The value of parm_in is passed to p_in. Control transfers to line 1 of Listing 20.2.

- In Listing 20.2, line 7 moves the value from p_in to the global variable g1. g1 is defined in the top include on line 2 of in Listing 20.14. That makes it visible to all function modules, and the value is persistent between calls to function modules of that group. Control returns to line 11 of Listing 20.1.

- In Listing 20.1, line 16 transfers control to line 5, then line 6, and then line 19. Line 20 calls function module z_tx_2003, which also exists in function group ztxb. Control transfers to line 1 of Listing 20.3.

- In Listing 20.3, line 7 moves the value from the global variable g1 to p_out. g1 still contains the value placed in it by the previous function module. Control returns to the calling program and the value is written out.

Passing an Internal Table to a Function Module

Passing an internal table to a function module follows the same rules as that of passing an internal table to a subroutine. There are two methods:

- Via the tables portion of the interface. This is equivalent to passing it via the tables addition to the perform statement.

- Via the importing or changing portion of the interface. The first is equivalent to using on the perform statement and the last is equivalent to changing on perform.

To return an internal table that originates from within a function module, use one of the following:

- The tables portion of the interface

- The exporting portion of the interface

Passing an Internal Table Via `tables`

If you use the `tables` portion of the interface, you can pass the internal table together with the header line. If it doesn't have a header line, it will automatically acquire one within the function module. `tables` parameters are always passed by reference.

To use this method, from the Function Library Initial Screen, choose the Table Parameters/Exceptions Interface radio button and then press the Change pushbutton. You will see the Table Parameters/Exceptions screen. In the upper-half of the screen under the Table Parameters column, type the names of internal table parameters.

If the internal table is a structured type, in the Ref. Structure column, you can optionally type the name of a DDIC structure. Only DDIC structure names can be entered here. If you don't specify a DDIC structure here, you will not be able to access any of the components of the internal table within the function module. To do so will cause a syntax error.

If the internal table is not a structured type, you can enter an ABAP/4 data type in the Reference Type column instead.

Passing an Internal Table Via `exporting`/`importing` and `changing`

If you use the `exporting`/`importing` or `changing` part of the interface, you can pass the body of an internal table only. However, these parts of the interface enable you to choose whether to pass the internal table body by value (the default) or by reference. When using this method, you must specify `table` in the Reference Type column.

Figures 20.1 and 20.2 and Listings 20.5 and 20.6 illustrate the ways of passing internal tables to a function module.

INPUT   **LISTING 20.5**   THIS PROGRAM PASSES INTERNAL TABLES TO A FUNCTION MODULE

20

```
 1 report ztx2005.
 2 tables ztxlfa1.
 3 data: it_a like ztxlfa1 occurs 3,   "doesn't have a header line
 4       it_b like ztxlfa1 occurs 3.   "doesn't have a header line
 5 select * up to 3 rows from ztxlfa1 into table it_a.
 6
 7 call function 'Z_TX_2006'
 8      exporting
 9           it1    = it_a[]
10      importing
11           it2    = it_b[]
```

continues

LISTING 20.5 CONTINUED

```
12      tables
13          it4     = it_a
14      changing
15          it3     = it_a[]
16      exceptions
17          others  = 1.
18
19 write: / 'AFTER CALL',
20         / 'IT_A:'.
21 loop at it_a into ztxlfa1.
22     write / ztxlfa1-lifnr.
23     endloop.
24 uline.
25 write / 'IT_B:'.
26 loop at it_b into ztxlfa1.
27     write / ztxlfa1-lifnr.
28     endloop.
```

FIGURE 20.1.

The Import/Export Parameters screen showing how to pass the body of the internal table.

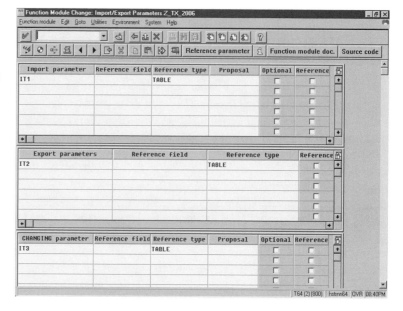

FIGURE 20.2.

*The Table Parameters/
Exceptions screen
showing how to pass an
internal table together
with its header line.*

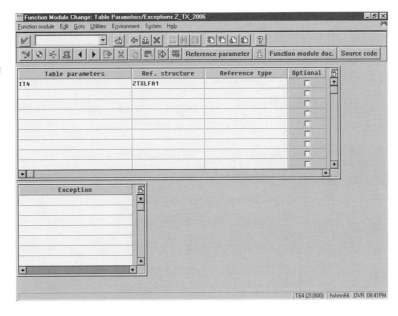

LISTING 20.6 THIS IS THE SOURCE CODE FOR THE FUNCTION MODULE CALLED
FROM LISTING 20.5

INPUT

```
 1 function z_tx_2006.
 2 *"----------------------------------------------------------
 3 *"*"Local interface:
 4 *"        IMPORTING
 5 *"             VALUE(IT1) TYPE  TABLE
 6 *"        EXPORTING
 7 *"             VALUE(IT2) TYPE  TABLE
 8 *"        TABLES
 9 *"             IT4 STRUCTURE  LFA1
10 *"        CHANGING
11 *"             VALUE(IT3) TYPE  TABLE
12 *"----------------------------------------------------------
13 data wa like lfa1.
14 write / 'IT1:'.
15 loop at it1 into wa.
16     write / wa-lifnr.
17     endloop.
18 loop at it3 into wa.
19     wa-lifnr = sy-tabix.
20     modify it3 from wa.
21     endloop.
22 uline.
23 write: / 'IT4:'.
```

continues

LISTING 20.6 CONTINUED

```
24 loop at it4.
25     write / it4-lifnr.
26     endloop.
27 uline.
28 it2[] = it1[].
29 endfunction.
```

The code in Listings 20.5 and 20.5 produce this output:

OUTPUT

```
- - - - - - - - - - -
IT1:
1000
1010
1020
- - - - - - - - - - -
IT4:
1000
1010
1020
- - - - - - - - - - -
AFTER CALL
IT_A:
1
2
3
- - - - - - - - - - -
IT_B:
1000
1010
1020
```

ANALYSIS

- In Listing 20.5, it_a and it_b are internal tables without header lines.

- Line 5 puts three rows into it_a.

- Line 8 passes the body of it_a to it1 by value, to it3 by value and result, and to it4 by reference with header line (it4 will acquire a header line within the function module).

- In Listing 20.6 and within the function module, it1 and it3 are independent copies of it_a. Line 13 defines a work area wa for use with it1 and it3 because they don't have header lines.

- Lines 15 through 17 write out the contents of it1 using the work area wa.

- Lines 18 through 21 modify the contents of it3. This table was passed by value and result, so the contents of the original will be changed when the endfunction statement executes.

- Lines 24 through 26 write out the contents of it4. Notice that line 25 accesses a component of it. This is only possible because the Ref. Structure column on the Table Parameters/Exceptions screen contains the name of the DDIC structure lfa1. This defines the structure of it within the function module. If the Ref. Structure column was blank, a syntax error would have occurred on line 25.

- Line 28 copies the contents of it1 to it2.

- Line 29 copies the contents of it3 back into it_a in the calling program and control returns to the caller.

- In Listing 20.5, lines 21 through 23 show that the contents of it_a have been changed by the function module.

- Lines 26 through 28 show that the contents of it_a have been copied to it_b by the function module.

Defining Subroutines in a Function Group

You can call internal and external subroutines from within function modules. Calls to external subroutines are the same for function modules as they are for reports. Internal subroutines should be defined within a special include: the F01.

The F01 is included into the function group by editing the main program and inserting the statement include Lfgid F01. Then, double-clicking on the name of the include will create it automatically. Within it, you can put subroutines accessible by all function modules within the group. There is, however, an easier way.

The easiest way to define the F01 is to code your call to the subroutine and then double-click on the subroutine name on the perform statement. The following procedure illustrates this process.

SCREENCAM　Start the ScreenCam "How to Create Subroutines within a Function Group" now.

20

1. Start from the Function Library: Initial Screen.

2. Select the Source Code radio button.

3. Press the Change pushbutton. The Function Module: Edit screen is shown.

4. Type a perform statement in the source code of the function module. For example, **perform sub1**.

5. Double-click on the subroutine name. In this example, you would double-click on sub1. The Create Object dialog box appears, asking you if you want to create the subroutine.

6. Press the Yes button. The Create Subroutine dialog box appears. The subroutine name appears in the Subroutine field. The include name lfgidf01 appears in the Include Choice box, and the radio button to its left is automatically selected.

7. Press the Continue button (the green checkmark). A Warning dialog box appears, indicating the main program will be modified and an include lfgidf01 statement will be inserted into it.

8. Press the Continue button (the green checkmark). You see the Exit Editor dialog box indicating that your source code has changed and asking you if you want to save the changes.

9. Press the Yes button. The Function Module Editor screen is shown. You are now editing the F01. Code the subroutine here.

10. When you have finished coding your subroutine, press Save and then Back. You are returned to the function module's source code where you began.

To see the include you just created, return to the Function Library Initial screen. Choose the Main Program radio button and press the Change button. You will see the Function Module: Edit screen. At the bottom will be the include lfgidf01 statement. This statement was inserted by step 7 of the above procedure. If you double-click on this line, you will see your subroutine.

Releasing a Function Module

NEW TERM   The release function adds a level of protection to the interface of a function module by protecting it from modification. If you have completed testing of your function module, you might want to *release* it to indicate that it is safe for other developers to use in their code. By doing so, you are essentially promising not to change the existing interface parameters in any way that would cause problems to any programs that will call your function module. You are promising interface stability.

For example, after releasing a function module, you shouldn't add a required parameter, change the proposals, or remove a parameter. If you did, any existing calls to your function module might fail or work differently.

After releasing, you can still change the interface, but you need to take an extra step to do it.

To release a function module, use the following procedure.

SCREENCAM   Start the ScreenCam "How to Release a Function Module" now.

1. Begin at the Function Library Initial Screen.

2. Choose the Administration radio button.

3. Press the Change pushbutton. The Function Module Change: Administration screen is shown. In the bottom right corner of the screen, at the bottom of the General Data box, you will see `Not Released`.

4. Choose the menu path Function Module->Release->Release. The message *Released* appears at the bottom of the window in the status bar. In the bottom right corner of the window, `Not Released` changes to `Customer Release On` and is followed by the current date.

If you try to change the interface after the function module has been released, the input fields on the interface screen will be grayed out. The message `Function module has been released` will also appear at the bottom of the window. However, if you want to change the interface, you only need to press the Display <-> Change button and you will be allowed to change it in any way you want. Remember, however, that you should not make changes that can cause existing programs to abnormally terminate or return different results.

| Tip | If you accidentally release a function module and want to cancel the release, go to the Function Module Display: Administation screen, press the Display <->Change button, and choose the menu path Function Module->Release ->Cancel Release. After choosing this menu path, press the Enter key to complete the cancellation process. |

Testing a Function Module

If you want to test a function module without writing an ABAP/4 program, you can do it using the test environment within the Function Library. Use the following procedure to access the test environment.

 Start the ScreenCam "How to Use the Test Environment for Function Modules" now.

1. Begin at the Function Library: Initial Screen. Type the name of the function module you want to test in the Function Module field.

2. Press the Test pushbutton. You will see the Test Environment For Function Modules screen (shown in Figure 20.3).

3. Type the parameters you want to supply for the test. To fill an internal table, double-click on the internal table name. A screen will be shown that enables you to

20

enter data into the internal table. (If you specified a Ref. Structure for the internal table, the columns of the structure will be shown.) Type your data and press the Enter key. You will be returned to the Test Environment For Function Modules screen.

FIGURE 20.3.

The Test Environment for Function Modules screen.

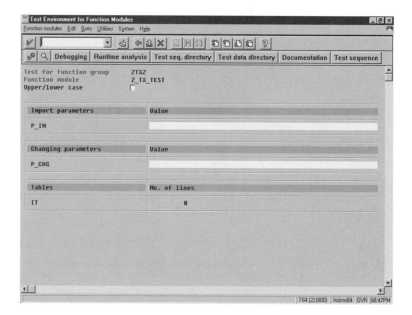

4. Press the Execute button on the Application toolbar to execute the function module. You will see the Test Function Module: Result Screen (see Figure 20.4). The output from `write` statements within the function module appear first. In Figure 20.4, `You passed A` is the result of a `write` statement within the function module. Then, the length of time taken to execute the function module (in microseconds) is shown. Following that, the values of the parameters are shown, and the `changing` and `tables` parameters have two values: the before and after. For `changing` parameters, the "before" value is shown first and the "after" value appears below it. For `tables` parameters, the "after" contents appear above the "before" (original) contents. In Figure 20.4, internal table `it` contained two lines after processing and three lines before. To see the before or after contents of the internal table, double-click on either line.

FIGURE 20.4.

The Test Function Module: Result screen showing the before and after values for the changing *and* tables *parameters.*

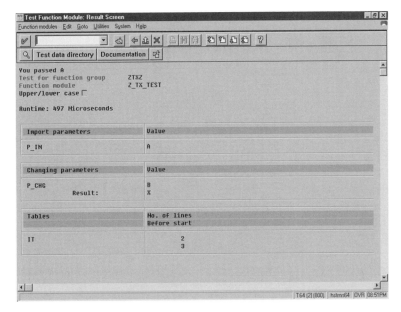

> **Tip**
>
> To save your test data and/or results, press the Save button either on the Test Environment screen or on the Result screen. To retrieve your saved information, press the Test Data Directory button on either screen. Test sequences can also be built using the Test Sequence button.

Finding Existing Function Modules

As stated before, SAP supplies more than 5,000 pre-existing function groups containing more than 30,000 function modules. Often the functionality you require is already covered by these SAP-supplied function modules—you only need to find the right one. To find an existing function module, use the Repository Information system. The following procedure shows you how.

SCREENCAM Start the ScreenCam "How to Search for Function Modules" now.

1. From the ABAP/4 Development Workbench screen, choose the menu path Overview -> Repository Infosys. You see the ABAP/4 Repository Information System screen shown in Figure 20.5.

20

FIGURE 20.5.

The ABAP/4 Repository Information System screen as it appears initially.

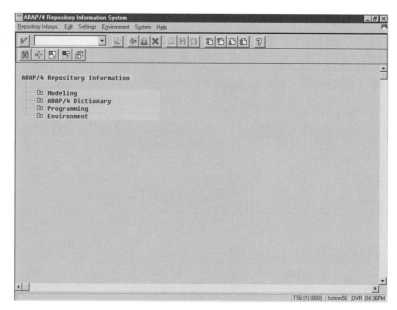

2. Expand the Programming line by clicking on the plus sign (+) to the left of it. A subtree is shown below it.

3. Expand the Function Library line by clicking on the plus sign (+) to the left of it. A subtree is shown below it. Your screen should now look like Figure 20.6.

FIGURE 20.6.

The ABAP/4 Repository Information System screen with the Function Modules left exposed.

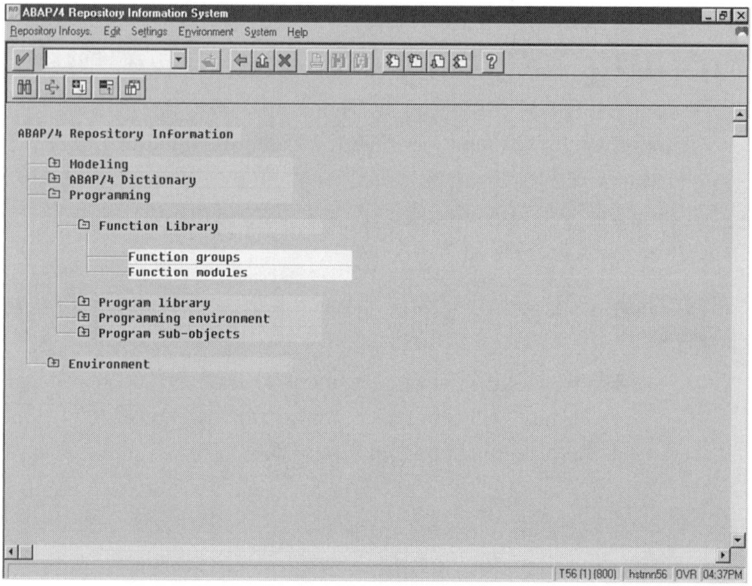

4. Double-click on the Function Modules line. The ABAP/4 Repository Information System: Function Module screen is shown. Press the All Selections button on the Application toolbar to display all possible selection fields. Your screen should now appear as shown in Figure 20.7. This is a selection screen in which you can enter search criteria for finding function modules. All fields are case-insensitive with the exception of the Short Description field, which is case sensitive!

FIGURE 20.7.

The ABAP/4 Repository Information System: Function Module screen with all selections shown.

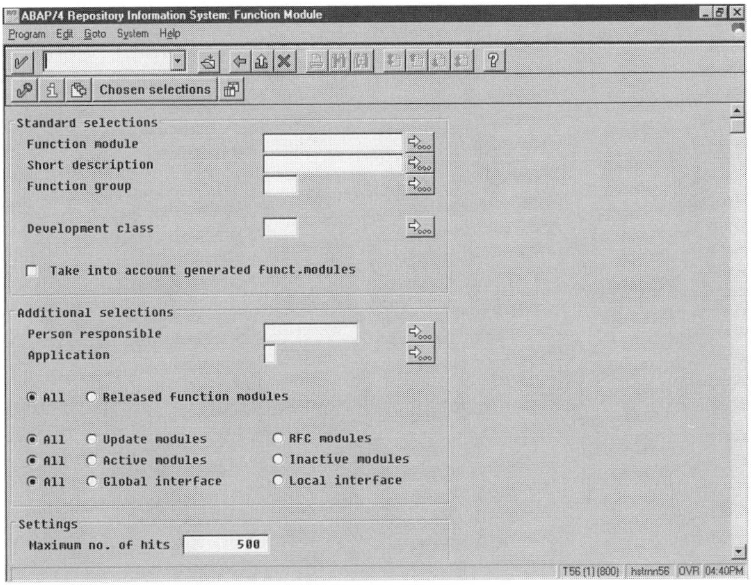

5. To search for a function module, either words or character strings might be entered in the search fields. Use + and * as wildcard characters. + will match any single character, and * will match any sequence of characters. For example, enter ***DATE***
in the Function Module field. This will find all function modules that contain the characters DATE anywhere in their name. Or, you might either enter ***Date*** or ***date*** in the short description field (only one string is allowed in this field).

6. To enter more than one value to search for, press the arrow at the end of the field. The Multiple Selection screen is shown (see Figure 20.8). The values you enter on this screen are ORed together. Type multiple selection criteria here. These values are known as the included values, or simply the "includes." (This is a different usage of the term than when it refers to include programs.)

7. Press the Options button to specify selection operators such as equal, not equal, greater than, less than, and so on. You will see the Maintain Selection Options screen, as shown in Figure 20.9. To be able to specify Pattern or Exclude Pattern,

20

your value must contain a pattern-matching character: either **+** or *****. Press the Copy button to return to the Multiple Selection screen.

FIGURE 20.8.

The Multiple Selection screen.

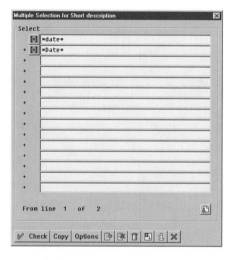

FIGURE 20.9.

The Maintain Selection Options screen.

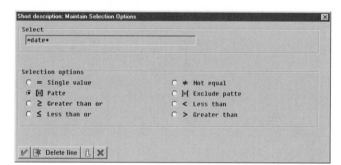

8. On the Multiple Selection screen, press the Complex Selection button. The Multiple Selection screen is reshown, but this time there is a scroll bar on the right side and Ranges fields appear (see Figure 20.10). To specify values that should be excluded from the search, scroll down and enter them within the box titled ...But Not (see Figure 20.11). These values are known as the excluded values, or more simply, the excludes.

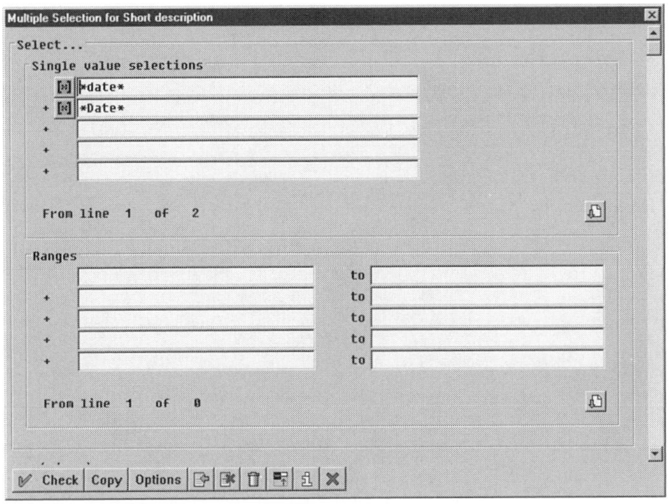

FIGURE 20.10.

The Multiple Selection screen with a scroll bar on the right side and Ranges fields.

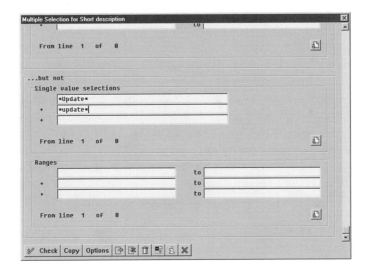

FIGURE 20.11.

The ...But Not box.

9. Press the Copy button to copy your selection criteria back to the selection screen. You are returned to the ABAP/4 Repository Information System screen, and if you entered multiple selection criteria, the arrow at the end of the line is green to show that more than one selection criterion exists (see Figure 20.12).

20

FIGURE 20.12.

The ABAP/4 Repository Information System screen. The green arrow at the end of the line shows that more than one selection criterion exists.

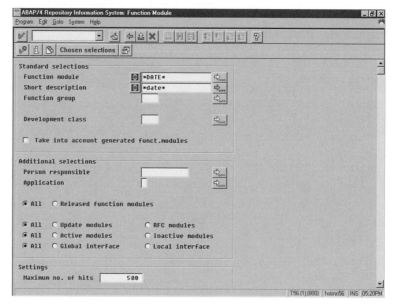

10. To begin the search, press the Execute button. The search results are determined as if separate searches had been done for all of the include criteria, and then the results ORed together. Then, if excludes have been specified, they are applied one entry after the other. For example, in the Short Description field, suppose you specified the includes *Date* and *date* and excludes of *Update* and *update*. All of the descriptions containing *Date* will be found, and then all of the descriptions contains *date* will be ORed with the first result set. Then all of the descriptions containing *Update* will be removed, and then all of those containing *update* will be removed. The result will contain the strings "Date" or "date" without "Update" and "update." You see the results on the Function Modules screen (see Figure 20.13). The number of function modules found is indicated in the title bar within parentheses.

11. To display a function module, double-click on it. The Function Module Display: Documentation screen is shown (see Figure 20.14). This screen shows you all the interface parameters and their documentation. To see more documentation, double-click on a parameter name (see Figure 20.15). To return to the interface documentation, press the Back button. To return to the function module list, press the Back button again.

12. To test a function module, put your cursor on it and press the Test/Execute button (it looks like a little monkey wrench). You will be shown the Test Environment Screen for that function module.

FIGURE 20.13.

The Function Modules screen.

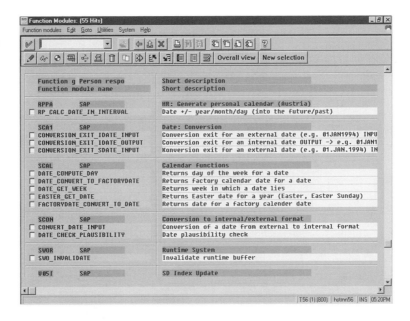

FIGURE 20.14.

The Function Module Display: Documentation screen.

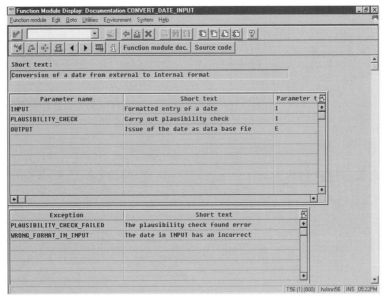

Note

Not all parameters have additional documentation. If the parameter you double-clicked on doesn't have any more documentation, nothing happens when you double-click on it.

20

FIGURE **20.15.**

*The additional
documentation for
a parameter.*

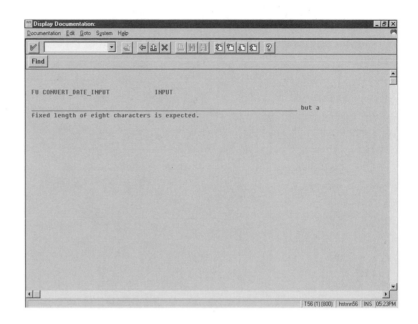

FIGURE 20.15.

*The additional
documentation for
a parameter.*

Tip

If, when you look at the title bar on the Function Modules screen, the number of function modules found is exactly 500, then you have probably hit
the maximum list size. Return to the selection screen and look in the
Maximum No. of Hits field. If it is also 500, you hit the maximum. You might
be tempted to increase the maximum number of hits, but this will rarely be
productive because you probably won't read an entire list of 500 function
modules. Refine your search criteria to reduce the number of hits.

Exploring the Components of Your Function Group

After creating your first function module, use the following procedure and take a few
minutes to explore the components of the function group. You should become familiar
with the structure that you have just created.

SCREENCAM   Start the ScreenCam "Exploring the Components of Your Function Group" now.

1. Begin on the Function Library Initial Screen. If it is not already there, type the
   name of your function module in the Function Module field.

2. Choose the Administration radio button and then press the Change pushbutton. The Function Module Change: Administration screen is displayed (see Figure 20.16). At the top of the screen in the Function Group field you can see the ID of the function group to which this function module belongs. In the bottom right corner in the Program field, you can see the name of the main program for the function group. In the Include field is the name of the `include` that contains the source code for the function module. The last field shows the status of the function module: Active or Inactive. Press the Back button to return to the Function Library Initial Screen.

FIGURE 20.16.

This is the way the Function Module Create: Administration screen appears after the function module has been created.

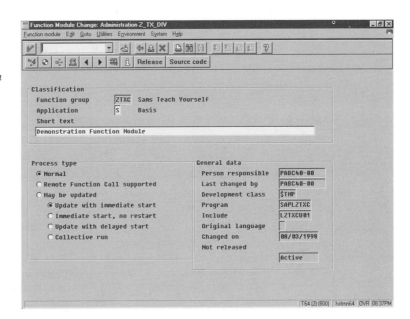

3. Choose the Import/Export Parameter Interface radio button and then press the Change pushbutton. The Import/Export Parameters screen is shown. Press the Back button to return to the Function Library Initial Screen.

4. Choose the Table Parameters/Exceptions Interface radio button and then press the Change pushbutton. The Function Module Change: Table Parameters/Exceptions screen is shown. Here you can enter or change internal table parameters and exception names. Press the Back button to return.

5. Choose the Documentation radio button and then press the Change pushbutton. The Function Module Change: Documentation screen is shown. Here you can enter a short description for each parameter and exception in the interface. Press the Back button to return.

20

6. Choose the Source Code radio button and then press the Change pushbutton. The Function Module: Edit screen is shown. Press the Back button to return.

7. Choose the Global Data radio button and then press the Change pushbutton. The Function Module: Edit screen is shown. This time, however, you are editing the top include. Notice the name of the top include in the title bar. It conforms to the naming convention lfgidtop, where *fgid* is the name of your function group. Here you can define global variables and tables work areas that are common to all function modules within the function group. If your function modules use the message statement, you can also define the default message class (on the function-pool statement). Press the Back button to return.

8. Choose the Main Program radio button and press the Change pushbutton. The Function Module: Edit screen is shown. This time, you are editing the main program (refer to Figure 20.17). Notice the name within the title bar begins with sapl followed by your function group ID. The two include statements incorporate the top include and the UXX into the main program. Double-clicking on the top include name will enable you to edit it. Press the Back button to return to the main program. Double-clicking on the UXX will display the include program source code—it contains the statements that include the function modules into the group. Their names are indicated within comments at the end of each include statement. You are not allowed to modify the UXX. Double-clicking on any of the include statements will display the source code for a function module within the group. Press the Back button to return.

FIGURE 20.17.

This is the main program for the z_tx_div *function module.*

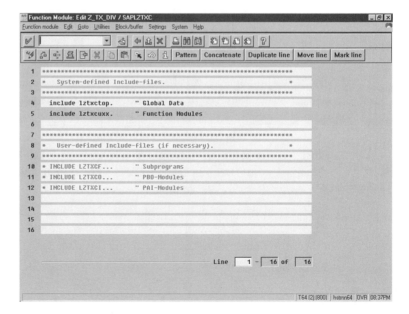

> **Tip**
>
> To copy, rename, or delete a function module, use the Copy, Rename, or Delete buttons on the Function Library: Initial Screen.

Finding and Fixing Errors in Function Modules

The easiest way to fix errors in a function module is to perform a syntax check when you are within the function module. You can do this on the Function Module Edit screen by pressing the Check button on the Application toolbar. Right now, you have only created one function module, so you know where to look if it doesn't work.

However, after you create many function modules, you might end up in the position where you are calling one or more function modules within a group and the system is telling you there is a syntax error somewhere. The error message you might see appears in a SAP R/3 dialog box such as the one shown in Figure 20.18.

FIGURE 20.18.

A syntax error detected at runtime within a function module.

Within this SAP R/3 dialog box is enough information to pinpoint the exact location and cause of the error. In Figure 20.18, the first field contains the program name lztxau02. This is the include program that contains the error. The second field tells you that the error occurred on line 10. At the bottom of the dialog box is the actual error. In this case the error reads "." expected after "P2".

To fix the error, use the following procedure.

SCREENCAM Start the ScreenCam "How to Fix an Error in a Function Module" now.

1. Begin at the ABAP/4 Editor: Initial Screen (transaction SE38).
2. In the Program field, type the program name from the first field of the dialog box, in this case **lztxau02**.

20

3. Press the Change pushbutton. This will show you the function module source code that contains the error.

4. Press the Check button on the Application toolbar. You should see the same error that was shown at the bottom of the SAP R/3 dialog box.

5. Correct the error. Often, you can simply press the Correct button and the system will automatically correct the error for you.

Setting the Value of `sy-subrc` On Return

Normally, after returning from a function module, the system automatically sets the value of `sy-subrc` to zero. Use one of the following two statements to set `sy-subrc` to a non-zero value:

- `raise`
- `message ... raising`

Using the `raise` Statement

Use the `raise` statement to exit the function module and set the value of `sy-subrc` on return.

Syntax for the `raise` Statement

SYNTAX

The following is the syntax for the `raise` statement.

`raise xname.`

where:

- `xname` is the name of the exception to be raised.

The following points apply:

- `xname` can be any name that you make up. It does not have to be previously defined anywhere. It can be up to 30 characters in length. All characters are allowed except `" ' . ,` and `:`.
- Do not enclose `xname` within quotes.
- `xname` cannot be a variable.

When the `raise` statement is executed, control returns immediately to the `call function` statement and a value is assigned to `sy-subrc` based on the exceptions you have listed there. Values assigned to export parameters are not copied back to the calling program. Listings 20.7 and 20.8 and Figure 20.19 illustrate how this happens.

Note   The code in the function module shown in Listing 20.8 is merely for sake of example; normally there would also be some code that does some real processing in there also.

FIGURE 20.19.

This illustrates raise statement processing.

```
call function 'Z_XXX'                    function z_xxx.
     exceptions
          error_A  = 1                    raise error_b.
          error_B  = 2  ← this value is
          other    = 3     assigned to    endfunction.
                           sy-subrc
```

LISTING 20.7   HOW TO SET THE VALUE OF sy-subrc FROM WITHIN A

INPUT   FUNCTION MODULE

```
 1 report ztx2007.
 2 parameters parm_in default 'A'.
 3 data vout(4) value 'INIT'.
 4 call function 'Z_TX_2008'
 5      exporting
 6           exname = parm_in
 7      importing
 8           pout   = vout
 9      exceptions
10           error_a = 1
11           error_b = 4
12           error_c = 4
13           others  = 99.
14 write: / 'sy-subrc =', sy-subrc,
15         / 'vout =', vout.
```

INPUT   **LISTING 20.8**   THIS IS THE FUNCTION MODULE CALLED FROM LISTING 20.7

```
 1 function z_tx_2008.
 2 *"----------------------------------------------------------------
 3 *"*"Local interface:
 4 *"       IMPORTING
 5 *"            VALUE(EXNAME)
 6 *"       EXPORTING
 7 *"            VALUE(POUT)
 8 *"       EXCEPTIONS
 9 *"            ERROR_A
10 *"            ERROR_B
11 *"            ERROR_C
12 *"            ERROR_X
```

continues

20

LISTING 20.8 CONTINUED

```
13 *"---------------------------------------------------------------
14 pout = 'XXX'.
15 case exname.
16   when 'A'. raise error_a.
17   when 'B'. raise error_b.
18   when 'C'. raise error_c.
19   when 'X'. raise error_x.
20   endcase.
21 endfunction.
```

The code in Listings 20.7 and 20.8 produce this output, if you specify a value of A for parm_in:

OUTPUT
```
sy-subrc =      1
vout = INIT
```

ANALYSIS
- In Listing 20.7, line 4 takes the value from parm_in and passes it to the function module z_tx_2007. Control transfers to line 1 of Listing 20.8.

- In Listing 20.8, line 14 assigns a value to the pout parameter. This parameter is passed by value, so the change is only to the local definition of pout. The original has not yet been modified.

- In Listing 20.8, line 15 examines the value passed via parameter exname. The value is B, so line 17—raise error_b—is executed. Control transfers to line 9 of Listing 20.7. Because the raise statement has been executed, the value of pout is not copied back to the calling program, thus the value of vout will be unchanged.

- In Listing 20.7, the system scans lines 10 through 13 until it finds a match for the exception named by the just-executed raise statement. In this case, it's looking for error_b. Line 11 matches.

- On line 11, the value on the right-hand side of the equals operator is assigned to sy-subrc. Control then transfers to line 20.

The special name others on line 13 of Listing 20.7 will match all exceptions not explicitly named on the exceptions addition. For example, if line 7 of Listing 20.8 were executed, exception error_x would be raised. This exception is not named in Listing 20.7, so others will match and the value of sy-subrc will be set to 99. You can code any numbers you want for exception return codes.

Caution

If you do not code `others` and an exception is raised within the function module that is not named on the `exceptions` addition, the program will be aborted and a short dump will result that has the runtime error `RAISE_EXCEPTION`.

If an export parameter is passed by value, after a `raise` its value remains unchanged in the calling program even if a value was assigned within the function module before the `raise` statement was executed. If the parameter was passed by reference, it will be changed in the caller (it has the Reference flag turned on in the Export/Import Parameters screen). This effect is shown in Listing 20.7. The value of pout is changed in the function module and, if a `raise` statement is executed, the changed value is not copied back into the calling program.

Note

`check`, `exit`, and `stop` have the same effect with function modules as they do in external subroutines. However, they should not be used within function modules. Instead, the `raise` statement should be used because it enables the caller to set the value of `sy-subrc` on return.

Using the `message ... raising` Statement

The `message ... raising` statement has two modes of operation:

- If the exception named after `raising` is not handled by the `call function` statement and `others` is not coded, a message is issued to the user.
- If the exception named after `raising` is handled by the `call function` statement, a message is not issued to the user. Instead, control returns to the `call function` statement and the exception is handled the same way as for the `raise` statement.

Syntax for the `message ... raising` Statement

The following is the syntax for the `message ... raising` statement

`message tnnn(cc) [with v1 v2 ...] raising xname`

where:

- *t* is the message type (e, w, i, s, a, or x).
- *nnn* is the message number.
- *(cc)* is the message class.
- *v1* and *v2* are values to be inserted into the message text.
- *xname* is the name of the exception to be raised.

20

▼ **SYNTAX**

▲

The following points apply:

- *xname* is an exception name as described for the `raise` statement.
- If the message class is not specified here, it must be specified on the `function-pool` statement in the top `include` for the function group via the `message-id` addition.
- The following `sy` variables are set: `sy-msgid`, `sy-msgty`, `sy-msgno`, and `sy-msgv1` through `sy-msgv4`. These can be examined within the calling program (after return).

When the `message ... raising` statement is executed, the flow of control depends on the message type and whether the condition is handled by the caller (specified in the exceptions list in the calling program).

- If the condition is handled by the caller, control returns to the caller. The values of the `sy-msg` variables are set. The values of exports passed by value are not returned.
- If the condition is not handled by the caller, and for message types `e`, `w`, and `a`, the function module is exited and the calling program is terminated immediately. The message is displayed and the output list appears blank. When the user presses the Enter key, the blank list is removed and the user is returned to the screen from which the program was invoked.
- If the condition is not handled by the caller, and for message type `i`, the message is displayed to the user in a dialog box. When the user presses the Enter key, control returns to the function module at the statement following the `message` statement. The function module continues processing and, at the `endfunction` statement, control returns to the calling program. The values of the `sy-msg` variables are set and the values of exports passed by value are returned.
- If the condition is not handled by the caller, and for message type `s`, the message is stored in a system area. Control continues within the function module at the statement following the `message` statement. The function module continues processing and, at the `endfunction` statement, control returns to the calling program. The values of the `sy-msg` variables are set and the values of exports passed by value are returned. When the list is displayed, the message appears in the status bar at the bottom of the list.
- If the condition is not handled by the caller, and for message type `x`, the function module is exited and the calling program is terminated immediately. A short dump is generated and displayed to the user.

Listings 20.9 and 20.10 illustrate the effect of the message ... raising statement.

INPUT   **LISTING 20.9**   USING THE message ... raising STATEMENT

```
 1 report ztx2009.
 2 parameters: p_etype default 'E',      "enter message types E W I S A X
 3             p_handle default 'Y'.     "if Y, handle the exception
 4 data vout(4) value 'INIT'.
 5
 6 if p_handle = 'Y'.
 7    perform call_and_handle_exception.
 8 else.
 9    perform call_and_dont_handle_exception.
10    endif.
11 write: / 'sy-subrc =', sy-subrc,
12        / 'vout =', vout,
13        / 'sy-msgty', sy-msgty,
14        / 'sy-msgid', sy-msgid,
15        / 'sy-msgno', sy-msgno,
16        / 'sy-msgv1', sy-msgv1.
17
18 *_____
19 form call_and_handle_exception.
20   call function 'Z_TX_2010'
21      exporting
22          msgtype = p_etype
23      importing
24          pout    = vout
25      exceptions
26          error_e = 1
27          error_w = 2
28          error_i = 3
29          error_s = 4
30          error_a = 5
31          error_x = 6
32          others  = 7.
33   endform.
34
35 *_____
36 form call_and_dont_handle_exception.
37   call function 'Z_TX_2010'
38      exporting
39          msgtype = p_etype
40      importing
41          pout    = vout.
42   endform.
```

20

LISTING 20.10   THE SOURCE CODE FOR THE FUNCTION MODULE CALLED FROM
LISTING 20.9

INPUT

```
 1 function z_tx_2010.
 2 *"----------------------------------------------------------------
 3 *"*"Local interface:
 4 *"          IMPORTING
 5 *"                  VALUE(MSGTYPE)
 6 *"          EXPORTING
 7 *"                  VALUE(POUT)
 8 *"          EXCEPTIONS
 9 *"                  ERROR_E
10 *"                  ERROR_W
11 *"                  ERROR_I
12 *"                  ERROR_S
13 *"                  ERROR_A
14 *"                  ERROR_X
15 *"----------------------------------------------------------------
16 pout = 'XXX'.
17 case msgtype.
18   when 'E'. message e991(zz) with 'Error E' raising error_e.
19   when 'W'. message e992(zz) with 'Error W' raising error_w.
20   when 'I'. message e993(zz) with 'Error I' raising error_i.
21   when 'S'. message e994(zz) with 'Error S' raising error_s.
22   when 'A'. message e995(zz) with 'Error A' raising error_a.
23   when 'X'. message e996(zz) with 'Error X' raising error_x.
24   endcase.
25 endfunction.
```

Using the default parameter values, the code in Listings 20.9 and 20.10 produce this
output:

OUTPUT

```
sy-subrc =       1
vout = INIT
sy-msgty E
sy-msgid ZZ
sy-msgno 991
sy-msgv1 Error E
```

ANALYSIS

- In Listing 20.9, when using the default values for the parameters line 6 is
  true, so control transfers to the subroutine call_and_handle_exception.

- Line 20 transfers control to line 1 of Listing 20.10.

- In Listing 20.10, line 16 assigns a value to the local parameter pout. This
  value is defined as pass-by-value, so the value of vout in the caller is not yet
  changed.

- Line 18 of the case statement is true and the message ... raising statement is executed. This triggers the exception error_e.

- The exception error_e is handled by the calling program, so the message is not displayed to the user. Control returns to line 25 of Listing 20.9. The value of vout is not changed; the sy-msg variables are assigned values.
- In Listing 20.9, line 26 assigns 1 to sy-subrc.
- Line 33 returns control to line 11 and the values are written out.

Try running program ztx2009. By specifying a p_handle value of N, you will see error messages produced.

Defining Exceptions in the Interface

Whenever you raise an exception in a function module, you should document that name in the function module's interface. The exception names will also automatically appear at the top of the function module source within the system-generated comments. The following procedure describes how to document your exceptions.

 Start the ScreenCam "How to Document Exceptions in the Function Module Interface" now.

1. Begin at the Function Library: Initial Screen.
2. Type your function module name in the Function Module field if it is not already there.
3. Choose the Table Parameters/Exceptions Interface radio button.
4. Press the Change pushbutton. The Function Module Change: Table Parameters/Exceptions screen is displayed.
5. In the bottom half of the screen, in the Exceptions section, type the names of the exceptions that appear in the source code of the function module.
6. Press the Save button and the Back button. You are returned to the Function Library: Initial Screen.

Automatically Inserting the `call function` Statement

20

Instead of typing the call function statement into your source code, the system can automatically generate it for you. When you do it this way, the exception names that you documented in the interface will automatically be inserted into your code as well.

 Start the ScreenCam "How to Insert a call function Statement into Your ABAP/4 Program" now.

To see the effects of your exception documentation, create an ABAP/4 program. Instead of coding the `call function` statement yourself, use the following procedure to automatically generate the `call function` statement:

1. Begin at the ABAP/4 Editor: Edit Program screen.

2. Position your cursor within the source code on the line after the one where you want the `call function` statement to appear.

3. Press the Pattern button on the Application toolbar. The Insert Statement dialog box appears.

4. The Call Function radio button should already be chosen. If it isn't, select it.

5. Type the name of your function module in the input field to the right of Call Function.

6. Press the Continue button (the green checkmark). You are returned to the Edit Program screen. A `call function` statement will appear in the source code on the line above the one you positioned your cursor on. The statement will begin in the same column as the column that your cursor was in. The parameters and exceptions that you named in the interface will appear. If a parameter is marked as optional in the interface, it will be commented out and the default value will appear to the right of it.

7. Fill in the values to the right of the equal signs. Feel free to change the code or remove any lines that follow the `importing` addition if you do not need those return values.

Caution

> An empty `importing` clause causes a syntax error. If there are no parameter names following the word `importing`, or if they are all commented out, you must remove the word `importing`. The same is also true for `exporting`.

Summary

- Global variables can be defined at two levels. When defined in the top `include`, they are global to all function modules within the group and remember their values between calls to function modules within the group as long as the calling program continues to execute. By globalizing the interface, parameters are visible within subroutines called from the function module.

- Subroutines defined within a function group are coded in the F01 include.

- Function modules can be released to denote that the interface is stable and no significant changes will be made to it. It is therefore released for general availability and is "safe" to use in production code.
- The test environment provides a convenient way of running function modules without writing any ABAP/4 code.
- Existing function modules can be found with the aid of the Repository Information System.

Q&A

Q Why would you pass an import parameter by reference? If you specify both import and export parameters should be passed by reference, aren't they the same? Why does the ability to do this exist?

A A pass by reference is more efficient than a pass by value. You should use it for efficiency. However, the words Import and Export provide important documentation regarding the role each parameter plays within the function module. You should not change Import parameters, they should always be passed in without being changed by the function module. Nor should you accept values into the function module via Export parameters. The value of an Export should always originate within the function module.

Workshop

The Workshop provides you two ways for you to affirm what you've learned in this chapter. The Quiz section poses questions to help you solidify your understanding of the material covered and the Exercise section provides you with experience in using what you have learned. You can find answers to the quiz questions and exercises in Appendix B, "Answers to Quiz Questions and Exercises."

Quiz

1. If a parameter with the same name exists in two function modules within a group and both interfaces are global, must the data definitions of both of these parameters be identical?

2. If you accidentally release a function module and want to cancel the release, what menu path can you use?

20

3. If you do not code others and an exception is raised within the function module that is not named on the exceptions addition, what happens?

4. Check, exit, and stop have the same effect with function modules as they do in external subroutines. Should they be used within function modules?

Exercise 1

Copy the z_tx_div function module, and modify it to raise the zero_divide exception if the value of p2 is zero. (To copy a function module, use the Copy button on the Function Library: Initial screen.)

DAY 21

Selection Screens

Chapter Objectives

After you complete this chapter, you should be able to

- Code selection screens that interact with the user.
- Understand how foreign keys can help validate user input.
- Understand how matchcodes are used in ABAP/4 programs.
- Use formatting elements to create efficient, well-designed selection screens.
- Use selection screens to maintain data integrity.
- Use messages to provide effective communication.

Event-Driven Programming

In this day and age, with the emergence of the World Wide Web and all that it entails, program code must be capable of interacting and communicating with the end user. This is done in ABAP/4 using events that are invoked by the users' actions.

NEW TERM Processing blocks are defined by *event keywords* and are thus executed on the invocation of certain relevant events.

By default, the event `start-of-selection` is attached to all events in ABAP/4. In your programs you can define a processing block and attach this block to an event keyword.

For generally easy-to-read code, it is good practice to define sequential processing blocks in the order by which they will most likely be triggered during selection screen execution. It is also good practice to utilize the most important events for selection screen programming. These events are as follows:

- The `initialization` event
- The `at selection-screen` event
- The `at user-command` event

Using the `initialization` Event

▼ SYNTAX

The following code shows the syntax for the `initialization` event:

```
report ywhatyr.
tables:  marc, mvke.
..
data: p_year for sy-datum.
initialization.
if sy-datum ge '01012000'
p_year = '2000'.
else.
p_year = 'Yesteryear'.
endif.
```

▲

In this example, when the program executes for which a selection screen is defined, this `initialization` processing block is executed, setting the parameter field `p_year` equal to a value depending on the system date at the moment of execution. It is this block in which you specify the initial default values of your selection screen based on whatever criteria is necessary to maintain data integrity of user input. Some examples include setting title bars, assigning text elements to graphical user interface (GUI) elements, and function code status.

You have seen how the `initialization` event works, so now it's time to take a closer look at some uses of the `at selection-screen` and `at user-command` events.

Using the `at selection-screen` Event

The `at selection-screen` event is processed after user input on the active selection screen. This can occur when the user presses a function key or clicks a pushbutton, as well as a host of other elements that can be interacted on by the user. In addition to data validation checks, warning messages, GUI status change, or even pop-up windows can be called using the at selection-screen event. You will look at more examples of these later in the chapter when you look at formatting selection screens and the events involved with screen formatting elements. For now, however, let's take a look at a pushbutton on a selection screen and how the events at selection-screen and at user-command are used with this next example.

Using the at user-command Event

Pushbuttons, as well as many other event-driven selection screen options, can be very useful in maintaining user interaction and validating user input. In this next section, you will explore how to use pushbuttons to invoke the at user-command event and look at an example of how pushbuttons can be used to process user input.

Syntax for the selection-screen pushbutton Event

The following code shows the syntax for the selection-screen pushbutton event:

```
selection-screen pushbutton example1 user-command 1234.
```

This statement, when used together with the at selection-screen command, is a great way to interact with the user as he enters data. The syntax is similar to that of a selection-screen comment except that data is passed when the user presses the button. Pushing the button triggers sccrfields-ucomm in the at selection-screen event and the input fields are imported. This data can then be validated and the user issued a message depending on the purpose of the button. This is an example of how you can use two pushbuttons to determine which language to report selected data in.

The following code shows the syntax for two pushbuttons that are used to choose a language:

```
selection-screen pushbutton 10(20) text-003 user-command engl.
selection-screen pushbutton 50(20) text-004 user-command germ.

at selection-screen.
at user-command.
case sy-ucomm.
when 'engl'.
    lang-english = 'Y'.
when 'germ'.
    lang-german = 'Y'.
endcase.
```

In this example, you can check which of the two pushbuttons were pressed by the user by using a case statement (see Figure 21.1). When the user triggers the at user-command event, the field sy-ucomm holds the unique four-byte name of the item that the user selected. In this way, you can code various data validations or command user input based on the combination of data entered and the items, in this case pushbuttons, selected by the user.

FIGURE 21.1.

A printout of the pushbuttons.

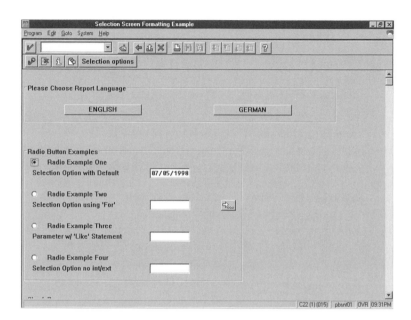

Note

You can also create up to five pushbuttons on the Application toolbar. These buttons on the Selection Screen toolbar are associated to specific function keys and are restricted to function keys 1 through 5.

NEW TERM   Now that you have learned a little about data validation using events in ABAP/4, it is time to look at some data validation techniques that are more system maintained and defined. You will first look at foreign keys. A *foreign key* is one or more fields that represent the primary key of a second table.

Data Validation Using Foreign Keys

The SAP environment's relational data model can contain many tables, views, structures, and linked tables. Foreign keys, it can be said, define these relationships between multiple tables. The functions that foreign keys perform include providing help data and creating dictionary objects, but the one that you will focus on will be in the data validation area. After all, maintaining data integrity is one of the main goals when defining selection screens and the most important use of foreign keys.

A foreign key field is, by definition, restricted to values that correspond to those of the primary key of the input field's check table. This is how the link between the two tables is made. One table, FORKEY1, can be thought of as the foreign key (or dependent) table mainly because it includes foreign key fields that are assigned to primary key fields in CHECK1, which is referred to as the check (or reference) table.

> **Note**
>
> The foreign key field and the primary key of a parent table must share the same domain and a value table for that domain must also be specified. This extends, in a way, the data integrity check usually provided by the value table alone.

Some check tables can have multiple primary key fields. In such cases, assignments must be made for each field when initiating a foreign key relationship. Three options are as follows:

- *Use a partial foreign key.* In this case, some fields will not be a factor when validating acceptable values for entries in the foreign key field. Certain fields are flagged as generic in this case and thus ignored by the system on validation.
- *Use a constant foreign key.* In order for the field input to be valid, the value must match that of the constant in the check table.
- *Create a field-to-field assignment.* This is the most thorough of the three choices. Every primary key field in the check table is matched with a field in the foreign key table and all key fields are then used to determine valid entries in the foreign key table.

Basically, the way a foreign key works resembles that of a direct select statement against the check table of the field with the foreign key. More specifically, when a foreign key check field is populated, the select statement that was generated by the SAP system when it defined the foreign key is sent by the program. If the table returns a value from that selection, the entry is valid. If the record is not found, the field input is invalid.

SYNTAX

The following code shows the syntax for a system-generated select statement:

```
select * from table_1 where table_1-exam1 = fk_exam1
                       and table_1-exam2 = fk_exam2.
```

21

This bit of code shows an example of a system-generated select statement that is called when data is entered into the field with the foreign key definition. In this scenario, an entry in this screen field is permitted only if the select statement produces valid data from the check table using the data entries made in fields fk_exam1 and fk_exam2 as keys.

Note

One thing that you must keep in mind while creating foreign key relationships is the cardinality. The cardinality of a foreign key, together with its type, is referred to as the semantic attributes of the foreign key. Each cardinality of a foreign key of these entries is optional. The cardinality should not be overlooked, however, because the entry is good practice and becomes necessary when you want to create certain types of aggregates such as help views, for example.

NEW TERM   *Cardinality* is a description of the relationship between one or more data elements to one or more of another data element. If a foreign key linking two tables has been defined, the record of the foreign key table refers to a record of the check table. This reference is constructed by assigning fields of one table, the foreign key table, to the primary key fields of the other table, the check table.

The relationship exists only if the foreign key fields are of the same data type and length as the corresponding primary key fields. A check or parent table is the table that is referenced by the foreign key itself. This is usually a *value* table, but it can also be a table consisting of a subset of the contents of a value table. A value table dictates the valid values that are assigned to the data element's domain.

In some cases, a constant foreign key might best suit your needs. This is the case when all valid entries in the input field contain a specific value in the key field of the cited check table. Upon the `select` statement's query, the constant field is checked against the primary key field that contains the fixed value.

Tip

It is good programming practice to utilize naming conventions that are descriptive and user friendly. In addition, SAP has agreed never to begin the name of a development object with the letters *Z* or *Y*. If you create all your objects with names that begin with one of these two letters, you will ensure that you will have no trouble with name conflicts when you upgrade your SAP system.

Data Validation Using Matchcodes

NEW TERM   Another useful way to maintain data integrity during user input is to use matchcodes. A *matchcode* is an object that is used to find data records in the SAP Data Dictionary. More specifically, matchcodes access data records in a way similar to an index in that all key fields are not necessary, but they differ from indexes in that matchcodes can contain more than one table in the selection range.

Here's how it works: First a matchcode object is defined with the pertinent primary and secondary tables and significant fields designated. This object then identifies all possible paths to the required data records. Next, matchcode IDs are created by mapping one path defined by the matchcode object. The only data fields that are allowable in this ID are based entirely on the matchcode object. At least one ID must be declared for each matchcode object. Matchcode objects are stored as a table pool, which is automatically generated for each matchcode ID that you declare.

NEW TERM   A *data pool* is a logical pooled table that is used by SAP to internally store control data. This data, which is not pertinent externally, is mapped as a number of database tables to one SAP table.

A matchcode can be assembled in two different fashions:

- *Physically.* In this setting, data is stored in a separate table in the SAP system. Update types A, P, and S are maintained in physical tables.

- *Logically.* This option sets up matchcode data temporarily on access to the matchcode. This access is managed by a database view. In this respect, the logical method is the same as transparent storage. This includes update types I and K only.

In the following task, you will learn how to follow 12 easy steps to create and maintain matchcode objects. Start at the Data Dictionary screen shown in Figure 21.2 and complete the following steps:

FIGURE 21.2.

The initial screen of Data Dictionary.

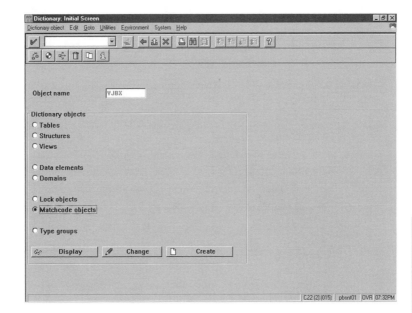

21

1. Enter a name for your new object, click on the Matchcode radio button, and press the Create button.

2. Enter descriptive text as you enter your primary table on the Attributes screen shown in Figure 21.3 and press the Save button. The primary table represents the primary source table for the subsequent field search. Secondary tables can also be maintained at this point by double-clicking on the primary table or pressing the Tables button. These tables must link to the primary table through foreign keys.

FIGURE 21.3.

The Maintain Matchcode Object attributes screen.

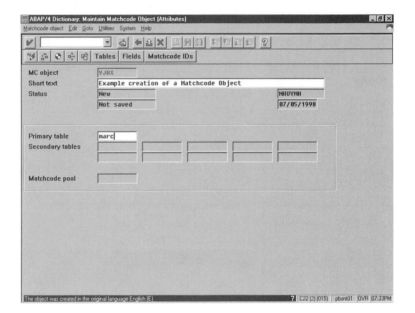

3. At this point you have the option of creating the matchcode as a local object or attaching it to a transport request. After you have done this, click on the Save button (see Figure 21.4).

4. As the status bar reflects, the mandatory key fields are transferred automatically (see Figure 21.5). If you want, you can press the Fields button and maintain any selection fields you want. At this point you need to click on the green arrow to go back to the Maintain Attributes screen.

5. The next step in the creation process is to activate the matchcode object. The status of the object is New and Saved (see Figure 21.6).

6. The status is now set to Active and Saved. Next you need to create a matchcode ID or your object will be incomplete (see Figure 21.7). To do this, click the Matchcode IDs button.

FIGURE 21.4.

The Create Object Catalog Entry screen.

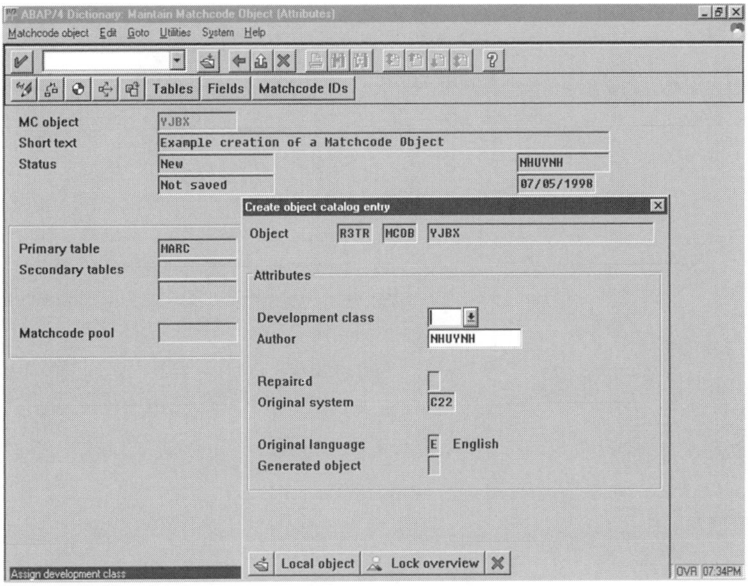

FIGURE 21.5.

The Maintain Matchcode Object (Fields) screen.

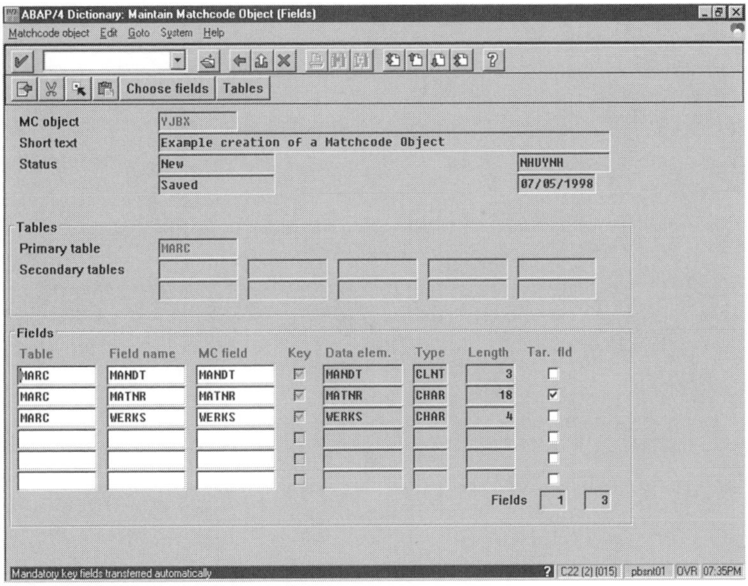

21

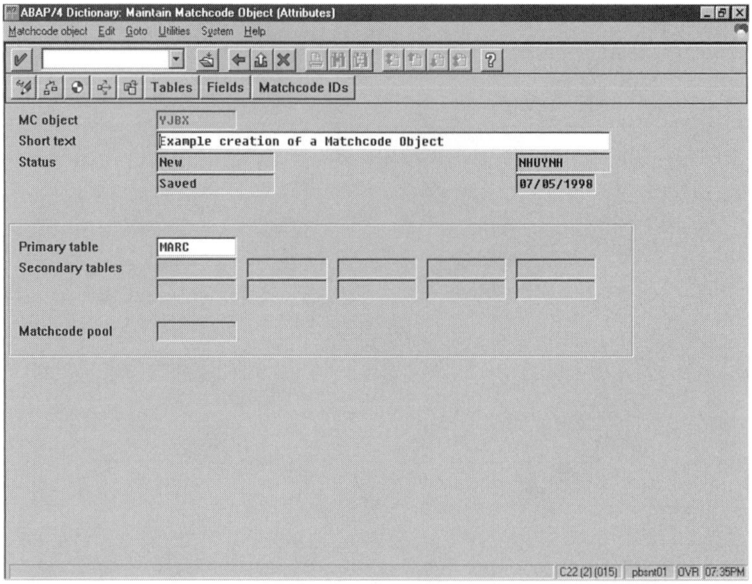

FIGURE 21.6.

The matchcode attributes prior to activation.

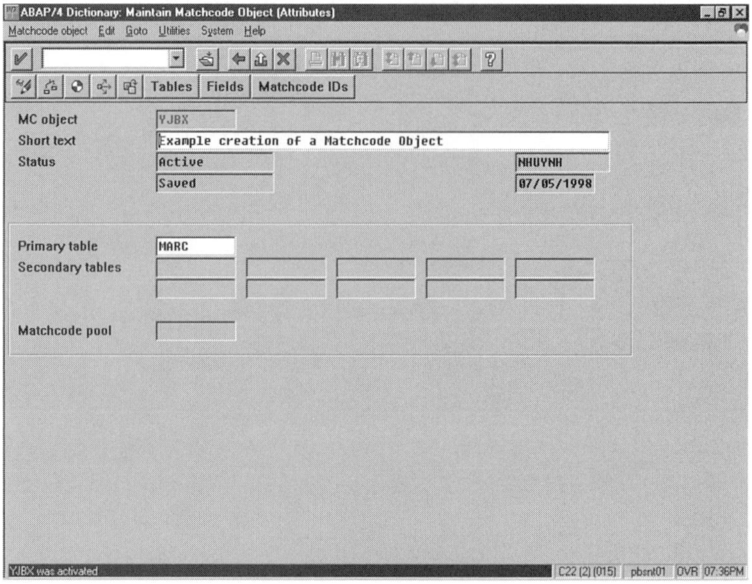

FIGURE 21.7.

The matchcode attributes after activation.

7. The system will prompt you to create a new ID if one does not exist (see Figure 21.8). To do this, click on the Yes button.

FIGURE 21.8.

A prompt to Create Object.

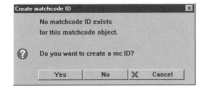

8. On the Create Matchcode ID screen shown in Figure 21.9, specify a matchcode ID number, valid input ranges from all of the alphabet, and any number. You can also click on the down arrow to view a range of valid entries.

FIGURE 21.9.

The Create Matchcode ID dialog box.

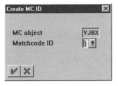

9. Let's view some possible entries (see Figure 21.10). As you can see, this list window shows a number of matchcode IDs and a short description of each. Choose one and click on the green arrow.

FIGURE 21.10.

A Matchcode hit list.

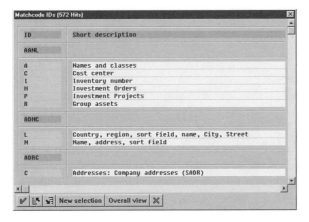

10. Follow these steps we learned to maintain selection fields for this matchcode ID, be sure to enter an Update type, and click on Save (see Figure 21.11). I will further discuss Update types later in this section. At this point, you can enter further selection criteria by pushing the Selection Criteria button.

21

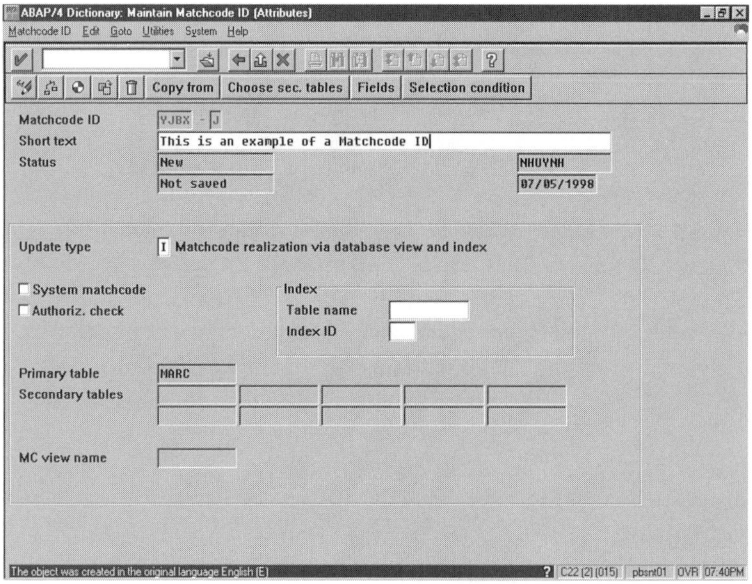

FIGURE 21.11.

*Maintenance of
matchcode attributes.*

11. In the Maintain Selection Conditions screen, you can enter and maintain fields and selection criteria for your matchcode IDs. Here is an example of a requirement of a Material Number *not* greater than the value of 8888 (see Figure 21.12). When finished, click Save and the green arrow to go back.

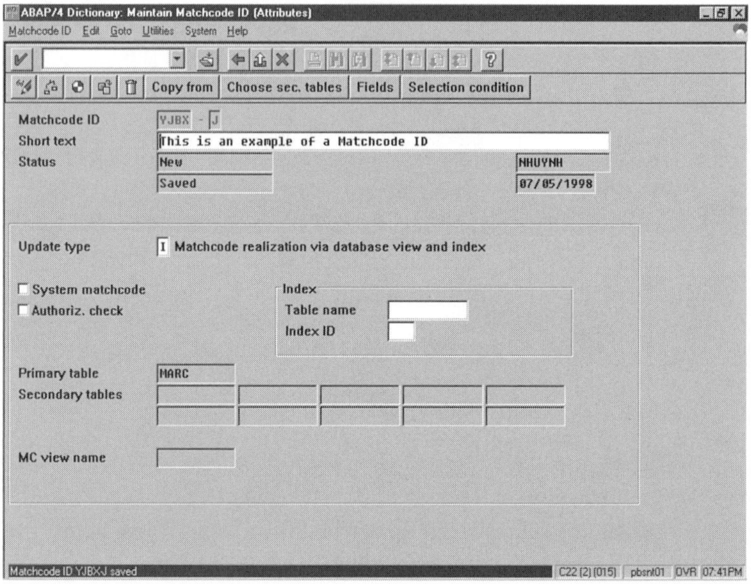

FIGURE 21.12.

*The Maintenance
Selection Conditions
dialog box.*

12. Now all you have to do is activate your matchcode ID and your new object is ready
    to use (see Figure 21.13).

FIGURE 21.13.

Generate and use the matchcode.

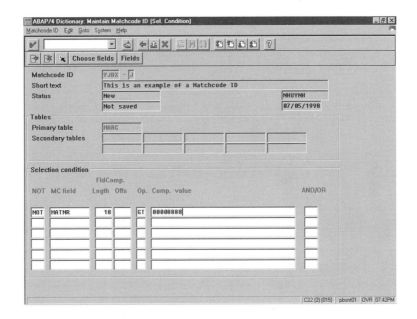

> **Note**
>
> The Index sub-screen doesn't need to be maintained because these charac-
> teristics are merely for documentation purposes in the current version of the
> SAP system. Just leave this blank and ignore the subsequent warning that
> appears in the log of your object activation.

In those 12 easy steps you created a matchcode that you can now use for maintaining
data integrity. You learned how the primary keys help you check possible values of
linked tables and the concept of a *pool* of data fields. Remember, the manner in which
the matchcode data is arranged varies according to which update type is selected during
initial creation. Here is a description of each of these five types:

- I—Arranged by the attributed database.
- S—Arranged by the database interface.
- A—Auto-arranged by the system program SAPMACO.
- P—Arranged by an application program.
- K—Also arranged by an application program.

21

Syntax for Using a Matchcode

The following is the syntax for using matchcodes for selection screen parameter input validation:

```
tables: saptab
parameter: example like saptab-field matchcode object exam.
select single field from saptab where field = example.
```

▲

This example uses the matchcode object exam, which has already been defined with a matchcode ID, to validate the data input into the parameter field example. This object exam holds the relationship data necessary to maintain the integrity of the user input.

Formatting Selection Screens

Now that you have explored some tools to validate input data in ABAP/4, let's take some time to learn more about designing effective selection screen formats. When defining input screens for the use of reporting on data, various selection elements can be combined to maintain data integrity and still be easy to use. These elements include standard input fields such as selection options and parameters, as well as others such as check boxes, radio buttons, and pushbuttons. The following section will take a look at each of these individually and give some examples of where they are best utilized. You will get a chance to combine them in Exercise 1 at the end of the chapter.

> **Note**
>
> Reports that have Logical Database attached to them are assigned pre-designed selection screens. These selection criteria can be modified to best suit your needs. Reports that do not have the screens pre-defined must be maintained by the programmer of the report. These custom user interfaces can take on any form and combine any elements that you, the programmer, want.

Using selection-screen Statements

Selection screen elements can be combined into cohesive units called *blocks*. These logical blocks are, in essence, a cosmetic screen feature that encapsulates a combination of screen input elements and can be created with a descriptive frame title. Logical blocks help to make the selection options easier to understand and use.

SYNTAX

Syntax for `selection-screen block with frame`

The following is the syntax for a `selection-screen block` with `frame`:

```
selection-screen begin of block block0 with frame title text-000.
```

ANALYSIS In addition to the `block` statement, selection screens can be customized by utilizing formatting elements such as the following `selection-screen` statements:

- `selection-screen comment`—This will place a comment on the selection screen.
- `selection-screen uline`—This will place an underline on the screen at a specified location for a specified length.
- `selection-screen position`—This is a very useful tool that specifies a comment for the next field parameter on the screen. This comes in handy for `selection-options` as well as `parameters`.
- `selection-screen begin-of-line` and `selection-screen end-of-line`— All input fields defined between these two statements are placed next to each other on the same line.
- `selection-screen skip` *n*—This statement creates a blank line for as many lines for *n* lines on the selection screen.

Most of the elements included in the previous section were of the cosmetic variety; in the next section you will look at some of the selection screen elements that are more specific to processing data input.

Selection Screen Parameters

The `parameter` statement on selection screens creates a data structure in the program that holds the input entered into the Parameter field by the user at runtime.

Parameters are best utilized when the field input required is a single value, as opposed to a range of values. The valid range of values can be determined by the user by clicking on the down arrow or by pressing F4 while the cursor is in the field generated by the `parameter` statement. This value table can be maintained by the programmer to include custom values for specific transactions or reports. The most straightforward way of setting up F4 help is by allocating a check table to the field domain in the ABAP/4 dictionary.

NEW TERM A *domain* describes the properties of the fields of a table. It defines the range of valid data values for a field and specific field characteristics.

21

Note Domains determine attributes such as field type, length, and possible foreign key relationships. Modifying a domain will automatically change the attributes of all data elements attached to that domain. This is due to the fact that data elements in a domain inherit all properties of the domain that they are referenced to.

To view or perform actions on a domain, start at the Data Dictionary screen (see Figure 21.14). Check the radio button corresponding to Domains and choose the button for the actions you want to invoke.

FIGURE 21.14.

The Domains initial screen.

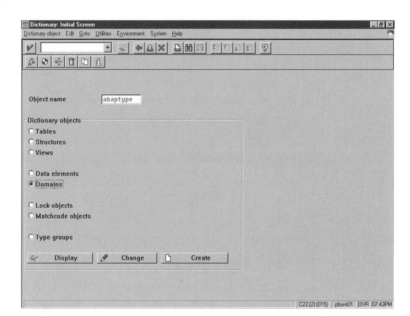

In this example, you have chosen display mode (see Figure 21.15). As you can see, the domain characteristics are displayed on the screen.

With the parameter statement, you can include keywords that can restrict the input with certain options. These three keywords are as follows:

- lower case—With this included in the selection statement, the lowercase value entered into the input field is not automatically converted to uppercase, which is what happens to all input fields in ABAP/4 at runtime.

- obligatory—This prohibits blank input fields.

- default—This term maintains an initial default value for the parameter.

FIGURE 21.15.

The Domains display screen.

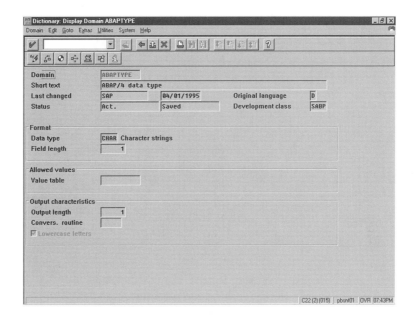

Tip

> Text elements should be maintained for screen elements such as Parameters to provide the user with a good explanation of what the Selection Screen input field represents in the context of the program. These text elements are language independent and are displayed in the language of the user's logon.

To maintain text elements for your selection screens, choose the menu path Goto->Text Elements from the ABAP/4 Editor. You can maintain all three text types for your program from here. We will now see an example of editing text symbols (see Figure 21.16).

Figure 21.17 shows the screen that enables you to edit the text symbols that you created in your program. If you want to add more, enter a number and text and click the Save button. Also note the Where Used feature, which really comes in handy.

Selection Screen checkbox

Parameters can be created as data fields that contain only one input value and they can also be created as check boxes. When Parameters take the form of check boxes, they are declared as type C and hold the value of X when checked and space when unchecked. A good use of the checkbox parameter is to prompt the user to signal if they want certain components of a report to be displayed.

21

FIGURE 21.16.

The Text Symbols initial screen.

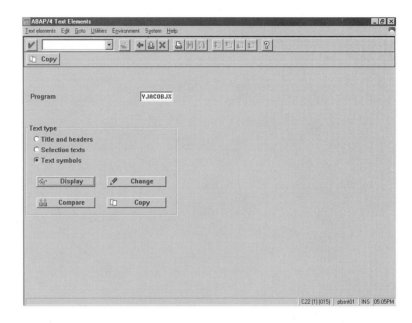

FIGURE 21.17.

Maintaining text symbols.

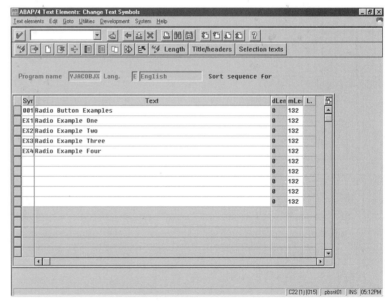

Syntax for `selection-screen checkbox`

The following is the syntax for a parameter that appears as a `checkbox`:

```
parameters: testparm as checkbox default 'X'.
```

In this example, the initial value is set to checked, or X for the logical processing of the program. Check boxes, unlike radio buttons, are not mutually exclusive so the user can have as many boxes checked as are generated on the selection screen.

As you have learned, the `parameter` statement is best utilized when soliciting a single input value. If the input required is better represented in a range of values, the `select-options` statement is a more efficient field to use.

 The `select-options` statement generates an internal selection table that contains the input for the attributed field entries.

Selection Screen `select-options`

The `select-options` statement is used similarly to the `parameters` statement in that it creates a selection criteria for a database field. The main difference between the two is that the `select-options` statement creates two input fields containing both a FROM and a TO field, as opposed to just a single field input.

Syntax for `select-options`

The syntax for this statement is as follows:

```
select-options ex sele for table-field default 'VALUELOW' to 'VALUEHI'.
```

ANALYSIS The `select-options` statement displays a line that usually has two fields for input data. This can be restricted to only one by using the `no-intervals` clause in the `select-options` syntax. For example, if your program does not require a TO field for entry in `select-options` statement line, but you still want to use the `select-options` statement, you would include this `no-intervals` clause. This clause, as well as the `no-extension` clause, will be further explored in the example at the end of this section. For now, however, we will turn to a discussion of the format of the `select-options` internal selection table.

This internal table is maintained with the following field format if the user clicks on the arrow to the right of the TO field of the `select-options`. Clicking on this arrow brings up a Multiple Selections input screen that fills the internal selection table. This table then holds the key attributes of the input data, including the SIGN, OPTION, LOW value, and HIGH value. These features of the `select-options` statement can have the following conditions:

- SIGN—Can signify INCLUSIVE, which is the default, or EXCLUSIVE, which can be flagged in the Complex Selections window.
- OPTION—Can hold values BT (between), CP (contains pattern), EQ (equal to), and GE (greater than or equal to).

21

- LOW—Holds the value input in the FROM field.
- HIGH—Holds the value input in the TO field.

> This multiple select-option can be excluded by using the no-extension clause as stated earlier in this chapter.

Selection Screen Radio Buttons

In addition to field parameters and select-options, the selection screen radiobutton statement is a great way to maintain data integrity while processing user input at runtime. In order to create Parameters as radio buttons, you must declare them using the radiobutton group clause.

Syntax for a radiobutton group

The following is the syntax for a radiobutton parameter group:

```
selection-screen begin of block rad_blk with frame title text-000.
parameters: rad_ex1 radiobutton group one,
            rad_ex2 radiobutton group one,
            rad_ex3 radiobutton group one.
selection-screen end of block rad_blk.
```

This example generates a group of three parameters as radio buttons. As you can see, these radio buttons are grouped in one block on the screen. This is good programming practice as it helps the user to realize that they all belong to the same input request group. These parameters are best utilized to select a single value from a multiple option setting and must contain at least two buttons per group.

Only one of these three example buttons can be checked at runtime due to its inclusion in group one. Data integrity is maintained because this is a great way to solicit mutually exclusive input from the user. This will be further demonstrated in the following section where there is an example of a simple selection screen that utilizes many selection screen elements that you have learned about.

Selection Screen Example Program

The following is example code for a selection screen consisting of most of the basic elements:

```
report YJACOBJX message-id Y6.
* Database Table Definitions
tables: mara.
```

```
selection-screen skip 1.
 selection-screen begin of block block0 with frame title text-000.
 selection-screen skip 1.
selection-screen begin of line.
selection-screen pushbutton 10(20) text-003 user-command engl.
selection-screen pushbutton 50(20) text-004 user-command germ.
selection-screen end of line.
 selection-screen end of block block0.
* Selection parameters
selection-screen skip 2.
selection-screen begin of block block1 with frame title text-001
                                             no intervals.
selection-screen begin of line.
parameters: p_ex1 radiobutton group rad1 .
selection-screen comment 5(30) text-ex1.
selection-screen end of line.
parameters: p_jdate1 type d default sy-datum.
selection-screen skip 1.
selection-screen begin of line.
parameters: p_ex2 radiobutton group rad1 .
selection-screen comment 5(30) text-ex2.
selection-screen end of line.
select-options: s_jdate2 for mara-laeda.
selection-screen skip 1.
selection-screen begin of line.
parameters: p_ex3 radiobutton group rad1.
selection-screen comment 5(20) text-ex3.
selection-screen end of line.
parameters: p_jdate3 like mara-laeda.
selection-screen skip 1.
selection-screen begin of line.
parameters: p_ex4 radiobutton group rad1 .
selection-screen comment 5(30) text-ex4.
selection-screen end of line.
select-options: s_jdate4 for mara-laeda no-extension no intervals.
selection-screen end of block block1.
selection-screen skip.
selection-screen begin of block block2 with frame title text-002
                                             no intervals.
selection-screen begin of line.
parameters: P_ex5 as checkbox.
selection-screen comment 5(30) text-ex5.
selection-screen end of line.
selection-screen skip.
selection-screen begin of line.
parameters: P_ex6 as checkbox.
selection-screen comment 5(30) text-ex6.
selection-screen end of line.
selection-screen skip.
selection-screen begin of line.
parameters: P_ex7 as checkbox.
```

21

```
selection-screen comment 5(30) text-ex7.
selection-screen end of line.
selection-screen end of block block2.
* AT selection-screen.
AT selection-screen.
  if ( p_ex1 = 'X' ) and
  ( ( p_jdate1 = 'IEQ?' ) or ( p_jdate1 is initial  ) ).
    message E017 with 'Selection Option with Default field has no value'.
  elseif ( p_ex1 = 'X' ) and
  not ( ( p_jdate1 = 'IEQ?' ) or ( p_jdate1 is initial  ) ).
    message I017 with 'We are now using Example 1'.
  endif.
  if ( p_ex2 = 'X' ) and
  ( ( s_jdate2 = 'IEQ?' ) or ( s_jdate2 is initial  ) ).
    message E017 with 'Selection Option using for field has no value'.
  elseif ( p_ex2 = 'X' ) and
  not ( ( s_jdate2 = 'IEQ?' ) or ( s_jdate2 is initial  ) ).
    message I017 with 'And now Example 2 is selected'.
  endif.
  if ( p_ex3 = 'X' ) and
  ( ( p_jdate3 = 'IEQ?' ) or ( p_jdate3 is initial  ) ).
    message E017 with 'Parameter w/ like statement field has no value'.
  elseif ( p_ex3 = 'X' ) and
  not ( ( p_jdate3 = 'IEQ?' ) or ( p_jdate3 is initial  ) ).
    message I017 with 'We are now using Example 3'.
  endif.
  if ( p_ex4 = 'X' ) and
  ( ( s_jdate4 = 'IEQ?' ) or ( s_jdate4 is initial  ) ).
    message E017 with 'Selection Option with no interval has no value'.
  elseif ( p_ex4 = 'X' ) and
  not ( ( s_jdate4 = 'IEQ?' ) or ( s_jdate4 is initial  ) ).
    message I017 with 'We are now using Example 4'.
  endif.
  if p_ex5 = 'X'.
  perform get_price_data.
  else.
    message I017 with 'No Pricing Data selected'.
  endif.
  if p_ex6 = 'X'.
  perform get_cost_data.
  else.
    message I017 with 'No Costing Data selected'.
  endif.
  if p_ex7 = 'X'.
  perform get_revenue_data.
  else.
    message I017 with 'No Revenue Data selected'.
  endif.
form get_cost_data.
...
endform.
```

```
form get_revenue_data.
...
endform.
form get_price_data.
...
endform.
```

ANALYSIS Because radio buttons are mutually exclusive, it is a good idea to keep them all in the same processing block on the selection screen. Notice, in Figure 21.18, how each group of field elements has been isolated to contain only those fields that are relevant to that decision block.

As you can see in Figure 21.19, it is harder to follow the requested data fields when they are not grouped into selection screen blocks.

Parameters that are defined with the `like` clause will appear with a down arrow, which can be clicked to view a list window of valid values (see Figure 21.20).

We can now click on our selection push the green check button. (see Figure 21.21). This will populate this parameter field with the value that you selected. This can be very helpful for helping a user become more familiar with your selection requirements.

When you create a `select-option` without using the `no-extension` clause, you have the ability to enter multiple selections or a range of selections. To enter multiple selections or range of selections, simply click on the white arrow button (see Figure 21.22).

FIGURE 21.18.

Selection screen with relevant decision block.

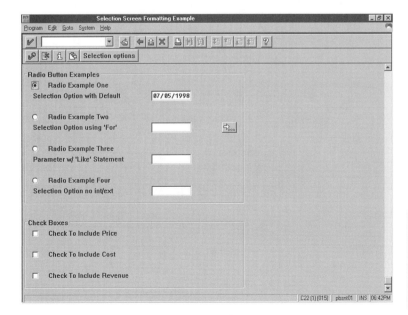

21

FIGURE 21.19.

Selection screen without blocks.

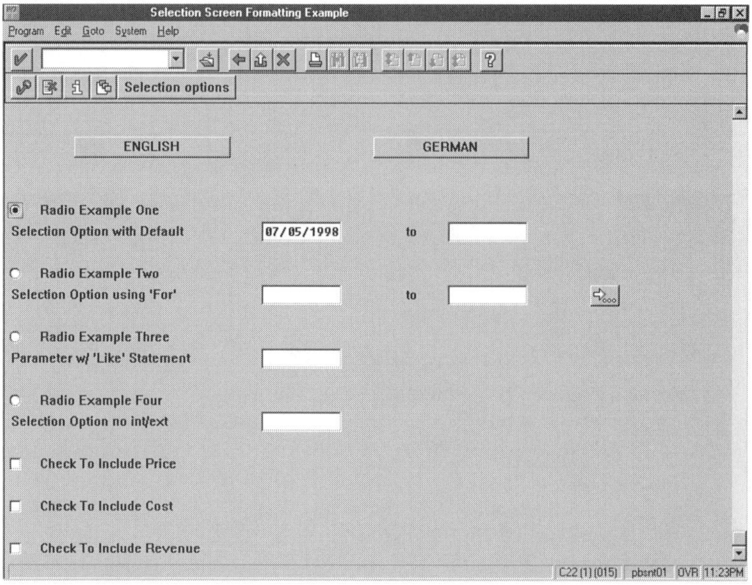

FIGURE 21.20.

Parameters and the down-arrow request.

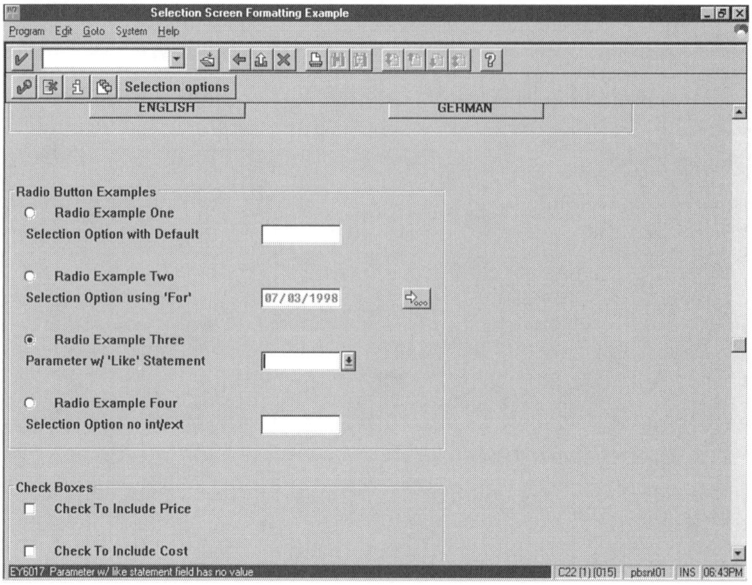

FIGURE 21.21.

Choose a valid value.

FIGURE 21.22.

Selection options with Extension.

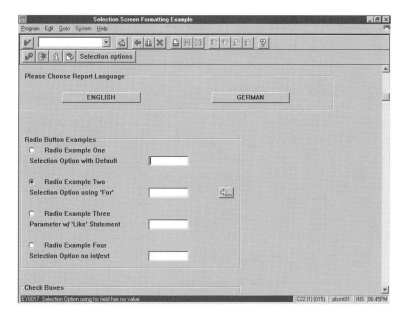

At this point, you can enter all of your selection criteria and click on the Copy button (see Figure 21.23).

As you can see, the arrow changes color, and is now green (see Figure 21.24). This reflects the fact that you have selected multiple selections for this field and these inputs will populate a selection table at runtime.

If you use the no-extensions and the no-intervals clauses in the select-options statement, you will get an input field that acts similar to a parameter field, complete with a down arrow key for viewing valid entries (see Figure 21.25).

21

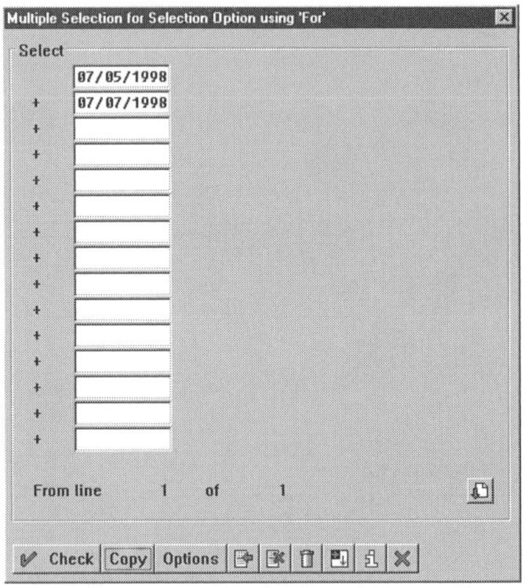

FIGURE 21.23.

Enter your selection requirements.

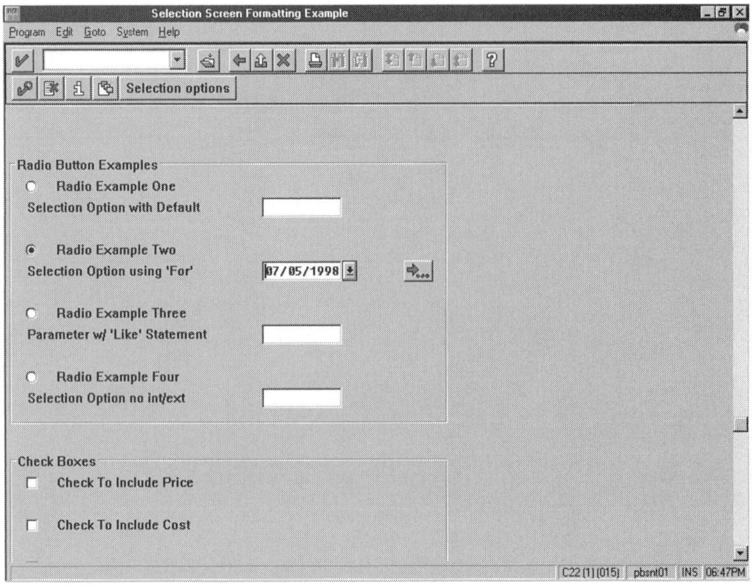

FIGURE 21.24.

Selection screen with green arrow enabled.

Be careful using default values for select-option fields. As you can see in Figure 21.26, if you populate a select-option field with a default value, the field will not allow you to view valid entries.

The following screen shows an example of a data validation routine that utilizes an information message in the form of a pop-up window that is merely informative and just pauses the program. This is best used to communicate status of events in the processing of data (see Figure 21.27).

FIGURE 21.25.

Selection screen without extension or intervals.

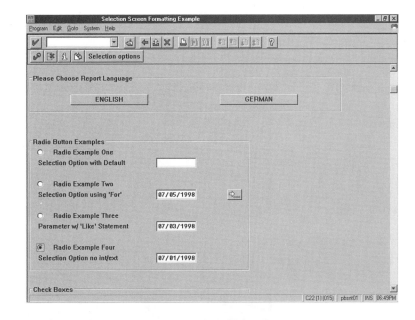

FIGURE 21.26.

select-option *with default value.*

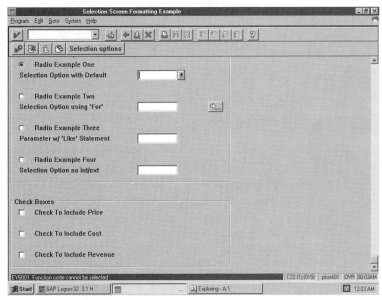

FIGURE 21.27.

Pop-up message used for data validation.

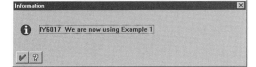

21

You can also utilize the error type of a message text. This type of message will append the program and issue a text message to the status bar. This is used primarily to validate data upon initial entry (see Figure 21.28).

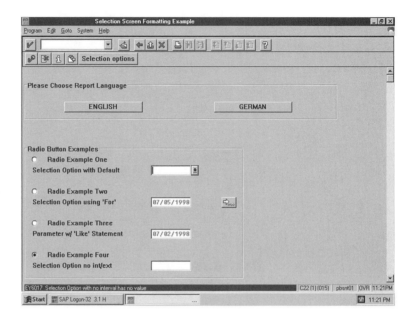

This example shows many elements of selection screens combined in an efficient and simple format. Please have a look at the code that created this selection screen in the paragraphs preceding this visual walkthrough.

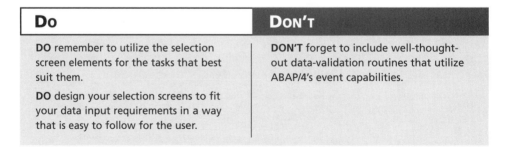

DO	**DON'T**
DO remember to utilize the selection screen elements for the tasks that best suit them.	**DON'T** forget to include well-thought-out data-validation routines that utilize ABAP/4's event capabilities.
DO design your selection screens to fit your data input requirements in a way that is easy to follow for the user.	

As mentioned in this last example, it is good practice to use message statements as input validation warnings at runtime.

Using the Message Statement

Messages are maintained and stored in the T100 table and can be accessed from the ABAP Workbench. An effective programmer issues messages that are descriptive and help the user understand the nature of the program flow.

Each individual message statement can be assigned message types that have various effects on the outcome of the program.

- S—Success, this message displays on the following screen in the status line.
- A—Abend, the current transaction is halted and a message is displayed until the user confirms it.
- E—Error, user must input data to continue.
- W—Warning, user can either modify input data or press Enter to proceed.
- I—Information, user must press Enter to continue at the same point in the program.

You must specify a message-id report statement at the beginning of your program.

Syntax for the message-id Statement

The following is the syntax for a message-id statement in a report:

```
report example line-count 65 line-size 132 message-id fs.
```

This two-character ID and a three-digit message number, together with the language, determine message classes. SAP has made including message statements in your program easy by using the insert statement command in the ABAP/4 editor.

Figure 21.29 is a quick by double-clicking on the message ID number in the ABAP/4 Editor.

Let's start at the Object Browser and choose Other Objects at the bottom of the list (see Figure 21.30). You can skip to the Maintain Individual Messages screen by double-clicking on the message ID number in the ABAP/4 Editor.

Next enter a message class and click on the icon for the action you want to perform. In this example, click on Create mode (see Figure 21.31).

Now you see the Maintain Message Class screen; it is here that you can enter the attributes of the message class that you are editing (see Figure 21.32). Click the Messages button to maintain individual messages.

You are now in editor mode, which corresponds to one item in a list of message text elements. After making necessary changes, click on the Save button and your message is ready to use.

SYNTAX

21

FIGURE 21.29.

Object Browser Initial Screen.

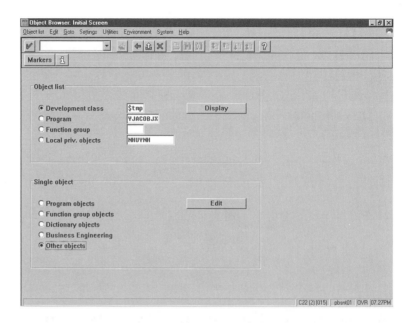

FIGURE 21.30.

Other Development Objects screen.

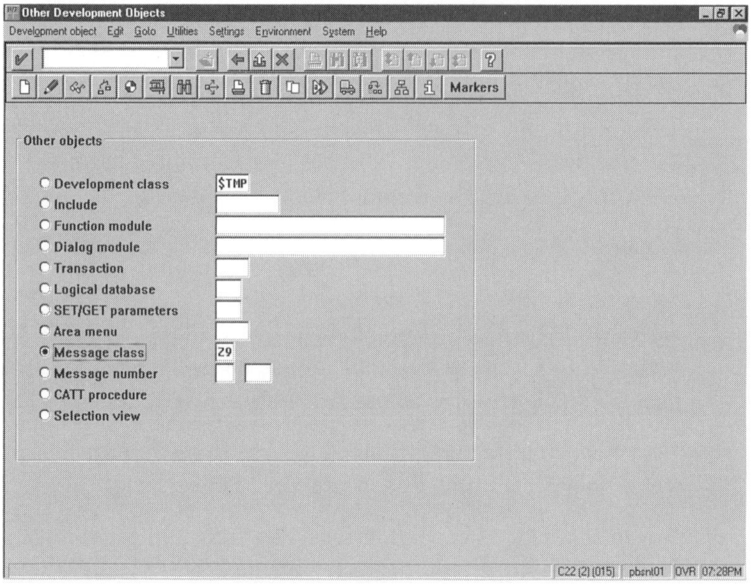

FIGURE 21.31.

*Maintain Message
Class screen.*

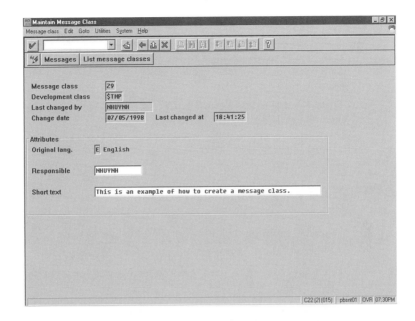

FIGURE 21.32.

*Maintain Individual
Messages screen.*

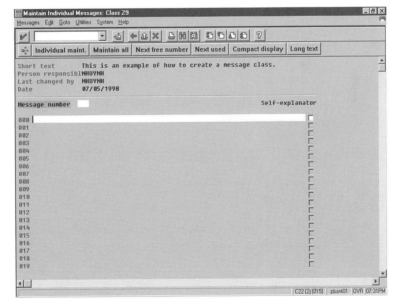

21

Do	Don't
DO remember to use messages in a way that helps the user input data more efficiently. **DO** make good use of the existing system message classes before creating your own.	**DON'T** forget to specify the correct `message-id` at the beginning of your report.

Summary

- ABAP/4 is an event-driven programming language, and you can take advantage of this fact by using the `at selection-screen` and `initialization` events, as well as the `at user-command` event, to validate user input using a number of techniques.

- Foreign keys can be used to check the integrity of input data using the primary key fields of a check table.

- Matchcodes use logically pooled data to validate user input based on specified selection criteria when used in conjunction with selection screen parameters and selection options.

- Messages can be used to communicate the status of the program and the validity of the data entered, as well as interact with the user in a way that can process data more efficiently.

- Text elements should be maintained for selection screen elements so that the user has a good understanding of the uses of the various selection criteria field objects.

- With ABAP/4 you can customize and modify existing logical database selection screens to suite your specific needs.

Q&A

Q What happens if a primary key field is added to a check table after a foreign key has been defined?

A Additional fields that are added to the primary key of a foreign key check table are flagged as *generic* and therefore ignored by the system when validating data entered into the foreign key field.

Q Is it possible to insert variables such as system error messages or return codes in a message text?

A Yes. If you place an ampersand in the place that you want the variable to appear in the message text and call the message passing the variable, similar to a perform statement.

Workshop

The Workshop provides you two ways to affirm what you've learned in this chapter. The Quiz section poses questions to help you solidify your understanding of the material covered and the Exercise section provides you with experience in using what you have learned. You can find answers to the quiz questions and exercises in Appendix B, "Answers to Quiz Questions and Exercises."

Quiz

1. How do the two flavors of matchcode assembly work in regard to the storage of matchcode data?

2. If you change the characteristics of a domain, do the characteristics of linked data elements change as well?

3. What is the primary rule for establishing a foreign key relationship?

Exercise 1

Create a selection screen report that lists all components of a bill of materials in multiple languages. Construct fields for selections from a range of material and plant combinations. Remember to utilize the elements that we have learned in this chapter for the tasks that best suit them.

21

Week 3

In Review

In the past week, you have accomplished the following tasks:

- produced reports that use graphical symbols and icons
- attached headings and footings to lists
- sent output to the print spool using `new-page print`
- became familiar with the `initialization`, `start-of-selection`, `end-of-selection`, `top-of-page` and `end-of-page` events
- coded internal and external subroutines and function modules, and passed typed and untyped parameters to them by value, value and result, and by reference
- raised exceptions within a function module to set the return value of `sy-subrc`
- created selection screens using the `select-options` statement

Appendix **A**

Naming Conventions

Program Naming Conventions

There are two program types:

- Reports
- Dialog programs

Each program type has its own naming conventions. Table A.1 contains the characters that are not allowed in program names.

TABLE A.1 INVALID CHARACTERS FOR PROGRAM NAMES

Character	Description
.	Period
,	Comma
	Blank
( )	Parentheses
'	Single quote

continues

TABLE A.1   CONTINUED

Character	Description
"	Double quote
=	Equal sign
*	Asterisk
_	Underscore
%	Percent sign
Ä ä Ö ö Ü ü ß	Umlaut and "scharfes s" characters

Naming Conventions for Reports

Customer report names follow the convention *Yaxxxxxx* or *Zaxxxxxx*, where:

- The first character must be a *Y* or *Z*.
- The second character represents the application area.
- The maximum program length is 10.

The second character is the short form for the application area (see Table A.2). For example, a customer report for Treasury would follow the convention *Z5xxxxxx*, while a logistics report would be named *Z21xxxxx*.

Each application area can be represented by a code. Each code has two commonly used forms, the short form and the long form. There is also a code used only for logical database names. These codes are shown in Table A.2.

TABLE A.2   CODES FOR THE APPLICATION AREAS IN R/3

Application Area	Long Form	Short Form	LDB Form
Financial Accounting	FI	1	F
Materials Management	MM	2	M
Sales and Distribution	SD	3	
Production Planning and Control	PP	4	
Treasury	TR	5	
Quality Management	QM	6	
Project System	PS	7	
Plant Maintenance	PM	8	
Warehouse Management	WM	9	

Application Area	Long Form	Short Form	LDB Form
Human Resources	HR	10	
Asset Accounting	AA	11	
Controlling	CO	12	
Process Industries	PI	13	
Investment Management	IM	14	
Logistics (General)	LO	21	
International Development	IN	22	
Cross Application Functionality	CA	23	

Naming Conventions for Dialog Programs

Customer dialog program names follow the convention *SAPMYxxx* or *SAPMZxxx*, where:

- The first four characters must be *SAPM*.
- The fifth character must be a *Y* or *Z*.
- The last three characters may be any valid characters.

Programs written by SAP follow the convention SAPMaxxx, where a is the short form for an application area.

Customer Name Ranges

The R/3 system contains many types of development objects. If you want to create a development object yourself, you must create it in the *customer name range*. The conventions for customer name ranges are shown in Table A.3.

TABLE A.3 CUSTOMER NAME RANGES FOR ALL R/3 DEVELOPMENT OBJECTS

Object Type	Max Length	Naming Convention	Notes
ABAP/4 Query			
Query	2	*	
Functional Area	4	*	
Function Group	3	*	
Append Structures			
Append Structure	10	Y* Z*	
Append Structure Fields	10	YY* ZZ*	

continues

TABLE A.3 CONTINUED

Object Type	Max Length	Naming Convention	Notes
Application Logs			
Object	4	Y* or Z*	
Sub-Object	10	Y* or Z*	
Area Menus	4	Y* Z*	
Authorizations			
Authorization	12	any	Not allowed in 2nd position
Authorization Class	4	Y* Z*	
Authorization Group	30	Y* Z*	
Authorization Object	10	Y* Z*	
CATT Flows	8	Y* Z*	
Change Document Objects	10	Y* or Z*	
Codepages	4	9*	
Data Elements			
Data Element	10	Y* Z*	
Data Element Supplement	4	*	If customer created the data element
SAP Supplement	4	9*	If SAP created the data element
Data Models			
Data Model	10	Y* Z*	
Entity	10	Y* Z*	
Development Classes	4	Y* Z*	
Dialog Modules	30	Y* Z* RP_* RH_INFOTYP_9*	
Documentation Modules			
General Text (TX)	28	Y* Z*	
Test Run Description	20	Y* Z*	
Main Chapter (BOOK)	20	Y* Z*	
Chapter of IMG	20	Y* Z*	
Chapter (CHAP)	20	Y* Z*	
Chapter Note (NOTE)	26	Y* Z*	
Release Information	20	Y* Z*	
Structure	12	Y* Z*	
Online Text	28	Y* Z*	

A

Object Type	Max Length	Naming Convention	Notes
Domains	10	Y* Z*	
Enhancements			
Enhancement	8	Y* Z*	
Enhancement Project	8	*	
Function Codes			
Function Code	4	Y* Z*	
Menu Exit	4	+*	
Function Library			
Function Group	4	Y* Z*	
User Exit Function Grp	4	XZ*	
Function Module	30	Y_* Z_*	
Field Exit Func Module	30	FIELD_EXIT_* FIELD_EXIT_*_x	
User Exit Func Module	30	EXIT_pppppppp_nnn	
Conversion Exits	30	CONVERSION_EXIT_xxxx_INPUT CONVERSION_EXIT_xxxx_OUTPUT	
GUI Status	8	*	
IDOCs			
Segment Type	7	Z1*	
Basis IDOC Type	8	Y* Z*	
Enhancement Type	8	*	
IDOC Type	8	Y* Z*	
Includes (DDIC)			
Customizing Includes	10	CI_*	Only used in an SAP-created table
Includes (Program)			
Include	8	Y* Z*	
Include for User Exits (function modules)	8	ZffffUnn	ffff = func group
Info Types	4	9*	
Lock Object	10	EY* EZ*	
Logical Databases	3	Y*a Z*a	a = app area (LDB form, see Table A.2)
Logistics Info System			
Event	2	Y* Z*	
Unit	2	Y* Z*	

continues

TABLE A.3 CONTINUED

Object Type	Max Length	Naming Convention	Notes
Maint. & Transport Objects	10	Y* Z*	
Matchcodes			
Matchcode ID	1	0-9	
Matchcode Object	4	Y* Z*	
Messages			
Message Classes	2	Y* Z*	
Message Numbers	3	*	
Module Pools			
Dialog Module Pools	8	SAPDY* SAPDZ*	
Screen Module Pools	8	SAPMY* SAPMZ*	
Info Type Module Pools	8	MP9*	
Subroutine Module Pools	8	SAPFY* SAPFZ*	
Update Pgm Module Pools	8	SAPUY* SAPUZ*	
Number Range Objects	10	Y* Z*	
Parameter Ids	3	Y* Z*	
Printer Macros	-	Y* Z* 9*	
Relation IDs	2	Y* Z*	
R/3 Analyzer Identifier	20	Y* Z*	
Reports			
Report Name	8	Y* Z*	
Report Category	4	Y* Z*	
Report Variant			
Transportable, Global	14	X* CUS&*	
Transportable, Local	14	Y*	
Not Transportable	14	Z*	
Report Writer			
Report	8	*	1st char not 0–9
Report Group	4	*	1st char not 0–9
Library	3	*	1st char not 0–9
Standard Layout	7	*	1st char not 0–9
SAPScript			
Layout Set	12	*	1st char not 0–9
Form	16	Y* Z*	
Standard Text ID	4	Y* Z*	
Standard Text Name	32	Y* Z*	
Style	8	Y* Z*	

Object Type	Max Length	Naming Convention	Notes
Screens	4	9* > 0	For screen exits for customer dialog programs
Spool			
Layout Type	16	Y* Z*	
Font Group	8	Y* Z*	
Device Type	8	Y* Z*	
Page Format	8	Y* Z*	
System Barcode	8	Y* Z*	
Standard Task	8	9*	
Standard Roll	8	9*	
Structure (DDIC)	10	Y* Z*	
SYSLOG Message ID	2	Y* Z*	
Tables			
Field Name	10	*	In append structures: YY* ZZ* only
Index Name	3	Y* Z*	
Transparent, Pool, Cluster Name	10	Y* Z*	
Pool Name		T9*	For pooled tables in the ATAB pool for
		P9*	customer info types
		PA9* PB9*	
		PS9*	
		HRT9* HRP9*	
		HRI9*	
Table Pool Name	10	Y* Z*	
Table Cluster Name	10	Y* Z*	
Titlebars	3	*	
Transaction Codes	4	Y* Z*	
Type Group	5	Y* Z*	
User Profiles	12	any	_ not allowed in 2nd position
Views			
View Cluster	10	Y* Z*	
View Name	10	*	
Help View	10	H_Y* H_Z*	

continues

TABLE A.3 CONTINUED

Object Type	Max Length	Naming Convention	Notes
View Maintenance Data			
View Content	-		reserved in TRESC
Table Content	-		reserved in TRESC
Workflow Object Type	10	Y* Z*	

You will find that a few SAP objects exist within customer name ranges and thus intrude on the above naming conventions. These objects were created before the preceding conventions were adopted. A list of these exceptions can be found in table TDKZ.

APPENDIX **B**

Answers to Quiz Questions and Exercises

Chapter 1

Quiz Answers

1. SM04 (use the menu path: *System->Status*)

2. S000

3. S001

4. Three. There is one database per R/3 system.

5. Three: two for the application servers, plus one for the database server.

6. Open SQL is SAP's dialect of ANSI SQL. It is a subset and variation of ANSI SQL.

7. Open SQL has three advantages:

   - It is portable because it is automatically converted into native SQL by the database interface component of the work process.

- It supports buffered tables, making the programs that use it run faster.
- It provides automatic client handling.

8. The database interface portion of the work process implements Open SQL.

9. A new roll area is allocated whenever a program is executed, and it is deallocated when the program terminates. The roll area contains the values of the variables for that program and the current program pointer.

10. A user context is allocated each time a user logs on, and deallocated when he or she logs off. It contains information about the user, such as authorizations, profile settings, and TCP/IP address.

11. The roll-out occurs at the end of a dialog step. It frees the work process to ready it for other requests, so that the program will not use CPU while waiting for user input.

Exercise 1 Answer

In Figures 1.28 and 1.31, the first field does not have type CLNT; therefore, the table is client-independent. Open SQL statements will operate on the all rows within these tables. In Figures 1.29 and 1.30, the first field in the table is type CLNT; therefore, the table is client-dependent. Open SQL statements will only operate on those rows having the same client number as your current logon client number.

Chapter 2

Quiz Answers

1. It allocates a default work area for the table and gives the program access to the database table of the same name.

2. The default table work area is the memory area allocated by a tables statement. This memory area has the same name and structure as the table named on the tables statement. The select statement uses it by default if there is no into clause.

3. Into the default table work area.

4. To the same line as the output from previous write statement.

5. sy-subrc

6. sy-dbcnt

7. Line 4 will be executed 30 times, once for each row retrieved.

8. Zero times. Line 4 will not be executed at all if the table is empty.

Programming Exercise Answers

1. This report displays all vendor numbers and company codes from table `ztxlfb1` where the company code is greater than or equal to `3000`. Note that `bukrs` is a character field. If you don't enclose the value `5000` in single quotation marks, the system automatically converts it to character for the comparison. There is no difference in the output for this program, whether you specify quotation marks or not. However, avoiding conversions is good programming practice and it makes the program more efficient.

```
1  report ztz0201.
2  tables ztxlfb1.
3  select * from ztxlfb1 where bukrs >= '3000'
4      order by bukrs lifnr descending.
5      write: / ztxlfb1-bukrs, ztxlfb1-lifnr.
6      endselect.
7  if sy-subrc <> 0.
8      write / 'no records found'.
9      endif.
```

2. Move the test for `sy-subrc` after the `endselect`, as shown here:

```
1  report ztz0202.
2  tables ztxlfa1.
3  select * from ztxlfa1 where lifnr like 'W%'.
4      write / ztxlfa1-lifnr.
5      endselect.
6  if sy-subrc <> 0.
7      write / 'no records found'.
8      endif.
```

3. There is a period missing at the end of the `tables` statement, and the vendor number must be padded on the left with zeros because it is a character field in the database. (This behavior is more fully explained in the chapter on conversions.)

```
1  report ztz0203.
2  tables ztxlfa1.
3  select * from ztxlfa1 where lifnr > '0000001050'.
4      write / ztxlfa1-lifnr.
5      endselect.
```

4. The last line of the output says `no records found`, even though records were found. The problem is on line 6. The test should be for equality, not inequality.

```
1  report ztz0204.
2  tables ztxlfa1.
3  select * from ztxlfa1 where lifnr > '0000001050'.
4      write / ztxlfa1-lifnr.
5      endselect.
6  if sy-dbcnt = 0.
7      write / 'no records found'.
8      endif.
```

B

5. The write statement should be inside the select loop.

```
1   report ztz0205.
2   tables ztxlfa1.
3   select * from ztxlfa1 where lifnr > '0000001050'.
4       write / ztxlfa1-lifnr.
5       endselect.
6   if sy-subrc <> 0.
7       write / 'no records found'.
8       endif.
```

6. Referring to the original program, table ztxlfc3 is not used; the definition for it can be removed from line 2. The into ztxlfa1 on line 4 is not needed, since ztxlfa1 is the default work area. Lines 5 and 6 can be chained together. The second expression using sy-dbcnt on line 8 is redundant and can be removed. Line 12 doesn't need an explicit work area, so it can be removed. Consequently, lines 13 and 14 must be changed to write from ztxlfb1, and line 3 is no longer needed. Lines 13 and 14 can be chained together. The simplified program follows:

```
1   report ztz0206.
2   tables: ztxlfa1, ztxlfb1.
3
4   select * from ztxlfa1.
5       write: / ztxlfa1-lifnr,
6                 ztxlfa1-name1.
7       endselect.
8   if sy-subrc <> 0.
9       write / 'no records found in ztxlfa1'.
10      endif.
11  uline.
12  select * from ztxlfb1.
13      write: / ztxlfb1-lifnr,
14                ztxlfb1-bukrs.
15      endselect.
16  if sy-subrc <> 0.
17      write / 'no records found'.
18      endif.
```

7. The syntax error is caused by the endselect on line 5. It should be removed. You could also correct the syntax error by removing the word single from the select statement on line 3. However, this is a less efficient solution since only one row is to be read. The comparison operator on line 3 is also incorrect. It should be =.

```
1   report ztz0207.
2   tables ztxlfa1.
3   select single * from ztxlfa1 where lifnr = '0000001000'.
4   write / ztxlfa1-lifnr.
5   if sy-subrc <> 0.
6       write / 'no records found'.
7       endif.
```

Chapter 3

Quiz Answers

1. The domain gives a field its technical characteristics, such as data type and length.

2. The data element contains a domain name, field labels for screens and lists, and documentation for F1 help.

3. Application data refers to data used by R/3 applications like SD (Sales and Distribution) or MM (Materials Management). There are two types: transaction data and master data. Examples of application data are purchase orders (an example of transaction data) or vendor information (an example of master data). There is also system data, such as configuration data or DDIC metadata, in addition to application data.

4. No, the location of the decimal point is part of the description of the field. It is contained in the domain, not stored with the value.

5. SE16, SE17, SM30 and SM31. SE16 is the most commonly used, and SE17 cannot be used to update data.

6. A transparent table has a one-to-one relationship with a table in the database. Pooled and cluster tables have many-to-one relationships with database tables.

Exercise 1 Answer

For this solution, refer to table ztz1fa1 in the R/3 system.

Exercise 2 Answer

To see the solution for the table •••kna1, refer to table ztzkna1 in the R/3 system. The solution for the report follows:

```
1    report ztz0302.
2    tables ztzkna1.
3    select * from ztzkna1.
4        write: / ztzkna1-kunnr, ztzkna1-name1,
5                  ztzkna1-cityc, ztzkna1-regio,
6                  ztzkna1-land1.
7        endselect.
8    if sy-subrc <> 0.
9        write / 'No rows found'.
10       endif.
```

Chapter 4

Quiz Answers

1. They must both use the same domain.

2. Within table zt1, type .INCLUDE in the field name field and zs1 in the data element name field at the point in the table where the structure should be included.

3. A text table provides descriptions for codes contained in a check table in multiple languages.

4. mandt, spras, f1 and f2.

5. Each field of type CURR must reference a currency key field (type CUKY).

Exercise 1 Answer

For the solution to this exercise, view the table ztzt005 online in the R/3 system.

Exercise 2 Answer

For the solution to this exercise, view the table ztzt005s online in the R/3 system. Don't forget to compare the cardinality and foreign key field type of the foreign key relationship with those specified online.

Exercise 3 Answer

For the solution to this exercise, view the table ztzlfa1 online in the R/3 system. Don't forget to compare the cardinality and foreign key field type of the foreign key relationships with those specified online.

Exercise 4 Answer

For the solution to this exercise, view the table ztzkna1 online in the R/3 system. Don't forget to compare the cardinality and foreign key field type of each relationship with the ones online.

Exercise 5 Answer

For the solution to this exercise, view the tables ztzt005h and ztzt005g online in the R/3 system. Don't forget to compare the cardinality and foreign key field type of your foreign keys with those online.

Exercise 6 Answer

For the solution to this exercise, view the structure •••tel and the tables ztzlfa1 and ztzkna1 online in the R/3 system.

Exercise 7 Answer

For the solution to this exercise, view the table ztzkna1 online in the R/3 system.

Chapter 5

Quiz Answers

1. No. You cannot "bind" an index to a select statement. The optimizer always chooses an index at runtime.

2. Yes, but you must apply for a modification key from SAP to do so. This can be done through OSS, the Online Service System.

3. Yes, you can use the runtime analysis tool to measure the difference.

Exercise 1 Answer

Go to the Data Dictionary transaction (transaction code SE12) and display the tables. Look at the technical settings.

The data class for the following:

MARA: APPL0 Master data, transparent tables (see Figure 5.21)

LFA1: APPL0 Master data, transparent tables (see Figure 5.22)

KNA1: APPL0 Master data, transparent tables (see Figure 5.23)

The size category for the following:

MARA: 4 Data records expected: 57,000 to 4,600,000 (see Figure 05.21)

LFA1: 3 Data records expected: 11,000 to 44,000 (see Figure 05.22)

KNA1: 3 Data records expected: 9,600 to 38,000 (see Figure 05.23)

The following figures help explain:

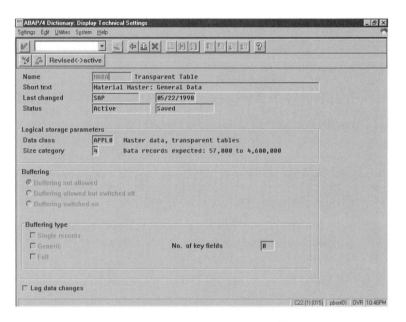

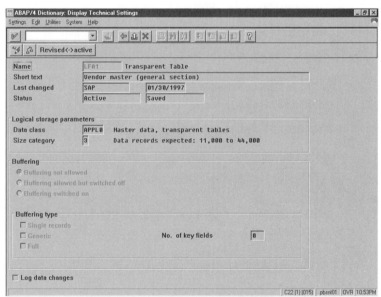

The size category determines the probable space requirement for a table in the database. Press F4 on the field size category to see the number of data records that can be maintained for your table's individual categories without complications. These complications could be, for example, a reorganization becoming necessary because the maximum space to be reserved for the table was exceeded due to the maintained size category.

Chapter 6

Quiz Answers

1. Yes. Any changes to the domain require that it be reactivated. The table should also be reactivated and a consistency check should be performed.

Exercise 1 Answer

1. In the database utility, click the Delete Database Table button. This "drops" the table and the table and content will be deleted. You can recreate the table by pressing the Create Database Table button. The table will be recreated using the active version of the table. You can use the database utility. Be cautious as you do this to a table in SAP.

Chapter 7

Quiz Answers

The solutions are as follows:

1. The correct definition is `'Don''t bite.'` It should have been enclosed in single quotation marks and it requires two consecutive quotation marks within.

2. The correct definition is `'+2.2E03'`. The exponent character is `E`, not `F`, and decimals are not allowed in an exponent.

3. The definition is correct.

4. The correct definition is `'00000F'`. There should not be a leading `x`. An even number of characters must exist, and they must be uppercase.

5. The correct definition is `'-9.9'`. Numeric literals containing decimals must be enclosed in single quotation marks, and the sign must lead.

6. Floating-point values cannot exceed `1E+308`.

7. `H` is not a valid hexadecimal character. The valid characters are `A–F` and `0–9`.

8. The definition is correct. A single quotation mark is represented. If written out, the output would be `'`.

9. The definition is correct. A double quotation mark within single quotation marks is represented. If written out, the output would be `'"'`.

The solutions are as follows:

1. The correct definition is `data st_f1(5) type c`. A dash should not appear in the definition of a variable name. The underscore character should be used instead.

2. The correct definition is `data f1 type c`. The data type for character is `C`.

3. The correct definition is `data f1(20) type c`. There should not be a space between the field name and length specification.

4. Variable names should not start with a numeric, and a length is not allowed with type `i`. The correct definition is `data a1 type i`.

5. The correct definition is `data per_cent type p decimals 1 value '55.5'`. A dash should not be used in a variable name. A decimal is specified in the value, but the `decimals` addition is missing. The value contains a decimal, but it is not enclosed in quotation marks.

6. The definition is correct. `f1` can hold three digits because `(L*2)-1 = (2*2)-1 = 3`.

Exercise 1 Answer

```
report ztz0707.
parameters: p_date like sy-datum default sy-datum,
            p_field1 type c,
            chckbox1 as checkbox,
            chckbox2 as checkbox,
            radbut1 radiobutton group g1 default 'X',
            radbut2 radiobutton group g1.
```

Chapter 8

Quiz Answer

1. The one predefined constant is SPACE and the equivalent literal format is ' '.

2. The types of statements that can be used are data and structure type. User-defined are defined in the Data Dictionary to help with maintenance and reduce redundancy.

Exercise 1 Answer

```
types: dollar(16)    type p decimals 2,
       point(16)     type p decimals 0.     "credit card points

data: begin of usd_amount,
            hotel       type dollar,
            rent_car    type dollar,
            plane       type dollar,
            food        type dollar,
            end of usd_amount,
        begin of amex_pt,
            hotel       type p decimals 2,
            rent_car    type point,
            plane       type point,
            food        type point,
            end of amex_pt.
```

Exercise 2 Answer

```
Output:

1 3 4 5
9 8 7 6
```

Chapter 9

Quiz Answer

1. You can use eq or =. For example, `move vara to varb.` is the same as `varb = vara.` or `varb eq vara`.

2. Operators and operands must be separated by spaces in order for the variables to be computed.

Exercise 1 Answer

1. `sperz`

2. `konzs`

3. `fdpos`

4. `msgid`

5. `matkl`

The two things wrong in the program are the table declaration of `ztxt005t` and the single quotation mark before the variable, `land1`. Declare the table `ztxt005t` and remove the single quotation mark before the `land1` variable.

Chapter 10

Quiz Answers

1. The answer is as follows:

```
case v1.
    when 5.        write 'The number is five.'.
    when 10.       write 'The number is ten.'.
    when others.   write 'The number is not five or ten.'.
    endcase.
```

2. The string operators are `CP` (contains pattern) and `NP` (does not contain pattern).

3. The three program control statements are `exit`, `continue`, and `check`:

   - The `exit` statement is used to prevent further processing from occurring in `loop`, `select`, `do`, and `while` statements and in subroutines introduced by `form`.

- The `continue` statement is used to skip all the statements in the current loop pass and go to the end of the loop. It can be used with `loop`, `select`, `do` and `while` statements.
- The `check` statement is like the `continue` statement but can contain a logical expression.

Exercise 1 Answer

```
report ztz1001.
data: l1(2) type c.
do 20 times.
    write / sy-index.
    do 10 times.
        l1 = sy-index.
        write l1.
        enddo.
    enddo.
```

Conversion occurs in the program as follows:

```
I --> C  ZTX1001 000060      L1 = SY-INDEX.
```

Chapter 11

Quiz Answers

1. In actuality, your Basis consultant sets a limit on the maximum amount of extended memory an internal table can allocate. If you exceed that amount, your program will allocate private memory from the work process and will no longer be able to roll your program out.

2. If you do, the system will allocate 8KB from the paging area. Memory will be wasted and paging could increase, resulting in poorer performance.

3. The `read table` statement can only be used to read internal tables. It doesn't work with database tables. Use `select single` instead.

Exercise 1 Answer

In systems prior, conversions were performed by converting from the value on the right to the data type and length of the component on the left.

B

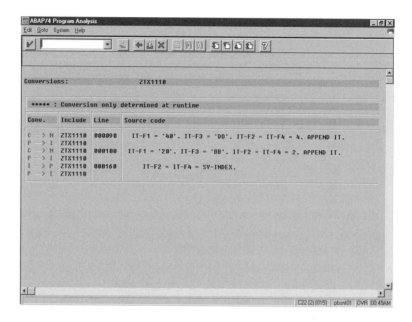

On lines 9 and 10, there was a conversion from c to n (character to numeric) and then a conversion from p to I (parameter to integer).

On line 16, there was a conversion from p to I (parameter to integer).

Chapter 12

Quiz Answers

1. Your change to sy-tabix is ignored and the statements would operate on the row in the work area. sy-tabix is like sy-index—modifying either does not affect loop operations. Also, the value of sy-tabix is reset at the endloop, and the next loop pass proceeds as if the value were never changed.

2. The only thing sy-toccu can tell you that other variables can't is whether your internal table is entirely in the paging area. If it is zero, it is entirely in the paging area. This has no use in a production system, but you might find it useful during development to confirm your expectation of how memory is allocated for an internal table. If, for example, you expect the internal table to be in the roll area, but sy-toccu contains zero (indicating that it's in the paging area), you might have another look at your occurs clause to determine whether it is correct.

Exercise 1 Answer

```
report ztz1201.
tables ztxlfa1.
data it like ztxlfa1 occurs 23 with header line.

select * from ztxlfa1 into table it.   "don't code an endselect
loop at it.
    write: / sy-tabix, it-land1, it-regio.
    endloop.
uline.
it-land1 = 'US'. modify it index 3 transporting land1.
it-regio = 'TX'. modify it transporting regio where regio = 'MA'.
loop at it.
    write: / sy-tabix, it-land1, it-regio.
    endloop.
free it.
```

Chapter 13

Quiz Answer

1. Numeric fields (types i p and f) are filled with zeros. The rest of the fields to the right of the control level are filled with asterisks.

Exercise 1 Answer

```
report ztz1301.
data: begin of it occurs 3,
        f1(2) type n,
        f2    type i,
        f3(2) type c,
        f4    type p,
        end of it.

it-f1 = '40'. it-f3 = 'DD'. it-f2 = it-f4 = 4. append it.
it-f1 = '20'. it-f3 = 'BB'. it-f2 = it-f4 = 2. append it.

sort it by f1.
do 5 times.
    it-f1 = sy-index * 10.
    it-f3 = 'XX'.
    it-f2 = it-f4 = sy-index.
    read table it
        with key f1 = it-f1
        binary search
        comparing f2 f3 f4
        transporting no fields.
    if sy-subrc = 2.
        modify it index sy-tabix.
```

B

```
    elseif sy-subrc <> 0.
        insert it index sy-tabix.
        endif.
    enddo.

loop at it.
    write: / it-f1, it-f2, it-f3, it-f4.
    endloop.
```

Exercise 2 Answer

Here is an efficient way to fix the problem:

```
report ztz1302.
tables: ztxlfa1.
data: begin of it occurs 10,
        lifnr like ztxlfa1-lifnr,
        land1 like ztxlfa1-land1,
        end of it.
select lifnr land1 from ztxlfa1 into table it.
loop at it.
    write: / it-lifnr,
            it-land1.
    endloop.
```

Chapter 14

Quiz Answers

1. You must sign off and sign back on again to the R/3 system before changes to user defaults take effect.

2. An edit mask beginning with a V, when applied to a numeric field (types i, p, and f), causes the sign field to be displayed at the beginning. If applied to a character field, a V is actually output.

3. The no-sign addition, when used with variables of type i, p, or f, suppresses the sign character's output. In other words, negative numbers will not have a sign and appear as if they were positive.

Exercise 1 Answer

```
1  report ztz1401.
2  write: /      '....+....1....+....2....+....3....+....4',
3         /      'First',
4         40     'December',
5         /16    'January',
6         /30    'First'.
```

Chapter 15

Quiz Answers

1. The three graphical additions are symbols, icon, and line. The program should have an include statement, include <...>, for each of the graphical additions in order to utilize it. For example:

```
include <symbol> for symbols,
include <icon> for icons,
include <line> for lines.
```

2. The two additions used with the report statement are line size and line count. The variables used for the additions must be numeric because they control the size of the page.

Exercise 1 Answer

```
report ztz1501.
include <symbol>.
write: /4 sym_filled_square as symbol, 'square',
       /4 sym_filled_diamond as symbol, 'diamond',
       /4 sym_filled_circle as symbol, 'circle',
       /4 sym_glasses as symbol, 'glasses',
       /4 sym_pencil as symbol, 'pencil',
       /4 sym_phone as symbol, 'phone',
       /4 sym_note as symbol, 'note',
       /4 sym_folder as symbol, 'folder'.
```

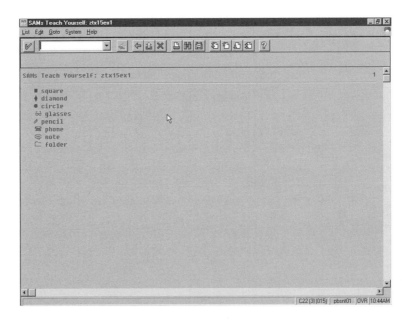

B

Chapter 16

Quiz Answers

1. The statement back can be used to return to the current output position.

2. Use the skip sy-linct instead of new-page when you want to set a new page and you want a footer at the bottom of that current page.

Exercise 1 Answer

- Line 3 begins a do loop. The first time through, the write statement on line 6 triggers the top-of-page event. The value of sy-linno always contains the current list line number. At this point, it is set to the line following the standard page headings. Line 13 assigns this value to variable *n*. Control returns to line 6 and A is written out. On each successive pass through the loop, line 8 increments the value of *n*, and line 9 sets the current output line. This results in the output being written on successive lines, beginning at the line following the standard headings.

- Line 4 begins a nested do loop. Each time through, line 5 sets the current output position equal to the current loop iteration. The current output position is set to 1 the first time through. The second time through it's set to 2, and so on. This causes line 6 to write the letter A four times, in columns 1–4.

Chapter 17

Quiz Answers

1. No.

2. Don't use stop in the following events: initialization, at selection-screen output, top-of-page, and end-of-page. Technically, it can work with top-of-page and end-of-page if you refrain from issuing write statements within end-of-selection afterward.

3. To be precise, a variable is only known within a program after the point at which it is defined. For example, if you define a variable on line 10, you would be able to access it on lines 11 and later, but not on lines 1–9. In the case of a local definition, you can access the global version of the variable at any point before the local definition.

Exercise 1 Answer

```
REPORT ZTZ1701 NO STANDARD PAGE HEADING.
TABLES ZTXLFA1.
PARAMETERS P_LAND1 LIKE ZTXLFA1-LAND1.

INITIALIZATION.
  P_LAND1 = 'US'.

START-OF-SELECTION.
  PERFORM CREATE_REPORT.

FORM CREATE_REPORT.
  SELECT * FROM ZTXLFA1 WHERE LAND1 = P_LAND1.
      PERFORM WRITE_REC.
      ENDSELECT.
  ENDFORM.

FORM WRITE_REC.
  WRITE: / ZTXLFA1-LIFNR, ZTXLFA1-NAME1, ZTXLFA1-LAND1.
  ENDFORM.

TOP-OF-PAGE.
  FORMAT COLOR COL_HEADING.
  WRITE: / 'Vendors with Country Code', P_LAND1.
  ULINE.
```

Chapter 18

Quiz Answers

1. Parameter names that appear on the `form` statement are called *formal parameters*. This term is easy to remember because formal starts with form. For example, in the statement `form s1 using p1 changing p2 p3`, the parameters p1, p2, and p3 are called formal parameters.

2. Passing a variable of the wrong data type or length to a typed parameter causes a syntax error.

3. New memory is not allocated for the value. A pointer to the original memory location is passed instead. All references to the parameter are references to the original memory location. Changes to the variable within the subroutine update the original memory location immediately.

4. The additions `using f1` and `changing f1` both pass f1 by reference—they are identical in function. The reason they both exist is that, used properly, they can document whether the subroutine will change a parameter or not.

Exercise 1 Answer

The following output is generated:

```
          Top of page, flag = S  ctr = 1
          --------------------------------
in Start-Of-Selection
          p1 =
```

The initialization section is not executed because no selection criteria is present in the program. The `Start-Of-Selection` event is executed. When the program gets to the first `write` statement, control in the program is passed along to the `Top-of-page` event. When the `Top-of-page` event is complete, control is passed back to the `Start-Of-Selection` event.

Chapter 19

Quiz Answer

1. True. You never need to specify a value for an import parameter that has a proposal.

2. True. You never need to code parameters that are exported from the function module.

Exercise 1 Answer

When the program executes the internal table is filled and the function module is called. A pop-up window with the contents of the internal table will appear. Depending on what entry was chosen by the user, it will then print out using the `write` statement.

Chapter 20

Quiz Answers

1. The data definitions of both of the parameters must be identical.

2. Use the menu path Function Module->Release->Cancel Release.

3. The program will be aborted and a short dump that has the runtime error `RAISE_EXCEPTION` will result.

4. They should not be used within function modules. Instead, the `raise` statement should be used because it enables the caller to set the value of `sy-subrc` on return.

Exercise 1 Answer

```
1  function z_tz_div.
2  *"----------------------------------------------------------
3  *"*"Local interface:
4  *"        IMPORTING
5  *"            VALUE(P1) TYPE  I DEFAULT 1
6  *"            VALUE(P2) TYPE  I
7  *"        EXPORTING
8  *"            VALUE(P3) TYPE  P
9  *"        EXCEPTIONS
10 *"            ZERO_DIVIDE
11 *"----------------------------------------------------------
12 if p2 = 0.
13    raise zero_divide.
14    endif.
15 p3 = p1 / p2.
16 endfunction.
```

Chapter 21

Quiz Answers

1. The two flavors of the matchcode assembled are physically and logically. Physically, the data is stored in a separate table. Logically, the data is managed by database view, which is the same as the transparent storage.

2. Yes, changes to the characteristics of a domain linked to data elements will also change, because data elements in a domain inherit all properties of a domain that are referenced.

3. The primary rule for establishing a foreign key relationship is to define and link a relationship between multiple tables.

Exercise 1 Answer

```
report ztz2101.
tables: mara, t001w.
* Selection parameters for BOMs
selection-screen begin of line.
selection-screen comment (33) text-bom.
parameters: bom like mara-matnr,
            spras like t002-spras.
selection-screen end of line.
selection-screen skip 1.
Select-options: matnr for mara-matnr,
                werks for t001w-werks.
```

B

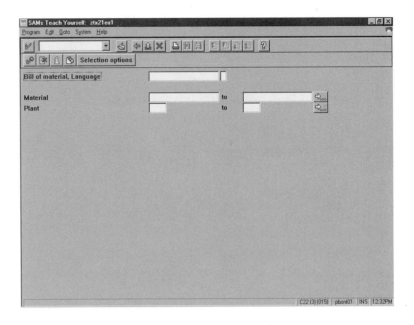

INDEX

M

What's on the CD?

The CD-ROM contains:

- The author's source code and examples from the book

- Lotus ScreenCams that demonstrate how to do various procedures described in the book, as well as the ScreenCam player itself

- Several utilities created by the author

- A 30-day trial version of Transcend, a German to English translation program by Transparent Language, Inc.

Installation Instructions

Windows 95/NT 4

1. Insert the CD-ROM into your CD-ROM drive.

2. From the Windows desktop, double-click on the "My Computer" icon.

3. Double-click on the icon representing your CD-ROM drive.

4. Double-click on the icon titled START.EXE to run the installation program.

If Windows 95/NT 4.0 is installed on your computer, and you have the AutoPlay feature enabled, the `start.exe` program starts automatically whenever you insert the disk into your CD-ROM drive.

Read This Before Opening Software